MW00784458

EXPOSITORY SERMON OUTLINES

CHARLES SIMEON

(From the painting by Sir William Beechey)

EXPOSITORY SERMON OUTLINES

CHARLES SIMEON
and Others

Baker Books
A Division of Baker Book House Co.
Grand Rapids, Michigan 49516

Reprinted 1995 by Baker Books
a division of Baker Book House Company
P.O. Box 6287, Grand Rapids, MI 49516-6287

Printed in the United States of America

ISBN 0-8010-9002-4

CONTENTS

PUBLISHER'S PREFACE

The book here reprinted as *Expository Sermon Outlines* has been assisting preachers in the preparation of sound, biblical sermons for much of the last 150 years. This work was originally published in three volumes under the title *Theological Sketch-Book: Skeletons of Sermons.* A two-volume edition was released, four years later, in 1848. This edition of *Theological Sketch-Book* carried an expanded subtitle:

> *Skeletons of Sermons, Carefully Arranged in Systematic Order So As to Constitute a Complete Body of Divinity; Partly Original but Chiefly Selected from Simeon's "Horae Homileticae"* and *"Skeletons."*

The anonymous editor of this compilation favored sermon "skeletons" (or outlines) written by Charles Simeon, an eminent Anglican preacher of the early nineteenth century. *Theological Sketch-Book* drew largely on the following two works by Simeon:

> *Horae Homileticae: Discourses (in the Form of Skeletons) upon the Whole Scriptures.* 17 vols. London, 1819–28.
> *Helps to Composition: 600 Skeletons of Sermons* . . . 5 vols. 2d ed. London, 1808.

Of the 202 outlines in volume 1 (reprinted here) of *Theological Sketch-Book*, 85 are drawn from Simeon's two multivolume sets.

The remaining outlines are drawn from the following sources: (1) *Joseph Benson's Sermons, and Plans of Sermons, on Many of the Most Important Texts of Holy Scripture;* (2) *The Pulpit Assistant: Containing 300 Outlines or Skeletons of Sermons, Chiefly Extracted from Various Authors;* (3) *The Pulpit: A Magazine of Sermons;* (4) *The Preacher: Containing Sermons by Eminent Living Divines; and* (5) *Sketches of Sermons, Preached to Congregations in Various Parts of the United Kingdom and on the European Continent.* (See Abbreviations of Sources.)

Who was Charles Simeon, the preacher whose work is featured in the *Theological Sketch-Book*? Simeon (1759–1836) was, with William Wilberforce, one of the two leading evangelicals in the Church of England during the early 1800s.

During his first year as a student at King's College, Cambridge, Simeon came under conviction of his sinfulness and his need of a Savior. By Easter morning, culminating months of seeking, he experienced the assurance of salvation. During Holy Communion that day he had "the sweetest access to God through my blessed Saviour."

Simeon became a Fellow of King's in 1782, and later that same year he was appointed to serve the Church of the Holy Trinity in Cambridge (the same pulpit that had been occupied by Puritans Richard Sibbes and Thomas Goodwin). Simeon remained in this parish for the rest of his life, despite many opportunities to accept more prestigious ecclesiastical posts.

Simeon's evangelical convictions were nurtured by his friendship with John Venn and his father, Henry. He did not mute these convictions when preaching, though evangelical preachers were a distinct minority in the Church of England and were granted no respect by the students and professors of Cambridge University.

Simeon suffered for his evangelical beliefs for many years, even at the hands of his parishioners. But he held firm and, after many years, finally earned the admiration of his parish, the university community, and the Church of England generally. Eventually he came to exercise greater influence in that church than any archbishop.

Simeon played a major role in the establishment of such evangelical organizations as the British and Foreign Bible society, Religious Tract Society, Church Missionary Society, and London Jews Society. He personally founded what came to be known as the Simeon Trust. He was also a pioneer in ministering to university students and in providing (however unofficially) theological and homiletical training to those planning to seek ordination.

According to Marcus Loane, "Simeon was a preacher of no mean fame in an age when preaching was too often defaced by artificial style and monotonous voice."His style, by contrast, was simple and direct. He aimed, above all, to be understood, to reach his hearer's heart and conscience. ". . . the gravity of that purpose and the dignity of his message kept his diction always free from tameness and raised it at times to noble heights of grandeur."

"His style of delivery as a young man," Loane continues, "was earnest and impassioned to a degree; it was still in old age lively and impressive in no common measure. Voice and gesture were marked by the natural and unstudied power of purest sincerity and strongest reality; he could not fail to hold his audience with the unlaboured utterance and the tremendous reverence with which he spoke."

The real secret of Simeon's effectiveness as a preacher, however, was his lifelong habit of arising early each morning and devoting four hours to prayer and the rigorous study of Scripture. At least twelve hours of work went into the preparation of each sermon.

According to Canon Smyth in *The Art of Preaching*, Simeon was "almost the first man in the history of the English pulpit since the Middle Ages to appreciate that it is perfectly possible to teach men how to preach." In 1792 Simeon began his sermon classes, which he held regularly for forty years. In each class fifteen to twenty undergraduates received instruction in the technique of constructing and delivering sermons.

To assist both his students and other preachers (most of whom had received no instruction in homiletics), Simeon began to publish shortened versions of his sermons. By the end of his life he had published more than 2,500 of these extended outlines in a final edition of *Horae Homileticae*, which, according to Kenneth Hylson-Smith, "were much appreciated by preachers and others in his day."

In the preface to *Horae Homileticae*, Simeon expressed the following concern: "Does it uniformly tend to humble the sinner, to exalt the Saviour, to promote holiness? If in one single instance it loses sight of any of these points, let it be condemned without mercy."

Was Simeon concerned about the outlines in *Horae Homileticae* becoming a crutch for preachers? "If it leads the ignorant to preach the truth, and the indolent to exert themselves, and the weak to attain a facility for writing their own, and the busy and laborious to do more and with better effect than they otherwise could have done," wrote Simeon, "I shall be richly repaid for my labour."

Baker Book House is pleased to make *Expository Sermon Outlines*, volume 1 of *Theological Sketch-Book*, available once again. In 1954 we released volumes 1 and 2 in a single binding under the title *Sermon Outlines*. We trust that this most recent reprint edition will be of real assistance to many preachers and that they will be inspired to preach in the enduring evangelical tradition of Charles Simeon.

FOR FURTHER READING

To learn more about Charles Simeon, one might next read Toon's article, Hylson-Smith's section, and Loane's chapter, in that order.

Hopkins, Hugh Evan. *Charles Simeon of Cambridge*. Grand Rapids: Eerdmans, 1977.

Hylson-Smith, Kenneth. *Evangelicals in the Church of England: 1734–1984*. Edinburgh: T. & T. Clark, 1989. Pages 70–76

Loane, Marcus L. *Cambridge and the Evangelical Succession*. London: Lutterworth, 1952. Pages 171–220.

Pollard, Arthur, and Michael Hennell, eds. *Charles Simeon (1759–1836): Essays Written in Commemoration of His Bi-Centenary by Members of the Evangelical Fellowship for Theological Literature*. London: SPCK, 1959.

Toon, Peter. "Charles Simeon." In *Who's Who in Christian History*. Edited by J. D. Douglas and Philip W. Comfort. Wheaton: Tyndale, 1992. Page 625.

ABBREVIATIONS FOR SOURCES

B. Benson, Joseph. *Sermons, and Plans of Sermons, on Many of the Most Important Texts of Holy Scripture.* 3 vols., 6 parts. London: Cadell, 1824–27.

H. *The Pulpit Assistant: Containing 300 Outlines or Skeletons of Sermons, Chiefly Extracted from Various Authors, with an Essay on the Composition of a Sermon by Thomas Hannam.* 5 vols. London, 1819.

H.H. Simeon, Charles. *Horae Homileticae: Discourses (in the Form of Skeletons) upon the Whole Scriptures.* 17 vols. London, 1819–28.

P. *The Pulpit: A Magazine of Sermons.* 8 vols. London, 1824ff.

Pr. *The Preacher: Containing Sermons by Eminent Living Divines.* London, 1831–35.

Sk. Simeon, Charles. *Helps to Composition: 600 Skeletons of Sermons . . .* 5 vols. 2d ed. London, 1808.

S.S. *Sketches of Sermons, Preached to Congregations in Various Parts of the United Kingdom and on the European Continent, Furnished by Their Respective Authors.* 8 vols. London, 1822–25.

Note: Two of the sermons are credited to Man., a source the publisher has been unable to identify.

CHAPTER I.

THE HOLY SCRIPTURES.

THE BOOK OF THE LORD.

Isaiah xxxiv. 16.—"Seek ye out of the book of the Lord and read." (Sk.)

THE text occurs nearly at the close of one of the most awfully sublime chapters that the language of man ever uttered, or the pen of inspiration ever wrote. A chapter in which JEHOVAH is represented as clothing himself with the garment of vengeance, and coming out of his place to punish the inhabitants of the earth for their iniquities; and a chapter, in which we not only discover the indignation of God displayed against sinners, so as utterly to effect their destruction; but where the very land that had nursed them in their crimes is made a standing monument of Divine vengeance. Can any thing within the whole compass of human language be more awful than the descriptions in ver. 9—16? It is not now necessary to say when these prophecies were fulfilled, or to what particular country they referred: what we have at present to regard is, the advice in the text; and here let us,

I. NOTICE THE OBJECT TO WHICH OUR ATTENTION IS DIRECTED—THE BOOK OF THE LORD. This phrase primarily meant the prophetic writings; but since the canon of Scripture has been filled up, we understand by the "book of the Lord," the whole Bible, consisting of the Old and New Testaments: these are called, "the book of the Lord."

1. *Because they were inspired by the Lord*, 2 Tim. iii. 16, 17. We infer this—from their wonderful preservation—from the exact fulfilment of the prophecies with which they abound—from the most stupendous and indisputable miracles recorded in them—from the grand and elevated subjects on which they treat—and especially from the moral influence of their doctrines in the salvation of mankind.

2. *They abound with the most correct and sublime descriptions of the Lord*. One of the ancients said, 'The Bible is the history of God.' It describes the nature of God—what he is in himself, and what he is to us—what he has been doing, and what he will do. It records the terrible acts of his justice—the grand displays of his mercy—his inviolate faithfulness, immaculate purity, and immutable goodness. There is scarcely a question which a serious mind may be disposed to urge relative to the Divine Being, which cannot be solved from the Old and New Testaments.

3. *They are sanctioned by the Lord, and he has set his seal to their truth*, Isa. lv. 10, 11; Rom. i. 16; 1 Thess. ii. 13. Oh! what great and glorious success attends the doctrines contained in the Bible, when preached in their purity. How many blind eyes are opened! How many hard hearts softened! How many inveterate prejudices subdued! How many wanderers reclaimed! How many penitents cheered! And how many immortal souls made wise unto salvation by the Holy Scriptures!

4. *They lead to the Lord*. They find us out in our state of estrangement and alienation from God; they teach us the way of access unto God, by the blood of the atonement; they mark the steps by which the prodigal returns to his Father; they encourage him by promises, and urge him by threaten-

ings; and their most obvious tendency and design is to lead us "to the rock that is higher than" ourselves.

II. ILLUSTRATE THE PURPOSES FOR WHICH WE ARE TO SEEK OUT OF THE BOOK OF THE LORD AND READ.

1. *To gain instructions.* The Bible is a book of knowledge. All the streams of sacred instruction, which have been flowing in every direction through all the Christian world, and fertilizing the waste and desolate places of the earth, have arisen from this source. Do we pant for knowledge? Here it spreads its ample page;

> 'Tis revelation satisfies all doubts,
> And solves all mysteries except its own;
> And so illuminates the path of life,
> That fools discover it and stray no more.'

A christian with a Bible in his hand resembles a man standing on the elevated summit of a mountain, "where ether pure surrounds him, and Elysian prospects rise." The dark clouds that hung over the past are all dissipated, and he views the birth of time, the formation of the globe, the origin of evil, and the long train of miracles, prophecies, and wonders, with which the Old Testament abounds. Nor is he less favored in looking through the bright vista of the future years.

2. *To gain examples.* The Bible is a book of models; here we see religion enlivened and embodied. The precepts of the Gospel describe what men ought to be, but in the living characters we see what they were; and there is not a single virtue that can adorn human nature, but what has been exemplified in some living characters, recorded in "the book of the Lord;" such as faith in Abraham, meekness in Moses, patience in Job, &c.

3. *To gain excitements.* The Bible is a book of motives.—Knowledge and practice do not always harmonize. Men know much; but how few live up to what they know! There are no motives equal to those which the Bible presents. Can love allure us? Here is love "no where to be found less than divine." Can terror awe us? Here are the terrors of the Lord most awfully displayed, in the punishments inflicted on the ungodly. Oh, what motives does "the book of the Lord" display! addressed to the understanding, to the conscience, and to the heart.

4. *To gain encouragements.* The Bible is a book of promises and consolations; they suit every case, meet every emergency, redress every grievance, scatter every doubt, and heal every wound; they are pure in their source, satisfying in their nature, and perpetual in their duration.

III. OFFER A FEW THOUGHTS AS TO THE MANNER, HOW WE SHOULD SEEK OUT OF THE BOOK OF THE LORD AND READ.

1. *We should do it with deep seriousness and holy awe resting upon our minds.* The very thought that we are about to consult the oracles of eternal truth, which came forth from God, and serve to describe his nature, ought to repress every feeling of levity, and every disposition contrary to serious godliness. Were God again upon earth in human form, and were we to consult him on the great business of our salvation, who can doubt but what we should do it seriously?—So read his word.

2. *We should "seek out of the book of the Lord, and read," with all the attention of which we are capable.* "*Search*," said our Saviour, "the Scriptures." This is a significant word, and is a metaphor taken from miners, who dig deep, and search for metals in the bowels of the earth. "The book of the Lord" has a rich vein of heavenly wisdom running through it, whose merchandise is better than silver; but this treasure lies deep, and

superficial observers never perceive it: while we read let us seek—bend the whole force of our minds—call in our attention—and repress every wandering thought.

3. *We should do it frequently.* If we cannot spare hours to do it, let us snatch moments; and if we cannot peruse many chapters, let us read single verses, and treasure them up in our memories. "Thy word have I hid in my heart," Psa. cxix. 11. Let our memories be sacred repositories for the words of God.

4. *We should do it with much prayer.* While you *read*, pray—pray for Divine illumination. "Holy men of old spake as they were moved by the Holy Ghost;" we need that same teaching, to understand what they wrote, Psalm cxix. 18; Prov. i. 23.

5. *We should do it practically.* Let us read, not merely to know, but to practise; all knowledge should be influential. "If ye know these things, happy are ye if ye do them," James i. 25.

Infer,

1. *The greatness of our privileges.* We live in a land of Bibles, we have "the book of the Lord;" and by the help of Sunday schools, &c., all may read.

2. *The greatness of our obligations*—to know, love, praise, and obey God.

3. *The greatness of our guilt*, if we abuse our privileges, and violate our obligations to God.

THE DIVINE AUTHORITY AND PERFECTION OF THE SCRIPTURES

2 Tim. iii. 16.—"All scripture is given by inspiration of God, and is profitable for doctrine, for reproof, for correction and instruction in righteousness." (H.)

THERE are but two possible ways of acquiring the knowledge of the mind of God, and these are *reason* and *revelation;* reason is that noble faculty of the soul by which man is distinguished from all inferior orders of creatures, and made capable of moral government. When our first parents were in a state of innocence, this alone was sufficient to acquaint them with every part of their duty; but upon their disobedience it was so far eclipsed, that from this time, the world, with all its wisdom has neither been fully acquainted with the perfections of the true God, nor with the right and acceptable manner of worshipping him; as appears from the history of those ages and nations, which have not had the advantage of revelation. The apostle Paul, speaking of the Gentile world, says, "they changed the glory of the incorruptible God into an image made like corruptible man." Rom. i. 23, &c. He admits they had some little acquaintance with God, but not sufficient to direct their practice; for even at Athens, the most learned city of Greece, there was an altar with this inscription, "To the unknown God." If we look abroad into the barbarous nations at this day, we shall find them buried in ignorance and superstition. How little do they know of the nature and perfections of the one living and true God, and of his reasonable service! and how dim are the remains of natural light, with regard to the terms of acceptance with him! all which demonstrates the necessity and usefulness of a Divine revelation, or of that clear and bright discovery of his will, contained in the scriptures of the Old and New Testament; which, according to the apostle, are given by the inspiration of God, and are profitable for doctrine.

I. THE SCRIPTURES OF THE OLD AND NEW TESTAMENT ARE GIVEN BY THE INSPIRATION OF GOD.

By the scriptures, the apostle, in our text, means chiefly the Old Testament, for the canon of the New was not yet finished; and by their being inspired, that those ancient prophecies came not by the will of man, but holy men of God spake as they were moved by the Holy Ghost.

In order to judge whether persons are inspired, we must,

1. Inquire into their moral character: Are they virtuous and holy persons? These dare not deceive, nor deliver any thing as a revelation from God, but what they are fully satisfied they have received from him. If a pretender to inspiration should denounce some remarkable judgment to be inflicted for our vile crimes, and should himself be notoriously guilty of those vices; it is not reasonable to suppose, we should receive him as a prophet sent from God.

2. We must examine into their doctrine. Is the doctrine they teach according to godliness? A Divine revelation must have a tendency to promote Divine knowledge and virtue, not only by teaching men to deny ungodliness, but also to live soberly, and righteously. Again, do they exalt the Divine glory and majesty, and abase the creature so far, as that no flesh should glory in his sight?

3. We must consider the credentials, or external proofs of their mission; which are principally,

1. Miracles. There can be no stronger evidence of a Divine mission than this. When Moses was sent with a massage to Pharaoh, the Lord said to Moses and Aaron, "When Pharaoh shall speak to you, saying, Show a miracle, then take your rod." Ex. vii. 9. By which it appears, that in those early times, miracles were esteemed a convincing proof of a Divine mission. Our Lord appeals, upon all occasions, to his miracles. When John the Baptist sent to inquire of him, "Whether he was the Christ?" He replies, "Go tell your master, that the blind receive their sight." Matt. xi. 5. How often did he point the scribes and pharisees to his mighty works, as well as his disciples? (John xiv. 11,) "Believe me that I am in the Father."

2. Fulfilment of prophecy. No mere man can foretell what shall be on the morrow, much less in ages far remote. This is the sole prerogative of the great God; as he alone searches and tries the reins and the heart, so he only can foretell the end from the beginning. When therefore a prophet speaks in the name of the Lord. Deut. xviii. 20.

Now all these marks and characters of inspiration are no where so conspicuous as in the Holy Scriptures. Moses, David, Solomon, Daniel, and the rest of the prophets, were pious and upright men, and it is no inconsiderable proof of their integrity, that they have left their own faults and infirmities on record. Their doctrines are reasonable, just, and good, tending to promote the glory of God and the happiness of men. What sublime strains of devotion are in the Psalms of David! What excellent rules for the conduct of life in the writings of Solomon! and how glorious does the God of Israel shine throughout all the prophets! how kind and gracious are his promises! how awful his threatenings! and how wonderfully is his majesty supported by the numerous representations of the infinite distance and disproportion between him and his creatures! These holy men believed themselves inspired, for they tell us the word of the Lord came unto them at such a time; and when they spake, it is with, "Thus saith the Lord."

And with regard to the New Testament, the evidence of its Divine authority is as strong as the nature of things will admit. The apostle tells us, "That God, who at sundry times, and in divers manners," Heb. i. 1. So that if Jesus Christ be the Son of God, it will certainly follow, that his doctrine could be no other than a Divine revelation. And this appears in many prophecies of the Old Testament. It was prophesied of the Messiah, "that he should be incarnate before the sceptre departed from Judah; that he should be born of a virgin; that he should be of the seed of David, and of the tribe of Judah; that the place of his nativity should be Bethlehem, a village of Judea; that his name should be Immanuel; that he should appear in the form of a servant, and after a mean and contemptible life, should be betrayed by one of his own household, and cut off for the sins of the people." It was therefore with the highest reason that our Saviour upbraided his countrymen for their unbelief. "O fools, and slow of heart." Luke xxiv. 25, 26.

Besides, how illustriously do the other characters of inspiration, already mentioned, shine forth in the person of Christ, who was holy, harmless, undefiled; whose doctrines were so rational and sublime, that the people wondered at the gracious words that proceeded out of his mouth. The miracles which he wrought in confirmation of his doctrine were so clear and surprising, that nothing but the extremest obstinacy and malice could withstand their evidence. But as there were many doctrines necessay to be known, which the apostles of our blessed Saviour could not receive from him in his state of humiliation and suffering; he therefore promised after his ascension into heaven, to inspire them with the extraordinary gift of the Holy Spirit, whereby they should be led into all truth, and qualified to declare to the Gentiles "the whole counsel of God." Accordingly, on the day of Pentecost, when the apostles were gathered together in one place, "the Holy Ghost came upon them, and enabled them not only to speak divers languages, but to confirm the doctrines they taught with signs and wonders."

II. The perfection or sufficiency of the scriptures.

It is said in the preceding verse, "that they are able to make us wise to salvation;" and in the text, "that they are profitable for doctrine, for reproof." By the sufficiency of the Holy Scriptures, we mean, that they contain all things necessary to be believed and practised; the law of Moses was so complete a direction of the faith and obedience of the Jews, that the addition of the Scribes and Pharisees were both useless and vain. Matt. xv. 29. In like manner the writings of the New Testament are a perfect standard to us Christians; for all things that our blessed Lord heard of his Father, he made known to his apostles, and the apostles to the churches. Acts xx. 26, 27, "I take you to record."

But the perfection of the Holy Scriptures may be farther illustrated from the particulars in my text, as,

1. They are profitable for doctrine; to acquaint us with our lost and miserable condition by sin, and the train of fatal consequences that attend it, with our recovery by Christ, the covenants of redemption and grace, the offices of Father, Son, and Spirit, in the work of our redemption, and with all those "other mysteries, which were kept secret since the world began." Rom. xvi. 25.

2. For reproof; or the discovery of our pernicious errors in doctrine and practice. When the gospel was first preached among the idolatrous nations

their dumb idols were thrown down, and their superstitious vanities fled before it, as the shadows of the night before the rising sun. The scriptures are now the standard of truth; and if men preach not agreeably thereto, it is because there is no light in them. A text of scripture, rightly explained and applied, is as full a confutation of error to a Christian, as a mathematical demonstration to a philosopher.

3. The scriptures are profitable for correction of vice and wickedness; "wherewithal (says the Psalmist) should a young man cleanse his way?" Ps. cxix. There we have a collection of all Christian graces and duties, with their opposite vices: the fruits of the Spirit and of the flesh are distinguished with the greatest propriety; and the most engaging motives to the practice of the one, and awful threatenings against the other, are represented with the greatest strength and advantage.

4. For instruction in righteousness; that is, either in the righteousness of God, which is by faith of Jesus Christ unto all, and upon all, that believe; or in the practice of moral righteousness, the nature and excellency of which are better explained and illustrated in the sermons of our blessed Saviour, than in all the writings of the ancient philosophers.

The precepts of the Bible are so many excellent rules for a holy life, and the promises are Divine encouragements to it: "Having therefore these promises, dearly beloved," 2 Cor. vii. 1. In a word, the Holy Scriptures are sufficient to all the purposes of religion.

III. Their clearness and perspicuity.

There are sublime speculations, which may employ the thoughts of the most learned inquirer after truth; as well as the deep things of God, which the angels are desirous to look into: and there are also the principles of the doctrine of Christ; that is, the "milk of the word," or the softest and gentlest food which is fit for babes, as the other is for strong men. The doctrines of the greatest consequence, such as repentance towards God, and faith in our Lord Jesus Christ, the certainty of a future state, of the resurrection of the dead, and of judgment to come, are most clearly revealed. The love of God, and of our neighbour; together with the necessity of universal holiness, charity, and good works, run through the whole of the New Testament, and are placed in so strong a light, that persons of the meanest capacities cannot but understand them. Besides,

1. The Holy Scriptures are written in the vulgar language, and therefore designed for the use of the common people. The Old Testament was written in the language of the Jewish nation, and a portion of it read in their synagogues every Sabbath-day. The New Testament was written in Greek, which was, at that time, the general language; and St. Paul's epistles were read in the churches. Now can we suppose, that the scriptures should be read to the common people, and they not capable to understand them? could not the Spirit of God write clearly; or would he not? To say the former is blasphemy; and to affirm the latter, is in effect to say, the scriptures are no revelation to the churches: for if they cannot understand them after their best inquiries, they might almost as well have been without them.

2. Our Saviour, in his sermons to the people, appeals to the scriptures, and exhorts his countrymen the Jews to search them. "Search the scriptures." John v. 39. The noble Bereans are commended for this practice, Acts xvii. 11; and young Timothy appears to have been acquainted with them from his childhood.

Remark,

Hence we may learn, that the religion of a Christian should be his

Bible; because it contains the whole revealed will of God, and is a perfect rule of faith and practice. It is also a more sure word of prophecy.

2. Let us be thankful that we have the scriptures in the vulgar language. Christianity was professed a thousand years in this island before the Bible was translated into English. This was one of the peculiar blessings of the Reformation.

3. Let us revive this neglected duty of reading the scriptures. It is both a delightful and useful employment. "Whatsoever things were written aforetime were written for our learning." It was enjoined the Israelites, upon their coming out of Egypt into the land of Canaan, that they should not only love the Lord their God, but "the words which I command thee this day." Deut. vi. 5—7.

4. When we read the scriptures, let us consider them not as the words of men, but as in deed and truth the word of God. If some things are above our capacities, let us remember, "that the foolishness of God is wiser than man." Let us read the scriptures therefore with reverence, and endeavor to understand them, as well as we can, by comparing spiritual things with spiritual.

5. In judging of controversies among Christians, let us not be carried away by the authority of great names or numbers. Councils, and fathers, and synods, may be mistaken in their decrees; but the word of God is infallible. Here we are safe, and no where else.

6. When we read the scriptures, let us pray for the instructions and teachings of the Holy Spirit; for it is not sufficient, that the light of the gospel shines around us, unless the Spirit of God, who once commanded light to shine out of darkness, shines in our hearts. "Then opened he their understandings, that they might understand the scriptures. Lord, open our eyes, that we may behold the wondrous things out of thy law."

ADVANTAGES OF POSSESSING THE SCRIPTURES.

Romans iii. 1, 2.—What advantage then hath the Jew: or what profit is there of circumcision? Much every way: chiefly, because that unto them were committed the oracles of God. (Pr.)

Paul's leading object in the whole of this epistle is to show that a sinner's justification with God is by faith in Jesus, in opposition to the works of the law. The Jews were for trusting in circumcision as the ground of acceptance; and the apostle admits, that if they had not sinned, circumcision as well as other acts of obedience might be pleaded; but that *having* sinned, their circumcision was nothing, and there was no justification with God on that ground: chap. ii. 25—29.

The words of the text are then introduced as containing an objection; to which the proper answer is given—

I. Consider the character here ascribed to the Holy Scriptures: they are "the Oracles of God."

1. Observe, an Oracle is the speech or *answer of a deity*, or of some supposed deity; as a temple is the residence of a deity, either real or imaginary. — — The heathens had their oracles, which they consulted on every occasion, though they were altogether a delusion, and a mere piece of priestcraft. — — But though all these were counterfeits, yet there were true oracles; and these are the Word of the true and living God.

The holy Scriptures are called oracles in other passages, as well as in this. In Acts vii. 38, they are denominated "the lively oracles." They are not an old dead history about persons and things long ago, but are what concern the living at this day. They are not like the dead languages, but are themselves a living language, in which every man hears in his own tongue the wonderful works of God.

God's precepts are the same now, as when they were delivered at Sinai. They are not grown obsolete, but are still in force, and are spoken to us as well as to them. Deut. v. 3. — — His threatnings are the same now as then, and God means the same by them as he ever did, and they are all equally in force. — — The promises are all the same: it is God that still invites us, saying, 'Come ye to the waters:' and the invitations are equally addressed to us as to those of old.

2. The Scriptures are called oracles as containing *the first principles* of religion: thus in Heb. v. 12. — — They contain indeed a fund of wisdom and knowledge, as well as first principles, and are therefore to be regarded as the standard of truth. Hence if any one speak or teach, let him do it as the oracles of God speak, and be careful that his doctrine corresponds with that rule. 1 Pet. iv. 11.

3. In some instances the oracles of God are *contrasted with the oracles of the heathen*, as in Isai. xlv. 19. — — The heathen oracles were chiefly distinguished by three things. — — They affected a mysterious concealment: but the oracles of God court examination. — — They disappointed those who trusted in them: but the Lord 'never said to the seed of Jacob seek ye me in vain.' — — They were of an immoral tendency, had no regard to righteousness, but taught and encouraged what was evil, and consulted only the sinful inclinations of the people: but the oracles of God declare 'the things that are right,' without consulting the sinful propensities of men, and whether they would regard it or not.

II. Consider the advantage of possessing the sacred writings; this is "much every way."

It was the distinguishing privilege of the Jews, that unto them were committed the oracles of God; and it is also one of our principle advantages. — — We cannot so well estimate the worth of any thing as by considering the condition of those who are without it; our commonest mercies are all undervalued, because they are common. — — The sun rises every day, and fills the world with light, and we think little of it; but if we were left in darkness for several months, we should then be taught to estimate its value.

Could we but see the state of the heathen world, and compare it with our own; could we but compare their general morals with those of christian countries, we should be more fully aware of the advantages which we enjoy. — — The Scriptures have an effect on men in general, who themselves have no love to righteousness; and they are compelled to act with some degree of decorum and good order. — — David having been driven away among the heathen, by the persecutions of Saul, and obliged to wander in the land of Moab, and among the Philistines, was led from hence to form an idea of the incomparable worth of the holy Scriptures; and then it was, very probably, that he wrote his encomiums in the nineteenth psalm, and also in the cxixth,

Some of the advantages of having the Scriptures will appear, if we consider more particularly the following things—

1. What a flood of light they pour upon that subject *which belongs to our best interests.* —— All men are convinced that they are sinners, for all have a conscience; yet by nature are wholly in the dark, not knowing whither they are going, nor what shall be hereafter. —— Oh the importance of that word, which shineth as a light in a dark place, and shows us the way of life! If heathens ask, what shall we do to be saved; none of their oracles, none of their priests can tell. Neither Greece nor Rome with all their learning, could answer such a question as this. But when the Philippian jailor proposed such a question to Paul and Silas, they could answer and say, Believe on the Lord Jesus Christ, and thou shalt be saved.
There is now no need to ascend into heaven, and descend into the deep: the word is nigh us, and it tells us all things. Rom. x. 6—9.

2. Consider how plain the directions are which the Scriptures give *on the subject of obedience.* The poor heathens are trying to please God, or rather their idols, in a thousand different ways, yet know not how: but the sacred oracles will tell us at once, and in one word, wherein the whole law is contained. —— God does not require such kind of sacrifices as their idols are supposed to do: his words are, 'My son, give me thy heart.' What does he require, but that we love mercy, and walk humbly with him.
The original inhabitants of this island had their wicked idols, like those of Moloch, in which they burned thousands of human beings alive, in honor of their deities.

Whatever use we may make of the oracles of God, and however much they may be abused, they are of the greatest importance in themselves, and it is our chief glory to possess them.

3. They are the principal means which God has used *in the conversion of sinners.* 'The law of the Lord is perfect, converting the soul; sure, making wise the simple.' The *works* of God did not convert men then, any more than they do now, though they declare his glory, and his handy work. Psal. xix.

It is by the truth that we are saved; the gospel is the power of God unto salvation; and whenever the time come that all shall know the Lord, and be made righteous, and when all the people shall praise him; it shall be by his way being made known upon earth, and his saving health among all nations. Psal. lxvii. 2. —— The history of the mission to India confirms this remark: from the time that they translated and circulated the Scriptures, the Lord began to bless them, and not till then.

III. Application of the subject.

1. If the oracles of God were of so much advantage to the Jews, they are *much more so to us.* We have also the New Testament, which is the accomplishment of the Old: such an addition to the sacred oracles is of infinite importance. —— If David could say so much of the five books of Moses, which were nearly all that was extant in his day; what would he have said of the whole Bible as we possess it in our day!

2. What a motive is presented for attempting to *diffuse the knowledge of the Scriptures all around us.* —— If we wish to see mankind blessed and made happy, let us give to them the words of eternal life

The instruction of the children of the poor is in this view a most desirable object. There are many public charities, and also charity schools, which have their use: but Sunday schools in particular have an object in view which distinguishes them from all the rest—that of giving access to the holy Scriptures. — — They give the key of knowledge, which is one of the chief advantages of true religion.

3. Let us remember that the oracles of God will be of no ultimate advantage to us, unless we are brought *truly to believe* and to embrace them, so as to live under their holy influence. — — Without this, they will only be a swift witness against us in the last day.

ON THE PERFECTION OF THE SCRIPTURES.

Psalms cxix. 96.—But thy commandment is exceeding broad. (H.)

By commandment, the Psalmist here means the whole will, word, and law of God, as it is contained in the Holy Scriptures. And I intend from these words to discourse concerning the fulness, perfection, and sufficiency of that word and law.

I. The perfection of the Holy Scriptures will appear, if we consider them with respect to their author and original.

This word the almighty God has spoken; this law, or this commandment, the infinite Jehovah has made and given. As the child bears the image of the parent, and the wax receives the impression of the seal, so these sacred oracles breathe forth the spirit of their great Author; and do in every page confess the likeness which they have to their Divine original.

The unparalleled excellence of the Divine nature, the glories of the supreme Majesty, are here expressed, as the features of a man's face are visible in the glass wherein he looks.

These scriptures are not of a common birth; "all scripture is given by the inspiration of God; and holy men spake as they were moved by the Holy Ghost."

Now there is, in the word and law of God, a perfection of holiness and purity; of truth and certainty; of righteousness and justice; of wisdom and knowledge; of mercy and goodness; of perpetuity and duration. Ps. xix. 7—9.

II. If we consider the subject matter.

It is said of the authority, excellency, and perfection of our Lord's doctrine, that "never man spake like this man." The gospel contains the words which our Lord spake: of which our Lord gives the truest and fairest description, when he says, "The words which I speak, they are spirit and they are life." There is that spirit of heavenly light, life, and love; there is that Divine virtue, and that exquisite beauty, in these sacred writings, that no other composure can parallel.

Here we have the nature of God discovered, the lines of sovereign power and wisdom drawn in the clearest brightness. Much of God may be read in his creatures; "the invisible things of him." Rom. i. 20.

But the most complete and attractive attributes of God, are nowhere so amply displayed, as in this revelation he has made of himself in his word: from this book do the brightest beams of Divine love break out upon us in the most astonishing manner. The perfection of the scriptures, will appear, if we consider the usefulness of the histories, the certainty of the prophecies, the wisdom of the laws, the sanctity of the morals, the loftiness of the mysteries, the brightness of the examples, the preciousness of the promises on the one hand, and the terror of the judgments on the other.

Here are contained the deep things of God, the unfathomable secrets of infinite wisdom. Here we have discovered to us the adorable mystery of the Trinity, the incarnation of the Son of God, the fall of man, and the corruption of our nature by it, the various windings of Providence, concerning which we have reason to break out with astonishment, "O the depth!"

How important are the discoveries of a future state of inexpressible rewards and punishments, of the solemn and august appearance of the great and last day. How admirable are the rules of life, how strict the precepts of virtue. What a complete treatise of practical religion have we given to us in our Saviour's sermon on the mount. There are such bright images of piety, such refined rules of holy living, such as by far outdo all the former institutions of religion and philosophy. They never taught the duty of loving our enemies, mortifying our anger, abstaining from revenge, the necessity of forgiving injuries. These are some of the peculiar perfections and excellences which belong to the laws of Christ.

III. THE NEXT INSTANCE WHEREIN THE PERFECTION OF THE SCRIPTURES CONSISTS, IS THE MANNER IN WHICH THEY ARE WRITTEN.

In the word of God there is not only a profound treasure of the most excellent matter, but those holy and heavenly truths are also delivered in the most majestic strains of oratory, and with all the ornaments of the most exalted rhetoric. Words are nowhere arranged in a more attractive order, nor do the triumphs of sacred eloquence shine in any author with greater splendour, nor flow with an evener stream. How wonderful and surprising are the descriptions which Job in chaps. xxxvii. xxxviii. and xxxix., gives us of the Divine power and providence! In how fine and poetical a strain are the songs of Moses and Deborah composed! and with how much beauty of style, as well as height of devotion, is the book of the Psalms replenished! How lofty and intricate are some of the prophets! how pathetical and terrible are others! and some, again, how mild and gentle! What refined wisdom, what deep experience, what admirable observations of human policy, have we in the writings of Solomon! What noble characters, and lively images of things, have we dispersed in those instructive pages! How inimitably is the passion of grief set forth in the Lamentations of Jeremiah!

"One would think," says Dr. South, "that every letter was wrote with a tear, every word was the sad accent of a breaking heart; that the penman was a man compacted of sorrows, and disciplined to mourning; that he never breathed but in sighs, nor spoke but in a groan."

How awful and dreadful is the account which Moses gives us of the publication of the law: God descended in fire and smoke, and the people did not only fear, but the hill shook, and the mountain did exceedingly quake and tremble. Nothing can give us a juster idea of omnipotent power, than that expression of Moses, when God says, "Let there be light, and there was light. He spake the word, and it was done; he commanded, and it stood fast."

How exactly, and with how much harmony, have the evangelists written of the life and passion of our Saviour! How strongly do the mysteries of Divine grace and goodness flow in the epistles! What a glorious description have we of the New Jerusalem. Rev. xxi. 23. Indeed, none can describe the excellency and dignity of the whole composition of the New Testament.

IV. THE EXCELLENCY OF THE SCRIPTURES WILL APPEAR, IF WE CONSIDER THE DESIGN FOR WHICH THEY ARE REVEALED.

The intent of their promulgation is glorious. There is no book in the world that is so adapted for the raising our minds, refining our judgments, spiritualizing our affections, and advancing our hearts to the imitation of God.

One great end of this inspired book is, to direct us to the knowledge of God, his being, nature, and attributes. God hath made himself known by his works; but he has done this more perfectly by his word. In the one, he has shown his back-parts, as once he did to Moses; but, in this, he has uncovered his face.

Another end of the Holy Scriptures is to lead us into the knowledge of the providence of God; his various dealings with his church and people in all ages; how he has protected them by his power, corrected them by his judgments, comforted them by his Spirit, ruled them by his laws.

To make us complete and universal in our obedience, that the uprightness which we lost by the fall, may be repaired and restored by the Spirit of grace.

To give us a true and just notion of ourselves, to abate our pride, to show us what we are, and from whom we have received our all.

To give us right thoughts concerning the world, the vanity and uncertainty of every creature.

They do in the best manner direct us to our great end, the glory of God, and the salvation of our souls. In all which particulars, we must say of the law of God,

"Thy commandment is exceeding broad," i. e. it is exceeding perfect, wanting nothing, either to declare the greatness of its Author, or to contribute to the happiness of man.

Observe,

If the scriptures are thus excellent and perfect, in their original composure and design; if we have in them so great and so worthy a rule and direction of life and manners; then from hence it will follow, that we cannot employ our time better than in searching this rule, than in reading and studying the scriptures, which are written for our learning, and which are so exceeding useful and profitable to us in every respect. Let us search, and diligently meditate on these sacred writings; and, since "we have so sure a word of prophecy, we should do well to take heed unto it."

THE WELLS OF SALVATION.

Isaiah xii. 3.—With joy shall ye draw water out of the wells of salvation. (H. H.)

WE wonder not that the Scriptures are read with so little interest by the generality: for, till persons know somewhat of their lost estate, and of the way of salvation provided for them, the Bible is to them a sealed book. But let them once experience a taste of the Redeemer's love, and instantly they will find in the Inspired Volume mines of wealth. Such a storehouse is that blessed book to the godly in this day: and such will it be to the Jewish Church, when once they shall be converted to the faith of Christ. "*In that day* they will say, O Lord, I will praise thee: though thou wast angry with me, thine anger is turned away, and thou comfortedst me." (Such will be the reflections at the time of their first discoveries of God's mercy to them in Christ Jesus. Then they will advance farther to express their full confidence in God.) "Behold, God is my salvation! I will trust, and not be afraid: for the Lord Jehovah is my strength and my song; he also is become my salvation." (Then will they be fully prepared to derive the richest benefit from the Scriptures: and) "*therefore* shall they draw water with joy out of the wells of salvation."

That we may form a just estimate of their privilege, let us consider,

I. THE CHARACTER BY WHICH THE SCRIPTURES ARE HERE DESIGNATED—

The expression, "wells of salvation," is supposed by many to be spoken of Christ: and doubtless it may be very fitly applied to him. But I rather understand it of the Scriptures, from whence, as from an inexhaustible fountain, all true comfort flows. They eminently deserve that name,

1. As containing in themselves all the blessings of salvation—

The whole of salvation as planned in the Divine counsels from all eternity, as executed for us by the Lord Jesus Christ in his incarnate state, as still carrying on by him at the right hand of his Father, and as offered through him to every child of man, is there fully contained. "This mystery of godliness was indeed kept secret since the world began; but now it is made manifest; and by the Scriptures of the Prophets, according to the commandment of the everlasting God, is made known to all nations for the obedience of faith." Rom. xvi. 25, 26.

Now let any one contemplate this mystery, and endeavor to explore the *wisdom*, the *love*, the *mercy*, and the *grace* contained in it: how surpassing all finite comprehension will they be found! Verily, the breadth, and length, and depth, and height of this mystery, and of the wonders contained in it, are utterly unsearchable; and the blessings flowing from it are a plenteous and perennial spring, for the refreshment of all on earth, and of all in heaven.

2. As revealing them for our use—

In the whole world besides, there is not to be found one drop of water to satisfy a thirsty soul. Where can one look that is oppressed with a sense of guilt? Where, one who is mourning over the corruptions of his nature? Go to those who have not the Scriptures: go to even the wisest philosophers of Greece and Rome; and see how vain were all their expedients for pacifying a guilty soul, or purifying a polluted soul. But in the Scriptures we find all that a sinner can desire; an atonement, sufficient for the sins of the whole world; and an Almighty Agent ready to dwell in the heart of all who seek him, and engaged to transform into the Divine image all who commit their souls to him. In them are promises suited to every condition incident to our fallen nature; as suited to refresh the soul, as water is to allay our thirst. Conceive of every want with which a sinner can be oppressed, and the appropriate relief will there be found.

3. As actually imparting them to our souls—

As a spring pours forth its waters, so do the Scriptures impart life, and peace, and strength to all who go to them as God's appointed channel of communication to their souls. They have within themselves a life-giving virtue; John iv. 10; so that, when brought home and applied by the Spirit of God, they quicken the dead, and give a vital energy to all our powers

They are able, not only to "make men wise unto salvation," but to impart salvation itself; being "like fire" to consume dross, Jer. xxiii. 29, and "a hammer to break the rock in pieces," ib., and "a two-edged sword to pierce the very inmost soul," Heb. iv. 12, and "a weapon to destroy every enemy." 2 Cor. x. 4, 5. They have a power to enlighten the darkest mind, Ps. xix. 7, 8, and to sanctify all on whom they operate aright; John xv. 3, and xvii. 19; and so to sanctify them, as to prepare them for the perfect fruition of their God. Eph. v. 26, 27.

Think then of,

II. The blessedness of having access to them—

Truly we should never contemplate them but with joy, on account of,

1. The freeness with which we may approach them—

There is no prohibition to any creature under heaven. About wells that have been dug for a supply of common water, there have been the fiercest contentions: Gen. xxvi. 18—21; but these are public property, and equally accessible to all: none have to "pay for this water," as Israel had: Numb. xx. 19; it is to be had "without money and without price." Isaiah lv. 1. True indeed it is that there are many, Protestants as well as Papists, who would bar our access to them: but God has given to all an equal right to come to them: for his invitation is, "Let him that is athirst come; and whosoever will, let him come and take of the water of life freely." Rev. xxii. 17.

2. The ease with which we may draw from them—

There are those who think it in vain for the poor to come to them, seeing that "the wells are deep, and they have nothing to draw with." John iv. 11. But be it known, that however valuable learning may be for the attaining a *critical* acquaintance with the holy Scriptures, it is not at all necessary for a *spiritual* perception of their truths. It is faith, and not learning, that is wanting for *that* end. All the learning in the universe will not impart to us a spiritual discernment, any more than it will furnish us with any corporeal organs. It is faith alone that will avail us here. That discerns the things which are not visible to mortal eyes; and will go to the very bottom of these wells, and draw from thence the most refreshing consolations.

3. The abundance that we may receive out of them—

When the rock was struck by Moses, the waters gushed out in such abundance, that the whole camp of Israel, with all their cattle, could drink thereof. And, if all the sinners in the universe will go to these wells, they shall find no lack for the supply of their most enlarged necessities. Our Lord says, "If any man thirst, let him come unto me and drink; and out of his belly shall flow rivers of living water." John vii. 37, 38. Indeed, the more intense and ardent your thirst is, the more abundant shall be the blessings which you shall derive from them.

4. The perfect satisfaction that we may find in them—

"Whoever drinks of other waters will thirst again: but whoever drinks of these wells, will never thirst: for the water which he has received will be in him as a well of water springing up into everlasting life." John iv. 13, 14; Isai. xlix. 9, 10. I may appeal to all, whether the most copious draughts of carnal pleasure are ever satisfied? Solomon, who drank as deep of it as a human being could do, pronounced it all to be vanity and vexation of spirit. "The eye was never yet satisfied with seeing, nor the ear with hearing." But he who has obtained the knowledge of Christ, and drunk deep of the promises of the Gospel, has no longer any relish for earthly vanities, nor any desire after them. Give him all the world, and he feels empty: give him the presence of God, and he desires no more.

ADDRESS,

1. Those who are going to broken cisterns—

What is the creature but "a broken cistern that can hold no water?" ———And will you for this forsake "the fountain of living waters?" Jer. ii. 13. Let me prevail on every one of you to go to God as your reconciled God in Christ Jesus, and to say with David, "All my fresh springs are in thee." Ps. lxxxvii. 7.

2. Those who are drinking from "the fountain of life"—Ps. xxxvi. 9.

Say whether you have not "a joy with which the stranger intermeddleth not?" Say whether the fountains do not richly supply you; and whether, even on the highest places, which, according to human apprehension, are inaccessible to rivers, the rivers do not follow you? Isai. xli. 17, 18. Yes, till you arrive at heaven itself, the streams shall never fail; and even there shall they run beside you for your comfort to eternal ages. Rev. vii. 17.

THE SPREAD OF THE GOSPEL.

2 Thess. iii. 1. Finally, Brethren, pray for us, that the word of the Lord may have free course and be glorified, even as it is with you. (H. H.)

THE light of the material sun is hailed and welcomed by every nation under heaven: but how much more is the light of the Sun of Righteousness to be desired! If the one be necessary for our comfort in this life, the other is necessary to guide us in the way to life eternal. Hence the Apostle not only labored to spread the Gospel himself, but endeavored to interest all the Lord's people in its behalf; that by their united supplications they might obtain from God whatever should conduce to its establishment in the world.

In this request of his we see,

I. WHAT WE SHOULD DESIRE FOR THE WORD OF GOD—

1. That it should "have free course"—

It is surprising that any should be averse to the circulation of the Scriptures; or should be jealous of the Scriptures, unless accompanied with human compositions to forestall and determine the judgment of the reader. What is this but to determine the judgment of the reader? What is this, but to return to Popery? The Papists locked up the Scriptures in an unknown tongue, and forbade the laity to read them; and sent forth among the people small portions of them only, and counteracted those portions by the most erroneous comments and grossest superstitions. Far be such conduct from Protestants: freely have we received, and freely we should give: nor should we relax our efforts to disseminate the Scriptures, till every human being shall have them in his possession, and be enabled to read in his own native language the wonderful works of God. See Ps. xix. 4, and Rom. x. 18.

II. THAT IT SHOULD "BE GLORIFIED"—

What is implied in this expression, we are at no loss to determine. We have only to see how it was glorified "*with them*," i. e. the Thessalonian converts, and we have the perfect model of its being glorified amongst ourselves.

In two ways is the word of God glorified; first, *in the conversion of sinners;* and, next, *in the edification and salvation of saints.*

How the Gospel wrought to *the conversion* of the Thessalonians, we are distinctly informed; They received it, "not as the word of man, but as the word of God:" it "came to *them*, not in word only, but in power;" and by it "they were turned from idols to serve the living God" 1 Thess. i. 5, 9, and ii. 13. ——— Similar effects were produced by it in other Churches. Acts vi. 7, and xix. 20. ——— And who must not confess that the word is glorified when such wonders are wrought by it? ——— But that it is so, is expressly affirmed by the voice of inspiration itself. Acts xiii. 48, 49.

Nor was the Gospel less powerful for their continued *edification.* This was greatly advanced among them, as the Apostle himself bore witness, 2 Thess. i. 3, 4, and ii. 13, 14. ——— Yet nothing but the pure word of God was, or could be, effectual for this end. 1 Pet. ii. 2. As the rod of Moses wrought all those miracles in Egypt and the wilderness, so was the Gospel "the rod of God's strength:" and in the production of such miraculous events, both the word itself, and God in it, were greatly glorified: Acts xxi. 19, 20, nor is it possible to see such effects yet produced in the hearts and lives of men, without acknowledging, that "he who hath wrought them to the self-same thing is God." 2 Cor. v. 5. ———

Let us next inquire—

III. How THAT DESIRE IS TO BE OBTAINED—

The Apostle speaks of himself and all his fellow-laborers, as instruments whereby the Gospel was propagated throughout the world. And the same is true of ministers in all succeeding ages, even to the present day: they are God's Ambassadors to a rebellious world. But the prayers of God's people are no less necessary than the efforts of his ministers: for it is God alone that can give effect to any exertions; and it is prayer alone that can interest him in our behalf—

It is God alone that can raise up ministers, or fit them for the work. Rom. x. 15, and 2 Cor. ii. 15, 16, and iii. 5. ——— Hence we are directed to "pray that *God would send forth* laborers into his harvest." Matt. ix. 38, Eph. iv. 12, 13.

It is God alone that can open places for them to labor in. Men universally of themselves reject the Gospel: but when God opens a door for his servants, no attempts of his enemies can shut it. Acts xviii. 10, 11; 1 Cor. xvi. 9, and Rev. iii. 8.———

It is God alone that can give success to their endeavors. That same divine power, which first opened the understandings of the Apostles, must open the hearts of others to attend to them. Luke xxiv. 45, with Acts xvi. 14 ——— And then only does the word effect any radical change in men, when it comes "in demonstration of the Spirit and of power." 1 Cor. ii. 4, 5, and iii. 5—7.

Hence St. Paul so earnestly intreated the prayers of the Thessalonian Church, and yet more earnestly the intercessions of the saints at Rome. Rom. xv. 30—32. God has in mercy made his servants and his people mutually dependent on each other: the people being quickened by the exertions of their ministers; and ministers being strengthened by the prayers of their people: and thus the builders and the building are advanced together, and all are edified in love.

We conclude this subject with,

1. A WORD OF ADMONITION.

Many who profess a reverence for the Bible, and even display a zeal for conveying the holy Scriptures to Heathen lands, who yet make but little use of it for themselves. But this zeal for the good of others will never be admitted as a substitute for personal religion——— Many of the religious world also, who study the Bible and profess to love the Gospel of Christ, are far from adorning that Gospel by holy tempers, and by heavenly lives ——— Let such persons look well to themselves; for "not he that saith Lord, Lord, shall enter into the kingdom of heaven; but he that doeth the will of our Father which is in heaven" ———

2. A WORD OF ENCOURAGEMENT—

Let any one see what was effected in the days of old by a few poor fishermen; and take courage to exert himself for God——— The same power that wrought effectually in that day will concur with us ——— Let us not then despond, as though our weakness were any obstacle to success; for God will display his own power by means of it, 2 Cor. xii. 9, and "ordain strength in the mouths of babes and sucklings." Whether therefore we address ourselves to the translation of the Scriptures into foreign languages, or labor for the circulation of them at home, let us only implore help from God, and we shall not be permitted to "labor in vain, or run in vain."

CHAPTER II.

THE TRINITY.

THE DOCTRINE OF THE TRINITY VINDICATED.

1 John v. 7.—There are three that bear record in heaven, the Father, the Word, and the Holy Ghost; and these three are one.* (H. H.)

Never was there any record so well attested, so worthy of acceptation, so necessary to be believed, as that which God has given of his Son. Upon the receiving or rejecting of it depends the eternal welfare of all mankind. The riches of wisdom, and love, and mercy that are contained in it, surpass all the comprehension of men or angels. With respect to the truth of it, every species of testimony that could be given to it by friends or enemies, by angels from heaven, by men on earth, yea even by devils themselves, has been given in the most abundant degree. But it has been confirmed by other testimony still, even by the Three Persons in the adorable Trinity.

From the words before us, we shall be led to shew,

I. WHO THEY ARE THAT ARE SAID TO "BEAR RECORD"—

We need not wonder at the zeal which has been shewn by the adversaries of the doctrine in our text, to discredit the authenticity of the text itself; since, if the genuineness of the text be admitted, that alone will put an end to all controversy on the subject of the Trinity. On the other hand, we need

* Any one who should preach on this subject can use his own discretion about the mode of introducing it. If he be perfectly assured that the words are an interpolation, he can state his views of that matter, and adopt the text, in order to shew, that, *though the words themselves are not authentic, the truths contained in them are truly scriptural, and important*: or he can take ver. 9 for his text.

not be anxious about the validity of this individual passage, as though the doctrine of the Trinity rested upon it; since, if the text were expunged from the Bible, there are a multitude of others which maintain most unequivocally the same important truth.

To establish the mysterious doctrine of a Trinity in Unity, we shall lay down, and substantiate, three positions:

1. There is but one God—

The unity of God may be deduced even from reason itself: but it is repeatedly affirmed in Scripture; compare Deut. vi. 4, with Mark xii. 29; nor must a doubt of it ever be suffered to enter into our minds. It is true, that in a subordinate sense there are gods many, and lords many; because angels, and magistrates, and the idols of heathens, are sometimes called by these names on account of the resemblance they bear to God in the authority vested in them, and the respect paid to them: but there is One Supreme Being, who alone is self-existent, and from whom all other beings, whether in heaven or earth, derive their existence. He, and he only, is God. 1 Cor. viii. 5, 6.

2. Though there is only one God, yet there are three distinct Persons in the Godhead—

In reference to this subject, we use the term *persons*, because there is no other so suitable: but we mean not that these persons are *in all respects* as distinct from each other as Peter, James, and John; but only that *in some respects* they are distinguished from each other, though they subsist together in one undivided essence.

It is certain that *there are three persons mentioned in the Scripture:* for baptism is ordered to be administered, not in the name of God merely, but in the name of "the Father, of the Son, and of the Holy Ghost." Matt. xxviii. 19. *These three are represented as distinct from each other;* for the Son has told us, that "he will send the Holy Spirit from the Father." John xv. 26. *They are moreover spoken of as performing separate offices in the work of redemption;* the Father elects; Eph. i. 4; the Son redeems; Eph. i. 7; the Spirit sanctifies; Rom. xv. 16; and St. Peter, comprising in few words the whole mystery of redemption, ascribes to each of these persons his proper office. 1 Pet. i. 2. *They are also declared to be sources of distinct blessings to the Church;* the Apostle prays, that "the grace of the Lord Jesus Christ, the love of God the Father, and the fellowship of the Holy Ghost, may be with us all. 2 Cor. xiii. 14.

3. Each of these persons is God without any difference or inequality—

We shall not occupy any time with proving the Godhead of the Father; but, taking that for granted, shall establish the Godhead of the Son and of the Holy Ghost.

To each of these belong the same *names* as unto the Father. Is the Father *God?* so is the Word, John i. 1, (as Christ is called in the text.) He is "Emmanuel, God with us," Matt. i. 23; God manifest in the flesh, 1 Tim. iii. 16; the mighty God, Isai. ix. 6; God over all, blessed for evermore. Rom. ix. 5. To Him is also given the incommunicable name, *Jehovah;* for we are to call him, "Jehovah our Righteousness." Jer. xxiii. 6. To the Holy Spirit also these names belong. Ananias, in lying unto the Holy Ghost, lied unto God. Acts v. 3, 4. And we, in being the temples of the Holy Ghost, are the temples of God. 1 Cor. iii. 16. The words also which were confessedly spoken by Jehovah to the prophet Isaiah, Isai. vi. 9, 10; are quoted by St. Paul as spoken by the Holy Ghost. Acts xxviii. 25.

To each of these the same *attributes* also are ascribed as characterize the Father. Is the Father *eternal*, *omnipresent*, *omniscient*, *almighty?* So is the Son (Mic. v. 2, and Heb. xiii. 8.—Matt. xviii. 20, and xxviii. 20.—John ii. 25, and xxi. 17.—John i. 3, and Matt. xxviii. 18.)— — — and so is the Holy Ghost (Heb. ix. 14.—Ps. cxxxix. 7, 8.—1 Cor. ii. 10.—Gen. i. 2, and Job xxvi. 13,)— — —

What now is the conclusion to be drawn from these premises, but that which is asserted in the text, that "there are THREE that bear record in heaven; and that those Three are ONE* ?"

Having shewn that by the Three witnesses we are to understand the Tri-une God, we proceed to shew,

II. WHAT THAT IS CONCERNING WHICH THEY BEAR RECORD—

We may well expect that the importance of the matter to which these Divine witnesses have borne record, is suited to the majesty of the witnesses themselves. Accordingly we find, that

Their testimony relates to the salvation that is in Christ Jesus—

God, who had passed by the angels that fell, has looked in mercy upon fallen man, and has given us eternal life, in and through his Son Jesus Christ. Ver. 11. He sent his dear Son to die in our stead, and, by his own obedience unto death, to work out a righteousness whereby we might be saved. The merit whereby we are to be justified, and the grace whereby we are to be renewed, he treasured up for us in Christ; and he calls all men to receive these blessings out of his fulness. This way of salvation is open for all, and sufficient for all: but, this rejected, no other remains for us.

This is the sum and substance of the Gospel; and this it is to which the sacred Three bear record.

Nor is their testimony at all more than the subject requires—

If God himself had not revealed such things, *who could ever have imagined them?* who could ever have thought of God becoming incarnate, and, by his own death, expiating the guilt of his own creatures? Who could ever have devised a plan so calculated to exalt the perfections of God; so suited to answer the necessities of man; and so efficacious to renew us after the Divine image? — — — Besides, supposing these things to have been reported, *who would ever have believed them*, if they had not been thus Divinely attested? Notwithstanding the testimonies given by the Sacred Three, there is yet reason to adopt that reiterated complaint, "Who hath believed our report?" Isai. liii. 1; John xii. 38; Rom. x. 16. Professions of faith indeed abound amongst us; but a true Believer, whose feelings and conduct accord with his professions, is "a sign and a wonder" in Christendom itself. Isai. viii. 18.

It remains yet to be declared,

III. IN WHAT MANNER THEY BEAR RECORD—

Each of these divine persons has borne record at divers times, and in different manners—

The Father thrice bore witness to Christ by an audible voice from heaven; declaring at the same time his acquiescence in him as the Saviour of men; and requiring us at the peril of our souls to "hear" and receive him in that

*Hence we see how properly we are taught to express our belief of this doctrine in the Athanasian Creed: "We worship one God in Trinity, and Trinity in Unity; neither confounding the persons, nor dividing the substance; for there is one person of the Father, another of the Son, and another of the Holy Ghost: but the Godhead of the Father, of the Son, and of the Holy Ghost is all one, the glory equal, the majesty co-eternal . . So that in all things the Unity in Trinity, and Trinity in Unity, is to be worshipped."

character. Matt. iii. 17, and xvii. 5, and John xii. 28. Moreover, in raising Christ from the dead, he yet more emphatically testified, that he had discharged the debt for which he had been imprisoned in the grave, and was "able to save to the uttermost all that should come unto God through him." Rom. i. 4.

The Lord Jesus Christ continually bore witness to himself. When asked, "If thou be the Christ, tell us plainly;" he answered, "I have told you, and ye believe me not." John x. 24, 25. "Before Pontius Pilate he witnessed the same good confession," 1 Tim. vi. 13; though he knew that it would issue in his death. After his resurrection, he called himself "the true and faithful witness," and testified, " am he that was dead and am alive again, and have the keys of death and of hell." Rev. i. 18, and iii. 14.

The Holy Spirit also bore witness to him, when he descended in a bodily shape, like a dove, upon him: And again, when he came down in the likeness of fiery tongues upon the Apostles, and converted three thousand to the faith of Christ. Similar testimonies he still continued to give; Acts x. 44, 45; and at this very day, when any are converted to the faith, it is owing to the testimony which the Holy Spirit bears to Christ; "the Spirit testifies of him," and thereby produces conviction or consolation in the soul. John xv. 26, and xvi. 7—11.

Thus the Sacred Three bear record in heaven, and by their united testimony encourage our acceptance of the salvation offered us in the gospel.

INFER,

1. How unreasonable and dangerous is unbelief!

If only men, who are credible and competent witnesses, attest a thing, we think it right to believe them. What an insult then is it to the Sacred Three to doubt their testimony! Yet this, alas! is the treatment which their record meets with in the world. Some reject it as "a cunningly-devised fable;" while others, professing a regard to it in general, deny the most important part of it, the necessity of being saved by Christ alone. Even those who in their hearts approve the gospel, are too apt to doubt the freeness and sufficiency of the salvation revealed in it. Let every one consider the extreme sinfulness of such conduct, and abhor the thought of "making God a liar,' ver. 9, 10.

2. What obligation lies upon believers to bear an open testimony to the truth!

It is evident how earnestly God desires that his dear Son should be known, and that the salvation wrought out by him should be embraced. Now believers are his witnesses in the midst of a blind deluded world. Ought they then to be ashamed or afraid to bear their testimony for God? What if the world agree to call the gospel a delusion, and to consider all as hypocrites or fanatics who embrace it? Should that deter us from making a public profession of his truth? Should we not rather be the bolder in confessing Christ, in proportion as others are bold in denying him?

But let us not confine our profession to creeds and forms: the best, and most acceptable way of declaring our affiance in Christ, is by manifesting to the world its efficacy on our hearts and lives. *This* will make them think that there is a reality in the gospel; and may contribute to win many who never would obey the written word.

3. How exalted must be the glory which believers still enjoy in heaven!

It cannot be conceived that the Three Persons of the Godhead would have devised and executed such a wonderful plan of salvation, if the end to be accomplished by it were not exceeding glorious. Surely all that the love of the Father can devise, all that the blood of Christ can purchase, all that the Holy Spirit can impart, is prepared for us in the eternal world, and shall be bestowed on us according to our measure and capacity to receive it. Yes, in heaven we shall see God as he is, and have the brightest discoveries of his glory: and, while we have the richest enjoyment of his presence and love, we ourselves shall be witnesses for him, how far his mercy could reach, what astonishing changes it could effect, and what blessedness it can bestow on the most unworthy of mankind.

CHAPTER III.

GOD.

THE SELF-EXISTENCE AND IMMUTABILITY OF GOD.

Exod. iii. 14.—And God said unto Moses, I AM THAT I AM: and He said, Thus shalt thou say unto the children of Israel, I AM hath sent me unto you. (H. H.)

It is of great importance that ministers should be considered as ambassadors of God—

And that they should deliver nothing which they cannot enforce with, Thus saith the Lord—

Without this, their word can have but little weight—

But ministrations thus supported will produce the happiest effects—

Moses was commissioned to offer deliverance to the oppressed Israelites—

But he rightly judged that they would ask, From whence he had his authority—

He therefore inquired of God, What answer he should return—

And received from God the direction recorded in the text—

To understand the words aright, we must consider,

I. The title God assumed—

The Deity had hitherto revealed himself to man by the name of God Almighty—

Though he had been called Jehovah, he was not fully known by that name, even to his most highly-favored servants—Exod. vi. 3.

He now was pleased to assume a title similar to that; but, if possible, of still plainer import—

The name, I AM THAT I AM, represents him to be

Self-existent—

Creatures have only a derived, and therefore a dependent, existence—

They are now what they once were not, and may again cease to be—

But God from all eternity was precisely what he now is—

To him therefore this august title may be properly applied—

Nor are there wanting other similar descriptions of him to confirm it—Ps. cii. 27; Rev. i. 4.

Immutable—

Every creature in earth and heaven is liable to change—

But "with God there is no variableness, neither shadow of turning"—

He himself claims immutability as his own peculiar prerogative—Mal. iii. 6.

And in this view, the title assumed in the text must ever belong to him—
Incomprehensible—
No words can convey, or imagination conceive, an adequate idea of God—Job. xi. 7; 1 Tim. vi. 16.
Hence God does not endeavor to explain his nature to Moses—
But, by declaring himself to be what he is, intimates, that he is what can neither be comprehended nor expressed—
His answer, in effect, was similar to that which he afterwards gave to Manoah—Judg. xiii. 17, 18.
The title thus explained, it will be proper to consider,
II. For what end he assumed it—
The Israelites were extremely debased by means of their long bondage—
It was necessary therefore to prepare their minds for the intended deliverance—
Though they groaned under their oppression, they were too much reconciled to their yoke—
They rather affected a mitigation of trouble, than the attainment of liberty—
Though the promises made to their fathers were not wholly forgotten, the accomplishment of them was not cordially desired—
Indeed, they scarcely conceived it possible that their emancipation should be effected—
Hence it was necessary to stimulate their desires, renew their hopes, and confirm their expectations, of a better country—
The title which God assumed was admirably adapted to this end—
If God was so incomprehensible a Being, he could easily devise means of executing his own sovereign will and pleasure—
If he was the one self-existent, independent Creator of the universe, all creatures must be wholly subject to his controul—
And if he were absolutely immutable, he could not recede from the covenant entered into with their fathers—
He therefore could not want either inclination or power to deliver them—
Yea, He could not but deliver them for his own great name's sake—
He could not be I AM, if his promised interposition should be either withheld or defeated—
Thus the declaration of his name must inspire them with confidence—
And induce them willingly to put themselves under the direction of Moses—
Infer,
1. What a solemn attention does the Gospel demand!—
The Gospel is a message of mercy to those who are in bondage to sin—
And they who preach it are ambassadors from the great I AM—
Jesus, who sends them forth, assumes to himself this very title—John viii. 58.
To the same effect also his character is drawn in the Epistle to the Hebrews—Heb. xiii. 8.
He has commissioned his servants to go forth into all the world—Mark xvi. 15.
And promised (as God did to Moses) to be always with them—Matt. xxviii. 20.
Shall we then make light of the mercy which He offers to us? —
Or doubt his power and willingness to fulfil his promises?—
Shall we thrust away his servants, saying, Why dost thou interfere with us?—Acts vii. 27.
Let us remember Who it is that speaks to us in the Gospel—Luke x. 16

Every faithful minister may say, I AM hath sent me unto you—
Nor, though miracles have ceased, shall signs be wanting to confirm the word—
The deaf shall hear, the blind see, the lame walk, the lepers be cleansed—
And blessed is he whosoever shall not be offended at the Redeemer's voice—Matt. xi. 5 6.
2. What encouragement is here afforded to those who are groaning under spiritual bondage!
God brought out his people safely, notwithstanding all their difficulties—
And in due time put them into possession of the promised land—
Shall the spiritual redemption offered by him be less effectual?—
Are not his power and faithfulness the same as in former ages?—Isa. lix. 1.
Will he not remove our obstacles, supply our wants, and destroy our enemies?—
Surely there are none so weak but they shall be made to triumph—Isaiah xlix. 24, 25.
Nor shall the Prince of Darkness oppose with more success than Pharaoh—Rom. xvi. 20.
Behold then, I AM hath sent me to proclaim these glad tidings—
Let all arise, and cast off their yoke, and burst their bands asunder—
Let not unbelief represent the obstacles as insurmountable—
Nor fear induce you to comply with the imperious dictates of the world*—
Behold! the Pillar and the Cloud are ready to conduct your path—
The great I AM is for you: who then can be against you?—
Go forth; and universal nature shall applaud your steps—Isa. lv. 12.

*Pharoah, after many successive plagues, agreed first that they should sacrifice to God *in the land, but not in the wilderness;* then that they should go *into the wilderness, but not far:* then that *the men* should go, but *without the women or children;* then that *the women and children, but not the flocks.* Exod. viii. 25, 28, and x. 11, 24. Thus the world would prescribe limits to the service we shall pay to God.

ON THE ETERNITY OF GOD.

Psalm xc. ii.—Before the mountains were brought forth, or ever thou hadst formed the earth, and the world; even from everlasting to everlasting, thou art God. (H.)

The title of this psalm is a prayer, the author Moses. There are two parts in this psalm; a complaint of the frailty of man's life in general, verses 3—6; and then a particular complaint of the condition of the church, verses 8—10; a prayer, verse 12. But, before he speaks of the shortness of human life, he fortifies them by the consideration of the refuge they had, and should find in God; verse 1, "Lord, thou hast been our dwelling-place." God is a perpetual refuge, and security to his people. His providence is not confined to one generation; it is not one age only that tastes his bounty and compassion. His providence is not wearied, nor his care fainting; he never wanted will to relieve us, for he hath been our refuge; nor ever can want power to support us, for he is a God from everlasting to everlasting. The church never wanted a pilot to steer her, and a rock to shelter her, and dash in pieces the waves which threaten her. How worthy is it to remember former benefits, when we come to beg for new. Never were the records of

God's mercies so exactly revised, as when his people have stood in need of new editions of his power; and though so much strength hath been upon various occasions manifested, yet his arm is not weakened: for, "from everlasting to everlasting, thou art God." God is of an eternal duration. The eternity of God is the foundation of the stability of the covenant, the great comfort of a christian.

I. How God is eternal, or in what respects he is so.

Eternity is a negative attribute, and is a denying of God any measure of time, as immensity is a denying of him any bounds of place; as immensity is the diffusion of his essence, so eternity is the duration of his essence.

1. God is without beginning. "In the beginning God created the world." God was then before the beginning of it; and what point can be set wherein God began, if he were before the beginning of created things! God was without beginning, though all other things had time and beginning from him. Gen. i. 1. Whatsoever number of millions of millions of years we can imagine before the creation of the world, yet God was infinitely before those; he is therefore called the Ancient of Days. Dan. vii. 9.

2. God is without end. He always was, always is, and always will be what he is; he remains always the same in being; so far from any change, that no shadow of it can touch him. James i. 17. "The Lord shall endure for ever." As it is impossible he should not be, being from all eternity; so it is impossible that he should not be to all eternity. He is said to live for ever. "The earth shall perish, but God shall endure for ever, and his years shall have no end." Ps. cii. 27. That which had no beginning of duration can never have an end, nor any interruptions in it. Since God never depended upon any, what should make him cease to be what eternally he hath been, or put a stop to the continuance of his perfections.

3. There is no succession in God. God is without succession or change; it is a part of eternity. "From everlasting to everlasting, he is God," *i. e.* the same. God doth not only always remain in being, but he always remains the same in that being. "Thou art the same." The creatures are in a perpetual flux; something is acquired, or something lost, every day. A man is the same in regard of existence, when he is a man, as he was when he was a child; but there is a new succession of quantities and qualities in him. Of a creature it may be said, he was, or he is, or he shall be; of God it cannot be said, but only he is; he is what he always was, and he is what he always will be.

There is no succession in the knowledge of God. The variety of successions and changes in the world make no succession or new objects in the divine mind; for all things are present to him from eternity. "Known unto God are all things from the beginning."

There is no succession in the decrees of God. He doth not decree this now, which he decreed not before. "He chose us in him before the foundation of the world, that we should be holy." Eph. i. 4.

4. God is his own eternity. He is not eternal by grant, and the disposal of any other, but by nature and essence. The eternity of God is nothing else but the duration of God; and the duration of God is nothing else but his existence enduring.

5. Hence all the perfections of God are eternal. In regard of the Divine eternity, all things in God are eternal; his power, mercy, wisdom, justice, knowledge.

II. God is eternal, and must needs be so.

The Spirit of God, in scripture, condescends to our capacities, in signify ing the eternity of God by days and years; but we must not conceive that God is bounded or measured by time. Ps. cii. 27. Though years are ascribed to him, yet they are such as cannot be numbered. "The number of his years cannot be searched out." Job xxxvi. 26, 27. Sometimes this eternity is expressed by parts, as looking backward and forward; by the difference of time, past, present, and to come; "which was, and is, and is to come." Rev. i. 8; and iv. 8. He always was, is now, and always will be.

1. His eternity is evident, by the name God gives himself. "And God said unto Moses, I AM THAT I AM; I AM hath sent me unto you." Ex. iii. 14. God only can be called "I AM;" all creatures have more of not being than being. If God, therefore, be properly "I AM," *i. e.* being, it follows, that he always was.

2. God hath life in himself. John v. 26. "The Father hath life in himself." He is the living God, therefore steadfast for ever. Dan. vi. 26. He hath life by his essence, not by participation; he is a sun, to give light and life to all creatures, but receives not light nor life from any thing; and therefore he hath an unlimited life: not a drop of life, but a fountain; not a spark of a limited life, but a life transcending all bounds: he hath life in himself: all creatures have their life in him, and from him. Since he hath life in himself, and there was no cause of his existence, he can have no cause of his limitation; and can no more be determined to a time, than he can to a place. What hath life in itself, hath life without bounds, and can never desert it, nor be deprived of it: so that he lives necessarily; all other things "live, and move, and have their being in him." Acts xvii. 28.

3. If God were not eternal, he were not immutable in his nature. It is contrary to the nature of immutability to be without eternity; for whatsoever begins is changed in its passing from not being to being. Mal. iii. 6. "I am the Lord, I change not." Job xxxvii. 23. "Touching the Almighty, we cannot find him out." God is a sun, glittering always in the same glory.

4. God could not be an infinitely perfect being, if he were not eternal. A finite duration is inconsistent with infinite perfection. God hath an unsearch able perfection. Job xi. 7. "Canst thou by searching find out God?" He cannot be found out; he is infinite, because he is incomprehensible. "He is blessed from everlasting to everlasting." Ps. xli. 13. Had he a beginning, he could not have all perfection without limitation; he would have been limited by that which gave him beginning.

5. God could not be omnipotent, almighty, if he were not eternal. The title of Almighty agrees not with a nature that had a beginning; whosoever hath a beginning, was once nothing; and when it was nothing, could act nothing. The almightiness and eternity of God are linked together: "I am Alpha and Omega, the beginning and ending, which was, and which is, and which is to come, the Almighty."

6. God would not be the first cause of all, if he were not eternal. But he is the first, and the last; the first cause of all things, the last end of all things. Rev. i. 8. This power cannot but be eternal; it must be before the world; the founder must be before the foundation; and his existence must be from eternity, or we must say nothing did exist from eternity. Nothing hath no faculties: so that it is necessary to grant some eternal being, or run into inextricable labyrinths and mazes. So then, if God were the cause of all things, he did exist before all things, and that from eternity.

III. Eternity is only proper to God, and not communicable.

It is as great a madness to ascribe eternity to the creature, as to deprive the Lord of the creature of eternity. It is so proper to God, that when the apostle would prove the deity of Christ, he proves it by his immutability and eternity, as well as his creating power. "Thou art the same, and thy years shall not fail." Heb. i. 10—12. Angels and souls have an immortality, but by donation from God, not by their own essence; dependant upon their Creator, not necessary in their own nature. Whatsoever is not God is temporary; whatsoever is eternal is God.

It is a contradiction to say a creature can be eternal; as nothing eternal is created, so nothing created is eternal. Eternity being the essence of God, it would be all one to admit many gods, as many eternals.

1. Creation is a producing something from nothing. What was once nothing, cannot therefore be eternal.

2. There is no creature but is mutable, therefore not eternal. It is as much the essence of a creature to be mutable, as it is the essence of God to be immutable.

3. No creature is infinite, therefore not eternal. To be infinite in duration is all one, as to be infinite in essence. This is the property of the Deity.

4. No effect of an intellectural free agent can be equal in duration to its cause. The producers of natural agents are as ancient often as themselves; the sun produceth a beam as old in time as itself; but who ever heard of a piece of wise workmanship as old as the wise artificer? God only is eternal, the first and the last, the beginning and the end; who, as he subsisted before any creature had a being, so he will eternally subsist, if all creatures were reduced to nothing.

IV. Use.

1. Of information.

1. If God be of an eternal duration, then Christ is God. Eternity is the property of God, but it is ascribed to Christ. "He is before all things," *i. e.* all created things. "All things were created by him." Col. i. 16. He hath no difference of time; for "he is the same yesterday, to-day, and for ever." Micah v. 2. "Whose goings forth have been of old." As the eternity of God is the ground of all religion, so the eternity of Christ is the ground of the christian religion.

2. If God be eternal, he knows all things as present. All things are present to him in his eternity; for this is the notion of eternity, to be without succession. "Known unto God are all his works, from the beginning." Acts xv. 18.

3. How bold and foolish is it for a mortal creature to censure the counsels and actions of an eternal God, or be too curious in his inquisitions? "Who hath enjoined him his way?" Job xxxvi. 23.

4. What a folly and boldness is there in sin, since an eternal God is offended thereby! All sin is aggravated by God's eternity. The blackness of the heathen idolatry was in changing the glory of the incorruptible God. Rom. i. 23.

5. How dreadful is it to lie under the stroke of an eternal God. His eternity is a great terror to him that hates him, as it is a comfort to him that loves him; because he is the living God, and everlasting king. "The nations shall not be able to abide his indignation." Jer. x. 10. He will "whet his glittering sword," and his "hand shall take hold of judgment," and he will "render vengeance to his enemies, and a reward to them that hate him;" a reward proportioned to the greatness of their offences, and the glory of an eternal God. "I lift up my hand to heaven, and say, I live for ever;" *i. e.* as surely as I live for ever, I will whet my glittering sword.

2. Of comfort. What foundation of comfort can we have in any of God's attributes, were it not for his infiniteness and eternity; though he be merciful, good, wise, faithful? What support could there be, if they were perfections belonging to a corruptible God?

1. If God be eternal, his covenant will be so. It is founded upon the eternity of God; the oath whereby he confirms it, is by his life: since there is none greater than himself, he swears by himself.

2. If God be eternal, he being our God in covenant, is an eternal good and possession. "This God is our God for ever and ever; he is a dwelling place in all generations." We shall traverse the world awhile, and then arrive at the blessings Jacob wished for Joseph, the blessings of the ever lasting hills.

3. The enjoyment of God will be as fresh and glorious after many ages, as it was at first. God is eternal, and eternity knows no change.

4. If God be eternal: here is a strong ground of comfort against all the distresses of the church, and the threats of the church's enemies. God's abiding for ever is the plea Jeremiah makes for his return to his forsaken church. The first discovery of the name I AM, which signifies the Divine eternity as well as immutability, was for the comfort of the oppressed Israelites in Egypt. Exodus iii. 14, 15. The church's enemies are not to be feared; they may spring as the grass, but soon after do wither by their own inward principles of decay, or are cut down by the hand of God. Psalm xcii. 7—9. They may threaten, but their breath may vanish, as soon as their threatenings are pronounced. Do the prophets and instructers of the church live for ever? No. Shall then the adversaries and disturbers of the church live for ever! They shall vanish as a shadow. He that inhabits eternity is above them that inhabit mortality, who must, whether they will or no, say to corruption, "Thou art my father, and to the worm, Thou art my mother, and my sister."

5. Hence follows another comfort: since God is eternal, he hath as much power as will to be as good as his word. Trust in the Lord for ever

THE OMNIPRESENCE OF GOD.

Psalm cxxxix. 7.—Whither shall I go from thy Spirit? (H.)

God is here; God is every where; veils of flesh and blood prevent our sight of him; these must fall, and we must open the eyes of our spirits, if we would see a God who is a spirit. Hear our prophet; hear his magnificent description of the immensity and omnipresence of God: "Whither shall I go from thy Spirit? or whither shall I flee from thy presence? If I ascend up into heaven, thou art there." 7—12.

In a text less abundant in riches, we might make some remarks on the terms spirit and presence; but we shall content ourselves at present with indicating what ideas we affix to them, by observing, that by the Spirit and presence of God, we understand God himself. The other expressions in our text, heaven, hell, the wings of the morning, are figurative expressions, denoting the rapidity of the light in communicating itself from one end of the world to the other; these expressions need no comment. The presence of God, the Spirit of God, signify then the Divine essence: and this assemblage of ideas, "whither shall I go from thy Spirit? whither shall I flee from thy presence?" means, that God is immense, and that he is present in every place. But wherein consists this immensity and omnipresence. We will content ourselves with giving you some light into the omnipresence of God:

I. By removing those false ideas, which, at first, seem to present themselves to the imagination.

II. By assigning the true.

I. Let us remove the false ideas.

When we say that God is present in any place, let none suppose we mean, that he is actually contained therein; as if, when we say, that God is in every place, we mean to assign to him a real and proper extension. Neither of these is designed.

1. "God is a Spirit." A spirit cannot be in a place, at least, in the manner in which we conceive of place.

But perhaps God, who is spiritual in one part of his essence, may be corporeal in another. No; for however admirable in man that union may be, and those laws which unite his soul to his body, nothing more fully marks his weakness and dependance, and consequently nothing can less agree with the Divine essence. If God be sometimes represented with feet, with hands, with eyes, these portraits are designed rather to give us emblems of his attributes, than images, properly speaking, of any parts which he possesseth. But there is a very just sense in which it may be said, that the whole universe is the body of the Deity. In effect, as we call this portion of matter our body, which we move, act, and direct, as we please, so God actuates by his will every part of the universe. "He weighs the mountains in scales."

2. But to prove that "God is a Spirit," and that he occupies no place, at least as our imagination conceives, is, in our opinion, to establish the same thesis.

It is difficult to make this consequence intelligible and clear. Yet, I think, whatever difficulty there may be in this system, there is a greater difficulty in the opposite opinion.

II. What notions then must we form of the immensity of God? In what sense do we conceive that the Infinite Spirit is every where present.

The bounds of our knowledge are so strait, our sphere is so contracted, we have such imperfect ideas of spirits, even of our own spirits, and for a much stronger reason of the "Father of spirits," that no genius in the world. however exalted you may suppose him, after his greatest efforts of meditation, can say to you, "Thus far extend the attributes of God; behold a complete idea of his immensity and omnipresence." Yet by the help of sound reason, above all, by the aid of revelation, we may give you, if not complete, at least distinct ideas of the subject. The omnipresence of God is that universal property by which he communicates himself to all, diffuses himself through all, is the great director of all, or, to confine ourselves to more distinct ideas still, the Infinite Spirit is present in every place:—

1. By boundless knowledge. 2. By a general influence. 3. By a universal direction.

1. The first idea of God's omnipresence is his omniscience. God is every where present, because he seeth all. This the prophet had principally in view. "O Lord, thou hast searched me, and known me," &c.

2. God knows all the effects of matter. He calls into being matter, without motion, and, in some sense, without form. He gives this matter

form and motion. He saw that a certain degree of motion, imparted to a certain portion of matter, would produce water; that another degree of motion, communicated to another portion of matter, would produce fire; that another would produce earth; and so of the rest. He foresaw, with the utmost precision, what would result from this water, from this fire, from this earth, when joined together, and agitated by such a degree of motion as he should communicate. By the bare inspection of the laws of motion, he foresaw fires, earthquakes. He foresaw all the vicissitudes of time; he foresaw those which must put a period to time, when "the heavens shall pass away." 2 Peter iii. 10.

3. But, if God could combine all that would result from the laws of motion communicated to matter, he could also combine all that would result from intelligence, freedom of will, and all the faculties which make the essence of spirits; and, before he had formed those spiritual beings which compose the intelligent world, he knew what all their ideas, all their projects, all their deliberations would be. He says, "he searcheth and knoweth them;" he foresaw, he foretold, the afflictions which Abraham's posterity would endure in Canaan; Gen. xv. 13, the infidelity of the Jews, the faith of the Gentiles, the crucifixion of the Messiah. On this article, we are obliged to exclaim, "Such knowledge is too wonderful for me; it is high, I cannot attain unto it." God is every where, because he veils the most impenetrable; darkness the most thick, distance the most immense, can conceal nothing from his knowledge. Soar to the utmost heights, fly to the remotest climates, wrap thyself in the blackest darkness, every where, every where thou wilt be under his eye. "Whither shall I go from thy Spirit?" But,

2. The knowledge of God is not a bare knowledge, his presence is not an idle presence; it is an active knowledge, it is a presence accompanied with action and motion. We said, just now, that God was every where, because he influenced all, as far as influence agrees with his perfections.

When new beings appear, he is there; he influences their productions. He gives to all life, motion, and being. "Thou, even thou, art Lord alone; thou hast made heaven." Neh, ix. 6. "O Lord, I will praise thee, for I am fearfully and wonderfully made. Ps. cxxxix. 14—16.

When beings are preserved, he is there; he influences preservation. "Thou preservest man and beast. When thou openest thy hands they are filled with good. The eyes of all wait upon thee."

When the world is disordered, he is there. He influences wars, pestilence. If nature refuse her productions, it is because he hath "made the heavens as iron, and the earth as brass." It is he who "makes the winds his messengers, and his ministers flames of fire."

When every thing succeeds according to our wisnes, he is there. He influenceth prosperity. "Except the Lord build the bouse, they labour in vain that build it." Ps. cxxvii. 1.

When our understanding is informed, he is there. He influenceth our knowledge. For "in his light we see light. He enlighteneth every man that cometh into the world."

When our heart disposeth us to our duties, be is there. He influenceth our virtues. It is he who "worketh in us, both to will and to do. Who giveth to all that ask liberally."

When grossest errors cover us, he is there. He influenceth errors. It is God who "sends strong delusions. Go, make the heart of this people fat." Isa. vi. 10.

When we live, when we die, he is there. He influenceth life and death. "Man's days are determined, the number of his months are with him. To God the Lord belong the issues of death. He bringeth down to the grave."

He influenceth the least events, as well as the most considerable. "The hairs of our head are numbered;" even "a sparrow cannot fall to the ground without his will." But,

3. When God communicates himself to all, when he thus acts on all, and diffuseth himself through the whole, he connects all with his own designs. God is present with all, because he directs all.

Doth he call creatures into existence? it is to manifest his perfections; it is to have subjects on whom he may shower his favours; it is, as it were, to go out of himself, and to form through the whole universe, a concert resounding the Creator's existence and glory: For the invisible things of God, even his eternal power and godhead, are understood by the things that are made. The heavens declare the glory of God." Ps. xix. 1—3.

Doth he preserve creatures? it is to answer his own designs; the depth of which no finite mind can fathom; but which we shall one day know, and admire his wisdom.

Doth he send plagues, war, famine? it is to make those feel his justice who have abused his goodness.

Doth he afford prosperity? it is to "draw us with the bands of love."

Doth he impart knowledge to us? it is to discover the snares that surround us, the miseries that threaten us, the origin from which we spring, the course of life we should follow, and the end at which we should aim.

Doth he communicate virtues? it is to animate us in our race; to convince us that there is a mighty arm to raise us from the abyss into which our natural corruption hath plunged us; it is that we may "work out our salvation with fear and trembling; knowing that God worketh in us."

Doth he send error? it is to make us respect that truth which we have resisted.

Doth he prolong our life? it is because he is long-suffering to us. He opens in our favour "the riches of his goodness and forbearance, to lead us to repentance."

Doth he call us to die? it is to open those eternal books in which our actions are registered; it is to gather our souls into his bosom, "to bind them up in the bundle of life;" to mix them with the ransomed armies "of all nations, tongues, and people."

Such are our ideas of the omnipresence of God. Then God seeth all, influenceth all, directeth all. In this sense we are to understand this magnificent language of scripture: "Behold, the heaven of heavens cannot contain thee. Thus saith the Lord, the heaven is my throne, and the earth is my footstool." This was our prophet's meaning throughout the Psalm, "O Lord, thou hast searched me," verse 1, &c.

Inference.

From this idea of God, we see all the virtues issue which religion prescribes.

If such be the grandeur of our God, what ought our repentance to be? who have provoked him to jealousy, as if we had been stronger than he; insulted that majesty which angels adore.

If such be the grandeur of God, what should be our humility? What are we? a grain of dust, a point, an atom, a nothing.

If such be the grandeur of God, what ought our confidence to be? "If God be for us, who can be against us?"

But, above all, if such be the grandeur of God, if God is every where present, what should our vigilance be? What impression should this thought make on reasonable souls, "Thou God seest me?"

THE POWER OF GOD.

Job. xxvi. 14.—Lo! these are parts of his ways: but how little a portion is heard of him? But the thunder of his power who can understand? (H.)

Bildad had, in the foregoing chapter, entertained Job with a discourse of the dominion and power of God, and the purity of his righteousness; whence he argues an impossibility of the justification of man in his presence, who is no better than a worm. Job, in this chapter, acknowledges the greatness of God's power, and descants more largely upon it than Bildad had done; but both preach it with a kind of ironical speech, as if he had not acted a friendly part, or said little to the purpose. The subject of Job's discourse was the outward prosperity of the wicked, and the afflictions of the godly; and Bildad reads him a lecture of the extent of God's dominion, the number of his armies, and the unspotted rectitude of his nature, in comparison of which the purest creatures are foul. Job therefore taxeth him, verses 1—4, that he had not touched the point, but rambled from the subject in hand: "How hast thou helped him who is without power?" Your discourse is so impertinent, that it will neither strengthen the weak, nor instruct the simple; but, since Bildad would take up the argument of God's power, Job would show that he wanted not his instructions on that subject, that he had more distinct conceptions of it than his antagonist had uttered, and therefore, from verse 5 to the end of the chapter, he treats the subject in a magnificent manner, and concludes in the words of the text, "Lo! these are parts of his ways."

I. The nature of God's power.

Power sometimes signifies authority; but the power of God in the text does not signify his authority, but his strength.

1. The power of God is that ability or strength, whereby he can bring to pass whatsoever he pleaseth, whatsoever his infinite wisdom can direct, and the unspotted purity of his will resolve. His counsel shall stand, and he will do all his pleasure. He hath done whatsoever pleaseth him.

2. The power of God gives activity to all the other perfections of his nature. As holiness is the beauty, so power is the life of his attributes in their exercise. God hath a powerful wisdom to attain his ends without interruption, a powerful mercy to remove our misery, a powerful justice to punish offenders, a powerful truth to perform all his promises.

3. This power is originally and essentially in his nature. The strength and power of princes is originally in their people, and only managed by their authority to command; but the power of God is not derived from any thing without him, but essentially in himself. Power belongeth unto God; and all the power that the creature possesses is derived from him.

4. Hence it follows, that the power of God is infinite, What is the exceeding greatness of his power? According to the working of his mighty

power. Nothing can be too difficult for the Divine power to effect. Is any thing too hard for the Lord? A power which cannot be opposed. None can stay his hand.

II. Wherein the power of God is manifested.

1. In creation. With what majestic lines doth God set forth his power in the works of creation. "The firmament showeth his handy work, and the heavens are the work of his fingers," therefore called the firmament of his power. And he only spake, and it was done; he commanded, and it stood fast. "Let there be light, and there was light."

2. The power of God is made manifest in the government of the world.

1. In preservation or natural government, God is the great Father of the universe, to nourish as well as create it. Thou, Lord, preservest man and beast. As they were created by his word, they are supported by the same. He openeth his hand, and satisfieth the desire of every living creature. It is by his power the heavenly bodies have rolled in their spheres, and the tumultuous elements have persisted in their order. He holds the waters in the hollow of his hand, and weighs the mountains in scales, and the hills in a balance; and in him we live, move, and have our being.

It is no small argument of omnipotence, to keep all the strings of nature in tune; to wind them up to a due pitch for the harmony he intended; and prevent those jarrings which would naturally result from their opposite qualities.

2. This power is evident in moral government.

1. In the restraint of the malicious nature of Satan. Since Satan hath the power of an angel and the malice of a devil, what safety would there be for our persons, did not the Lord restrain his malice? It is a part of the strength as well as the wisdom of God, that the deceived and the deceiver are his. Wisdom to defeat, and power to over-rule, the malicious designs of Satan to his own glory.

2. In the restraint of the wickedness of man, what havoc has this made in the world! "From whence come wars?" But had not the Lord, by his power, restrained these, how would the world be drenched in blood? The Lord not only restrains, but overrules the wickedness of man. "Surely the wrath of man shall praise thee."

3. In his gracious government.

1. In the deliverance of his church. He is the strength of Israel. He hath preserved his little flock in the midst of the wolves, and maintained their standing, when the strongest kingdoms have been sunk, and the best jointed states have been broken in pieces. This power shone forth in the deliverance of his people in the Red Sea; and also in the destruction of their enemies. "He showed strength with his arm; he scattered the proud in the imagination of their hearts."

2. In effecting his purposes by small means. As he magnifies his wisdom, by using ignorant instruments, so he exalts his power by the weak. By the motion of Moses' rod he works wonders in the court of Pharaoh. The walls of Jericho, falling at the sound of the rams' horns, was a more glorious display of the power of God, than if Joshua had battered them with the engines of war. Goliah, a giant, levelled with the ground by the force of a sling from the hand of a stripling, is a more glorious character of the power of God, than if a warlike Israelite in Saul's armour had hewed him to pieces

3. In the work of our redemption. As Christ is called the wisdom of God, so he is called the power of God. The arm of power was lifted up as high

as the designs of wisdom were laid deep; as this way of redemption could not be contrived but by an infinite wisdom, so it could not be accomplished but by infinite power. This will appear,

1. In the person redeeming. The union of the two natures in the person of Christ. "The seed of David according to the flesh," An immortal spirit and dying flesh. Infinite purity and a reputed sinner. Omniscience and ignorance. Immutability and changeableness. Human weakness and almighty power. A God of blessedness and a man of sorrow. "The Word made flesh." When we consider the power of God manifested in this union, we are lost. That God upon a throne should be an infant in a cradle. The thundering Creator be a weeping babe and a suffering man.

2. In the progress of his life. In the miracles he wrought. How did he expel the powers of darkness? By a word and touch, sight is restored to the blind, hearing to the deaf, healing to the sick, life to the dead.

3. In his resurrection. The unlocking the belly of the fish for the deliverance of Jonah, the rescue of Daniel from the den of lions, and the three Hebrew worthies from fire, were signal declarations of his power, yet but faint representations of the resurrection of Jesus. This was an hyperbole of power. The exceeding greatness of power, according to the working of his mighty power, which he wrought in Christ, when he raised him from the dead.

2. In the publication of it.

1. The power of God was manifested in the instruments. Men of a low condition, meanly bred, so far from any splendid estates, that they possessed only their nets; without credit or reputation in the world; without comeliness or strength; as unfit to conquer the world by preaching, as an army of hares were to conquer it by war. Not learned doctors, bred up at the feet of the famous rabbins at Jerusalem, whom Paul calls the princes of this world, nor nursed up in the school of Athens. Not the wise men of Greece, but the fishermen of Galilee, are employed to publish the gospel of Christ. The heavenly treasure was placed in these earthen vessels; as Gideon's lamps in empty pitchers; that the excellency of the power might be of God

2. In the success of their ministry, These poor fishermen, tent makers, ignorent men, without letters, without arms, without power, without intrigues, without human help, without philosophy, without eloquence, contemptible and persecuted people, triumphed over the whole world with the sound of their voice. Idols fell, temples were demolished, oracles were struck dumb, the reign of the devil was abolished, the strongest inclinations of nature were diverted, people's ancient habits were changed, they flocked in crowds to adore Jesus; whole provinces presented themselves at the foot of the cross. This is the finger of God; nay, more, this is the outstretched arm of Jehovah.

To conclude.

1. Here is comfort in all afflictions. Our evils can never be so great to distress us, as his power is to deliver. "If God be for us, who can be against us?"

2. This doctrine teaches us the fear of God. "Who would not fear thee, O thou King of nations?" for, if God be against us, it matters not who they be that are for us. Fear him, therefore, who hath power to cast into hell.

THE WISDOM OF GOD.

Rom. xvi. 27.—To God only wise. (H.

Wisdom is a transcendent excellency of the Divine nature. Most confound the knowledge and wisdom of God together; but there is a manifest distinction between them in our conception.

I. Show what wisdom is; wisdom consists

1. In acting for a right end, and choosing proper means. To shoot at random is a mark of folly. As he is the wisest man that hath the noblest end and the most proper means, so God is infinitely wise; as he is the most excellent being, so he hath the most excellent end. "Of him, and through him, and to him, are all things."

2. Wisdom consists in observing all circumstances for action. He is counted a wise man that lays hold of the fittest opportunities to bring about his designs. God hath all the circumstances of things in one entire image before him. It is impossible he should be mistaken, or miss of the due season of bringing about his own purposes. The time of our Saviour's incarnation is called the fulness of time, the proper season for his coming.

3. In willing and acting according to the right judgment. We never count a wilful man a wise man. The resolves and ways of God are not mere will, but well guided by the reason and counsel of his own infinite understanding. Who worketh all things. Eph. i. 11. All his ways are judgment. Deut. xxxii. 4.

There is an essential and personal wisdom of God. The essential wisdom is the essence of God; the personal wisdom is the Son of God. 1 Cor. i. 24. God is originally wise. "Who hath been his counsellor?" Rom. xi. 34. God is perfectly wise. There is no cloud upon his understanding. Job iv. 18. God is perpetually wise. His counsel stands like an immoveable rock. God is incomprehensibly wise. His thoughts are deep. Ps. xcii, 5. His judgments unsearchable. Depths that cannot be fathomed. Rom. xi. 33. O the depth. Job xi. 6, 7. God is infallibly wise. The wisest men meet with rubs in the way. God always compasses his ends. There is no wisdom. Isa. lv. 11. His word that goeth forth. Isa. xiv. 24, 27. As he thinks, so shall it come to pass.

II. Wherein the wisdom of God appears.

1. In creation. The whole creation is a poem, every species a stanza, and every individual creature a verse in it. Prov. iii. 19. "The Lord by wisdom, hath founded the earth." Jer. x. 12. "He hath established the world by his wisdom." There is not any thing so mean, so small, but shines with a beam of Divine wisdom. Ps. civ. 24. "In wisdom hast thou made them all." This wisdom of the creation appears,

1. In the variety. "O Lord, how manifold are thy works!" How great a variety is there of animals, plants, colours. Gen. i. 11, 20, 24.

2. In the beauty and order. Eccles. iii. 11. "He hath made every thing beautiful." All the creatures are as so many pictures, or statues, exactly framed by line. Ps. xix. 4. "Their line is gone."

3. In the fitness of every thing for its end. After the most diligent inspection, there can be found nothing unprofitable. The earth is fitted into his parts; the valleys are appointed for granaries, the mountains to shadow them; the rivers, like veins, carry refreshment. Ps. civ. 14. "There he causes the grass to grow." The sea is fitted for its use; it is a fish pond for

the nourishment of man; it joins nations: a great vessel for commerce. Ps. civ. 26. "There go the ships." Showers are appointed, to refresh the bodies, to open the womb of the earth. Ps. civ. 3. "To make it fruitful." Winds are fitted to purify the air, to carry the clouds, to refresh the earth. Ps. civ. 3. "He walketh on the winds." Rivers are appointed to bathe the earth: they are the water pots of the earth. Ps. civ. 10, 12, 13. Trees are for the habitations of birds. The seasons have their uses. The days and nights have also their usefulness. Ps. lxxiv. 16, 17; civ. 23.

4. This wisdom is apparent in the linking all those useful parts together. All parts are exactly suited to one another, and every part to the whole. "The heavens hear the earth." Hos. ii. 21, 22.

III. In his government, especially of man.

I. In his government of him as a rational creature, in the law he gives him.

1. It is suited in the nature of man.

2. To his happiness. "Rejoicing his heart." Ps. xix. 7, 8; Deut. iv. 8.

3. In suiting his laws to his conscience. "The Gentiles do by nature." Rom. ii. 14. Conscience dictates that the law is worthy to be observed.

4. In the encouragement he gives. "In keeping thy commandments." Ps. xix. 11.

II. God's wisdom appears in the government of man as a fallen creature.

1. In the bounding of sin. "The wrath of man." Ps. lxxvi. 10.

2. In overruling it to his own glory and our good. "As sin reigned unto death." Rom. v. 21.

3. In the work of redemption. In which he manifested the greatest hatred to sin, and the greatest love to the sinner. "Herein is love—God so loved the world."

4. In overturning the empire of Satan. "Through death." Heb. ii. 14. Thus the devil ruined his own kingdom, whilst he thought to establish it

5. In the manner of publishing the doctrine of redemption. In the general discoveries of it to Abraham and Moses; the time and circumstances of the first publication of the gospel by the apostles. Acts ii. 1—12. In the instruments employed: he did not employ philosophers, but fishermen. "The foolishness of God is wiser than men." In the ways and manner: by ways seemingly contrary; by scattering of the disciples, it inflamed their courage, and spread their doctrine. "Many shall run to and fro." Dan. xii. 4. The flames of the martyrs brightened the doctrine. Religion grew stronger by sufferings; making the "wisdom of this world foolishness with God."

To conclude—we may hence see,

1. The right and fitness of God for the government of the world. Power and wisdom are the two arms of authority.

2. That God is a proper object for our trust and confidence. "The Lord knoweth how to deliver." Job v. 13. He taketh the wise.

3. Meditate on the wisdom of God, as manifested in creation. Ps. viii. 4, 5. "When I consider the heavens." In redemption, shall the angels be ravished with it, and bend themselves down to study it, and shall not we admire it! Prov. ii. 1—6.

4. Let us seek to God for wisdom. "If any man lack wisdom." James i. 17. There is a spirit in man. Job xxii. 8.

Submit to the wisdom of God in all cases; he is a God of judgment.

ON THE HOLINESS OF GOD.

Exodus xv. 11.—Who is like unto thee, O Lord, among the gods? Who is like unto thee, glorious in holiness, fearful in praises, doing wonders? (H.)

THIS verse is one of the loftiest descriptions of the majesty and excellence of God in the whole scripture. It is a part of Moses' triumphant song, after a great, and real, and a typical victory; in the womb of which all the deliverances of the church were couched. It is the first song upon holy record, and it consists of gratulatory and prophetic matter. It casts a look backward, to what God did for them in their deliverance from Egypt; and a look forward, to what God shall do for the church in future ages.

It consists of, 1. A preface, verse 1—"I will sing unto the Lord."

2. An historical narration of matter of fact, verses 3, 4, "Pharaoh's chariots and his host hath he cast into the Red Sea."

Let these two things be considered. If any, this attribute hath an excellency above his other perfections; none is sounded out so loftily, with such solemnity, and so frequently by angels, as this. Isa. vi. 3. "Holy, holy, holy." Rev. iv. 8. He singles it out to swear by. Ps. lxxxix. 35. "Once have I sworn by my holiness." Amos iv. 2. "The Lord will swear by his holiness;" it is glory and beauty. Power is his hand and arm, omniscience his eye, mercy his bowels, eternity his duration, his holiness is his beauty. 2 Chron. xx. 21. "Should praise the beauty of holiness." It is his very life. So it is called. Eph. iv. 18. "Alienated from the life of God;" that is, from the holiness of God. "Be ye holy, as I am holy."

I. THE NATURE OF DIVINE HOLINESS.

The holiness of God, negatively, is a perfect and unpolluted freedom from all evil; as we call gold pure that is not embased by any dross.

Positively, it is the rectitude or integrity of the Divine nature; or that conformity of it in affection and action of the divine will, whereby he hath a delight and complacency in every thing agreeable to his will.

As there is no darkness in his understanding, so there is no spot in his will. Ps. xi. 7. "The righteous Lord loveth righteousness."

This property of the Divine nature is,

1. An essential and necessary perfection; he is essentially and necessarily holy. His holiness is as necessary as his being.

2. God is only absolutely holy: "There is none holy as the Lord." It is the peculiar glory of his nature; he is not only holy, but holiness. Holiness, in the highest degree, is his sole prerogative.

3. God is so holy, that he cannot possibly approve of any evil done by another, but doth perfectly abhor it; would not else be a glorious holiness. Ps. v. 4. "He hath no pleasure in wickedness."

1. He abhors it necessarily. Holiness is the glory of the Deity, therefore necessarily. The nature of God is so holy, that he cannot but hate it. Hab. i. 13 "Thou art of purer eyes than to behold evil." He is more opposite to it than light to darkness; and therefore it can expect no countenance from him.

2. Therefore intensely. Nothing do men act for more than their glory. He hates the first spark of it in the imagination. Zach. viii. 17. With what variety of expressions doth he repeat his indignation at their polluted services; Amos v. 21, 22; so Isa. i. 14; it is the abominable thing that he hates; Jer. xliv. 4; he is vexed and fretted at it; Isa. lxiii. 10; Ezek. xvi. 43; he abhors it so, that his hatred rebounds upon the person that commits it. Ps. v. 5. "He hates all workers of iniquity."

3. Therefore universally, because necessarily and intensely. He doth not hate it in one, and indulge it in another, but loathes it wherever he finds it; not one worker of iniquity is exempt from it. Ps. v. 5. "Thou hatest all workers of iniquity."

4. Perpetually. This must necessarily follow upon the others. He can no more cease to hate impurity, than he can cease to love holiness. James i. 17. God is always the same, without any shadow of change; and "is angry with the wicked every day," Ps. vii. 11, *i. e.* uninterruptedly.

5. God is so holy, that he cannot but love holiness in others. Not that he owes any thing to his creatures, but from the unspeakable holiness of his nature. Ps. xi. 7. "The righteous Lord loveth righteousness."

6. God is so holy, that he cannot positively will or encourage sin in any. How can he give any encouragement to that which he cannot in the least approve? Light may sooner be the cause of darkness, than he that is the fountain of good should be the source of evil. James iii. 11.

1. God cannot commit any unrighteousness.

2. Nor can God secretly inspire any evil into us.

3. Nor can God necessitate man to sin. Indeed sin cannot be committed by force; there is no sin but is in some sort voluntary.

II. The demonstration of it.

1. His holiness appears as he is Creator, in framing man in a perfect uprightness. Angels, as made by God, could not be evil; for God beheld his own works with pleasure, and could not have pronounced them all good, had some been created pure, and others impure; two moral contrarieties could not be good. Human nature was well strung and tuned by God, according to the note of his own holiness. Eccles. vii. 29. "God hath made man upright." Other creatures were his footsteps, but man was his image. "Let us make man in our image, after our likeness;" which, though it seem to imply no more in that place, than an image of his dominion over the creatures, yet the apostle raises it a peg higher, and gives us a larger interpretation. Col. iii. 10. "And have put on the new man, which is renewed in knowledge, after the image of him that created him;" making it to consist in a resemblance to his righteousness.

2. His holiness appears in his laws; and he is a law-giver and a judge. Man was bound to be subject to God, as a creature, and had a capacity to be ruled by the law. Deut. iv. 8. "What nation hath statutes and judgments so righteous?" They are compared to fine gold, that hath no speck nor dross. Ps. xix. 10.

This purity is evident,

In the moral law; which is therefore dignified with the title of holy twice in one verse. Rom. vii. 12. "Wherefore the law is holy."

1. The purity of the law is seen in the matter of it. It prescribes all that becomes a creature towards God, and all that becomes one creature towards another. "Wherefore the law is holy." The purity of this beam and transcript of God, bears witness to a greater clearness and beauty in the sun and original. Undefiled streams manifest an untainted fountain.

2. It is seen in the manner of his precepts. As it prescribes all good, and forbids all evil; so it doth enjoin the one, and banish the other, as such. The laws of men command virtuous things; not as virtuous in themselves, but as useful for human society. But God commands that which is just in itself; enjoins virtues as virtues, and prohibits vices as vices.

3. In the spiritual extent of it. It frowns upon all stains and pollutions of the most retired thoughts; hence the apostle calls it a spiritual law. Rom vii. 14

4. In regard to the perpetuity of it. The purity and perpetuity of it are linked together by the Psalmist. Ps. xix. 9. "The fear of the Lord is clean, enduring for ever."

5. This holiness appears in the allurements annexed to the law for keeping it, and the affrightments to restrain from the breaking of it: both promises and threatenings have their fundamental root in the holiness of God. "Having these promises, let us cleanse ourselves from all filthiness of flesh and spirit, perfecting holiness in the fear of God."

6. His holiness appears in the judgments inflicted for the violation of the law. Divine holiness is the root of Divine justice, and Divine justice is the triumph of Divine holiness. Ps. ciii. 6: Dan. ix. 7; Ps. xi. 6, 7.

1. How severely hath he punished his most noble creatures for it?

2. How detestable to him are the very instruments of sin. Gen. iii. 14; Lev. xx. 15; Deut. vii. 25, 26. So contrary is the holy nature of God to every sin, that it curseth every thing that is instrumental in it.

3. How detestable is every thing to him that is in the sinner's possession. The very earth, which God had made Adam the proprietor of, was cursed for his sake." Gen. iii. 17, 18. It lost its beauty, and lies languishing to this day. Rom. viii. 20—22.

4. What design hath God in all these acts of severity and vindictive justice, but to set off the lustre of his holiness?

III. The holiness of God appears in our RESTORATION. It is in the glass of the gospel we behold the glory of the Lord; 2 Cor. iii. 18; that is, the glory of the Lord, into whose image we are changed; but we are changed into nothing, as the image of God, but into holiness. Isa. i. 27.

1. This holiness of God appears in the manner of our restoration, viz. by the death of Christ. Not all the vials of judgments that have, or shall be poured out upon the wicked world, nor the flaming furnace of a sinner's conscience, nor the irreversible sentence pronounced against the rebellious devils, nor the groans of the damned creatures, give such a demonstration of God's hatred of sin, as the wrath of God let loose upon his Son.

It appears the more, if you consider,

1. The dignity of the Redeemer's person. One that had been from eternity, had laid the foundations of the world; had been the object of the Divine delight: he that was "God blessed for ever," becomes a curse. One equal to him in all the glorious perfections of his nature, Phil. ii. 6, dies on a disgraceful cross, and is exposed to the flames of Divine wrath, rather than sin should live.

2. The near relation he stood in to the Father. He was his own Son, that he delivered up. Rom. viii. 32. His essential image, as dearly beloved by him as himself; yet he would abate nothing of his hatred of those sins imputed to one so dear to him.

3. The value he puts upon his holiness appears farther, in the advancement of this redeeming person after his death. Our Saviour was advanced, not barely for his dying, but for the respect he had in his death to this attribute of God. Heb. i. 9. "Thou hast loved righteousness, and hated iniquity."

4. It may be farther considered, that in this way of redemption his holiness in the hatred of sin seems to be valued above any other attribute. He proclaims the value of it above the person of his Son. In this way of redemption the odiousness of sin is equally discovered with the greatest of his compassions: an infinite abhorrence of sin, and an infinite love to the world, march hand in hand together Sin is made the chief mark of his displeasure,

while the poor creature is made the highest object of Divine pity; in this way mercy and truth, &c. Ps. lxxxv. 10.

II. The holiness of God in his hatred of sin appears in OUR JUSTIFICATION, AND THE CONDITIONS HE REQUIRES OF ALL THAT WOULD ENJOY THE BENEFIT OF REDEMPTION. Our justification is not by the imperfect works of creatures, but by an exact and infinite righteousness. Faith is the condition God requires to justification; but not a dead, but an active faith; such a "faith as purifies the heart." James ii. 20; Acts xv. 9. He calls for repentance, which is a moral retracting our offences. He requires mortification, which is called crucifying; whereby a man would strike as full and deadly a blow at his lusts, as was struck at Christ upon the cross. There is no admittance into heaven of a starting, but a persevering holiness, Rom. ii. 7, "a patient continuance in well-doing."

III. It appears in the ACTUAL REGENERATION OF, AND A CARRYING IT ON TO A FULL PERFECTION. Our pardon is the fruit of his mercy, our knowledge a stream from his wisdom, our strength an impression of his power; so our purity is a beam from his holiness. "Holy Father, keep them through thy own name, and sanctify them through thy truth;" as the proper source whence holiness was to flow to the creature: as the sun is the proper fountain whence light is derived, both to the stars above and bodies here below. Hence he is not only called holy, but the "Holy One of Israel." Isa. xliii. 15.

To conclude.

1. There can be no communion between God and unholy spirits. Can there be any delightful communion between those whose natures are contrary? Darkness and light may as soon kiss each other, and become one nature; God and the devil may as soon enter into an eternal league and covenant together; for God to have pleasure in wickedness, and to admit evil to dwell with him, are things equally impossible to his nature.

2. Hence it will follow, there is no justification of a sinner by any thing in himself. Eph. i. 6. "Who hath made us accepted in the Beloved." The infinite purity of God is so glorious, that it shames the holiness of angels, as the light of the sun dims the light of the fire.

3. This attribute renders God a fit object for trust and dependance. The notion of an unholy, and unrighteous God, is an uncomfortable idea of God, and beats off our hands from laying any hold of him: Isa. xli. 14; "Fear not, thou worm Jacob;" he will be in his actions what he is in his nature.

4. A sense of this will render us humble in the possession of the greatest holiness a creature is capable of. We are apt to be proud with the Pharisee; but let any clap their wings, if they can, in a vain boasting and exaltation, when they view the holiness of this God. "Who can stand before this holy Lord God?"

5. This would make us full of an affectionate reverence in all our approaches to God. By this perfection God is rendered venerable, and fit to be reverenced by his creature; and magnificent thoughts of it in the creature would awaken him to an actual reverence of the Divine Majesty. Ps. cxi. 9. "Holy and reverend is his name." Ps. xlvii. 8.

6. A due sense of this perfection would inflame us with a vehement desire to be conformed to him. Contemplating it as it shines forth in the face of Christ will transform us into the same image.

7. Let us seek for holiness to God, the fountain of it. As he is the author of bodily life in the creature, so he is the author of his own life, the life of

God in the soul. By his holiness he makes men holy, as the sun by his light enlightens the air. He is not only the Holy One, but our Holy One. Isa. xliii. 15. The Lord that sanctifies us. Lev. xx. 8. As he hath mercy to pardon us, so he hath holiness to purify us; the excellency of being a sun to comfort us, and a shield to protect us, giving grace and glory. Ps. lxxxiv. 11.

ON THE GOODNESS OF GOD.

Mark x. 18.—And Jesus said unto him, Why callest thou me good? There is none good but one, that is God. (H.)

Truly "God is good." Ps. lxxiii. 1. All nations in the world have acknowledged this truth. The notion of goodness is inseparable from the notion of a God. We cannot own the existence of God, but we must confess also his goodness.

I. What this goodness is?

There is a goodness of being, which is the natural perfection of a thing; there is the goodness of will, which is the holiness and righteousness of a person; there is the goodness of the hand, which we call liberality, or beneficence, a doing good to others.

1. We mean not by this, the goodness of his essence, or the perfection of his nature. God is thus good, because his name is infinitely perfect; he hath all things requisite to the completing of a most perfect and sovereign being. All good meets in his essence, as all water meets in the ocean.

2. Nor is it the same with the blessedness of God, but something flowing from his blessedness. Were he not first infinitely blessed, and full in himself, he could not be infinitely good and diffusive to us.

Had not the sun a fulness of light in itself, and the sea a vastness of water, the one could not enrich the world with its beams, nor the other fill every creek with its waters.

3. Nor is it the same with the holiness of God. The holiness of God is the rectitude of his nature. The goodness of God is the efflux of his will, whereby he is beneficial to his creatures: "The Lord is good to all."

4. Nor is the goodness of God the same with the mercy of God. Goodness extends to more objects than mercy; goodness stretcheth itself out to all the works of his hands; mercy extends only to a miserable object.

By goodness is meant,

1. The bounty of God. This is the notion of goodness in the world; when we say a good man, we mean either a holy man in his life, or a charitable and liberal man in the management of his goods. As God is great and powerful, he is the object of our understanding; but as good and bountiful, he is the object of our love and desire.

2. The goodness of God comprehends all his attributes. All the acts of God are nothing else but the effluxes of his goodness, distinguished by several names, according to the objects it is exercised about. As the sea, though it be one mass of water, yet we distinguish it by several names, according to the shores it washeth and beats upon. When Moses longed to see his glory, God tells him he would give him a prospect of his goodness. Ex. xxxiii. 19. "I will make all my goodness." The whole catalogue of

"mercy, grace, long-suffering," Ex. xxxiv. 6, all are streams from this fountain. When it confers happiness without merit, it is grace; when it bestows happiness against merit, it is mercy; when he bears with provoking rebels, it is long-suffering; when he performs his promise, it is truth; when it commiserates a distressed person, it is pity; when it supplies an indigent person, it is bounty; when it succours an innocent person, it is righteousness; and when it pardons a penitent person, it is mercy; all summed up in this one name of goodness. Ps. cxlv. 7, 8. "They shall abundantly utter the memory of thy great goodness."

II. The nature of this goodness.

1. He is good by his own essence. God is not only good in his essence, but good by his essence. Hence his goodness must be infinite, and circumscribed by no limits; the exercise of his goodness may be limited by himself, but his goodness, the principle, cannot; for since his essence is infinite, and his goodness is not distinguished from his essence, it is infinite also. He is essentially good by his own essence, therefore good of himself, therefore eternally and abundantly good.

2. God is the prime and chief goodness. Being good by his own essence, he must needs be the chief goodness, in whom there can be nothing but good, from whom there can proceed nothing but good, to whom all good whatso ever must be referred, as the final cause of all good. As he is the chief being, so he is the chief good. Ps. xvi. 2. Our goodness extends not to him; wickedness may hurt a man, as we are, and our righteousness may profit the son of man; but, if we be righteous, "what give we to him, or what receives he at our hands?" Job xxxv. 7, 8. God is all good; other things are good in their kind, as a good man, a good angel. He is no less all good than he is almighty.

3. This goodnes is communicative. None so communicatively good as God. As the notion of God includes goodness, so the notion of goodness includes diffusiveness; without goodness he would cease to be a Deity, and without diffusiveness he would cease to be good. Ps. cxix. 68. "Thou art good and doest good."

4. God is necessarily good. None is necessarily good but God; he is as necessarily good as he is necessarily God. His goodness is as inseparable from his nature as his holiness.

5. Though he be necessarily good, yet he is also freely good. The necessity of the goodness of his nature hinders not the liberty of his actions. It would not be a supreme goodness, if it were not a voluntary goodness. It is agreeable to the nature of the highest good, to be absolutely free, to dispense his goodness in what methods and measures he pleaseth.

6. This goodness is communicated with the greatest pleasure. Moses desired to see his glory, God assures him he should see his goodness; Ex. xxxiii. 18, 19; intimating, that his goodness is his glory, and his glory his delight also. He prevents men with his blessings of goodness. Ps. xxi. 3. He is most delighted when he is most diffusive. He is not covetous of his own treasures. It is the nature of his goodness to be glad of men's solicitations for it.

III. The manifestation of this goodness.

1. In creation. His goodness was the cause that he made any thing, and his wisdom was the cause that he made every thing in order and harmony; he pronounced "every thing good."

1. The creation proceeds from goodness. Because God is good, things have a being; if he had not been good, nothing could have been good; nothing could have imparted that which it did not possess.

2. Creation was the first act of goodness without himself. Creation was the first efflux of his goodness without himself; and therefore it was the speech of an heathen, "That when God first set upon the creation of the world, he transformed himself into love and goodness."

3. There is not one creature but hath a character of his goodness. The whole world is a map to represent, and a herald to proclaim, this perfection. Ps. cxlv. 9. "He is good to all;" he is therefore good in all; not a drop of the creation, but is a drop of his goodness. These are the colors worn upon the heads of every creature. As in every spark the light of the fire is manifested, so doth every grain of the creation wear the visible badges of this perfection.

But, let us see the goodness of God in the creation of man.

1. How much of goodness is visible in his body? How neatly hath he wrought this "tabernacle of clay, this earthly house?" as the apostle calls it. A curious wrought-piece of needle-work, a comely artifice; an embroidered case for an harmonious lute. It is a cabinet fitted by Divine goodness, for the enclosing a rich jewel; a palace made of dust, to lodge in it the viceroy of the world.

2. But what is this to that goodness which shines in the nature of the soul? Who can express the wonders of that comeliness that is wrapt up in this mask of clay? A soul endued with a clearness of understanding and freedom of will. A soul that excelled the whole world, that comprehended the whole creation. In the ruins of a palace we may see the curiosity displayed, and the cost expended in the building of it; in the ruins of this fallen structure, we still find it capable of a mighty knowledge.

3. Besides this, he did not only make man so noble a creature in his frame, but he made him after his own image in holiness. He imparted to him a spark of his own comeliness, in order to a communion with himself in happiness. He made man after his image, after his own image.

4. The goodness of God appears in the conveniences he provided for, and gave to man.

1. The world was made for man. God put all things under his feet, and gave him a deputed dominion over the rest of the creatures under himself, as the absolute sovereign. Ps. viii. 6. "Thou madest him to have dominion over the works of thy hands."

2. God richly furnished the world for man. He did not only erect a stately palace for his habitation, but provided all kind of furniture, as a mark of his goodness, for the entertainment of his creature man: he arched over his habitation with a bespangled heaven, and floored it with a solid earth. Ps. civ. 14.

3. The goodness of God appears in the laws he hath given to man, and the covenant he hath made with him.

1. In the fitting the law to the nature of man. It was rather below than above his strength; he had an integrity in his nature to answer the righteousness of his precept. Eccles. vii. 29. "God created man upright;" his nature was suited to the law, and the law to his nature.

2. In fitting it for the happiness of man. For the satisfaction of his soul, which finds a reward in the very act of keeping it. Ps. cxix. 165.

3. In engaging man to obedience by promises and threatenings. A threatening is only mentioned, Gen. ii. 17, but a promise is implied.

2. In redemption. The whole gospel is nothing but one entire mirror of Divine goodness: the whole of redemption is wrapt up in that one expression of the angel's song, Luke ii. 14, "Good will towards man."

1. Goodness was the spring of redemption. All and every part of it owes only to this perfection the appearance of it in the world. 1 John iv. 8.

2. It was a pure goodness. He was under no obligation to pity our misery, and repair our ruins; he might have stood to the terms of the first covenant and exacted our eternal death, since we have committed an infinite transgression.

3. Hence we may consider the height of his goodness in redemption to exceed that in creation. His goodness in the latter is more astonishing to our belief, than his goodness in creation is visible to our eye. There is more of his bounty expressed in that one verse, John iii. 16, "God so loved the world, that he gave his only begotten Son," than there is in the whole volume of the world. In creation, he formed an innocent creature of the dust of the ground; in redemption, he restores a rebellious creature by the blood of his Son.

4 The goodness of God in his government. That goodness that despised not their creation, doth not despise their conduct. The same goodness that was the head that framed them, is the helm that guides them.

1. This goodness is evident in the care he hath of all creatures. There is a peculiar goodness to his people; but this takes not away his general goodness to the world. Ps. civ. 24. "The earth is full of his riches." The whole world swims in the rich bounty of the Creator. The goodness of God is the river that waters the whole earth. His goodness is seen in preserving all things. Ps. xxxvi. 6. "O Lord, thou preservest man and beast." He visits man every day, and makes him feel the effects of his providence in giving him "fruitful seasons, and filling his heart with food and gladness," Acts xiv. 17, as witnesses of his liberality and kindness to man. "The earth is visited and watered by the river of God; he crowns the year with his goodness."

The goodness of God is seen in taking care of the animals and inanimate things. Divine goodness embraceth in its arms the lowest worm as well as the loftiest cherubim; he provides food for the crying ravens, Ps. cxlvii. 9, and a prey for the appetite of the hungry lion. Ps. civ. 21. He clothes the grass, and arrays the lilies of the field with a greater glory than Solomon Matt. vi. 26—30.

Again, the Divine goodness is evident in providing a scripture, as a rule to guide us, and continuing it in the world. The scripture was written upon several occasions, yet, in the dictating of it, the goodness of God cast his eye upon the last ages of the world. 1 Cor. x. 11. They are written for our admonition, upon whom the ends of the world are come. It was given to the Israelites, but Divine goodness intended it for the future Gentiles. Thus did Divine goodness think of us, and prepare his records for us, before we were in the world. It is clear, to inform our understandings, and rich, to comfort us in our misery; it is a light to guide us, and a cordial to refresh us; it is a lamp to our feet, and a medicine for our diseases; a purifier of our filth, and a restorer of us in our faintings. He hath by his goodness sealed the truth of it, by its efficacy on multitudes of men: he hath made it the word of regeneration. James i. 18. The Divine goodness doth appear in answering prayers. He delights to be familiarly acquainted with his people, and to hear them call upon him. He indulgeth them a free access to him, and delights in every address of an upright man. Isa. lxv 24. The goodness of God is seen in bearing with the infirmities of his people, and accepting imperfect obedience. He takes notice of a sincere, though chequered obedience, to reward it. The goodness of God is seen in afflictions and persecutions; if it be good for us to be afflicted, for which we have the Psalmist's vote, Ps. cxix. 71. "What is man that thou shouldst magnify him?" Job vii. 17.

To conclude.

1. If God be so good, how unworthy is the contempt or abuse of his goodness. Jer. ii. 5. By a forgetfulness of his benefits, we enjoy the mercies and forget the donor; we take what he gives, and pay not the tribute he deserves. The Israelites forgot God their Saviour, by a distrust of his providence; Num. xiv. 3; thus the Israelites thought their miraculous deliverance from Egypt. In sinning more freely upon the account of his goodness; in ascribing our benefits to other causes than Divine goodness. Thus Israel ascribed her felicity, plenty, and success, to her idols, as rewards which her lovers had given her. Hos. ii. 5, 12. "Thou hast praised the gods of silver, and gold, and brass." Dan. v. 23. This was the proud vaunt of the Assyrian conqueror, for which God threatens to punish the fruits of his stout heart. Isa. x. 11—14. "By the strength of my hand I have done it."

2. It is matter of comfort in afflictions. What can we fear from the conduct of infinite goodness? Can his hand be heavy upon those that are humble before him? They are hands of infinite power indeed, but there is not any motion of it; Ps. lxxxiv. 11. "Grace and glory will he give, and no good thing will he withhold."

3. Imitate this goodness of God. Mat. v. 44, 45. "Do good to them that hate you, that you may be the children of your Father, which is in heaven." Verse 48, "Be not overcome of evil."

ON THE DOMINION OF GOD.

Psalm ciii. 19.—The Lord hath prepared his throne in the heavens, and his kingdom ruleth over all. (H.)

"THE Lord hath prepared;" the word signifies established, as well as prepared. Due preparation is a natural way to the establishment of a thing. Hasty resolves break and moulder. This notes,

The infinity of his authority. He prepares it, none else for him. Readiness to exercise it upon due occasions. He hath prepared his throne; he hath all things ready for the assistance of his people. Wise management of it; it is prepared: preparations imply prudence; the government of God is not a rash and heady authority. Successfulness and duration; he hath prepared, or established. It is fixed, not tottering; it is an immoveable dominion, all the struggles of men and devils cannot overturn, nor so much as shake it. As his counsel, so his authority shall stand, and "he will do all his pleasure." Isa. xlvi. 10.

"His throne in the heavens." This is an expression to signify the authority of God; for as God hath no member properly, though he be so represented to us, so he hath properly no throne. It signifies his power of reigning and judging.

"His throne in the heavens," notes,

"The glory of his dominion." The heavens are the most stately and comely pieces of the creation; his majesty is there most visible, his glory most splendid. Ps. xix. 1. The heavens speak out with a full mouth his glory; it is therefore called, "The habitation of his holiness and of his glory" Isa. lxiii. 15. The supremacy of his empire; they are elevated above all earthly empires. Peculiarly of this dominion; he rules in the heavens alone. The vastness of his empire; the earth is but a spot to the heavens. The easiness of managing this government; his being in the heavens renders him capable of doing whatsoever he pleases. Ps. cxv. 3. Duration of it; the heavens are incorruptible. His kingdom rules over all; he hath an absolute right over all things, within the circuit of heaven and earth. 1 Chron. xxix. 11, 12.

Jehovah's dominion is here proclaimed as universal. A dominion over the whole world.

I. I SHALL STATE SOME GENERAL PROPOSITIONS FOR THE CLEARING AND CONFIRMING OF THIS GLORIOUS FACT.

1. We must know the difference between the power of God and his authority. We commonly mean, by the power of God, the strength of God, whereby he is able to effect all his purposes. By the authority of God, we mean the right he hath to act what he pleases. Among men, strength and authority are two distinct things. A subject may be a giant, and be stronger than his prince, but he hath not the same authority. Worldly dominion may be seated, not in a brawny arm, but a sickly and infirm body. A greater strength may be settled in the servant, but a greater authority resides in the master. As God is Lord, he hath a right to enact; as he is almighty, he hath a power to execute. His strength is the executive power belonging to his dominion.

2. All the other attributes of God refer to this perfection of dominion. His goodness fits him for it, because he can never use his authority but for the good of the creatures. His wisdom can never be mistaken in the exercise of it; his power can accomplish the decrees that flow from his absolute authority. Without this dominion, some perfections, as justice and mercy, would lie in obscurity, and much of his wisdom would be hid from our sight.

3. This of dominion, as well as that of power, hath been acknowledged by all. The high-priest was to wave the offering, or shake it to and fro, Ex. xxix. 24, which, the Jews say, was customary from east to west, and from north to south, the four quarters of the world, to signify God's sovereignty over all the parts of the world. And some of the heathens, in their adorations, turned their bodies to all quarters, to signify the extensive dominion of God throughout the whole earth. It is stamped upon the conscience of man, and flashes in his face in every act of self-judgment.

4. This notion of sovereignty is inseparable from the notion of God. To acknowledge the existence of a God and to acknowledge him a rewarder are linked together. Hebrew xi. 6. To acknowledge him a rewarder, is to acknowledge him a governor: rewards being the marks of dominion. We cannot suppose God a Creator, without supposing a sovereign dominion in him. No creature can be made without some law in its nature; if it had not law, it would be created to no purpose. It is so inseparable, that it cannot be communicated to any creature. No creature is able to exercise it, every creature is unable to perform all the offices that belong to this dominion.

II. WHEREIN THE DOMINION OF GOD IS FOUNDED.

1. On the excellency of his nature. God being an incomprehensible ocean of all perfection, and possessing infinitely all those virtues that may lay a claim to dominion, hath the first foundation of it in his own nature. On this account God claims our obedience. Isa. xlvi. 9. "I am God, and there is none like me;" and the prophet Jeremiah on the same account

acknowledgeth it. **Jer. x. 6, 7.** "Forasmuch as there is none like **unto** thee."

2. In his act of creation. He is the sovereign Lord, as he is the almighty Creator. The relation of an entire Creator induceth the relation of an absolute Lord. His dominion or jurisdiction results from creation. When God himself makes an oration in defence of his sovereignty, Job xxxviii., his chief arguments are drawn from creation, and Ps. xcv. 3—5, "The Lord is a great king above all gods." And so the apostle. As he "made the world and all things therein," he is styled, Lord of heaven and earth. Acts xvii. 24. His dominion also of property stands upon this basis. Ps. lxxxix. 11. "The heavens are thine, the earth also is thine." On this title of forming Israel as a creature, or rather as a church, he demands their service to him as their sovereign. "O Jacob and Israel, thou art my servant: I have formed thee." Isa. xliv. 21.

3. "As God is the final cause, or end of all, he is Lord of all." God, in his actual creation of all, is the sovereign end of all, "for thy pleasure they are and were created. Rev. iv. 11. "The Lord hath made all things for himself." Prov. xvi. 4.

4. "The dominion of God is founded upon his preservation of things." Ps. xcv. 3, 4. The Lord is a great king above all gods. Why? In his hand are all the deep places of the earth. While his hand holds things, his hand hath a dominion over them. The master of this great family may as well be called the Lord of it, since every member of it depends upon him for the support of that being he first gave them. As the right to govern resulted from creation, so it is perpetuated by preservation.

5. The dominion of God is strengthened by the innumerable benefits he bestows upon his creatures. The beneficence of God adds, though not an original right of power, yet a foundation of a stronger upbraiding the creature, if he walk in a violation and forgetfulness of those benefits. Isa. i. 2. "Hear, O heavens, and give ear O earth!" Thus the fundamental right as a creator is made more indisputable by his relation as benefactor. The benefits of God are innumerable. But that benefit of redemption doth add a stronger right of dominion to God; since he not only as a creator gave being, but paid a price of his Son's blood for their rescue from captivity, so that he hath a sovereignty of grace as well as nature. 1 Cor. vi. 19, 20. "Ye are not your own."

III. The nature of this dominion.

1. This dominion is independent. His throne is in the heavens; the heavens depend not upon the earth, nor God upon his creatures. Since he is independent in regard of his essence, he is so in his dominion, which flows from the excellency and fulness of his essence.

2. Absolute. If his throne be in the heavens, there is nothing to control him. His authority is unlimited.

1. Absolute in regard of freedom and liberty. Thus creation is a work of mere sovereignty; he created, because it was his pleasure to create. Preservation is the fruit of his sovereignty. Redemption is a fruit of his sovereignty.

2. His dominion is absolute in regard of unlimitedness by any law without him. He is an absolute monarch, that makes laws for his subjects, but receives no rules nor laws from his subjects for the management of his government.

3. In regard of supremacy and uncontrollableness. None can implead him, and cause him to render a reason of his actions. "Who may say unto

him, What doest thou?" Eccles. viii. 4. It is an absurd thing for any to dispute with God. Rom. ix. 20. "Who art thou, O man!" In all the desolations he works, he asserts his own supremacy to silence men. Ps. xlvi. 10. "Be still, and know that I am God."

4. In regard of irresistibleness. His word is a law, he commands things to stand out of nothing. "He commands light to shine out of darkness." 2 Cor. iv. 6. There is no distance of time between his word. "Let there be light, and there was light." Gen. i. 3. If the Lord will work. "Who shall let it?" Isa. xliii. 13. He sets the ordinances of the heavens, and the dominion thereof in the earth. And sends lightnings, that they may go, and say unto him, Here we are. Job xxxviii. 35.

5. Yet this dominion, though it be absolute, is not tyrannical. If his throne be in the heavens, it is pure and good. This dominion is managed by the rule of wisdom. What may appear to us to have no other spring than absolute sovereignty, would be found to have a depth of amazing wisdom. His sovereignty is managed according to the rule of righteousness. Worldly princes often fancy tyranny and oppression to be the chief marks of sovereignty, and think their sceptres not beautiful till dyed in blood, nor the throne secure till established upon slain carcasses. But justice and judgment are the foundation of the throne of God. Ps. lxxxix. 14. In all his ways he is righteous. Psalm cxiv. 17. His sovereignty is managed according to the rule of goodness. Some potentates there have been in the world, that have loved to suck the blood and drink the tears of their subjects, that would rule more by fear than love. God's throne is a throne of holiness, so is it a throne of grace. Heb. iv. 16. A throne encircled with a rainbow. Rev. iv. 3. In sight like to an emerald. An emblem of the covenant, that hath the pleasantness of a green color, delightful to the eye betokening mercy. If he bind them in fetters, it is to show them their transgressions, and open their ear to discipline, and renewing commands in a more sensible strain, to depart from iniquity.

6. This sovereignty is extensive. He rules all, as the heavens do over the earth. He is king of worlds, king of ages. Earthly kings may step out of their own country into the territory of God. He hath prepared his throne in the heavens, and his kingdom rules over all. The heaven of angels and other excellent creatures belong to his authority. He is principally called the Lord of Hosts, in relation to his entire command over the angelic legions. And the inanimate creatures in heaven are at his beck, they are his armies in heaven, disposed in an excellent order in their several ranks. Ps. cxlvii. 4. He calls the stars by names. The stars by their influences fight against Sisera. Jud. v. 20. And the sun holds in its reins, and stands still, to light Joshua to a complete victory. Josh. x. 12. They are all marshalled in their ranks, to receive his word of command, and fight in close order. And those creatures which mount up from the earth, and take their place in the lower heavens, vapors whereof hail and snow are formed, are part of the army, and do not only receive, but fulfil his word of command. Ps. cxlviii. 8. These are his stores and magazines of judgment against a time of trouble, and a day of battle and war. Job xxxiii. 22, 23. The hell of devils belong to his authority. They have cast themselves out of the arms of his grace, into the furnace of his justice; they have by their revolt forfeited the treasure of his goodness, but cannot exempt themselves from the sceptre of his dominion. The earth of men and other creatures belong to his authority. Ps. xlvii. 7. God is king of all the earth, and rules to the ends of it.

But his dominion extends,

1. Over the least creatures. All the creatures of the earth are listed in Christ's muster-roll, and make up the number of his regiments. He hath a host on earth as well as heaven. Gen. ii. 1. The heavens and the earth were finished, and all the hosts of them. And they are all his servants. Ps. cxix. 91, and move at his pleasure. And he vouchsafes the title of his army, to the locust, caterpillar, and palmer worm. Joel ii. 25. And describes their motions by military words, climbing the walls, marching, not breaking their ranks, ver. 7. He hath the command as a great general over the highest angel, and the meanest worm. Not a spot of earth, nor air, nor water, in the world, but is his possession; not a creature in any element but is his subject.

2. His dominion extends over men. It extends over the highest potentate, as well as the meanest peasant; the proudest monarch is no more exempt than the most languishing beggar. He accepts not the persons of princes, nor regards the rich more than the poor. Job xxxiv. 19.

3. But especially this dominion in the peculiarity of its extent, is seen in the exercise of it over the spirits and hearts of men. Earthly governors have by his indulgence a share with him in a dominion over men's bodies, upon which account he graceth princes and judges with the title of gods. Ps. lxxxii. 6. But the highest prince is but a prince according to the flesh. God is the sovereign; man rules over the beast in man, the body; and God rules over the man in man, the soul.

IV. Wherein this dominion and sovereignty consists, and how it is manifested.

1. The first act of sovereignty is the making laws. This is essential to God; no creature's will can be the first rule to the creature, but only the will of God. Hence the law is called the royal law. James ii. 8; Isaiah xxxiii. 22. The Lord is our lawgiver, the Lord is our king.

The dominion of God in this regard will be manifest,

1. In the supremacy of it. The sole power of making laws doth originally reside in him. James iv. 12. There is one lawgiver, who is able to save and to destroy.

2. The dominion of God is manifest in the extent of his laws. As he is the governor and sovereign of the whole world, so he enacts laws for the whole. The heavens have their ordinances. Job xxxviii. 33. All creatures have a law imprinted on their beings, rational creatures have Divine statutes copied in their heart. Rom. ii. 15.

3. The dominion of God appears in the moral law, and his majesty in publishing it. As the law of nature was writ by his own fingers in the nature of man, so it was engraven by his own finger in the tables of stone, Ex. xxxi. 18.

4. The dominion of God appears in the obligation of the law, which reacheth the conscience. The laws of every prince are framed for the outward conditions of men. Conscience hath a protection from the King of kings, and cannot be arrested by any human power. The conscience is intelligible to God in its secret motions, and therefore only guidable by God.

2. His sovereignty appears in a power of dispensing with his own laws It is as much a part of his dominion to dispense with his laws, as to enjoin them. Positive laws he hath reversed; as the ceremonial law given to the Jews; the very nature of that law required a repeal, and fell of course. Eph. ii. 14.

3. His sovereignty appears in punishing the transgression of the law.

1. This is a breach of God's dominion as lawgiver. As a lawgiver he saves or destroys. James iv. 12.

2. Punishing the transgression of his law. This is a necessary branch of dominion. Surely there is a God that judgeth the earth. Ps. lvii. 9. 11. He reduceth the creature by the lash of his judgments, that would not acknowledge his authority and his precepts.

3. This of punishing was the second discovery of his dominion in the world. His first act of sovereignty was the giving of a law, the next, his appearance in the state of a judge.

4. The means whereby he punisheth shows his dominion. Sometimes he musters up rain and mildew, sometimes he sends regiments of wild beasts; so he threatens Israel. Lev. xxvi. 22. Sometimes he sends out a party of angels, to beat up the quarters of men, and make a carnage among them. 2 Kings xix. 35. Sometimes he mounts his thundering battery, and shoots forth his ammunition from the clouds; as against the Philistines. 1 Sam. vii. 10. Sometimes he sends the slightest creatures to shame the pride, and punish the sin of man; as lice, frogs.

4. The dominion of God is manifested as a governor as well as a lawgiver and proprietor.

1. In disposing of states and kingdoms. Ps. lxxv. 7. God is judge, he puts down one and sets up another. In wars, whereby flourishing kingdoms are overthrown, God hath the chief command. God is called the Lord of Hosts 130 times. It is not the sword of the captain, but the sword of the Lord, bears the first rank. The sword of the Lord and of Gideon. Judges vii. 18. The sword of a conqueror is the sword of the Lord. He looseth the bond of kings, and girdeth their loins with a girdle.

2. The dominion of God is manifested in raising up and ordering the spirits of men according to his pleasure. He doth, as the Father of spirits, communicate an influence to the spirits of men as well as an existence. There are many examples of this part of his sovereignty. God by his sovereign conduct ordered Moses a protectress as soon as his parents had formed an ark of bulrushes, wherein to set him floating on the river. Ex. ii. 3—6. Thus he appointed Cyrus to be his shepherd, and gave him a pastoral spirit for the restoration of the city and temple of Jerusalem. Isa. xliv. 28, and xlv. 5. Tells them in the prophecy, that he had girded him, though Cyrus had not known him.

3. The dominion of God is manifest in restraining the furious passions of men, and putting a block in their way. Sometimes God doth it by a remarkable hand, as the Babel builders were diverted from their proud designs by a sudden confusion; sometimes by ordinary, though unexpected means: as when Saul, like a hawk, was ready to prey upon David, whom he had hunted as a partridge upon the mountains.

4. The dominion of God is manifest in defeating the purposes and devices of men. God often makes a mock of human projects. Job v. 12. He disappointeth the devices of the crafty. The cunningest designs baffled by some small thing intervening, when you see men of profound wisdom infatuated, mistake their way, and grope in the noonday as in the night. Job v. 14.

5. The dominion of God is manifest in the means and occasions of men's conversion. Sometimes one occasion, sometimes another; one word lets a man go, another arrests him, and brings him before God and his own conscience.

6. The dominion of God is manifest in disposing of the lives of men He keeps the key of death, as well as that of the womb, in his own hand; he hath given man a life, but not power to dispose of it, nor lay it down at his pleasure.

To conclude,

1. How great is the contempt of this sovereignty of God? Man naturally would be free from God's empire, to be a slave under the dominion of his own lust. The sovereignty of God as a lawgiver is most abhorred by man. Lev. xxvi. 41; Prov. i. 25. Ye have set at naught all my counsels. All sin is in its nature a contempt of the divine dominion.

2. How dreadful is the consideration of this doctrine to all rebels against God. Punishment is unavoidable. None can escape him. He hath the sole authority over hell and death, the keys of both are in his hand.

3. What matter of comfort and strong encouragement for prayer. My king, was the strong appellation David used in prayer. Ps. v. 2. "Hearken to the voice of my cry." Here is comfort in afflictions. As a sovereign, he is the author of afflictions; as a sovereign, he can be the remover of them. In the severest tempest the Lord that raised the wind against us, which shattered the ship, and tore its rigging, can change that contrary wind for a more happy one, to drive us into the port. It is a comfort to the church in times of public commotions. The consideration of the divine sovereignty may arm us against the threatenings of mighty ones, and the menaces of persecutors. Prov. xxi. 30.

THE LONG-SUFFERING OF GOD.

2 Peter iii. 9.—The Lord is long-suffering to us-ward. (H.)

It is a shocking disposition of mind, which Solomon describes in that well-known passage in Eccles, "Because sentence against an evil work is not executed speedily, therefore the heart of the sons of men is fully set in them to do evil."

It seems, at first sight, as if the wise man had rather exceeded in his portrait of the human heart.

God is patient towards all who offend him; then let us offend him without remorse, let us try the utmost extent of his patience. God lifteth over our head a mighty hand, armed with lightenings and thunderbolts, but his hand is usually suspended awhile before it strikes; then, let us dare it while it delays, and till it moves to crush us to pieces, let us not respect it. What a disposition, what a shocking disposition of mind is this.

Could we have the madness to add sin to sin, if we were really convinced that God entertained the formidable design of bearing with us no longer?

And shall we "despise the riches of the long-suffering of God?" What! because a space to repent, shall we continue in impenitence?

"The Lord is long-suffering to us-ward, not willing that any should perish, but that all should come to repentance."

Consider,

I. The nature of this long-suffering.

1. It is part of the Divine goodness and mercy, yet differs from both The Lord is full of compassion, slow to anger. Long-suffering differs from

mercy in respect to the object; mercy respects the creature as miserable: patience, or long-suffering, respects the creature as criminal: mercy pities him in his misery; long-suffering bears with the sin, and waits to be gracious.

Patience or long-suffering differs also from goodness, in regard to the object. The object of goodness is every creature, from the highest angel in heaven to the meanest creature on earth; goodness respects things in a capacity, or in a state of creation, nurseth and supporteth them as creatures. Long-suffering considers them as already created and fallen short of their duty; goodness respects persons as creatures; long-suffering as transgressors.

2. Since it is a part of goodness and mercy, it is not insensibility. He is slow to anger. The Lord considers every provocation, but is not hasty to discharge his arrows on the offenders; he sees the sin with an eye of abhorrence, but beholds the sinner with an eye of pity; his anger burns against the sin, whilst his arms are open to receive the sinner.

3. As long-suffering is a part of mercy and goodness, it is not constrained or faint-hearted patience. Patience or long-suffering in man, is often a feebleness of spirit and want of strength. But it is not from the shortness of the divine arm, that he cannot reach us, nor from the feebleness of his hand that he cannot strike us. He can soon level us with the dust, dash us in pieces like a potter's vessel, or consume us as a moth.

4. Since it is not for want of power over the creature, it is from a fulness of the power over himself. The Lord is slow to anger, and great in power. As it is the effect of his power, so it is an argument of his power. As the more feeble any man is in reason, the less command he hath over his passions. Revenge is a sign of a childish mind. He that is slow to anger is better than the mighty. The long-suffering of God towards sinners, manifests his power, more than the creation of a world.

5. As long-suffering is a branch of mercy, the exercise of it is founded on the death of Christ. It is in Christ we find the satisfaction of justice; and it is in and through Christ the long-suffering of God is manifested to man

2. How this long-suffering or patience is manifested.

1. To our first parents. The patience or long suffering of God was manifested in not directing his artillery against them, when they first attempted to rebel. He might have struck them dead when they began to hearken to the tempter. And after our first parent had brought his sin to perfection, God did not immediately send that death on him, which he had merited, but continued his life to the space of 930 years.

2. His long-suffering is manifested to the Gentiles. What they were, we need no other witness than the apostle, who sums up many of their crimes, Rom. i. 29—32, being filled with all unrighteousness. And he concludes with these dreadful aggravations, they not only do the same, but have pleasure in them that do them. They were so naturalized in wickedness, that they delighted in nothing else. They were plunged into idolatry and superstition. Yet, did the Lord appear against them with fire and sword? "At the times of that ignorance he winked."

3. The long-suffering of God was manifested to the Israelites. He suffered their manners forty years in the wilderness. He bore with that people above 1500 years from their coming out of Egypt to the destruction of their commonwealth.

In particular this long-suffering of God is manifested,

1. In his giving warning of judgments before they are commissioned to go forth. The Lord speaks before he strikes, and speaks that he may not strike.

Wrath is published before it is executed, and that a long time; the old world were warned 120 years before the deluge came on them.

The Lord does not come unawares. I will chastise them as their congregation hath heard. The Lord summoned by the voice of his prophets, before he confounded by the voice of his thunders. He seldom cuts men down by his judgments, before he hath hewed them by his prophets. Not a remarkable judgment but was foretold; the flood, by Noah; the famine to Egypt, by Joseph; the earthquake, by Amos; Amos i. 1; the storm from Chaldea, by Jeremiah; the captivity of the ten tribes by Hosea; and the total destruction of Jerusalem and the temple, by Christ. And he thus warns, that men may take the warning, and thunders again and again, before he crushes with his thunderbolt.

2. The long-suffering of the Lord is manifested in his unwillingness to execute his threatened judgments, when he can delay no longer. He doth not afflict willingly nor grieve the children of men. He takes no pleasure in it. When he came to reckon with Adam, he walked, he did not run with his sword, and that in the cool of the day. His exercising of judgment, is a coming out of his place. Isa. xxvi. 21; Micah i. 3. Hence every prophecy loaded with a threatening is called the burden of the Lord. When the Lord punishes, he doth it with some regret; when he hurls down his thunders, he seems to do it with a backward hand. He created, saith Chrysostom, the world in six days, but was seven days in destroying one city, Jericho. When the Lord strikes, it is with a sigh. "Ah! I will ease me of my adversaries, and avenge me of my enemies. Oh Ephraim, what shall I do unto thee? How shall I give thee up, oh, Ephraim! And many a time (says the Psalmist) turned he his anger away."

3. His long-suffering is manifested, in that when he begins to send out his judgments, he doth it by degrees. His judgments are as the morning light. He doth not thunder all his judgments at once. First the palmer-worm, then the locust, then the canker-worm, then the caterpillar. Joel i. 4. A Jewish writer says, these came not all in one year, but one year after another.

4. His long-suffering appears, by moderating his judgments. He stirreth not up all his wrath. He doth not empty his quivers, nor exhaust his magazines of thunder. "He rewardeth us not according to our iniquities."

5. His long-suffering farther appears, in giving great mercies after provocations. He is so slow to anger, that he heaps many kindnesses on a rebel; instead of punishment, there is prosperous wickedness. Israel quarrelled with his servant Moses at the Red Sea; yet then the Lord stretched forth his hand and delivered them.

6. The long-suffering of God appears also when we consider the greatness and multitude of our provocations. Men drinking in iniquity like water. Rushing into sin. The imaginations of the thoughts of the heart only evil.

III. The ground and reason of this long-suffering to us-ward.

1. As a testimony of his reconcileable and merciful nature towards sinners. "Howbeit, for this cause I obtained mercy, that in me Jesus Christ might show forth all long-suffering."

2. That sinners may be brought to repentance. "Not knowing," says the apostle, "that the riches of his forbearance and goodness leads thee to repentance." The Lord is long-suffering to us-ward. "The long-suffering of God is salvation," i. e. hath a tendency to salvation.

3. For the continuance of his church. "As the new wine is found in the cluster, and one saith, Destroy it not, for a blessing is in it." Isa. lxv. 8, 9

4. That his justice may be clear when he condemns the impenitent. "I gave her space to repent of her fornication, and she repented not."

5. In answer to the prayers of his people, his long-suffering is exercised towards sinners. "Except the Lord of hosts had left unto us a very small remnant, we should have been as Sodom."

To conclude.

1. How is the long-suffering of God abused! May we not say to the Lord as Saul said to David, "Thou art more righteous than I; thou hast rewarded me with good."

2. Is the Lord long-suffering? How much better, therefore, is it to fall into the hands of God, than into the hands of man: the best of men. Moses, a meek man, once cried, Ye rebels.

3. We may infer from the Lord's long-suffering towards sinners, the value of the soul; he not only died to redeem it, but waits with unwearied patience and forbearance to receive it. "Behold, I stand at the door."

Lastly, If the Lord be thus long-suffering to us-ward, who have so long and repeatedly rebelled against him, ought not christians to exercise forbearance and long-suffering one towards another? "Walk worthy of the vocation wherewith ye are called, with all lowliness and meekness, with long-suffering." Eph. iv. 1—6.

GOD'S COMPASSION.

Hos. xi. 7—9.—My people are bent to backsliding from me: though they called them unto the Most High, none at all would exalt him: [yet] how shall I give thee up, Ephraim? how shall I deliver thee, Israel? how shall I make thee as Admah? how shall I set thee as Zeboim? mine heart is turned within me, my repentings are kindled together. I will not execute the fierceness of mine anger. (S. S.)

The riches of Divine grace are manifest in all the promises—

But they are more eminently displayed in the manner in which the promises are given—

God often introduces them after an enumeration of his people's sins—

The passage before us well exemplifies this remark—See similar instances, Isa. xliii. 22—25, and lvii. 17, 18.

God has been contrasting his kindness to Israel, and their ingratitude towards him—

In the text he sets forth their wickedness with all its aggravations—

Yet all this is preparatory, not to a heavy denunciation of his wrath, but to the tenderest expressions of paternal love—

I. The conduct of men towards God.

The ten tribes, since their separation from Judah, had become idolators—

Yet God calls them his people because they had been admitted into covenant with him, and still professed to be his—

Thus all who call themselves Christians are "God's people"—

But they "are bent to backsliding from him"

The ungodly are justly compared to an unruly heifer—

They will not submit to the yoke of God's laws—

Their whole spirit and temper is like that of Pharoah—Exod. v. 2.

The "bent" and inclination of their hearts is wholly towards sin—

An outward conformity to God's will they may approve—
But they have a rooted aversion to spiritual obedience—
Nor can they by any any means be prevailed on to "exalt and honor him —
They are "called" frequently by God's ministers—
They are exhorted and intreated to return to the Most High—
But neither promises can allure nor threatenings alarm them—
They turn a deaf ear to all admonitions—
They will not "exalt" God in their hearts and lives—
This is almost universally the conduct of mankind
There are a few indeed who desire and delight to serve God—
They wish him to be the sole Lord and Governor of their hearts—
It is their study to exalt him both in their words and actions—
But these are few in every age and place—
So few, that, in comparison of the rebellious, they may be said to be "none at all"—
What might such persons expect at the hand of God?
II. GOD'S CONDUCT TOWARDS THEM
How different are God's ways from the ways of man!—
Instead of executing vengeance in a moment,
He deliberates
Admah and Zeboim were cities destroyed with Sodom and Gomorrah—
And such monuments of wrath do the unregenerate deserve to be—
But God knows not, as it were, how to inflict the deserved punishment—
He calls to mind that they are *his* people*—
He hesitates, like a parent, that is about to disinherit his son—
Thus is he distracted between his affection for them, and his regard for his own honor—Thus also in Hos. vi. 4.
He relents
To accommodate himself to our weak comprehensions he speaks of himself after the manner of men—
He cannot endure the thought of making men the objects of his everlasting displeasure—
Thus did Jesus weep over the murderous Jerusalem—Luke xix. 41.
And thus do the bowels of our Father yearn over us—Jer. xxxi 20.
He resolves
Often has "the fierce anger" of the Lord been kindled against us—
Yet many times has he turned away from his wrathful indignation—Ps. lxxviii. 38.
Often, when his bow was bent, has he forborne to strike—Ps. vii. 11, 12.
He waits, in hope that he may yet return to him—
His language to his rebellious creatures is the same as ever—Jer. ii. 12, 13.
Infer,
1. How precious in the sight of God are the souls of men!—
When it was necessary for man's salvation, God gave his Son—
Nor did he then *deliberate*, "how shall I do this?"—Rom viii. 32.
Neither did he *relent*, when he laid our iniquities on him—Mark xiv. 35, 36
Yea, he was even *pleased* in bruising his own Son for us†—
But when a sinner seems irreclaimable, every tender emotion is excited—

* The repitition of their names, "*thee* Ephraim, and *thee*, Israel," seems to import tenderness and affection towards them.
† This is the proper sense of Isa. liii. 10.

God sustains a conflict in his mind, and cannot give him up—
O that men would duly estimate the worth of their own souls!—
2 How just will be the condemnation of the impenitent!
This compassion of God greatly aggravates their backsliding —
And at last it will give way to wrath and indignation—Gen. vi. 3,
Soon God will not deliberate, but decide; not relent, but laugh at their calamity; not resolve to pardon, but swear they shall not enter into his rest—
Then how just will their condemnation appear?—
May this goodness of God now lead us to repentance!—
3. How certainly shall the returning sinner find mercy!
If God feel thus for the rebellious, how much more for the penitent!—
Let all then seek him with humble confidence in his mercy—
Let them offer their supplications like those of old—Isa. lxiii. 15.
So shall that song of praise succeed their present disquietude—Isa. xii 1

THE MERCY OF GOD.

Micah vii. 18—20.—Who is a God like unto thee, that pardoneth iniquity, and passeth by the transgression of the remnant of his heritage? He retaineth not his anger forever, because he delighteth in mercy. He will turn again, he will have compassion upon us; he will subdue our iniquities; and thou wilt cast all their sins into the depths of the sea. Thou wilt perform the truth to Jacob, and the mercy to Abraham, which thou hast sworn unto our fathers from the days of old. (S. S.)

Every work of God should lead our thoughts up to its great author—
The prophet had prayed that the Jews might be restored to their own land—Ver. 14.
God had promised that he would grant them such a deliverance from Babylon as he had before given to their ancestors from Egypt—Ver. 15—17.
The prophet immediately elevates his thoughts from the deliverance to the author of it, and breaks forth in admiration of his mercy—
His devout acknowledgments lead us to consider God's mercy
I. In its rise
God has had at all times a people in the world
They were very few in the days of Noah, or of Abraham—
In our Lord's day they were but a "little flock"—
The apostle's description of them is still as true as ever—Rom. xi. 5.
These, however, are esteemed as God's "heritage"—Ps. xxxiii. 12.
Towards these he exercises peculiar mercy
He "passes by their transgressions" with much long-suffering—Ps. ciii. 10.
Though he feels anger against them, Ps. vii. 11. "he retains it not for ever"—
He "pardons their iniquities," giving them repentance unto life—
In so doing he is actuated only by his own love and mercy
There is not any thing in his elect that can merit his favor—
But "he delighteth in mercy," and would gladly exercise it towards all*—
The iniquities of the wicked are a burthen to him Isa. i. 14, 24. Amos ii. 13.
He waits to be gracious unto them—Isa. xxx. 18.

*Judgment is called "his *strange* work, his *strange* act." Is. xxviii. 21. Ezek. xxxiii. 11

He deliberates long before he casts them off—Hos. vi. 4.
When he rejects them finally, he does it with reluctance—Luke xix. 41.
He is often so troubled for the obstinate, that he resolves for his own sake to reclaim them by a sovereign exercise of almighty power—Jer. iii. 19.
When he has prevailed on a sinner, he exults for joy—Zeph. iii. 17. See also the parables of the shepherd, the woman, the father, Luke xv.
And thus it is that he saves the remnant of his heritage—Isa. xliii. 25.
What reason then have they to exclaim, "Who is like unto thee?"
The mercy thus freely manifested is worthy of admiration also
II. In its progress.
God continues to act with astonishing forbearance towards them
They are, alas! too prone to backslide from him—
They often provoke him to withdraw himself from them—Deut. xxxii. 20
But he leaves them not eternally to take the fruit of their misconduct—
He has "compassion on them," remembering they are but dust—Ps. ciii. 14
He "turns to them again" after hiding himself for a little season. Isa liv. 7, 8. See a striking declaration to this effect, Isa. lvii. 16—18.
He restores to them the light of his countenance—
How interesting and endearing is this description of his character!—
How must every saint adopt the church's confession!—Lam. iii. 22.
He pledges himself not only to pardon, but to "subdue their iniquities"
He will not suffer sin to have dominion over them—Rom. vi. 14.
He hides his face in order to embitter sin to them—
He turns to them again to encourage their opposition to it—
He renews their strength when they are fainting—Isa. xl. 29—31.
And gradually perfects in them the work he has begun—
Who can survey this progress of mercy, and not exclaim "Who?" &c.—
But the full extent of God's mercy can only be seen
III. In its consummation.
Sin cleaves to the Lord's people as long as they are in the body—
Hence they have daily occasion for renewed forgiveness—
But soon their pardon shall be final and complete
God overthrew the Egyptian host in the Red Sea—
"There was not so much as one of them left"—
So will God "cast his people's sins into the sea"—
He will cast them "all" without one single exception—
And *that* "into the depths" from whence they shall never rise—
If the Israelites so rejoiced in seeing their enemies dead on the shore, how will christians in their final victory over sin—
God will fulfil to them his promises in their utmost extent
The promises as made to Abraham and his seed were "mercy"—
The confirmation of them to Jacob and to the church was "truth"—
They have been established with the sanction of an "oath"—
And these "promises" will be fulfilled "to all the seed"—
Soon will "the head-stone be brought forth with shoutings," &c.—Zech. iv. 7.
How will every glorified soul *then* admire the divine mercy!—
What energy will a sight of sins forgiven, of backslidings healed, of glory bestowed, give to the exclamation in the text!—
May this view of the subject be realized in our experience!—
Application
Let *the careless* consider against whom their sins are committed—
Will they never pause, and exclaim like Joseph—Gen xxxix, 9.

Let *the penitent* reflect on the descriptions given of God in scripture—Neh. ix. 17. Isa. lv. 7.

Nor let them judge of him by the dictates of sense—Isa. lv. 8, 9.

Let *the sincere believer* apply to himself that congratulation—Deut. xxxiii. 29.

And let him adopt that triumphant boast—Isa. xxv. 9.

THE KNOWLEDGE OF GOD BY THE LIGHT OF NATURE.

Acts xiv. 15—17.—The living God, which made heaven and earth, and the sea, and all things that are therein, &c. (H.)

When the apostle Paul gave authority to his ministrations at Lystra, by working a miraculous cure on a man who was born a cripple, the inhabitants imagined that he and Barnabas were gods, and were immediately preparing a sacrifice for them: but to divert this madness and superstition of paying Divine worship to the creatures, the apostles, with holy jealousy and indignation, ran into the midst of them, and preached to them the living and the true God. "We," say they, "are utterly unworthy of these Divine honors; for we are men of such flesh and blood as yourselves, and are liable to the like infirmities: we preach to you, that ye should turn from these vanities to the living God who made heaven and earth," &c.

From which words we may raise the following observations:

I. The light of nature may teach us, that there is one Supreme Being.

He hath not left himself without witness. The Being which made all things, or the first cause of all. And when I say, God may be known by the light of nature, I mean, that the senses and the reasoning powers, which belong to the nature of man are able to give him so much light in seeking after God, as to find out something of him thereby, or to gain some knowledge of him. Rom. i. 19, 20. "That which may be known of God is manifested."

1. By the light of nature we may come to the knowledge of his existence. It is evident, that nothing could make itself. It is impossible that any thing which once had no being should ever give being to itself. Since, therefore, there is a world with millions of beings in it, which are born and die, it is certain there is some Being who had no beginning. This is the being whom we call God.

Of all the visible beings that we are acquainted with, man is the highest and most noble; but he is forced to confess he is not his own maker. Our parents, or our ancestors, were no more able to make themselves than we are.

Or if some atheist should say, We must run up from son to father, and from father to grandfather, in endless generations without a beginning, and without any first cause. This is impossible; for if ten thousand generations cannot subsist of themselves without dependance on something before them, neither endless generations. Suppose a chain of ten thousand links hung down from the sky, and could not support itself, unless some mighty power upheld the first link; then it is certain, a chain of ten thousand times ten thousand links, or an endless chain, could never support itself. There must be, therefore, some first bird, some first beast, some first man.

2. What God is, viz. that he is a spirit, perfect in wisdom and perfect in power. The amazing work of God in the heavens, the sun, the moon, the stars, their regular and unerring motions, for so many thousand years; the progress of the hours, the changes of day and night, winter and summer, which depend on these motions and revolutions; they all abundantly discover that the maker of them was wise, and skilful beyond all our conceptions. If we observe the operations of a clock or watch, which doth but imitate the motions of these heavenly bodies, and point out to us the day and the hour, we say, it is impossible this curious engine could be made without great wisdom and skill in some artificer who contrived it; and can we be so foolish as to imagine, that this vast and glorious engine of the heavens, with all its bright furniture, which makes times and seasons, day and night, could ever come into being by chance?

The wonderful production of plants, herbs, trees, and flowers, and astonishing operations of living creatures, and their several parts and powers, discover to us the deep wisdom and knowledge of the Being that made them. Let us consider but our own natures, our parts, and powers, what wonders are contained in every sense? Can all these be formed without infinite wisdom? I might demand of the sons of atheism, in the language of the Psalmist, Ps. xciv. 9, 10, "He that planteth the ear, shall not he hear?" And as the wonders of contrivance in the works of God declare his depth of wisdom, so the difficulty of creating them out of nothing argues his almighty power. "When we survey the heavens, the work of his hands," what a glorious and powerful Being must that be, which formed these vast bodies at first, and which upholds their stupendous frame? Man can only change the shapes and qualities of things; he can make a clock, but he must have brass and iron given him, for he cannot create these materials: but God's huge and astonishing engine of the heavens, whereby hours and days, seasons and ages, are made and measured out, were all formed by him without any materials: he made all the materials himself. A creator must be almighty, he must be God.

Again, Let us think within ourselves, what a powerful Being must that be, who can make a soul, a spirit, a thinking being to exist, so nearly like himself, with an understanding capable of knowing the works of God, and of knowing God himself? We are his image, "we are his offspring;" thus sang Aratus the heathen poet, Acts xvii. 28, 29, and spoke like a christian.

And thus it appears beyond all controversy, that the light of nature finds there is a God, and that this God is an all-wise and almighty spirit. If we were in doubt about his existence or being, these reasonings would assure us of it; and if we seek after his nature, and his perfections, these his works discover them.

3. His supreme and absolute dominion over all things, that God is the sovereign lord and possessor of heaven and earth, Gen. xiv. 19, and consequently that he hath a right to dispose of all things as he pleases. Rom. ix. 20. "Who therefore shall say to him, What dost thou?"

4. That though God be the absolute and natural lord of all things that he hath made, yet he is pleased to deal with his rational creatures in a way of moral government. The conscience which he hath formed in man may discover in him so much of the natural law and will of his God, as a righteous governor of the world, if it be properly and wisely employed. Rom. ii. 14, 15. "The Gentiles which have not the written law," which not only teaches them that adoration and worship, prayer and praise, are duties which they owe to God; but it instructs them also to distinguish between vice and virtue. Acts xxviii. 4. "Surely this man is a murderer."

Reason and conscience might teach mankind that since God has given them an understanding and freedom of will to choose or refuse good or evil, he will certainly call them to account for their behaviour. In their own consciences there is a kind of tribunal erected, "their conscience excusing or accusing them."

5. That God is a universal benefactor to mankind, even above and beyond their deserts, and notwithstanding all their provocations. That though they walked in their own idolatrous ways, yet God left them not without witness of his goodness, giving them fruitful seasons.

II. What are the various uses of this knowledge of God, which is attainable by the light of nature.

In general, it is to bear witness for God in the world. More particularly,

1. This knowledge of God, as our maker and governor, by the light of nature, is useful, not only to show men their duty, but to convince them of sin. The apostle Paul begins with this doctrine in the first chapter of his Epistle to the Romans, where his great design is to show mankind the guilt and wretchedness of their state.

2. As it is a design to awaken men to the practice of their duty. This natural conscience is the candle of their Lord, which he has set up in the heart of man; and though it shines but dimly, yet it has sometimes kept them from being more vile.

3. Gives some encouragement to guilty creatures to repent of their sins, and to return to God by a general hope of acceptance, though they had no promise of pardoning grace. And this was the very principle on which some of the Gentiles set themselves to practise virtue, to worship God, and endeavor to become like him. I do not say, that natural religion can give sinful men a full and satisfying assurance of pardon on their repentance; for the deepest degrees of penitence cannot oblige a prince to forgive the criminal: but still his overflowing goodness may evidently and justly excite in their hearts some hope of forgiving grace. The Ninevites themselves, when threatened with destruction, "repented in sackcloth and ashes." Jonah iii. 5—10. And there is yet a more express text to this purpose. Rom. ii. 4. "Despisest thou the riches of his goodness?"

4. Serves to vindicate the conduct of God as a righteous governor. This will leave them without excuse in "the great day, when God shall judge the secrets of all hearts." Their own consciences will accuse them. Rom. i. 20, 21; ii. 15. "Is God unrighteous, who taketh vengeance on such sinners? God forbid." Rom. ii. 5, 6. In the world to come, not one condemned sinner shall be able to say, God is unjust. "Every mouth shall be stopped, and the heavens and the earth proclaim his righteousness."

5. Prepares the way for preaching and receiving the gospel of grace: and that many ways.

We see the apostle wisely managing his ministry to the Athenians, of which we have but short hints in Acts xvii. 22, &c. By discoursing first on natural religion, and agreeably to this method of propagating the gospel among the heathen nations, we find, in fact, that where there was any thing of the knowledge of the true God, either by the light of nature, or by tradition, there the gospel was soonest received.

III. The defects or imperfections of it.

1. It is but a small portion of the things of God, which the bulk of mankind can generally be supposed to learn merely by their own reasonings. This is sufficiently evident by the history of past times and ancient nations, as well as by present observation of the heathen world. Though some of

the philosophers attained considerable knowledge of the nature of God and clearly saw his eternal power and godhead, Rom. i. 20, yet these were but very few in comparison of the rest.

2. It is but dim and feeble, and leaves mankind under many doubts and uncertainties in matters of importance. A short lesson of knowledge in the heathen schools was obtained with long toil and difficulty: their philosophy was rather a feeling after God in the dark, than a sight of him in daylight: so the apostle expresses himself, Acts xvii. 27, "That they should seek the Lord." What feeble words are these! how doubtful a knowledge is represented by them! how generally, and almost, without exception, did their philosophers comply with the idolatry of their country, and "worship God in the form of beasts and birds."

In some countries, the youth and flower of conquered nations were doomed a sacrifice to their idols: and sometimes filthy and abominable lewdness were the ceremonies of their worship. How blind was the eye of their reason, not to see this madness! and how feeble its power, that it made no remonstrance against these lewd and bloody scenes of degenerated piety!

All these instances indeed do not effectually prove, that reason could not possibly teach them better; but the experience of long ages and of whole nations sufficiently shows us, that their reason neither did inform them better, nor was ever likely to do it. 1 Cor. i. 21. "The world by wisdom knew not God."

3. All the knowledge of God which they arrived at, by the light of nature, had actually but little influence to reform the hearts or the lives of mankind. I say, it had but little influence in comparison of what it might or should have had, Acts xiv. 16; Rom. i., "latter end."

4. It doth rather serve to show men their sin and misery, than discover any effectual relief; and in this respect it comes infinitely short of what the revelation of the gospel of Christ hath done.

1. The light of nature of itself gives no assurance or forgiveness to the repenting sinner. "Who can tell but the Lord may turn away from his fierce anger?" is but a feeble motive to repentance and new obedience, in comparison of such a word from God himself, as Ex. xxxiv. 6. "And the Lord passed by before him, and proclaimed, The Lord, the Lord God, merciful and gracious." Prov. xxviii. 13. "He that confesseth and forsaketh."

2. The light of nature discovers no effectual atonement for sin, nor relief to a guilty conscience, by all the costly sacrifice and blood of animals; but the gospel points us to the "Lamb of God that taketh away the sins of the world," John i. 29, and assures us, that if we confess our sins, 1 John, i. 6.

3. The light of nature points us to no effectual mediator, or advocate in heaven; but the gospel leads us to "Jesus the righteous as our advocate with the Father." 1 John ii. 1, 2.

4. The light of nature and our daily experience discover to us our weakness to subdue sin within us, to restrain our unruly appetites, to mortify our corrupt affections, to resist the daily temptations that surround us; but it points us not to the fountain of strength, even the promised aids of the Holy Spirit, these are the peculiar glories and blessings of the gospel of Christ.

5. The light of nature and continual observation show us, that we must die, but give us no clear and certain evidence of happiness after death. But the gospel sets these future glories in a Divine and certain light before every man, who reads or hears it. It encourages us to repentance of sin, to diligence, patience, and perseverance, in the ways of faith and holiness, by the joys unspeakable, which are set before us, and builds our hope of eternal life on the well-attested promises of a God who cannot lie.

Reflections.

1. Since the rational knowledge of God and natural religion had its proper uses, and especially to lay a foundation for our receiving the gospel of Christ, let it not be despised nor abandoned by any of us. There may be some necessary occasions for our recourse to it. St. Paul made glorious use of it in his discourse with the Athenian infidels.

2. Since this knowledge of God, which is attainable by the light of nature, has so many defects, let us never venture to rest in it. Dare not content yourselves with the lessons of the book of nature. The sun in the firmament, with the moon and all the stars, can never give the light to see God, which is derived from the Sun of Righteousness.

What a deplorable thing is it, that multitudes in our nation, where the glory of the blessed gospel shines with such brightness, should be running back to the glimmering light of nature, and satisfy themselves with heathenism and philosophy! that they should choose to walk in twilight, and refuse to be conducted by the blaze of noon. "The God of this world hath blinded the eyes of them that believe not."

3. Since the nations, which have only the light of nature, and forced to feel out their way to God through such dusky glimmerings, let us bless the Lord with all our souls, that we are born in a land of clear light, where the gospel shines in all its beauty. How should we value the Bible as our highest treasure, which gives us such blessed discoveries of God and his wisdom and power, and his mercy in Christ, which infinitely exceed all the doubtful twilight of nature. O, may the blessed Bible lie next our hearts, and be the companion of our bosoms.

4. Pity and pray for the heathen world, the dark corners of the earth, the benighted nations, where the Sun of Righteousness never rose, and were they can but feel after God through the mists of ignorance and error. Let us remember these ancient times, when our forefathers in this nation were led away into the same errors and gross idolatries, and lift up one compassionate groan to heaven for them. When shall the ends of the earth learn to know thee? When shall all nations, people, and languages, begin their songs of salvation to him that sits upon the throne, and to the Lamb?

THE GOSPEL PRODUCTIVE OF GOOD WORKS.

1 Timothy, vi. 3.—The doctrine which is according to godliness. (H. H.)

THE objections which men urge against the doctrines of the gospel, originate for the most part in their aversion to its precepts. The restraint which it imposes on their actions is irksome to them. They wish to follow the impulse of their passions, or the dictates of self-interest: and when they are checked in their progress, they complain, that the path marked out for them is too strait, and the yoke which we would put upon them is too heavy.

St. Paul is giving directions for the conduct of masters and servants towards each other: but, however "wholesome his words" were, he foresaw that some would "not consent to" them, notwithstanding they were "the words of Christ himself," and in perfect unison with the gospel, which was in that, as well as in every other respect, "a doctrine according to godliness He then proceeds to animadvert upon such characters, and to shew that their dislike to the injunctions given them was owing only to their own pride, and ignorance, and love of sin.

The expression contained in the text is peculiarly worthy of our attention. It gives a just, and very important view of the gospel; to illustrate and confirm which is the intent of this discourse.

In order to prove that the gospel is indeed "a doctrine according to godliness," let us consult,

I. Its doctrines,

We might, if our time would admit of it, illustrate this in every one of the doctrines of our holy religion. But we shall confine ourselves to,

1. The representations which it gives us of God—

The systems of religion which obtained among the heathen, were calculated rather to promote, than to repress, iniquity: for even their gods themselves, according to their own representations of them, were monsters of iniquity. But our God is holy and just; so holy, that he cannot look upon sin without the utmost abhorrence of it. Hab. i. 13. And so just, that he will never suffer it to pass unpunished. Exod. xxxiv. 7.

If indeed these were his only attributes, men might set down in despair, and take their fill of sin, because they would have no encouragement to depart from it. But "there is mercy also with him, that he may be feared;" yea, so "rich is he in mercy," that "none shall ever seek his face in vain."

How must the contemplation of such perfections tend to deter men from the commission of evil, and to foster in them every holy sentiment and desire!

2. The means which it prescribes for our reconciliation with him—

The leading feature of the gospel is, that it proclaims pardon to penitent sinners, through the blood and righteousness of the Lord Jesus Christ.

Let any one reflect on this stupendous mystery, the incarnation and death of the Son of God; let him consider, that no less a sacrifice than that made by our incarnate God was sufficient to atone for sin; and will he then be willing to incur all the penalties of sin, and to bear them in his own person? Will not the tears and agonies of an expiring Savior compel him to exclaim, "If such things were done in the green tree, what shall be done in the dry?" and will not the love of Christ in submitting to such an ignominious death, on purpose that he might redeem him from iniquity, have any influence on his mind? Will he readily trample on the blood that was shed for him, and crucify his Lord afresh by continuing in sin.

Let us prosecute the same inquiry, in relation to,

II. Its precepts—

View the precepts relating to God and our neighbor—

The two great commandments of the law are confirmed and ratified by the gospel, "Thou shalt love the Lord thy God with all thy heart, and thy neighbor as thyself," Now can any man love God, and not endeavor to do his will? Or, if he make his own self-love the rule and measure of his love to others, can he willingly injure them in any thing, or forbear to do them good? Would not an unfeigned love to these commands lay the axe to the root of all sin, and transform men into the very image of their God?

View the directions which it gives for self-government—

The gospel does not regulate the actions only, but the heart: it extends its dominion over all the most secret motives and inclinations; and requires every thought to be brought into captivity to the obedience of Christ. It makes no allowance for temptations, as though they extenuated the guilt of sin, or were an excuse for the commission of iniquity; but teaches us to "heap coals of fire on the head of an enemy" by acts of kindness, and "not to be overcome of evil, but to overcome evil with good." It tolerates no kind or degree of sin, but enjoins us to "cleanse ourselves from all filthiness both of flesh and spirit, and to perfect holiness in the fear of God." It requires us to "be holy as God himself is holy," and "perfect, even as our Father which is in heaven is perfect."

Can any one that considers these precepts, doubt what is the nature and tendency of the gospel?

Let us examine further,

III. Its examples—

It calls us to an imitation of,

1. Our blessed Lord—

He was virtue itself embodied. Neither friends nor enemies could ever find in him the smallest spot or blemish. Under circumstances the most trying that can be imagined, he preserved the same serenity of mind, the same meek and heavenly disposition. While he was suffering the most injurious treatment, he was like a lamb led to the slaughter: and in the very agonies of death, he prayed for nothing but blessings on the head of his cruel murderers. Now we are told, that in all this "he set us an example, that we should follow his steps:" and that all his followers must "walk even as he walked."

2. His holy Apostles—

These were far inferior indeed to their Divine Master; yet were they bright patterns of every thing that was excellent and praise-worthy. As being men of like passions with us, they manifested on some occasions their infirmities: and, in these instances, they are warnings to us, and not examples. But, for the most part, they conducted themselvs in a way that excites our highest admiration. And though, on account of their defects, we cannot follow them in every thing, yet we are called on the whole to tread in their steps, and to "be followers of them, as they were of Christ"

Are not these sufficient proofs of the holy tendency of the gospel?

Infer,

1. How little reason is there for objecting to the gospel as unfriendly to morality!

Men ground this objection upon the doctrine of our being "justified by faith only, without the works of the law." But if they would consider that that faith is always preceded by repentance, and followed by obedience, they would see that there was no foundation at all for their objection. If we said that people might live and die in an impenitent and disobedient state, and yet be saved by their faith, then there were good reason to condemn the gospel which we preach: but while we maintain the character of God as it is exhibited in the gospel, together with the obligation of its precepts, and the purity of its examples, no man need to tremble for the ark of God. A roof is not the less necessary to a house, because it is not to be laid as a foundation: nor are works less necessary because they cannot justify us before God. Let them but stand in their proper place, and they are as necessary as faith itself.

2. How deluded are they who hold the truth in unrighteousness!

There are doubtless many who profess to believe in Christ, while yet by their works they utterly deny him. There was one of this description even in the family of Christ himself. But will the faith which they exercise, be sufficient to save them? No: their faith is dead, being alone: it is no better than the faith of devils: nor will it be productive of any benefit to their souls: yea rather, inasmuch as it argued light and knowledge, it will only enhance their guilt, and aggravate their condemnation. Let those who are not occupied in a careful imitation of their Lord, and an unreserved obedience to his will, know assuredly, that if, on the one hand, he that believeth shall be saved, so, on the other hand, "the unrighteous shall not inherit the kingdom of heaven."

3. How great are the obligations of God's people to walk circumspectly! The world will judge of the gospel, not so much by what they hear, as by what they see. Now, though they have no right to act thus, we should be careful not to lay a stumbling-block before them. We should endeavor rather to make a good impression on their minds, and to give them no occasion from our conduct to speak evil of the truth itself. We should shew them by our lives, that their fears respecting the licentious tendency of the gospel are groundless. By walking as it becometh saints, we should put to silence their ignorant objections, and constrain them to confess, that, however the gospel may be dishonored by its friends, or calumniated by its enemies, it is indeed a doctrine according to godliness.

OF GOD AND HIS NATURAL PERFECTIONS.

John iv. 24.—God is a spirit. (H.)

The existence of God, and several of his perfections, open themselves with shining evidence in his works, and in his word; but the manner of his existence, and the eminent perfections, as they really exist in him, are wrapped up in thick and awful darkness, as a pavilion round about him. These are far, infinitely far, above our reach; "who by searching can find out God?" Job vi. 7. We can easier say what he is not than what he is. O, may he assist our thoughts, lest we darken counsel by words without knowledge while we speak concerning him!

I. That there is but one God, or one Divine Being.

That there is only one God is the concurring language of the genuine light of nature, and of scripture revelation. We are led into this sentiment,

1. By the light of nature.

The very notion it gives us of a God, and the very same arguments by which it proves that there is a God, must, if duly pursued, necessarily lead us into the thought, that there can be no more gods than one; for there can be but one necessarily existent Being, one first Cause, one absolutely infinite, one Supreme. Hence, though the rude, unthinking multitude among the pagans were led, perhaps chiefly by the wild fictions of the poets, into the absurd notion of gods many, and lords many, yet the soberer and wiser of their philosophers had their one supreme God, and all the rest were looked upon but as petty deities. Their most celebrated writers go into this way of representing things; and it is notorious, that Socrates fell a sacrifice to Athenian fury, for asserting the doctrine of one God. But we are still more abundantly assured of this important doctrine.

2. By scripture revelation.

The great and blessed God himself has given us the clearest evidence of his unity in his word. "I, even I, am he. Deut. xxxii. 39. Before me there was no God formed. Isa. xliii. 10. I am the first" Isa. xlvi. 6.

And the sacred writers, under Divine inspiration, have said of him, 'The Lord he is God." Deut. iv. 35. And, "Hear, O Israel (Deut. vi. 4;) and, Thou art great," says the Psalmist. Ps. lxxxvi. 10.

All this is evidently brought over by our Lord into the doctrine of the New Testament; he told the scribe that came to question him, The first of all the commandments. Mark xii. 29. And he spoke with high approbation of the answer, ver. 32. 34.

II. That this God is a Spirit, or that he is a Spiritual Being.

God is a Spirit. This relates to the nature of God, and as a spirit is the most excellent of beings that we have any notions of, God is represented under this character, to heighten our thoughts of him. We indeed know but little of the nature of spirits. The most natural obvious thought that arises in our minds about a spirit is that it is an incorporeal and invisible being, with life and action, understanding and will.

Let us then a little consider these, as applicable to God.

1. He is incorporeal and invisible.

All corporeal beings consist of parts, and so are in their own nature capable of separation or dissolution, of alterations, additions, or diminutions, and of different figures, sizes, shapes or forms; but all this argues composition and imperfection.

God can indeed, by his infinite power, make what visible appearances he pleases, as he did in various forms under the Old Testament, and at Christ's baptism and transfiguration, in the New; but these were not appearances of the essence of God itself, they were only outward symbols, which he occasionally formed to notify his presence for special purposes; but as to his own nature, or essence, he is the "invisible God, whom no man has seen, nor can see." Col. i. 15; 1 Tim. vi. 16. Accordingly our Lord says of his Father, "Ye have neither heard his voice. John v. 37.

Whenever therefore we read in scripture of any representations of God, as having eyes, ears; or, as seeing, hearing, we are by no means to imagine, that he hath such bodily organs, or acts by them; for, "To whom will you liken God?" Isa. xl. 18.

2. He lives and acts, or is a being that has life and action.

He is usually styled, by way of eminence, the living God: he has life in himself and with him is the fountain of life." John v. 26; Ps. xxxvi. 9. All the life of the vegetative, animal and rational world; the life of nature, and the life of grace here, and the life of glory hereafter, are of him, and derived from him; and therefore he himself must live,

And as he is a living, so he is an active spirit; he is ever active within himself, in the communion of the sacred Three with each other in the one undivided Godhead, ever active in his purposes and designs to display his own glory, and particularly the riches of his glory in and through a Redeemer. And he is ever capable of acting out of himself. He hath been, is, and ever will be, incessantly active, in upholding, exciting, or restraining, guiding, and governing all that he has made, to the glory of his own great name; for, "Of him, through him," Rom. xi. 36.

3. He has an understanding and will.

Had not God an understanding, he could never have designed any thing; and had he not a will, he could never have determined upon the execution of any design. "How manifold are his works!" Ps. civ. 24. "And he works all things," Eph. i. 11. "He is wonderful in counsel," Isa. xxviii. 29. "And he does according to his will." Dan. iv. 35.

III. That God is an infinitely perfect Spirit.

By his being an infinitely perfect Spirit, we may understand, that he is a Spirit, possessed of all possible perfections.

1. God is an infinite Spirit.

Nothing short of infinity can be ascribed to God; for he can neither limit his own being and perfections, nor can he be limited by any other. The farther our notions go to inquiries after him, the more they lose themselves in solemn wonder at his unsearchable greatness. But, O! how do we feel ourselves ingulphed, and, as it were, blinded with dazzled light, and lost in our darkness and nothingness, when we read the magnificent accounts the sacred oracles give of him! "Behold the nations are as a drop of a bucket." Isa. xl. 15. 17.

2. He is a self-sufficient, independent Spirit.

His existence is of himself, not as an effect from its cause; but he is of himself, as necessarily existing by the essential perfection of his own nature, without dependance on any other being. His name is, "I AM THAT I AM;" and "He only has immortality, in and of himself." 1 Tim. vi. 16. And as he is, by the perfection of his nature, self-sufficient for his own being, so he is for his own glory and blessedness. He is "exalted in himself above all blessing and praise." Neh. ix. 5. His name is El Shaddai, God all-sufficient, and he is "the Lord that maketh all things." Isa. xliv. 24. "For his pleasure they are and were created. But none can be profitable to God." Rev. iv. 11.

3. He is an eternal Spirit.

His self-sufficiency and independency make it impossible that he should ever begin to be, or cease from being. "Before the mountains were brought forth." Ps. xc. 2. He is without beginning, and without succession, of time or age. "The Lord shall endure for ever." Ps. ix. 7, and cii. 27.

4. He is an unchangeable Spirit.

"With him there is no variableness, nor shadow of turning." James i 17. There can be no change in him, as to posture, situation, or place.

He is unchangeable in his being and perfections.

He is unchangable in his glory. Though the manifestations of his glory, and due ascriptions of it to him, may vary; yet he is, and ever was, infinitely glorious in himself.

His blessedness is as unchangeable as his glory; for as this consists in the enjoyment of himself, so it neither can be increased nor lessened. "Look into the heavens and see. Job xxxv. 5—7. And it may be said of our Lord's own mediatorial goodness, that it "extendeth not to him," so as that he should be a real gainer by it. Ps. xvi. 2.

He is unchangeable in his decrees. "He is of one mind, who can turn him? The counsel of the Lord standeth forever." Ps. xxxiii. 11. And he has proclaimed with the majesty of a God, "My counsel shall stand." Isa. xlvi. 10. 11.

And he is unchangeable in his covenant, love and promises, to his people; for, "The mountains shall depart." Isa. liv. 10. "I am the Lord, I change not." Mal. iii. 6.

Whenever therefore, we read in scripture of God's repenting, and the like, it is not to be understood, of any alteration in his purposes; but all such expressions are to be understood with relation to his outward dispensations. All those affections of love, joy, grief, and hatred; that are ascribed to God· these are not properly affections, that take their turns in his heart, as they do in ours; but they are expressions of the agreeableness, or disagreeableness, of persons and things to his holy nature.

5. He is an omnipresent Spirit.

His infinite essence spreads, in an inconceivable manner through infinite space, without any parts or bounds: it is intimately near to, and in all creatures, in all places, in heaven, earth and hell, and in all possible space that is between and beyond them. "Do not I fill heaven and earth, says the Lord? He is not far from any of us, for in him we live. Wherever we are, whatever we do, and whithersoever we go, there is no flying away from God, "Though they dig into hell, thence shall mine hand take them; though they climb up to heaven, thence will I bring them down." Amos ix. 2, 3. And the Psalmist, in his elegant description of him says, "Whither shall I go from thy Spirit." Ps. cxxxix. 7—10.

Whenever, therefore, we read of God's dwelling in the heavens, coming down from thence, and drawing near to us; or, of forsaking us, and returning to his place, and the like; such expressions are not to be understood as if, in his natural being, he were more in one place than another; but they are to be understood of his actions, and manifestations of himself, in a way of mercy or judgment.

6. He is an all-knowing Spirit.

His omnipresence is with all intelligence attending it, because he is an omnipresent Spirit. "His understanding is infinite. There is not any creature that is not manifest in his sight." Heb. iv. 13. He knows all our works and ways. "His eyes are upon the ways of man, and he seeth all his goings." Job xxxiv, 21, 22. He knows all the secret thoughts of our hearts, all our inmost principles. "The righteous God trieth the hearts and reins." Hence Peter could make this humble appeal to Christ, "Lord, thou knowest all things. John xxi. 17.

And as to all things past, and to come, he challenges the gods of the heathen, as incapable of knowing them like him. "Let them show the former things, what they be." Isa. xli. 22. 23. But known unto the Lord are all his works." Acts xv. 18. And he "calls those things that are not as though they were."

All these things he knows of himself without information from others, and without any external medium to assist him; for "who has taught him knowledge? Isa. xl. 14. "He that teacheth man knowledge, shall not he know?" He knows every thing perfectly and distinctly with the utmost accuracy "Yea, the darkness hideth not from him." Ps. cxxxix. 12. "The very hairs of our head are all numbered." His knowledge is ever the same; it is perpetual and everlasting. "He neither slumbers nor sleeps;" and "a thousand years in his sight are but as yesterday." Ps. cxxi. 4; xc. 4.

7. He is an almighty Spirit.

He is able to do all that can be the object of power, and that is every thing that does not imply a contradiction, either to his own perfections, or to the nature of things themselves. "By the word of the Lord were the heavens made." Ps. xxxiii. 6. 9. And, "he is able to do exceeding abundantly, above all that we can ask or think." Eph. iii. 20.

Application.

1. How absurd and abominable are all pretended images or pictures of God.

None can draw the figure, or carve the image of his own soul. How monstrously foolish, then, must it be, to offer any visible portraiture of the invisible God. Jer. x. 8—14. It changeth the truth of God into a lie, and degrades the glory of the incorruptible God into the likeness of corruptible creatures. Rom. i. 23—25. What awful sentiments should we entertain of the great God, and what solemn regards to him!

With what serious attention and spiritual frames of heart, should we worship! with what adoring reverence and profound humility should we ever think and speak of him! With what subjection, resignation and obedience, should we yield up our souls without reserve to him? With what solemnity should we consider ourselves, as his entire dependents, as always in his sight and presence, as accountable to him for all that we think, say, or do.

3. What a dreadful enemy, and what a comfortable friend, must this great God be?

It is a fearful thing to fall into the hands of the living God, Ezek. xxii. 14. "Who can stand before his indignation?" But O, who can rate the happiness of having an interest in the favor of the infinite, eternal, unchangeable, and almighty God! In his favor is life, and his loving kindness is better than life. The eternal God is the people's refuge; and, "If God be for us, who can be against us?"

4. How thankfully should we embrace a gospel revelation, which opens the way of sinful creatures access to God and acceptance with him through a Redeemer.

Without this discovery of him, every thought of his greatness must make creatures, conscious of guilt, tremble before him; but in Christ we may behold him as a Father of mercies, and a God of all consolation.

THE MORAL PERFECTIONS OF GOD.

Matt. v. 48.—*Your Father which is in heaven is perfect.* (H.)

THE knowledge of God being necessary to the practice of true religion it greatly concerns us to form just apprehensions of him. The natural perfections of the Divine Being have been represented; those that are commonly called moral are the subject of the present. Moral perfections are the same in God and creatures, as to kind, though infinitely different, as to degrees; what we read in the verse of the text plainly supposes this, "Be ye perfect, even as your Father which is in heaven is perfect."

The perfections of the moral sort, which we find ascribed to God in his word, may be reduced to these; wisdom, goodness, holiness, justice, and truth. These shall be now distinctly considered; and under each particular, I shall endeavor to show what practical improvement should be made of it by us; then conclude with some general reflections.

I. GOD IS PERFECTLY WISE.

Wisdom implies knowledge; it is the right use of knowledge; it lies not only in the understanding, but in the will. He acts wisely, whose will is directed by right reason, who does that which is fit to be done. This excelleth folly as far as light excelleth darkness. Nor is it less evident, that wisdom belongs to God. With what brightness does his wisdom shine in his works! How vast are his schemes of creation, providence, and redemption! With what exquisite skill are their various parts contrived and adjusted, to promote his grand design! The Psalmist was thrown into a rapture at the contemplation of some of God's works here below; when he viewed their beautiful order, he cried out, "O Lord, how manifold are thy works! in wisdom hast thou made them all." The consideration of a particular branch of Divine Providence, had the same effect upon the apostle, which he thus expressed: "O the depth of the riches!" How has he abounded towards us in all wisdom and prudence in the contrivance of the method of our redemption by Christ Jesus! The publication of this is spoken of as a discovery of God's manifold wisdom. Eph. iii. 10.

It has pleased the Father of lights to "teach us more than the beasts of the earth." Job xxxv. 11. He has communicated much larger measures of his wisdom to the angels, who dwell in the regions of light; yet the scripture speaks as if the character of wise was peculiar to him: he is styled again and again, "The only wise God, who is wonderful in counsel."

The practical improvement.

1. We should be hereby excited to seek wisdom. To this we are exhorted: "Get wisdom, get understanding." Prov. iv. 5—7. Let this engage our greatest care and most diligent application. There is hardly any thing of which men are more ambitious, than to be thought wise: it would be happy for them if they were as much concerned to obtain true wisdom. The fear of the Lord is the beginning, or the principal part of wisdom; and the knowledge of the holy is understanding.

2. Is God perfectly wise? then we should ask wisdom of him. "If any man lack wisdom, let him ask of God." Would you be made wise unto salvation, apply to Christ Jesus, "in whom are hid all treasures of wisdom. He is made of God wisdom to those that are in him."

3. Is God perfectly wise? then certainly it becomes us to resign to his will, and acquiesce in his appointments. What can be more reasonable than that we leave him to govern the world, who made it so wisely.

II. God is perfectly good.

His other attributes are rendered amiable and engaging to us by his goodness: it is upon the account of this, that he bears the endearing character of Father, in relation to us, which is given him in the text; "Your Father which is in heaven." It was goodness that moved him to create the world; and as the good pleasure of God raised the universe out of nothing, so is his goodness poured out, as it were, upon all his works.. Moses, when he writes the history of the creation, closes his account of every day's work with this expression, "God saw that it was good."

How extensive is the Divine goodness! "The Lord is good unto all. Ps. cxlv. 2—15. The earth is full of the goodness of the Lord." It is said to be great above the heavens. Ps. cviii. 4. It shines in the upper world with amazing lustre; there is no exhausting of this, it endureth for ever.

1. Is God perfectly good? then all our powers ought to be awakened to bless his name. The sense which the Psalmist had of God's goodness, made him press his soul with great earnestness to offer praise unto him upon this account. "Bless the Lord, O my soul." Ps. ciii. How often does he repeat that wish in Ps. cvii. 21. "O that men would praise the Lord for his goodness."

2. Is God perfectly good? how hateful then should sin be unto us. As our sinfulness illustrates the goodness of God, their being committed against an infinitely good God, adds an inconceivable weight to our guilt. The riches of God's goodness leads men to repentance; not only as they encourage their return to God, but as they manifest the great evil of their transgressions.

3. Is God perfectly good? Ought it not to be our ambition to imitate his goodness? "To do good, forget not. Do good to them that hate you."

III. God is perfectly holy.

To be holy doth often signify in the scriptures to be set apart from a common and ordinary, to a peculiar and excellent use. In this sense the Sabbath-day is styled holy; and the character of holy may be given to God, to denote the transcendant excellencies of his nature, whereby he is infinitely separated and distinguished from all other beings. Again, by holiness, the word of God frequently means a separation from moral evil. "As he that has called you is holy." 1 Pet. i. 15. Perfecting holiness in the fear of God, stands in opposition to all filthiness both of flesh and spirit. Without doubt, God is infinitely holy in this respect. "God is light, and in him is no darkness at all," *i. e.* no moral imperfection. He is without iniquity. "He is of purer eyes than to behold evil." But there is something positive in God's holiness. The beauty of holiness, which is a description given of God, must needs signify not only a freedom from all blemishes, but the possession of every thing that is excellent and amiable.

The holiness of God is a perfection, for the honor of which he has a very high regard; therefore he swears by it. "Once have I sworn by my holiness." Ps. lxxxix. 35. It is his most distinguishing style, that he is glorious in holiness. The seraphim cried one to another, "Holy, holy, holy, is the Lord of Hosts."

Use.

We should press it on our conscience, as a most powerful argument to induce us to follow after holiness. Thus God condescends to reason with us; "Be ye holy, for I am holy." They and they only are blessed who dwell in his presence; this shall be the felicity of those who are truly sanctified. "Blessed are the pure in heart, for they shall see God." If we would not be debarred a blissful sight of God, let us "follow after holiness." Heb. xii. 14.

IV. God is perfectly just.

Justice is commonly distinguished into commutative and distributive. Commutative justice lies in an equal exchange of benefits; and ought to be observed by us in our dealings with each other. But such are the perfections of God, so entire is our dependance upon him, that it is impossible we should lay any obligations on him; therefore this sort of justice can have no place in his transactions with us. "Who hath first given unto the Lord?"

Distributive justice, which ought to be exercised by rulers towards their subjects, consists in the equitable distribution of rewards and punishments. We may be sure, that God is a righteous governor. Men, notwithstanding their most careful inquiries, may be imposed on by false evidence. But all things are naked and open unto God.

Again, the great God cannot be awed by any power to pervert judgment. "Surely the Almighty will not pervert judgment." Job xxxiv. 11, 12.

God cannot be biassed by the prospect of any profit to depart from that which is right; this is a spring of a great deal of injustice among men. But the Most High is infinitely above every temptation of this kind "The Lord your God is God of gods. Deut. x. 17. He is a righteous Lord, and he loveth righteousness."

The judgments of God are a great deep; they cannot be fathomed by us at present: but his righteousness is like the great mountains, very obvious "Righteous art thou, O Lord." How we ought to be affected with this perfection of God!

1. Should not the consideration of God's justice awaken in us an holy awe of him? The Psalmist declares, that his flesh trembled for the fear of God: he was afraid of his judgments.

2. Is God perfectly just? Is it not then of the greatest concern to us guilty creatures, that we be found in Jesus Christ. Should we not, without delay, apply ourselves to Christ, "whom God hath set forth to be a propitiation through faith in his blood." Rom. iii. 25, 26.

Perfectly true, which is the

V. and last, of the DIVINE PERFECTIONS.

This, as it is a moral virtue, signifies a conformity of words to thoughts, then it is styled veracity; and a conformity of actions to words, then it is called faithfulness. God is perfectly true in each of these respects: as it is impossible for him to be deceived, so it is certain that he will not deceive. "A God of truth. Deut. xxxii. 4. His faithfulness shall never fail. The mountains shall depart. Isa. liv. 10. It is impossible for God to lie." Heb. vi. 18. Nor is God liable to a change of mind. "He is not a man, that he should lie."

1. We may hence learn, that we ought heartily to embrace whatever God has revealed to us: though our reason cannot comprehend it, yet if we have sufficient evidence of its being spoken by God, we may be sure it is true.

2. We may hence infer the reasonableness of a steadfast reliance on God's promises. Great is the guilt of those who will not believe God; they are said to make him a liar.

Reflections.

1. It should yield us great satisfaction to consider, that such a perfect being as God is, governs the world; who is infinitely wise, good, holy, just, and true.

2. We should, in our contemplations of God, and conduct towards him, have a strict regard to the harmony of his attributes. He never displays any one of his excellences, but in a consistence with the honor of the rest.

3. Blessed are they, who upon good grounds can call this perfect Being their Father and their God. That this may be our happiness, let us sincerely give up ourselves to God, through Christ, and take him to be our portion for ever. "Whom have I in heaven but thee?"

THE PROVIDENCE OF GOD IN THE NATURAL WORLD.

Psalm ciii. 19.—The Lord hath prepared his throne in the heavens, and his kingdom ruleth over all. (H.)

THIS is a very grand representation of the majesty of the great God. As an earthly monarch sits upon his throne, and keeps his court in some one capital city, and from thence extends his dominion and government over the whole kingdom; so, in allusion hereunto, the great and mighty God, who is King of kings, and Lord of lords, is here represented as having prepared his throne in the heavens, and from thence extending his sovereign dominion and influence as wide as universal nature, over all creatures, and over all worlds. By the kingdom of God, we are here to understand his providence, or his preserving and governing all his creatures, and all their actions. The subjects of this universal kingdom may be distinguished into natural and moral:—by the moral world, we mean, the rational part of the creation, or those creatures who are fit subjects of a moral law, as angels and men, considered as reasonable creatures. By the natural world, we understand the whole mass of matter, which is variously disposed into a multitude of shapes and forms, and different sorts of creatures, as sun, moon, and stars, air, earth, and sea; with all the vast variety with which they are stored, and by which they are inhabited. God's providential kingdom is absolutely universal, and over all. But at prevent, consider the providence of God, as the preserver and sovereign disposer of all things, in the natural world only.

I. To prove that there is a PROVIDENCE, which presides over the whole course of nature, and all the world of creatures. This may be argued,

1. From the perfections of God: and of those we need only single out his knowledge and his wisdom, his goodness and his power; for if we believe that God is infinitely possessed of such perfections as these, it will hardly be possible for us to stop short of believing his providence. For will not his wisdom and goodness incline him to take care of his creatures, and govern them in the best manner? Can we suppose the universal Parent of all creatures and worlds, to be like the foolish ostrich? Job xxxix. 16. And since God is almighty, no reasonable doubt can remain of his providence.

2. One may produce many express testimonies out of scripture, for the proof of a Providence. It is said, that God upholdeth all things; and that they continue according to his ordinance. "He appointeth the moon for seasons. Ps. civ. 19. He bringeth the winds out of his treasure." Ps. civ. 24, 25, 27. God is the supreme governor among the nations. This providence of God presides not only over great and important affairs, but it reaches to the minutest creatures. As in Matt. x. 29, 30—"Are not two sparrows sold for a farthing?" But I should transcribe a great part of the Bible, should I collect all the proofs. I will only farther hint to you one article of the doctrine of providence, which we learn from scripture, viz. "That the kingdom of Providence is administered by Christ our Saviour. It is by him that all things consist. Col. i. 17. And to him is all power given." Matt. xxviii. 18. The whole administration of Providence, over all creatures, and all worlds, is committed into the hands of the Mediator, Jesus Christ; which speaks both the dignity of his person, and the safety and happiness of his friends and people. If any farther proof were wanting, one might,

3. Appeal to the appearance of things: to the frame of nature, and the continued order and harmony of the whole creation; where we have as good testimonies to a providence, as to the very being of a God. Can it be only by chance, that day and night, and summar and winter so regularly succeed to one another? Did all things happen by mere chance, it would be altogether uncertain when spring or the autumn season would come; or whether either of them would come any more; nay, it would be ten thousand times more likely, that all things would presently run into confusion and disorder. It is, therefore, most reasonable to ascribe it to the providence of God, that "seed time and harvest." Gen. viii. 22.

II. To explain and illustrate the PROVIDENCE OF GOD IN THE NATURAL WORLD, by some of the principal acts of it.

1. The providence of God is exercised in preserving his creatures.

1. In the preservation of the several species or kinds of animal creatures; so that though all the individuals die, one after another, yet no species, is lost out of the creation, but most probable, and as far as we can learn from the most ancient account of things, there are all sorts of creatures still in the

world, that were at first. And this is truly wonderful, if we consider what a natural enmity there is betwixt some animals, and others, and with what diligence men have endeavored, in all ages to destroy some whole kinds of them. The due proportion of the various inhabitants of the world to one another; and especially of the males to the females, which is so constantly preserved throughout the animal creation, is a very sensible instance of providential care.

2. God preserves them by his providence in their individual beings, until the end has been answered for which he made them. It is God that holdeth our soul in life. In him we live. We are the living instances of Divine preservation: hitherto God has helped us. Nor is God's providential care confined to man. "He heareth the young raven cry. Not a sparrow falls to the ground."

2. As God preserves, so he also disposes of, and governs his creatures, and their actions by his providence.

1. The inanimate creatures. He who fixed the laws of nature in the first creation, does still by his providence continue their force and power. "He binds the sweet influences of Pleiades, and looses the band of Orion. Job xxxviii. 31, &c. He giveth the former, and the latter rain; and he stays the bottles of heaven." Thus does God keep the springs of universal nature in his own hand, and turns them which way soever he pleaseth.

2. The whole animal creation. "The beasts of the forest are his, and the cattle upon a thousand hills;" they are all his creatures, and the subjects of his providence. What but a Providence could direct every beast, bird, and insect, where to seek its food, and its habitation? Or teach every parent-animal, how to take the properest care of its young? Or, what is it that conducts those birds, who shift their country and climate at certain seasons of the year, in their passage to some distant land, where multitudes of them never were before? "The stork in the heavens knoweth her appointed times." Jer. viii. 7. Had they reason like men, how little would it help them to find their way through the pathless air, without needle or compass? What is their guide, but Providence.

III. To lay before you some of the most REMARKABLE PROPERTIES OF GOD'S PROVIDENCE, as it appears in the natural world.

1. The wisdom of Providence. A property so remarkable, that one may apply those words of the apostle to the mysteries of Providence, as well as those of grace: "O the depth of the riches!" How is the wisdom of God displayed in his preserving and governing the whole frame of nature! It is by this the "sparrow is directed to find a house, and the swallow a nest for herself." How admirably is the wisdom of Providence displayed in the different instinct of the various tribes of animals! Can we observe these things, and a thousand more of the same kind, and not confess and admire the wisdom of Providence.

Or, if we hearken to the voice even of storms and tempests, they will farther declare to us the admirable wisdom of that God, whose word they obey, and whose designs they execute. Who, upon a view of the wisdom of Providence in the natural world, can forbear saying, "O Lord, how manifold are thy works!"

2. The goodness and kindness of it. And we need not go far for instances and proofs of this; for "the earth is full of the goodness of the Lord." Ps. xxxiii. 5. There is not a creature that lives in all the world, but bears a testimony to the goodness of Providence. "These all wait upon God, and he giveth them their meat in due season." Ps civ 27, 28. God extends his

kind regard to many thousands of creatures, who have no capacity of knowing and praising their Benefactor. "Shall not I spare Nineveh (saith God,) that great city?" Jonah iv. 11. "He causeth the grass to grow for the cattle." Ps. civ. 14, 15. And as God has plentifully stored the earth with the blessings of his goodness, so his providence kindly directs us to find out the various uses, whether for food or physic, for necessary support, or for convenience, and delight.

3. It is very powerful. God upholdeth all things by the word of his power. The continued harmony of nature and the constant and regular revolutions of seasons, are sensible demonstrations of the power of God. "Thou hast established the earth." Ps. cxix. 90, 91. God brings forth Mazaroth in his season, he guides Arcturus with his sons. He reneweth the face of the earth after the dearth of winter. And the same almighty God, who created this world at first, and still upholds the whole frame of nature, will one day display his mighty power, by dissolving it again, and changing it into another form. "The day of the Lord will come as a thief in the night." 2 Pet. iii. 10—13.

Improvement.

1. To raise our admiring thoughts to the great God. What a great and mighty Being must he be, who is able thus to wield and manage the whole frame of nature! "How large and manifold is his wisdom. He satisfieth the desire of every living thing."

2. We may infer, how terrible the wrath of this great and mighty God must be, and of what importance it is to secure his favor. So Pharoah and the Egyptians found it a very dreadful thing to have that God against them, "whose kingdom ruleth over all;" who had beast and insects, hail and fire, &c., absolutely at his disposal. Only to be without God in the world, to be without his favor, is a very sad circumstance; how much worse to have him for our enemy. How much is it to our interest, while as yet there is hope, to seek after reconciliation and peace with this great and terrible God! And if we return to him, in his appointed way, he will be at peace with us, yea he will "delight over us, to bless us." Rom. viii. 28.

3. Let the reconciled friends and people of God learn from hence to trust and acquiesce in Providence: "It is the Lord that gives, and the Lord that takes away. He that spared not his own Son."

4. Let us learn to observe and adore the providence of God in all that befalls us, and to bless him for all our enjoyments and comforts. What love, and duty, and honor, do all men owe to him, "whose tender mercies are over all his works!"

THE GOVERNMENT OF THE LORD GOD OMNIPOTENT.

Revelation xix. 6.—And I heard as it were the voice of a great multitude, and as the voice of many waters, and as the voice of mighty thunderings, saying, Alleluia: for the Lord God omnipotent reigneth. (Sk.)

The total overthrow of Babylon, or papal Rome, is predicted in the preceding chapter; and, on the fall of that apostate church, the inhabitants of heaven unite in a song of praise in which they ascribe salvation, and glory, and honor, and power unto the Lord their God, whose judgments are true and righteous. In consequence of that event, the four and twenty elders and the four beasts fall down, and worship God on his throne, saying, "Amen, Alleluia;" and a voice came out of the throne, saying, "Praise our God, all ye his servants, and ye that fear him, both small and great." Then the beloved John heard as it were the voice of a great multitude, and as the voice of many waters resembling the roaring of the sea, and as the voice of mighty thunderings, or loud peals of thunder, saying, "Alleluia: for the Lord God omnipotent reigneth."

I. The Lord God omnipotent reigneth.

1. *The church of Rome reigned over the nations many ages.* Her government was so strong, that no power less than Omnipotence could overthrow it. She ruled with a rod of iron—shed the blood of saints—trampled princes under her feet—and lived in honor, ease, and luxury. Her policy was as deep as hell, her works resembled those of the devil, and her end was a lake of fire, ver. 3.

2. *But the time is at hand when it will be said.* "Babylon the great is fallen, is fallen;" her *power* is *broken*, her *glory* is *faded*, her *wealth* has taken its flight, Prov. xxiii. 5; her oppressions have ceased, and she is now utterly burned with fire, chap. xviii. 8. Thus every thing which exalted itself against God, or against truth and holiness, shall be destroyed, 2 Thess. ii. 4—8.

3. *Then this song shall be sung,—"The Lord God omnipotent reigneth."* He has reigned in the heavenly world, and over the system of nature, ever since he created the holy angels, and the material world; but now he reigneth over men, whose rebellion against his high authority has come to an end. He reigneth in the hearts of believers; in the church, which is his spiritual kingdom; and men of every rank and degree bow down to his authority, Ps. ciii. 19.

4. *It is fit and right that the Lord God omnipotent should reign.* To prove this great truth, let us state, with clearness, the following observations. All things were *created* by the Lord God omnipotent, Rev. iv. 7;—his *wisdom* is a depth which cannot be fathomed, Rom. xi. 33;—his *power* is uncontrollable, Ps. cxxxv. 5. 6;—his *presence* is unlimited, Ps. cxxxix. 7—12; —his *justice* never swerves from what is right, Gen. xviii. 25;—his *purity* is as the light of heaven, 1 John i. 7;—his *goodness* extends to all, Ps. cxlv. 9;—and his *truth* endureth for ever, Ps. c. 5. On a view of these adorable perfections, who would not devoutly pray, "Thy kingdom come!"

5. *The government of the Lord God omnipotent is absolute.* Absolute monarchies among men are *absurd*, because all human beings are *imperfect;* but as every possible perfection meets and unites in Jehovah, it is highly proper that the whole power of government should be placed in his hands. He may employ agents and instruments to carry on his great designs; but he should hold the reigns of government, that he may guide and direct all things in wisdom and goodness, to their proper ends.

6. *And of his government there will be no end.* Mighty empires among men have come to an end. The *Assyrian*, founded by Nimrod, continued about fourteen hundred years; the *Persian*, established by Cyrus, son of Cambyses, continued about two hundred years; the *Grecian*, founded by Alexander the Great, lasted about three hundred years; the *Roman* was more extensive, and endured much longer: but they all "passed away as a flood, or as a tale that is told." Blessed, then, be the Most High, who liveth for ever, and "whose dominion is an everlasting dominion," and whose "kingdom is from generation to generation," Dan. iv. 34; Ps. cxlvi. 10.

II. His subjects should praise him, and sing alleluia.

1. The Hebrew word literally signifies, "Praise ye the Lord." It was often sung by the Jews in the synagogue, but is now transferred to the Christian church. An eminent writer observes, that 'this is the first time the word occurs in the New Testament;' and that 'this word being Hebrew, may be taken for the Christian church's invitation of the Jews, or Hebrews, to join with them in praising God; and being so often used here, implies that Christ shall be praised by the Jews also, now, after Rome's destruction.'

2. *The government of the Lord furnishes matter of praise to all his subjects.* It puts an end to war, and restores *peace* and order among men; it promotes human *happiness* in every possible degree; it puts an end to the *tyranny* of wicked men, sin, and the devil: it places men under the secure *protection* of almighty power: it is a *mild*, *equitable* and *holy* government; it is *firm* and stable: and its foundations are "righteousness and judgment," Ps. xcvii. 2.

3. *He should be praised for condescending to govern men.* Some men have denied the being of God, Ps. liii. 1, and others, his knowledge of human affairs, Ps. lxiii. 11; but we have indubitable proofs of his being, and comfortable assurances of his watchful care, 1 Pet. iv. 7. We admit that he is *inconceivably* great and glorious, and that it is *infinitely* condescending in him to notice the highest order of celestial spirits; but he is mindful of man, Ps. viii. 4, and he knoweth them that trust in him, Nahum i. 7.—"Praise ye the Lord."

4. *Praise him for receiving you into his kingdom.* You were strangers and foreigners, but are now "fellow citizens with the saints," Eph. ii. 19; you entered into the kingdom by regeneration, which was a work wrought in you by the Spirit of God, John iii. 3, 6; and you now share all the privileges of the kingdom. You are highly honored, and greatly blessed; give God the glory, and praise his holy name, Ps. cxvii.

5. *Endeavor to praise him in lofty and exalted strains.* To this end charge your memory with those Scripture phrases which express the high praises of your God. The inspired songs of Zion far exceed all other compositions in clearness, strength and sublimity. Angels praise the Lord in lofty strains; try to imitate them, Luke ii. 14; and, ere long, you shall praise him in a higher key, with all the redeemed of the Lord. Isa. lxi. 11.

6. *Employ all your powers in his praise.* Praise him in your *hearts*, by cherishing honorable thoughts of his majesty and glory, by warm affections of love and gratitude, and by inward expressions of his goodness and mercy, Ps. ciii. 1, 2; praise him with your *lips*, by speaking honorably of his attributes, works, and ways, Ps. xxxiv. 1; and praise him in your lives, by living in all things to his honor and glory. The inanimate works of creation may be said to praise God by showing forth his greatness and glory; and when our lives abound in good works, every action speaks his praise, Ps. cxlviii. 4, 8, 9.

7. *Offer up united and loud praises.* Let these resemble "the voice of many waters," and "the voice of mighty thunderings." There is a true sublime in sound. 'The burst of thunder or of cannon, the roaring of winds, the shouting of multitudes, the sound of vast cataracts of water, are all incontestibly grand objects.'* The united praises of *one* large congregation are awfully grand: what then will be the united praises of all the servants of God, both small and great! May the whole earth *ring* with the high praises of this great and glorious Being!

* Blair's Rnetoric.

8. *When the prophecy to which our text refers is accomplished, the church will praise the Lord for the utter destruction of papal tyranny.* That glorious event will put an end to dangerous error and delusion—to degrading superstition—to proud intolerance—and to vile oppression. Then truth will triumph over error, and *Dagon* fall before the ark of God; tormenting fear will be cast out; and persecution, in all its forms, will cease for ever.—" Praise ye the Lord."

9. *But even now let us praise the Lord in every state and circumstance of life.* David said, "I will bless the Lord at all times;" let us follow his example. We may see times of peace, and times of war; times of joy, and times of grief; times of ease, and times of pain; times of wealth, and times of want; and times of honor and times of disgrace. Our circumstances in life are ever varying; but still the Lord God omnipotent reigneth. ALLELUIA.

10. *Thus employed on earth, we shall be prepared to praise the Lord for ever in the realms of light and glory.* Happy spirits in that world may serve the Lord God in ten thousand different ways; but every thing will be begun, carried on, and ended in praise. This exalted work will be an honor to the arch-angel; and the pleasure attending it will be pure and elevated beyond conception.

"What a rapturous song, when the glorified throng
  In the spirit of harmony join;
Join all the glad choirs, hearts, voices and lyres,
  And the burden, is "Mercy divine!"
Hallelujah, they cry, to the King of the sky,
  To the great everlasting I AM;
To the Lamb that was slain, and that liveth again,—
  Hallelujah to God and the Lamb!"

GOD'S APPROBATION OF HIS WORKS.

Gen. i. 31.—And God saw every thing that he had made, and behold it was very good. (Sk.)

NOTWITHSTANDING the oppressive load of labor, and care, and sorrow, and temptation, by which we are usually burdened, and the attention we are constrained to bestow on matters which concern food and raiment, and other supplies necessary for ourselves and our dependants, while passing through the present life; the vigorous and immortal mind sometimes disengages herself from her encumbrances, and spurning the low and grovelling pursuits in which she has been detained, plunges into the future; and either anxiously inquires, 'Through what variety of untried being, through what new scenes and changes must I pass?'—or expatiates on the bright and blissful prospects which revelation offers to the eye of faith, and anticipates the period when those prospects shall be realized.

Nor are such excursions confined to the future. Man's future destiny is closely connected with his past and present circumstances. It is therefore natural for us to desire to inform ourselves concerning that part of the history of our species which relates the most important events of former times. Here again revelation comes to our assistance; and in its sacred pages, and particularly in the chapter in which our text is found, carries us back, through a variety of most interesting occurrences, even to the birth of time itself. In this light our text appears to be of considerable consequence: for while it furnishes matter of history the most ancient aud venerable, it asserts some important natural truths, and suggests by way of inference, several others of the moral kind. Let us consider,

I. THE NATURAL TRUTHS ASSERTED. Among these the text asserts,

1st. *The true origin of all things.* "And God saw every thing that *he had made.*" Of this, plain as it may now appear, it is highly probable we should have no conception, but for what the Bible has taught us; for though it may be easily demonstrated, that matter cannot have created itself, yet it will not so easily follow, that it must have had a creator. We acquire our stock of ideas by experience; and a creation out of nothing is so different from all the experience of mankind, that some philosophers, as Aristotle and his followers, supposed the world to have been eternal; while others, as the Epicureans, conjectured that the matter, the atoms only of which it was composed, was eternal, and that they happened by chance to fall into their present form and order. And even to this day, the worshippers of Budhoo, perhaps the most numerous sect of idolators in the world, though they acknowledge "*gods many,*" have no notion of a Supreme Creator. "The world by wisdom knew not God." But the Scripture assures us, that the universe is the production of a Being, who is *infinitely free and powerful:* not overruled by a fatal necessity; but whose will is the *law,* as it was the *cause* of nature, verse 1; Ps. xxxiii. 9: Dan. iv. 35; James i. 18: who is *infinitely wise;* whence those works of design and arrangement we every where perceive, Ps. civ. 24, and even that intellect by which we are capable of the perception, and which is only a feeble emanation from the source of intelligence, Job xxxii. 8; Isa. xl. 28: who is *infinitely good;* not a mere intelligence, wise to design and powerful to execute, yet destitute of every thing like moral excellence, but ever respecting what is *right and holy:* and what is *good,* is *best* for his rational creatures. Agreeably to this, our text asserts,

2d. *The original perfection of all things:*—"And God saw *every thing* that he had made, and behold it was *very good.*"

1. *It was very good, as being well adapted to answer its particular intention.* Instance the suitable instrumentality of the heavenly bodies in the diffusion of light; and the adaptation of the eye to receive, by means of that light, impressions of surrounding objects, ver. 14—17. Instance again, the correspondence between the structure of fishes and the waters in which they are to live; and between that of fowls and the lighter element in which they have to fly, ver. 20, 21; and, in short, we might instance all the numerous subjects of what are called astro and physico theology. In this sense it is said concerning the distribution of almost every day, "*it was good,*" ver. 1, 10, 12, &c.

2. *It was very good, as being conducive to the perfection and welfare of the whole.* Here it may be necessary to distinguish between the world as it now is, and as it came out of its Maker's hands. All its glory, beauty, utility, &c. are *remaining* glory, &c.—all its deformity and disadvantages are superinduced. Sin produced a most disastrous change both in the *constitution* and in the *residence* of man. At first there was nothing parched or dreary in the earth, pestilential or tempestuous in the air, scorching in the sun, ferocious in the animal tribes, &c. but the reverse of this. And man especially, was nobly *free, wise* as needful, *righteous* and truly *holy;* Eph iv. 24; Col. iii. 10. Hence,

3. *It was very good as being well calculated to promote the glory of its Maker.* This was the design of the first, as well as of the *new* creation, Eph. iii. 10; Rev. iv. 11. And in the contemplation of themselves and the universe, God's rational offspring found abundant matter of wonder and praise, Job xxxviii. 7. Even now, in this state of disorder which sin has introduced, to minds rightly disposed, "the things that are made" powerfully declare "the invisible things of God, even his eternal power and Godhead," Ps. xix. 1; Rom. i. 20; and prompt the pious reflection,

> "These are thy glorious works, Parent of good,
> Almighty! thine this universal frame,
> Thus wondrous fair! thyself how wondrous then!"

We are therefore, not surprised that the text asserts,

4. *God's approbation of his work.* He saw it "*very* good;" *supertatively* so. This is affirmed of "*every* thing that he had made." We do not say that all parts of the creation are equally *valuable;* see Matt. x. 29—31; yet God *approves* of what is *good* in its *place and nature;* approves as much of the "green herb" or the tuft of "grass," or even of the rock which furnishes moisture for its support, as of the "living creature" which feeds upon it. He is present to every part of his creation; sees the dependance of the parts on each other; and regards them accordingly. Man, in particular, possessed all the perfections consistent with his nature and his circumstances. And to object on the one hand, that he had better not have been blessed with liberty seeing he has abused it, is to say, in effect, that a mere machine is more excellent than an angel?—and on the other to ask, "Why were not all men made angelic or super-angelic beings?" is to propose a foolish question. In the case proposed, there would have been a different class of entities; but we, as men, should have had no existence at all. When any creature has all its powers and properties in perfection, then it is "very good." Such was creation; and such it was in its Maker's esteem. Let us hear,

II. The moral truths suggested. Here we may observe,

1. Seeing that God had done for man the utmost that his case admitted, both as respected himself and as respected the world around him, the blessings of which were given him "richly to enjoy," it follows that *man was under the greatest obligations possible*, in his then present circumstances. He might, indeed, become more indebted for a *continuance* and *increase* of unmerited blessings. And *we* have the obligation of *redemption*, in addition to every other, 1 Cor. vi. 20. Hence,

2. *Sin is at once the vilest injustice and the basest ingratitude, imaginable.* It is an unwarrantable appropriation of *time*, and *talents*, and *property*, not our own but another's, and a foul abuse of favors conferred, to the disadvantage and grief of our best benefactor, Isa. i. 2; Mal. i. 6.

3. *A continuance in sin is the most daring imprudence.* According to that constitution of things which was "very good," holiness and happiness went together. Sin, by violating that constitution, 'brought death into the world, with all our wo.' It is an outrage on the principles of our nature; and the ardent flame might as soon cease to burn, as sin to produce misery This is abundantly confirmed by the threatenings, Prov. xi. 21; 2 Thess. i, 7, 9;—the entreaties, Ezekiel, xviii. 30—32, and xxxiii. 11—and even the promises of God's word, Isa. lv. 6, 7; Jer iii. 12, 22.

4. *Reformation is well-pleasing to God.* He approved of things in their original state. He is unchangeable; and therefore must disapprove of the

derangement which sin has occasioned; consequently a restoration to their former order must be highly acceptable in his sight. In proof of this, he has provided ample means of moral renovation.—His Son, John iii. 16; 1 John iii, 3.—His word, Ps. xix. 7—10; John xx. 31.—His ministers, 2 Cor. v. 18—20; Col. i. 25—28.—His Spirit, to convince, intercede, strengthen, comfort, &c. John xvi. 8; Rom. viii. 26; Luke xi. 13.

5. *The text suggests a lesson of humility.* "How is the gold become dim!" the divine image effaced! Humility becomes every rational creature, on account of its *debt* and its *dependance.* Unfallen intelligences feel it; much more should we. "The crown is fallen from our head: wo unto us that we have sinned!" Lam. v. 16; Dan. ix. 7. Yet,

6. *The text furnishes ground of hope and encouragement.* It proclaims the *goodness* of him with whom we have to do; and therefore encourages us to hope in his *mercy.* Let us remember however, that it is to the Gospel we are indebted for improving hope into assurance, Rom. viii. 32. And while we cautiously avoid sin, the pest of happiness and the abhorrence of God, let us gratefully acknowledge, as our surest ground of hope, for grace here, and for "the blissful seat" hereafter, that

> "'Twas great to speak a world from nought,
> 'Twas *greater* to *redeem!*"

GOD'S DELIGHT IN SAVING SINNERS.

Zeph. iii. 17.—The Lord thy God in the midst of thee is mighty: he will save, he will rejoice over thee with joy; he will rest in his love, he will joy over thee with singing. (S. S.)

A KNOWLEDGE of ourselves will shew us how much need we have of repentance; and a knowledge of God will encourage us to repent. Many are the descriptions which we have of God in the inspired volume; but none deserves our attention more than that before us. In it we behold

I. GOD'S POWER TO SAVE.

We shall not speak of God's power in general, but as it is manifested in the salvation of his church and people. He dwelt "in the midst" of his people in the wilderness; Exod. xl. 38; and displayed his "power to save them" by delivering them from all their enemies, Exod. xiv. 27, 28, and xvii. 14, and supplying all their wants. Ps. lxxvii. 15, 16, 24, 25. Thus is he in the midst of his church at this time; Matt. xviii. 20, and xxviii. 20; and is as able as ever to save his people. For this end he orders every thing by his providence, Rom. viii. 28, and makes his word effectual through the almighty operations of his Holy Spirit. Heb. iv. 12. 2 Cor. x. 4, 5.

II. HIS DETERMINATION TO SAVE.

If he should leave us to ourselves none of us would be saved. We all say to him, "Depart from us;" Job xxi. 14, 15; nor do we ever turn effectually to him till he has made us willing in the day of his power. John vi. 44. Ps. cx. 3. On this account he takes the matter into his own hands, and determines to save those whom he has given to his Son. John vi. 37. See this exemplified, Jer. iii. 19. Having bought us with the blood of his Son, he will secure us to himself, by the operation of his Spirit. He does not indeed destroy our free agency; but he overcomes our reluctance, Phil. ii.

13, and draws us to himself by an operation not less powerful than that, which he exerted in raising his Son, Jesus Christ, from the dead. Eph. i. 19, 20.

III. His delight in saving.

There is not any thing so delightful to God as the work of saving sinners. Nor will he merely feel an inward pleasure; but, as a man, overjoyed at any event, involuntarily expresses his joy by singing, or some other outward token, so will God manifest his pleasure to the returning soul. Luke xv. 23, 24. Man by nature knows no greater happiness than that which a bridegroom feels, when, after long suspense and many fears, he is united to his bride. Yet such is the image which God himself uses, to illustrate his joy over returning sinners. Isai. lxii. 5.

IV. His immutability towards those whom he intends to save.

Man is often alienated from the object of his affections, either by means of some unexpected evil he has discovered, or through his own fickleness and inconstancy. But God changeth not. Mal. iii. 6. Jam. i. 17. Whom he loveth he loveth to the end. John xiii. 1. He hateth putting away. Mal. ii. 16. And, as he loved his people from eternity, Jer. xxxi. 3, and chose them without any reference to good either seen or foreseen in them, Deut. vii. 7, 8, and ix. 5, 6; so will he not forsake them on account of their infirmities. Isai. liv. 7—10. He will indeed punish their transgressions with all needful severity; Ps. lxxxix. 30—34; but his gifts and callings are without repentance; Rom. xi. 29; nor will he cast off the people, whom he has chosen in Christ, and given to him. 1 Sam. xii. 22. Hos. ii. 19, 20.

Uses—In this glorious character of God we may see

1. The evil of sin

Sin, under whatever circumstances it may be committed, is directly levelled against him. Gen. xxxix. 9. Ps. li. 4. And, if our consciences be not seared as with an hot iron, the thought of having so often committed that, which militates against the honor, the authority, and the very existence of such a God, must render us loathsome in our own eyes, and cause us to abhor ourselves in dust and ashes. Ezek. xxxvi. 28, 31. Job xlii. 6.

2. The danger of dying in an unconverted state.

Those to whom our Lord preached, and amongst whom he wrought his miracles, had a far heavier condemnation than they would have received, if they had never enjoyed such advantages. John xv. 22. Matt. xi. 20—24. And will it be no aggravation of our guilt in the day of judgment to have despised such a loving and gracious God? Surely, he will then shew himself mighty to destroy such obdurate rebels; and will feel an abiding satisfaction in vindicating the honor of his insulted majesty, Luke xii. 20; Prov. i. 24—30; Deut. xxviii. 58, 63; as he now would in displaying the riches of his mercy. It will be "a fearful thing to fall into his hands" under such aggravated guilt.

3. The obligation that lies upon believers to serve the Lord.

Have you been selected by God as objects of his unmerited love? Have you been redeemed with the blood of his dear Son? And have you a good hope, that you shall be made eternal monuments of his power and grace? What should you render to the Lord for such benefits? O love him; rejoice in him with joy unspeakable; and rest in your love to him; having no end, no aim, no wish, but to please and honor the God of your salvation.

GOD'S CARE FOR THE RIGHTEOUS.

Prov. x. 3.—The Lord will not suffer the soul of the righteous to famish. (S. S.)

God, who is the author and giver of al good, dispenses his blessings no less to the evil and unjust, than to the good and just. But he promises to those who seek first his kingdom and his righteousness, that all other things shall be added unto them. To this effect he speaks also in the passage before us. But though this be the primary import of the text, we must not exclude its relation also to the concerns of the soul.

To elucidate this blessed promise, we shall shew

I. What reasons the righteous have to apprehend that their souls may famish.

A sense of weakness and of guilt may greatly discourage them: for

1. They cannot secure provisions for themselves:—

The word of God, and Christ in the word, is the proper food of the soul: and, if a person can read, he need not be wholly destitute. But it is by the public ministration of the word that God principally confirms the souls of his people. Now in many places where Christ should be preached, his name is scarcely heard; and, instead of children's bread, little is dispensed besides the husks of heathen morality. Even where some attention is paid to christian doctrines, there is often much chaff mixed with the wheat; and "the trumpet that is blown, gives but an uncertain sound." Those therefore who by reason of distance, or infirmity, or other insurmountable obstacles, cannot have access to the purer fountains of truth, have great reason to fear that their souls will famish.

2. They cannot, of themselves, feed upon the provisions set before them. Where all the treasures of the gospel are fully opened, it is God alone that can enrich any soul by means of them: even "Paul may plant, or Apollos may water, but it is God alone that can give the increase." The very same word is often made a peculiar blessing to one, that was altogether useless to another. God reserves the times and the seasons in his own hands; and "gives to every one severally as he will." When therefore the righteous hear of the effects wrought on others, and feel conscious that they themselves reaped no benefit from the word, they are ready to fear that their souls will famish even in the midst of plenty.

3. They well know that they deserve to be utterly abandoned by their God:—

It is not only for their sins in general, that the righteous find occasion to humble themselves before God, but more particularly for their misimprovement of divine ordinances. Perhaps there is not any other more fruitful source of self-condemnation to the godly than this. When therefore they see how many opportunities of improvement they have lost, and how much guilt they have contracted by their deadness and formality in the worship of God, they are sensible that God may justly "remove their candlestick," and leave them to experience "a famine of the word."

But lest a dread of famishing should oppress the minds of the righteous, we shall proceed to shew

II. What grounds they have to hope, that God will never suffer such a melancholy event to happen.

However great the grounds of fear may be which the righteous feel within themselves, they have abundant reason to "encourage themselves in the Lo: ' their God"

1. He has bountifully provided even for the ungodly

The gospel is "a feast of fat things full of marrow, and of wines on the lees well refined;" and God has "sent out into all the highways and hedges to invite the poor, the halt, the lame, and the blind," and has commissioned his servants to compel men, by dint of importunity, to accept his invitation. Now has he shewn such concern for the wicked, and will he disregard the righteous? Will he not rather "cause the manna to fall around their tents," and "the water to follow them" through all this dreary wilderness? Yes; he would rather send a raven to feed them, or sustain them by a continued miracle, 1 Kings xvii. 6, 14; than ever suffer their souls to famish.

2. He is peculiarly interested in the welfare of the righteous

The righteous are God's "peculiar treasure above all people;" they are even "his sons and daughters." If they were left to perish, Jesus would lose the purchase of his blood, and the very members of his body. And can we imagine that God will be so unmindful of them as utterly to forsake them? Did he not on many occasions vouchsafe mercy to his chosen people *for his own name sake*, when their backslidings had rendered them fit objects of his everlasting displeasure? Thus then will he still be actuated by a regard for his own honor, and "not forsake his people, because it hath pleased him to make them his people." 1 Sam. xii. 22.

3. He has pledged his word that they shall never want any thing that is good

"Exceeding numerous, great, and precious are the promises which God has given to his people." "He will supply all their wants, according to his riches in glory by Christ Jesus: he will give them grace and glory; and will withhold no good thing:" their souls "shall be even as a well watered garden:" "bread shall be given them; and their water shall be sure." And will he violate his word? he may leave his people in straits, as he did the Israelites of old: but it shall be only for the more signal manifestation of his love and mercy towards them. Let them only trust in him, and he "will never leave them, never, never forsake them." Heb. xiii. 5; see the Greek.

We shall conclude with a word

1. Of reproof

It is certain that many do not "make their profiting to appear" as they ought. To such therefore we must say, "Wherefore art thou, being a king's son, lean from day to day?" 2 Sam. xiii. 4. Why art thou crying continually, "Woe is me, my leanness, my leanness!" Isai. xxiv. 16; when thou shouldest be "growing up as the calves of the stall?" Mal. iv. 2. Some part of the blame perhaps may attach to him who dispenses the ordinances among you, as wanting more life and spirituality in his ministrations; yet even this would be no excuse to you, since if your hearts were more spiritual, God would render your mean fare as nutritious as the richest dainties. Dan. i. 12—15. If God should even "give you your desire, yet would he also send leanness into your souls," Ps. cvi. 15; while you continued to loathe the heavenly manna. Learn then to come with more eager appetite— — —Be more careful to digest the word afterwards by meditation and prayer— — —And look, not so much to the manner in which the word is preached, as to Christ in the word; since HE is that bread of life which alone can nourish your souls; and which, if eaten by faith, will surely nourish them unto life eternal— — —John vi. 51.

2 Of consolation

Some may put away from them this promise, under the idea that they are not of the character to whom it belongs. Now though we would by no means encourage any to apply the promises to themselves in a presumptuous manner, and thereby to deceive their own souls with ungrounded expectations, yet we would not that any should refuse the consolation that properly belongs to them. Suppose then that any cannot absolutely number themselves among the righteous, yet, "if they hunger and thirst after righteousness, they are blessed, and shall be filled." Matt. v. 6. This is the word of God to their souls; and we would have them expect assuredly its accomplishment in due season— — —Let them "desire the sincere milk of the word, and they shall grow thereby"— — —1 Pet. ii. 2.

GOD'S TREATMENT OF US AS BRANCHES OF THE TRUE VINE.

John xv. 1, 2.—I am the true vine, and my Father is the husbandman. Every branch in me that beareth not fruit, he taketh away; and every branch that beareth fruit, he purgeth it, that it may bring forth more fruit. (S. S.)

The union which subsists between Christ and his church is mysterious—

The scripture sets it forth both in figurative and plain expressions—

It is spoken of not as a speculative or doubtful point, but as well known—John xiv. 20.

It is declared in the text under a beautiful similitude—

Christ is the true vine

If this was a continuation of our Lord's discourse, the idea of a vine might arise from what he had just before said respecting the fruit of the vine—Luke xxii. 18.

If it was spoken in his way to the mount of olives, it might be suggested by his passing through a vineyard—

The representation respects Christ not personally, but as united to his church—

In this view it fitly exhibits *our union with him*

This union is not natural to any—

We are, by nature, plants of a degenerate vine—Jer. ii. 21.

We are, however, separated from it by Almighty power—Eph. i. 19, 20.

And are made willing to be united to Christ—Ps. cx. 3.

We are then engrafted into Christ by the Spirit on God's part, and by faith on ours—Eph. iii. 16, 17.

Thus we become branches of the true vine—

And the union, when formed, is intimate and inseparable—1 Cor. vi. 17. Rom. viii. 35, 39.

It expresses, moreover, *our dependence on him*

A branch derives all its fructifying power from the root—

So believers receive all their grace out of Christ's fulness—John i. 16.

Hence it is that Christ is so precious to them—1 Pet. ii. 7.

Hence, too, they determine to live entirely by faith on him—Gal. ii. 20.

The Father is the husbandman

The husbandman has many offices to perform—

He engrafts the scions, digs about them and dungs them, guards them from the weather, prunes the luxuriant branches, &c.—

The Father performs these offices
He chooses (but not for their superior goodness) what scions he will—
He separates them from their stock by the means he judges best—
He engrafts them, in his own time and manner, into the new stock—
He continues to promote their good by his word, his Spirit, and his providence—
He separate or combines, renews or changes, the various means of culture, as he sees occasion—
His treatment of the branches is suited to their state—
There are "branches in Christ," which are so only in appearance
They have never been thoroughly separated from their old stock—
They have never been truly engrafted into Christ—
The change wrought in them has been only partial—
They bring not forth such fruit as the living branches do—
These the Father "taketh away"—
They are a disgrace to the vine, and to the husbandman himself—
He, however, exercises forbearance towards them—Luke xiii. 8, 9.
His culture of them, in the mean time, shews their unfruitfulness to be of themselves—Isa. v. 4.
But he will ere long separate them from the others—
He will take them away, in order to burn them, ver. 6.—
How fearful should we be lest we be found such branches at last!—
And how carefully should we examine our fruit, in order that we may not be self-deceived!—Matt. vii. 17—20.
There are other branches, which are vitally united to Christ
They manifest that they are so, by the fruits which they produce—
These the husbandman purges and prunes
Notwithstanding their fruitfulness, they need the pruning-knife—
Afflictions have a tendency to make them more fruitful—
God therefore sends them afflictions of various kinds—
This he does to "every one of them"—Heb. xii. 6—8.
He even promises affliction to them as a blessing—Jer. xxx. 11, with Heb. xii. 10, 11.
Let us then enquire whether we be living branches of the true vine—
Let us study to answer the ends of all his care—
If we be indeed fruitful branches, let us welcome affliction as a blessing in disguise—
Let us, above all, seek to be confirmed in our *union to Christ*, and *our dependence on him*—Col. ii. 6, 7.

THE PRESENCE OF GOD WITH HIS PEOPLE.

Exodus xxxiii. 14.—And he said, My presence shall go with thee, and I will give thee rest. (Sk.)

THE preceding context clearly discovers the deep concern which Moses felt for the children of Israel. Having according, to divine appointment, conducted them from Egyptian bondage to mount Horeb, there the Lord communed with him, and gave him special directions for his future guidance and encouragement. But being 'tremblingly alive' to the awful responsibility of his high and important situation, he was on various accounts greatly perplexed and discouraged. This was particularly the case when he was commanded to proceed on the journey to Canaan; and yet the Lord threatened, that he would not go with them. This deeply affected the tenderest sympathies of his heart, and rendered his prospects exceedingly gloomy and distressing. But he gave himself unto prayer, and obtained, in the text, an assurance that the divine presence would accompany them through the trials of the wilderness, and bring them to the promised rest;—"And he said, My presence," &c. As these words are applicable to the people of God in every succeeding age, they will lead us to observe, The journey they pursue,—The privilege they possess,—and the happiness they enjoy.

I. The journey the people of God pursue. There is a striking analogy between the *literal* history of the children of Israel, and the *spiritual* history of the members of the Christian church. As the former were delivered from Egyptian bondage, and travelled through the wilderness to the land of Canaan; so the latter are redeemed from sptritual thraldom,—are strangers and pilgrims on the earth,—and are travelling to the land of eternal rest.

1. *They are delivered from spiritual bondage.* Once they were willingly captivated by sin and Satan, and deeply enslaved by the fascinating snares and corruptions of the world. They were the bond slaves of their spiritual enemies, 'tied and bound with the chain of their sins,' John viii. 34. But by the mercy of God, they are happily "delivered from the power of darkness, and stand fast in the liberty wherewith Christ hath made them free," John viii. 36; Gal. v. 1. This glorious emancipation of the soul is eminently the work of God, and is the high calling and common privilege of all his believing people, Luke i. 74, 75: Rom. vi. 22.

2. *They are strangers and pilgrims on the earth.* Such were the children of Israel *literally*, while journeying through the toils of the wilderness; and such is *morally* the state of Christians as travellers to the heavenly Canaan. They are not of the world, but seek "a city which hath foundations, whose builder and Maker is God," Heb. xiii. 14. Like the ancient patriarchs, they desire a better country, for this is not their rest. Heaven is their home, and the world is the house of their pilgrimage. Their portion is above, and they are hastening on to glorious mansions, "not made with hands, eternal in the heavens," John xiv. 1—3; 2 Cor. v. 1.

3. *They are travelling to the land of promise.* The earthly Canaan was, in many respects, a striking emblem of the heavenly rest that remains for the people of God. The former was promised to Abraham and his seed, as a goodly and permanent possession; and the latter is promised as an incorruptible and unfading inheritance, to all the saints, 1 Pet. i. 3—5; 1 John ii. 25. For such characters it is prepared, and kept in reserve. They are heirs of the promises, and "have respect unto the recompense of reward." It is the glorious object of their hope and pursuit: and being faithful unto death, they will receive the crown of life, Rom. ii. 7; Luke xii. 32.—Let us then consider,

II. The privilege the people of God possess. "My *presence* shall go with thee." Not only his *general* or *universal* presence which fills all space; but his *special* and *manifested* presence, to guide, protect, support, and constantly to abide with them.

1. *His guiding presence is with his people.* He led the children of Israel forty years in the wilderness, "that he might bring them to the city of habitation," Deut. viii. 2. He still guides his faithful servants in "the right way," both of providence and of grace. By his word and Spirit, he directs

their steps, and leads them into all truth, Isa. xlii. 16. He is continually with them, to instruct them in every difficulty,—encourage them in every trial,—and prepare them for his eternal kingdom, Ps. lxxiii. 24.

2. *His protecting presence is with his people.* Like the Jews, they are travelling through "a terrible wilderness." They are pursued by enemies and beset with snares. But as the Lord led and protected his ancient people, "by day in a pillar of a cloud, and by night in a pillar of fire;" he is still the refuge and strength of them that put their trust in him. Ps. xlvi. 1; he is with them in all their troubles, and they are perfectly secure under the shadow of his wing. They "shall be as mount Zion, which cannot be moved, but abideth forever, Ps. cxxv. 2; 1 Pet. iii. 13.

3. *His sustaining presence is with his people.* They feel their entire dependance upon him; and as their gracious benefactor and Savior, he richly supplies all their wants, and satisfies them with his goodness, Ps xxxiv. 10. As he anciently fed the Israelites with manna from heaven, and gave them water to drink from the smitten rock; he will ever continue to spread a table in the wilderness for his beloved people, Exod. xvi. 35, xvii. 6. He grants them the bread and the water of life, "and withholds no good thing from them," Eph. iii. 20; Phil. iv. 19.

4. *His abiding presence is with his people.* "I will *go* with thee." He will not merely send a messenger, or visit them occasionally; but will continually *abide*, and *go* with them, to the end of their journey, Ps. xlviii. 14. He will be with them in all their afflictions, temptations and trials; and will manifest himself unto them, as he does not unto the world, John xiv. 32. Human friends may fail, and worldly comforts be withdrawn; but God is "a friend that sticketh closer than a brother," and will never leave, nor forsake us, Ps. lxxiii. 26. And hence we may discover,

III. The happiness the people of God enjoy. "And I will give thee *rest*." This is always the certain result of the divine presence, and is the peculiar privilege and blessedness of the saints.

1. *His presence gives them rest in the present life.* In coming to Christ they find rest for their souls, and have joy and peace in believing. They rest from the terrors of a guilty conscience, and from the painful distractions of an impenitent and unbelieving heart. "We which have believed," says the Apostle, "do enter into rest, and have peace with God through our Lord Jesus Christ," Isa. xxvi. 3. But though they have spiritual rest of mind, it is not perfect and uninterrupted. In the world they have tribulation, and are called to war a good warfare; but in Christ they have peace which passeth all understanding, John xvi. 33.

2. *His presence gives them rest in the hour of death.* It was this consideration that induced the Psalmist joyfully to anticipate the period of his approaching dissolution, and exclaim with holy confidence, "Though I walk through the valley of the shadow of death, I fear no evil; for thou art with me; thy rod and thy staff they comfort me." He delivers his people from the fear and sting of death, and enables them to triumph over their last enemy, which shall certainly be destroyed, 1 Cor. xv. 55—57 Though the final exit of the righteous is not *equally* triumphant and glorious, it is *always* peaceful and safe, for they "die in the Lord, and rest from their labors," Ps. xxxvii. 37.

3. *His presence gives them rest in the world to come.* Their bodies shall rest in certain hope of a glorious resurrection to eternal life; and their spirits shall enter into the joy of the Lord, 2 Cor. v. 8. His immediate presence will constitute their perfect and everlasting rest, dignity, and blessed-

ness, Ps xvii. 15. There they will rest from every enemy, affliction, and trouble; for "in his presence there is fulness of joy, and pleasures for evermore," Rev. vii. 14—17.

From this subject we may learn.

1. The *character* of God's people. They are redeemed and saved by grace, and are heirs of immortal bliss. Rom. viii. 17.

2. The *encouragement* of the saints. It is their ineffable consolation to know, that "the Lord of hosts is with them, and the God of Jacob is their refuge," Deut. xxxiii. 29.

GOD'S CARE FOR HIS PEOPLE.

Isaiah xliii. 2, 3.—When thou passest through the waters, I will be with thee; and through the rivers, they shall not overflow thee: when thou walkest through the fire, thou shalt not be burned; neither shall the flame kindle upon thee: for I am the Lord thy God, the Holy One of Israel, thy Saviour. (S. S.)

God's goodness to his people never appears more wonderful than when contrasted with their conduct towards him

The history of the church in all ages attests the truth of the apostle's assertion—Rom. v. 20.

We have a remarkable instance of this in the passage before us—

The Israelites were utterly incorrigible—Isai. xlii. 24, 25.

Yet God forebore to "make a full end of them"—

On the contrary, to display the riches of his grace, he promised them his continued care and protection, ver. 1, 2.—

The text suggests to our consideration

I. God's care for his people

God's people are subjected to many and great troubles

"Fire and water" are emblems of heavy calamities—

God's people are often brought into them—

All are taught to expect them in their way to heaven—

The most eminent saints have usually the greatest share—Job—Asaph—Heman—David—Paul—

But God takes peculiar care of them in that state

He represents himself as watching them in the furnace like a refiner—Mal. iii. 3.

He has promised they shall not be overwhelmed by temptation—1 Cor x. 13.

He vouchsafes his special presence at those seasons—

Even when he has withdrawn himself apparently from his people, he secretly and imperceptibly upholds them—

The burning bush was intended to teach us this—Exod. iii. 2.

It has been experienced by the saints in all ages—

David bears testimony to this fact—Ps. lxvi. 10—12. "*We went through fire and through water.*"

The history of the Hebrew youths also attests it—Dan. iii. 25, 27.

The passage of the Jews through the Red Sea, and through Jordan, confirms it—Isai. li. 10.

There are also many living witnesses for the truth of it—

However great this mercy is, we are at no loss to assign

II. The reason of it.

God is the Covenant God and Saviour of his people

God has given himself to his people by covenant—Jer. xxxi. 33.

Hence he assumes the titles "the God of Israel," "the Holy One of Israel"—

This implies that all his perfections shall be employed for their good—

This is the reason of his peculiar care for them

On account of this relation he *feels for* them

God represents himself as tenderly feeling for his people—

His compassion towards them is like that of a parent—Ps. ciii. 13.

He bears them, like a nursing mother, in his arms—Isai. lxiii. 9.

He considers every injury done to them, as done to himself—Zech. ii. 8.

He sympathizes thus on account of his relation to them—Jer. xxxi. 20.

On this account also he is *interested in* them

He has purchased and redeemed them by the blood of his Son—

Hence he calls them his "purchased possession"—

He regards them as his "peculiar treasure," the "lot of his inheritance"—

He promises to take care of them as *his* vineyard—Isai. xxvii. 3.

Hence Moses made God's interest in his peeple a plea for his forbearing to destroy them—Exod. xxxii. 11.

Hence David also urged this plea on his own behalf—Ps. cxix. 94.

On this account also he is *bound to* them

God has pledged himself that "he will not forsake his people"—

He has assured them, that no weapon formed against them shall prosper—

He never will break the covenant he has entered into—Ps. lxxxix. 34, 35.

This affords a sure ground of hope to his people—

The church of old urged it as a reason for his return to them—Is. lxiii. 15—19. *This is remarkable strong.*

And every believer may adopt the patriarch's plea—Gen. xxxii. 12.

Infer,

1. Of what importance is it to know that we are interested in Christ!

We cannot claim God for our God unless we have believed in Christ—

If therefore we have not an evidence that we have indeed believed, we can derive no comfort from these promises—

Yea, rather, we have reason to fear that we shall be overwhelmed with God's wrath, and be made to "dwell with everlasting burnings"—

Let us then not leave this matter in doubt and suspense—

Let us "flee to Christ for refuge, as to the hope set before us"—

We may then assuredly expect these promises to be fulfilled to us—

2. What consolation does the gospel of Christ afford!

Every man must expect to "pass through fire and through water"—

It is our appointed way to the kingdom of heaven—Acts xiv. 22.

In the hour of death, if not before, we shall feel need of support—

But God has provided in the text abundant consolation—

We need not fear any thing whilst we can rest on this promise—

Let us then adopt the triumphant language of the Psalmist—Ps. xxiii. 1, 4.

GOD'S DARK DISPENSATIONS TO HIS SAINTS.

Gen. xlii. 36.—And Jacob their father said unto them, &c. (H.)

THESE are the words of Jacob, in great perplexity and distress; the occasion of which we are acquainted with in the foregoing verses of this chapter. He concluded Joseph to be dead, and looked upon Simeon as lost; in both which he was mistaken: and the thoughts of parting with Benjamin cut him to the heart, as if it were to send him to the grave; and therefore he cries out, "All these things are against me." But Joseph was safe in honor, Benjamin would be so too, and well received; Simeon would be set at liberty, all the family would be kindly entertained, and the father sent for, to be nourished by his beloved son; and thus all was making for his comfort and advantage, that appeared so black and dismal, and from whence he expected nothing but ruin. And, as Jacob's is not a singular case, I shall endeavor,

I. To show GOD'S DEALINGS WITH HIS PEOPLE, even when he is working their deliverance, and designs their good, are often dark and intricate.

1. This was the case with Jacob. God designed the preservation of him and his family in Egypt, by Joseph's advancement there; but how unlikely the means he made use of, in order to it, and yet how wonderfully was the end proposed, accomplished.

2. Thus it was with the deliverance of Israel from Egypt, four hundred and thirty years after. They were exceedingly oppressed by Pharaoh; see the complaints of the people to Moses and Aaron; Ex. v. 21; and the complaint of Moses before the Lord, on the same occasion; ver. 22, 23; and after they were brought a little on their way out of Egypt, their danger was increased, chap. xiv. 8, 9. The pursuing army was behind, the sea before, on either hand mountains, that forbade their flight or escape; to all appearance, every thing was working towards their destruction; and yet this was the way that God took to accomplish their deliverance, by opening the sea to give them passage, and drowning their enemies, who ventured to follow them. Ver. 26—28.

3. Thus it was with Daniel, and the three Hebrew worthies. God resolved to deliver and save them: but the way in which he chose to do it, was by suffering the first to be cast into the lions' den, and the others into the fiery furnace, and yet by keeping them unhurt, to the confusion of their enemies.

4. David was designed for a throne, and anointed to it: but, before he reached it, he was driven from place to place, as a partridge upon the mountains; and reduced to that distress, that he seemed to conclude his case desperate, and his destruction certain. 1 Sam. xxvii. 1.

5. Such also were God's dealings with Job: he resolves to bless Job's latter end more than his beginning, but how unlikely a way to this, to be stripped of all, and reduced to the deepest distress; to be plundered by his enemies, censured by his friends, Satan let loose in the sorest manner to afflict him, and God writing bitter things against him. Who could have thought, that saw him in his low condition, that the issue would have been so bright and blessed.

Thus God's dealings with his servants have often a sad aspect, as if he was set on their destruction; when he is consulting their truest advantage, and promoting their salvation. Verily he is a God that hideth himself, when he is at the same time the God of Israel, the Saviour. Wraps himself in clouds and darkness, before he shines through to their comfort. But this leads me to consider,

II. Whence it is that a CHILD OF GOD may be ready to conclude that to be against him, which is really for him.

1. This proceeds from their weakness of faith, as to God's wisdom and power, faithfulness and love. We are slow of heart to believe, that he is able to bring good out of evil, and light out of darkness; that he hath hidden designs to serve by all his dealings with his servants, which he knows how to bring about, and will not fail to do in the appointed way and time, which are always to be left to him, who is wonderful in counsel, and excellent in working.

2. By looking to Providence, and loosing sight of the promise. Rom. viii. 28.

3. Judging by sense. When afflicted and pained, we are apt to feel and complain, that "all these things are against us;" but faith speaks in a very different language. Ps. lxxiii. 1.

4. By looking down to the present world, and our interest in it. When this is chiefly regarded, that which tends to lessen our comforts in it may be thought to make against us; but that which is contrary to our temporal welfare, may promote our everlasting happiness.

5. Through rashness; viewing only a part of his work, and not waiting for the issue. Jacob, who cried out so passionately, "all these things are against me," in the end discovered his mistake.

6. Through not attending to the usual method of God's dealing with his people, and our own, and others' experience of the happy purposes he has served by it. He makes rich, by first making poor: he heals by wounding and making them sick: he quickens in the way to heaven, and better prepares them for it, by all the sufferings of the present life. 2 Cor. iv. 17.

III. The grounds upon which we may conclude that what the CHRISTIAN apprehends to be against him, shall in the end terminate in his favor.

1. From God's relation to him: God is his Father; Rom. viii. 15; and is particularly concerned for his good and happiness, even in affliction and distress. Heb. xii. 10.

2. From God's love to him. See his language to his people; Isa. xliii. 4; and this love will engage all his perfections for them.

3. From his express promises. Rom. viii. 28. Things shall have a better issue than they expected. He that dwelleth in the secret place of the Most High shall abide under the shadow of the Almighty, and there be safe from fear of evil. Isa. xl. 1, 2.

IV. Why is it that the LORD CHOOSES this way to promote the best interests of his followers.

That he really does so, is clear from Jacob's case; and what we sometimes think to be a judgment, is a mercy. The fish that swallowed Jonah was a mean to bring him to shore. This way the Lord chooses,

1. For his own glory, as appears from the case of Lazarus. John xi. 4.

2. To discover their corruption, and to try their graces. Deut. viii. 2.

3. To quicken, and make them more earnest in prayer. The more dark his dispensations are, the more fervent and enlarged we should be in prayer.

4. To sweeten and endear the mercy he grants them, after all their fears and doubting to the contrary.

5. To heighten their thanksgiving for the mercy bestowed. How thankful must Jacob have been, after all his difficulties, to find his children all alive and well. How was the thanksgiving of Israel enlarged, upon their deliverance from danger at the Red Sea! It produced the song, Ex. xv.

Application.

1. Let us be anxiously careful to assure ourselves, as to our special relation to God, as his children in covenant with him, devoted to his service.

2. Let us be aware of judging God's purposes of grace by the external dispensations which make way to bring them into effect. The promise is often just about to be fulfilled, when, to an eye of sense, it seems at the greatest distance. In the evening-time, when least expected, it shall be light. Wherefore,

3. Beg that faith may not fail, when surrounding circumstances seem dark and dismal. In every place he can come to us, and in the deepest distress he can relieve us. Isa. xli. 10.

4. Beware of entertaining narrow thoughts of God in the deepest distress. Believe him always the same whatever changes you meet with.

Lastly, While you are apt to say on earth, "all these things are against me," press on with greater earnestness to heaven. There all your tears shall be wiped away; and there you shall have "fulness of joy, and pleasure for evermore."

THE LOVE OF GOD TO THE WORLD.

John iii. 16.—"God so loved the world," &c. (P.)

In the former part of this chapter, we have an interesting conversation recorded between our Lord and Nicodemus, an eminent Jew. He instructs him respecting the nature of the new birth, his design in coming into the world, and the happiness of those who receive him.

Let us contemplate,

I. The unspeakable love of God. "God so loved the world."

Man, in consequence of his apostacy from God, had fallen into an abyss of misery, from which he could never have extricated himself; but "God so loved the world," &c. What world? The expression admits of different acceptations: sometimes it is applied to the universe, the heavens, the earth, the sea, the elements, angels, men, animals, &c. Sometimes it is used in scripture, when speaking of the Roman empire, as Matt. iv. 8; at other times the Jewish nation, Luke ii. 1; but here it means the world of his intelligent creatures, the human race, 1 John, ii. 2. "God so loved," &c.; how much, the Apostle could not tell. "There is," (as an eminent commentator justly observes,) "an eternity of meaning in the word 'so,' which we must die to know." The expression is most vehement and forcible—"God *so* loved," &c., *so* richly, *so* freely, *so* inexpressibly, *so* infinitely.

His love to the world was,

1. Unmerited. There was nothing in man to attract it, much less to merit it. We were guilty, and rebellious against him; but notwithstanding this, "God so loved," &c.

2. Universal.—"The world." It was designed and intended for the world. Hence our Lord's final commission to his disciples was, "Go ye in to all the world," &c. Mark xvi. 15.

3. Unsolicited—Though a blessing so rich and valuable, and so much needed by man, yet it was never implored by him. For we were not only enemies, but in a state of spiritual darkness, when we were reconciled to God by the gift of his Son. It was,

4 Unparalleled. No human being could have equalled this act of mercy.

"Love so amazing, so divine, demands," &c.

5. Incomprehensible.

"God only knows the love of God."

II. THE EVIDENCE OR MANIFESTATION OF THAT LOVE. "He gave his only," &c.

1. Intentionally. "He was the Lamb slain from the foundation of the world," Rev. xiii. 8. When man sinned, it was promised "the seed of the woman shall bruise the serpent's head," Gen. iii. 15. This promise was renewed to Abraham, Isaac and Jacob, as well as to most or all of the prophets—"And in thy seed shall all the nations of the earth be blessed." Gen. xxii. 18.

He gave his Son,

2. Typically. Under types, and shadows, and emblematical representations. Isaac, and Jacob, and Joseph, and Jonah, were all types of Christ, Matt. xii. 40. The rock, the manna, the brazen serpent, were each of them typical of him who "came into the world to save sinners." He gave his Son,

3. Prophetically. "A prophet shall the Lord your God raise unto you; him," &c. "Behold, a virgin shall conceive," &c., Isa. vii. 14. "His name shall be called, Wonderful," &c. Isa. ix. 6. "Behold I lay in Zion for a foundation," &c., Isa. xxviii. 16. "He is despised and rejected of men," &c., Isa. liii. 3. "Rejoice greatly, O daughter of Zion," &c., Zech. ix. 9.

4. Actually. "When the fullness of the time was come, God sent forth," &c., Gal. iv. 4. He was born in Bethlehem, fled to Egypt from the rage of Herod, returned back again to Nazereth, and continued there till he commenced his public ministry.

III. THE GRAND DESIGN INTENDED: "That whosoever believeth," &c. Thus faith is the key by which we unlock all the divine promises, and by which we become interested in all the blessings of the gospel. It implies,

1. The assent of the understanding. "Rabbi, thou art the Son of God," &c., John i. 49.

2. That we receive him in all his offices, as our teaching prophet, our atoning priest, and our ruling king. And, "as many as received him, to them," &c. John i. 12.

8. That we rely upon him for the pardon of our sins, the acceptance of our persons, and the sanctification of our natures. Such is the faith that is necessary to salvation; the object of which is Christ, and the end of which is full salvation.

1. "That we might not perish." The meaning of this emphatic expression is the same as "losing the soul," Matt. 16, 26. It means to be eternally lost—to be ruined—to be damned; for "he that believeth shall be saved; but he," &c. Mark, xvi. 16. It is to sink into everlasting darkness—to endure unquenchable fire—to bear inexpressible misery. It is

"To writhe, to pant, to toss beneath the load,
And bear the weight of an offended God."

It is banishment from the presence of the Lord, and from the glory of his power; for "the wicked shall be turned into hell,"

2. "That we might have everlasting life." He came, that he might PUR-

CHASE "everlasting life;" and this life begins in the soul on earth; for what is grace, but glory begun; and glory but grace consumated and perfected? He came to give a LEGAL TITLE to eternal life. "Eye hath not seen, nor ear heard, nor heart conceived, what God hath prepared for them that love him." He came that he might become an expiatory sacrifice for sin. None could accomplish this grand design but him. "He that spared not his own Son, but freely delivered," &c., Rom. viii. 32. He came that he might exalt us to glory. Hence, he is not only "the author, but the finisher of our salvation. He not only begins, but carries on the work, till the top stone is brought forth with shoutings of "Grace, grace unto it."

Improvement,

1. Address those who disregard and slight this love. The greatest blessing God bestowed upon the world, will be to you the greatest curse. O harden not your hearts against his love, but melt beneath its influence

> "His offered benefits embrace,
> And freely now be saved by grace."

Some may limit the mercy of the Holy One; but listen to his own word, and hear the rich encouragement he offers you himself—"Ho every one that thirsteth," &c.

2. Let those who enjoy the benefits of Christ's atonement, and who feel his love shed abroad in their hearts, "hold fast the beginning of their confidence, steadfast unto the end," Heb. iii. 14. And, finally, brethren, "be ye steadfast and unmoveable, always abounding in the work of the Lord; for as much as ye know that your labor shall not be in vain in the Lord," which may God of his infinite mercy grant, for his name's sake, Amen.

THE NAME OF THE LORD A STRONG TOWER.

Prov. xviii. 10.—The name of the Lord is a strong tower: the righteous runneth into it, and is safe. (H. H.)

IN the Proverbs of Solomon we must not expect to find long and accurate statements of Divine truth, nor elevated strains of devotion founded upon it: the scope of the book is rather by brief sentences to fix upon the mind truths already acknowledged, and to shew the excellency of them in their effects. The passage before us is very instructive in this view, namely, as illustrating the blessedness attendant on true piety. But it commends itself to us yet more forcibly, by exhibiting a contrast between the dispositions and habits which religion inspires, and those which are indulged by the whole ungodly world. The text informs us what "the righteous man" does: the verse following our text informs us what the worldling does: the one makes God his refuge; the other trusts in his wealth, or some other idol equally vain: the one founds all his hopes on God, as made known to us in the Scriptures of Truth; the other, on some vanity, that has no title to confidence but "in his own conceit."

It was to mark this contrast that the blessedness mentioned in our text was confined to "the righteous." Solomon did not mean to intimate, that an unrighteous man, if he would flee to this tower, should be shut out: for the most unrighteous man in the universe is invited to come to it; and, like the cities of refuge, its gates stand open day and night for the admission of all who desire to flee to it for refuge. But the truth is, that none but the righteous will run to it: none but they who are sensible of their guilt and danger, and are fleeing in earnest from the wrath to come, will enter in. All others deny the necessity of submitting to so humiliating a measure: they think they are safe enough without it. The believing penitent, on the contrary, is thankful for such a refuge, and is in the habit of running to it on every occasion: and therefore to him, and to him alone, is the security confined.

To elucidate the passage, we will endeavor to unfold,

I. The character of God—

By "the name of the Lord" we are not to understand the mere *word*, Jehovah, as though that would afford us any security. This is a vain and foolish superstition, that has no foundation whatever in the Oracles of God. But, by "the name of the Lord" we must understand his character; as we learn from that expression of David, "They that know thy name," *i. e.* thy character, "will put their trust in thee." Ps. ix. 10. Consider then the character of Jehovah,

1. As described by himself—

God, in infinite condescension, was pleased to make known himself to Moses, and by an audible voice to "proclaim his name:" Exod. xxxiv. 5; "The Lord passed by and proclaimed, The Lord, the Lord God, merciful and gracious, long-suffering, and abundant in goodness and truth; keeping mercy for thousands, forgiving iniquity, transgression and sin, and that will by no means clear the guilty." Exod. xxxiv. 6, 7. Now we would ask the trembling sinner, What character he would wish Jehovah to bear? Would he wish God in no instance to testify his displeasure against sin, but to treat all men alike, putting no difference between "the guilty" who are going on in all manner of wickedness, and the penitent, who are turning from all iniquity? No: there is not a penitent in the universe that would wish God to act in a way so unworthy of his divine majesty. But if he desire to be assured of mercy to returning penitents, it is not possible that any words he could devise could more richly portray this attribute, than those which God himself has used. Consider them distinctly and separately, — — —and see how constantly they have been verified towards you hitherto, and how abundantly they contain all that you can desire.

2. As revealed to us in Christ Jesus—

The Lord Jesus Christ is "Emmanuel, God with us;" and he is particularly called, "The image of the invisible God," because in him the whole character of the Deity is made, as it were, visible to mortal men. He is "the brightness of his Father's glory, and the express image of his person;" and his whole character is marked in the name given him before he was conceived in the womb. Matt. i. 21, 23. The name "Jesus" is the same with Joshua, or "Jehoshua," that is, Jah Osea, Divine Saviour. What a glorious and comprehensive name is this! All that he has done and suffered for us, and all that he has promised to us, is contained in it; together with his perfect sufficiency for all that he has undertaken to effect. The trembling sinner finds in the very name of Jesus a pledge of all that he wants. Besides, whilst we contemplate him in the whole of his work and offices, we are expressly authorized to apply to ourselves the benefit of them all, and to call him, "The Lord our Righteousness." Jer. xxiii. 6. Follow this idea in all its bearings, and what unsearchable mysteries of love and mercy will it unfold to our view!

Such being the name and character of God, let us contemplate,

II. The interest we have in it—

It is indeed "a strong tower"—

Consider every perfection of the Deity: there is not one which is not "a chamber where we may hide ourselves till every calamity be overpast." Isa. xxvi. 20. The wisdom, the goodness, the love, the power, the faithfulness of Jehovah; who that is encompased by them does not feel himself in an impregnable fortress? Truly they are not merely a wall, but "a wall of fire" round about the righteous; of fire, which whilst it protects the fugitive, will devour the assailant.— — —What a tower too is the Lord Jesus Christ in the whole of his work and offices! Well is he said to be "a strength to the poor, a strength to the needy in his distress, a refuge from the storm, a shadow from the heat, when the blast of the terrible ones is as a storm against the wall." Isai. xxvi. 4. Yes, "the man" Christ Jesus, in his Mediatorial character, is such "a hiding-place," Isai. xxxii. 2; where no adversary shall "ever penetrate."

All who run to it shall "be safe"—

Who shall ever approach "to harm" those who are thus protected? 1 Pet. iii. 13; Surely "they shall be kept in perfect peace." They are "safe:" safe from the curses of the broken law; for "there is no condemnation to them that are *in Christ Jesus*" Rom. viii. 1;— — —They are safe too from the assaults of Satan; for "their lives are hid with Christ in God," where Satan can never come, Col. iii. 3, 4,— — —In a word, they are safe from every kind of evil; for God has said of those who make the Most High their habitation, that "no evil shall befall them" Ps. xci. 9, 10;— — The persecutor may touch their body, but cannot reach their soul: Luke xii. 4, 5; they shall sooner be fed with ravens, than be suffered to "want any manner of thing that is good." Ps. xxxiv. 9, 10. And if any thing occur that has the semblance of evil, they may be assured that it shall work for their present and eternal good. Rom. viii. 28. 2 Cor. iv. 17, 18. Like Elisha, they are surrounded with horses of fire and chariots of fire; 2 Kings vi. 14—17; and any assaults made upon them shall only terminate, as in Elijah's case, with the confusion and ruin of their enemies. 2 Kings i. 9—14.

Suffer now a word of exhortation—

1. Study much the character of God—

"To know God, and Jesus Christ whom he hath sent, is, as our Lord informs us, "eternal life." All other knowledge is mere vanity in comparison of this. Without this we have nothing to warrant our hopes or to dissipate our fears— — —"Acquaint then yourselves with God, and be at peace"— — —

2. Maintain constant and intimate communion with him—

You know how a child runs to his parent on every occasion: do ye in like manner run unto your God. This is the very character of the true christian; "The righteous runneth unto God as his strong tower." Get to him under every fear, and every want, and every distress: and "cast your care on Him who careth for you"— — —

3. Assure yourselves of the safety which you are privileged to enjoy—

Well may you say, "If God be for me, who can be against me?" See how David exulted in his security! Ps. xviii. 1, 2, and xxvii. 1;— — — and learn like him to glory in your God: for it is God's desire that you should enjoy all possible consolation. Heb. vi. 18. Your Saviour has assured you, that "none shall pluck you out of his hands:" lie there then in peace and safety, "knowing in whom you have believed, and that he is able to keep that which you have committed to him"— — —When he has lost his power to save, then, and not till then, shall any enemy prevail against you.

GOD'S FAITHFULNESS TO HIS PROMISES.

Joshua xxiii. 14.—Behold, this day I am going the way of all the earth: and ye know in in all your hearts and in all your souls, that not one thing hath failed of all the good things which the Lord your God spake concerning you: all are come to pass unto you; and not one thing hath failed thereof. (H. H.)

It has been common in all ages to pay peculiar attention to the words of dying men: and the more eminent their characters were, the more regard has been shown to their last instructions or advice. The person speaking in the text, was, in some points of view, distinguished even above Moses himself: for though Moses was the appointed instrument of bringing the Israelites out of Egypt, he was forced to leave them to the care of Joshua, who alone was commissioned to settle them in Canaan: and who was therefore a more illustrious type of Jesus, whose name he bore,* and whose character he prefigured. The dying words of such a person, when speaking too, the dictates of inspiration, may well be considered as calling for more than ordinary attention; especially when the scope of them was to vindicate the honor of God, and they were delivered in a way of solemn appeal to the whole nation of the Jews. But they have yet a further claim to our regard, because, though primarily applicable to those to whom they were immediately addressed, they are equally applicable to the Lord's people, in every place, and every age.

To illustrate them in this view, we shall,

I. Notice some of those good things which the Lord our God has spoken concerning us—

In order to mark what we are principally to insist upon, the faithfulness of God in performing his promises, we will specify some that were made,

1. To the Church at large—

God promised to the Church the gift of his dear Son. Gen. iii. 15. Gen. xxii. 18. Deut. xviii. 18. Isa. vii. 14, and ix. 6, and liii. 6. Dan. ix. 24. Jer. xxiii. 6. — — — the abiding presence of his Spirit. Prov. i. 23. Isa. xxxii 15. Ezek. xxxvi. 25—27. John xv. 26. John xvi. 14. Ib. ver. 8. Zech. xii. 10. Rom. v. 5. 2 Cor. i. 22. — — — and a final triumph over all her enemies. Isa. xxvii. 2, and xxxiii, 20, and liv. 17. Jer xxxi. 35—37. Matt. xvi. 18.

To individual members in particular—

Though the names of individuals are not specified, their characters are delineated, and that too in such a way, that all who study the sacred oracles may read, as it were, their names in them. There are distinct promises made to the humble. Isa. lxvi. 2. Jam. iv. 6. Isa. lvii. 15. — — — the weak. Isa. xlii. 3, 4, and xl. 11, and xli. 14, 15, 17, 18. 2 Cor. xii. 9. Amos ix. 9. — — — the tempted. 1 Cor. x. 13. Heb. ii. 18. — — — the backslidden. Jer. iii. 14, 22. Hos. xiv. 4. — — — and especially to them that trust in God. Isa. xxvi 3. Ps. cxxv. 1. Jer. xvii. 7. 8. — — — In that class is every rank and order of true Christians comprehended, "Verily it shall be well with the righteous." Isa. iii. 10.

These are "great," "exceeding great and precious promises:" 2 Pet. i. 4. and the persons who correspond with the different characters, are at full liberty to apply them to themselves.

Having taken a short view of the promises we may proceed to,

II. Show the faithfulness of God in fulfilling them—

* The names *Joshua* and *Jesus* are the same in Greek.

There is in the minds of all who have heard the Gospel, a general conviction of the truth and faithfulness of God—

It is seen that God has already fulfilled all that he has promised in reference to the Church at large. Besides what he did for the Jews, Josh. xxi. 43—45, he has sent his Son; he has poured out his Spirit; he has maintained his Church, notwithstanding all the efforts that have been used both by men and devils to destroy it. And from hence we feel a persuasion, that his word shall be fulfilled in other respects also. We do not indeed suffer our convictions to operate as they ought; yet we revolt at the idea that "God should lie. Numb. xxiii. 19, and we know that "he cannot deny himself." 2 Tim. ii. 13. — — —

All who have ever sought after God at all, have had proofs of his veracity to their own experience—

The Israelites "knew in all their hearts, and in all their souls," that God had fulfilled his promises to them. And are there any who have ever called upon him, or trusted in him, and not found him ready to hear their prayers, and to supply their wants? If we look back to seasons of peculiar trial, shall we not find some manifestations of his mercy, sufficient to shew, that, if we have not received more from him, it has been owing to our own backwardness to ask, rather than to any unwillingness in him to give — — —

Nor can the whole universe produce one single instance wherein his promises have failed—

We can make the same appeal to you, as Joshua, after sixty years' experience did to the Israelites. Bring forth every promise from the Bible; then search the annals of the world: and inquire of every creature in it, to find one single instance of God's violating or forgetting a promise; and if one instance can be *proved*, we will consent that his word shall henceforth be called in question. Tell us then, To whom has he "been a wilderness?" Jer. ii 31. What penitent, believing, and obedient soul hath he ever forsaken? Heb. xiii. 5. Isa xlix. 14, 15, and liv. 7—10. He himself bids you "testify against him." Mic. vi. 3. But we defy the whole world to impeach his veracity, or to contradict our assertion, when we say, that "*all* which he has promised us is come to pass; not one thing hath failed thereof" — — — God may have delayed the accomplishment of his promises, or fulfilled them in a way that was not expected: but not one of them has ever failed.

Address,

1. Those who have not considered the faithfulness of God—

In spite of the general conviction of God's truth that floats upon our minds, there is a proneness in us to indulge a thought, that his mercy will in some way or other interpose to prevent the execution of his threatenings. But the veracity of God is pledged as much for the accomplishment of his threatenings as of his promises: and of this he *labors in the most earnest manner* to persuade us. Ezek. xxiv. 13, 14. How many, alas! are now experiencing in hell what they would not believe when they were on earth! Let us learn to "tremble at God's word." Let us remember, that though the antediluvian scoffers said, as others now do, "Where is the promise of his coming?" 1 Pet. iii. 3—4, he did come at last, though he bore with them a hundred and twenty years. And in like manner he will overwhelm us also at last with the deluge of his wrath, if we enter not into the ark before the door be shut against us — — —"We are going the way of all the earth," whether we be old or young, rich or poor: and as death finds us, so shall we remain forever. Stay not then till death overtake you; but join yourselves to the Lord, and to his people. "Come with us, and we will do you good; for *the Lord hath spoken good concerning Israel*." Numb. x. 29.

2. Those who are tempted to doubt his faithfulness—

Let not delays lead you to harbor unbelieving fears. God sent not his Son till four thousand years after he had announced his purpose to the world: nor did he bring Israel out of Egypt till the time fixed in his promises was just expired. If a few more hours had elapsed, his promise to Abraham had been broken: but God remembered the very day; and then inclined the rebellious Pharaoh to submit: yea he disposed the Egyptians to "*thrust his people out*" from their land, on "*the self-same day*" that he had fixed 430 years before. Exod. xii. 51. Tarry then the Lord's leisure. Take the promises of God as your support, and "claim them as your heritage forever." Ps. cxix. 111. Be not hasty in concluding that God will not accomplish them. 1 Sam. xvii. 1. Ezek. xxxvii. 11. But take them with you to a throne of grace, and plead them as the saints of old were wont to do. Gen. xxxii. 12. Then you shall find them all to be "yea, and amen, in Christ." 2 Cor. i. 20. "If things be marvellous in your eyes, do not imagine that they must therefore be so in the eyes of God, Zech. viii. 6; for as "there is nothing too *hard* for him" *to do*, so there is nothing too *great*, or too *good*, for him to *give* to his believing people.

3. Those who are relying on his faithfulness—

It cannot but be a source of unspeakable comfort to observe, in how many passages the faithfulness of God is expressly pledged for the performance of his promises. Does he promise to forgive our sins, 1 John i. 9; to deliver us from temptation, 1 Cor. x. 13; to further in us the great work of sanctification, 1 Thess. v. 23, 24; and to preserve us to the end? 2 Thess. iii. 3. We are told in each, that he is "*faithful* to do it" for us. It is also delightful to reflect, that "his word is *tried*. 2 Sam. xxii. 31. Solomon's testimony was precisely that which is given in the text, 1 Kings viii. 56: and the more we trust in God, the more evidence shall we have that "he keepeth covenant and mercy to a thousand generations." Deut. vii. 9. But remember that his fidelity to you requires in you fidelity to him: it lays you under a tenfold obligation to "hold fast the profession of your faith without wavering." Heb. x. 23. See then that ye bear in mind the vows that are upon you, and that ye execute all that ye have undertaken in your baptismal covenant. Labor to be found "children that will not lie; so will He be" your faithful and almighty "Savior." Isa. lxiii. 8.

CONFIDENCE IN GOD A SOURCE OF CONSOLATION.

2 Tim. i. 12.—I know whom I have believed; and I am persuaded that he is able to keep that which I have committed unto him against that day. (H. H.)

MAN is born to trouble: and it is of the greatest importance to him that he should know where to turn his eyes in the day of adversity. The gospel directs us to a reconciled God in Christ Jesus, who has engaged to be our support and comfort under every distress. The christian has many trials peculiar to himself: but the gospel is fully adequate to his necessities. Its power to support him may be seen in the passage before us. St. Paul is exhorting Timothy to stedfastness in the cause of Christ: ver. 8; and, for his encouragement, he tells him what was the ground of his own consolations under the heavy afflictions which he was now enduring for the sake of Christ. He tells him, that, notwithstanding he was immured in a dungeon, and in daily expectation of a violent and cruel death, he was neither "ashamed" nor afraid: for that he had a firm persuasion of God's ability to keep him; and that persuasion afforded him ample support.

To illustrate the text, we may observe,

I. THE CHRISTIAN COMMITS HIS SOUL TO GOD—

The apostle doubtless committed unto God the concerns of the church: but it is rather of his soul that he is speaking in the words before us, because it was *that* which alone could be in danger at the day of judgment. In like manner,

Every christian commits his soul to God—

We know what it is to commit a large sum of money to the care of a Banker: and from thence we may attain a just notion of the christian's conduct. He has a soul which is of more value than the whole world: and he feels great anxiety that it should be preserved safely "against that day,' when God shall judge the world. But to whom shall he entrust it? He knows of none but God that can keep it; and therefore he goes to God, and solemnly commits it into his hands, intreating him to order all its concerns, and, in whatever way he shall see best, to fit it for glory.

To this he is prompted by manifold considerations—

He reflects on the fall of man in Paradise, and says, 'Did Adam, when perfect, and possessed of all that he could wish, become a prey to the Tempter, when the happiness of all his posterity, as well as his own, depended on his stedfastness; and can such a corrupt creature as I, surrounded as I am by innumerable temptations, hope to maintain my ground against my great adversary? O my God, let me not be for one moment left to myself; but take thou the charge of me; and let "my life be hid with Christ in God:" then, and then only, can I hope, that at the last coming of my Lord I shall appear with him in glory.' Col. iii. 3, 4.

He bears in mind also his own weakness and ignorance.—He is conscious that "he has not in himself a sufficiency even to think a good thought;" and that "it is not in him to direct his way aright." Hence he desires to avail himself of the wisdom and power of God; and cries, "Lead me in the right way, because of mine enemies:" "Hold thou me up, and I shall be safe."

But more especially he considers the gracious commands of God.—God has not only permitted, but enjoined, this surrender of our souls to him. 1 Pet. iv. 19, and Isa. xxvi. 20. O what a privilege does the christian account it to obey this divine injunction! How thankful is he that God will condescend to accept this deposit, and to take care of this charge! Hence he avails himself of this privilege, and says, "Hide me under the shadow of thy wings!" "O save me for thy mercy's sake!"

Whilst he acts in this manner,

II. HE IS PERSUADED OF GOD'S ABILITY TO KEEP HIM—

He does not merely presume upon God's sufficiency: he is well persuaded of it,

1. From the report of others—

He is informed by the Inspired Writers, *that God created the world out of nothing; and that he upholds and orders every thing in it;* insomuch that not a sparrow falls to the ground without his express permission. Hence then he argues; 'Did God create my soul, and can he not uphold it? Did he form my enemies also, and can he not restrain them ?* Has he numbered even the hairs of my head, and will he overlook the concerns of my soul

He is told *that God is ever seeking opportunities, not only to exert, but also magnify, his power in his people's cause.* 2 Chron. xvi. 9. This is meant by "shewing himself strong." Shall all that vigilance, then, be exercised in vain? or shall any be able to prevail against him?

He is assured also *that God never yet lost one whom he had undertaken to keep:* he never suffered "one of his little-ones to perish." Matt. xviii. 14. "None was ever plucked out of his hand;" John x. 28, 29; not the smallest grain of wheat, however agitated in the sieve, was ever permitted to fall upon the earth." Am. ix. 9. "The gates of hell have never been able to prevail against his church." Then, says the christian, "I will trust, and not be afraid." My Saviour, in the days of his flesh, "lost none that had been given him:" John xviii. 9; "Whom he loved, he loved to the end;" John xiii. 1; and therefore I am persuaded he will perfect that which concerneth me, Ps. cxxxviii. 8, and "complete in me the good work he has begun." Phil. i. 6.

2. From his own experience—

The christian well remembers what he was by nature; and knows by daily experience what he should yet be, if Omnipotence were not exerted in his support. And hence he argues thus; 'Has God created me anew, and by an invisible, but almighty, influence turned the tide of my affections, so that they now flow upward to the fountain from whence they sprang; and can he not keep me from going back? Has he kept me for many years, like the burning bush, encompassed, as it were, with the flame of my corruptions, yet not consumed by it; and "can any thing be too hard for him?"———

These arguments are indeed of no weight for the conviction of others; but to the christian himself they are a source of the strongest conviction, and of the richest consolation: yea, from these, more than from any others, he is enabled to say, "I *know* whom I have believed."

Moreover,

III. THIS PERSUASION IS A STRONG SUPPORT TO HIM UNDER ALL HIS TRIALS—

Many are the difficulties of the christian's warfare: but a persuasion of God's ability to keep him,

1. Encourages him to duty—

The path of duty is sometimes exceeding difficult: and too many have fainted in it, or been diverted from it. But we may see in the Hebrew youths what a persuasion of God's power will effect. They braved the furnace itself, from the consideration that God could deliver them from it, or support them in the midst of it. Dan. iii. 17, 18. And thus will every christian "encourage himself in God," and "be strong in the Lord and in the power of his might."

2. Strengthens him for conflict—

Under temptations of Satan, or the hidings of God's face, the most exalted christian would sink, if he were not supported by this hope: "I had fainted," says David, "unless I had believed verily to see the goodness of the Lord in the land of the living." But the thought that the grace of Christ is sufficient for him, will turn all his sorrows into joy: 2 Cor. xii. 9, and Rom.

*See this argument suggested by God himself, Isaiah liv. 15—17. *q. d.* "Your enemies are forming weapons; but I formed *them;* and whatever skill they exercise, I will defeat their attempts."

vii. 24; he will chide his dejected spirit, Ps. xlii. 11, and return again to the charge, knowing that at last "he shall be more than conqueror through Him that loved him." Rom. viii. 37.

3. Enables him to endure sufferings—

Many and great were the sufferings of St. Paul; yet says he, "None of these things move me, neither count I my life dear unto myself." Thus every christian must "go through much tribulation in the way to the kingdom:" but he learns, not only to bear, but to "glory in tribulation," because it gives him a more enlarged experience of God's power and grace, and thereby confirms his hope, which shall never make him ashamed. Rom. v. 3—5.

4. Assures him of final victory—

Those who have not just views of God are left in painful suspense: but they who know whom they have believed, are as much assured of victory, as if all their enemies were lying dead at their feet. Compare Isa. l. 7—9, with Rom. viii. 33—39.

We shall further IMPROVE the subject,

1. For conviction—

All persons are ready to think that they are possessed of true and saving faith. But faith is not a mere assent to the truths of the gospel, or even an approbation of them. It includes three things; *A committing of the soul to Christ; a persuasion of his ability to save us; and a determination to go forward in dependence upon him, doing and suffering whatever we are called to in the path of duty.*

Have we *this* faith?— — —

2. For consolation—*

If there be any amongst us weak and dejected, let them turn their eyes to God as their almighty friend. Let them know that "He is able to make them stand:" Rom. xiv. 4; he is "able to make all grace abound towards them, that they, having always all-sufficiency in all things, may abound unto every good work." 2 Cor. ix. 8. It is God himself who suggests to the fainting soul these very considerations; and he requires nothing, but that we wait on him in order that we may experience their truth and efficacy— — — Isai. xl. 27—31.

"Now unto Him that is able to keep us from falling, and to present us faultless before the presence of his glory with exceeding joy, to Him be glory and dominion for ever and ever, Amen." Jude, ver. 24, 25.

*If this were the subject of a FUNERAL SERMON, the excellencies ef *the deceased* might here be enumerated, and *the survivors* be comforted by the consideration that THEIR KEEPER lives for ever.

LOVE TO GOD, THE GREAT COMMANDMENT.

Mark xii. 28—30.—And one of the Scribes came, and having heard them reasoning together, and perceiving that he had answered them well, asked him, Which is the first commandment of all? And Jesus answered him, The first of all the commandments is, Hear, O Israel, The Lord our God is one Lord: and thou shalt love the Lord thy God with all thy heart, and with all thy soul, and with all thy mind, and with all thy strength: This is the first commandment. (H. H.)

IT is no uncommon thing for those who plainly declare the truth, to be beset by cavillers—

Our Lord who spake as never man spake, endured continually the contradiction of sinners against himself—

He had been captiously interrogated by Pharisees, Herodians, and Sadducees: and having silenced all of them, was again attacked by one of the Scribes, who either was, or thought himself, more subtle than the other Pharisees who had already been confounded. Verse 13, 18, 28., with Matthew xxii. 34, 35.

The answer of our Lord to him, will lead us to shew,

I. Who is the Christians' God—

Our Lord being questioned respecting the law, answered him out of the law. Deut. vi. 4, 5.

His answer which is given more fully than in St. Matthew's Gospel, intimates,

1. That we must know God before we can love him—

Our love to God must be founded on what he is himself, and what he is, and will be, to us—

Without such a knowledge of God, all our pretences to love him must be vain—

2. That there is but one God—

The heathen in general worshipped a multitude of gods—

Some, who were better instructed, supposed that there were two powerful Beings; the one the author of all good, the other of all evil—

Our Lord declared, in opposition to all such erroneous notions, that there was but One self-existent Jehovah, who made and governed all things—

3. That that God exists in Three Persons—

Some of the Jews, before the time of Christ, thought there was a deep mystery contained in these words of their law, Bp. Patrick on Deut. vi. 4.

Many early Christians were persuaded, that in these words God had given to the Jews an intimation of his subsistence in Three Persons. Bp. Patrick on Deut. vi. 4.

This is certainly the scriptural view of God, Matt. viii. xxviii. 19; and we may well take occasion from the text to speak of it; though it would not be prudent to found the doctrine altogether on the words before us—

Having called our attention to the One object that is worthy of our affections, he shews us,

II. Our duty towards him—

We must not only love God, but our love to him must be,

1. Supreme—

Our esteem of God should be so exalted, our desire after him so intense, and our delight in him so exquisite, that no created good should rival him for one moment in our affections—

Our love to him should destroy all love to what is evil, and both limit and regulate all our lawful attachments. Luke xiv. 26.

2. Abiding—

If we are to love him with *all* our heart, &c., there is no time when we are at liberty to offer him only a *divided* heart—

His excellencies never vary; and therefore our love to him should not change—

3. Operative—

Love to a fellow-creature is a mere pretence, if it do not approve itself to him in our actions—

Our love to God should make us exert all our powers for him,* and seek his glory in all we do. 1 Cor. x. 31.

In further elucidating our Lord's answer, we shall endeavor to explain,

III. WHY THAT DUTY IS CALLED "THE FIRST AND GREAT COMMANDMENT"—

The Jews doubted whether the moral law, or the ceremonial rites of circumcision and sacrifices, were the greater—

Our Lord tells them that the duty of love to God was beyond comparison greater than any, or all others together—

1. It is the noblest exercise of our faculties—

Love, towards whomsoever it be exercised, whether friends or enemies, is a noble affection, and assimilates us to "God, who is Love"—

But the exercise of this affection towards God is suited to beings who are endowed with reason, and destined to immortality—

Such an employment is an anticipation of heaven itself—

2. It is the foundation of all our other duties—

Let the best services of a fellow creature be divested of this principle, and they are good for nothing even in our eyes—

How worthless then must all our actions be in the sight of God, if they do not originate in a regard for him, and in a zeal for his glory!—

Surely love to God, as our Creator, Redeemer, and Sanctifier, ought to be the one principle from which every thing else should flow—

Nor will any sacrifice go up with acceptance before God, unless it be inflamed with this heavenly fire—

INFER,

1. How dreadfully are we fallen!

Man originally fulfilled this command, just as they are now doing in heaven—

But how far are we from such a state—

What base and vile things have usurped the throne of God in our hearts—

Let us humble ourselves in dust and ashes—

2. How impossible is it that we should ever be justified by the works of the law!

If we would be justified by the law, we must *perfectly* fulfil this duty from the earliest to the latest period of our existence—

But who has fulfilled it *perfectly?* or does? or can?—

Let us then renounce all dependence on the law—

3. What reason have we to be thankful for the blood of Jesus!

The guilt we have contracted is more than words can express or imagination conceive—

Yet it may all be washed away in the fountain opened for sin—

O let us flee to Jesus, and bless God for such an all-sufficient Saviour—

4. How should we value "the glorious Gospel of the blessed God!"

The scope and intent of the Gospel is to restore us to our primitive state—

To bring us to love God with all our hearts is the end of of all its declarations and precepts, its promises and threatenings.

Let us then close with its offers, and shew forth its fruits—

* This is implied in the word *strength.*

GOD'S ADOPTING LOVE.

1 John iii. 1.—" Behold what manner of love the Father hath bestowed upon us, that we should be called the sons of God." (Sk.)

When the Danish missionaries, stationed in Malabar, set some of their converts to translate a catechism, in which it was asserted that christians become the sons of God, one of the translaters was startled, and said, "It is too much! Let me rather render it, 'they shall be permitted to kiss his feet.'" We cannot wonder at this, since even St. John appears quite overpowered by the same sentiment, and filled with rapturous amazement at the love of God therein exhibited.—"Behold," he exclaims, "what manner of love," how vast, unparalleled, and transcendent, "the Father hath bestowed upon us, that we should be called," and constituted—not dazzling geniuses, renowned philosophers, invincible heroes, imperial monarchs,—no, but "sons of God," the high, the omnipotent, the everlasting Jehovah!—But this high title, together with the privileges of adoption, belong exclusively to believers in Christ. In John i. 12, 13, we see that men do not become the sons of God, by being naturally descended from this or that father, nor by having the title conferred on them by men like themselves, but by God's granting them that privilege through faith.

In order to enter into the apostle's views and feelings, let us consider,

I. The original state of those whom God adopts.—What were they? They were "children of wrath even as others." As men, they were the creatures of God, but as sinners, they were,

1. *Criminals*, guilty both in principle and practice of rebellion against God. Traitors to the Majesty of heaven. Hating, spurning, and violating all the divine laws, they robbed their Maker and Benefactor of his just due, and exposed themselves to his righteous displeasure.

2. *Servants, slaves, and captives of sin.* "His servants ye are to whom ye yield yourselves to obey," &c. "Whoever commiteth sin is the servant of sin." The word rendered servant signifies a *slave*, and justly denotes that bondage in which the unconverted are held, while enslaved by their own lusts, appetites, and passions.—Yea, they are represented as captives serving under their enemies, and wearing the chains of their oppressors.

3. *Children of Satan, and heirs of hell.* "Ye are of your father the devil," &c.—"Children of Belial."—"Children of wrath." "The wages of sin is death." They had no lot nor portion with the saints, but were liable to eternal misery, 1 Cor. vi. 9; Psa. ix. 17; Rev. xxi. 8.

4. *Spiritually dead.* Not only legally dead, as condemned to eternal death, but actually dead, as being destitute of all spiritual life and energy; dead in trespasses and sins, rotting as it were in the grave of corruption, &c. Can such as these become sons of God? Yes, for such were all who can now call God, "Abba Father."—We now consider,

II. The method by which he brings them into his family. This method may justly increase our admiration. Three things were necessary in order to their adoption:—

1. *To provide a pardon for them.* As they were criminals, this was the first step towards their salvation, for while the curse hung over their heads, they could not participate the divine favor. Hence, to satisfy the claims of justice, honor the violated law, and open the door of mercy, Jesus is sent to die, the just for the unjust, to propitiate for their sins and take away the

curse, so that God may be just, and yet the justifier of those who believe Behold! believe! adore!

2. *To subdue their hearts*, so that they may be disposed to receive the mercy of God. To effect this, the Spirit of grace is sent to enlighten, soften, humble, and afflict—to apply the word of truth—to strip them of all their fancied worth and righteousness—then to lead them to the cross—to dispose and enable them to lay hold on the atoning sacrifice by faith. By this act of faith they obtain justification, and God, according to the gospel constitution, receives them as his children. "Ye are all the children of God, by faith in Christ Jesus."—"Whosoever believeth is born of God."

3. *To liberate them from the bondage of sin, and infuse a new principle of life*. This is done at the same time that they obtain pardon through Christ—they then are set free, they awake to righteousness, the love of God is shed abroad in their hearts, and becomes thenceforth the vital, actuating, governing principle of their souls.

Such is the method by which sinners are brought into the family of God. Let us now regard,

III. The dignities and privileges of their adoption.

The sons of earthly grandees value themselves highly upon their birth and parentage, although they neither inherit their ancestors' virtues, nor thereby become wiser or more happy. But what is it to be a son of the greatest potentate, compared to being a son of God! The believer may boast a higher descent than the proudest monarch that ever filled a throne. Nor is it an empty boast; for all the sons of God,

1. *Inherit their Father's nature, and moral perfections;* i. e. they resemble him in all his imitable attributes. They are just, upright, true, merciful, generous, loving, compassionate, &c. They are renewed in the spirit of their minds, in knowledge after the image of him by whom they are created, and begotten anew. And, oh, how amiable, how noble, how sublime, is this heaven-born nature!

2. *They are united by the nearest and tenderest relations to Jesus Christ* "He is the first-born among many brethren." "He is not ashamed to call them brethren, saying," &c. This elder brother is their representative, their husband, and their head. He dwells in their hearts by faith, and he ever liveth in heaven to intercede for them.

3. *They have free access unto the Father on all occasions*, Eph. ii. 18; Rom. v. 2.

4. *They enjoy their heavenly Father's approbation.* His Spirit bears witness to their spirits, that they are his children, Rom. viii. 15, 16; Gal iv. 6.

5. *They are heirs of God, and joint heirs with our Lord Jesus Christ*, Rom. viii. 17. If each had been made heir of a world—a universe, it would have been a trifle compared to this! "To be heirs of God," &c. What is this but to be entitled to all that the Deity has, or is, or can do, to render them happy? To be heirs of the God of the universe, and joint heirs with Jesus his only Son, who inherits all; this is to reach the highest eminence to which creatures can be elevated, and to be only less than God!

Hence the lofty titles given them. Priests, princes, kings. "Ye are a chosen generation," &c. "Unto him who hath loved us, &c., and made us kings and priests unto God and his Father," &c.

In life or death, time or eternity, height or depth, they are secure, blessed, and inexpressibly happy.

View all these things in connexion—their original state—the astonishing method adopted towards them—and above all the transcendent privileges of their adoption, and you will exclaim, "Behold what manner," &c.

Our subject leads,

1. To correction of the false opinions formed by the world concerning the pious, whom it supposes miserable, low-spirited, unworthy. But "the world knoweth us not, because it knew him not."

2. To self-examination—are *we* the sons of God?

3. To excitement;—let the sons of God live suitably to their dignity.

GOD'S VISIT TO HIS PEOPLE.

Luke vii. 16.—God hath visited his people. (Sk.)

The text is connected with an interesting narrative circumstantially detailed by the evangelist in the preceding verses. The Lord Jesus "went about doing good;" in the course of his travels he came to a city called Nain; many disciples and much people were with him. Some to gratify curiosity, others perhaps to entangle him in his talk, others to imbibe instruction. Near the gate of the city, they met a funeral procession, a young man cut down in the prime of life—a mother's only son, and she was a widow. A widow is a solitary character; the prop that once supported her is withdrawn; she has sometimes indeed the melancholy pleasure of beholding in her offspring the resemblance of him whose memory is ever dear to her; but in the widow before us, this slender consolation was denied her; she was following her only son to the grave. Jesus Christ compassionated her circumstances, and he drew near and said, "Young man, I say unto thee, Arise: and he that was dead sat up," &c. "And there came a fear on all, and they glorified God, saying, That a great prophet is risen up amongst us, and that God hath visited his people." We will state,

I. The nature of this visit.

1. *It was not an abrupt or unexpected visit, but a visit previously and variously intimated.*—God was accustomed to visit man in his primitive innocency; and the visits of Jehovah were sources of inexpressible joy to our first parents: but when man revolted from God, he no longer desired his presence. "I heard thy voice in the garden, and I was afraid." God however did not abandon man, but gave him a promise, Gen. iii. 15.

2. *It was a visit long and ardently expected.*—The words of Christ sufficiently prove this: "Verily I say unto you, that many prophets and righteous men have desired to see the things which ye see," Matt. xiii. 17.—"Your father Abraham rejoiced to see my day," &c. John viii. 56.

3. *It was a visit personally and punctually paid.*—Personally, as to the manner, "For in the fulness of time God sent forth his Son, made of a woman," &c. And punctually as the period. Daniel had referred to this, "Seventy weeks are determined upon thy people," &c. Dan. ix. 24.

4. *It was a visit generally known, and widely and extensively spread.*—John the Baptist did all that he could to give publicity to the character of Christ, and Christ himself "went about all Galilee teaching in their synagogues," &c. Matt. iv. 23. But,

5. *It was a visit almost generally disregarded.*—A few reverenced and adored the Savior, and exclaimed, "Never man spake like this man;" but the great mass of the Jewish people rejected him. "He came unto his own, but his own received him not." View the insults they offered unto his person, and the contempt they cast upon his doctrines and miracles.

II. THE PURPOSES FOR WHICH THIS VISIT WAS PAID.

1. *To display the divine glory.* Every thing that God does in the kingdom of nature, providence, and grace, must in a certain sense refer to himself. "The heavens declare the glory of God," the glory of his natural perfections; but the visit which God in the person of Christ paid to his people, was to display the glory of the moral perfections of the Deity—wisdom, love, power, and mercy.

2. *To make an atonement for sin.*—God is the moral governor of the world.—When he made man he placed him under a law, a law whose penalty was death.—This law was violated—justice demanded punishment. No creature could make an expiation. God revealed himself in human nature. to make an atonement for sin. Hence "He was wounded for our transgressions," &c.—"He gave his life a ransom for many," &c.—"He was made sin for us," &c.

3. *To reveal a comprehensive and complete system of religious truth.*—Divine truth was sparingly and cautiously revealed under the Old Testament dispensation; it was here a little and there a little; and that which was revealed, was corrupted by the artifice or ignorance of men. But Christ declared, "To this end was I born, and for this cause came I into the world, that I should bear witness unto the truth," &c. John xviii. 37.

4. *To exhibit a perfect model of virtue.*—The Old Testament saints were patterns of piety—Joseph of chastity. Moses of meekness, Job of patience, Daniel of courage—but Christ was all perfection. See his submission to parental authority, his humility, his sympathetic feeling for the afflicted, his zeal for his Father's glory, his love, his patience, &c.

III. THE RETURNS WE SHOULD MAKE TO GOD FOR FAVORING US WITH SUCH A VISIT.

1. *We should admire aud adore the condescension of the visitant.*—Never was there such a visit paid before;—so voluntary;—so little was there on the part of man to invite such a visitant;—the treatment he was to meet with from the parties visited: all serve to excite our astonishment, and lead us to adore the condescension of our God and Saviour.

2. *We should form our lives upon the model of his.*—Let us study his character, let us imbibe his disposition, and let us copy his life, 1 John iv. 17.

3. *We should avail ourselves of all the advantages which God's visit to our world was designed to procure.*—He came to save sinners—to destroy the works of the devil—"that we might have life, and have it more abundantly." Let us seek salvation, &c.

4. *As God has visited us, let us visit him in return.*—He comes among us when we assemble in his name.—Let us meet him in his house—in our closets—at his table, and let us anticipate the time when we shall visit him in his kingdom. When he will send his flaming messengers to shout us welcome to the skies. "He is gone to prepare a place for us, and he will come again, and receive us unto himself." Amen. "Even so, come. Lord Jesus."

THE GOD OF OUR SALVATION DAILY LOADETH US WITH BENEFITS.

Psalm lxviii. 19.—Blessed be the Lord, who daily loadeth us with benefits, even the God of our salvation." (Sk.)

"O Lord how manifold are thy works!" What a diversity prevails in all the walks of nature! How multiform are the operations of God in the church! What a variety of truths is displayed in the Bible! But were we to analyze the sacred volume, we should not find one sentiment of more frequent occurrence than that with which our text commences: "Blessed be the Lord!"—How proper then for our consideration! Nothing can be more calculated to inspire us with this sentiment, than the subject before us. Here we have,

I. What God is:—He is "the God of our salvation."

II. What God does:—He "daily loadeth us with benefits."

III. What we should do in return.—"Bless the Lord."

I. What God is.—"The God of our salvation;" salvation is deliverance from danger; the term is sometimes applied to deliverance from human enemies, then we call it a temporal salvation. It is generally however applied to the soul. Man is a sinner, and sin exposes him to danger; for "the wages of sin is death," and "the soul that sinneth it shall die." But there is deliverance from this danger; this is attributed to God.

1. *The scheme of salvation* originated in God. When man sinned, he could not restore himself to the forfeited favor and image of God. He had no desire for salvation—he could make no atonement for his sin—he could not extricate himself from the power of his enemies. But God pitied him in all his wretchedness; and "God sent not his Son into the world," &c. John iii. 17.

2. *The means of salvation are afforded us by God.* God sends us his gospel, containing good news of salvation; his ministers to declare the way of salvation. He gives us a day of salvation. He affords us Christian sabbaths, religious ordinances, and various means of grace in order to promote our salvation.

3. *The work of salvation is accomplished in the human soul by God's immediate agency.* "Behold God is become my salvation!" The Holy Ghost convinces of sin, and shows us the need of salvation; witnesseth with our spirits that we are saved; sanctifies the soul, and makes it his holy habitation; and seals it unto the day of redemption.

4. *The sole glory of our final salvation will endlessly redound to God.* In heaven we shall have clearer discoveries of the greatness, extent, and freeness of our salvation; we shall see the evils from which we have been delivered, and the hell we have escaped, and we shall feel how deeply we are indebted to God for our salvation, and sing "Salvation to our God," &c. Rev. vii. 10.

II. What God does for us;—He "daily loadeth us with benefits." Three things we notice here,

1. *The nature of God's gifts;*—they are "benefits;" a benefit is a kind ness, a favor conferred, an act of love. God's gifts are benefits, not deserts; were God to deal with us according to our demerit, we should be loaded with punishments rather than benefits. Even our afflictions are benefits, as they "work for us," &c. 2 Cor. iv. 17; Heb. xii. 10.

> "Crosses from his sovereign hand,
> Are blessings in disguise."

2 *Their number.* We are loaded with benefits. Here we may enumerate the intellectual powers we possess—the health we enjoy—the age of the world in which we live—the country we inhabit—the civil and religious advantages with which we are favored, and especially the spiritual privileges which God has so graciously conferred upon us.

3. *The frequency of their communication.* He "*daily* loadeth us," &c. God's benefits come to us daily, they are new every morning; great is his faithfulness.

> "Each evening shows his tender love,
> Each rising morn his plenteous grace;
> His waken'd wrath doth slowly move,
> His willing mercy flies apace."

And these benefits flow to us *freely*, unsolicited, unemployed, unsought. *Seasonably*, exactly as we need them. Critics state, that instead of "daily loadeth us with benefits," it should be read, "who bears our burdens, or supports us every day." This is an interesting truth! In the wilderness God bare Israel as a man doth bear his son, Deut. i. 31. Or as an eagle bears her young on her wings, Deut. xxxii. 11. The promise is, "Even to hoary hairs will I carry you," Isa. xlvi. 4. We have our cares, and burdens, and anxieties, but God invites us to cast them upon him. Ps. lv. 22.

III. WHAT WE SHOULD DO IN RETURN.—"Blessed be the LORD." To bless, signifies to extol, exalt, or speak well of a person; and to bless the Lord is to speak good of his name.

1. *We should bless the Lord sincerely.*—Hypocrisy is hateful to God. What our lips express, our hearts should feel. In order to this, we should meditate on God's benefits, and on our unworthiness, sinfulness and great demerit.

2. *We should bless the Lord affectionately.*—Our gratitude should be the effusion of love. How pleasing is the exercise of praise when love tunes our hearts.

3. *We should bless the Lord constantly.* "I will bless the Lord at all times." The benefits of God are incessantly flowing to us, and our gratitude should be as constantly returned to him.

4. *We should bless the Lord practically.*—To say, "We praise thee, O God, we acknowledge thee to be the Lord;" while we practically violate his laws, must be abominable in his sight. Let us "praise him not only with our lips, but by our lives," &c. Conclusion,

1. *Is the Lord the God of our salvation?*—Are we saved from sin? from the dominion of sin? from our easily besetting sin? Salvation from sin is essential to our being saved from hell. God is the Saviour, and the only Saviour. He invites us to look to him, and be saved. O let us avail ourselves of his kind invitation! How desirable it is to be saved! May God be our Saviour, even the God of our salvation.

2. *Does he daily load us with his benefits?*—What a lesson for humilty? What have we that we have not received? What an excitement for love to him who deals so bountifully with us! Does God bear our burdens! Let us learn to depend upon him. He will never suffer the righteous to be moved

3. *Are we saying "Blessed be the Lord."*—Are his statutes our songs in the house of our pilgrimage? Let us anticipate the period when we shall join the society of angels, and rival them in the chorus of praise.

> "Thee they sing with glory crown'd,
> We extol the slaughter'd Lamb;
> Lower if our voices sound,
> Our subject is the same."

ENCOURAGEMENT IN GOD.

1 Samuel xxx. 6.—But David encouraged himself in the Lord his God. (S. S.)

In seasons of prosperity the superior happiness of a christian is not visible to all—

But in adverse circumstances he has a manifest advantage over others—

The ungodly, when the cisterns from whence they draw their water are broken or emptied, have no comfort left—

But when every stream is dried up, the godly have still access to the fountain itself—

This was experienced by the church of old—Hab. iii. 17, 18.

And it is beautifully exemplified in the history before us—

David was in great trouble, being suspected by the Philistines—Plundered by the Amalekites—and threatened by his own soldiers—

But in the midst of all he encouraged himself in God—

We shall shew

I. What reason he had to do so.

Though reduced to the greatest extremities, he derived encouragement

1. From the perfections of God as revealed in the word.

He was no stranger to the character of God as it was revealed to Moses—Exod. xxxiv. 6, 7.

Or to the unnumbered illustrations of it which the history of his nation afforded him—

Consequently he knew that there was nothing too hard for God to effect, or too great for him to give—

2. From the experience which he himself had had of God.

The lion, the bear, the Philistine giant, and the murderous rage of Saul had given him abundant proofs of God's superintending providence—1 Sam. xvii. 37, xviii. 11, and xix. 10, 11.

These he called to mind in this season of trial and distress—Ps. xlii. 6, lxxvii. 10, 11.

And wisely judged that, with such a friend on his side, he had no cause for fear—2 Cor. i. 10.

3. From the covenant which God had made with him.

God had covenanted with him to give him the throne of Israel—

Hence he was assured that his life should be spared till this promise was accomplished—

It was in this view that he was enabled to call God his God—

And the thought of this relation to God added tenfold confidence to his soul—

While we admire the conduct of David in this particular, let us consider

II. What reason we have to do likewise.

Certainly the grounds of David's encouragement are equally calculated for our support.

God is still the same almighty and gracious Being as ever—

His arm is not shortened, nor is his ear heavy with respect to us—

We may also see much of his goodness *in our own experience*—

Wonderful have been the ways in which he has dealt with us for the awakening, preserving, and sanctifying of our souls—

He has *also covenanted with us* that "he will never leave us nor forsake us"—Heb. xiii. 5.

Nor shall one jot or title of his word ever fail—

Are not these then grounds of encouragement to us as well as to David?—

But we have far greater reason to encourage ourselves in God than David had—

We have seen more stupendous displays of God's *power*.

David had read of the wonders wrought in Egypt and the wilderness—

But what were these wonders when compared with the victories gained over all the passions and prejudices of the world by the preaching of a few poor fishermen?—

We have beheld more astonishing exercises of his *love*.

The history of the Jews records many instances of God's love towards them—

But what were these when compared with the gift of his dear Son to die for us, and of his holy Spirit to renew us?—

These things are as much beyond any thing that David had ever seen, as the substance is beyond the shadow—

We have experienced more abundant proofs of his *faithfulness*.

How many promises, made to the church at large, have been accomplished by the mission of Christ, and the gift of the Holy Spirit!—

And all the members of the church, from its first establishment to the present moment, have found the promises of the gospel fulfilled to them in their season!—

In proportion therefore as God's faithfulness has been tried and ascertained, our confidence in him must be increased—

Application.

1. Let us endeavor to secure God as *our* God.

Unless God be ours, we can have but little reason to encourage ourselves in him—

Let us then look to Christ, that through him we may find acceptance with God—

So shall God be our friend, our father, and our "eternal great reward"—Gen. xv. 1; John i. 12; 2 Cor. vi. 18.

2. Let us encourage ourselves in God.

We must expect to meet with many difficulties and troubles—

Nor can we find any grounds of encouragement in ourselves—

But in God there is all that we can either need or desire—

Are we then discouraged by outward difficulties or inward corruptions? let us direct our eyes to him, as our compassionate, almighty, and ever faithful friend—

Let us, like David, chide our unbelief, Ps. xliii. 5; and henceforth say with him, "In the day of my trouble I will call upon God"—Ps. lxxxvi. 7

GOD AND THE REDEEMER MUTUALLY GLORIFIED.

John xvii. 1.—Father, the hour is come: glorify thy Son, that thy Son also may glorify thee. (Pr.)

We here find our Lord Jesus in a most solemn and affecting situation. He had often said that his hour was not yet come; but now it is fully arrived. Having comforted his disciples by an inimitable farewell address, he here concludes it by a prayer, which was offered in their hearing.

It does not seem that our Lord had in these words an immediate respect to his sufferings: he appears rather to look through them, to the joy that was set before him. We have other instances of this, especially in John xii. 23, 24, 31.

The prayer presented in our text is intended to intimate, that the honor conferred on the Redeemer, in the establishment of his kingdom, would redound to the glory of God the Father.

I. Enquire in what respects GOD HAS GLORIFIED, and does still glorify his Son.

Whatever tends to raise him in the esteem of intelligent beings, or to exhibit the excellence of his character, is the means of glorifying him.

God is said to have 'magnified' his servant Joshua, when he wrought by him before the face of all Israel. Josh. iii. 7. So Christ was glorified from his first coming into the world: angels worshipped him: witness was borne to him at his baptism, also on the mount of transfiguration, and by the miracles which he wrought.— — —But the principal part was to follow upon his sufferings and triumphs on the cross, as David was honored when he had killed the uncircumcised Philistine: then they sung his praises in their song

More particularly—

1. God has glorified his Son *in granting him the desire of his heart.*

It was an honor to Esther to be asked what was her petition, and what was her request; when she asked her own life, and the life of her people. — — —This honor was conferred on Christ; and he asked the life of his enemies, that he might be made a covenant for the people: their salvation was all that he desired. Isai. xlix. 8; liii. 11; Psa. ii. 8; xxi. 1, 2.

2. In bestowing mercy upon sinners *only in his name, and for his sake.* — — —It was an honor conferred on Joseph that he should have all things in his hand, and that all Egypt should be dependent upon him. It was also a great honor conferred on Job that he should be made a mediator, and that God should accept his three friends for his sake: this was more than enough to do away his reproach. Job xl. 8.— — —But to Jesus is given superior honor: God hears no prayer but in his name, gives no blessing but for his sake: and through his name the greatest sinners are pardoned, justified, and eternally saved.

3. God has glorified his Son in pouring forth *a richer effusion of grace* at the time of his ascension, than at any former period.— — —The mercy was to begin at Jerusalem, but to go on to the ends of the earth. Luke xxiv. 47.— — —It was at his coronation, that the captives among the Gentiles were set free: God reserved that honor to grace his triumph.— — —All the blessings that have since been given to the church, are given with a view of honoring him, and in consequence of his intercession.

4. In investing him with *the government of the world,* in subservience to the great ends of his mediation: ver. 2.— — —All that is going on in the earth is only making way for his kingdom, and the accomplishment of his designs. Ephes. i. 20—23.

II. In what respects the GLORY OF CHRIST redounds to the glory of the Father.

Wherein the Son is glorified, the Father is glorified also, and that by the same means. It is the office of the Holy Spirit to glorify Christ, and his work is to glorify the Father.— — —The honor of the Son does not disagree with that of the Father: there is no jealousy here, though some have affected to be very jealous for the Father's honor. John v. 23.— — —The interests of the Lawgiver do not suffer by those of the Saviour: they are inseparably blended together, and cannot exist apart.

1. The gospel provides for *the honor of God*, in such a way as nothing else could have done. The moral law glorifies him in asserting his authority: the sacrifices under the ceremonial law glorified him, as containing a virtual acknowledgment that sinners deserved to die for their offences.— — But the Son of God magnifies the law by his obedience, and makes it honorable; satisfies divine justice by his atonement, and glorifies the name of the Lord.

2. The mediation of Christ exhibits *the divine character* as infinitely glorious.— — —All other mediums afforded only a partial view of his perfections; but his entire glory is seen in the face of Jesus Christ. The light of nature was insufficient to show the path of life, and it effected no moral change in the state of the world.— — —But wherever the doctrine of the cross is made known, idolatry and iniquity fall before it. God is glorified in the highest; on earth there is peace, and good will towards men.

3. Wherever Christ is believed in, the name of the Lord *is loved and feared*.— — —The Lawgiver is adored wherever the Mediator is embraced. All the christian graces do honor to God: repentance bears respect to his authority, faith implicitly obeys the dictates of his word, hope lifts up its eyes to his mercy seat, love cleaves to him as our portion, and his law is our delight.— — —The believer is of the same mind as Christ, making the divine glory the ultimate end of all.

We learn from hence—

1. What encouragement there is for sinners to *come to Christ*. The glory of God was the great hinderance in the way of acceptance: now it admits of a free salvation, and God is more abundantly glorified than he would have been in our condemnation. He can now pardon the greatest sins: look to him therefore, and be saved.

2. The motives that should urge us to pray for *the success of the gospel*. It is Christ's own prayer, and we may unite with him in it: "Father, glorify thy Son!"— — —Let us lay hold of this plea: it has always been successful, and always will. If we love God and the Redeemer, we shall pray and labor to promote their mutual glory in the world.

CHAPTER IV.

CHRIST.

CHRIST ONE WITH THE FATHER.

John x. 30.—I and my Father are one. (H. H.)

It might well be expected, that, if God should reveal his will to man, there would be many things disclosed by him, which exceed the narrow limits of human reason. This might more particularly be expected in whatsoever related to his own person and character: for, as we can know nothing of him any farther than he is pleased to reveal himself to us; and as we cannot even comprehend our own nature, or discover how the soul is united to the body;

it would be strange indeed if we could comprehend the mode of God's existence, and explain how there should be an union of Three Persons in the Godhead. In relation to such a mysterious subject, our wisdom is to ascertain what God has revealed concerning himself, and to receive it on the testimony of his word. This is the office of reason, as well as of faith: for reason requires, that we submit our understandings to the dictates of His wisdom, no less than our wills to the influence of His authority. That a Trinity of Persons in the Godhead is revealed, cannot reasonably be doubted, as long as the baptismal rite shall continue to be administered "in the name of the Father, and of the Son, and of the Holy Ghost:" for to imagine, that a creature is here associated with Almighty God in the highest possible act of Divine worship, were the height of absurdity, and impiety. The subject before us relates only to the union subsisting between Christ and his Father: to that therefore we shall confine our attention. We begin with,

I. The assertion of Christ—

Our Lord says, "I and my Father are one." Now it must be remembered, that the same expressions are used, as in human compositions, so also in the holy scriptures, sometimes in a metaphorical and figurative sense, and sometimes in a plain and literal sense; and their true import must always be judged of by the context. This is particularly the case with respect to the expression before us; which is elsewhere used in reference to the saints, to mark the exalted state to which they are raised by their connexion with Christ, and the mutual interest which they should feel in each other's concerns: "I pray for them, that they all may be one; as thou, Father, art in me, and I in thee, that they also may be one in us; that the world may believe that thou hast sent me. And the glory which thou gavest me, I have given them; that they may be one, even as we are one: I in them, and thou in me, that they may be made perfect in one." John xvii. 20—23. Here the sense is obvious: no one could conceive for a moment that the union here spoken of is *personal*, as though the saints could be one *person* with God, or one *person* in their collective capacity: it simply means, that the saints are to enjoy an union with God and with each other, as nearly resembling that which subsists between Christ and his Father, as their situation and circumstances will admit of, namely, an union of sentiment, of affection, of will, and of operation. But, in the passage under our consideration, more is evidently intended: in that is implied, not merely a figurative, but a *real* and *personal* union, an union of nature and of essence. In proof of this, we must refer you to,

1. The whole scope of the passage—

Our Lord is speaking of the security which his sheep enjoyed; that "He gives unto them eternal life, and that they shall never perish, nor shall any one ever pluck them out of his hand." But, because he was speedily to be taken from them, and might therefore be supposed incapable of fulfilling this promise, he says, that "his Father was confessedly greater than all" created powers, yea, greater than he himself was in his human or Mediatorial capacity; and that "none should ever be able to pluck them out of his Father's hand." Yet, that they might know that he would not on account of his removal from them remit his care of them, he added, "I and my Father are one;"—'we are one, as in will, so in power; as in operation, so in nature and in essence: and consequently my sheep have a double pledge of their security.'

This is the plain meaning of the passage; and that it is so, may be clearly seen from.

2. The construction which the Jews put upon his words—

They took up stones immediately, to stone him: and when he inquired, for which of all his good works they were about to stone him, they replied, that it was "not for any good work, but for blasphemy; because that He, who was only a man like themselves, made himself God." Verses 32, 33. Now this shews incontestably what meaning *they* affixed to his words: it was not an ignorant individual, or persons ill acquainted with the received import of the words, that so interpreted them; but the whole audience. who perfectly understood what meaning his expressions were suited to convey.

The Jews were taught by God himself to be particularly jealous on the subject of idolatry; and to put to death any person who should, whether openly or in secret, attempt to seduce them to it. When therefore they heard our Lord arrogate to himself divine honors, they resented it, as they had done repeatedly before, by taking up stones to stone him as a blasphemer. John v. 17, 18, and viii. 58, 59. We do not say, that they were right in expressing their abhorrence of idolatry in this way; because they should have had the matter examined before a magistrate, and have acted according to evidence, and not according to the impulse of their blind passions: but we do say, that Jesus was justly accused of blasphemy, if he was not God; and that there was just cause for the indignation which his audience expressed.

But perhaps they were mistaken in their construction of his words: in which case we may be assured that Jesus would carefully rectify their error. But do we find that he did disclaim the assertion which they called blasphemy? No;

In his answers to them we find only,

II. His confirmation of it—

They had just complained that he kept them in suspense; and had desired that he would tell them plainly, who, and what, he was. He, in reply, declares that he had told them, and that they would not believe. Ver. 25. Had he told them that he was a mere man like themselves, they would readily enough have believed *that:* but when he tells them again that he was "one with his Father," they go about to stone him for blasphemy. Nevertheless, instead of revoking his word, he vindicates his claim; and establishes the justice of it,

1. By an appeal to the Sacred Writings—

Magistrates, he tells them, were in the Inspired Volume frequently dignified with the name of gods: Exod. vii. 1, and xxii. 28; and he refers them to one passage in particular well known to them all, "I have said, Ye are gods." Ps. lxxxii. 6. Now these were called gods on two accounts; first, because they were Jehovah's Representatives and Vice-gerents upon earth; and next, because *they were types of the Messiah, who was to be really and truly God,* even "Emmanuel, God with us." Isai. vii. 14. Matt. i. 23. 'Now,' says our Lord, 'if these persons, *in order to prepare you for the reception of your incarnate God,* were honored with the name and title of gods, and you readily acquiesced in it, with what reason can you, when your incarnate God appears, accuse him of blasphemy, because he assumes that title, or calls himself by a name which you justly consider as equivalent to it? You are looking for your Messiah; and that Messiah is expressly foretold under the character of "Jehovah's fellow," Zech. xiii. 7, who is "David's Lord as well as David's Son:" Ps. cx. 1, with Matt. xxii. 42—45; such therefore the Messiah *must* be; for "*the Scriptures cannot be broken:*" why then do you not acknowledge the justice of my claim? If indeed I do not give evidence enough that I am the Messiah, you may justly dispute my title to be regarded as God; but if I do, then you are the blasphemers, who rob me of my proper honor. Know ye then, that I am the Person, "whom the Father hath sanctified" and set apart from all eternity to the office, "and now hath sent into the world" to execute it: know also, that, instead of retracting any thing I have said, I repeat my assertions, and demand your acknowledgment of me in my true character.'

Thus our Lord confirms his assertion by an appeal to scripture. He next proceeds to confirm it,

2. By an appeal to his own works—

'I do not desire to be credited in such an assertion upon my bare unsupported word, without any corroborating evidence;' says our Lord: '"If I do not the works of my Father, believe me not: but, if I do, though ye believe not me, believe the works; that ye may know and believe, that the Father is in me, and I in him." Ver. 37, 38. Consider my works, both *the matter*, and the *manner* of them, and see if they do not justify every assertion I have made. Did ever *man* perform such miracles as I have done, so many, so great, so benevolent, so demonstrative of a divine agency? Moses indeed and the prophets wrought some few miracles: but *how?* they wrought them uniformly by application to Jehovah for the intervention of of his power: but look at my miracles: on some occasions indeed, I also, acting in my Mediatorial capacity, have acknowledged my dependence on him, and have acted "in his name," as his servant; Luke xi. 41—43; (for as Mediator, I *am* his servant:) but, as being *One* with the Father, I have wrought in instances without number by that power and authority which I possess in common with the Father. Whence had I the power to still the elements, as I have done; Mark iv. 39; or to expel Satan, Mark ix. 25, or to raise the dead? Mark v. 41; Luke vii. 14. When the leper justly acknowledged my power to effect whatsoever I *would;* to whom was I indebted for power to heal him, when I said, "I *will*, Be thou clean?"' Matt. viii. 3.

Such an appeal as this was sufficient to convince the most incredulous: and it receives much additional light from the manner in which the apostles wrought their miracles: they wrought them invariably *in the name of Jesus;* Acts ix. 34, and xvi. 18; and disclaimed all idea of any inherent power in themselves, or even of any goodness on account of which God had wrought by them; so fearful were they, lest by any means they should rob the Lord Jesus of the honor due unto his name. Acts iii. 6, 12, 16, with iv. 9, 10, 12.

Shall it be said that our Lord did not mean in this appeal to assert his true and proper Godhead? Then see both his words, and the sense in which his enraged adversaries continued to understand them: "Though ye believe not me, believe the works; *that ye may know and believe*, that the Father is in me, and I in him.—*Therefore they sought again to take him.*" Here are two things demonstrated; first, that his enemies understood him to affect equality with God: and next, that He, knowing that they did so understand him, renewed and confirmed the assertions which they had so interpreted. A clearer explanation of what he affirmed, or a stronger proof of WHAT HE IS, we cannot reasonably desire.

We are the more earnest in establishing the divinity of our blessed Lord, because it is intimately connected with every fundamental truth of our holy religion. LEARN then from it.

1. The dignity of his person—

Because God condescended to take our nature upon him, we requite his love by denying him to be God. But know that Jesus Christ is indeed "the true God," 1 John v. 20, "the mighty God," Isai. ix. 6, "the great God and our Saviour," Tit. ii. 13, "God over all blessed for evermore." Rom ix. 5. He is "the brightness of his Father's glory, and the express image of his person;" Heb. i. 3; yea, in him dwelleth all the fulness of the God head bodily." Col. ii. 9. Hear what he himself saith unto Philip: Philip, having heard him speaking of the Father, as actually known to his disciples, and already seen by them, saith, "Lord, shew us the Father, and it sufficeth us." To this Jesus replies, "Have *I* been so long with you, and hast thou not known *me*, Philip? He that hath seen *me*, hath seen *the father;* and how sayest thou then, Shew us the Father? Believest thou not that I am in the Father, and the Father in me? Believe me, that I *am* in the Father, and the Father in me; or else believe me for the very works' sake." John xiv. 7—11. Now, I ask, if Jesus had not been really "one with the Father, would he have dared to use such language as this? And, if his disciples were guilty of idolatry in worshipping him, was not the fault altogether *his?* Were not his words and his arguments expressly calculated to mislead and deceive them? But there is no room for doubt on this head. We never can entertain too high thoughts of him; nor can we ever honor him as we ought, unless we "*honor him, even as we honor the Father.*" John v. 23.

2. The virtue of his sacrifice—

On the dignity of his person depends the whole value of his atonement. The apostle justly observes, that "it is not possible for the blood of bulls and of goats to take away sin:" and the same observation may with justice be applied to every creature, however exalted. But when we are assured that it was "*God* who was manifest in the flesh," 1 Tim. iii. 16, that it was "*the Lord of Glory* that was crucified," 1 Cor. ii. 8, and that it was "*God* who purchased the church with his own blood," Acts xx. 28, we no longer hesitate to declare that his death was "a full, perfect, and sufficient sacrifice, oblation, and satisfaction for the sins of the whole world." The Communion Service; and 1 John ii. 2. He was, it is true, "in the form of a servant; but he was also in the form of God, and thought it not robbery to be equal with God;" Phil. ii. 6—8; and therefore we may be assured that "his blood will cleanse us from all sin." 1 John i. 7. The ransom he has paid for us, is fully equal to the redemption of a ruined world: and the righteousness which he has wrought out for us by his obedience unto death, is all that is wanted for the justification of those who trust in it. The very name given him by the prophet declares this; for we are taught to "call him, JEHOVAH OUR RIGHTEOUSNESS." Jer. xxxiii. 16. Here then "the weary and heavy-laden may find rest unto their souls."

3. The sufficiency of his grace—

If Jesus were only a creature, those who trust in him might be addressed like the worshippers of Baal, "Cry aloud, for he is a god: either he is talking, or he is pursuing, or he is on a journey; or peradventure he sleepeth, and must be awaked." 1 Kings xviii. 27. He could not attend to the concerns of the whole universe at once; and therefore could not be a suitable object of our trust and confidence. But he is infinitely above all creatures, being "King of kings, and Lord of lords." Rev. xix. 16. He could truly say to Paul, and to every suppliant in the universe, "My grace is sufficient for thee." Let not any one then despond, as though his corruptions were irremediable, or his enemies invincible; for "God hath laid help for us upon

One that is mighty;" Ps. lxxxix. 19; and the weakest of the human race that relies on him, may confidently say, "In the Lord have I righteousness and strength:" Isai. xlv. 24; "The Lord Jehovah is my strength and my song; he also is become my salvation:" Isai. xii. 2; "The Lord is my shepherd; therefore can I lack nothing." Ps. xxiii. 1.

4. The excellency of his salvation—

If we consider the price that has been paid, we may judge of the value of that redemption which has been purchased for us. Even in relation to the present life, we are told that "eye hath not seen, nor ear heard, nor hath it entered into the heart of man to conceive, the things which God hath prepared for them that love him." Isai. lxiv. 4; 1 Cor. ii. 9, 10. Under whatever figure they are spoken of, they are represented as exceeding all human apprehension: "the gift of them is unspeakable:" 2 Cor. ix. 15; "the riches of them unsearchable:" Eph. iii. 8; "the peace that is enjoyed by means of them, passeth understanding;" Phil. iv. 7; and "the joy which they produce, is unspeakable and glorified:" Eph. iii. 18; the love that bestowed them has "a height and depth, and length and breadth" that can never be explored. Eph. iii. 18. Respecting the future life, we are still further from being able to appreciate the glories of it. The description of heaven, as a city paved with gold, and enriched with every thing magnificent or good, affords but a faint idea of that blessed place; Rev. xxi. 10—23; as the songs and music of its inhabitants very inadequately represent their blessedness and joy. Rev. v. 8—14, and xiv. 1—3. But this we know, that, both on earth and in heaven, the felicity of the saints shall be worthy of the sacrifice that was made to obtain it. Let not any one then seek it in a listless and lukewarm manner, as though it were of little value; for it is a "great salvation," Heb. ii. 3, which the tongues of men and angels can never worthily describe, nor can the ages of eternity suffice to enumerate its blessings.

THE FIRST PROMISE.

Genesis iii. 15.—And I will put enmity between thee and the woman, and between thy seed and her seed: it shall bruise thy head, and thou shalt bruise his heel. (Sk.)

THE former part of this chapter is truly awful! It contains a melancholy account of the introduction of evil into our world, and of man's apostacy from the Lord his God; but here we find the first promise: and when that was made, the gospel day began to dawn. From that time to the present, all men have been placed in the hands of a Mediator: for Jesus was then appointed to redeem man, to avenge his wrongs, and to save him from the sad effects of sin. Our first parents understood this promise in *part;* but we understand it *fully*. They knew that a deliverer would come to bruise the head of their envious and malicious foe; but we know by subsequent events, the character of this deliverer, and the means which he used to accomplish his plans of grace and mercy. The words of our text may be divided into two parts:—first, the Lord put enmity between the serpent and the woman, and between his seed and her seed;—and, secondly, the seed of the woman was to bruise the serpent's head, and the serpent was to bruise his heel.

I. The Lord put enmity between the serpent and the woman, and between his seed and her seed.

1. *The serpent is addressed, but the devil is intended.* He is called, "the dragon, that old serpent, the devil," Rev. xx. 2. Three reasons may be assigned why he is called a serpent;—first, he assumed that form when he tempted "the mother of all living," ver. 1.—Secondly, he is crafty, subtle, and cunning, 2 Cor. xi. 3.—And, thirdly, his influence on man resembles the deadly bite of a serpent, Gen. xlix. 17.

2. *The woman is named.* She was made "a help-meet for man," chap. ii. 18: but she yielded to temptation, and drew her husband into sin. "Adam was not deceived, but the woman being deceived, was in the transgression." This is an *humbling* reflection to the female sex; but let it be remembered, to their *honor*, that the Saviour is the seed of the woman.

3. *Wicked men are the seed of the serpent.* The devil is their father, and they are his children, by wicked works. This may be proved by what our Lord said to the Jews: "Ye are of your father the devil, and the lusts of your father ye will do," John viii. 44. The old serpent is an enemy of God, and this may be affirmed of all his children, without exception, Rom. viii. 7.

4. *The seed of the woman is Christ Jesus our Lord.* He was born of a pure virgin, without the concurrence of man, Matt. i. 23; and was made of a woman; for, "when the fulness of time was come, God sent forth his Son, made of a woman, made under the law," Gal. iv. 4. But he who was made of a woman, was "Immanuel, which being interpreted, is, God with us," Matt. i. 23; and when the devil contended with him, he contended with God incarnate, 1. Tim. iii. 16.

5. *God put enmity between these parties; and they can never be reconciled.* This will not be doubted, when we consider their opposite characters:—the devil is *polluted* and *defiled*, but Christ is *pure* and *holy*;—the devil is a *destroyer*, Christ is Saviour;—the devil is a *merciless tyrant*, but Christ is a *mild pacific Prince.* A war was about to commence between them, in which the one was to conquer, and the other to be destroyed, Heb. ii. 14. For,

II. The seed of the woman was to bruise the serpent's head, and the serpent was to bruise his heel.

1. *By the head of the serpent, we are to understand the mischievous power of the devil;* and the figure is very appropriate, because the life and power of the serpent lie in his head. His bite leaves a poisonous liquor in the wound, which quickly mixes with the blood, and produces speedy death.

2. *To bruise his head, is to crush his power.* All his power has been employed in doing mischief; and among his other works, we may reckon error, unbelief, sin, misery, and death: and therefore we rejoice in hope of that day, when his power shall be wholly destroyed, and when his deadly influence shall cease, Rev. xx. 10.

3. *Jesus came into the world, to bruise his head.* The first conflict between these parties, of which we have any account was in the wilderness of Judea; and there our Lord was more than conqueror, Matt. iv. 1—11: afterwards the almighty power of Jesus appeared, on many occasions, in casting devils out of the bodies of men; so that they trembled before him, and asked if he were come to torment them before their time, Matt. viii. 29.

4. *The head of the serpent was bruised by the death and resurrection of Jesus.* Under the influence of the devil, his impure seed, the wicked Jews, "killed the Prince of Life," Acts iii. 15; but in death, he made atonement

for sin, redeemed man, and gave a death blow to the serpent: and in his resurrection, he conquered death and the grave, and "became the first fruits of them that slept," 1 Cor. xv. 20.

5. *And he is now bruising the serpent's head, in the exercise of his grace and mercy.* After his resurrection he appointed a gospel ministry, Mark xvi. 15; ascended into heaven, till his enemies should be wholly subdued, Heb. ix. 12, 13; sent down his Holy Spirit, Acts ii. 1—4; and by the ministry of his word, and the agency of his Spirit, he bruises the head of the serpent in the hearts of all true believers.

6. That the serpent still exercises considerable power, is a fact which we cannot deny; but we may safely affirm, that *he has received incurable wounds*, and that his destruction is certain. Our Glorious Redeemer reigns and "must reign, till he hath put all enemies under his feet," 1 Cor. xv. 25; and then glorious times will follow to his church, and to the world, Isa. xi. 5—9.

7. *But the heel of Jesus was bruised by the serpent.* He suffered greatly in his human nature, while he tabernacled on earth, and his holy seed have suffered much from their adversary the devil; but it has only been a bruising of the heel, which is not a vital part. When Satan obtained leave to attack Job, the Lord said unto him, "Behold he is in thine hand: but save his life," Job ii. 6; and it is a pleasing thought, that this wicked and malignant spirit could never touch the life of our great Deliverer. It is true his body died, but that was only the heel or inferior part of his nature.

Inferences.

1. The influence of this serpent has been vast and extensive, the mischief which he has done is incalculably great; and even now, "he worketh in the hearts of the children of disobedience," Eph. ii. 2.

2. But it is matter of rejoicing, that we have a Saviour, and a Great One, who is both able and willing to deliver all who put their trust in him; and if we commit ourselves to his care, he will keep us safely against that day, when the serpent and all his seed shall be cast into hell, 2 Tim. i. 12.

2. That we may be *safe* and *happy*, we should "renounce the devil and all his works:" embrace the offers of the gospel; and place ourselves under the government and protection of the woman's conquering seed.

4. Placed under the banner of our Redeemer, let us not fear the *wicked one*, but constantly and courageously resist him, under an assurance that he will flee from us, James iv. 7. Soon we shall be out of his reach, and all the sad effects of his malice will be done away for ever. Amen.

ABRAHAM'S PROMISED SEED.

Gen. xxii. 18.—In thy seed shall all the nations of the earth be blessed. (S. S.)

There is nothing in man which can merit the divine favor: the promises of God to us are altogether free, resulting wholly from his sovereign grace: yet does God frequently *manifest* his love towards us in consequence of something done by us. Abraham, it should seem, was an idolater, when God first made himself known to him in his native land: and *then* did the Almighty promise, that in him should all the families of the earth be blessed. But, in the passage before us, Abraham is recorded to have performed the most extraordinary act of obedience that ever was known from the foundation of the world: and God takes occasion from that to renew his promise and, for his more abundant consolation, to confirm it with an oath. To ascertain the full import of this glorious prophecy, it will be proper to inquire

I. WHO IS THE SEED HERE SPOKEN OF.

It is not to all the natural descendants, or to that part of them that composed the Jewish nation, or even to the spiritual seed of Abraham, that these words refer: they speak of one particular individual, the Lord Jesus Christ.

1. To him all the types direct our attention.

The temple with all its utensils, the priests with all their habits and services, the sacrifices and oblations of every kind, all shadowed forth his work and offices. The principal events in the Jewish history, together with the great persons engaged in them, their lawgiver, their commanders, judges, kings, and prophets, prefigured him in different points of view, and, as so many lines, meet in him as their common centre. On this account we have reason to think that the prophecy before us relates to him.

2. In him all the prophecies receive their accomplishment.

However some of the prophecies might be partially fulfilled in Solomon or others, it is certain that all of them together were never accomplished in any one but Jesus. They were intended to designate HIM, that, when he should arrive, there might be no doubt of his being the very person foreordained of God to be the Saviour of the world. The minute description of the promised Messiah, together with the marvellous combination of circumstances that marked Jesus as the person foretold, lead us further to believe that the text had particular respect to him.

3. To him *exclusively* the text is applied by God himself.

St. Paul tells us that *the blessing of Abraham* was to come on the Gentiles through Jesus Christ; Gal. iii. 14; and that the words of the text related, not to others, but to Christ alone. Ib. 16.

This point being ascertained, let us inquire

II. IN WHAT RESPECT ALL NATIONS ARE BLESSED IN HIM.

The full accomplishment of the text will not take place till that glorious period when the knowledge of the Lord shall cover the earth, as the waters cover the sea. Yet, in a limited sense, all nations have experienced the truth of this prophecy already.

1. They are reconciled to God through him.

Christ died not for one nation only; he was a propitiation for the sins of the whole world. Many of all nations have already believed in his name, and rejoiced in his salvation: and in every place they who believe in him shall find acceptance with their God. Col. i. 20—22.

2. They are united in one body in him.

He has broken down the middle wall of partition that divided the Jewish and Gentile world, and, having reconciled both unto God in one body by the cross, he has slain the enmity thereby. Eph. ii. 14—16. All mankind are now brought into one family, and are taught to regard each other as brethren: and in proportion as the religion of Jesus gains the ascendant over our hearts, we are united in love to every member of his mystical body.

3. They are blessed with all spiritual blessings.

There is not any thing that can conduce to our present or future happiness which Jesus will not bestow on his believing people. Adoption into his family, peace in our consciences, holiness in our hearts, and an eternity of glory in the Father's presence, are the certain portion of all his faithful followers. There is no difference between Jew and Gentile; all are admitted to the same privileges, and all shall participate the enjoyments.

INFER,

1. The antiquity of the gospel.

The sum and substance of the gospel is, that Christ is the only source of all spiritual and eternal blessings. Wherever this truth is strongly urged, men are ready to cry out against it as a *new* doctrine. But we can trace it, not only to the reformers of our church, but to the apostles, yea to Abraham also: for St. Paul declares, that when God spake the words to Abraham, he "*preached the gospel to him*," even that very gospel, whereby he and all the nations of the earth must be saved. Gal. iii. 8. Let this truth then no longer be reviled as novel, but be received as the one ground of all our hopes.

2. The importance of faith.

Abraham's faith in this gospel was imputed to him for righteousness: Gal. iii. 6, and by believing the same divine record we also must be justified. Ib. 7, 9. No doctrine whatever is more explicitly declared in scripture than this. Let us then acknowledge the necessity of faith, and look to the Lord Jesus Christ as that promised seed, through whom alone the blessings of Abraham can flow down upon us.

3. The connection between faith and works.

Faith was that principle which produced in Abraham such exemplary obedience: Heb. xi. 17, and the same root will bear similar fruits wheresoever it exists. Acts xv. 9. Indeed the pardon of past sins would be utterly insufficient to make us happy, if it were not accompanied with the renovation of our natures. To this effect St. Peter expounded, as it were, the very words of the text, declaring to the Jews, that conversion from sin was one of the first blessings which the Lord Jesus was sent to bestow. Acts iii. 25, 26 Let us then not consider faith and works as opposed to each other, but as possessing distinct offices, the one to justify our souls, the other to honor God, and to manifest the sincerity of our faith.

ISAIAH'S VISION OF CHRIST.

Isaiah vi. 5—7.—Then said I, Wo is me! for I am undone; because I am a man of unclean lips, and I dwell in the midst of a people of unclean lips: for mine eyes have seen the King, the Lord of hosts," &c. (Sk.)

THIS prophet was peculiarly favored by the Lord, and has ever been distinguished as the most eminent of the Jewish seers. He was singularly honored with clear and comprehensive views of the person and character of the Messiah; and minutely predicted the circumstances of his incarnation, and the triumphs of his kingdom. In this chapter, he was highly privileged, by having a distinct and glorious vision of the Son of God. It took place when he was in the temple, where "he saw the Lord sitting upon a throne, high and lifted up," attended by numerous seraphims, who were perpetually employed in rendering him their profoundest homage, and devoutly adoring his holy name, ver. 2, 3. The effects which these things produced on his mind, and what occurred on this interesting occasion, he informs us in the language of the text; from which we may learn, that this vision was,—glorious in its object,—instructive in its design,—and gracious in its influence.

I. THE PROPHET'S VISION WAS GLORIOUS IN ITS OBJECT:—"Mine eyes have seen *the King, the Lord of hosts.*" The dignified person whom he saw was the promised Messiah. This is evident from the testimony of St. John, who when referring to this chapter, expressly declares, "These things said Esaias, when he saw his glory, and spake of him." It is certain that "no man hath seen God," or the divine *essence* at any time, but his "only begotten Son hath declared him." When the prophet saw him "in the bosom of the Father;" he appeared in the two-fold character of *essential God* and an *Almighty Sovereign.* Hence he justly specifies,

1. *The divinity of his person:*—"The Lord of hosts," or according to Lowth, "*Jehovah* God of hosts." This language is certainly a legitimate and powerful argument, in proof of the deity of the Lord Jesus Christ. To deny this would be equally opposed to just reasoning and sound criticism. The prophet actually *saw* his *personal glory*, even the glory of the "only begotten of the Father;" and boldly asserts his essential divinity, as the second person of the triune Godhead. And this character of the Saviour perfectly accords with the descriptions given of him throughout the sacred writings. The eternity of his existence fully proves that he is absolutely God, and equal with the Father, John viii. 58, xvii. 5; Heb. xiii. 8. He is therefore justly called "both Lord and Christ,—the Lord of glory,—the Lord of all,—the Lord of hosts," Phil. ii. 11.

2. *The sovereignty of his character:*—"Mine eyes have seen *the King.*" Christ's kingly office is clearly revealed in the Scriptures, and is highly encouraging to his people, Ps. cxlix, 2. He is *a supreme king;* even "the King of kings and the Lord of lords," Prov. viii. 15. *A universal king;* whose kingdom ruleth over all things, both visible and invisible, Col. i. 15—18; Rev. i. 18. *A spiritual king;* whom God has set upon his holy hill of Zion, to be the head and governor of his church, and reign in the hearts of his people, Ps. ii. 6; Luke xvii. 21: Col, i. 13. *An everlasting king;* who shall continue to reign and prosper when all other kings and their dominions shall be destroyed, "but of his kingdom there shall be no end," Dan. vii. 14; Heb. i. 8. How glorious is the Redeemer's character! Let us adore his name and gladly bow to his sceptre. Observe,

II. THE PROPHET'S VISION WAS INSTRUCTIVE IN ITS DESIGN;—"Then flew one of the seraphims," &c. As no scripture is of private interpretation, this vision was, no doubt, intended not only for the personal benefit of the prophet, but also for the general instruction of mankind. It evidently illustrates,

1. *The nature of salvation;*—"Thine iniquity is *taken away*, and thy sin *purged.*" We are not only actually guilty, but morally polluted. When God therefore saves sinners, he takes away their guilt by his mercy, and purifies their hearts by his grace. Both pardon and purity are equally necessary for our present and final happiness. They are freely promised in the gospel, and are happily enjoyed by all the righteous, 1 Cor. vi. 11. This was certainly the blessed experience of the prophet, and such is still the salvation of all true believers.

2. *The medium of salvation;*—"Then flew one of the seraphims unto me," &c. Here God employed one of his angels as a messenger of his grace to the prophet. He came flying with a live coal in his hand, which was taken from off the altar. This was most probably the altar of burnt offering, which had always coals of fire burning upon it, Lev. vi. 12, 13. This manifestly typified the Lord Jesus Christ, as the atoning sacrifice for our sins, and the high-priest over the house of God for ever, Heb. ix. 14, xiii. 10: 1 John iv. 10. The seraphs laying the live coal upon the prophet's mouth, might represent the necessity of a personal application of Christ's

atonement as the only medium of pardon, purity, and every spiritual blessing, Heb. xii. 24. It might also point out the sanctifying influence of the Holy Ghost, as a "spirit of burning and refining fire;" and is in the whole, an instructive and emblematical representation of the divine method of saving sinners to the end of time, Matt. iii. 11; John xiv. 6; Heb. iv. 14—16.

3. *The assurance of salvation.* This was unquestionably the privilege of the prophet. He was assured of it by the declaration of the seraph, and the sign which he received, verse 7. This, without doubt, was highly consolatory to his mind, and greatly encouraged him in his work. And though we cannot expect to receive it in the same way, it is still a possible privilege, and is enjoyed by many, who can declare, like David, what God has done for their souls. The Lord communicates it by his word and Spirit, and gives his people "the knowledge of salvation by the remission of their sins,' Rom. viii. 15, 16; 1 Thess. i. 5. This will lead us to consider,

III THE PROPHET'S VISION WAS GRACIOUS IN ITS INFLUENCE;—"Then said I, Wo is me! for I am undone," &c. All spiritual intercourse with God is profitable to the soul. This was manifestly the case in the instance before us. The prophet was both powerfully affected, and greatly profited by this heavenly vision.

1. *It was deeply humbling;*—"Wo is me! for I am undone," &c. I am struck dumb, "because I am a man of unclean lips," &c. He had such a discovery of the infinite splendor and purity of the Lord of hosts, that he was more than ever convinced of his own personal pollution, and of the sinfulness of the people among whom he dwelt. These things deeply humbled him before God, and filled him with unfeigned repentance and self-abasement. The manifestation of God to the soul is always productive of genuine humility and contrition of heart; and leads the penitent believer to exclaim, "Wo is me! I abhor myself, and repent in dust and ashes," Job xlii. 5, 6.

2. *It was personally sanctifying.* Whilst the prophet was abashed and humbled, on account of his uncleanness, he received a comfortable assurance of his pardon and acceptance with God. His sin was also purged, and he was made "a vessel unto honor," more deeply and fully "sanctified and meet for the master's use." By communion with God we feel his transforming power, and are changed into the same image, 2 Cor. iii. 18. A believing discovery of his glory and purity is always assimilating and hallowing in its influence, Ps. lxiii. 2, 3; 2 Cor iv. 6.

3. *It was highly encouraging.* The prophet was called to the painful task of addressing the Jews, who were "a disobedient and gainsaying people." He deeply felt the importance of his office, and the difficulty of his work; and humbled under a sense of his own inability to discharge the duties of his high commission. But by this divine vision his fears were instantly removed, and he was greatly encouraged to engage in the work which God appointed him to do, with great delight. When the Lord said, "Whom shall I send, and who will go for us?" the prophet immediately said, "Here am I, send me." Nothing is deemed hard or unreasonable by the believer, that appears to be the will of God, Phil. iv. 11—13.

To conclude,

1. Let us carefully search the Scriptures which testify of Christ, and reveal the way of salvation.

2. Let us diligently improve the privileges we enjoy, till we obtain the perfect vision of the "King eternal," 1 John iii. 2.

THE JOYFUL PROCLAMATION.

Isaiah lxii. 11.—Behold the Lord hath proclaimed unto the end of the world, Say ye to the daughter of Zion, Behold, thy salvation cometh; behold, his reward is with him, and his work before him. (Sk.)

From the very nature of prophecy, it must generally involve a degree of obscurity, which can only be fully removed by its accomplishment. But it is evident, that all the prophetic testimonies are not *equally* mysterious and difficult to comprehend. Some of them are *comparatively* plain and intelligible to the weakest capacity, and leave no reasonable doubt of their precise import and application. This is particularly observable in many of Isaiah's predictions of the promised Messiah, and the inestimable blessings of his kingdom. And though he frequently employs the most beautiful imagery, and describes with inimitable sublimity of language, the most glorious and important events, yet his writings in general are more distinct and perspicuous than the other prophets.—This chapter *primarily* predicts the deliverance of the Jews from the Babylonish captivity; and very probably refers to their *final restoration* as the people of God. But it also manifestly announces the propagation and triumphs of the gospel; and contains the most encouraging promises of the universal diffusion of divine knowledge, and the future prosperity of the christian church.—The text may therefore be regarded as the Lord's general commission to the prophet, and to all his faithful ministers, to proclaim the glad tidings of salvation throughout the world, both to Jews and Gentiles, "Behold the Lord hath proclaimed it." &c. Let us observe,

I. This proclamation exhibits a glorious object.

"Behold thy *salvation* cometh." Such is the distinguished character of the Messiah. He is a *Saviour*. He *saves his* people from their sins, and is therefore called *their salvation*. For this purpose he came into the world —was delivered for our offences—and now ever liveth to make intercession for us. His saving character is perfectly such as our necessities require.

1. *He is the appointed Saviour*. When we had destroyed ourselves, in God was found help. He loved the world and sent his only begotten Son, that we might live through him. As the mediator of the new covenant, Jesus is frequently called God's *servant*, because he assumed humanity, that he might accomplish his *will*, and finish the *work* which he had given him to do, Isa. liii. 11; Heb. x. 5—7; John iv. 34. "The Lord laid on him the iniquity of us all," and exalted him with his right hand, to be a prince and a *Saviour*. It thus "pleased the Father, that in him should all fulness dwell," for the salvation of perishing sinners.

2. *He is the all-sufficient Saviour*. He is both divinely authorized, and infinitely qualified, to execute his saving office. He is "the propitiation for our sins," and hath obtained eternal redemption for mankind." In him, there is an inexhaustible plenitude of grace and truth. Millions have put their trust in him, and have proved the virtue of his name, Rev. vii. 13, 14: —and he is "the same yesterday, to-day, and for ever." He can save the vilest sinners, and will cast out none that come unto him. However *multiplied* our crimes—however *aggravated* our guilt—and however *deep* the *stains* of our depravity may be, Jesus is *able* and *willing* to redeem us from all iniquity, and save us to the uttermost, Psa. cxxx. 7, 8; Matt. xi. 28; Heb. vii. 25.

3. *He is the only possible Saviour.* There is no other way to the Father; nor any other mediator between God and man; 'For other foundation can no other man lay than that is laid, which is Jesus Christ." He alone has bought with a price, and can save us from wrath to come. He has been the *only Saviour* of his people in every age, Isa. xlv. 21, 22. Salvation is not the scheme of angelic wisdom, nor the production of human energy; but the special purchase of Christ's infinite merit, and the sovereign achievement of his omnipotent power, Titus iii. 4—7. No other Saviour is *necessary*, nor can any other be *found;* for "there is none other name under heaven given among men whereby we must be saved." *Behold thy salvation!*

II. THIS PROCLAMATION CONTAINS A GRACIOUS MESSAGE.

"Say ye to the daughter of Zion, Behold," &c. Whatever reference these words might have to Cyrus, who proclaimed liberty to the captive Jews, they more eminently describe the *office* and *work* of Christ, as the Redeemer and Saviour of sinners. Observe,

1. *His mysterious advent;*—"Behold he cometh." He had long been promised as the seed of Abraham, in whom all nations should be blessed. To him gave all the prophets witness, and greatly rejoiced in the anticipation of his manifestation in the flesh, 1 Pet. i. 10. 11.—Behold, now he *is come!* "The Word was made flesh, and dwelt among us." He is Immanuel, God with us.—'God with God, is man with men.' Glorious mystery! Infallible truth! Matchless love! 1 Tim. iii. 16; 2 Cor. viii. 9.

2. *His important mission;*—"*His work* before him." What an infinite work did he engage to accomplish! It includes all that he has *done* and *suffered* to redeem and save the world. His human incarnation—perfect righteousness—atoning sacrifice—triumphant resurrection—glorious ascension—and prevailing intercession, Rom. viii. 3, 34.—The work of *redemption* he gloriously *finished* in the days of his flesh, Heb. ix. 4.—But the work of *salvation* is still *before him*, in which he is *perpetually engaged*, and will not cease to carry it on, till he has *fully* accomplished all the designs of his mediatorial engagements, 1 Cor. xv. 24—28.

3. *His glorious recompence;*—"His *reward* is with him." In him are hid all the treasures of wisdom and knowledge, and all the unsearchable riches of salvation. From his infinite fulness, he freely and abundantly communicates the richest blessings to his believing people;—he enlightens their minds—justifies their persons—liberates their souls—purifies their hearts—and inspires them with "joy unspeakable and full of glory;"—he graciously bestows an inestimable treasure of *grace* here, and an ineffable reward of *glory* hereafter, 1 John iii. 2. This message must be published in all nations;—"The Lord hath proclaimed," &c.

III. THIS PROCLAMATION DEMANDS SPECIAL ATTENTION.

The threefold repetition of the term *behold*, in the text, intimates the vast *importance* of the subject introduced, and the absolute *necessity* of attentively regarding the Saviour as proclaimed by the prophet. We should beho him,

1.. *With devout admiration.* He is the most *glorious* and *interesting* object. He is altogether lovely in his person, character, works, and offices How great is his beauty, and how infinite his goodness! Behold his astonishing love, his attractive dignity, and his captivating grace! Embrace his truth—bow to his sceptre—and imitate his example;—supremely adore his exalted name—and affectionately exclaim, "This is my *beloved*, and this is my *friend* "

2. *With believing application.* The Saviour is not an object of *sight*, but of *faith*. Beholding him, therefore, is an *act* of the *mind*, under the influence of his Spirit. By faith we *look* to him—*come* to him—*receive* him—and *trust* in him, as "the Lamb of God, which taketh away the sin of the world," John i. 12; Eph. i. 13. *Such* a beholding Christ, is always accompanied with a personal interest in his merits, and a participation of present salvation.

3. *With joyful anticipation.* "Faith is the substance of things hoped for, and the evidence of things not seen."—It looks to the unseen Saviour, and joyfully expects his *second appearing*, without sin unto salvation. The believer looks through all sufferings and discouragements, and greatly rejoices in hope of the glory of God—having a "desire to depart and be with Christ which is far better," Phil. iii. 20, 21; Col. iii. 3, 4. May all mankind speedily hear the joyful proclamation of the gospel—behold the ineffable glories of the Redeemer—and participate the exceeding riches of his grace!

CHRIST'S NATIVITY.

Luke ii. 8--11.—And there were in the same country shepherds abiding in the field, keeping watch over their flock by night. And lo, the angel of the Lord came upon them, and the glory of the Lord shone around about them; and they were sore afraid. And the angel said unto them, Fear not: for, behold, I bring you good tidings of great joy, which shall be to all people. For unto you is born this day, in the city of David, a Saviour, which is Christ the Lord. (Pr.)

In the circumstances attending the birth of Christ, we see much of the hand of God. The decree of Cæsar Augustus, which directed the Virgin mother to Bethlehem, is employed for the accomplishment of ancient prophecy: ver. 1—3. Mic. v. 2.— — —The low and humble state in which the Saviour was born, ver. 7, serves as a specimen of the treatment he should meet with from the world in general, while the ministry of attendant angels indicated the honor which God would put upon him notwithstanding. John i. 10, 11.

Let us notice some of the particulars of the history, before we enter on the immediate subject of the text—

1. Observe the interest which the *angels* felt on the occasion.— — —The minds of men were wholly occupied with the 'taxing,' and the decree of the emperor; but *their* thoughts are full of Christ.— — —The rulers and principal inhabitants of Jerusalem overlooked what had happened at Bethlehem, as scarcely deserving of regard, while the humble shepherds in the field are visited by an angel from heaven.

2, Not only did an angel appear to them, but "the glory of the Lord shone round about them."— — —Angels sometimes made their appearance in human form, as in the instance of Abraham and Lot; and then they excited no particular fear or dread. But on this occasion, so great and interesting, they appear in all their native dignity and glory, that it might be seen they brought a message immediately from God.

3. The effect it had upon the shepherds: "they were sore afraid," but were afterwards cheered by the heavenly messenger.— — —Mary Magdalene also was greatly alarmed at the appearance of the angel at the sepulchre

and as both these visions took place amidst the darkness of the night, it must have added a terrific grandeur to the scene.— — —Yet in this awful manifestation of the divine glory, there is a mixture of tender mercy; and the shepherds are filled with fear and hope, a presentiment of the feelings which the gospel should inspire.

4. The object proclaimed is the "Saviour."— — —When an angel turns preacher he does not speak of himself, nor draw the attention to that quarter, but to Christ, as the supreme object of regard. What an example to all who engage in the sacred ministry!

5. The good news was common to "all people," and not to one nation only.— — —The highest and best source of consolation is that which is common to all christians, and consists in the common blessings of salvation; and not that which distinguishes one people or one christian from another. David's principal desire, and also Paul's is equally the desire of all that truly believe. Ps. xxvii. 3; Phil. iii. 8.

6. The good news, though common to all people, was more immediately addressed to the shepherds, who like many others were waiting for the consolation of Israel. "To you" is born a Saviour, which is Christ the Lord. — — —The gospel also is as much addressed to individuals, as if they only were the objects of it.

7. In this heavenly message particular attention is paid to time, place, and other circumstances, to show their agreement with ancient prophecy: ver. 11. Not an angel from heaven must be permitted to speak any thing contrary to what is written in the scriptures of truth. Gal. i. 8.

I. Consider the subject of the angelic message, and see what "good tidings" are contained in it.

1. The *birth of Jesus Christ* was itself good news.— — —This was the great object of prophecy from the beginning of the world, and the hope of the church in all ages. Zion was bid to rejoice in it, Zech. ix. 9; and the whole creation to be glad, Ps. xcvi.— — —God was now manifest in the flesh, even Immanuel, God with us. The Word was made flesh, and dwelt amongst us, the only-begotten of the Father, full of grace and truth.

2. The *gracious design* of his incarnation imported good tidings to a guilty and ruined world.— — —He came to do the will of God, to die as a ransom for us, to rise from the dead, to ascend into heaven, and make intercession for us.— — —The Son of God was manifested to destroy the works of the devil, to bring glory to God in the highest, on earth peace, and good will to men.

3. The *way of salvation*, which was effected by the coming of Christ, forms an essential part of the good tidings brought to us by the angel. To us is born "a Saviour," which is Christ the Lord.— — —Repentance and remission of sins are now preached among all nations; a free, full, and eternal salvation. These in effect are the tidings announced by the celestial messenger.

II. These tidings are matter of joy, "of great joy to all people."

The term here employed is strong, and never used but on great occasions; for the joy of harvest, or an important victory; but is fully applicable to the subject under consideration.

1. The coming of Christ was the joy of *the old-testament church*, while they lived only in the hope of this great event. Isai. xxv. 9; John viii. 56. How much more when it is fully realised.

2. All the joy of believers, *during the lifetime of our Saviour*, centred entirely in him.— — —Mary and Elizabeth, Simeon and Anna, and all that looked for redemption in Jerusalem, rejoiced and triumphed in the incarnation, when they saw the mercy promised to the fathers, and the performance of the holy covenant. Christ was the joy of his immediate disciples and followers, and his presence the only happiness they knew on earth.

3. All the joy *in the times of the apostles*, had an immediate reference to Christ and his salvation.— — —Jerusalem, which had been the scene of his deepest abasement, was afterwards filled with peace, and joy, and gladness, and resounded with the triumphs of the ascended Saviour. There was great joy also in the city of Samaria, but it was through the doctrine of the cross. The apostles triumphed in every place, but it was because the savour of his name was spread abroad. Whom having not seen, says Peter, ye love: in whom, though now ye see him not, yet believing, ye rejoice with joy unspeakable and full of glory.

4. Christ and his salvation made all their *troubles and sorrows light and momentary;* yea they counted not their lives dear for his sake. The history of the primitive church is a history of sufferings in the cause of Christ, and of joy and rejoicing in his holy name. This also is the way for us to bear up under all the sorrows of the present life.

III. Enquire what is necessary to render these good tidings a matter of real joy to us.

It is an undoubted fact, that they do not produce joy in all. They did not then, and they do not now.— — —Many think the tidings of the gospel not worth hearing.— — —Many who hear, neglect them, or feel no interest in them.— — —Some who seem to rejoice for a time become indifferent; and afterwards wither away.

To become the subject of real joy, these tidings require to be believed as true, and to be received with the utmost cordiality.— — —Christ was in the world, and the world knew him not; he came unto his own, and his own received him not. Those who did receive him were such as believed on his name, being born again.

In particular, it includes a deep conviction of our guilty, lost, and ruined state, which is pre-supposed by the gospel; and which must be felt and realized, before it can convey to us tidings of great joy.

Also a cordial reception of the gospel itself, as revealing the only way of salvation; obeying it from the heart, and receiving the truth in love.

OF THE INCARNATION OF CHRIST.

1 Timothy, iii. 16.—God manifested in the flesh. (H.)

The incarnation of Christ is a most extraordinary and amazing affair; it is wonderful indeed, that the eternal Son of God should become man; that he should be born of a pure virgin, without any concern of man in it; that this should be brought about by the power of the Holy Ghost, in a way unseen, imperceptible, and unknown, signified by his overshadowing; and all this in order to effect the most wonderful work that ever was done in the world, the redemption and salvation of men: it is a most mysterious thing, incomprehensible by men, and not to be accounted for upon the principles of natural reason; and is only to be believed and embraced upon the credit of Divine revelation, to which it solely belongs.

I. The subject of the incarnation, or the Divine Person that became incarnate.

The evangelist John says it was the Word, the essential Word of God; "The Word was made flesh, and dwelt among us," John i. 14; and he is said to be the "Word with God;" that is, with God the Father; and therefore must be distinct from him, Rev. xix. 13; Acts xx. 32; John i. 1. Wherever we read of any visible appearance of a Divine person in the Old Testament, it is always to be understood, not of the first, but of the second person. The Father prepared a body, a human nature in his purpose, council, and covenant, and not for himself, even for his Son, as he acknowledges; "A body hast thou prepared me." Heb. x. 5. That Divine person who came in the flesh, or became incarnate, is always distinguished from the Father, as being sent by him; "God sending his own Son," Rom. viii. 3. "God sent forth his Son," Gal. iv. 4, that is, God the Father, in both passages; as appears from the relation of the person to him, sent in the flesh, his Son. If the Father had been incarnate, he must have suffered and died; for that is the end of the incarnation, that the person incarnate might obey, suffer, and die, in the room of sinners; so Christ suffered in the flesh, and was put to death in the flesh. Nor is it the Holy Spirit that became incarnate, for the same reasons that the Father cannot be thought to be so; and besides, he had a peculiar hand, and a special agency, in the formation of the human nature, and in its conception and birth: when Joseph and Mary were espoused, before they came together, "she was found with child of the Holy Ghost:" and Joseph was told, in order to encourage him to take her to wife, that what was "conceived in her was of the Holy Ghost;" and therefore he himself was not incarnate. See Luke i. 35; Matt. i. 18—20. It remains that it is the second person, the Son of God, who is meant by "the Word that was made flesh," or became incarnate; and indeed, it is explained of him in the same passage; for it follows, "And we beheld his glory, the glory, as of the only-begotten of the Father." When this mystery of the incarnation is expressed by the phrase, "God manifest in the flesh:" not God the Father, nor the Holy Ghost, but God the Son is meant, as it is explained; 1 John iii. 8; for "this purpose the Son of God was manifested."

II. To observe in what sense the Word, or Son of God was made flesh.

John i. 14; Heb. ii. 14; 1 John iv. 2, 3; 1 Tim. iii. 16; signify, that he who is truly God, really became man, or assumed the whole human nature, as will be seen presently, in union with his Divine person.

1. What is meant by *flesh*, in the phrases and passages referred to, is a whole individual of human nature, consisting of soul and body, as when it is said, "There shall no flesh living be justified in his sight;" and again, "That no flesh shall glory in his presence," Rom. iii. 20; 1 Cor. i. 29, with many other passages; see Gen. vi. 12; Luke iii. 6; for such acts as being justified and glorying, can never be said of the flesh nor body, abstractedly considered; but of the whole man, or of individuals of human nature, consisting of soul and body; and in this sense are we to understand it, when it is used, of the incarnation of the Son of God, who took upon him the whole nature of man.

He took a true body, not a mere phantom, spectre or apparition, the appearance of a body, and not a real one. It is certain that Christ partook of the same flesh and blood as his children: and therefore if theirs be real, his must be so. Likewise, his body is called the body of his flesh, his fleshly body, Col. i. 22, to distinguish it from the token of his body in the supper; and from his mystical and spiritual body, the church; all his actions, and what is said of him, from his birth to his death, and in it, and after it, show it was a true body that he assumed. The very infirmities that attended him, though sinless, were proofs of his body being a true and real one; such as his fatigue and weariness in travelling, John iv. 6, his tears at the grave of Lazarus, and over Jerusalem, and his sweat in the garden, John xi. 35; Luke xix. 41, xx. 44. In short, it was through weakness of the flesh that he was crucified; which was not in appearance, but in reality.

2. Christ assumed a reasonable soul, with his true body, which made up the nature he took upon him, and are included in the flesh he was made. Christ asserts that he had a soul, and which, he says was exceeding sorrowful; and which was an immaterial and immortal spirit; and which, when his body died, and was separated from it, he commended into the hands of his Divine Father, Matt. xxvi. 38; Luke xxiii. 46.

2. In what sense the Word, or Son of God, was made flesh, and so became incarnate.

The Word could not be made at all, that is, created, since he is the maker and creator of all things; and therefore, he himself could not be made, nor created. But as other scriptures explain it, God the Word, or Son, was made and became "manifest in the flesh;" the Son that was in the bosom of the Father, the Word of life, that was with him from all eternity, was manifested in the flesh in time to the sons of men; and that in order to take away sin, and to destroy the works of the devil. 1 John i. 2, and iii. 5, 8.

III. The causes of the incarnation.

1. The efficient causes of it, God, Father, Son, and Spirit. The Father prepared a body for the Son in his purpose, and proposed it to him in council and covenant to assume it; and he sent him forth in the fulness of time. Heb. x. 5; Gal. iv. 4; Rom. viii. 3. The Son having agreed to it, being sent, came in the flesh, by the assumption of it; "he took unto him the form of a servant." Heb. ii. 14, 16; Phil. ii. 7, 8. The Holy Ghost had a very great concern in this affair; for that which was conceived in the virgin, was of the Holy Ghost. Matt. i. 20. Now, though all the three persons in the Deity had a hand in the wondrous incarnation, yet only one of them became incarnate; only the Son assumed the human nature. Some have illustrated this by three virgins concerned in working a garment, when only one of them puts it on and wears it.

2. The moving cause of the incarnation of Christ is the love of the Father, and of the Son, to mankind. "God so loved the world; herein is love, that God sent." John iii. 16; 1 John iv. 9, 10; And such was the love and condescending grace of the Son, that though he were in the form of God, of the same nature with him. Col. ii. 6—9; 2 Cor. viii. 9.

3. The final cause, or for whose sake, and for what the Son of God became incarnate. It was for the sake of lost sinners: "To us," or for us, for our sakes "a child is born, a Son is given." See Isa ix. 6; Luke ii. 10, 11; Matt. i. 21.

IV. The parts of the incarnation are next to be considered, conception and nativity.

1. Conception. This is a most wonderful, abstruse, and mysterious affair, and which to speak of is very difficult.

1. This conception was by a virgin; "Behold, a virgin!" this was a new thing, unheard of, and astonishing, which God created in the earth, in the lower parts of the earth, in the virgin's womb: a woman compassed or conceived, a man, without the knowledge of man. Isa. vii. 14; Jer. xxxi. 22. This was not natural, but supernatural.

2. This conception was through the power and influence of the Holy Ghost overshadowing the virgin.

3. It was a nature, not a person, that Christ assumed so early as at its conception; it is called the "Holy Thing," and not a person. The seed of Abraham; the form and fashion of a man, that is, the nature of man; as the form of God, in the same passage, signifies the nature of God. See Luke i. 35; Heb. ii. 16; Phil. ii. 6—8.

2. Nativity,

1. Of whom born,

1. Of a virgin: "a virgin shall conceive and bear a Son." See Matt. i. 18—23.

2. Christ was born of a virgin of the house of David, as in Luke i. 27. For the phrase, "of the house of David," is equally true of the virgin, as of Joseph, and may be connected with her. Acts xiii. 23; Rev. xxii. 16.

3. He was born of a virgin of the tribe of Judah; as she must be, since she was of the house of David, which was of that tribe. Gen. xxx. 10 Heb. vii. 14.

2. The place of his birth was Bethlehem, according to the prophecy in Micah, v. 2. See Matt. ii. 4—6; John vii. 42.

3. The time of his birth was as it was fixed in prophecy; before the sceptre, or civil government, departed from Judah. Herod was king in Judea when he was born, before the second temple was destroyed; for he often went into it, and taught in it: and it was at the time pointed at in Daniel's weeks. See Gen. xlix. 10: Mal. iii. 1; Hag. ii. 6, 7, 9; Dan. ix. 24. &c.

V. THE ENDS OF CHRIST'S INCARNATION ARE MANY; THERE IS A CLUSTER OF THEM IN THE SONG OF THE ANGELS. Luke ii. 14.

1. One end of Christ's incarnation was, to show forth the glory of God in it. The glory of his grace, kindness, and goodness to men, in the mission of his Son in this way; the glory of his faithfulness in fulfilling his promise of it: the glory of his power, in the miraculous production of Christ's human nature; and the glory of his wisdom, in bringing it into the world in such a manner as to be free from sin, and so fit for the purpose for which it was designed.

2. To make peace with God for men on earth; to make reconciliation for sin, was the work appointed him in covenant; and to do this was the reason of his being made, in all things, like unto his brethren; and make peace by the blood of his cross.

3. That man might receive the fruit of God's good will and favor towards them; even all the blessings of grace.

4. Particularly, Christ became man that he might be our God, our near kinsman, and might appear to have a right to redeem us; and he was, in the fulness of time, made of a woman, to redeem men from the law, its curse, and condemnation, &c.

5. Christ became man, that he might be a Mediator between God and men; and, the better to perform several parts of his office as such, he took upon him the nature of man, that he might have something to offer, as a priest, to be a sacrifice for sin, and make a satisfaction for it in that nature that sinned; and be a prophet like unto Moses.

THE JOY OF ANGELS AT THE INCARNATION.

Luke ii. 13, 14.—And suddenly there was with the angel a multitude of the heavenly host, praising God, and saying, glory to God in the highest, and on earth peace, good will toward men. (P.)

In this divine Anthem we are taught,

I. That the incarnation of the Saviour was a bright exhibition of the glory of God.

For thousands of years angels had beheld the unveiled glory of the deity; but they never saw the divine glory with any thing like the clearness with which they saw and felt the subject now. They had seen the glory of the divine *justice* in the punishment of their compeers; and something like *mercy* in the suspension of the sentence pronounced on guilty man. But O, when they saw Christ, the coequal and coeternal Son of God, take upon him a body that he might suffer and die to atone for the sins of men, and redeem them from the curse of the law, when they could not be redeemed by silver and gold—by human blood, by angelic interference, or by any thing short of the inestimably precious blood of the Son of God; here they saw justice shining in all its awful brightness, tremendous glory, and affecting majesty, in a way they had never seen it before. And when they saw that the love of God was ready to make such a sacrifice, that he spared not his own Son, but began to give him up for all; here was a display of mercy indeed; here mercy appeared to be his darling attribute; here mercy flowed in a deeper, wider, more majestic channel, than they had ever before formed any just conception of. From this anthem we learn

II. That the incarnation of Jesus Christ was the means of bringing peace upon earth.

Sin had created on earth a most horrible war; a threefold war, dreadful and interminable, to which Jesus came to put an end.

1. *It had created war in every man's own bosom.* The passions were tumultuous: the mind of man was the erena of perpetual discord: he was ever at variance with himself. Now Christ came to put an end to this war, by procuring pardon for sin, peace for the conscience, tranquility for the passions, subordination for the appetites; reconciling reason to the conscience, and conscience to the law of God. Man, before, was constrained to cry out, if he felt his situation, "O wretched man that I am! who shall deliver me!" But redeemed man, man under a proper, believing view of the christian scheme as exemplified in our incarnate God, can say, "I thank God through Jesus Christ our Lord."

2. *Sin had created a horrible war between man and man.* It armed every man against his brother, strife, envy, jealousy, oppression, ambition, had caused a thousand interferences, jars, discords, and hostilities, and had made man a wild beast to his brother. But Christ came to put an end to this war; he came to preach the doctrine of universal charity; he came to exemplify universal charity. He came to proclaim that peace with God in the conscience, and that work of the mighty Spirit on the heart of man, that should tear from every breast, and extirpate from the very soil, all that was there of enmity, and sweetly constrain him to love his neighbor as himself.

3. *Sin had caused war between man and his* Maker. Man was in rebellion with his Maker, and the Maker with man. But when Ch ist appeared in our nature, "God was in him, reconciling the world to himself, not imputing their trespasses unto them;" mercifully pardoning them on a plan

consistent with the strictest claims of his justice, and affording them grace to help in every time of need. And so amazing, so transforming is a proper view of his love, that they are brought to love him with a love like his own.

Well then, was Jesus designated "*the* PRINCE of PEACE!" Whatever of strife may be discovered in his kingdom, "an enemy hath done this." He does all to suppress it; and when his kingdom shall be fully established upon earth, wars shall terminate.

III. THAT THE INCARNATION OF THE DIVINE REDEEMER WAS A MARVELLOUS DISPLAY OF THE GOOD-WILL OF GOD TO MAN.

Good-will, in the abstract, nothing but good-will; love for love's sake. The angels had seen much of God's goodness to man *in the creation;* and *in providential dispensations.* They had seen that God had "not left himself without witness" of his benignant dispositions, continually giving them "rain from heaven, and fruitful seasons, filling their hearts with food and gladness;"—pouring from heaven, blessings, year after year, on the evil and on the good. But there were characters in this exhibition of God's good-will; there was a height, a length, a depth, a breadth, in this manifestation, which angel minds had never seen before.

In this was *most astonishing condescension.* That he was in "the form of God, and thought it no robbery to be equal with God, should be found in fashion as a man, and take upon himself the form of a servant;" that the "Ancient of Days," should become an infant;—that he who fills immensity, should be contracted, in appearance, to a span; that he, whom "the heaven of heavens cannot contain," should be born a babe in a manger; is an instance of condescension that proclaims this act of good-will to man, to be most unparalleled.

It was *altogether unmerited.* He shewed good-will to man; what for? Was there any thing in man to deserve it? No! He became incarnate for a race of rebels in arms against him; a rebel universe! then on the very core of whose heart was engraven, the deepest, deadliest animosity to that being, who left his own glory that he might wrap it around them

The most unparalleled love. The loftiest idea man can ever form of love, is, that a man lay down his life for his friend. But, in this instance, God lays down his life for us! God, the great law-giver, lays down his life for the most inveterate enemies, and for the foulest transgressors of that law which is "holy, just, and good."

Finally, it is "*good-will to men;*" that is, to human nature, to our fallen nature. There is a character of *universality* in it. Shew me the greatest sinner out of hell, and if he be *a man*, he is interested in this event. "He spared not his own Son, but delivered him up *for us all.* He took our common nature: "he gave himself, by the good-will of God, a ransom for all." The best cannot go to heaven any other way than through the Mediator; and, thank God, the worst, on repentance, may go to heaven by that way. We learn,

FINALLY. From the persons who sang this anthem, and the manner in which this event was celebrated, WHAT OUGHT TO BE OUR VIEWS, AND FEELINGS, AND CONDUCT.

1. *It should be laudatory.* We should tune up our feelings to the highest pitch, to celebrate a display of love, an act of mercy, which has no parallel in the universe. Angels had but little interest in it compared with us; had Jesus never become incarnate, they had been angels still. But if he had not come to take our nature, and to undertake our cause, we should have been ruined, lost, damned Shall *they* celebrate in strains like these, this

glorious event, and shall *our* lips be sealed up in silence, or opened only in Bacchanalian sports! Shall *they* be so rapt, and *we* so dead and dull?—God forbid! Let us celebrate it in psalms, and hymns, and spiritual songs. If we be silent—if we mourn and complain, and think we have nothing to thank God for on all other days; let our hearts be touched, our lips opened; let us muse over the glorious scene, till our hearts burn within us, and all we have and all we are, becomes sacred to the praise of God! We are taught,

2. From the example of the angels, *that we should proclaim the* SAVIOUR *to others.* They were not contented to enjoy this themselves, but wished the whole creation to be vocal, and every thing that hath breath to praise the name of the Lord; and especially every sinner, every fallen man, every one in danger of sinking into hell-fire, but now about to be raised to the means of obtaining heaven. They wished by every means in their power, to excite men to unite with them in praising and celebrating the great God of love. Go, you, and do likewise. Proclaim the Saviour to Christless, prayerless, sensual, debauched, wicked sinners. And O, invite, entreat, persuade, with prayers, with tears, if it were possible, if it were needful, *with tears of blood,* to unite with you—to taste and see for themselves that God is love—that religion is happiness—that religious people have *two* heavens: one here, and another hereafter. Angels deemed it no disparagement to be thus employed, and it will be an honor to *you;* and your tongues will never be a greater glory to you, than when you plead for Christ with success. But it will not be in vain; should you fail to kindle up the slumbering embers of love in the lukewarm—should you fail to swell the praises of the church to a more rapturous height;—yet, in watering others, you shall be watered *yourselves.* Angels never felt so much of heaven on earth, as when they thus sang; and you will never feel so much of the joy of angels, as when you are thus piously acting. You will then, indeed, have *a joyful* CHRISTMAS and *a happy* NEW YEAR. WHICH MAY GOD GRANT YOU ALL, FOR HIS MERCIES SAKE. AMEN.

THE IMPORT OF THE NAMES GIVEN TO CHRIST.

Matt. i. 21—23.—Thou shalt call his name Jesus: for He shall save his people from their sins. (Now all this was done that it might be fulfilled which was spoken of the Lord by the prophet, saying, Behold, a virgin shall be with child, and shall bring forth a son, and they shall call his name Emmanuel, which being interpreted is, God with us.) (S. S.)

THE dispensations of Providence are extremely dark and intricate—

The things which appear most afflictive often prove to be the richest mercies that could have been vouchsafed to us—

This was remarkably verified in the history before us—

Joseph was espoused to a virgin of consummate piety—

But, before their nuptials, she proved to be in a state which gave him reason to suspect her fidelity—

Desiring to exercise all the lenity which the case would admit of, he determined to put her away privily—

How distressing must such a state have been to this holy man!—

But God sent an angel to unfold to him the mystery, to declare the ends for which the child should be born, and to impose on the infant a name, that should mark his office in the world.

I. THE APPOINTMENT OF THE NAME.

God had often condescended to assign names to men—

Sometimes he had made an alteration in their names;* and sometimes totally changed them—†

Sometimes he had assigned a name before the child was conceived—John, Luke i. 13.

In these things he always acted with unerring wisdom—

When men have attempted to give significant appellations, they have only manifested how ignorant they were of futurity—‡

But God sees all things from the beginning to the end—

And his designation of Christ's name was a prognostic of his character—

The appellation given to the virgin's son was peculiarly suitable—

"Jesus" simply means a *Saviour;* Acts xiii. 23; and was a common name among the Jews—

It was sometimes assigned to those who were great deliverers—Neh. ix. 27.

It had been given in a peculiar manner to the son of Nun—Num. xiii. 16. Which name is precisely the same with "Jesus," and is so translated Acts vii. 45, and Heb. iv. 8.

He was eminently a Saviour, as leading the Israelites into the promised land, which Moses was not permitted to do—Deut. i. 37, 38.

But Christ, whom he typified, is a far greater deliverer—

He "does that for us which the law could not do"—Rom. viii. 3; Acts xiii. 39.

He leads the true Israel of God into their heavenly Canaan—

So remarkable an event may justly lead us to enquire into

II. THE REASON OF THAT APPOINTMENT.

Waving all other reasons, we notice two before us

1. To fulfil a prophecy.

Isaiah had foretold that the Messiah should be called Emmanuel—Isaiah vii. 14.

From the event it appears, that God did not intend this prophecy to have a *literal* accomplishment—

We may expect however that *the spirit of it* should be accomplished—

Now the name "Jesus" was in fact equivalent to Emmanuel—

"Jesus" means "divine Saviour;" and Emmanuel, God with us—See Bp. Pearson on the Creed, p. 70, 71.

And the evangelist himself tells us, that the imposition of *that* name was in order to the fulfilment of *this* prophecy—Matt. i. 22, 23.

2. To declare the infant's office and character.

The virgin's child was to be the Saviour of the world—

He was to save his people *by price*, and *by power*—

They were under sentence of eternal condemnation—

His life was the ransom to be paid for their souls—Matt. xx. 28.

*Abram and Sarai to Abraham and Sarah. †Jacob to Israel.

‡Eve named her first child, "Cain," which signifies, *getting;* thinking perhaps that she had now gotten the promised seed: having probably soon discovered her mistake, she called her second son "Abel," which signifies, *vanity*. But how misnamed were both! *This* proved a martyr for his God; and *that*, a murderer of his own brother.

Hence they are called his purchased possession—Eph. i. 14. **See also 1** Cor. vi. 20, and 1 Pet. i. 18, 19.

They were also in bondage to sin and Satan—Luke xi. 21. 2 Tim. ii. 26. •

And he was to make them a peculiar people, zealous of good works—Tit. ii. 14.

Yea, he was ultimately to place them beyond the reach of all the penalties and pollutions of sin—

It was of importance that this great work should be represented in his very name—

And the text informs us that the name was given him for this very purpose—

Infer,

1. How precious aught the name of Jesus to be to all his followers!

What benefit can be bestowed like salvation from sin?—

A deliverance from its dominion is an unspeakable blessing—

The godly desire it no less than deliverance from hell itself—

And how delightful is pardon *to a burdened conscience!*—

How sweet is a sense of God's favor *in a dying hour!*—

What joy must the glorified soul possess *in the day of judgment!*—

Yet Jesus has bought it all with his own most precious blood—

He has bestowed it freely on all his faithful followers—

He will impart it liberally to all who will believe on him—

Is there not reason then for that divine anathema?—1 Cor. xvi. 22.

Will not the very stones cry out against those who refuse to praise him?—

Let Jesus then be precious to us all—

Let us adopt the grateful strains of that sweet Psalmist of Israel—Ps. ciii. 1—4.

2. How vain is it to expect salvation in the ways of sin!

Sinners seem to entertain but little fear about their souls—

They even encourage one another to commit iniquity with greediness—

But they cannot possibly be saved in such a state—

If they could, the angel should have assigned a very different reason for the appointment of Jesus' name—*

In that case, Christ would have been a minister of sin—

But who must not, with the apostle, express his abhorrence of such a thought?—Gal. ii. 17.

Our Lord has plainly told us what shall ere long be his address to self-deceiving sinners—Matt. vii. 23.

Let us then "flee for refuge to the hope set before us"—

And tremble lest we provoke *the Saviour* to become our *destroyer*—

*He should rather have said. "He shall save his people in their sins."

A SKETCH OF CHRIST'S NATIVITY.

Isaiah ix. 6.—For unto us a child is born, unto us a son is given; and the government shall be upon his shoulder: and his name shall be called Wonderful, Counsellor, the Mighty God, the everlasting Father, the Prince of peace. (Sk.)

Our text is an ancient prediction of Christ's nativity, and a comprehensive outline of his glorious character, both in his humanity and in his divinity. After the lapse of many years, this prophecy was accomplished at Bethlehem in Judea. There the Messiah appeared as a child, and as the mighty God; for while he was laid in a manger, angels came down from heaven to adore him, Heb. i. 6. Let us join the Christian church in a cheerful and pious commemoration of that astonishing event; let us, on this glad day, call to mind the condescension of our blessed Saviour, and examine, with modesty and humility, his character and designs. This fine passage of Scripture will furnish our thoughts with rich materials: let us consider it in the order it stands before us.

I. Unto us a child is born.

1. The prophet had an eye to the child Jesus, whose birth, in many points of view, *was an exact accomplishment of ancient prophecy.* It had been foretold that he should be born of a virgin, and he was born of the virgin Mary, Isa. vii. 14; Matt i. 22, 23—that he should come forth out of Bethlehem, the place where he was born, Mic. v. 2; Matt. ii. 1:—and that he should appear in low and mean circumstances, or "as a root out of dry ground," and he was born in a stable, because there was no room for Joseph and Mary in the inn, Isa. liii. 2; Luke ii. 7,

2. *Remarkable circumstances attended his birth.* He was made known, by an angel, to poor shepherds, who were watching their flocks by night, Luke ii. 11;—his birth was celebrated by a song of angels, chap. ii. 13, 14;—and the world, when the Prince of Peace came into it, was in a peaceful. tranquil state.

3. But the most important consideration is, *he was born unto us*, and for our salvation; for though this was spoken by a Jewish prophet, to the Jewish nation, yet we are assured, that in him all the families of the earth should be blessed, Gen. xii. 3. "He took not on him the nature of angls, but the seed of Abraham," Heb. ii. 16. Good angels did not need his mediation, and bad ones were not to share the benefits of his redeeming love; but he became man, that he might redeem and save sinners of the human race, 1 Tim. i. 15.

II. Unto us a son is given.

1. *Our blessed Saviour is the Son of God.* He is called the Son of God in reference to his miraculous conception in the womb of Mary, Luke i. 35;—he was the son of God by commission, being sent of God, John x. 36;—he was declared to be the Son of God, by his resurrection from the dead, Rom. i. 4;—and he is the only begotten Son of God in his divine nature. John iii. 16; Heb. i—3.

2. *Unto us this Son was given:* and he was the greatest gift that heaven could bestow on man, Rom. viii. 32. He was given to enlighten the world, John viii. 12;—to be a propitiation for sin, 1 John ii. 2;—to make reconciliation for iniquity, Dan. ix. 24;—to save the world, John iii. 17;—and to bring many sons unto glory, Heb. ii. 10.

III. The government shall be upon his shoulder.

1. This does not refer to the *political government* of the Jews. In their depraved state, they expected such a Messiah, and in their pride and vanity, they desired a great temporal king; but the kingdom of Jesus, which had been foretold by the prophets, was not of this world, John xviii. 36.

2. The *spiritual government* of the church, in all its vast and weighty concerns, was laid upon his shoulder: he is the head of the church, Eph. iv. 15; Col. i. 18; and his faithful followers dare not acknowledge any other Lord or master, Matt. xxiii. 8.

3. He is *able to bear the weight of government*, having all power both in heaven and in earth, Matt. xxviii. 18;—he is sufficiently wise to manage and direct all the affairs of this spiritual kingdom, as in him are "all the treasures of wisdom and knowledge," Col. ii. 3;—and he now rules, and ever will rule in righteousness, Heb. i. 8.

IV. And his name shall be called Wonderful.

1. *He shall be what his name imports.* The Hebrews gave names which expressed the qualities of things, and the characters and offices of persons. Thus Jesus was callled "Emmanual, which being interpreted, is, God with us;" and for this plain reason, he was God with men, Matt. i. 21.

2. He was *wonderful* in his *person:* a child born, and yet the mighty God; the offspring of David as a man, and the root of David as God, Rev. xxii. 16; the son of David in his human nature, but his Lord in the divine nature, Matt. xxii. 45. He was wonderful in his love, 1 John iii. 16; and wonderful in all his undertakings. Who can comprehend his nature? Who can fully understand his great and merciful designs? Why do we ask after his name, and attempt to pry into inconceivable mysteries? Gen xxxii. 9; Judges xiii. 18. Oh let us stand, and wonder, and adore!

V. Counsellor.

1. *A revealer of secrets.* He revealed the gospel, which is called the counsel of God, Acts xx. 27; the hidden wisdom, 1 Cor. ii. 7; but is now made manifest to all nations for the obedience of faith, Rom. xvi. 21; "even the mystery" which hath been hid from ages and generations, but now is made manifest to his saints, Col. i. 26. He is called the Word of God, because God speaks by him to the sons of men, Heb. i. 1.

2. *One who gives counsel*, Rev. iii. 18. Jesus gave counsel to men in the days of his flesh; and he now gives counsel by his Holy Spirit, by his written word, and by his faithful ministers. His counsel is *safe*, may be had on *easy terms*, James i. 5; and, if followed, will guide us to glory, Ps. lxxiii. 24.

VI. The mighty God.

1. The *titles* of God are given to Jesus. He is called God, John i. 1;—the great God, Tit. ii. 13;—the true God, 1 John v. 20;—and Lord, or Jehovah, Isa. xl. 3.

2. The *attributes* of God are ascribed to him. Eternity, Mic. v. 2;—omnipotence, Rev. i. 8;—omnipresence, Matt. xviii. 20;—and immortality, Heb. xiii. 8.

3. He *created* all things. The visible world, John i. 3;—the invisible world, including thrones, dominions, principalities and powers, Col. i. 16.

4. Divine *worship* has been paid to him; by angels at his birth, Heb. i. 6;—by Stephen, the first martyr, Acts vii. 59;—by all who baptize in his name, Matt. xxviii. 19;—and by heavenly hosts, Rev. v. 13.

VII. The everlasting Father.

1. This clause, in the *Septuagint*, is, *the Father of the age, or world to come;* and in allusion to this, the gospel dispensation, under the reign of the Messiah, is called *the world to come*, Heb. ii. 5.

2. Jesus is *a Father to his people.* As a father, he *loves* them, *protects* them, and supplies their wants. He is the author of salvation to all who obey him, Heb. v. 9;—he was the founder of the new and eternal age; he is the father of a new race, the head of a new family which will never be extinct; and all believers are his seed, or children, Isa. liii. 10: for by his obedience to the law, the atonement which he made, and the influences of his Holy Spirit, they are brought into life, and into a new state, Gal, ii. 20.

3. And he will be the *everlasting* Father of his people. Earthly fathers die; but Jesus says, "I am alive for evermore," Rev. i. 18; and he will be as a Father to them, and they will be as sons and daughters to him in the eternal world, Rev. xxi. 7.

VIII. The Prince of peace.

1. Our Lord is a Prince. He is the Prince of the kings of the earth, surpassing them in all that is great and excellent, Rev. 1. 5: and by him "kings reign, and princes decree justice," Prov. viii. 15. He is the Prince of life, or the author of all life, whether temporal, spiritual, or eternal, Acts iii. 15; for he created us at first, is the author of our new creation, and conducts us safely to eternal life, Eph. iii. 9, ii. 10; John x. 27, 28.

2. But here he is called the "Prince of *Peace*." By him, all who believe have peace with God, Isa. xii. 1; Rom. v. 1;—he plants peaceable dispositions in the hearts of his subjects, James iii. 17;—his government promotes peace in the world, Heb. xii. 14;—and when the nations of the earth bow down to him, and acknowledge him as their Sovereign, they shall learn war no more, Isa. ii. 4.

Inferences.

1. Admire and adore the Saviour of the world; and instead of prying into the profound mysteries of his nature, bow the knee to him, and pay him homage, Ps. ii. 12; Phil. ii. 10.

2. Trust in him with an unshaken confidence for pardon, peace, holiness, and heaven, Matt. xii. 21.

3. Look to him in all difficulties and dangers for counsel and support; and ever give him the glory that is due to his holy name, Isa. xliii. 2, 3; John v. 23

4. Honor him, especially, on this festival, by temperance and sobriety, by praise and thanksgiving, and by acts of charity to his suffering saints, Gal. vi. 10.

5. And lastly, commit to his care your bodies and souls, your families and friends, and all your affairs; that he may have you and yours in his holy keeping against that day, when he will "judge the world with righteousness, and the people with equity," Ps. xcviii. 9.

CHRIST THE LIGHT AND SALVATION OF THE GENTILES.

Isaiah xlix. 6.—And he said, It is a light thing that thou shouldest be my servant to raise up the tribes of Jacob, and to restore the preserved of Israel: I will also give thee for a light to the Gentiles, that thou mayest be my salvation unto the end of the earth. (S. S.)

That the Gentiles were to be received into the church of God, was a truth which the Jews were backward to admit—

Several years after the gospel had been preached to the Jews, Peter declined visiting the Gentiles, and was afterwards called to an account by the apostles themselves for going to them—Acts xi. 1, 2. This was six or seven years after Christ's ascension.

Nor could any thing but repeated miracles in their favor overcome the prejudices which he entertained respecting them—

Not but that the conversion of the Gentiles had been very frequently and plainly foretold—

The very passage before us, if there had been no other, was quite sufficient to raise an expectation of that event—

In the context there is a conversation between Jehovah and his Son—

The Messiah announces to the Gentiles his qualifications for the work to which he was called—Ver. 1—3.

But at the same time complains that his labors among the Jews were almost in vain—Ver. 4.

Nevertheless He declares his unshaken confidence that Jehovah would not leave him without ultimate success—Ib.

Jehovah then, in answer to his Son, assures him, that however he may be treated by the Jews, he shall be upheld and accepted in his work—Ver. 5.

And that his failure among the Jewish nation shall be far overbalanced by his success among the Gentiles—

To elucidate this prophecy we shall consider

I. The characters here given to Christ.

There can be no doubt but that the words of the text relate to Christ

They are far too strong to be applied to Isaiah himself—

Nor could they with propriety be spoken of any but the Messiah—

The expressions here used are similar to those which the prophet elsewhere uses in reference to him—Isa. xlii. 1, 6, and lx. 3.

They were evidently alluded to by the patriarch when he took up the infant Jesus in his arms—Luke ii. 30—32.

And are expressly quoted by St. Paul as having received their accomplishment in Christ—Acts xiii. 46, 47.

To him the characters, there specified, most eminently belong—

He is "the Restorer of Israel," having reconciled "many myriads" of them to serve God—

He is also the "Light of the Gentiles"—

Another prophet describes him as "the sun of righteousness"—Mal. iv. 2.

In the New Testament also he is repeatedly called "the Light of the world"—John i. 4, 9.

Others have enlightened the world by revealing the will of God—

But He alone reveals it by his Spirit to the souls of men—

He only, who opened Lydia's heart, can have access to ours—Acts xvi. 14.

He only, who opened the understanding of his disciples, can illumine our benighted minds—Luke xxiv. 45.

And this he does for them that lie in darkness and the shadow of death—

While his once favored people the Jews are blinded, he takes the veil from our hearts, and guides us into all truth—

Thus does he abundantly fulfil to us his gracious promise—John viii. 12.

He is moreover "the salvation of men even to the ends of the world."

Many of the judges and kings of Israel were Saviours in a temporal view—

But Jesus imparts to his followers a far more glorious salvation—

By his own blood he has "obtained an eternal redemption" for them—
And by his meritorious obedience he renders them completely righteous—
He is not merely a Saviour to them, but "salvation" itself—
As he procured, so he imparts, maintains, and perfects the salvation of those who trust in him—
There are none so remote but he extends to them the benefits of his death—
"He came to save the lost," in whatever quarter of the globe they be—
For this very end was he sent into the world by his heavenly Father—
And, as being expressly appointed to this office, he is called *God's* salvation—
In fulfilling these characters he displays
II. THE EXCELLENCE OF THE DISPENSATION COMMITTED TO HIM.
The dispensation of the law to the Jews was glorious.
There was much of the gospel communicated in and with the law-
The ceremonial rights were altogether "shadows of the good things which were afterwards to be more fully revealed—
The moral law itself, while it condemned the Jews, was intended to promote their salvation—
And many, in different ages, were guided to heaven by the light which was then afforded them—
The Mosaic law therefore was a rich blessing to that nation—
And the salvation of a remnant from among them clearly manifested the efficacy of the great sacrifice—
But the dispensation of the gospel to the whole world is incomparably more glorious—
It brings far greater good to men.
We must not disparage the salvation of one single soul—
Much less should we undervalue the mercy shewn to so many of the Jews—
But still, the Jews were a small body when compared with the Gentile world—
And it was but a little remnant, even of them, that obtained mercy—
But the publication of the gospel to the Gentiles has been the means of saving unnumbered myriads—
There are persons in every quarter of the globe who experience the efficacy of the Redeemer's blood—
Yea, every day and hour are multitudes ascending from the darkest corners of the earth to swell the chorus in heaven—
How much more glorious then is the dispensation which diffuses its blessings so extensively, than that which confined them to such a narrow sphere!—
Surely it would have been "a light thing to save the Jews" in comparison of such a multitude—
We may well therefore apply to this subject those words of the apostle—2 Cor. iii. 9—11.
It brings also far greater glory to the Saviour himself.
Had none but Jews been saved by him, he might have appeared partial in his regards—
Or it might be thought that his sacrifice was but of a limited value—
But the extension of mercy to the Gentiles displays "the exceeding riches of his grace"—
And shews that his death is a sufficient "propitiation for the sins of the whole world"—

How transcendent is the Redeemer's glory in this view!—

And how glorious will he appear, when all that he has redeemed from every nation of the earth shall unite in ascribing salvation to him!—

The saving of a few from one nation only would not have been a suitable recompence for his work—

He might well have complained that he had "spent his strength for nought"—

But he will be fully "satisfied with the travail of his soul," because "the birth of his womb will be as the dew of the morning"—Ps. cx. 3.

We shall conclude with a word or two of ADVICE:—

1. Welcome the Saviour under the characters which are here given him—

We all need him as the light of our minds, and the Saviour of our souls—

Let none then boast of the light of reason, or "lean to their own understanding"—

Nor let us trust in our own goodness to merit, or strength to work out salvation—

Let us rather look to Jesus for the teaching of his word and Spirit—

And unite our acknowledgments with those of the saints of old—Isaiah xlv. 24.

Let us rejoice exceedingly that "help is laid upon One so mighty"—Ps. lxxxix. 19.

And let us receive him for all the ends for which he is offered to us—1 Cor. i. 30.

Let none say, I am so far off, I can never hope for salvation by him—

His exhortation recorded by the prophet yet sounds in our ears—Isaiah xlv. 22.

Nor shall any be ashamed who put their trust in him—

2. Do not attempt to separate his characters, but unite them—

In vain shall we hope to be saved by Christ, if he have not enlightened our understandings—

Though he gives not to all his people the same degree of knowledge, he invariably instructs them in the most important truths—

And if we have no views of the evil of sin, the deceitfulness of the heart, the beauty of holiness, and the suitableness of his salvation, we are still in a lost and perishing condition—

The text itself informs us that Christ becomes our salvation by being our light—

On the other hand, let us not rest in a speculative knowledge of these things—

We must manifest the practical and sanctifying effects of what we know—

We must be delivered from the love and practice both of open and secret sin—

Without this, the clearest perception of divine truths will be of no avail—

Let us unite in our experience what is thus united in Christ—

And seek to grow as well in gracious affections, as in the knowledge of our Lord and Saviour—2 Pet. iii. 18.

"THE CHILDREN OF ZION SHALL BE JOYFUL IN THEIR KING."

Psalm cxlix. 2.—Let the children of Zion be joyful in their King. (Sk.)

THE first and purest form of government which the world ever knew, was a theocracy. But in proportion as the minds of men became degraded and sensualized, this got into disrepute; and the *beau ideal* of polity was human monarchy. To have the source of legislation in one of their own species appeared desirable to the thinking part of the community; places of emolument and exaltation presented themselves to the minds of the avaricious and aspiring; while the multitude were allured by a prospect of unbounded license, and by the hope of pomp and show. Thus were the minds of all prepared to second the designs of any daring adventurer, who might aim at the usurpation of sovereign power. The consequence was, that divine government was soon postponed to human; and from that time to the present, this example has been almost universally followed. Theocracy is no more. There is however a freedom, and volatility about the human mind, which human laws cannot destroy, or even suppress, and hence the great desideratum in jurisprudence is, what can perhaps never be known, and certainly never reduced to practice, except by Him who first breathed into man a living soul. Of his power in spiritual government, believers are illustrious monuments, as a consideration of our text will serve to prove. The first thesis with which this passage furnishes us is,

I. BELIEVERS ARE "THE CHILDREN OF ZION."

1. *Zion is often used as an emblem of the church of God.* Psa. ii. 6; Isa. xxviii. 16; Rom. ix. 33; 1 Pet. ii. 6. It was stable, Psa. cxxv. 1; so is the church, Matt. xvi. 18. It was secure, Psa. xlviii. 3, 11, 12; so is the church, Eph. v. 29. The situation of Zion was exceeding beautiful, Psa. xlviii. 2; so is that of the church. It is elevated above the din of the world, and "breathes the spirit of a purer air," Matt. v. 14. Zion was a holy mountain; because on mount Moriah, which joined it on the north-east, the temple of God was built, 2 Chron. iii. 1; Psa. xlviii. 1; the church is holy also, Eph. v. 27. Mount Zion was peculiarly loved by God, Psa. lxxxviii. 2; so is the church, Eph. v. 25.

2. *Believers are children of Zion by birth.* Naturally we are all "aliens from the commonwealth of Israel, and strangers to the covenants of promise," Eph. ii. 11, 12. We can obtain no entrance into spiritual Zion except by spiritual birth, John iii. 5, 6. This birth is effected through faith in Christ, by the influence of the Holy Ghost, John x. 9; Rom. v. 1, 2; Eph. ii. 13; Tit. iii. 5, 6. It is frequently preceded by deep anguish, and distressing solicitude, Jer. i. 4, 5; Acts ii. 37, ix. 6, xvi. 29, 30.

3. *Believers can continue children of Zion no longer than while they retain faith*, Heb. x. 38. By the retention of that faith which first introduced them into Zion, they still continue members of Christ's mystical body. Hence the exhortation of the apostle Paul, Col. iii. 6, 7. They therefore dwell in Zion, knowing that destruction attends their leaving it, John xv. 6. And from the public treasury of Zion they receive their support, they are fed and clothed, Luke xv. 22; John vi. 35, 51, 53—58.

4. *Zion is often emblematic of heaven*, Heb. xii. 22: Rev. xiv. 1. If the church below be so secure, though still militant, and encompassed by enemies; so lovely, though surrounded by the clouds of sense; and so sacred, though environed by the unclean and polluted; who can describe or even imagine the security, the beauty, and the sanctity of the church of the

first-born in heaven; around which no night ever closes, on which no cloud ever rests, over which no wind ever blows, and towards which no sin ever approaches! 1 Cor. ii. 9; Rev. xxii. 4, 10—27.

5. *Believers are children of Zion by a title to heaven*, Acts xxvi. 18; Eph. i. 18; Col. i. 12; 1 Pet. i. 3, 4. The title to earthly inheritances is often very obscure and uncertain, and consequently not unfrequently the subject of protracted litigation; the title of believers to heaven is clear, and indisputable, Eph. i. 13, 14. The title to an earthly estate may be cut off. The title of believers to heaven is indefeasible. It is founded upon the promise, nay, upon the oath of God, Heb. vi. 17, 18; and though the grass may wither, and the flower may fade, yet the word of the Lord remaineth for ever. The second thesis presented by our text is,

II. Believers have a "King."

1. *Royalty is the centre of supremacy.* A king is a supreme governor. God in this sense is the king of believers. The pope is the head of the Romish church. Civil governors are the heads of national churches, but God is the head of his own, the true church; and consequently, all authority in that church is communicated from Him. Its officers and laborers are of his appointment. To some he grants the commission, "Go ye into all the world," &c., Mark xvi. 15; and to others, a more circumscribed commission. How great then is the impiety of those, who assume the garments of God's priesthood; professing the call of the Holy Ghost, without being even the subjects of God's spiritual kingdom!

2. *Royalty is the source of legislation.* God is the legislator of his people. His code is more pure than any ever conceived by the human mind, for the perfection of human jurisprudence, Rom. vii. 12. It does not result contingently from any thing like an arbitrary constitution of the divine will, but necessarily from the purity and wisdom of the divine mind. It does not merely refer to outward conduct, but extends itself to a cognizance of the thoughts and intents of the heart, Psa. cxix. 96. The revelation of it is clear, nor is an extraordinary extent of intellect necessary for its comprehension, Isa. xxxv. 8; for even those parts of it which defy unaided human research, are made known to man by the teachings of the Spirit, John xiv. 26; 1 Cor. ii. 13. For its requirements see Matt. xxii. 37—39.

3. *Royalty is the fountain of protection.* Probably, the ostensible reason for the appointment of a supreme governor, has been almost universally founded upon this principle. Thus the children of Israel, 1 Sam. viii. 19, 20. Their first reason for demanding a king, was, "that our king may judge us," *i. e.* protect us from the wrongs which may be inflicted by those who live under the same government; their second, "that he may go out before us, and fight our battles," *i. e.* protect us from the ambitious and unjust designs of surrounding nations. In the first of these senses, the protection of God over his subjects is not required, because the kingdom of God is "peace;" but in the second he exercises his royal power, far more completely and effectively than consists with the ability of any human monarch, Job i. 10; Psa. v. 12, xxvii. 1, xxxvii. 17, 39, lv. 22, cxviii. 8—12, cxlvi. 3—6. The third thesis, which our text presents us, is,

III. Believers should be "joyful in their King."

1. *Because he is the most glorious and dignified of all beings.* Consider his nature. He is the independent Jehovah, who was, Psa. xc. 2, xciii 2; who is, Exod. iii. 14; who shall be, Deut. xxxii. 40; Psa. xlv. 6. He is immutable, Psa. cii. 25—27; Mal. iii. 6; Heb. xiii 8; James i. 17. He is omnipresent, and omniscient, 1 Kings viii. 27; 2 Chron. ii. 6, vi. 18;

Psa. cxxxix. 1—12; Jer. xxxiii. 23, 24. He is almighty, Gen. xviii. 1, xxxv 11; Rev. iv. 8. Consider his moral attributes, his benevolence, Exod. xxxiv. 6; Psa. lxxxvi. 5, cxlv. 8, 9; 1 Tim. ii. 3, 4; James v. 11; 1 John iv. 8. His justice, Deut. xxxii. 4; Psa. lxxxix. 4; Rev. xv. 3. His wisdom, Psa. civ. 24, cxxxvi. 5; Prov. iii. 19; Rom. xi. 33; Col. ii. 3; 1 Tim. i. 17. His truth, Psa. xxv. 10, lxxxvi. 15, c. 5, cxvii. 2, cxlvi. 6; Rev. xix. 11. Consider his works, and kingdom of nature, Gen. i. 1, xiv. 19, 22; Deut. x. 14; Psa. cxv. 16; Isa. xxxvii. 16; John i. 3; Acts xvii. 24. Consider his retinue, Psa. lxviii. 17, civ. 4; Heb. i. 6, 14. How closely the honor and joy of a nation are connected with the dignity of their monarch, will be evident without any attempt at illustration.

2. *Because by his charter they enjoy great privileges and immunities.* Whether any human monarch should be absolute, is a question which does not demand much discussion, as most men are agreed to decide it in the negative; for on the one hand a monarch is not always solicitous for the advantage of his subjects; and on the other, if he were, his capacities would not be equal to his wishes. But, the absolute sovereignty of God is justified by his independence, his benevolence, and his wisdom. He gains no advantage from his subjects; he is benevolently disposed towards them, and he knows how to put his designs into execution most advantageously for them; hence he communicates to them through his Spirit an evidence of their acceptance, Rom. viii. 16; and through his word exceeding great and precious promises, 2 Pet. i. 4. They possess peace and joy, Rom. xiv. 17, xv. 13. They have the privilege of rejoicing even in affliction, Rom. v. 3; 2 Cor. vi. 10. They enjoy a freedom from condemnation, John iii. 18, v. 24; Rom. viii. 1; and a well grounded hope of everlasting enjoyment, Rom. v. 2; Col. i. 5, 27; Tit. ii. 13, iii. 17; Heb. vi. 19. Nor is there any possibility for their charter to be revoked or taken away.

3. *Because the monuments of their great men are protected.* The Bible is a record of the saints. In it are contained monuments of their patience, meekness, courage, faith, and heavenly mindedness. Here we are taught to admire their virtues, and excited to follow their example, Heb. xi. and vi. 12.

4. *Because their enemies are totally inefficient to disturb his government*, Deut. xxxiii. 26—29; Psa. xciii. 1.

5. *Because his kingdom will ultimately be universal. and all opposing powers will be destroyed*, Psa. lxxii. 17, cx. 1; Isa. ii. 4, ix. 6, 7, xi. 9, xlv. 23; Jer. xxiii. 5; Hab. ii. 14; Mic. iv. 1—3; 1 Cor. xv. 25; Rev. xi. 15. Human enemies shall either be subdued by the influences of his grace, or destroyed by the power of his anger; and diabolical enemies shall be bound in chains of darkness, Rev. xx. 1—3.

'Come, then, and, added to thy many crowns,
Receive yet one as radiant as the rest;
Due to thy last, and most effectual work,
Thy word fulfilled, the conquest of a world.'

REMARKS.

1. How great and glorious is the moral elevation of a believer, and how insignificant does the honor of this world appear contrasted with the dignity of a Christian!

2. How great should be our solicitude to become subjects of the spiritual kingdom of Jehovah.

3. How indefatigable should we be in spreading the knowledge of God, by personal instruction,—by example,—and by the dedication of property, talents, and influence!

CHRIST'S LOVE A PATTERN FOR OURS.

Eph. v. 2.—Walk in love, as Christ also hath loved us, and hath given himself for us, an offering and a sacrifice to God for a sweet-smelling savour. (H. H.)

To restore us to the divine image is one great end of all that the Lord Jesus Christ has done and suffered for us. There are indeed perfections in the deity which are incommunicable to any creature: but his moral perfections admit of imitation and resemblance: and therefore we are exhorted to "be followers, or imitators, of God, as dear children." Ver. 1. But in the person of our blessed Lord and Saviour, Jehovah is brought nearer to us, so that we may trace his very steps, and learn to follow him in every disposition of the mind, and every action of the life. Hence in the passage before us, whilst we are particularly informed of the manner in which he has displayed his love to man, we are exhorted to "walk in love, as he has loved us."

In our further elucidation of these words, we shall be led to speak of the Lord Jesus Christ in a two-fold view;

I. As a sacrifice to God—

It was not merely as a martyr that Jesus died, but as a sacrifice for sin. This appears,

1. From all the sacrifices of the Mosaic law—

For what end were these instituted, but to prefigure him? These beyond a doubt were offerings for sin, the victims dying in the place of the offerer and making an atonement for him by their blood: and if the Lord Jesus Christ did not correspond with them in this particular, and actually fulfil what those prefigured, they were all instituted in vain, and were shadows without any substance at all.

2. From the declarations of the prophets—

The prophet thus plainly speaks of Christ as dying for the sins of men, "He made his soul an offering for sin:" "He bare the sins of many:" "On him were laid the iniquity of us all." Isa. liii. 6, 10, 12. What is the import of these testimonies, if Christ did not offer himself a sacrifice for sin?

3. From the testimony of John the Baptist—

It was in reference to the lambs that were offered every morning and evening for the sins of all Israel, that the Baptist spake, when he pointed out the Lord Jesus as "the Lamb of God that taketh away the sins of the world." If Christ were not a sacrifice for sin, this testimony was not founded in truth.

4. From the declarations of Christ himself—

He constantly affirmed, that "he came to give his life a ransom for many:" that his blood should be shed for the remission of sins; and that by being "lifted up upon the cross, he would draw all men unto him."

5. From the united testimony of all the apostles—

All with one voice represent him as redeeming us to God by his blood, and offering himself as "a propitiation, not for our sins only, but also for the sins of the whole world." In a word, the whole tenor of the Sacred Writings proves, that "he bare our sins in his own body on the tree," and "died, the just for the unjust, that he might bring us to God."

But in all this he was further designed,

II. As an example to us—

In the circumstance before noticed, we cannot resemble him; for "no man can redeem his brother, or give to God a ransom for him." Nevertheless in the love which instigated him to this we may resemble him. Our love, like his, should be,

1. Disinterested—

It is not possible for us to add any thing to him: we cannot make him more happy or more glorious by any thing that we can do: "our goodness extendeth not to him;" "nor can we by any means profit him:" yet did he in this astonishing manner display his love to us. Thus in the exercise of our love we should not consider whether the objects of it will ever be able to make us any suitable return: we should shew love in every possible way, without so much as desiring any return from man, or even desiring that our exercise of it should be known; yea, even though we knew that it would only be requited with evil. We should love our very enemies; and, "instead of being overcome of evil, should strive incessantly to overcome their evil with good."

2. Generous—

What unsearchable riches has he purchased even for his bitterest enemies! He would not that any one of them should fall short of all the glory of heaven. True it is, that we cannot thus enrich the objects of our love: yet we should do all we can towards it, by providing for them not only the things needful for the body, but, above all, the things that may promote the welfare of the soul. Here the poor may be on a par with those who are able to give out of their abundance: for if they are constrained to say, "Silver and gold have I none," they may add, "but such as I have, give I unto thee;" and then may proceed to speak to them of the Saviour, through whom they may obtain all the blessings of salvation. Thus, "though poor, we may make many rich."

3. Self-denying—

Our blessed Lord "emptied himself of all the glory of heaven," and endured all the wrath of an offended God; and became a curse himself, in order to deliver us from the curse which our iniquities had deserved. And shall we decline exercising our love, because it may be attended with some pain or difficulty on our part? No: we should not hesitate even to lay down life itself, if by so doing we may promote the eternal welfare of our brethren. 1 John iii. 16.

4. Constant—

"Whom our Lord loved, he loved to the end." There were many occasions whereon his immediate disciples displeased him: but he did not therefore "withdraw his mercy from them, or shut up his loving-kindness in displeasure." There are occasions also whereon we shall be called to exercise forbearance and forgiveness one towards another; and we ought to meet those occasions with love proportioned to them. We should strive with all our might to "follow peace with all men," and to "keep the unity of the Spirit in the bond of peace."

Address—

1. Be thankful to Christ for all the wonders of his love—

Think how unworthy you were of all his love: for, it was "when you were yet enemies, that he died for you." Think too what must have been your state to all eternity, if he had not so "undertaken for you:" his sufferings under the hidings of his Father's face, and under the strokes of divine justice, shew what miseries awaited you in hell for ever, if he had not become your substitute and surety to discharge your debt. Oh! never for a moment lose sight of the obligations you owe to him for that "love of his, which passeth knowledge."

2. Present yourselves as living sacrifices to him—

This *may* be done; and it is the very end for which such astonishing mercies have been vouchsafed to you. Rom. xii. 1. Consider all that you are, and all that you have, as his; and let it all be devoted henceforth to the glory of his name.

3. Endeavor to resemble him more and more—

Whatever attainments you may have made, you must still be aspiring after higher degrees of love. 1 Thess. iv. 9, 10. Look at him then, not only as the ground of your hopes, but as the pattern for your imitation. Trace him in all the labors of his love: trace him from heaven to earth, and from earth to heaven: trace him in all that he either did or suffered: and study to resemble him in the whole of his spirit and deportment. In all his labors "God smelled a sweet savour;" even as he had done in those offerings and sacrifices by which Christ had been shadowed forth: Gen. viii. 21; Lev. i. 9; and though your labors of love can never resemble his, as making an atonement for sin, they shall, like his, come up for a memorial before God, and be accepted as well-pleasing in his sight. Heb. vi. 10, and xiii. 16.

CHRIST THE DAY-SPRING.

Luke i. 78, 79.—Through the tender mercy of our God; whereby the day-spring from on high hath visited us, to give light to them that sit in darkness and in the shadow of death, to guide our feet into the way of peace. (Pr.)

These words contain an animated but highly figurative description, of our Lord Jesus Christ. He is, indeed, the bright and glorious day-spring from on high which hath visited us. The word here translated "day-spring," occurs also in the Old Testament, where it is considered "the branch;" but the most literal interpretation of the Greek word is "the East," or the place whence the light comes. This expression may intimate the pre-existence of our Lord Jesus Christ: as we well know, that the sun exists before he arises upon us, so Christ also existed, before he appeared upon our earth in the form of sinful man; and it may also refer to the high and exalted station of the Redeemer of mankind. Our text contains,

I. A very moving or affecting view of the state of mankind, without the Lord Jesus Christ:—"They are sitting in darkness and the shadow of death."

II. A very interesting description of our Lord Jesus Christ,—he is, "The day-spring from on high,"

III. A very encouraging representation of the design of our Saviour's mission into our world, "to give light" and "to guide our feet," &c.

I. A very moving or affecting view of the state of mankind without the Lord Jesus Christ.

In Scripture, *darkness* sometimes means the judgments of God—sometimes the afflictions of God's people—sometimes sin, (as, for instance, men love *darkness* rather than light, that is, they love sin rather than holiness,)—sometimes it means the grave—sometimes hell itself; but it is frequently used in Scripture with regard to the moral state and condition of mankind by nature, which is darkness indeed; and then, (as in the text,) it means the absence of that knowledge of Christ which is essential to impart comfort to the human mind, or bring to a saving acquaintance with him as the only way of salvation. This absence of the knowledge of Christ leaves us in darkness—as to *the moral character of God*—as to *the purity of his law*—as to *the evil nature and dreadful consequences of sin*—as to *the genuine source of happiness to the human mind*—and, finally, as to *a future state.*

But without the knowledge of the Lord Jesus Christ, mankind are not only sitting in darkness, but in the *shadow of death.* The Scriptures contemplate death as spiritual, temporal and eternal. If you ask me, whether there is such a thing as spiritual death in this world, I answer, yes, there is, and it consists in that separation of the best affections of the soul from God, which is so evident in every unregenerate mind. When man transgressed the commands of his Creator, his desires after his God became paralysed, and death—a spiritual death—passed upon all his affections, and upon all those enjoyments he had hitherto experienced in communion with him.

Notice three particulars in the phraseology of this part of our text,

I. A shadow always supposes the existence of the substance. And do we not behold every day on our right hand and on our left the ravages of death? and are not the mourners which go about our streets continually, sufficient to satisfy us that he is abroad in the world, and busily engaged on every side?

2. The object which creates a shadow in which we are sitting must be very near. And who can tell how near death may be to each one of us, or how soon we may have to pass through the dark valley. But,

3. A shadow even of the most terrible object, is a very inoffensive thing. A lion, with his savage aspect, his ferocious countenance, his glaring eyes, his erect mane, apparently ready to pounqe upon you for his prey, is certainly a formidable object; but the *shadow* of a lion, thus savage and ferocious, is as harmless as the shadow of a lamb. Thus death, however formidable he may really be to the wicked, is stripped of all his terrors, and becomes only a *shadow* to the believer in Jesus.

II. Our text contains a very interesting description of the Lord Jesus Christ.—He is *the day-spring,* &c. This we shall attempt to illustrate and to justify.

1. The day-spring, or the sun is *the great source of light;* so is the Lord Jesus Christ: he is the great source of *natural* light, for he first formed and still commands the rising and the setting sun—of *intellectual* light, for it is he who forms our mind as well as our bodies—of *rational* light—of *spiritual* light—and of all those beams of light which, shooting their radiance over our present path, afford us also some bright glimpses of the glory of a future state.

2. The day-spring is *gradual and progressive.* And how gradually has spiritual light dawned upon our world, if we take a review of the history of our species from the morning of time to the present moment! The light which the patriarchs posesssed may be compared to the grey shadows of twilight, or as the morning spread upon the mountains. When we say that the light of the gospel has increased since the days of the apostles, we mean not

that the gospel, as preached by them, was incomplete or ineffectual; but, that holy men, by more copious effusions, and fuller manifestations of the Holy Spirit, and by events and circumstances which are continually transpiring, are enabled more thoroughly to understand and consequently more clearly to preach and to explain the grand truths it contains. But the increase of spiritual light in the mind of man is also gradual. Conviction of sin is the first dawning of this light; and as he proceeds in the divine life, he becomes more and more enlightened, and is continually making new discoveries, and increasing in knowledge, holiness, and the fear of the Lord; "for the path of the just is as the shining light, increasing more and more unto the perfect day."

3. The day spring is *certain and irresistible.* When the proper time arrives, what can prevent the rising of the sun? The darkest, densest clouds, storms or tempests, or the most violent agitations of the atmosphere, cannot prevent or hinder him from arising in his majesty, and shedding his beams through the heavens; and the incarnation of Christ, or the rising of the spiritual day-spring was certain, and had been long predicted; but what clouds of opposition strove against its rising, and endeavored at once to extinguish its glorious, its delightful beams!

4. The day-spring or the light of the sun, is *free and common to all;* so it is with Christ and his gospel; by this, we mean to say that the atonement of Christ is sufficient for all; that there is efficacy enough in his righteousness for all; that there is an abundant sufficiency of the influences of his spirit for all; that the invitations of the gospel are freely addressed to all; and that the blessings of the gospel are offered to all. At the same time, it must be admitted, that they only can be benefitted who *accept* these blessings thus freely offered; and that those who receive not, must bear upon their own heads the guilt and punishment which must inevitably follow their rejection of them.

III. Our text contains a very encouraging representation of the design of our Saviour's mission into our world. The Lord Jesus Christ is the sum and substance of all that is contained either in the Old or the New Testament. Take him away, and we may fairly ask, what is there left? there may, indeed, be the shadow, but the substance is gone; there may be the breathless corpse, but the animating spirit is fled, and no real life remains. This head divides itself into the two following particulars. He came,

1. To give *light.* But before Christ could be known and acknowledged as the light which was to enlighten the world, it was necessary that he should show himself amongst us in the same way as the natural sun must arise and shine upon the world before he can impart light to the world; and in order, therefore, that Jesus might appear as this spiritual light, he has shown himself in the dignity of his *person,* in the perfection of his *atonement,* in the fulness of his *grace,* in the *willingness* he has manifested to save unto the uttermost all that come unto God by him, and in the *discovery* he has made of the way in which moral pollution may be purged from the heart of man. Repentance and faith are not in any way meritorious in themselves; and yet they are inseparably connected with every sinner's salvation. Thus we see how Christ has become a light unto the world, and what discoveries he has made to us of things which belong unto our eternal salvation; but of which, without him, we should have remained in total darkness.

2. He came to *guide our feet into the way of peace.* He is himself the very Prince of Peace. By nature we are enemies to God by wicked works, consequently far from every source of peace But the design of his mis-

sion into our world was to guide our feet again into the way of peace, by effecting our reconciliation with his Father, through the shedding of his most precious blood, and hereby making peace. Thus the apostle declares, "For he is our peace;" and again, "We have peace with God, through our Lord Jesus Christ."

But peace in Scripture is also frequently to be understood in a very extended sense. It was a common form of salutation, and intends "all good." Thus it was used by Boaz to his reapers, and by Christ himself to his disciples. And Christ came to guide our feet into the ways of all good, which, without him, would have continued in the ways of all evil.

There are four things we shall notice by way of improvement to the whole:—

1st. The infinite condescension of Jehovah in interposing in our behalf. Eternity will be quite short enough to unravel this mysterious and delightful theme, if we consider from what misery it raises, and to what glories it exalts us.—2ndly. The Christian's duty and privilege. It is his duty to trust in the word of the Lord in the times of darkness. There are times when the natural sun does not shine upon the world; and it is the believer's privilege sometimes to walk in the light of God's countenance.—3rdly. Notice the miserable state of those who hear the sound of the gospel, and yet remain at a distance from this light; and, lastly, If the pleasures of religion be so great upon earth, what must be the enjoyment of believers in the upper world?

CHRIST A GREAT SAVIOUR.

Isaiah xix. 20.—They shall cry unto the Lord because of the oppressors, and He shall send them a Saviour, and a great One, and he shall deliver them. (S. S.)

God usually vouchsafes his mercies when we are reduced to the greatest straits—

This is manifest in his most remarkable dispensations of providence and of grace—

In the greatest extremity God promised to send a deliverer to Egypt—*

But there is a further reference to Christ as the Saviour to the Gentile world—†

And it is in seasons of heavy dejection that He reveals himself to them—

To him therefore we must look as the Saviour foretold in the text—

I. In what respects He is "a great Saviour."

It is justly said by the Psalmist that "his greatness is unsearchable"—Ps. cxlv. 3.

Nevertheless we may, not unprofitably, endeavor to illustrate it.

*In this view it seems applicable to the angel who slew 185,000 of Sennacherib's army: for, though that deliverance was more immediately vouchsafed to the Jews under Hezekiah, yet in its consequences it extended to Egypt. Sennacherib had before conquered and ravaged Egypt; and it was most probable that if he had taken Jerusalem he would have again proceeded thither with his victorious army, and reduced that already desolated kingdom to the lowest ebb of misery. But perhaps there may be a further reference to some other deliverers.

†This appears from the whole context, ver. 18—25.

He is great when considered *in his own person.*

He has a name above every name either on earth or in heaven—

He is exalted to be a prince that can give repentance and remission of sins—Acts v. 31.

The voice of inspiration calls him, "the great God and our Saviour"—Tit. ii. 13.

He speaks of himself in terms of similar import—Isa. xlv. 22.

Nor can any thing be more glorious than the description given of him by the prophet—Isa. ix. 6.

He is also great in respect of the *salvation he has wrought out for us.*

Who can count the number of the sins from which he has delivered us?—

Or estimate the misery from which he has redeemed us?—

Through our whole lives we have been heaping up treasures of wrath—Rom. ii. 5.

Yet there is no condemnation to us if we be interested in him—Romans viii. 1.

Besides, he has purchased for us an eternal inheritance in heaven—

We must know all the glories of heaven and the horrors of hell, before we can fully appreciate the greatness of his salvation—

But before we speak peace to ourselves it becomes us to inquire

II. FOR WHOSE DELIVERANCE HE IS SENT.

Great as his mercy is, it will not indiscriminately extend to all—

They, for whose relief he comes, are "oppressed" with the burthen of sin—

The generality, alas! are well contented with their bondage—

If he should offer to deliver them they would thrust him from them—Acts vii. 37, 39.

But there are some who mourn like the saints of old—Isa. vi. 5. Rom. vii. 24.

They desire nothing so much as to be delivered from their corruptions—

For these Jesus came down from heaven, and died upon the cross—

Nor, though they be lawful captives, will he leave them in the hand of their enemies—Isa. xlix. 24, 25.

They at the same time "cry earnestly to the Lord" for deliverance.

There are some, it must be confessed, who are uneasy in their sins, yet do not with fervor and constancy implore his mercy—

Such therefore, notwithstanding their uneasiness, obtain no help from him—

His mercy is promised to those alone who seek it with importunity—Matt. vii. 7; Ezek. xxxvi. 37.

But humble and believing suppliants shall never be rejected by him—

They shall find him a great, compassionate, and all-sufficient Saviour—

APPLICATION:—

Let *those who are unconcerned about their sins* reflect on their state—

Would God have sent them *such* a Saviour if their condition had not required it?—

Or, will they take occasion from this grace to live more securely in their sins?—

Let them consider that their cries, however available now, will soon be of no effect—Luke xvi. 24, 25

Let *those who are conflicting with sin and satan* lift up their heads with joy—

However desperate their state may seem, their redemption draweth nigh—
Nor shall all the powers of darkness rescue them from their Redeemer's hands—John x. 28.
Let *those who have experienced deliverance* adore their Lord—
Let them still go on, "strong in the grace that is in Christ Jesus"—
And soon they shall join in eternal Hallelujahs to God and to the Lamb.

WHAT WE OUGHT TO THINK OF CHRIST.

Matt. xxii. 42.—What think ye of Christ? (Sk.)

1. It is certain that the most correct views of Christ may be obtained from the Holy Scriptures, for these testify of him, John v. 39. The Old Testament testifies of Christ, in a great variety of promises, types, and prophecies. Luke xxiv. 44; Acts x. 43. The New Testament testifies of Christ, by recording the history of his life; by inculcating his doctrines; and by exhibiting the blessings of his kingdom. Christ is therefore the sum and substance of the inspired writings.

2. The testimony thus given is most highly creditable; for it is the testimony of *infinite knowledge*, which cannot mistake, Acts xv. 18, and the testimony of *unbounded goodness*, which will not deceive, Deut. xxxii. 4. Under the guidance of these divine oracles, let us observe,

I. What we ought to think of Christ. That we may entertain distinct ideas of this interesting subject, let us consider,

First, What we ought to think of Christ's *person*.

1. We ought to think that *he is truly man*, possessed of a human body, and a human soul, by which that body is animated. He is repeatedly *denominated* man. Thus he is called by Peter, in his sermon on the day of Pentecost, Acts ii. 22, and by Paul in his epistles, see 1 Cor. xv. 21—47; 1 Tim. ii. 5. And he is *described* as man, in his birth. "When the fulness," &c., Gal. v. 4, 5. In his *growth;* "and Jesus increased," &c., Luke ii. 52. And in the common *infirmities;* through bodily exercise, he felt weary. That he might be prepared for renewed labors of piety, and benevolence, he took rest in sleep. His mind was the subject both of grief and joy; and his body, of pain and death. It behoved him in all things to be made like unto his brethren, Heb. ii. 17.

2. We ought to think that *he is also truly God.* This appears,—From his *names*, he is called "The mighty God," Isa. ix. 6. He is also called, Immanuel. God with us," Isa. vii. 15; Matt. i. 23. "The Lord our Righteousness,' Jer. xxiii. 6. "God," John i. 1; Acts xx. 28. "God over all," Rom. ix. 6. "The great God and our Saviour," Tit. ii. 13. "The true God, and eternal life," 1 John v. 20.—From his *works;* he is "the Creator of the universe," John i. 3; Col. i. 16; Heb. ii. 8—10. And the preserver of it, in its existence, and in its order, Col. i. 17; Heb. i. 3.—From his *perfections;* he is eternal, without beginning, Mic. v. 2. He is omnipresent, John iii. 13; Matt. xviii. 20; omniscient, John xxi. 17; Heb. iv. 13; omnipotent, Psa. xlv. 3; Rev. i. 8, and immutable, Heb. ii. 12, and xiii. 8.—From his *pre-existent glory*, which he enjoyed from eternity, John xvii. 5. This glory was seen by Isaiah, chap. vi. 1—3 and is ascribed to

our Lord, see John xii. 41.—From the *worship* paid him by God's approved servants; by Christians on earth, 1 Cor. i. 2; by angels, Heb. i. 6, and by glorified saints, Rev. vii. 9, 10.—And from the *gifts* conferred by him; as forgiveness of sins, Acts v. 31; adoption into God's family, John i. 12; the gift of the Holy Ghost, Acts ii. 33, and eternal life. This he engages to give his followers, John x. 28; Rev. ii. 10, and this they expect from him, 2 Tim. iv. 3.

3. We ought to think that *Christ is God and man united in one person*, John i. 14; 1 Tim. iii. 16. This thought of Christ, renders all assertions respecting him perfectly consistent and harmonious. Thus we perceive how truly he is both the child born, and the mighty God. The Son, and the Lord of David, Matt. xxii. 45. The Root and the offspring of David, Rev. xxii. 16. Having considered what we ought to think of his person, let us consider,

Secondly, What we ought to think of his *name;* "Christ."

1. *This name is usually connected with that of Jesus.* Under this conjunct name of Jesus Christ, he is represented as coming into the world to save us, 1 Tim. i. 15.—Under this name he is preached to us, by his servants, 2 Cor. iv. 5; 1 John i. 2.—And under this name we must, as Christians, believe on him, Acts xvi. 31.

2. We should think, *how this name, thus connected, is expressive of his great work, and the various offices by which he effects it.* The name Jesus, signifies a Divine Saviour; and is expressive of his *great work.* This is to save mankind, Matt. i. 21; John iii. 17. To save them, by redeeming them from all sin, Psa. cxxx. 8. By restoring them to all the blessings forfeited by sin, 1 Pet. iii. 18. And by preserving them unto eternal life, Jude 24, 25.—The name of Christ, signifies *anointed*, and is expressive of those *various offices* which he sustains in effecting his work of human redemption. Of his *prophetic* office; as anointed to teach us, Isa. lxi. 1; Acts iii. 22.—Of his *kingly* office; as anointed to govern, protect, and reward us, Psa. ii. 6. Of his *priestly* office; as anointed to atone for our sins; to make intercession for us; and to bless us, Heb. iii. 1, and ix. 26, and vii, 25, 26, and ix. 28.—Those who desire to become interested in him as their Saviour, are required to receive him in all his offices, as the Lord's anointed, John i. 11, 12.—And all who thus receive him, are blessed by him, Psa. ii. 12. Hence let us consider,

Thirdly, What we ought to think of the *privileges* enjoyed by his subjects.

1. *These are various;* they include illumination, John viii. 12,—liberty, John viii. 32,—rest, Matt. xi. 28,—purity, John xiii. 8; 1 John i. 7,—protection, Isa. xl. 11; 1 Pet. i. 5,—provision, Matt. vi. 33. And eternal glory, John xii. 26.

2. *They are exactly adapted to our natural state and exigencies.* We are ignorant, and want illumination; enslaved, and want liberty; burdened, and want rest; defiled, and want purity; defenceless, and want protection; needy and immortal, and want eternal enjoyments.

3. *They are amply sufficient* to fulfil all our desires, Col. i. 19; Psa. cxlv. 19.

4. *And they are certain*, to all who obey him, Heb. v. 9. Let us consider,

Fourthly, What we ought to think of his *demands.*

1. *These are most graciously proposed by himself*, Matt. xi. 28, 29.

2. *They are highly reasonable.* We should learn of him; for he is an infinitely wise and kind teacher, Isa. xlviii. 17. We should obey him; for he is our rightful sovereign, having redeemed us by the price of his blood, 1 Cor. vi. 19, 20, and by the power of his grace, Psa. cxvi. 16. We should confide in him, for he is an all-sufficient, and never-failing friend, Isa. xxviii. 16, and xii. 2.

3. *They are truly pleasant to those who are endued with his grace.* For his grace enables us to do his will, Phil. ii. 12. And it inspires us with love, which makes our duty our pleasure, 1 John iv. 4; Matt. xi. 30. Thus we ought to think of Christ. And let us now observe,

II. Why we should thus think of Christ. We should thus think of him,

1. *Because those views of Christ are true and correct.* They are those views which we know God has of him. And these views must be adopted by us, if we would choose the way of truth, Psa. cxix. 30.

2. *Because we must think aright concerning Christ, that we may act aright towards him;* for ignorance of Christ must ever prevent a due acknowledgment of him.—If we do not think aright concerning his *offices;* we shall never learn of him as our Prophet; we shall never obey him as our King; nor trust in him as our High Priest, John i. 10, 11. If we do not think aright concerning his *divinity;* we shall not duly honor him, John v. 23. The Samaritan woman, not knowing him, omitted prayer to him, John iv. 10. The princes of this world not knowing him, put him to death 1 Cor. ii. 8.

3. *Because we must act aright towards Christ, or we cannot be saved by him.* Those who will not hear him will be destroyed, Acts iii. 23; Heb. xii. 25. Those who will not obey him, must be executed as his avowed enemies, Luke xix. 27; Rom. ii. 8, 9; 2 Thess. i. 7—9. Those who do not trust in him, remain under God's curse, Jer. xvii. 5. And those who deny his divinity and atonement, destroy themselves, 2 Pet. ii. 1. Having thus considered what we should think of Christ, and why we should thus think of him, let us

III. Apply the question. "What think ye of Christ?"

1. *Do you think him an imposter*—one who deceives the people? John vii. 12.—Then consider the *prophecies* which have been fulfilled in him, 2 Pet. i. 19.—Consider the *predictions* spoken by him, Matt. xvii. 22, 23; Luke xxi. 12, and xix. 41—44.—Consider the *miracles* wrought by him; consider, and believe, John xiv. 11; 2 Chron. xx. 20.

2. *Do you think him a mere man, and not God?* If so,—Consider, his names, works, attributes; his former glory, honors, and donations.—Consider these proofs of his divinity, and submit to his authority; by engaging in his service, and confiding in his mediation, Psa. ii. 12.

3. *Do you think little or nothing concerning him?* Is he not in all your thoughts? Psa. x. 4. If thus forgetful of him,—Consider his gracious remembrance of you, Psa. cxxxvi. 23; Luke i. 78, 79; Psa. viii. 4.—Consider this, and lament your ingratitude, Isa. liii. 4; Zech. xii. 10.

4. *Do you now think less of Christ than you formerly did?* Jer. ii. 32. If so—consider your fall; and return to him as at first, Rev. ii. 5; Hos. xiv 1, 2.—Consider his unwearied kindness, and hope in his mercy, 1 John ii. 1; Psa. cxxx. 7.

5. *Do you think Christ desirable*, and long to find him? Job xxiii. 2, 3. If so, then now open your hearts to receive him, Rev. iii. 20,—and now you will find salvation ready for you, Luke xiv. 17.

6. *Do you think and find Christ an inestimable treasure?* 1 Pet. ii. 7 Then carefully abide in him, 1 John ii. 28,—steadily walk in him, Col. ii 6.—and hope for his beatific presence, John xiv. 2, 3; 1 John iii. 2.

THE FOUNTAIN OPENED.

Zech. xiii. 1.—In that day there shall be a fountain opened to the house of David and to the inhabitants of Jerusalem for sin and for uncleanness. (Sk.)

An inspired apostle assures us, that to Christ, "give all the prophets witness;" and their various testimonies concerning him, are highly descriptive of his character and work, as the Redeemer and Saviour of his people. He is distinctly represented by a rich variety of metaphors and figures, which strikingly illustrate the nature of his offices, and the operations of his grace. He is the *Sun of Righteousness*, to enlighten our minds—an *infallible physician*, to heal the maladies of our souls—a *spiritual refiner*, to purify our hearts—and an *inexhaustible fountain*, to supply all our hearts, by "the exceeding riches of his grace." He possesses an infinite plenitude of blessings, which he is ever ready to communicate to perishing sinners. In the text, the prophet evidently "testified beforehand the sufferings of Christ, and the glory that should follow;" prophetically anticipating the personal manifestation of the Messiah, and the unspeakable benefits resulting to mankind from his atoning sacrifice, he exclaims with holy joy and gratitude, "In that day," &c. Let us pray that we may comprehend the import, and realize the truth of these words, while we consider,

I. The fountain that is opened. The term *fountain* is a metaphor, and is used in the text to represent the mediatorial character of Christ, as the *source* and *medium* of salvation to the human race. The figure is highly appropriate and instructive. "A fountain opened," implies,

1. *The plenitude of Divine grace.* It is not a *wasting stream*, that soon exhausts its store; but a *never-failing fountain*, ever flowing in plenteous supplies for every demand. The Lord Jehovah is emphatically styled, "The fountain of living waters, and the God of all grace." The saving influences of the Holy Ghost are figuratively called *water;—water of life;*—and the *washing of regeneration*, John iv. 14; 1 Cor. vi. 11. And the Lord Jesus Christ as the Author of salvation, graciously exclaims to a perishing world, "If any man thirst, let him come unto me, and drink." In him there is an unlimited fulness of "grace and truth," Col. i. 19; John i. 16. Millions have been refreshed by this fountain, and still it is undiminished. There is "enough for all, and enough for evermore."

2. *The freeness of Divine grace.* It is not a fountain *sealed up*, and *forbidden;* but freely *opened* and *accessible* to all. None are excluded from participating its richest blessings, Rev. xxii. 17. No personal merit, or moral worthiness, is required in its willing recipients. All are invited, and are welcome, to drink the living streams of bliss, "without money, and without price." The Saviour will not cast out any that come unto him. He opened a fountain of *life* by his *death*, and in infinite compassion, declares, "I will give unto him that is athirst, of the water of life freely.—Blessed are they which do hunger and thirst after righteousness, for they shall be filled." Observe,

II. THE PERIOD WHEN IT WAS OPENED. "In that day," &c. When this expression occurs in the prophetic writings, it generally refers to the *actual appearing*, or *spiritual reign* of the Messiah In this sense we understand it in the text, as referring to Christ's assumption of our nature, and sacrifice for our sins. But we ought to notice respecting this fountain, that,

1. *It was virtually opened in the original scheme of redemption.* According to God's gracious promise to mankind, Christ is called, "The Lamb slain from the foundation of the world." When the counsel of peace was between them both; the covenant of redemption was made in Jesus Christ, as the Mediator between God and man, Rom. iii. 24—26. This scheme of reconciliation was, in due time, announced to the world; and the fountain of grace *gradually revealed* and *opened* in the various promises of the Redeemer to the patriarchs, the emblematic shadows of the Mosaic dispensation, and the inspired predictions of the holy prophets, John viii. 56; Rom. iii. 21, 22.

2. *It was actually opened in the mediatorial work of the Redeemer.*— When the fulness of time was come, Christ was manifested in the flesh, to accomplish the will of God, and procure the salvation of sinners. He then *fully opened* this fountain, by fulfilling all righteousness in his own person —becoming the propitiation for our sins—rising again for our justification— ascending to heaven to be our Advocate with the Father—and diffusing an enlarged dispensation of the Holy Ghost; it was ministerially opened in the labors and writings of the apostles, as "ambassadors for Christ," 1 Cor. i. 23, 24, 30. And it still continues *open*, issuing in copious streams through all the doctrines, promises, and ordinances, of the Gospel, to satisfy the thirsty souls of them that repent and believe, John vii. 38. Consider,

III. THE PEOPLE TO WHOM IT IS OPENED. "The house of David, and the inhabitants of Jerusalem." It is very evident,

1. *This fountain was primarily opened to the Jews.* This is the express declaration of the text. To the *Jews* Christ was promised, and to them he came as his own people, according to the flesh. His personal ministry was generally confined to them; and though they crucified him as an impostor, his blood was shed for their sins; and he commanded his apostles to open their commission at Jerusalem, and preach the gospel *first* to the "lost sheep of the house of Israel," Luke xxiv. 46, 47, &c.

2. *This fountain is now graciously opened to the Gentiles.* The blessings of the Messiah were not to be confined to the Jewish church.—He was sent "to be a light of the *Gentiles*, and for salvation to the *ends of the earth*." "By the grace of God he tasted death for every man;" and his "unsearchable riches" are to be preached in "every nation, and to every creature." Jews and Gentiles are equally welcome, for there is now no difference, Rom. x. 12, 13; Eph. ii. 14—18. Unnumbered millions of Gentiles have proved the cleansing power of this *fountain*, which is *rapidly opening* and *extending* its healing virtues to "every kindred, tongue, and people." Our text also specifies,

IV. THE PURPOSE FOR WHICH IT IS OPENED. It is "for sin and for uncleanness." This implies,

1. *A fountain is opened for the expiation of sin.* The death of Christ was a *perfect sacrifice*, by which an *atonement* was made for the sins of mankind. The Divine perfections *harmonized*, and a new and living way of salvation opened to fallen sinners, Psa. lxxxv. 10 Heb. x. 18—22. *Such an expiation* was absolutely necessary—was typified by the Jewish sacrifices

—was announced by the prophets—and was ultimately accomplished, when Christ was "wounded for our transgressions, and his soul was made an offering for sin," John i. 29; 1 John iv. 10.

2. *A fountain is opened for the destruction of sin.* It must not only be *sacrificially expiated*, but *personally destroyed;* and "for this purpose the Son of God was manifested, that he might *destroy* the works of the devil." He effects this *destruction* by the merit of his death, and the operation of his grace, Tit. ii. 14. All sin is *moral uncleanness*, and spreads its infectious disease through every power, both of body and soul. The ceremonial purifications under the law were *emblematic* of the *efficacy* of *this fountain*, Heb. ix. 13, 14. The blood of Christ cleanseth from all sin, 1 John i. 8, 9. Have we come to this living fountain? It is *open* and *free* for all "Believe, and be saved." "Come drink, aud thirst no more."

NOAH'S ARK A TYPE OF CHRIST.

1 Peter iii. 21.—The like figure whereunto, even baptism, doth now save us. (S. S.)

God has marked the necessity of holiness no less by the dispensations of his Providence than by the declarations of his grace. His destroying of the whole world for their iniquity, evinced, as strongly as any thing could, that sin should never go unpunished, and that the righteous only should be saved. In this view St. Peter introduces the mention of that well attested fact, and declares that the salvation, experienced by Noah in the ark, was typical of that which we experience by Christ, and into which we are brought by our baptism. The text is by no means free from difficulties: to render it as intelligible as we can, we shall consider

I. The typical salvation here referred to.

God had determined to overwhelm the world with a deluge.

Though there had been so few generations upon earth, that Noah's own father (Lamech) had been contemporary with Adam for sixty years, and lived till within five years of the flood, so that Noah, and the people of that generation, had, for no less than six hundred years together, received instruction only at second hand from Adam himself, yet had "all flesh corrupted their way," insomuch that "God repented that he had made man," and resolved to destroy him from off the face of the earth.

But for the preservation of the righteous he instructed Noah to make an ark.

This vessel was not constructed according to man's device, but by the special direction of God himself. To the eyes of man it doubtless seemed an absurd attempt: but "the foolishness of God is wiser than man;" and the event justified the hopes and expectations of Noah.

In the mean time he called the people to repentance by the ministry of Noah.

God exercised forbearance towards them 120 years. But they "received his grace in vain." And the means used for their salvation only ripened them for destruction.

When the appointed time was come, he ordered Noah and his family to go into the ark.

The symptoms of the flood did not yet appear, but these favorites of heaven were to condemn the world, not in word only, but in deed. By manifesting their faith, their fear, and their obedience, they were practically to condemn the world's unbelief, security, and disobedience. Heb. xi. 7. And, upon their entrance into the ark, "God shut them in" with his own hand, that the door might be secure against the violence of the wind and waves.

Then the waters, that destroyed all the world besides, bore them up in perfect safety.

Every other refuge now proved vain. The unbelievers found to their cost the truth of God's threatenings. Their numbers did not screen them from his judgments. Nor was the fewness of the elect any bar to their acceptance and salvation. They rose, while others sank in the mighty waters. Nor, if any cleaved to the ark, did that avail them. The very builders of the ark perished. They, and they only, who were in the ark, were made the monuments of saving mercy.

This history being altogether typical, we shall consider.

II. THE CORRESPONDENT SALVATION WHICH WE ENJOY.

Baptism is spoken of in the text as the *antitype*,* of which Noah's flood was the type. But we apprehend the apostle's meaning to be, that Noah's salvation in the ark was typical of our salvation under the christian dispensation.† This subject will be best understood, not by drawing the parallel between the flood and baptism, or between the ark and Christ, but by exhibiting *the fact* of our salvation as corresponding with that of Noah.

God has determined to punish the world with an everlasting destruction.

His word bears frequent and most undeniable testimony to this solemn truth— — —Matt. xxiv. 37—39. 2 Peter ii. 5, 9. Psalm xi. 6 and 9, 17.

But he has prepared a Saviour for those who repent and turn unto him.

Human sagacity never could have devised a way of saving sinners consistently with the honor of God's perfections. But God has sent and qualified his only begotten Son, that, through him, all who believe might be justified from all things. And though salvation through the death of Christ be "to the Jews a stumbling-block, and to the Greeks foolishness," yet to them that are called to partake of it, it has invariably proved the power of God and the wisdom of God. 1 Cor. i. 23, 24.

Ever since the method of salvation has been announced to the world, God has been inviting sinners to embrace it.

The first plank of this ark was laid, if we may so speak, when God promised to Adam a "Seed, who should bruise the serpent's head,"—From that day, it has been erecting visibly in the world, in order that, while men were warned of their danger, they might see their remedy: and now, for nearly six thousand years, has God exercised forbearance towards an impenitent and unbelieving world.

By "baptism" we embark, as it were, on board this divinely constructed vessel.

When we are baptized into the faith of Christ, we profess our persuasion that "there is salvation in no other," and our desire "to be found in him,"

* Ἀντίτυπον. †The relative ᾧ cannot agree with κιβωτȣ, which is feminine, but must agree with ὕδατος, or rather perhaps with the whole sentence; this last construction renders the sense of the passage incomparably more clear; on which account it is here preferred.

not having our own righteousness, but that which is of God by faith in him Acts iv. 12; Phil. iii. 9. Thus we come to be *in him*, as a branch in the vine, as a man-slayer in a city of refuge, as Noah in the Ark. Not that this benefit is annexed to the mere outward form of baptism, but to that baptism which is accompanied with "the answer of a good conscience towards God."*

Being then *in* Christ, we are saved "by his resurrection."†

It should seem, that Noah's inclosure in the ark for so long a period was a kind of sepulture; and his elevation on the waters, till he afterwards came forth from the ark, was a kind of resurrection, when he took possession of a new world. Thus, according to St. Paul, "we are buried with Christ by baptism into death, that like as Christ was raised up from the dead by the glory of the Father, even so we also should walk in newness of life: for if we have been planted in the likeness of his death, we shall be also in the likeness of his resurrection." Rom. vi. 4, 5. This appears to be *intended* by St. Peter in the text, and to be, on the whole, the most natural, as well as most beautiful, construction of it: as Noah entered into the ark, and was saved by its elevation above the water-floods, so we, by baptism, enter into Christ, and are, by his resurrection, saved from sin and Satan, death and hell; yea, like Noah too, we are brought safely to the possession of a new and heavenly world.‡

INFER,

1. How deeply should we reverence the ordinances of God!

What is said of baptism is true, in a measure, of every other ordinance: yet how shamefully is both that, and every other ordinance, profaned amongst us! Let us remember, that all the institutions of God are intended to help forward our salvation: but, if trifled with, they will fearfully aggravate our condemnation.

2. How careful should we be to obtain "the answer of a good conscience!"

In the apostles days, as well as in ours, they, who applied for baptism, were *interrogated* with respect to their faith and practice: nor could the mere ablution of the body profit them, if they had not a correspondent purity of soul. Thus it is with us: we shall in vain receive the rite of baptism, or partake of the Lord's Supper, if we cannot *declare, as in the presence of God*, that it is our desire and endeavor to be holy as God is holy. Let us then not lay an undue stress upon outward observances of any kind; but rather seek a conformity to the divine image; for it will surely be found true at the last, that "the pure in heart shall see God," but that "*without holiness no man shall see the Lord.*"

*See the words following the text. †Ib.

‡If the opposition between διεσώθησαν δι' ὕδατος and σώζει δι' ἀναστάσεως be marked the sense of this difficult passage will be more apparent.

ISAAC A TYPE OF CHRIST.

Gen. xxii. 6—10. And Abraham took the wood of the burnt-offering, and laid it upon Isaac his son: and he took the fire in his hand and a knife: and they went both of them together. And Isaac spake unto Abraham his father, and said, My father: and he said, Here am I, my son. And he said, Behold the fire and the wood: but where is the lamb for a burnt-offering? And Abraham said, My son, God will provide himself a lamb for a burnt-offering. So they went both of them together. And they came to the place which God had told him of, and Abraham built an altar there, and laid the wood in order, and bound Isaac his son, and laid him on the altar upon the wood. And Abraham stretched forth his hand, and took the knife to slay his son. (S. S.)

Many and wonderful are the instances of faith and obedience recorded in the scriptures. But no action whatever (those only of our Lord himself excepted) has at any time surpassed or equalled that related in the text. It justly obtained for him who performed it, the honorable title of The Father of the Faithful, and, The Friend of God. Jam. x. 21, 23. We shall find it profitable to consider,

I. The history itself.

Abraham had often enjoyed intimate and immediate communion with the Deity. But now he heard the command which was of a most singular and afflictive nature.

God in some way clearly intimated to Abraham his will: nor left him to doubt one moment, whether it were his voice or not. He commanded Abraham to take his only, his beloved son Isaac, and to offer him up as a burnt-offering in a place that should afterwards be pointed out. How strange the order! How difficult to be complied with! How well might Abraham have said, "Would to God I might die for thee, O Isaac, my son, my son!"

Instantly, however, and without reluctance, he arose to execute the will of God.

Had he presumed to reason with God, what specious arguments might he have adduced for declining the way of duty! The certainty of his being reproached by Sarah, "A bloody husband art thou to me:" Exod. iv. 25, 26, the offence that would be taken by all the neighboring nations against him, his religion, and his God: the counteracting and defeating of all the promises which had been made by God himself, and which were to be accomplished solely in and through his son Isaac: Gen. xvii. 19: all this, with much more, might have been offered in excuse for his backwardness, if indeed he had been backward, to accomplish the will of God. But he conferred not with flesh and blood. Gal. i. 16.

Nor was he diverted from his purpose during the whole of his journey.

Having prepared the wood, he proceeded instantly, with Isaac and his servants, towards the place, that God had pointed out. Nor did he open his intentions to Sarah, lest she should labor to dissuade him from his purpose But what must have been his thoughts every time that he looked on Isaac? Yet never for one moment did he relax his determination to execute the divine command. Having come in sight of the mountain, he ordered his servants to abide in their place, lest they should officiously interpose to prevent the intended offering. He put the wood on his son, and carried the fire and the knife in his own hands. Affecting as these preparations must have been to a father's heart, how must their poignancy have been heightened by that pertinent question, which was put to him by his son! Ver. 7. His answer, like many other prophetical expressions, conveyed more than he himself probably was aware at the moment. Without giving a premature disclosure of his intention, he declares the advent of Jesus, that Lamb of God, who in due time should come to take away the sin of the world. Ver. 8. John i. 29. Thus for three successive days did he maintain his resolution firm and unshaken.

Having arrived at the spot determined by God, he with much firmness and composure proceeded to execute his purpose.

He built the altar, and laid the wood upon it in due order. Then with inexpressible tenderness announced to Isaac the command of God. Doubtless he would remind his son of his preternatural birth; and declare to him God's right to take away, in any manner he pleased, the gift he bestowed. Job i. 21. He would exhort him to confide in God as a faithful and unchangeable God; and to rest assured, that he should, in some way or other, be restored, after he was reduced to ashes, and have every promise fulfilled to him. Having thus gained the consent of his son, he binds him hand and foot, and lays him on the altar; and, with a confidence unshaken, and obedience unparalleled, holds up the knife to slay the victim. Whether shall we more admire the resolution of the father, or the submission of the son? O that there were in all of us a similar determination to sacrifice our dearest interests for God; and a similar readiness to yield up our very lives in obedience to his will!

Nothing but the interposition of God himself prevented the completion of this extraordinary sacrifice.

God had sufficiently tried the faith of his servant. He therefore, by a voice from heaven, stopped him from giving the fatal blow; ordered him to substitute a ram in the place of Isaac; renewed to him with an oath his former promises; rendered him a pattern to all succeeding generations; and, no doubt, is at this instant rewarding him with a weight of glory, proportioned to his exalted piety.

Almost every circumstance in this narrative deserves to be considered in,

II. Its typical reference.

Waving many less important points, we may observe that Isaac was a type of Christ.

1. In his appointment to be a sacrifice.

Isaac was a child of promise, born in a preternatural way, of a disposition eminently pious; yet him did God require for a burnt-offering: it must not be Abraham's cattle, or his son Ishmael, but his beloved Isaac. Thus was Jesus also the promised seed, named, like Isaac, before he was conceived in the womb: He was born, not after the manner of other men, but of a pure virgin: He was that only, that beloved son, in whom the Father was well pleased: yet him did God appoint to be a sacrifice. A body was given him for this very purpose. Heb. x. 4. 5. He was ordained from eternity to be a propitiation for sin: Rom. iii. 25: nor did the Father recede from his purpose for 4,000 years. Having set apart his son for this end, he changed not: and Jesus, at the appointed time, became obedient unto death, even the death of the cross. Phil. ii. 8.

2. In the manner of being offered.

Isaac bore the wood on which he was afterwards to be lifted up; and voluntarily yielded up his body to be bound, and his life to be destroyed in God's appointed way. Thus did Jesus bear his cross to the place of his crucifixion; and, having been bound was lifted up upon it. On the very spot where Isaac had been laid upon the altar, was Jesus (most probably) offered in sacrifice to God.* And by whose hand was Isaac to bleed, but by that of his own Father? By whom too did Jesus suffer, but by Jehovah's sword? Zech. xiii. 7; Isa. liii. 10. It was not *man* who made him so to agonize in the garden; nor was it man that caused that bitter complaint upon the cross. Luke xxii. 44; Mark xv. 34. Nevertheless it was with the perfect concurrence of his own will that he died upon the cross; "He *gave himself* an offering and a sacrifice to God of a sweet smelling savor." Eph. v. 2.

There is one point however, wherein the resemblance does not appear.

For Isaac was found a substitute; for Jesus none. Neither the cattle on a thousand hills, nor all the angels in heaven, could have stood in his place. None but Jesus could have made a full atonement for our sins. He therefore saved not himself, because He was determined to save us.

INFER,

1. How marvellous is the love of God to man!

We admire the obedience of Abraham: but God had a right to demand it: and Abraham knew, that he was about to give his son to his best and dearest friend. But what claim had we on God? Yet did he give up his Son for us sinners, rebels, enemies; nor merely to a common death, but to the agonies of crucifixion, and to endure the wrath due to our iniquities. Isa. liii. 6. What stupendous love! Shall any soul be affected with a pathetic story, and remain insensible of the love of God? Let every heart praise him, trust him, serve him: and rest assured that He who delivered up his Son for us, will never deny us any other thing that we can ask. Rom. viii 32.

2. What an admirable grace is faith.

The faith of Abraham certainly had respect to Christ, the promised seed. Heb. xi. 17—19. And, behold how it operated! So will it operate in all who have it. It will keep us from staggering at any promise, however dark or improbable; and will lead us to obey every precept, however difficult or self-denying. Let us seek his faith: and while we are justified by it from the guilt of sin, let us manifest its excellence by a life of holiness.

JOSHUA A TYPE OF CHRIST.

Deut. iii. 28.—Charge Joshua, and encourage him, and strengthen him; for he shall go over before this people, and he shall cause them to inherit the land which thou shalt see. (S. S.)

JOSHUA was a very eminent type of Christ. The text naturally leads us to shew this: and we shall trace the resemblance of Joshua to Christ.

I. IN HIS NAME.

The name of *Joshua* was intended to designate his work and office.

His name originally was Osea, but was altered by Moses to Joshua. Num xiii. 16. This, doubtless, was of God's appointment, that he might be there-

*Mount Calvary was one of the mountains in that small tract of country called the land of Moriah: and from verse 2, it can scarcely be doubted, but that it was the very spot pointed out by God. It could not possibly be far from the spot; and therefore, when the place for the sacrifice of Isaac was so accurately marked, it can scarcely be thought to be any other, than the very place where Jesus was offered 2,000 years afterwards.

by rendered a more remarkable type of Jesus. This name imported, that he should be *a divine Saviour;** and though, in the strictest and fullest sense, it could not properly belong to him; yet, as he was to be such a distinguished representative of Jesus, it was very properly given to him.

The name of *Jesus* still more fitly characterized the work that was to be performed by *him*.

This name is precisely the same with Joshua in the Greek language; and repeatedly do we, in the New Testament, translate it, "Jesus," when it ought rather to have been translated, "Joshua." Acts vii. 45; Heb. iv. 8. It was given to our Lord by the angel, before he was conceived in the womb: Matt. i. 21; and the express reason of it was assigned, namely, that "he should *save* his people from their sins." To him it is applicable in the fullest extent, because he is "God manifest in the flesh," "Emmanuel, God with us;" and because he is the author, not of a typical and temporary, but of a real and eternal salvation, to all his followers. Heb. v. 9.

This striking coincidence, with respect to the name, may prepare us for fuller discoveries of a resemblance.

II. In his office.

Joshua was appointed to lead the Israelites into the promised land.

Moses was certainly intended to represent the law, which was admirably calculated to lead men through the wilderness, but could never bring them into the land of Canaan: one offence against it destroyed all hope of salvation by it: Gal. iii. 10; it made no provision for mercy: its terms were simply, Do this and live: Rom. x. 5; and, for an example of its inexorable rigor, Moses himself was, for one unadvised word, excluded from the land of promise. The office of saving men must belong to another; and, for this reason, it was transferred to Joshua, who had been both appointed to it, and thoroughly qualified by God for the discharge of it. Deut. xxiv. 9.

Jesus also was commissioned to bring his followers into the Canaan that is above.

He, probably in reference to Joshua, is styled the Captain of our salvation: Heb. ii. 10; and he appeared to Joshua himself in this very character, proclaiming himself to be the Captain of the Lord's host. Josh. v. 13—15. "What the law could not do, in that it was weak through the flesh," the Lord Jesus Christ came to effect. Rom. viii. 3. He has been divinely qualified for the work; and, like Joshua, was "encouraged to it, and strengthened in it," by an assurance of God's continual presence, and support. Isaiah xlii. 1, 4, 6. He leads his people on from grace to grace, from strength to strength, from victory to victory. Ps. lxxxiv. 7; 2 Cor. iii. 18; Rev. vi. 2. Nor will he ever desist from his work, till he shall have subdued his enemies, and established his people in their promised inheritance.

Happily for us the resemblance may be likewise traced.

III. In his success.

Nothing could oppose any effectual bar to Joshua's progress.

Though Jordan had overflowed its banks, its waters were divided, to open him a path on dry land. Joshua iii. 17. The impregnable walls of Jericho, merely at the sound of rams' horns, were made to fall. Josh. vi. 20. Confederate kings fled before him. Josh. x. 16. City after city, kingdom after kingdom, were subjected to his all-conquering arms: and almost the whole accursed race of Canaanites were extirpated, and destroyed. Joshua xii. 7, 24. The promised land was divided by him amongst his followers: Joshua

**Jah*, which was prefixed to his name, is the name of God.

xi. 23, and xviii. 10; and he appealed to them with his dying breath, that not so much as one, of all the promises that God had given them, had ever failed. Josh. xxiii. 14.

And shall less be said respecting our adorable Emmanuel?

He "triumphed over all the principalities and powers" of hell; and causes his followers to trample on the necks of their mightiest foes. Rom. xvi. 20, with Josh. x. 24. He leads them safely through the swellings of Jordan, when they come to the border of the promised land; Isa. xliii. 2; and, having given them the victory, he divides among them the heavenly inheritance. Matt. xxv. 34. When he comes to number them at last, even though they may have sustained the sorest conflicts, it will be found, that not so much as one of them is lost: Numb. xxxi. 49, with John xvii. 12; and he will be able to appeal to the whole assembled universe, that not so much as one jot or title of God's word hath failed of its accomplishment. Thus will all of them be put into possession of "that rest, which remained for them," in the hope and expectation of which, they endured the labors of travel, and the fatigues of war. Heb. iv. 1, 9, 11.

INFER,

1. How earnestly, and how humbly, should all submit themselves to Jesus!

Notwithstanding Joshua's commission was, utterly to destroy the inhabitants of that sinful land, yet he both spared the Gibeonites, and made a league with them, when they humbled themselves before him; Josh. ix. 15; he, moreover, gave a special charge respecting the perservation of the harlot Rahab, who, in faith, had concealed his spies. Josh. vi. 22, 25. But resistance to him was vain: there were none that could stand before him. Thus must all thine enemies, O Lord, perish, if they do not prostrate themselves before thee in humility and faith. Shall we not then believingly receive his messengers, and, *in the use of his appointed means*, expect his mercy? Shall we not go and make a covenant with him, and yield up ourselves, with unreserved submission, to his commands? Yes: and if this conduct provoke the world to combine against us, we will call him in to our aid, and despise the assaults of earth and hell. Josh. x. 4.

2. How confidently may the very weakest christians go forth to their future conflicts!

Though Canaan was promised to the Israelites, yet they were all to fight for it: so neither is heaven to be gained without many severe conflicts. But what have we to fear, when we have such a Captain? "If he be for us, who can be against us?" Did he ever yet suffer one of his faithful followers to perish? If they have been wounded, has he not healed their wounds? If they have fainted, has he not renewed their strength? Has he not made them conquerors, yea, "more than conquerors?" Rom. viii. 37. What then, though we have mighty Anakims to contend with, and their fortresses be walled up to heaven? Let us "be strong and very courageous;" and we shall find that "the weapons of prayer and faith, though weak and contemptible to a carnal eye, are mighty through God to the casting down of strong holds, and every high thing that exalts itself against the knowledge of God." 2 Cor. x. 4, 5. Let us then "be strong in the Lord, and in the power of his might." Let us "put on the whole armor of God." Eph. vi. 10, 11 And let us look forward with confidence to the joyful period, when we shall receive our portion in the promised land, "the land that floweth with milk and honey"

CHRIST THE FOUNDATION.

1 Cor. iii. 11.—For other foundation can no man lay, than that is laid, which is Jesus Christ. (P.)

It is not here alone, but in many other scriptures, both in the Old and New Testament, that our Lord Jesus Christ is held forth under the notion of a foundation. We shall,

I. Show the properties of Christ as a foundation; what kind of a foundation he is; and, 1st. He is a *laid* foundation—"Behold I lay in Zion for a foundation a stone" Isa. xxviii. 16. "Behold I," *i. e.* God the Father; one that knew well enough how to do it; a God of infinite wisdom and power. The Lord Jesus Christ did not take upon himself this honor of being a mediator; no, he was called to it, appointed of God for such a purpose; and this is our comfort and joy. He that could best tell what would best serve to satisfy his offended justice, pitched upon his own Son for that purpose: this was the ransom he found for man. Job xxxiii. 24. "I have laid help upon one that is mighty; I have exalted one chosen out of the people." Ps. lxxxix. 19. 2nd. A *low* foundation—low laid; foundations are wont to be laid low; the lower the surer. So the Lord Jesus Christ, as a foundation, was laid very low, that he might be a meet foundation for us. He was "in the form of God, and thought it not robbery to be equal with God: but he made himself of no reputation, and took upon him the form of a servant, and was made in the likeness of man," &c. Phil. ii. 6—9. There were several steps of his humiliation. 1. Into the human nature. He condescended to be made a man; this was a long step downward. That the Word should become flesh was more than if a star should turn into a cloud. 2. Into subjection under the laws. "When the fulness of time was come, God sent forth his Son, made of a woman;" made *under the law*—the moral law; nay, the ceremonial law. He was to be circumcised—presented in the temple—redeemed and ransomed with two turtles—bound to go up to all the feasts. 3. Into poverty and persecution, contempt and contradiction; to be spurned and trampled on. 4. To death itself: "he became obedient unto death, even the death of the cross," a most painful, shameful, and ignominious death. This is called *a lifting up*, John xii. 32, but it was *humiliation*. 5. To the grave. When he was buried, he was, as other foundations, laid under ground; and there was a necessity for all this; without it, there could have been no atonement, no reconciliation. 3rd. Christ is a foundation of *stone*. Isaiah xxviii. 16. A stone is the fittest thing of all others to make foundations of, because it is hard and firm, and yet easily hewn. Now Jesus Christ is a stone—a foundation—a rock. 1 Cor. x. 4. Observe again, 4th. He is a foundation *out of sight*. All foundations are so; we see the building, but we do not see the foundation: such a foundation is the Lord Jesus Christ. He is out of sight. Not below, as he once was, under the earth, but above, in glory. His *person* is out of sight, yet we love him. 1 Peter i. 8. His *presence* is invisible. He is with us every where, especially in his ordinances, but it is in an invisible way: we feel it, but we do not see it. Matthew xviii. 20, and xxviii. 20. His *proceedings* are invisible. The proceedings of his grace within—the proceedings of his providence without; Psalm lxxvii. ult. 5th. He is a *precious* foundation; Isaiah xxviii. 16. Though all stones in their places be useful, yet they are not all precious stones. Few buildings are built upon precious stones, but the church of Christ is precious *in himself;* he is of great worth and value.

"The chief among ten thousand, and altogether lovely." He is precious *in the account and esteem of his disciples.* To others he is a stone of stumbling, and a rock of offence; but unto them which believe, he is precious. 1 Peter ii. 7. Moreover, 6th. He is a *permanent* foundation; Isaiah xxvi. 4. He is the rock of ages, from everlasting to everlasting. The saints have been building on him from the beginning, and will build on him to the end of time. He is "the same yesterday, to-day, and for ever." His righteousness is everlasting; his promises are unchangeable. 7th. He is an *elect*, or *chosen* foundation, Isaiah xxviii. 16, chosen of God, and precious—"Behold my servant, whom I have chosen, mine elect, in whom my soul is well pleased," Isaiah xlii. 1. Once more, 8th. He is an *experienced* or *tried* foundation. He was tried by *God*, who laid upon him the iniquities of us all. He was tried by *men* and *devils*, who did their best against him, but all to no purpose. He has been tried by the *saints*, who have had occasion to make use of him, and he has never failed them.

II. WHAT IS OUR DUTY IN REFERENCE TO THIS FOUNDATION? It is our duty, 1st. To *believe all this concerning him.* That God hath laid him purposely for a foundation; anointed and appointed him to be a Prince and a Saviour, and given him to the world, that "whosoever believeth in him, might not perish, but have everlasting life." 2nd. To *behold and see our need of him.* There is no rearing a building without a foundation. We have each of us a building to rear, and what foundation have we? None in ourselves—no righteousness of our own to commend us to God—no strength or ability to any thing that is good. 3rd. To *renounce all other foundations.* They are but sand; and he that builds on the sand, his building will fall; Matthew vii. 24, *ad finem.* 4th. To *repair* to him. In the way of faithful and fervent prayer tell him you are sensible of your need of him, and that you are undone without him. 5th. To *build* upon him: in the great business of *justification;* to rest our souls by faith upon his meritorious righteousness. None but Christ! None but Christ! In all our *perils* and *dangers*, personal or public, we should fly to him, trust in him, rely upon him: "Faithful is he that hath promised," Psalm xlvi. 1, and lxii. 1, 2; and it is our duty, 6th. To *beware what we build* upon this foundation, in *opinion* and in *practice*, 1 Cor. iii. 12, 13, 14, 15. If we build loose, careless walking, our hopes built, will be accordingly wood, hay, stubble, &c.

CHRIST'S DILIGENCE IN SERVING GOD.

John iv. 34. Jesus saith unto them, My meat is to do the will of him that sent me, and to finish his work. (S. S.)

OUR blessed Lord throughout his whole life, was the most illustrious pattern of condescension to man and of fidelity to God. Both these dispositions were eminently displayed in the history before us. Notwithstanding he was already exhausted with a long and fatiguing journey, he had been laboring for the salvation of a most abandoned adultress: and when urged to intermit his exertions for a little while in order to recruit his strength by some necessary refreshment, he declared, that food was not so delightful to a famished body, as the prosecuting of the great ends of his ministry was to his soul.

From his words we shall take occasion to,

I. CONSIDER OUR LORD'S EXAMPLE.

Jesus in his human and mediatorial capacity, was the Father's servant. And the work assigned him was, to reveal in a more perfect manner the will of God, and to save mankind by his own obedience unto death.

In this work he engaged,

1. With fervent affection.

Nothing could exceed the delight with which he *undertook* this arduous task; Ps. xl. 7, 8; nothing the zeal with which he *accomplished* it. Luke xii. 50. Whether we view his private addresses to God, Heb. v. 7, or his public ministrations among men,* we shall see that in him was that prophecy accomplished, "The zeal of thine house hath eaten me up." John ii. 17.

2. With indefatigable diligence.

From the commencement of his ministry to the end of it not a day was unemployed. Frequently, after having labored all the day, he spent the night in prayer, and resumed his labors with the returning light. Like the sun in the firmament, he proceeded in one steady course through all the cities, towns, and villages; nor ever ceased from his work, till he could say, "It is finished."

3. With undaunted resolution.

What "continual opposition" did he endure! He was truly "a sign spoken against," or a butt of contradiction. Luke ii. 34. There was not any thing however perverse, scandalous, or contemptuous, but his ears were assailed with it from day to day. From the very first discourse he uttered till the hour of his crucifixion, his enemies never ceased to seek his life. John xi. 8. Yet did he persevere in the face of every danger, and at last complete his obedience, by surrendering up his life on the cross.

That we may profit from this great example, we will,

II. Propose it for your imitation.

We also have a work to do for God.

Our work is great; but O! how different from that which was committed to our Lord! We have not to satisfy the demands of justice, or to endure the wrath due to sin: blessed be God! *that* was the Redeemer's work; and it has been finished by him on our behalf. The work which we have to do, is to believe in Christ, John vi. 29, and, from a sense of his love to us, to devote ourselves unreservedly to his service. Rom. xii. 1.

Let us then engage in it,

1. Heartily.

"Whatever our hand findeth to do, we should do it with all our might." Eccl. ix. 10. A lukewarm service is unacceptable, yea, hateful, to God. Rev. iii. 15, 16. Let us then first labor to know the will of God, and then endeavor to do it with our whole hearts. Let us be "fervent in spirit, while we serve the Lord." Rom. xii. 11.

2. Uniformly.

It is not an occasional act of zeal that will please God, but a steady, conscientious, uniform discharge of our duty. Our spirit, alas! is often faint; and even when "the spirit is willing, our flesh is weak." But we must counteract our sloth, and "give all diligence to make our calling and election sure." 2 Pet. i. 10.

3. Courageously.

*He was filled with joy at the least prospect of success, verse 35, and grieved and wept when he could not succeed. Mark iii. 5; Luke xix. 41.

We shall surely meet with reproach and persecution, if we set ourselves in earnest to serve the Lord. 2 Tim. iii. 12. But let us "remember him who endured such contradiction of sinners against himself. Heb. xii. 3. Woe be to us, if we draw back through the fear of man. Heb. x. 38. We must hate, not only father and mother, but even our own life also, if we would be Christ's disciples. Luke xiv. 26. Let us then "take up our cross daily" after Christ's example, and "suffer with him, in order that we may be also glorified together." Rom. viii. 17.

ADDRESS,

1. Those who are unconcerned about the work of God.

Has not God appointed you a work to do; and ought you not to have begun it long ago? Is it expedient to leave it to a dying hour? What if you should die before it is finished? O begin instantly; for the "night cometh, wherein no man can work."

2. Those who do his work deceitfully.

God has pronounced such persons accursed, no less than if they did nothing for him. Jer. xlviii. 10. His service must be your "meat" and drink; the joy of your souls, and the business of your lives. See then that ye "approve yourselves to God as servants that need not to be ashamed." 2 Tim. ii. 15.

3. Those who are in a measure conformed to their Saviour's image.

Bless your God, who has thus far enabled you to serve him. But O! think how much you fall short of your heavenly pattern! Forget then what is behind, and press forward for that which is before you; Phil. iii. 13—15; so shall you in due season "rest from your labors," and be welcomed as good and faithful servants to the joy of your Lord. Matt. xxv. 21

CHRIST, HE THAT SHOULD COME.

Luke vii. 19.—*Art thou he that should come? or, look we for another?* (Sk.)

THESE words were addressed to our Lord by two disciples of John the baptist, who sent them to Jesus, and instructed them to make these inquiries for the confirmation of their faith.

1. The question could not be proposed on John's account, for he was fully convinced that Christ was the true Messiah. Of this he was assured by divine revelation, and the testimony of God the Father at our Lord's baptism, John i. 32; Matt. iii. 17. And that Jesus was the Messiah John uniformly testified, by speaking of him as the Son of God, as incomparably superior to himself, as the Lamb of God, and as come to baptize with the Holy Ghost.

2. But though John believed in Jesus, and thus bore witness to him, yet it seems these disciples and their brethren were led to doubt even the testimony of their master. It is probable they thus doubted, because they did not find Jesus setting up a splendid earthly kingdom, such as they expected the Messiah would establish; because our Lord was not so rigidly abstemious as their master was; and because no miracle was wrought to deliver John out of prison; which they concluded the Messiah would certainly be both inclined and able to work, on such an occasion.

3. For the kind purpose of removing their doubts, and satisfying their minds, John therefore prudently sent them to hear, and see, and judge for themselves; and with this view he taught them to make the inquiries now before us, "Art thou," &c. The purport of these questions may be expressed thus, 'Sacred prophecy leads us to expect that the Messiah, the Lord's anointed, will appear in this land about this time. We entreat thee therefore to inform us whether thou art this great expected personage or not; that we may respect thee according to thy proper character.' To these inquiries our Lord wisely answers by actions, rather than words, verse 21. Then he requires the messengers to go and inform John what they had seen and heard, ver. 22, 23. Hereby Jesus evidently referred to sacred prophecy for an answer to these important questions. And as we are no less interested in this answer than John's disciples, let us consider,

I. THE TESTIMONY OF SACRED PROPHECY CONCERNING THE MESSIAH.

1. *Respecting the Person who should come under this character.* He is spoken of and described as David's *Son*, and *Lord*, Psa. lxxxix., 29, and cx. 1; as Immanuel, Isa. vii. 14; the Child born, and the Mighty God, Isa. ix. 6.

2. *Respecting the time when he should come.* This was to be before the sceptre departed from the tribe of Judah, Gen. xlix. 10; within the seventy weeks of Daniel, or 490 years after the Persian decree which was passed for rebuilding Jerusalem, Dan. ix. 24—26; and during the continuance of the second temple, Hag. ii. 7, 9.

3. *Respecting the purposes of his coming.* These were to guide as a Prophet, Deut. xviii. 18; to govern as a King, Psa. ii. 5; to save us as our Redeemer, Isa. xxxv. 4; to feed us as a Shepherd, Isa. xl. 11; and to reward us as our Judge, Isa. xl. 10, and xxxiii. 22.

4. *Respecting some remarkable circumstances which would attend his coming.* As the performance of various benevolent miracles, Isa. xxix. 18, and xxxv. 5, 6; silent modesty in working these miracles, Isa. xlii. 2, 3; a gracious reception of the poor by him, Isa. xxix. 19, and lxi. 1; and the reception of him by the Jewish nation, Isa. viii. 14, and liii. 1. This is the testimony of prophecy, which St. Peter informs us is sure in its accomplishment, and should engage our attention, 2 Pet. i. 19. Let us therefore notice,

II. THE FULFILMENT OF PROPHECY IN THE PERSON OF CHRIST. Here observe,

1. *These prophecies must be fulfilled in some person;* as the time specified for their accomplishment has long been past. For the sceptre departed from the tribe of Judah, and the second temple was destroyed, about seventeen hundred and fifty years since; and Daniel's seventy weeks expired about forty years before these events took place. In other words, our Jesus, the Messiah, was cut off by death just when those weeks were expiring; and about forty years before the destruction of the temple. Observe,

2. *These prophecies have been exactly fulfilled in Jesus Christ.* Witness his *two natures*, human and divine, Rom. ix. 5; hence he was David's Lord; and Immanuel; the Child born, and the Mighty God. The *time of his coming;*—he came when the sceptre was about to depart from the tribe of Judah: as a proof of which, just at the time of his birth a decree for taxing the land of Judea was passed by Augustus, the Roman emperor, Luke ii. 1, 2, 5. He came just exactly at the end of Daniel's seventy weeks, or four hundred and ninety years after the commandment or decree given to Ezra to rebuild Jerusalem. And he came while the second temple stood:

and cleansed it, and taught in it. His *various offices:*—he is our Prophet, John vi. 14, and viii. 12; our King, Luke i. 33; Acts v. 31; our Saviour, Matt. i. 21; 1 Tim. i. 15; our Shepherd, John x. 11, 27, 28; and our Judge, Acts xvii. 30, 31. And *the circumstances attending his coming.* Was the Messiah to work benevolent miracles? Christ wrought such, as here in the presence of John's disciples. Was the Messiah to be Modest in performing them? so was our Lord, Matt. xii. 16—21. Was the Messiah to teach the poor? so did Jesus, Luke iv. 18, 21. Was the Messiah to be rejected by the Jews? so was Jesus, John i. 11. As all these prophecies have been fulfilled in our Lord, so we observe,

3. *They have been fulfilled in no other.* This is evident from the appeal of Christ's friends, the advocates of Christianity, who challenge the world to produce any person besides our Lord, in whom these predictions have been accomplished. And from the concessions of Christ's enemies, the Jews; who can produce no person besides our Jesus, whom they reject, and still perversely look for another. Hence let us consider,

III. The conclusion we should draw from this accomplishment of prophecy in the person of our Lord. We should conclude,

1. *That our Jesus is certainly the true Messiah.* For infinite wisdom could not mistake in its prophetic descriptions; and infinite truth cannot mislead us, Deut. xxxii. 4.

2. *That we should look for no other Saviour.* To look for another would be *impious*, by discrediting God himself, 1 John v. 10; it would be *ungrateful*, by slighting the richest love, John iii. 16; it would be *unreasonable*, opposed to the clearest evidence, 2 Thess. iii. 2; it would be *unnecessary*, for Christ is all sufficient to save, Heb. vii. 25; it would be *vain*, for no other Saviour will come, Heb. x. 26; it must be *destructive*, Christ being our only remedy, Prov. xxix. 1.

3. *That we should see experimental proofs of Christ's divine authority.* The proofs arising from the fulfilment of prophecy are *rational* ones, and of no small importance; but those most satisfactory to us are experimental ones, resembling our Lord's miracles; including spiritual life, sight, strength, purity, health, and comfort. Seek these as of the first importance, Prov. iv. 7; Matt. vi. 33; seek them with confidence, for Christ is come for the purpose of bestowing these blessings on mankind, Isa. lx. 1, 2, 3; John iii. 17.

4. *That Christ's coming should engage Christians in the practice of holy duties.* As, compassion for lost sinners, Luke xix. 10; Phil. ii. 5; as evidence of this, pray and labor for their conversion, James v. 16, 19, 20; beneficence to the poor, 2 Cor. viii. 9; hope of perfect purity, 1 John iii. 8; and grateful adoration, Luke i. 68.

THE GLORY OF CHRIST.

Zech. ix. 17 —How great is his goodness, and how great is his beauty? (S. S.)

The glory of Christ is manifested throughout all the holy scriptures—

This is attested both by the apostles and by our Lord himself, Acts x. 43, Luke xxiv. 27, John v. 39.

In the New Testament he shines like the sun in an unclouded atmosphere—

In the Old, though generally veiled, he often bursts forth as from behind a cloud with astonishing beauty and splendor—

Such a view of him is exhibited in the chapter now before us*—

Nor could the Prophet himself forbear exclaiming with wonder and admiration, "How great is his goodness!" &c.

We cannot have our minds more delightfully occupied than in contemplating,

I. The goodness of our Lord.

In the context he is set forth as the God of providence and of grace—

And in order to behold his goodness we must view him in both respects,

1. As the God of providence.

As all things were created, so are they upheld and governed by him—

To him we owe the preservation of our corporeal and intellectual powers.

We are continually fed by his bounty, and protected by his arm—

The meanest creature in the universe has abundant reason to adore him—

His own people in particular may discern unnumbered instances of his goodness in his dispensations towards them—

His most afflictive as well as his more pleasing dispensations afford them much occasion for gratitude and thanksgiving, Ps. cxix. 75.

2. As a God of grace.

Jesus is the one fountain of spiritual blessings to his church, Eph. i. 22.

Neither prophets nor apostles had any grace but from him, John i. 16.

To him must we ascribe every good disposition that is in our hearts, Phil ii. 13, Heb. xii. 2.

What reason then have his faithful followers to bless his name! —

How thankful should they be that he called *them* by his grace!—

That he so distinguished them, not only from the fallen angels, but from multitudes of the human race!—

With what gratitude should they acknowledge his continued kindness!—

Though they have often turned back from him, he has not cast them off—

Yea rather, he has "healed their backslidings and loved them freely"—

Surely, every blessing they receive, and every victory they gain, should fill them with admiring thoughts of his goodness, 2 Cor. ii. 14.

Let every soul then comply with that injunction of the Psalmist, Psa cxlv. 7.

And, like him, repeat the wish, which a sense of his mercies must inspire, Ps. cvii. 8, 15, 21, 31.

If we have just conceptions of his goodness we shall be more able to behold,

II. His beauty.

The world behold "no beauty nor comeliness in" the face of Jesus—

But the saints of "old saw his glory as the glory of the only-begotten of the Father"—

This we also may see, if we survey him,

1. In this divine character,

"We cannot by searching find out the Almighty to perfection"—.

* After foretelling the preservation of the Jews amidst the destruction of surrounding nations, the prophet called their attention to Christ, as their lowly but triumphant king (ver. 9,) who should redeem them by his blood, (ver. 11,) be a strong hold to all who should turn unto him, (ver. 12,) and save then with an everlasting salvation, (ver. 16.)

Little do we know of the greatness of his *majesty*, or the thunder of his power, Job. xxvi. 14.

We cannot comprehend his unsearchable *wisdom*, his unspotted *holiness*, his inviolable *truth* and *faithfulness*—

We can scarcely form any idea of the inflexibility of his *justice*, the extent of his *mercy*, or the heights and depths of his *love*, Eph. iii. 19.

We know that Jesus is the brightness of his Father's glory, and the express image of his person, Heb. i. 3.

But when we attempt to delineate that image, we only "darken counsel by words without knowledge," Job. xxxviii. 2

His glory is more than the feeble language of mortality can express—

2. In his human character.

Here we look at him, as the Jews at Moses when his face was veiled—

And can cantemplate him more easily, because he shines with a less radiant lustre—

Doubtless while he lay in the manger the virtues of his mind beamed forth in his countenance—

Nor is it to be wondered at that the Jewish doctors were so filled with admiration at him while he was yet a child, Luke ii. 46, 47.

But principally must we view him during the course of his ministry—

What marvellous *compassion* did he manifest to the souls and bodies of *men!*—

Not one applied to him for bodily or spiritual health without obtaining his request—

And when many were hardened in their sins he wept over them, Luke xix. 41.

Yea, he even pleaded the cause of those who mocked and reviled him on the cross, Luke xxiii. 34.

His *zeal for God* was ardent and unremitted—

It was "his meat and drink to do the will of his heavenly Father"—

Nor could any thing for one moment divert or deter him from the prosecution of his work—

His *meekness*, *patience*, *fortitude* were altogether invincible—

Whatever was amiable and excellent in man abounded in him, Ps. xlv. 2.

He was not merely virtuous, but virtue itself incarnate—

Nor, though continually tried in the hottest furnace, was there found in him the smallest imperfection or alloy, John xiv. 30.

3. In his mediatorial character.

With what readiness did he become a surety for sinful man, Ps. xl. 7, 8.

What astonishing condescension did he manifest in uniting himself to our nature!—

How cheerfully did he go forth to meet the sufferings that were appointed for him—

In the garden and on the cross, when to the eye of sense "his visage was marred more than any man's," his beauty was most conspicuous to the eye of faith—

His obedience unto death was the fruit of his love, and the price of our redemption—

How beautiful is he *now* in the eyes of those who behold his glory!—

And how will he "be admired and glorified by all" in the last day!—

Satan must have blinded us indeed if we be yet insensible to his charms, 2 Cor. iv. 4.

If we be true believers, he cannot but be precious to our souls, 1 Pet. ii. 7

APPLICATION.

1. To those who have never yet beheld the gooodness and beauty of the Lord:—

We speak not *now* to those who seek his face, and long to enjoy him—

For though their sorrow endure for a night, joy will come to them in the morning—

But they, who pant not after him, are miserably ignorant of his excellency—

Their views of Christ are different from those of the most competent judges*—

And different from what they will shortly be in the eternal world—

Let such persons diligently consider the Saviour's character—

And cry to God for that Spirit whose office it is to reveal Christ unto us—

Then shall they both see the King in his beauty, and be changed into his image, Isa. xxxiii. 17, 2 Cor. iii. 18.

2. To those whose eyes have been opened to behold him,

Let your meditations of him be more sweet and frequent—

However much you know of him, there are unsearchable depths unfathomed—

Let your determination therefore accord with that of David, Ps. xxvii. 4.

View him as appointing your trials, and dispensing your mercies—

Consider him as the fountain from whence you are to have supplies of grace—

Look to him as the example which you are continually to follow—

Above all, rely on him as expiating your guilt, and interceding for you—

Thus will you glory in him as your "friend and your beloved"—

And at last will see him as he is and be like him forever.

CHRIST THE LIGHT OF THE WORLD.

John xii. 46.—I am come a light unto the world, that whosoever believeth on me should not abide in darkness. (Sk.)

THERE is no subject more interesting to the Christian, than the character of Jesus Christ. He is not only infinitely glorious in his person, but exceedingly precious to his believing people. He sustains every character, and fills every office, that can possibly endear him unto them, and render him the supreme object of their attachment and delight. In him, therefore, they glory, and count all things but loss for the excellency of his knowledge. Through him they receive every blessing, and trust in his name for complete and eternal salvation. He reigns in their hearts by his grace, as their sovereign; and is the High Priest of their profession, by whom they draw near to God, and are cleansed from all unrighteousness. He is also their *infallible* teacher, imparting heavenly instruction to their minds, and delivering them from the fatal delusions of sin and Satan. This is the *specific*

*To the Father he is "chosen and precious," 1 Pet. ii. 4; to the angels, the subject of their praise, Rev. v. 11, 12; to saints of old, an object of great desire, Hag. ii. 7, John viii. 56; to all pious men at this time, their supreme good, Phil. iii. 7, 8.

character he assumes in the text, in which he declares to the Jews, "I am come a light into the world," &c. In these words the Saviour distinctly represents,

I. The design of his mission. "I am come a light," &c. He is *perfect* and *essential light* in his own essence; and like the sun of nature, he sheds his enlightening beams to disperse the condensed darkness that envelopes mankind. He is the *source* and *medium* of all divine knowledge, and came a "light into the world" by his office—by his gospel—and by his Spirit.

1. *By his office.* He had long been announced in the vision of prophecy, as a divine prophet, "the sun of righteousness," and "a light to lighten the Gentiles," &c. And when he assumed human nature, he was recognised as a "teacher come from God;" and "never man spake like this man," was the encomium bestowed on his teaching. He taught the most *sublime* and *important* doctrines: explained the law and the prophets; more clearly revealed the perfections and will of God—the redemption of the world—the way of salvation—the certainty of a future state, &c., John i. 18, iii. 16; Mark i. 15; Matt. vii. 13, 14; verse 28, 29. Such was the *prophetic office* and work of Christ, when he came "to give light to them that sat in darkness and in the shadow of death."

2. *By his gospel.* It is therefore emphatically called, "*the light* of the glorious gospel of Christ." The Mosaic dispensation was *comparatively* dark and obscure; it was only the general *outline* and *shadow* of the more glorious revelation of "grace and truth, by Jesus Christ." *Now*, "life and immortality are" *fully* "brought to light by the *Gospel*." It clearly unfolds the *whole system* of Divine truth, in its connection with the salvation of mankind; it discovers the nature, blessings, and privileges of the covenant of grace; and infallibly teaches the only way to happiness and heaven, 1 Cor. i. 21; Rom. i. 16. Wherever, therefore, the Gospel is disseminated, either in its *written* or *ministerial revelation*, it is graciously designed to "turn men from darkness to light, and make them wise unto salvation."

3. *By his Spirit.* A *measure* of the Holy Ghost has been given to mankind in all ages, Gen. vi. 3; Job xxxii. 8. But the most *enlarged diffusion* of his influence, is the distinguishing glory and promise of the Christian dispensation. When Jesus therefore was "glorified," he, according to his word, poured out of his Spirit more abundantly "on all flesh," to convince the world of sin, and guide his people into all truth, John vii. 39. As a Spirit of "wisdom and understanding," he dissipates darkness and error, and communicates all spiritual knowledge and holiness to them that believe, 1 Cor. ii. 10—15; 2 Cor. iii. 18. Thus Christ is the *true light of the moral world*, which, he assures us in the text, was *one important design* of his manifestation in the flesh. We shall now consider,

II. The principle of salvation. "That whosoever believeth on me." It must be acknowledged that faith, as an *abstract principle*, is difficult to define; but when it is considered in connection with its *object* and *effects*, it is comparatively easy to comprehend, and hence, it is *thus* represented throughout the Scriptures. In the passage before us,

1. *The object of faith is specified.* "Whosoever believeth on *me*." Christ is not the *exclusive*, but the *concentrating object* of Christian faith. We must believe in the triune God, and all revealed truth. But saving faith *principally* regards Jesus Christ as the Redeemer of the world, and the Saviour of sinners. We should believe in the divinity of his person—the au-

thority of his mission—the efficacy of his sacrifice—the dignity of his offices—and the sufficiency of his grace, &c.

2. *The nature of faith is implied.* "Whosoever *believeth*," &c. The personal exercise of faith is a *complex act* of the mind, by which we *fully credit* the record which God has given of his Son—*cordially approve* the appointed method of salvation—and *actually embrace* Jesus Christ as our all-sufficient Saviour. The different acts and operations of faith are *metaphorically* represented by *looking* and *coming to*, *receiving from*, and *trusting in* Christ, for every promised blessing of the gospel, &c., Isa. xlv. 22; Matt. xi. 28; John i. 12; Eph. i. 12, 13.

3. *The necessity of faith is suggested.* It is here made the condition of participating an interest in Christ. He *only* who believes in him as the light of the world, shall be delivered from darkness. He that *believeth not* is condemned already, and abides in the gross darkness of sin and death. But living faith receives all the personal benefits of redemption, and is the *only instrument* by which we can possibly obtain salvation and eternal life, Mark xvi. 16; John iii. 36. As closely connected with this principle, we may regard,

III. The privilege of believers. "They *shall not abide in darkness.*" The christian's privileges are exceeding great and glorious. That which is mentioned in the text is highly desirable, and is graciously promised to all the subjects of saving faith.

1. *They shall not abide in mental darkness.* They are naturally "alienated from the life of God through the *ignorance* that is in them." But by divine grace the eyes of their understanding are enlightened, and they receive correct and comprehensive views of the whole science of godliness. Being made "light in the Lord," they have new conceptions of every subject. Their former darkness is passed away, and "the light of the knowledge of the glory of God shines into their hearts through Jesus Christ," Isa. lx. 1; 1 Peter ii. 9.

2. *They shall not abide in spiritual darkness.* Sin and misery are justly represented by a state of *darkness*, Col. i. 13. But the Saviour delivers his people from guilt and condemnation, purifies their hearts, and fills them with joy and peace through believing, Eph. iv. 14. As God is light, they receive the impress of his moral image, which is "righteousness and true holiness." The light of grace both *illuminates* the mind, and *sanctifies* the soul, Psalm xcvii. 11.

3. *They shall not abide in practical darkness.* They shall no longer wander in the forbidden paths of sin and error, under the galling yoke of the prince of darkness. Being saved from the broad road of destruction, "they walk in the light as God is in the light," and their path shineth more and more unto the perfect day of ineffable bliss, ch. viii. 12; Col. i. 12. Let us then adore the Saviour's character, believe in his holy name, and "walk as children of light."

THE BENEVOLENT CONDUCT OF JESUS.

Acts x. 38.—Who went about doing good. (Sk.)

The Lord Jesus Christ, our adorable Saviour, had glory with the Father before the world was; but he laid aside that glory, and came into our world on an errand of love, John xvii. 5. But how did he spend his time on earth? Very little is known of his early life. The whole of what is recorded on that subject may be summed up in a few particulars; he was strong in spirit; he was filled with wisdom; the grace of God was upon him; when he was twelve years old, he sat in the temple with the Jewish doctors, and asked questions which astonished all who heard him; he was obedient to his parents; and he grew in wisdom and stature, and in favor with God and man, Luke ii. 40—52. But after he entered on his public ministry, to which he had been anointed by the Holy Ghost, he went about doing good, Matt. iii. 16, 17. Let us consider his conduct in the walks of life,—and endeavor to imitate him.

I. The conduct of Jesus. He "went about doing good."

1. Jesus did good to the *bodies* of men. He opened the eyes of the blind; he gave hearing to the deaf; and he raised the dead, Matt. xi. 5. Those miracles were truly benevolent; they promoted human comfort; and, perhaps, may be considered as emblems of those spiritual blessings which are bestowed on all true believers: whether they are designed to be viewed in this light or not, certain it is, that they point out the saving power of our glorious Redeemer.

2. He did good to the *souls* of men. The ignorant were instructed by him, in the essential doctrines and duties of religion, Matt. v. 1, 2; Luke xix. 47; John viii. 2. He reproved the guilty and warned the careless, that they might amend their ways and turn to God by true repentance, Matt. xxiii. 13—31. He preached good tidings unto the meek; he bound up the broken hearted; he proclaimed liberty to the captives; and the opening of the prison to them who were bound, Isa. lxi. 1. He strengthened the weak and wavering, and comforted mourning penitents, Matt. v. 4, xi. 28.

3. Our Lord *went about* doing good. He was an itinerant preacher. When persons in want applied to him for special blessings, he granted their requests, and sent them away rejoicing. But he did not wait for such applications. He went forth, with the finest feelings of pure benevolence and love, to seek and to save that which was lost, Luke xix. 10. And to accomplish his merciful designs, he frequently visited large and populous places, and places of public resort.

4. The motives of our Lord, in doing good, were *pure and perfect*. He was moved by the transcendent goodness of his nature to acts of kindness; the pressing wants and painful sufferings of men excited his pity and tender compassion; and all his works were directed to the glory of his Father, John xiii. 4. How widely different are the motives of many, in the exercise of charity, from those of our blessed Saviour! they seek the praise of men; he sought the honor of God: and they aim at their own glory; but he at his creatures good: they are partial to a few; but he was good to all.

5. Jesus *persevered* in doing good. It was his constant employment, and he was never weary of it. Even when he hung upon the cross, he prayed for his murderers, and saved the penitent thief, Luke xxiii. 34—43. And his death on the accursed tree, where he suffered as a sacrifice for sin, was an act of sublime and unparalleled love.

6. In all the works, and in all the ways of our Saviour, *his lovely temper and amiable conduct shone with resplendent glory*. How unlike the renowned conquerors and tyrants of the world, whose glory has been acquired by blood and slaughter! Nothing exalts the human character more than acts of disinterested benevolence; but Jesus was more than human. He was God and man; and yet it is the temper of the man Christ Jesus which we now contemplate.

II. We should endeavor to imitate the conduct of Jesus.

1. *That we may do so, let us study the character and conduct of our great Exemplar*. To this end we should carefully read his public and private discourses, examine his temper, and weigh his conduct. There are three infallible sources of information on this subject: the ancient prophecies; the holy gospels; and the apostolical epistles. The prophets foretold his character; the evangelists have recorded it with artless simplicity; and the apostles, who knew him well, have confirmed the whole. By this course of study, we shall gain a clear, correct, and complete knowledge of the temper and conduct of our Lord.

2. *But those who copy after his blessed example, must have the mind which was in him*, Phil. ii. 5. Without this, there can be no successful imitation of his conduct; for the source of outward action is in the inner man. To have his mind, we must be born again of the Spirit of God, John iii. 3. All who are born from above. receive those principles of grace, which produce every thing that is excellent in the conduct of man. They are new creatures in Christ Jesus, and grace reigns in their hearts: they are influenced in all things by real goodness; by soft pity and tender compassion to the wretched; and by an ardent desire to promote the honor and glory of God.

3. *Having acquired the mind of Jesus, let us endeavor to imitate his conduct*. We cannot imitate his miracles; the attempt would be presumption; but we should endeavor to copy his benevolent actions. Particularly, let us go about, as far as opportunity may serve, to seek the sons and daughters of affliction; when we find them in their wretched abodes, let us pity them; and there let our pity be shown in acts of kindness. Feed the hungry; clothe the naked; instruct the ignorant; comfort the mourners; visit the sick, the prisoner, the fatherless, and the widow. Jesus will reward these works as if they were done to himself, Matt. xxv. 40.

4. *Let us proceed in these works of love, as the Lord may enable us*. More than this is not required; and less than this will not be accepted. The means of some are limited; but they must do what they can. Others abound in means: let these proceed on a liberal plan. It is recorded of the woman who anointed the head of Jesus, "She hath done what she could," Mark xiv. 8. No person will perish who does what he can. It was the opinion of pious Matthew Henry, that 'there is not a damned sinner in hell, but if he had done well, as he might have done, had been a glorified saint in heaven.' Note on Gen. iv. 7.

5. *This conduct will please the Lord, who is good to all, and whose tender mercies are over all his works*, Psa. cxlv. 9. He blesses us that we may be a blessing, Gen. xii. 2. This conduct accords with the spirit of the gospel, which breathes pure benevolence, and introduces "peace on earth, and good will towards men," Luke ii. 14. It resembles the employment of angels, who come down from heaven, on errands of love to the heirs of salvation, Heb. i. 14. And has been practised by the greatest and best of men in all ages.

1. In the world, and in the visible church, we have many bad examples; but we must not follow a multitude to do evil, Exod. xxiii. 2.

2. There are a few in the church who may be followed in some things; but whatever their excellencies are, we cannot safely follow them in all their ways.

3. But we have a perfect example in the conduct of our Saviour; and we are bound by the most sacred ties to walk in his steps, 1 Pet. ii. 21. May the Lord enable us to do so, for his name and mercies' sake!

THE COMPASSION OF CHRIST TOWARDS THE WEAK.

Matt. xii. 18—21.—Behold, my servant whom I have chosen; my beloved in whom my soul is well pleased: I will put my Spirit upon him, and he shall shew judgment to the Gentiles. He shall not strive nor cry; neither shall any man hear his voice in the streets. A bruised reed shall he not break, and smoking flax shall he not quench, till he send forth judgment unto victory. And in him shall the Gentiles trust. (S. S.)

One might gather almost as complete a character of Christ from the prophecies as from the gospels themselves—

Not only the great incidents relating to his life and death were foretold, but his spirit and conduct were most minutely delineated—

He had just withdrawn himself from the Pharisees who sought to destroy him—

And had strongly enjoined his attendants not to make known his miracles—

This conduct appeared strange to those, who were expecting him to erect a temporal kingdom—

But the Evangelist declares that these very things had been made the subject of prophecy many hundred years before—

The passage quoted by him from Isaiah is recorded, not with literal exactness, but according to its true import—It declares,

I. The commission given to Christ.

Christ was the Father's ambassador to our ruined world.

However, in his divine nature, Christ was equal to the Father, yet, in his mediatorial capacity, he was the Father's servant—

The office assigned him was to shew judgment, that is, the way of righteousness and salvation both to Jews and Gentiles—

And for this he was qualified by an immeasurable communication of the Spirit to him, John iii. 34, Isa. xi. 2, 3.

In this view the Father exceedingly delighted in him.

The Father doubtless regarded him as his beloved *for his own sake*—

But was peculiarly pleased with him as having undertaken the work of man's redemption—

In him he saw, as it were, all his own perfections glorified, and the thrones of apostate angels occupied by sinners of the human race—

Hence in triumphant exultation he declares his acquiesence in him, and calls every human being to "behold" him—

The prophet further specifies,

II. The manner in which he should execute it.

He was to accomplish his work,

1. Silently.

There was to be nothing in him ostentatious, contentious, or clamorous—

Together with firmness and fidelity, he exercised continued gentleness and meekness*—

Would to God that many who bear a similar commission would learn of him to execute it in a similar way!—

2. Tenderly.

The terms here used seem to be proverbial—

The former metaphor is taken from reeds, which were used as musical instruments by shepherds, and which, when bruised, could no longer emit any melodious sound—

The smoking flax alludes to the wick of a lamp which, when the flame is extinct, produces an offensive smell—

Both these metaphors fitly represent the state of a soul bruised under a sense of sin, and lamenting that its grace is nearly extinguished while whole clouds of corruption are arising from it—

But Jesus, instead of despising its low estate, will rathar fan the spark into a flame, and cause the worthless reed to send forth melody that shall delight the ears of God himself—

3. Successfully.

However gentle his exertions, he shall never ultimately fail—

As his forbearance towards his enemies gave them a momentary appearance of triumph, so he sometimes delays his aid even to his most favored people—

But he will at last prevail, and make his grace victorious in their souls—

To this description of the Saviour the prophet naturally subjoins,

III. Our duty towards him.

Blessed be God, our duty is our highest privilege—

We are commanded to trust in him,

1. For instruction.

Jesus is both qualified and commissioned to enlighten the Gentiles, Luke i. 78, 79, and ii. 32.

Nor are there any so weak and ignorant but that he can make them wise unto salvation, Matt. xi. 25.

Let us then, "not lean to our own understanding," but seek to be "taught of him," Eph. iv. 20, 21.

2. For acceptance.

It is not merely in his individual capacity, but as the head of the elect world, that he is so pleasing to his heavenly Father—

We therefore, if we believe on him, may be certain of acceptance through him, Eph. i. 6, 10.

Yea, God will not behold a spot in the most polluted soul, if it be only washed in his blood, and clothed in his righteousness, Eph. v. 27, Jude 24.

3. For victory.

None have need to despond on account of their own weakness and corruptions—

The "grace of Christ is sufficient," and shall prove so to all who trust in him—

"Wherever he has begun the good work he will carry it on unto the end," Phil. i. 6, Rom. viii. 37.

Application.

* His conduct, as related in the context, strongly illustrates this

1. The text is addressed to *all the sinners of the Gentiles.*
How gracious is God in thus inviting sinners to "behold" his Son —
And *how powerful the recommendation that is thus enforced by the example of God himself!*—
But can any thing be a stronger reproof to those, who, instead of choosing Christ, and being well pleased with him, have uniformly despised and rejected him?—
Say then, ye ungrateful world, whom will ye condemn; yourselves, or God?—
Still however, the invitation is addressed to you, "Behold my Son"—
O that ye may behold him now to your joy, and not hereafter to your confusion!—
2. But the words are more eminently suited to *the weak and desponding.*
More consolatory declarations could not have been desired by man, or given by God—
The lowest possible state of grace is here described in most appropriate terms—
And an assurance given that it shall prove victorious in the issue—
Let the desponding soul then learn to "trust" in Jesus—
And even in the midst of conflicts sing, "Thanks be to God, who giveth us the victory through our Lord Jesus Christ."

CHRIST AND THE BRAZEN SERPENT COMPARED.

John iii. 14.—As Moses lifted up the serpent in the wilderness, even so must the Son of Man be lifted up. (P.)

The great object of revelation. is to display the work and character of Christ. He is exhibited by symbolical representations, in all the characters, places, sacrifices, and events, described in the Old Testament.

This is particularly the case, in reference to the brazen serpent, the lifting up of which, in a remarkable manner typified the death of the Son of God.

We now propose to point out the resemblance between the type and the anti-type.

I. They correspond with each other, in THE OCCASION OF THEIR INSTITUTION. The Israelites in the wilderness, murmured for want of water, and loathed the manna which came down from heaven.

For this, God sent fiery serpents among them, and many of the people died.

Nor was there any remedy for those who had been wounded—they, therefore cried unto GOD, and intreated Moses to intercede for them, and in answer to their prayer, the serpent was ordered to be erected. We are wounded by the more deadly sting of sin, its poison has pervaded all our faculties, and is bringing a speedy and everlasting destruction on our souls; but GOD in his own mercy, appointed his Son to suffer in our stead.

II. There is an agreement between them in THEIR QUALITIES. 1. The serpent was made of brass. This is an inferior metal, and of little value, and in this respect, it represented the human nature of Christ, for he was as a root from the dry ground, without form or comeliness. 2. There was only one brazen serpent for the whole of the Jewish camp; the camp was no doubt large, and extended for many miles, yet this sufficed for all; there is only one mediator between God and man, Jesus Christ the righteous; there is only one way to the Father, and that is by him; there is only one remedy for sin, and that is the precious blood of Jesus. 3. This serpent was appointed by God: if Moses had devised it himself, the wounded Israelites would have looked in vain for a cure.

Christ has not taken the office of a Saviour upon himself without authority; he has been appointed by the father, and qualified for it, by the outpouring of the Holy Spirit. All attempts therefore to look to any thing short of Christ, instead of healing our wounds, will aggravate our disorder. 4. When the brazen serpent was prepared, it was publicly lifted up. Moses would have acted most criminally, if he had kept it within his own tent: by so doing, the death of all the Israelites might have been laid to his charge.

The ministers of the gospel are to exhibit Christ to a sick and dying world, and "*woe, woe* be to them," if they are not "instant in season and out of season," in pointing sinners to the "lamb of God that taketh away the sins of the world," and the blood of those they warn not. will be upon their heads. It is fully the design of Christ, and the will of the Father, that even the ends of the earth, should look to him and be saved.

III. There is a resemblance in the MANNER IN WHICH BENEFIT IS DERIVED, both from the type, and the anti-type. 1. The Israelites were commanded *to look to it*. It was not sufficient that they heard about this remedy, that they understood its nature, or that they sent others to look to it; they were required to have a personal view of it, or they died miserably in the wilderness.

Religion with us is a *personal* thing; if we do not feel the wounds of sin, and if we have not a personal view of Christ as our Saviour, all the external means which we possess will be of no avail. 2. The Israelites were required to look to the brazen serpent *instantly;* procrastination would have been immediately fatal in their case, and not less fatal will it be to us, if we delay looking to the adorable Jesus. "Now is the accepted time, now is the day of salvation." 3. They were required to look *steadily* and *constantly* upon the serpent. A mere glance would not suffice, their disease was too deeply imbedded to be removed in an instant—our eyes should always be directed to calvary, and while looking upon him, who is hanging upon the accursed tree, we may expect, that the power of sin will be destroyed within us, and that our souls will be purified by that healing power which proceeds from the cross. 4. If any in the Jewish camp disbelieved in the efficacy of the remedy provided, alas, there was no other means to procure a restoration to health; and there is reason to suppose that many did refuse to participate in this remedy, for it is added, "and many of the people died." So it is at the present day; there is *balm in Gilead, and a physician there;* but they will not come to him, that they may have life.

IV. There is a further agreement in THE EFFECTS THEY PRODUCE. 1. The brazen serpent effected a complete cure in every stage of disease; it mattered not whether they were just bitten, whether they were suffering great pain from the power of the disorder, or whether they were in the agonies of death; if they looked to the brazen serpent they lived.

All those who look to Christ shall be saved, notwithstanding the vileness of their moral characters, or the number of years they have lived in sin. The same blood which cleansed a cruel Manassah, a persecuting Saul, and a dying thief, is quite sufficient to remove every stain from our souls. 2. The number of those who were healed by looking to the brazen serpent was great; the princes and the people, children and their parents, came crowding to that part of the camp, where this wonderful remedy was found.

Neither is the number *small* who look to Christ; they already exceed the number of the stars; and the day will arrive, when those who are "ready to perish shall come from Assyria, and the outcasts from the land of Egypt, and shall worship the Lord in his holy mount at Jerusalem." 3. Moreover, the lifting up of the brazen serpent, in the end recovered the whole of the camp, so that a diseased person was not found; and by this circumstance, we are reminded of that period, when all nations, and kindreds, and tongues, and people, shall bow down and worship at the feet of the Messiah. From this subject learn, 1. How plain and simple is the way of salvation;—we simply look by faith to a crucified Saviour, and are healed. 2. How injurious to our welfare, is unbelief;—if we despise this ordinance of God, we perish.

CHRIST THE AUTHOR OF OUR SANCTIFICATION.

Rom. viii. 3, 4.—What the law could not do, in that it was weak through the flesh, God, sending his own Son in the likeness of sinful flesh, and for sin, condemned sin in the flesh; that the righteousness of the law might be fulfilled in us, who walk not after the flesh, but after the Spirit. (H. H.)

The necessity of holiness is allowed by all: the means of attaining it are known by few. Christ is regarded as the meritorious cause of our justification before God; but he is not sufficiently viewed as the instrumental cause of our deliverance from sin. He is represented in the scriptures as "our sanctification," no less than "our wisdom and our righteousness:" 1 Cor. i. 30, and we should do well to direct our attention to him more in that view. In the preceding context he is spoken of as delivering his peop from condemnation, and many judicious commentators understand the text as referring to the same point: yet, on the whole, it appears more agreeable both to the words of the text, and to the scope of the passage, to understand it in reference to the work of sanctification.* St. Paul had just said that "the law of the Spirit of life in Christ Jesus," that is the gospel, "had made him free from the law of sin, as well as of death." He then adds, that on account of the insufficiency of the law to condemn and destroy sin, God had sent his own Son to effect it; and that through his incarnation and death its power should be effectually broken.

From this view of the text, we are led to consider,

I. The end and design of Christ's Mission.

God's desire and purpose was to restore his people to true holiness—

Sin was the object of his utter abhorrence: it had marred the whole creation: it had entered into heaven itself, and defiled the mansions of the Most High: it had desolated the earth also, and all that dwelt upon it. To remedy the miseries introduced by it, and to root it out from his people's hearts, was a design worthy of the Deity; since, if once they could be brought to "fulfill the righteousness of the law," by walking, in their habitual course

* See Doddridge on the place.

of life, no longer after the flesh, but after the Spirit, eternal honor would accrue to him, and everlasting happiness to them.

The law was not sufficient to effect this—

The law was indeed perfectly sufficient to direct man, while he remained in innocence; and it was well adapted to reclaim him when he had fallen; because it denounced the wrath of God against every transgression of its precepts, and set forth a perfect rule of duty. But "it was weak through the flesh:" man was deaf, and could not hear its threatenings; dead, and could not execute its commands. Hence, as to any practical effects, it spake in vain.

God therefore, in order that his purpose might not fail, sent his only dear Son—

He sent his co-equal, co-eternal Son, "in the likeness of sinful flesh," and to be a sacrifice "for sin;"* that through his obedience unto death, he might "deliver those who had been, and must for ever have continued, subject to bondage." How this expedient was to succeed, will come under our consideration presently; we therefore only observe at present, that it was a plan which nothing but infinite wisdom could have devised. It could no have entered into the mind of any finite Being, to subject God's only dear Son to such humiliation; to make him a partaker of our nature, with all its sinless infirmities; to substitute him in our place, and, by his vicarious sacrifice, to restore us to the image and favor of God; this does, and must for ever, surpass all finite comprehension.

But though we cannot fathom all the depths of this mystery, we may shew,

II. In what way it is effectual for the end proposed.

We speak not of the way in which the death of Christ obtains our justification, but of the way in which it is instrumental to our sanctification. In reference to this, we say,

1. It displays the evil and malignity of sin—

The evil of sin had been seen in a measure by the miseries which it had introduced, and by the punishment denounced against it in the eternal world. But in what light did it appear, when nothing less than the incarnation and death of Christ was able to expiate its guilt or destroy its power! Let any person behold the agonies of Christ in the garden, or his dereliction and death upon the cross, and then go and think lightly of sin if he can. Surely if men were more habituated to look at sin in this view, they would be filled with indignation against it, and seek incessantly its utter destruction.

2. It obtains for us power to subdue sin—

Though man is in himself so weak that he cannot, of himself, even think a good thought, yet through the influence of the Holy Spirit he can "fulfil the righteousness of the law," not perfectly indeed, but so as to walk altogether in newness of life.† Now, by the death of Christ the promise of the Spirit is obtained for us; and all who seek his gracious influences, shall obtain them. Thus the axe is laid to the root of sin. "The weak is enabled to say, I am strong:" and he, who just before was in bondage to his lusts, now casts off the yoke, and "runs the way of God's commandments with an enlarged heart."

* This is the meaning of περὶ ἁμαρτίας. See Heb. x. 6, and 2 Cor. v. 21.

† There is a two-fold fulfilling of the law mentioned in the Scriptures; the one *legal*, the ther evangelical. Compare Matt. v. 17, with Rom. xiii. 8, and Gal. v. 14.

3. It suggests motives sufficient to call forth our utmost exertions—

The hope of heaven and the fear of hell are certainly very powerful motives; yet, of themselves, they never operate with sufficient force to produce a willing and unreserved obedience. While the mind is wrought upon by *merely* selfish principles, it will always grudge the price which it pays for future happiness. But let the soul be warmed with the love of Christ, and it will no longer measure out obedience with a parsimonious hand: it will be anxious to display its gratitude by every effort within its reach. "The love of Christ will constrain it" to put forth all its powers; to "crucify the flesh with its affections and lusts," and to "perfect holiness in the fear of God."

INFER,

1. How vain is it to expect salvation while we live in sin!

If we could have been saved *in* our sins, can it be conceived that God would ever have sent his own Son into the world to deliver us from them; or that, having sent his Son to accomplish this end, he would himself defeat it, by saving us in our iniquities? Let careless sinners well consider this; and let the professors of religion too, especially those in whom sin of any kind lives and reigns, lay it to heart: for if sin be not "condemned in our flesh," our bodies, and souls too, shall be condemned for ever.

2. How foolish is it to attack sin in our own strength!

A bowl, with whatever force it be sent, and however long it may proceed in a right direction, will follow at last the inclination of its bias, and deviate from the line in which it was first impelled. Thus it will be with us under the influence of legal principles: we shall certainly decline from the path of duty, when our corrupt propensities begin to exert their force. Our resolutions can never hold out against them. We must have a new bias; "a new heart must be given us, and a new spirit be put within us," if we would persevere unto the end. Let us not then expect to prevail by legal considerations, or legal endeavors. Let us indeed condemn sin in the purpose of our minds, and sentence it to death: but let us look to Christ for strength, and maintain the conflict in dependence on his power and grace. Then, though unable to do any thing of ourselves, we shall be enabled to "do all things."

3. How are we indebted to God for sending his only Son into the world!

If Christ had never come, we had remained for ever the bond-slaves of sin and Satan. We had still continued, like the fallen angels, without either inclination or ability to renew ourselves: whereas, through him, many of us can say, that we are "made free from the law of sin and death." Let us then trace our deliverance to its proper source; to the Father's love, the Saviour's merit, and the Spirit's influence. And let us with unfeigned gratitude adore that God, who "sent his Son to bless us, in turning away every one of us from our iniquities." Acts iii. 26.

UNION WITH CHRIST.

Eph v. 30 —We are members of his body, of his flesh, and of his bones. (H. H.)

That the eternal Son of God assumed our nature, and lived and died for the salvation of men, is doubtless the fundamental truth on which we are to build our hopes. But we shall have a very partial view of that truth, if we consider it merely in reference to our acceptance with God. The apostles state it as the strongest of all motives to obedience, and as the pattern which, as far as circumstances will admit of it, we are bound to imitate. To go no further than the context; St. Paul is stating the duties of husbands and wives: and, having observed that wives are to be as obedient to their husbands, in all lawful things, as the church is to Christ, he shews, that husbands are not, however, at liberty to act the tyrant; but that they should at all times be influenced by love, and consult the good and happiness of their wives, as much as Christ himself does of the church, to whom he stands in a similar relation. Ver. 22—30.

The words before us are, in this view, deserving of the deepest attention; since they not only unfold a most mysterious and important truth, but tend in the highest degree to meliorate our tempers, and to diffuse universal happiness. Let us consider then,

I. The union which subsists between Christ and his Church—

There is a *personal* union which Christ has with our nature, by means of his incarnation, John i. 14, and which was necessary for the executing of the great work which he had undertaken. Heb. ii. 11, 14, 16. But in this the whole human race participate, without any distinction. The union which Christ has with the church is distinct from that, and is,

1. Legal—

There is, among men, an union between a debtor and his surety; insomuch, that if a debt be not discharged, the surety is as much answerable for it as if he had contracted it himself: and if, on the contrary, it be discharged by the surety, the creditor has no further claim on him that contracted it. Thus it is with respect to Christ and his church. He is the surety of the new covenant: Heb. vii. 22; having undertaken for us, he was charged with our debt; "it was exacted of him, and he was made answerable." Isa. liii. 7. Bp. Lowth's version. Having paid the debt, his payment is put to our account; "By his obedience we are made righteous." Rom. v. 19. In a word, "He who knew no sin, was made sin for us, that we (who had no righteousness) might be made the righteousness of God in him." 2 Cor. v. 21.

2. Spiritual—

Very much is spoken in scripture respecting the spiritual union which subsists between Christ and his people. To mark that they stand by him alone, it is compared to a foundation and the superstructure. Eph. ii. 20—22. To shew that he is the one source of vital influence to them all, it is illustrated by a root and the branches. John xv. 5. To intimate that one spirit pervades both him and them, 1 Cor. vi. 17, it is set forth under the image of a body; he being the Head, and they the members. Eph. iv. 15, 16. To convey some idea of the tender endearments with which it is accompanied, it is shadowed forth by a marriage union. This is the representation given in the text. He is our husband; Isa. liv. 5; and we are his bride: Rev. xxi. 9; and, as Adam said of Eve when she was brought to him, "She is flesh of my flesh, and bone of my bones," Gen. ii. 23, so may we say respecting the Lord Jesus Christ, "We are members of his body, of his flesh, and of his bones."

Whatever beauty there is in all the other figures, methinks there is a peculiar propriety in that which is now under our consideration, because it marks that volition, yea, and those means also whereby the union is effected. The Lord Jesus Christ displays before our eyes his excellency and glory, his suitableness and sufficiency; and, by the constraining influence of his love inclines us to leave all that has hitherto been esteemed by us, in order to connect ourselves with him, and enjoy his presence. Ps. xlv. 10, 11. Mark x. 29, 30. We accept that gracious proposal, "Thou shalt not be for another man; so will I also be for thee:" Hos. iii. 3; and being thus engaged by a solemn covenant, we surrender up ourselves to him, whether it be for better or for worse in this world, determining through grace to "be faithful unto him, even until death."

We prosecute the idea of a marriage union no further at present, because it will be more fully opened, while we shew,

II. The blessings resulting from it—

It is needless to expatiate upon the comforts and benefits of that relation among men: but we cannot be too minute in specifying the blessings that result from an union with Christ. The chief of them will come under our review, while we observe, that,

1. He has communion with us in all our trials—

One who understands the duties of a husband, and labors faithfully to discharge them, is ever ready to sympathize with his partner in her afflictions of whatever kind, and solicitous to the utmost to relieve them. What is done to her, whether it be good or evil, he considers it as done to himself. Thus it is with our blessed Lord. Are we tempted?— — —a consciousness of his relation to us calls forth his sympathy, and engages his utmost exertions on our behalf, Heb. ii. 17, 18, and iv. 15,— — —Are we persecuted? He feels in his inmost soul the dagger that pierces us, Zech. ii. 8, Acts ix. 4, — — —Do we labor under distresses of any kind? "In all our afflictions he is afflicted;" Isa. lxiii. 9; and every attempt made to mitigate our trouble, he accepts, as if he himself were personally relieved— — —Matt. xxv 35—40.

2. We have communion with him in all his benefits—

A woman, from whatever rank she be taken, is no sooner united in the marriage-bond, than she is exalted to a participation of all the honors and possessions of her husband. Thus it is with the church when united unto Christ. Is he possessed of a perfect righteousness, commensurate with the highest demands of law and justice? They who are joined to him by faith, are partakers of it all, and may boldly call him, "The Lord our Righteousness." Jer. xxiii. 6. However sinful they may have been in former times, "in him shall they be justified, and in him may they glory"— — —Isai. xlv. 24, 25. Has he within himself an inexhaustible fountain of grace? Col. i. 19. They may receive it out of his fulness: John i. 16; and having had a measure of it communicated to them, they may go to him for more: Jam. iv. 6; yea, whatever supplies they may need, they shall have sufficient for them; 2 Cor. xii. 9; sufficient to mortify every sin, Rom. vi. 14, to fulfil every duty, Phil. iv. 13, to triumph over every enemy— — —Rom. viii. 37. Is he enthroned on high, the heir, and Lord of all things? Heb. i. 2. Let not his people think that even these things are too great for them: for they shall have a throne like unto his throne, Rev. iii. 21, a kingdom like unto his kingdom, Luke xxii. 29, a glory like unto his glory— — —John xvii. 22.

ADDRESS,

1. Those who have reason to believe that they are "married to Christ"—Jer. iii. 14; Isa. lxii. 5.

If we congratulate our friends when they are settled in life with a fair prospect of happiness, shall we not much more congratulate you; you, who by your connection with Christ are become children of the living God? John i. 12. What earthly advancement can be compared with this? Who among the children of men is so wise to discern, so tender to regard, so able to relieve, your every want? We hope that you know your union with him. It is certainly your privilege to know it, and to rejoice in it. John xiv. 20. "Rejoice then in the Lord alway, and again I say. Rejoice"— — —Phil. iv. 4. But together with your privileges, remember also the duties which this high relation bringeth with it. Would you be unfaithful to him, or grieve him in any thing? God forbid. Remember the fervent attachment, Tit. ii. 4, the humble reverence, Eph. v. 33, the unreserved submission, ib. ver. 22, 24; 1 Pet. iii. 1, 5, 6, which a dutiful wife feels towards her husband: and let these feelings be transferred in the highest possible degree to your august "Head," Eph. v. 23; 1 Cor. xi. 3, and be exercised towards him without any intermission or alloy— — —*

2. Those who have no evidence that such an union has been formed—

They who have felt no need of an union with Christ, will be ready to say, like Ezekiel's hearers, "Ah! Lord God, doth he not speak parables?" Ezek. xx. 49. But indeed "we speak forth the words of truth and soberness." Acts xxvi. 25. You hope to bring forth fruit to God in some other way than by an union with Christ: but you may as well expect a branch to be fruitful, when separated from the vine. John xv. 4, 5. The image in the text is applied by St. Paul in reference to this very thing: he tells us, that "we must be married unto Christ, that we may bring forth fruit unto God." Rom. vii. 4. Moreover, if you be not united to Christ in this world, you will in vain hope for an union with him in the world to come. This is the time wherein you are to be betrothed to him. Seek then to know him: seek to become an object of his regard: seek to be united to him as intimately as he is to his Heavenly Father. John xvii. 21, and vi. 56, 57. Be not contented with *seeking*, but *strive;* strive to obtain an interest in his favor; nor cease from your labor till you can say, "My Beloved is mine, and I am his." Cant. ii. 16. Then shall you have the most delightful fellowship with him: 1 John i. 3; you shall have such manifestations of his regard, as the world can neither know nor receive: John xiv. 21, 22; ib. ver. 17; and, when all earthly connexions shall cease, your happiness shall be consummated in the everlasting fruition of his love. 1 Thess. iv. 17.

*If this were preached on the occasion of *a Marriage*, it would be proper to shew to the parties present, that their cheerful performance of their relative duties is indispensable, as an evidence of their union to Christ.

JESUS CHRIST, THE MOST EXCELLENT OF ALL TEACHERS.

John vii. 46.--Never man spake like this man. (H.)

So said the officers, whom the Pharisees and chief priests had sent to take Jesus Christ into custody, assigning this as a reason why they had not executed their commission.

When these officers went to take Jesus Christ, he was standing in the temple, and speaking boldly of the Spirit, which they that believe on him should receive, when the Holy Ghost should be given, after he was glorified: very likely our Lord was expounding some of the prophecies, for he said, "if any man thirst, let him come unto me and drink: he that believeth on me, as the Scripture hath said, out of his heart shall flow rivers of living water."

It must have been very delightful to hear Jesus Christ explain the prophecies, and particularly such as are contained in the 35th and 44th of Isaiah, the 2d chapter of Joel, and other places, where the Holy Spirit is spoken of under the similitude of a well, or a spring in the minds and hearts of inspired men; the mouth of a righteous man is a well of life, and Christian knowledge is a well of water springing up into everlasting life.

Many of the people when they heard this discourse, were persuaded that the speaker was an extraordinary person, and others thought he was the promised Messiah; many said, Of a truth, this is the Prophet, i. e. the Prophet spoken of by Moses. Others said, This is the Christ; the officers ventured to say, in general, Never man spake like this man. We unite these opinions, and affirm, Jesus is the Prophet like Moses, he is the Christ, he is the man who spoke as no man ever did speak, Jesus Christ is the most excellent of all teachers. They who were so happy as to attend his ministry, as it is written in the prophets, were all taught of God, and they who are so happy as to hear his doctrine now, though not honored to hear it from his own lips, may truly say, "Master, we know thou teachest the way of God in truth." Blessed is the man, O Lord, whom thou teachest out of thy law, though not out of thine own mouth!

I. With reference to what he taught.

Jesus Christ had a full and perfect knowledge of what he taught.

1. He understood the subject of religion; herein he differed from those, 1 Tim. i. 4, 6, 7; Acts xvii. 23; Matt. xi. 27.

2. Understood the whole of religion perfectly; his understanding of religion was clear, complete, full, and without any defect; and there is not, in all his instructions, one line of guess-work; he hath built the whole of the Christian religion on certain principles, beyond all conjecture and peradventure. Hence the Scriptures are called lively oracles, the first principles of which were committed to the Jews, and perfected by the apostles. Acts vii. 38; Heb. v. 12; Rom. iii. 2; Heb. vi. 1; 1 Peter iv. 10.

3. He knew the perfections of God, the nature of man, the laws of Providence, which govern this world, and all the distributions of happiness and misery which shall take place in the next. Wisdom, in him, was natural, perfect, eternal, and out of his fulness all receive. If we ask, from whence the followers of Christ have their knowledge, the Jews, even Priests, Captains, and Sadducees, can tell us. Acts iv. 13; 1 Cor. xv. 10; Gal. ii. 20; 2 Cor. xii. 11.

II. As to the choice of his subjects.

Our heavenly Teacher, out of the rich abundance of his knowledge, made a judicious choice of the subjects of his ministry. He was governed in this by the condition of his disciples. (John xvi. 12.) As if he had said, I perfectly understand every thing; but I love you, I know the infancy of your faith, the strength of your temptations, &c. I therefore will adapt my instructions to your present condition. Our Lord hath discovered eminent prudence in the choice of his subjects.

1. The subjects taught by Jesus Christ are strictly and wholly true, he was opposed to those mentioned. Hab. ii. 18; Isa. ix. 15, 17. He taught the perfections, government, and worship of the true God, without mixing the traditions of men.

2. Important; there is nothing trifling, every thing is of the utmost consequence; how important to devotion is the knowledge of God, to the exercise of repentance; the knowledge of ourselves, for our faith; the knowledge of the true and real character of Christ; in all these articles Jesus Christ hath instructed us; our Lord did not waste his time, or the attention of his disciples, about articles of no consequence. John xvi. 21, 22.

3. Propriety; every thing he taught was proper for him to teach, and suitable for his disciples to learn; were they in danger, he gave them friendly warning; did they sin, he gave them reproof; were they inquisitive on proper subjects, he poured forth instructions; and when idle curiosity put them on asking questions, he turned their attention; when they were in trouble, he comforted them; and when attacked by their enemies, he showed them how to defend themselves. And, though he was always humble, yet he was never mean; always zealous, never frantic; always kind, never fond; always firm, never sour; always various, yet always the same, as to the choice of his subjects. "Never man spake like this man."

III. The manner.

1. Plainness and simplicity. There are none of what the apostle calls "great swelling words of vanity;" no fine terms, taken from the court of Herod. Matt. xi. 4, 5; Psa. lxxii. 1, 4, 6; Matt. xxi. 16. A plainness that could not but be understood by people the most likely to misunderstand it: "Never man spake like this man."

The subject he taught was stated simply, without mixture, or being rendered abstruse, by needless arguments. Prov. viii. 9. All the words of the law were written plainly. Deut. xxvii. 8; Hab. ii. 2. The apostles used plainness of speech. 2 Cor. iii. 12. But for this excellency Jesus Christ exceeded all, "and never man spake so plainly as this man."

1. The affecting manner in which he proposeth all his instructions to us. For example, in the parable of the prodigal son, we have the almighty, who is represented Nah. i. 3, 5, 6; Ps. lxxvii. 18, 19, pictured in one word, *Father*. A Father, patient and silent during all the provocations of a son; a Father seeing, when he was a great way off, melting with compassion for him, running, falling on his neck, &c.

2. What a picture of sin and wretchedness doth the life of the prodigal afford! A son, a son of such a Father, a younger son, going from home. with all his fortune, into a far country, wasting his substance, &c.

3. Repentance described in a very pathetic manner. "The son came to himself," &c.

4. The joy there is in heaven and in the church, at the repentance of a sinner, is set forth by the pleasure of the servants. All this is not only

clear and cold, like a sharp, frosty night, but clear and affecting: "Never man spake like this man."

IV. Consider one excellency more; THEY WERE ALL CONFIRMED BY HIS OWN EXAMPLE.

Many describe the road to heaven, but tread the way to hell; but he never did any thing to render his religion suspected. John i. 14; viii. 46. Hence it is said, "He began to do and to teach." Acts i. 1

Sum up all these together. A perfect knowledge of all truth: a wise choice of such truths: a clear manner of stating them, to carry conviction to the mind, to obtain assent and belief, and affecting the emotions of the heart with piety towards God and love to all men, together with example. Surely then we may say, Jesus Christ is the first and most excellent of all teachers, "Never man spake like this man."

CHRIST'S PERSONAL MINISTRY, MIRACLES, AND PROPHETIC OFFICE.

John i. 18.—He hath declared him. (H.)

THE verse, of which these words are the close, is part of John the Baptist's testimony concerning our Lord; it contains three propositions. "No man hath seen God at any time." Neither Moses, nor any other of the prophets, hath ever seen God as he is. "The only begotten Son is in the bosom of his Father." He, as the eternal, only begotten Son of the Father, is, and ever was, intimately present with him; he knows him as he is. "He hath declared him." He, as the prophet of the church, has made such discoveries of God, as never were made before, and has given us a plain and complete revelation of his mind and will in all things necessary to salvation.

I. CONSIDER CHRIST'S MINISTRY.

1. The contents of his ministry.

The principal subject of it was, that he, the promised Messiah, was come to set up his kingdom in the world. "He came preaching the gospel of the kingdom of God." Mark i. 14, 15.

In pursuit of this design, he set himself against human traditions, hypocrisy, and superstition; explained and vindicated the moral law. He introduced the everlasting gospel, as the last dispensation. "The Spirit of the Lord," said he, "is upon me." Luke iv. 18, 20, 21.

He declared God's nature and perfections, authority and government; opened the eternal counsels of his will for the salvation of lost sinners; displayed the riches of his free and sovereign grace, and proclaimed the wonders of his love. He intimated the saving design of his incarnation, life, obedience, sufferings, and death; cleared up the spiritual nature of his kingdom; insisted on the necessity of regeneration and repentance, &c.

He instructed his disciples in the great doctrines of mortification to this world, and heavenly-mindedness; of self-denial, humility, and Christian contentment; of brotherly love, meekness, patience, &c.

He delivered various prophecies of things to come, concerning his own death, resurrection, ascension to heaven, intercession, and exaltation: the effusion of his Spirit; the publication and success of his gospel among the

Gentiles; the infidelity and rejection of the Jews; the destruction of Jerusalem; his coming to raise the dead, to judge the world. To all this he added the doctrine of the sacraments, baptism, and the Lord's supper, as the ordinances of his kingdom, the seals of God's covenant, and the visible badges of discipleship to him.

2. The manner of Christ's fulfilling his ministry.

"Never man spake like this man;" the officers themselves being judges, who came to apprehend him; and the common people could not but observe, that he "taught like one having authority," and could not but "wonder at the gracious words." He spake with the majesty and authority of a God; not like the prophets of old, with a "Thus saith the Lord," but with a "Verily, verily, I say unto you:" and yet he did not seek his own glory, nor aim at ostentation and applause.

Zeal for the glory of God, detestation of all iniquity, and good will to men, breathed through all its holy ministrations. With what strength and evidence did he support his Father's honor, and confute the cavils of his adversaries! With what undaunted courage did he reprove the vices and errors of the age, never fearing the faces of men! With what admirable skill did he point or soften his reproofs, as the occasion of things required! With what compassion, condescension, and meekness, did he mourn over his obstinate hearers, and "grieve at the hardness of their hearts!" Matt. xxiii. 37; Mark iii. 5.

How tenderly did he expostulate with sinners of all ranks and degrees! How graciously did he invite and encourage the weary and heavy laden! "The bruised reed he did not break." Matt. xii. 20. "He gathered the lambs with his arms." Isa. xl. 11. And he had "the tongue of the learned." Isa. l. 4

"The words he spake were spirit and life." John vi. 63. He could add a quickening virtue and commanding energy to them; hence, when he said to one and another, "Follow me," immediately they left all and followed him. And as soon as he spoke to Nathaniel, the woman of Samaria, and Zaccheus; the first said, "Rabbi, thou art the Son of God." John i. 49. The second said, "Come see a man, which told me all things that ever I did." Chap, iv. 29. And the third "made haste, and came down." Luke xix. 5, 6.

3. The credentials of Christ's ministry.

Among these we might reckon the exact accomplishment of many remarkable types and ancient prophecies in him; his miraculous birth subsequent to that of John the Baptist, his forerunner; the extraordinary star, that appeared to the wise men of the east; the glory of the Lord, that shone round about the shepherds in the field, and the attestation of the heavenly host concerning him; the visible descent of the Holy Ghost upon him, at his baptism; and his Father's public testimony to him, "This is my beloved Son.' Matt. iii. 16, 17.

1. His ministry appeared to be Divine by the miracles he wrought, whilst he was employed in it.

These were innumerable, and of various kinds, and not done in a corner; but before the learned, friends, and enemies. "He healed all manner of diseases, opened the eyes of the blind, unstopped the ears of the deaf, loosed the tongues of the dumb, cured cripples, cast out devils, and raised the dead."

2. At the close, &c. by miracles.

Surprising signs and wonders were seen at his death; all nature seemed to be flung into confusion. Luke xxiii. 45. "The sun was darkened at noon-day; the veil of the temple was rent in twain." Matt. xxvii. 45—51. And he rose again from the dead on the third day, according to his own prediction. John ii. 20, 21. This great event was attended with the "resurrection of many bodies of saints," Matt. xxvii. 52, 53, and with the testimony of angels, saying, "He is not here." Luke xxiv. 6. And when he had "shown himsel: alive to his disciples," Acts i. 3—11, he ascended up to heaven in their sight, and ten days afterwards shed down his Spirit abundantly upon them, according to his promise, Acts ii. 1—4.

II. Take a more comprehensive view of Christ's prophetic office.

1. Christ teaches by the ministry of inspired men.

During the time of his personal ministry, he spake the word to his auditors, as they were able to bear it. Mark iv. 33. And he said to his own disciples, "I have yet many things to say unto you." John xvi. 12, He promised that, upon his departure, he would send his Spirit: "When he, the Spirit of truth, is come." John xvi. 13, 14.

And by this Spirit "he brought all things to their remembrance." John xiv. 26. He also revealed new doctrines to them, and "showed them things to come." Acts xxvii. 11, 16, 17. "He gave them the Spirit of power." 2 Tim. i. 7. It was likewise under his inspiration and influence, that they committed so much of the gospel revelation to writing. They therein "declared the testimony of God." 1 Cor. ii. 1—13.

2. He teaches by the ministry of others, who are not inspired.

As, "When he ascended up on high, he gave apostles, prophets, and evangelists," which were extraordinary officers, endued with miraculous gifts; so he gave pastors and teachers, to be standing officers in the church, for the "perfecting of the saints." Eph. iv. 1, 11—13. And his promise, to be with his servants always, Matt. xxviii. 20, looks forward to the ministers of the gospel till time shall be no more.

3. He teaches by an internal illumination, by means of all these external teachings.

By his external teachings he takes off the veil from our hearts, or removes their natural depravity and prejudices. This internal illumination teaches us to profit, there is something efficacious in it, for every man. John vi. 45. But without this internal work upon the heart, all external revelations would be ineffectual, as to any saving purpose: "Who hath believed our report?" Isa. liii. 1; 1 Cor. ii. 12, 14.

Our Lord Jesus, in the discharge of his prophetic office, undertakes the work of opening the heart, as he did the heart of Lydia. Acts. xvi. 14. He, by his Spirit, "convinces the world of sin." John xvi. 8. Hence the apostle John says, "The Son of God is come." 1 John v. 20. And, "Ye have an unction from the Holy One." 1 John ii. 20.

To conclude.

1. This shows the excellence and necessity of Christ's teachings.

With what light and authority, condescension, grace, and efficacy, does he teach us the way to pardon, peace, &c.

O, how thankful should we be for this great Prophet of the church!—"Blessed be the Lord God of Israel." Luke i. 68, 77—79.

2, The danger of refusing to hearken to this Divine teacher.

"For him," says God, "shall ye hear in all things." Acts iii. 22, 23. O, solemn injunction! and, O, dreadful ruin, to such as turn a deaf ear to him! "How shall we escape?" Heb. ii. 3. "See, then, that ye refuse not him that speaketh." chap. xii. 25

THE CHARACTER AND WORK OF JESUS CHRIST.

Matt. xxi. 10.—And when he was come into Jerusalem, all the city was moved, saying Who is this? (H.)

When any person of a singular character, and who is represented as having done some remarkable works, makes his appearance in any age or country, he usually engages the attention of mankind. If he has achieved some great thing for the good of the human race, or of his country, he readily becomes an object of admiration, and receives the applause of the multitude; many of whom perhaps will afterward, from various considerations, commence his enemies, and persecute him with a hatred and rancour, equal, if not superior, to their former admiration and applause: so variable are the tempers of men, and of so little importance are their professed admiration and regard. This was evidently the character and behaviour of that multitude, who followed our Saviour in his progress to Jerusalem. And when he was come into Jerusalem, &c. It is intended by divine assistance,

I. To suggest several ANSWERS TO THIS QUESTION, put by the people of Jerusalem, concerning Jesus Christ.

1. Who is this? He is the glorious Personage who was typified and promised to the church as the true Messiah, and the Saviour of sinners. He is the great antitype of all the typical persons, places, and things, appointed to prefigure him, under the Old Testament. He was promised as the woman's seed. Gen. iii. 15. As Abraham's. Gen. xii. 3. In the character of Shiloh. Gen. xlix. 10. In his prophetical character he was foretold by Moses. Deut. xviii. 15. He was to be of the family of David. Jer. xxiii. 5. He was to be born of a virgin. Isa. vii. 15. Bethlehem was foretold as the place of his birth. Micah v. 2. It was foretold that he was to perform wonderful works. Isa. xlii. 7; xxxv. 5, 6. Had the Jewish nation paid proper attention to these things, they would not have rejected Christ, but hailed him as the true Messiah.

2. Who is this? He is a person of infinite dignity, the only begotten and eternal Son of God. John i. 14—18; iii. 16. He is the Son of God, as begotten by the Spirit of God. Luke i. 35. As being raised immediately from the dead by God. Acts xiii. 33. It is so said of others, much more so of Christ. Luke xx. 36. In his resurrection he was declared to be such: and as being made heir of all things in his Father's house. Heb. i. 4, 5. But more especially, he is the only begotten Son of God by nature, of the same essence with his Father, the eternal Son of God, who, when he became incarnate, came forth from the Father; John xvi. 27, 28; who was before Abraham. John viii. 58. Who preached to the antediluvians. 1 Peter iii. 18—20. Who made the world. John i. 3; Col. i. 14—18. And is God. Heb. iii. 4. God manifest in the flesh. 1 Tim. iii. 16. Possessing all the perfections of God, is the brightness of his glory, and the express image of his person.

3. Who is this? He is the only mediator between God and man. 1 Tim. ii. 5. Man in his primitive innocence, required no mediator; but when man sinned, a mediator was essentially necessary, to interpose between an offended God, and offending sinners. No angel was equal to the arduous undertaking; the Son of God, alone, was found equal to the work; hence the Father, in his infinite wisdom and love, appointed him to the service. Ps. lxxxix. 19.

4. Who is this? He is Head of the church by the Father's appointment. Ps. ii. 6; Luke i. 32, 33; Eph. i. 22, 23. He is her head, as it respects representation, being the second Adam, the first being the figure of him who was to come. Of government, as her King and Lawgiver, the scriptures being the great standing statute-book of his kingdom; which none must add to or diminish, at the peril of his salvation. Of saving influence, and the fountain of spiritual life to all her members. And of example, 1 Pet. ii. 21.

5. Who is this? He is that glorious Personage to whom the whole administrations of divine providence are committed. He is the Governor of the world. The Father has put all things under his care and management. He moves and directs the whole frame of nature, he directs the motions and propensities of his creatures, so as to render them subservient to his will. He appoints and conducts all the changes and revolutions of empires, raises some, and depresses others. He sits invisible at the helm of the great providential dispensations, and tremendous scenes of Providence which appear in our own day, and will bring glory to his name, good to his church, and destruction to his enemies out of them all. We may exclaim here, with Paul, on another occasion, "O! the depth," &c. Rom. xi. 33.

6. Who is this? He is the dignified and glorious Person, who is appointed by Jehovah the Father, to be the Judge of the world, and to pass the decisive and unalterable sentence, which will fix the conditions of all mankind through eternity. John v. 22; Acts xvii. 31; Rom. xiv. 10; Rev. xx. 12. Jesus will then appear in circumstances of awful and tremendous majesty. The whole race of mankind will be assembled at his tribunal, from hoary Adam to his youngest son. He will possess a perfect knowledge of all the characters and causes which will come before him, whether good or bad, and the final sentence will proceed accordingly. O! what a dreadful day will that be to the wicked, and how terrible their sentence! Matt. xxv. 41. But what an auspicious and joyful day to the righteous! They will lift up their hands with joy, to hear their gracious welcome to the Lord. Matt. xxv. 34.

7. Who is this? It is he who is appointed to be the blessed medium through which the happiness of the redeemed will come into their possession to eternity. In the state of primitive innocence, all blessings flowed immediately from God, in the channel of absolute love and goodness; but this channel of communication was shut up by sin; and after the introduction of moral evil, Jehovah could hold no gracious intercourse with man, but through a mediator. It is in this way, and in this only, that all the blessings of grace and glory can be obtained by them who believe. Of this David says, this is all my salvation, and all my desire. And Paul says to believers, ye are complete in him; for, in him all fulness dwells; and, my God shall supply all your wants, according to his riches in glory by Jesus Christ. And the burden of the song of the redeemed will be, unto him that loved us, &c. Rev. i. 5, 6.

The improvement.

1. How great and wonderful are the love and wisdom of God displayed in the scheme of redemption! Hence it is called, "the wisdom of God in a mystery; and the manifold wisdom of God."

2. How inexcusable are all those who reject the Redeemer, and despise the great salvation set before them in the word of God, and the preaching of the glorious gospel! Such, particularly, are all infidels, who reject the gospel revelation; all worldly professors, who love their farms and merchandise above God, and the word of truth. Matt. vii. 21.

3. Let christians daily implore the Redeemer by faith in his mediatorial character and offices. Believe on him, trust in him, depend upon him, as made of God unto them wisdom, &c. 1 Cor. i. 30.

4. Dwell much on the glorious excellency of Christ, and on the work he has performed, and will still perform, for you, and for his whole church. In your serious contemplations, often put the question to yourselves, "Who is this?" and study to consult suitable answers, according to the information already given. This is he, "who is the eternal Son of God, who hath loved me, and given himself for me," &c. &c.

5. Amidst the present convulsions of the nations, console your minds with the reflection, that Jesus is the Governor of the nations: and that he will order all things for the good of his church; and he, himself, "will be a wall of fire round about her, and the glory in the midst."

6. In an age like the present, when error, infidelity, and every vice abound, let me direct you, O believer, to stand fast in the faith and holiness of the gospel. "Contend for the faith once delivered to the saints." Live down all reproaches and aspersions cast upon your character, or religion, by the most exemplary purity and godliness; "For this is the will of God your Saviour, that by well-doing you may put to silence the ignorance of foolish men. Be steadfast and unmoveable, always abounding in the work of the Lord, forasmuch as ye know that your labor shall not be in vain in the Lord."

JESUS CHRIST IS THE WAY, THE TRUTH, AND THE LIFE.

John xiv. 6.—Jesus saith unto him, I am the way, the truth, and the life; no man cometh unto the Father, but by me. (Sk.)

The prospect of our Lord's departure out of the world, filled the hearts of his disciples with trouble, because they had long enjoyed his gracious presence, and had indulged a hope that he was about to "restore again the kingdom to Israel;" but he comforted them with an assurance that "he was going to his Father's house to prepare a place for them, and that he would come again, and receive them to himself," ver. 1—3. When he had stated this. he added, "Whither I go ye know, and the way ye know," ver. 4. Bu Thomas, who was slow of apprehension, and apt to doubt, saith unto him, "Lord, we know not whither thou goest, and how can we know the way?" ver. 4. Then Jesus said, "I am the way, and the truth, and the life: no man cometh unto the Father but by me."

I. "I AM THE WAY."

1. As a way, or road, leads to a certain place, and as means lead to certain ends, so our Lord Jesus Christ is the way to all the blessings of grace on earth, and to all the glories of the upper and better world. Particularly,

2. He is the way to *pardon*. Through him our sins are remitted, when we believe in his name, Acts x. 43; and through him, the ministers of his word preach the forgiveness of sins, Acts xiii. 38.

3. Jesus is the way to *peace*. Wicked men are at war with God; but he is the medium of reconciliation, 2 Cor. v. 19; and all true believers have peace with God, through our Lord Jesus Christ, Rom. v. 1.

4. Christ is the way to *holiness*. "His blood cleanseth from all sin," 1 John i. 7; his Spirit sanctifies the soul by an application of that blood, 2

Thess. ii. 13; and he "gave himself for us, that he might redeem us from all iniquity, and purify unto himself a peculiar people, zealous of good works," Tit. ii. 14.

5. And our blessed Lord is the way to *heaven*. His merit gives us a title to it; his grace works in us a fitness for it; his Holy Spirit leads us to that happy world, Rom. viii. 14; and by his blood we shall enter with boldness into the holiest place, Heb. x. 19.

II. "AND THE TRUTH."

1. Jesus is the *fountain* of truth. All truth is known to him, John xxi. 17; all the treasures of wisdom are hid in him, Col. ii. 3; and all the divine truth that is known in the world has flowed from him.

2. He is the *revealer* of truth: he revealed truth, in former times, by his holy prophets; he revealed truth himself, in the days of his flesh, John viii. 12; and he sent his apostles to reveal the truth to a dark and erring world, Acts xxvi. 18.

3. He is the constant *patron* of truth. The friends of truth are his friends; and the enemies of truth are his enemies. His cause is the cause of truth; he contends for it; and his truth must finally triumph: for "he shall bring forth judgment unto truth," or "victory," Isa. xlii. 3; Matt. xii. 20.

4. And he is the truth of all those promises, prophecies, and types of the Messiah which are recorded in the Old Testament; for they also had their accomplishment in him, John i. 17.

III. "AND THE LIFE."

1. Our blessed Lord has life in *himself*, John i. 4; and he is the author of life to all created beings, both in heaven and on earth, visible and invisible, John i. 3; Col. i. 16, 17.

2. He is the *spiritual life* of believers. They were quickened by him, Eph. ii. 1; they live by faith in him, Gal. ii. 20; and the constant supplies of their life are derived from him, as those of the branch are derived from the vine, John xv. 5.

3. Our Saviour is the life of the *body*, which "is dead because of sin," Rom. viii. 10; but he will raise it from the dead at the last day; for he is "the resurrection and the life," John xi. 24, 25; his resurrection is a pledge of ours, and because he lives we shall live also, ver. 19.

4. And he may be called the life, as he gives *eternal life* to all who hear his voice and follow him, John x. 27, 28. Through him, "the gift of God is eternal life," Rom. vi. 23; and "he that believeth on the Son, hath everlasting life," John iii. 36; he hath an undeniable claim to it, and a sweet foretaste of it in his heart.

IV. "NO MAN COMETH UNTO THE FATHER BUT BY ME."

1. Men have no intercourse with the Father, in *this world*, but by Jesus Christ; but through him both Jews and Gentiles have free access, by one Spirit, Eph. ii. 18. In his name they offer up prayer and praise, and through him the choicest blessings are sent down from the *throne of grace*, Heb. iv. 16.

2. No man when he departs this life, can go to the Father in *the heavenly* world, but by Jesus Christ. He is gone before to prepare the place for us; he will receive us to himself; and in that world, he will make us kings and priests unto God and his Father for ever, Rev. i. 6.

3. Jesus as *our Mediator, stands between us and the Father*, 1 Tim. ii. 5. He brings the offender and the offended together; and is the instrument of restoring us to the divine favor by the death of the cross, Eph. ii. 16.

4. This proves that the mediatorial plan is the only way of salvation to a sinful world; and no man ever was saved, and no man ever will be saved, on any other plan, 1 Cor. iii. 11. The law cannot save us, and therefore salvation must be by grace; and if by grace, then by Jesus Christ, Eph. ii. 13

INFERENCES.

1. We should be thankful for Christ, and gratefully bless God, for the unspeakable gift of his Son, 2 Cor. ix. 15.

2. It is our duty, and our privilege, to receive Christ, in all his sacred offices and characters, John i. 11.

3. Having received him, we should abide in him, John xv. 4; and we should walk in him, in holiness and righteousness all the days of our life Col. ii. 5.

4. Then we shall live with him, and reign with him, when time shall be no more; and, with all the redeemed of the Lord, sing "blessing, and glory, and wisdom, and thanksgiving, and honor, and power, and might, be unto our God for ever and ever. Amen," Rev. vii. 12.

CHRIST IN HIS ORDINANCES.

Matthew xviii 20.—*For where two or three are gathered together in my name, there am I in the midst of them.* (Sk.)

The Saviour delivered these words for the instruction and encouragement of his people, in every succeeding age of the church. In the preceding context he supposes the case of personal offence among his followers, and gives special direction for the amicable adjustment of such offences. The offended brother is directed to endeavor to convince, and reclaim the offender, by first going to him alone, and telling him of his fault; but if he will not hear him, he must take with him two or three witnesses; and if he refuse to hear them and the church, he must be expelled their communion as an incorrigible transgressor, ver. 15–17. And to encourage their exertions in the exercise of Christian discipline, the Redeemer informs them, that all their faithful reproofs and decisions, in conformity to his instructions, would be highly approved and ratified in heaven, ver. 18. He also assures them, that their united prayers for the divine blessing in this and every case, would certainly be heard and answered; assigning as a reason, his own omnipresence, which extends to all the assemblies of his saints;—"For where two or three," &c. In this interesting declaration we shall notice—the duty it prescribes—the instruction it suggests—and encouragement it affords.

I. The duty the text prescribes;—It is to "gather" ourselves "together in Christ's *name*." This is evidently an important obligation; and implies that we should meet,

1. *For the purposes of his worship.* When we worship the holy Trinity, in the unity of the Godhead, it should be with profound reverence, and godly fear, Psa. lxxxix. 7. We should not carelessly rush into his sacred presence; but diligently seek a necessary preparation of heart, for the hallowed solemnities of devotion, Prov. xvi. 1; Eccl. v. 1, 2. As professing Christians we should faithfully attend the instituted ordinances of Christianity, to

confess our sins;—to acknowledge the divine goodness;—to call upon his holy name;—to hear the instructions of his word;—to commemorate the dying love of the Redeemer;—and to receive the communications of his grace, Psa. xxvii. 4, and lxiii. 2-5.

2. *On the ground of his mediation.* We cannot approach the Almighty in our own names, because we are sinners, and enemies to him in our minds, and by wicked works, Rom. viii. 7, 8. Nor is there any name either in heaven or on earth, by which we can come to God, or be saved, but the all-prevailing name of Jesus Christ, Acts iv. 12. Through his atonement and intercession, "a new and living way is consecrated for us," to the "Father of mercies," John xiv. 6; Heb. x. 19-22. Whenever therefore we meet together in his name, we must have special reference to his character and office; and entirely trust in his merits and mediation, for acceptance with God, and the attainment of every blessing, John xvi. 23, 24; Eph. ii. 12.

3. *Under the influences of his Spirit.* No worship can be acceptable to God, but that which is sincere and spiritual. "God is a Spirit, and they that worship him, must worship him in spirit and in truth." We must not only draw near to him with our spirits, in the sincerity of our hearts, but we must also worship him under the enlightening, enriching, and hallowing influence and power of the Holy Ghost, Jude 20. And hence he is given to help our infirmities,—to teach us how to pray,—and to make intercession for us; that we may "worship God in the spirit, rejoice in Christ Jesus, and have no confidence in the flesh," Rom. viii. 26, 27; Eph. ii. 18. Such is our duty; let us therefore consider,

II. The instructions the text suggests;—These are various and important; but the following points are clearly implied, and consequently claim our particular attention. We learn,

1. *The essential Godhead of Jesus Christ.* His human nature is necessarily *local* in its situation, and therefore can only be in *one place* at the *same period* of time. But the Saviour promises to be in the midst of all his assemblies, however numerous, and in any and every part of the world at the *same moment;* which evidently proves that he must refer to his character as *God*, for in this sense only can his promise be true. As an infinite Spirit, his presence "fills both heaven and earth," Matt. xxviii. 20. And if he were not essential God, why should we meet in his name? But because "in him dwelleth all the fulness of the Godhead bodily," we must worship and "honor the Son, even as we honor the Father," John v. 23.

2. *The divine origin of religious ordinances.* This appears from the institution and design of the Sabbath, Gen. ii. 3.—The positive injunctions of the moral law, Exod. xx. 8-11.—The Mosaic dispensation of ceremonies, Deut. xvi. 16. The example of Christ in the days of his flesh, Luke iv. 16.—The united testimonies and examples of the holy patriarchs, prophets, apostles, and primitive Christians, Psa. lxxxiv. 2—4; Mal. iii. 16; Luke xxiv. 53. Our moral obligations to God,—the general voice of Scripture,—the sacred character of religion,—and the instructive language of the text, in which the Saviour directs and encourages his people to "gather" themselves "together in his name."

3. *The comparative indifference of outward modes of worship.* Under the law, the Lord particularly appointed the various ceremonies to be used by the Jews in his worship; but that dispensation is abolished by the coming of Jesus Christ. And though the Saviour taught the necessity and spirituality of the worship of God as a pure spirit, he did not enjoin any *external rites*, as essential to the acceptance of true devotion, Luke xviii. 1;

John iv. 23.—In the text, he does not fix the *time when*, or *place where* we should assemble in his name. Nor does he limit the *number*, or prescribe the particular *ceremonies* or *forms*, to be adopted by his worshippers. These things are *comparatively indifferent*, though many attach great importance to them, John iv. 20. But the Lord looks at the heart, and *whenever*, *wherever*, and *however* his people "worship him, in the beauty of holiness," he is in the midst of them, and will show them his salvation. This will lead us to observe,

III. The encouragement the text affords. It is the compassionate language of the Saviour, in which he assures his followers of his presence in all their religious assemblies. And according to this gracious promise, we are still encouraged,

1. *By the infinity of his presence.* His omnipresence is a doctrine highly consolatory to his people. By his *general* or *universal presence*, he fills all space, and exists in all duration, Heb. xiii. 8.—But in the text he means his *special* and *gracious presence*, which ever accompanies the saints, and inspires them with joy and gladness in his ways, Exod. xxxiii. 14,15; Luke xxiv. 32. He particularly manifests himself unto them in his worship, and is perfectly acquainted with the respective characters, motives, desires, and necessities of them that wait upon him, John xx. 19–22.

2. *By the certainty of his presence.* His promise is infallible. It was not limited to the apostolic age, but has been happily realized in every succeeding period of the church. He is never absent from his ordinances, for nothing can prevent his being present with his devout worshippers. And how encouraging is the reflection, that he is with them on every occasion, and in every place, whether they may be *many* or *few!* He does not despise the day of small things. Where even "*two* or *three* are gathered together in his name," whether they be rich or poor, learned or illiterate, he is certainly "in the midst of them."

3. *By the efficacy of his presence.* Without the presence of Christ, the assemblies of his followers would ever be barren and unprofitable. But according to his word, he is always with them, and that to do them good. He assists their devotions—answers their prayers—and fulfils their desires. He possesses an infinite plenitude of grace, and in his ordinances he communicates his blessings to them that unite in his worship. He enlightens the ignorant—pardons the penitent—strengthens the weak—succors the tempted—comforts the sorrowful—establishes the wavering—and renders to all a portion of grace in due season, which frequently induces them to exclaim, "Lord, it is good for us to be here."

We may infer from this subject,

1. The public means of grace are inestimable privileges, Psa. lxxxiv. 1.
2. The sin and folly of neglecting the worship of God, Heb. x. 25. And,
3. The duty and blessedness of meeting in Christ's name, Isa. xl. 31.

CHRIST'S TRANSFIGURATION.

Matthew xvii. 1, 2.—And after six days, &c. (H.)

Jesus Christ appeared in this world in the form of a servant; yet sometimes the rays of his divine glory shone forth with peculiar splendor, and declared him to be the Prince of Life and the Lord of Glory. This was the case at his transfiguration on the mount, in the presence of Peter, James, and John. "His face shone as the sun, and his raiment as white as the light."

Let us consider,

I. Some important facts which are established by the TRANSFIGURATION OF CHRIST.

1. That he is the Son of God, and a Mediator between God and sinners. At his transfiguration, a voice was heard out of the cloud, saying, This is my beloved Son, &c.; Matt. xvii. 5; a plain intimation that Christ is a divine person, and the Saviour of sinners.

There are three Persons that have communion in the same Divine Nature, and are one God; and the distinction between the first and second Persons of the Trinity is set forth in scripture by the relation of Father and Son. The Son is of the same substance with the Father, and has communion with him in all his infinite perfections: he is his only begotten Son; John i. 14; and the Jews attempted to kill him, because he called God his Father, &c. John v. 18.

God here calls him "his beloved Son," and he takes the highest complacency and pleasure in him; he was with him from eternity, and daily his delight. Prov. viii. 23, 30, 31. He loveth him, &c. John iii. 35.

He is well pleased with him in the accomplishment of our salvation: it is in Christ that God reveals his justice, wisdom, and love, in the highest perfection: he has obeyed the law in precepts and penalties, and made full satisfaction to God for the sins of mankind. It pleased the Lord to bruise him, &c. Isaiah liii. 10. How divine and able a Saviour is Christ! He is Emanuel, &c. Heb. i. 3.

He is the messenger of his Father's love; we are to "hear him." He has revealed to us the Father's intentions to save mankind by the merit of the cross; John iii. 16; he has declared that the greatest sinners may be pardoned and saved; he has promised the Holy Ghost to assist us in the work of salvation; John xvi. 7, 8; he has told his followers that they shall have his presence with them upon earth; that after death they shall be advanced to the kingdom of heaven; that their bodies shall be raised from the grave, and clothed with the robes of immortality and glory; and that they shall be for ever with the Lord. John xiv. 3.

The great God is well pleased with all those who fly to Christ for salvation. John vi. 40.

2. His transfiguration is an evidence that he will come from heaven at the last day, with great power and majesty. 2 Peter i. 16, 17, 18. Though Christ is man, yet the fulness of the Godhead bodily dwells in him: and if the Godhead diffused such a lustre over his body at his transfiguration, what superior brightness will it spread over his humanity when he comes to judge the world!

When Christ was transfigured, Moses, the giver of the Jewish law, and Elias, the restorer of it from many gross corruptions, appeared with him in glory, to teach us that the gospel is a more excellent institution than the law;

and that Christ will be attended with millions of angels and saints when he comes to judge he world. Luke ix. 30, 31.

Though Christ lived in low circumstances while he was upon earth, accompanied by poor fishermen, yet the glorified saints and angels will attend him at the last great day. Matt. xxv. 31; Jude, verse 14. Then he will raise the bodies of the saints, publicly own them for his people, and put them in possession of eternal life. Matt. xxv. 34.

He will judge the wicked, and condemn them to eternal torments. Matt. xxv. 41.

O what a joyful and terrible day will this be! How will the awful solemnities of it turn to the honor of Christ our Redeemer! 2 Thess. i. 10.

3. His transfiguration is a pledge and emblem of the future glorification of the saints; he is their pattern and example, both in their sanctification and glorification.

Though their bodies turn to dust, they shall be raised, and richly endowed with divine and heavenly qualities; he himself is the first fruits from the dead. 1 Cor. xv. 20.

What divine beauty and lustre shall the bodies of the saints be clothed with, when they shall resemble the body of Christ, the Lord of glory! Phil. iii. 21. They shall be so refined from all gross qualities, as to resemble a spirit in their nature: they shall be strong, lively, and active, and no hinderance to the soul in its holy desires and operations.

They shall see Christ in his glory. Col. iii. 4. They now see him by faith, and in the ordinances of the gospel: but then, face to face. 1 Cor. xiii. 12.

II. Make some observations upon the event, and the circumstances attending it.

1. God is sometimes pleased to grant unto his children very blessed manifestations of his presence and love, before he brings them into a state of peculiar suffering. God here owns Christ for his Son, before he suffers and dies.

2. The sight of Christ's glory is delightful to the saints. All the perfections of God shine with the brightest lustre in the person of Christ. Col. i. 15. The disciples were delighted with the views of his glory, and said, It is good for us to be here; and wished to make three tabernacles, and there to abide. Verse 4.

3. When the Lord reveals the divine glory to his saints, their minds are impressed with a holy awe of his greatness and majesty.

When God revealed himself in a vision to Jacob, "he was afraid," &c. Gen. xxviii. 17.

At such seasons the saints behold his all-sufficiency, and sink into their own nothingness: his majesty and greatness, which fills them with humility and self-abasement; his perfect purity, filling them with a sense of their own vileness.

When the disciples saw the cloud which overshadowed them, and heard God's voice, they fell on their face, and were sore afraid. Verse 5, 6.

4. The Saviour delights in comforting his people upon earth, as well as to save and bring them to heaven.

When the disciples were terrified at the displays of divine majesty upon the mount, Jesus came to them, and said unto them, Arise, be not afraid. Verse 6, 7.

The heart of Christ is full of tenderness towards his children, and he delights in speaking peace to them. Be of good cheer, said he. Matt. xiv.

27. Fear not, little flock. Luke xii. 32. Let not your heart be troubled. John xiv. 1. And, Peace I leave with you, &c. John xiv. 27.

Though Christ is now absent from his saints, as to his bodily presence, yet he often comforts them in the ordinances of the gospel, and revives them with the sweet promises of his grace; he speaks to them by his Spirit, and conveys peace and comfort to their hearts.

After these things, Jesus and his disciples came down from the mountain: the vision was at an end, and the glorious scene was finished. Matt. xvii. 9.

5. The presence of Christ with his saints here is but of short duration, and subject to many interruptions.

Having enjoyed the presence of Christ for a season in his ordinances, they come down from the mount of vision, into the valley of the world, and are employed about the concerns of life.

This glimpse of the Redeemer's glory, is an emblem of that immediate, full, and everlasting vision of his glory, with which the saints shall be blessed in the kingdom of God. For,

6. Their enjoyment of his presence there will be everlasting: it will never be interrupted by sin. They shall be so filled with a sense of his love to them, that they will always love and serve him with the greatest vigor; and their hearts will never wander from him. They shall be for ever with him. 1 Thess. iv. 17.

III. Apply what has been delivered.

1. If Christ is the Son of God, and the Saviour of sinners, we may infer the happiness of those who trust in him by faith. As God and man, in one person, he is a glorious Saviour, suited to the wants and necessities of guilty sinners.

As their Priest, he has satisfied divine justice for their sins: they are united to Christ, and their sins are pardoned.

As their Prophet, he teaches them divine things; yea, the whole will of God. And,

As their King, he guards them in all dangers, and enables him to overcome sin, Satan, and the world.

They have peace with God, through the atonement of Christ.

They are the sons of God, through faith in his blood.

And in virtue of that blood, they shall have admission into the beatific presence of God in heaven, where there are fulness of joy, and pleasures for evermore.

2. If the transfiguration of Christ is a pledge of the saint's future glory, the consideration of it should raise them superior to the sorrows of the present state.

How happy are they who are one with Christ, and are the heirs of salvation! They shall be enriched with the same glory which Christ now possesses in heaven.

Their number upon earth appears to be but few; but in heaven there will not only be Moses and Elias, a few humble worshippers, but the "general assembly," and whole "church of the first born," even an "innumerable company," saying, Salvation to our God, who sitteth upon the throne, and unto the Lamb for ever. Rev. vii. 9, 10.

CHRIST THE ONLY SOURCE OF LIFE AND BLESSEDNESS.

John xi. 25.—Jesus said unto her, I am the resurrection and the life. (Pr.)

Few families, even among the godly, have been so eminently distinguished as was the family at Bethany. There it was that Lazarus and his sisters lived, whom Jesus loved, and where he spent many a happy hour.

In this beloved family, the brother was sick, and tidings were sent to Jesus. The disciples did not wish to visit Bethany for fear of the Jews; but Jesus went: and the text relates a part of his conversation with Martha, as he approached the village.

There is a great depth in many of the sayings of our Lord, which renders them difficult to be understood; and it seems by Martha's answer, that she did not wholly comprehend his meaning on the present occasion, verse 27.

I. Endeavor to explain the subject.

The general design of our Lord was to fix the faith of Martha on himself, as the fountain of life, of all life, both natural and spiritual.

More particularly—

1. The words were designed to *correct an error* in Martha's judgment; for she spoke as if his power was limited to *time*.— — —It was his intention to raise Lazarus, and he desired to do it in answer to faith; but her expectations seemed to be very low.— — —"If thou hadst been here, my brother had not died: but I know that even now, whatsoever thou wilt ask of God, God will give it thee:" ver. 21, 22.— — —This was saying little more of Jesus, than might have been said of another prophet: he therefore leads her to consider himself not merely as the medium, but the fountain of life, and the author of eternal salvation.— — —She believed that he would raise him up at the last day; but our Lord intimates that he could at any time raise him up; and she was required to believe this.

2. His calling himself *the resurrection*, was designed to correct another error which she seemed to entertain, as if his power could only have *prevented* the death of her brother Lazarus.— — —This Mary dwelt upon, as well as Martha, and the Jews likewise with unbelief: ver. 32—37.— — — But his calling himself "the resurrection," was like saying, My power is not limited merely to prevention; I come not so much to prevent as to restore.— — —Christ did not interpose to prevent the fall, but to restore us from its ruins; to seek and to save the lost.— — —He does not prevent our dying; but he brings us back from death and the grave. Hos. xiii. 14.

3. In calling himself *the life*, he intended to carry the idea still farther. The first means restoring to life, but the last the perpetuity of that life.— — —Christ not only raises his people from the dead, but he is their life when raised. He is not only the way to heaven, but the very life of heaven itself. John xiv. 6, Col. iii. 4.

4. The *resurrection and the life* of which he speaks, represents more than the simple fact of raising Lazarus.— — —The life which he received on his resurrection was only corporeal, and he was still liable to die again: but that of which our Lord speaks is common to all believers as the two following sentences explain it.— — —"He that believeth in me, though he were dead, yet shall he live; and whosoever liveth, and believeth in me, shall never die." It therefore means a resurrection to immortal life.

II. Contemplate the leading truth in the text; namely, that Christ is the only source of life to fallen creatures.

God is the fountain of life to creatures, considered merely as such; but where that life is forfeited and lost, Christ is the only restorer of it.— — — He is described as that life which is the light of men, ch. i. 4. He quickeneth whom he will, v. 21: and those who live, must live by faith in him. Gal. ii. 20.

The world since the fall is like the valley of vision, or a field of slaughter, some years after a battle, covered with the slain. Ezek. xxxvii. Angels might ask, can these dry bones live? If they can, it must not be by any human power, oh Lord God thou knowest!— — —Prophets, angels, ministers would despair; but Jesus is the resurrection and the life.

In various senses we may be said to be dead: more particularly—

1. We are *spiritually* dead, as the Prodigal was when lost to his father. "This my son," said he, "was dead, and is alive again; was lost, and is found."— — —By nature we are like dead bodies, without any soul for what is good and heavenly; we have no desire after God, or spiritual objects. Ephes. ii. 1.

But Christ's death brings life to the soul; through his atoning sacrifice, the Spirit of life in Christ Jesus breathes upon the dry bones, and they live; and there was no other consistent way in which this life could be imparted. — — —God would not have given his Holy Spirit, but for Christ's sake: if I go not away, said he, the Comforter will not come. Hence the great effusion on the day of pentecost. Acts i. 4, 8.

2. We are dead *legally*, as well as spiritually, dead in law as well as in fact.— — —As sinners we were under the sentence of death and condemnation, to be banished forever under the curse, and all the threatnings of God's righteous law stood against us. Gal. iii. 10.

But through the mediation of Christ, those who believe in him shall not come into condemnation, but are passed from death unto life. John v. 24.— — —They come out of their graves, like Lazarus; and their being forgiven all trespasses, is equivalent to the command, "Loose him and let him go." — — —Christ was treated for our sake as if he had been a sinner, and that we for his sake might be treated as righteous. 2 Cor. v. 21.

3. We are all subject to *corporeal* death; and though we should have been raised, whether Christ had died or not, yet not to life, but to endure the second death; to be carried from prison to judgment, and there to receive our everlasting doom. John v. 29.

But believing in Christ, and receiving the atonement, we are made one with him, and shall rise with him, and sit with him in heavenly places. Ephes. ii. 6.— — —Our resurrection to eternal life is a part of his mediatorial undertaking, and is secured by the promises which he has made to them that love him. John v. 27—29, vi. 39.

4. Through the mediation of Christ, each of these kinds of life becomes *perpetual*.— — —Our being delivered from the *curse* will be perpetual: "There is no condemnation to them that are in Christ Jesus—they shall never come into condemnation."— — —Being *quickened* also from a death in sin, we shall die no more: "because I live, ye shall live also."— — —Being *raised* up at the last day, we shall live for ever. There is "no more death," no sorrow or pain, but all tears shall be wiped away. Rev. xxi. 4.

If we wish to die and be lost, therefore, we shall turn away from Christ, and make light of him; shall prefer the things of the present world to his gospel and salvation, and depend on our own righteousness, to the rejection of his righteousness.

If we desire to live, we must believe in Jesus, come to him, and make him our all in all. John iii. 36.

CHRIST'S FAREWELL TO HIS DISCIPLES.

John xvi 16.—A little while and ye shall not see me: and again, a little while and ye shall see me, because I go to the Father. (Pr.)

THIS is part of the last tender discourse of our Lord to his disciples, which was omitted by the other Evangelists, but is given us by John. His design throughout the whole of his address is to reconcile their minds to his departure, and to arm them against future troubles. Such also is the kind intention in the words of our text.

Our Lord's meaning, however, was not plain to the disciples; for they did not fully understand him. He therefore took occasion to explain himself; and the explanation extends to ver. 27.

I. ENDEAVOR TO ILLUSTRATE THE SUBJECT—

In general, it has a double aspect, a dark side, and a bright one—

1. Notice *the dark part* of the subject. Our Lord's first sentence seems plainly to refer to his death: "ye shall not see me." In the course of five or six days at most he would be taken from them, and they would be left alone.— — —His farther explanation of this is given in ver. 20: they should "weep and lament." This indeed they did, not only as having lost him whom their souls loved, but as being nonplused as to all their future hopes and prospects.— — —Their feelings must have been what ours would be, if something were to transpire which would seem to prove that there was nothing true in religion.— — —They walked about, not knowing what to do with themselves: they communed, and were sad. Luke xxiv. 21.— — — While this was the case, the world triumphed, the enemy rejoiced, and were ready to say, See now what is become of your Messiah—where now is your God!

2. Let us view *the bright part* of the subject.— — —Though the situation of the disciples was very painful, it should not be of long continuance: "a little while and ye shall see me."— — —Does he mean at his resurrection? It would seem so but for the last clause, and the context—"because I go to the Father."— — —If it be understood of their seeing him with their bodily eyes after his resurrection, his going to the Father would rather be a reason of the reverse, as in ver. 10. It is not therefore with their bodily eyes that they were to behold him, though that was true for a little time, but with the eyes of their mind which from that time should be greatly irradiated: on his departure a flood of light should be poured upon them. In confirmation of this sense of the passage, the enjoyment promised was to remain with them; "no man shall take it from you."— — —The whole context agrees with this construction: when the eyes of their understanding were opened, this promise was fulfilled,

3. Observe *the similitude* by which the whole subject is illustrated, verse 21, 22.— — —The joy that should follow on Christ's going to the Father should be so great, that it should make them forget as it were their sorrow. — — —The little church of Christ was then like a woman in travail; it was also the hour of Christ's travail, and they must be in travail with him. — — —But when they come to see the fruits of all, they remember no more the anguish. Their natural attachments to him after the flesh, were henceforth swallowed up in spiritual and holy joy. 2 Cor. v. 16.

4. The *advantages* arising from Christ's going to the Father, are also exhibited for the purpose of reconciling the disciples to his departure, ver. 23

—27.— — —There are three things in particular respecting our **Lord's departure**, that are worthy of notice—

1. Our being allowed and directed henceforward to *make use of his name* in our approaches to the Father.— — —While he was upon earth, the disciples presented all their requests to him; or if to the Father, no special mention was made of the name of Jesus.— — —But now, after his soul had been made an offering for sin, his name shall be the plea: and thus we are furnished with a plea the most powerful and efficacious.

2. *A flood of light* was from hence poured upon the church.— — —A fulfilment of the prophecies would elucidate the various important events that had taken place, and the Holy Spirit was also given them in great abundance.

3. *Christ's intercession* on our behalf is also promised as one of the benefits consequent on his departure, ver. 26, 27; and hence the comfort it was intended to impart.

II. Apply the subject to ourselves.

1. We may expect, in common with the disciples of Jesus, to have *a portion of tribulation*, or a time to weep and lament.— — —There are also special times for this, and when the world rejoice: times when the cause of Christ seems to be run down and going to ruin, through persecutions from without, or contentions from within.— — —The whole of the christian life is in some degree a time of weeping and mourning, while the men of the world appear to be cheerful and happy.

2. We may take comfort in this, it is *but for a little time*. At most it cannot be long, and God shortens many of our sorrows even here.— — — The disciples did not leave the world, till they had their sorrow turned into joy; and we may also live to see many of our troubles end. Psa. xl. 1.

3. It is our duty and happiness to *believe the promise*, without knowing how it shall be accomplished.— — —The disciples knew not how, but they were told that their sorrow should be turned into joy, and it was so.— — — We know not the ways of this world, nor the ways of God, and less still of the world to come: yet we are required to believe.

4. All the advantages arising from Christ's going to the Father, *apply to us* as well as to the primitive disciples; and it is our duty and interest to avail ourselves of them.— — —To make use of Christ's name, in praying for our own souls, or for his cause; to walk by the light which is now shed abroad, to pray for large measures of the Holy Spirit; and to take encouragement from his intercession to pray for spiritual blessings, assured that him the Father heareth always.

What an awful reverse to all this, is the state of the unbelieving sinner. John xii. 35.

OUR LORD'S DESIRE TO BE GLORIFIED IN HEAVEN.

John xvii. 4, 5.—I have glorified thee on the earth: I have finished the work which thou gavest me to do. And now, O Father, glorify thou me with thine own self, with the glory which I had with thee before the world was. (S. S.)

The promises of God do not supersede the use of prayer—

They are rather encouragements to it, as being a guide to our desires, and the ground of our hopes—

It is necessary on our part in order to obtain the performance of them—Ezek. xxxvi. 37.

The necessity was laid upon our Lord himself—Ps. ii. 7.

Hence, in his last moments, he prays for his promised reward—

I. OUR LORD'S APPEAL.

Christ acted in the capacity of a servant—

He considers now his work as completed, and speaks of it in that view—

He appeals to the Father.

1. That he had "glorified him on earth"—This he did.

In his life.

The whole of his life was conformed to the divine will—

Not the smallest blemish could be found in it—

In his doctrine.

He declared the Father to the world—

He directed persons to himself only as *the way* to the Father—

In his miracles.

These, though wrought by his own power, were ascribed to the Father—John xiv. 10.

Hence the Father was particularly glorified by them—Matt. ix. 8.

In his death.

In this he most eminently glorified the Father—John xiii. 31, 32.

Even Peter in his death is said to glorify God—John xxi. 19.

Much more did Jesus both in the manner and end of it—

2. That he had "finished the work which had been given him to do."

He had fulfilled the law.

This was part of his commission—

It was necessary that he should fulfil it, both that the law might be honored, and that a righteousness should be wrought out for us—

He did fulfil it in every point—

He had satisfied the demands of justice.

He had undertaken to expiate sin by the sacrifice of himself—

It was necessary he should do so as our surety—

He did it by bearing our sins in his own body on the tree—

He paid our debt to the uttermost farthing—

He had introduced a new dispensation.

He had fulfilled and abrogated the Mosaic ritual—

He had set up the kingdom of God among men—

He had commissioned and qualified men to carry it on—

This appeal afforded him just ground for the petition he proceeded to offer.

II. THE PETITION HE GROUNDS UPON IT.

He had before prayed to be glorified on earth, ver. 1.—

He now prays to be glorified in heaven—

He had a glory with the Father before the world was.

He was from eternity with God—John i. 1.

As God he had equal glory with the Father—

This glory he had laid aside.

He veiled his godhead in human flesh—

Being in the form of God he took on him the form of a servant—

Hence he is said to have "made himself of no reputation"—

He now desired to resume it.

The ends for which he had laid it aside were accomplished—

It was therefore expedient that he should resume it—

He prayed that his human nature might be exalted to a participation of i

This had been promised to him—Ps. xvi. 10, 11.
And it was now about to be conferred upon him—Phil. ii. 9.
This petition was highly reasonable as grounded on the foregoing appeal.
He had left heaven to promote the Father's glory—
He ought therefore to return to it for his own glory—
It was right that his body, which had been the instrument whereby the Father was glorified, should itself be glorified with the Father—

INFER,

1. How easy is it to see who are real christians!
Every true christian follows Christ, and walks as he walked—
But the end and aim of Christ's life was to glorify the Father—
Here then is a plain line of distinction whereby we may judge—
May we all dread the doom of the unprofitable servant!—
May we begin the work assigned us in good earnest!—
May we on our death-bed be able to make the same appeal, and offer a similar petition to that in the text!—

2. What ground of consolation is there for true penitents!
The work assigned to Christ was to redeem a lost world—
He perfected that work, so that nothing need or can be added to it—
Let penitents then confide in him, and rejoice in his salvation—

3. How blessed is the end of the christian's labors!
He here labors much and suffers much for God's glory—
But soon he shall be glorified with God himself—
He shall continue to enjoy that glory when the world shall be no more—
Let christians then look forward to the end with joy.

DEITY AND ATONEMENT OF CHRIST.

Heb. i. 3.—Who being the brightness of his glory, and the express image of his person, and upholding all things by the word of his power, when he had by himself purged our sins, sat down on the right hand of the Majesty on high. (Pr.)

Some of the earliest corruptions of christianity consisted in entertaining low thoughts of the person and work of Christ: had it been otherwise, much that is found in this epistle would have been irrelevant. We have cause however to be thankful for what rose out of these corruptions, both in this epistle and the gospel of John.

The text contains a divinely magnificent account of the person and work of Christ, partly in relation to his antecedent character, or what he was originally; partly to his taking on him the office of a priest, to purge away our sins; and partly also to his consequent exaltation at the right hand of God. Let us briefly review each of these great and important subjects.

I. Consider what is said of the person of Christ, PREVIOUS TO HIS BECOMING OUR SAVIOUR.

He is "the brightness of the Father's glory, the express image of his person, and he upholds all things by the word of his power"—

If this be not descriptive of his being *truly God*, it is not in the power of language to convey such an idea. There is a great resemblance between this passage and that in Phil. ii. 6, where he is represented as being originally "in the form of God, and thinking it no robbery to be equal with God:"

and as that passage was intended to show the deep humiliation of Christ, in taking on him "the form of a servant," so the description in the text is designed to show what it is that gives value to his sacrifice, and dignity and importance to the whole of the christian revelation.

The antecedent *glory of Christ* is a subject on which the Scriptures delight to dwell, as may be seen in various passages. Mic. v. 2; John i. 1—3; 1 John i. 1,2. It is on this principle that all the reasoning in this epistle rests, for this it is that places him infinitely above angels, i. 6—8; above Moses the lawgiver, iii. 4—6; and above Aaron the high priest, v. 4—6. The pre-existence of Christ was necessary to his assumption of our nature, and his pre-existent and essential glory rendered that assumption an act of infinite condescension. Heb. ii. 14—16; 2 Cor. viii. 9.

Let us attend to the meaning of the terms employed in the text, as far as we can comprehend them, for the subject is great and overwhelming.

1. Christ is here called *the brightness of the Father's glory*. The description is metaphorical, for it is not in the power of language to express what God really is, or to give a literal account of the divine nature. The allusion here is to the sun, sending forth its beams throughout the wide creation; and Christ is the emanation or effulgence of the divine glory. This perhaps is as just an idea as can be conveyed to us, of the union and distinction between the Father and the Son. He is in the Father, and the Father in him. God never was without a Son, any more than the sun in the heavens can exist without its beams; yet they are not so one as to admit of no proper or personal distinction. Christ is not the Father, yet there is such an equality, that he is emphatically "the brightness of his glory."—— —It is also through him that the glory of the divine nature is revealed and made manifest. God made the world by him, and by him he saved it: the Lord Jesus is therefore the shining forth of all this glory.

2. He is *the express image of his person*, the image of the invisible God. Col. i. 15. This also is figurative, alluding to the likeness of a son to a father, only this likeness is perfect. There is not an attribute or a feature in the character of the Father but what is also in the Son. Here is likewise a personal distinction consisting with a oneness of nature, and without any other subordination than that which is relative, as between a Father and a Son.

3. Christ *upholdeth all things by the word of his power*. Nothing can be more expressive of his godhead, for this is claimed as the special prerogative of God alone. Psa. lxxv. 3. Such then is the character of him with whom we have to do, as the apostle and high priest of our profession.

II. Observe what is said of his work in undertaking the office of a priest. "HE BY HIMSELF PURGED OUR SINS"—

This is expressive of the great object of his incarnation and coming into the world; and there are two things which demand attention—

1. *The efficacy of his sacrifice:* "he purged our sins." The term alludes to the ceremonial cleansings under the law, which were effected by sacrificial blood: ch. ix. 22. Hence David prayed, "Purge me with hyssop, and I shall be clean." Psa. li. 7. Our being cleansed by the blood of Christ is the substance of all these typical purifications. 1 John i. 7, 9. By his eeath he removed the penal effects of sin, and through the application of it by faith, the conscience is purified. The gospel therefore connects repentance and the remission of sins, and proclaims forgiveness amongst all nations. Luke xxiv. 47.

2. The ground or *reason of this efficacy:* "He by Himself purged our sins." When the Scriptures speak of Christ's miracles, they usually ascribe them to the power and authority of the Father, rather than the divinity of the Son. So also in his sufferings he was succored by the ministry of angels, and upheld by the power of God, seeing he had taken upon him the form of a servant, which required that he should act in subordination to him that sent him. Isa. xlii. 1; xlix. 8. But the scriptures as uniformly ascribe the efficacy of his sacrifice to the divinity of his person, as giving value and virtue to his sufferings. It is the blood of Jesus Christ, as he is the Son of God, that cleanseth us from all sin. 1 John i. 7. He hath purged our sins by the sacrifice of "himself," and hence we see the necessity of Christ's divinity in order to the atonement.

III. The exaltation which followed upon his offering himself as a sacrifice for us. "HE SAT DOWN ON THE RIGHT HAND OF THE MAJESTY ON HIGH."

1. By "right hand of God" is meant the *first place in his favor.* None are so high in the esteem of the Father, either in heaven or earth, as Christ; none have such honors conferred upon them, or such favors granted at their intercession. In all things he is to have the pre-eminence, for he is before all things, and by him all things consist. Col. i. 17, 18.

2. This is mentioned as *an honor which became him.* Conscious that he had done the will of God, and finished the work which he had given him to do, the Lord Jesus went and took the place which belonged to him. He sat down on the right hand of God, angels and authorities and powers being made subject unto him. 1 Peter iii. 22. While all in heaven cry, Thou art worthy to receive power, and riches, and wisdom, and strength, and honor, and glory, and blessing. Rev. v. 12.

IMPROVEMENT.

1. Seeing that God hath provided for us an all-sufficient Saviour, let us learn to trust him, and to call upon his holy name, remembering that there is salvation in no other. John iii. 35; Acts ii. 21; iv. 12.

2. We see the way in which our sins are to be expiated and removed; not by tears or sufferings of our own, but by the precious blood of Christ, and that alone. Nevertheless sin must be lamented and confessed, or it cannot be forgiven. 1 John i. 9.

3. The exaltation of Christ, as the reward of his humiliation, is to us a source of great encouragement. He is exalted as a Prince and a Saviour, to give repentance and the remission of sins; and is able to save all that come unto God by him.

4. The conduct of Christ in doing and suffering the will of God, and then entering into his glory, is given as an example for our imitation. Heb. xii. 2.

NECESSITY OF THE ATONEMENT.

Luke xxiv. 46, 47.—Thus it is written, and thus it behoved Christ to suffer, and to rise from the dead the third day: and that repentance, and remission of sins should be preached in his name, among all nations, beginning at Jerusalem. (Pr.)

IT is remarkable how low the disciples were sunk, before the resurrection of Christ. That event was like a resurrection to them, and by it they were begotten again to a lively hope. 1 Pet. i. 3.

1. Observe, the words of our Lord, addressed to his disciples, were intended to *set their hearts at rest;* by showing them that nothing had taken place but what was foretold in the scriptures, and predetermined of God. — — —His plan was going on, whatever were the designs of men. This was like setting their feet on a rock when they were sinking: this truth they also remembered, and afterwards employed to an important purpose. Acts ii. 23; iv. 28.

2. The words were also designed to *explain to them* so much as they immediately needed, and no more.— — —There were other things that it behoved Christ to do, as well as to suffer: it behoved him to ascend to heaven, to reign, to intercede, to come again. But this was not their present concern, and therefore his death and resurrection only are mentioned.

I. Notice the GREAT AND INTERESTING FACTS which had lately transpired, and had filled the minds of the disciples with so much distress.

It was a fact then, that Christ had suffered—had risen again—and furnished them with a message of salvation.

1. *Christ had suffered*, had expired on the cross. This was an event on which all our salvation depended.

How did he suffer, and in what capacity? As a *martyr?* This is true, though not the whole truth. He did suffer indeed that he might bear witness to the truth, and for this cause came he into the world. John xviii. 37.

But this was not the principal cause of his sufferings and death: he suffered and died as a *substitute* in our stead. He was made sin for us, who himself knew no sin: he died for us, and bore our sins in his own body on the tree. 1 Cor. xv. 3; 2 Cor. v. 21; 1 Peter ii. 24.

As a martyr only, he suffered from the hands of wicked men; but as a substitute, he suffered from the hands of God.— — —"It pleased the Lord to bruise him, and put his soul to grief:" he bore the divine displeasure due to us.— — —He complained not of the former, but "endured the cross, despising the shame:" but in the latter case he felt and expressed himself in the strongest language. Matt. xxvi. 38, 39.— — —Job complained that his grief was heavier than the sand; and the church in captivity exclaimed, What meaneth the heat of this great anger. But all this was as nothing, compared with what Christ suffered, for he was made a curse for us. Deut. xxix. 23, 24; Lam. iii. 1; Gal. iii. 13.

2. *He had risen again.* This was another fact which had taken place: he had obtained a victory over the grave, and was loosed from the bands of death.— — —God had raised him up, according to the working of his mighty power, and this in token of his approbation, and acceptance of his sacrifice.— — —Yes, he is risen indeed, and hath appeared unto Simon This was the source of a lively hope, and an example of our own resurrection.

3. He had furnished his apostles with a *message of salvation.* This is called "preaching repentance, and remission of sins, among all nations." This was another important fact, which should soon be realised.

1. Observe, *repentance* was not itself followed by *remission*, as a necessary consequence: sin was too heinous to be thus atoned for.— — —Repentance is the duty of all mankind, as being a branch of the moral law and required by it, antecedently to all consideration of the coming of the gospel. But through the mediation of Christ, repentance and remission are now joined together.— — —Now, if we confess our sins, he is faithful and just to forgive us our sins: but this connection is all of grace.

2. The remission of sins is joined with repentance, for the honor of God's righteousness: yet it is not for the sake of repentance, but through the name of Jesus, that remission of sins is granted, and there is none in any other way. 1 John i. 7, 9.

3. This message of mercy is sent to *all nations*, "beginning at Jerusalem. This was now the worst city in all the world, for there they had crucified the Lord of life and glory.— — —Yet there the mercy was to begin, though it was not to end there. Such was the fulness of Christ's sacrifice, that its blessings should be extended to all nations: all men are now commanded every where to repent, because now mercy may be extended to all.

II. Consider the necessity there was for these things taking place.

It was necessary, in particular, that Christ should suffer, and rise again from the dead, and that on two accounts—

1. It was necessary *from the scriptures of truth:* "thus it is written." — — —Moses and the prophets had all foretold that he should suffer and rise again,. ver. 44. ——— The seed of the woman, Gen. iii. 16; Abraham's lamb for sacrifice, the prophecies of David in Psa. xxii. lxix., and those of Isaiah liii. all predicted this event. ——— So also his resurrection had been foretold, Psa. xvi. He should see his seed, prolong his days, and the pleasure of the Lord should prosper in his hands.

2. It was also necessary *from the nature of things.* "It behoved him to suffer;" it was not possible that the cup should pass from him. Matt. xxiv. 39; Luke xxiv. 26; Heb. ii. 17, x. 4. ——— Yet it may be asked, in what sense did it behove him to suffer? Certainly he was not originally obliged to it: no, it behoved us as sinners to suffer, and not him. We should have suffered justly, had we been consigned to punishment: but this cannot be said of our Surety. It is only in consideration of two things, that it behoved him to suffer—

1. His own voluntary *engagements.* There was a necessity for his going through with the work which he had begun: he had sworn as it were to his own hurt, but repentance must be hid from his eyes.

2. Our *salvation* made it necessary. If we be saved, the cup must not pass from him; otherwise God would have spared his own Son.— — —He must bear the curse, or it must fall upon us: he must drink the cup, or we cannot be exempt.

It was also fit that he should *rise again:* for if not risen, we are yet in our sins. ——— His sacrifice would not have availed, had he not risen to carry it into effect: hence it is said that he died for our sins, and was raised again for our justification: and hence it is that he is able also to save to the uttermost. Rom. iv. 25, v. 10; Heb. vii. 25.

There was likewise a propriety in *repentance being preached in his name.* It was fit that pardon should then be proclaimed: the jul ilee followed on the great day of atonement. Lev. xxv. 9. ——— It was not for the sake of repentance, but for his name's sake: yet without repentance there is no remission.

IMPROVEMENT.

1. We learn from hence the *way of salvation:* "repent and believe the gospel." This is the way for all men and for all nations to the end of time, and no other way will do.

2. We see the *allsufficiency* of salvation for the chief of sinners. The gospel might first have been sent to other nations, and last of all to the Jews: but to display its fulness it was to "begin" at Jerusalem.

3. The deplorable condition of those who perish in *unbelief*, and from under the sound of mercy. Matt. xxiii. 37.

CHRIST'S AGONY IN THE GARDEN.

Matt. xxvi. 38.—My soul is exceeding sorrowful, even unto death. (P1.)

The sufferings of Christ contain one of the great mysteries of godliness. It is a subject of which we know but little, and cannot fully comprehend; but it would be happy for us if we were better acquainted with it. It was Paul's prayer, that he might know the fellowship of his sufferings, and be made conformable unto his death.

The manner in which our Lord spent the last night, the night before his suffering, is highly impressive. He went with his diciples to the house of a friend in Jerusalem; and when evening was come, they entered an upper room to eat the passover; after which the supper of the Lord was instituted. Judas left the room, and had an interview with the Jews, according to a previous appointment. When he was gone, Jesus delivered his farewell discourse to his disciples, which is given in the 14th to the 17th chapter of John. At the close of this affecting address, Jesus offered up his intercessory prayer, in the hearing of his disciples. Taking with him his confidential friends, Peter, James, and John, he entered into the garden of Gethsemane; and here he began to be "very heavy, and sore amazed." The disciples who were with him beheld his agony, and heard the distressing words recorded in our text. Let us,

I. Attentively consider the fact: "His soul was exceeding sorrowful."

It was so indeed, and to such a degree as exceeded all his former sufferings. Christ's own testimony is sufficient to prove this: he never affected grief, nor magnified his sufferings. Men are apt indeed to represent their afflictions as greater than they are, and to complain too much; but it was not so with our blessed Lord. Great sorrows generally prevent loud complaints, and are like deep waters, which run the stillest. It was thus with Job, and also with Jesus.— — —He made no great complaint: a few words to his friends, and a few to his heavenly Father, are all that dropped from his lips. Isa. liii. 7; 1 Pet ii. 23.

Nearly all the evangelists have given an account of his sufferings in the garden, which they describe in various affecting forms of speech. Mark tells us that he begins to be "sore amazed:" ch. xiv. 33.— — —Luke that he was "in an agony, sweating as it were great drops of blood, falling to the ground."— — —Matthew tells us that he was "exceeding sorrowful even unto death."— — —What a scene was this?

Sorrow is the fruit of sin; but here was no sin, though he was treated as if he had been the chief of sinners, yea the only sinner in the world; as if divine vengeance had forgotten to run in its usual channels, it concentrated all in him. Blessed Saviour! Why art thou cast down, and why is thy soul disquieted within thee?— — —Considering the infinite dignity of his person, and how much he was the object of the Father's delight; the scene is full of awful grandeur, and such as was never before exhibited.

II. Endeavor to account for it.

If Christ died merely as a martyr, as some have pretended, the overwhelming nature of his sufferings could not be accounted for. On this scheme, he would appear very inferior to many of his followers, who have suffered death for his sake with heroic fortitude. ——— Some indeed who deny the deity and atonement of Christ, have endeavored to remove the difficulty, by allowing that Christ is not only a mere man, but a very imperfect one, and bring this transaction in the garden as an instance of his timidity and want of resolution! Thus has the Saviour of the world been degraded by his followers, and betrayed by his professed friends. —— Our blessed Lord challenged the Jews, saying, "which of you convinceth me of sin?" But it seems as if some of his pretended followers would accept the challenge, which even his enemies declined. Let us dread dishonoring the Saviour, by attempting to account for his agony in such a way as this.

In general, we may observe, it was now that the Father *withdrew himself* from his beloved Son: and what that would be to him, who can tell? "My God! My God! why hast thou forsaken me!"

It was now also that he poured out *his wrath* to the uttermost upon him —— —As he had become the sinner's Surety, he must feel the weight of that curse which the sinner had deserved: and who knoweth the power of thine anger! ——— Who can estimate the tremendous evil and demerit of sin? Even Jesus himself was "sore amazed."

Now it was that the *prince of this world* came to make his last desperate attack upon him: this was the hour and the power of darkness. ——— The enemy had before tried what he could do by temptation; and now he will try what the most awful terrors may accomplish. John xiv. 30. All these things meeting together, his soul became "exceeding sorrowful, even unto death."

More particularly—

1. The *greatness of his mind* rendered him more susceptible of grief than we can possibly experience or imagine. ——— As man, his intimate union with the divine nature, gave an enlargement to his powers beyond our highest conceptions. ——— It was no small part of Job's affliction that he was to be set at nought by persons so inferior to himself, and towards whom it would have been an act of condescension to have noticed them in any other circumstances.

2. His *infinite purity* freed him from all partiality. He therefore saw things as they were, and had a full view of the infinite evil of sin, as it affected the righteous government of God; and this would render him susceptible of the greatness of his displeasure against it. ——— It is this which gives an edge to punishment: if God's displeasure against sin had been arbitrary, or severe beyond measure, even hell itself would be tolerable, and Christ would not have felt what he did. ——— We can bear con

tempt or suffering much better when we know they are undeserved, than when it is otherwise. ——— All that Christ felt, he knew to be the just desert of sin; and this it was that gave poignancy to his sufferings.

3. His *love to the Father* was such that it must necessarily have affected him in an unknown degree, to be forsaken and put to grief by him. Isa. liii. 10. ——— The frowns of any one may be endured, excepting those of a friend: oh why hast "*thou* forsaken me!"

4. The love he bore *to the souls of men*, made their conduct towards him exceeding grievous. Had it been an enemy that should crucify and put him to open shame, he could have borne it: but he was wounded in the house of his friends, he was put to death by those whose life he came to seek. ——— When Satan came against him, it did not grieve him, but raised his abhorrence: but the prospect of suffering by the hands of men, filled him with bitterness of soul. Heb. v. 7.

III. Improvement.

1. What a motive is here for *gratitude*, when we consider the results of this dismal hour. From hence it is that the curse is removed, and that the sorrows of the believer have nothing penal in them. Since he has drunk the bitter cup, there is nothing left for us: the means is now prepared for turning our sorrows into endless joys, and our tears into rivers of delight. John xvi. 20; 2 Cor. iv. 17.

2. What a motive for *repentance*, to think of the sorrows which he endured- ——— What has sin done: how evil in its nature and how bitter in its consequences.

3. Let the example of the suffering Saviour teach us *sympathy* towards the afflicted. ——— He bore our sorrows, and carried our griefs: in all our afflictions he himself was afflicted. Let us learn to bear each other's burdens, and so fulfil the law of Christ. Isa. lxiii. 9; liii. 4; Gal. vi. 2.

4. Let us also learn *patience* from his example, and consider him who endured the cross for us, lest we be weary and faint in our minds. Heb. xii. 2, 3; 1 Pet. ii. 21—23.

5. From his sufferings we may learn what will be the portion of the finally *impenitent*, who reject his salvation. Their sorrows will be insupportable, and unavailing. Matt, xiii. 42.

CHRIST'S INTERCESSION ON THE CROSS.

Luke xxiii. 34.—Then said Jesus, Father, forgive them; for they know not what they do. (Pr.)

What a surprising contrast, between the treatment which the blessed Saviour received from his enemies, and that which they received from him in return, ver. 33.

We here see the wisdom of God overruling the enmity of wicked men. They crucify Jesus, to render his name infamous; and place him between two malefactors, to cover him with reproach. But by this lingering, painful, and shameful death, an opportunity was given for the Saviour more fully to express his love. While suspended on the cross he uttered many things and all of them highly interesting and important. Here also he made intercession for the transgressors.

I. OBSERVE THE PETITION ITSELF: "FATHER, FORGIVE THEM."

How well this agrees with the language of prophecy. Isa. liii. 12.

1. Notice *the magnitude of the blessing* prayed for, even "forgiveness." — — —This includes all other blessings, and an interest in eternal life. Sin is the great mountain that stands between God and us, and prevents the manifestation of his favor: if that be removed, all is removed. It is forgiveness that extracts the sting of death, and calms the terrors of a future judgment; for if God forgives, who is he that shall condemn. Forgiveness takes away the curse of the law, and the bitterness of all affliction in this life. In the present instance especially, it is a blessing greater than could be asked or thought, by any other than the blessed Redeemer himself.

2. Consider *the extreme unworthiness of the objects.*— — —Surely, if such be pardoned, it must indeed be according to the riches of his grace. They were not common sinners, nor had they committed any common offence: they had killed the Prince of life, and crucified the Lord of glory. They had put him to open shame whom God had made heir of all things, and by whom also he made the worlds.— — —To pray for such sinners was love operating against hatred, and doing good against evil in the highest sense possible. He had met with enough from their hands to turn his heart against them; but his was love that many waters could not quench, neither could the floods drown it.— — —Such is his love to us also; for when we were enemies he died for us, and it is wholly owing to his intercession that we are spared and pardoned Rom. v. 10.

3. The *heinous nature of their offence:* "they know not what they do." — — —This very plea implies that it was an awful sin they were committing, though they were blinded to it; it was one on which the heavens frowned with preternatural darkness, and the earth trembled while they perpetrated the dreadful deed. It was such as might have awaked the vengeance of God, to send out evil spirits and destroy them. For offering insult to an angel in human form, the inhabitants of Sodom were smitten with blindness; but the guilt of the inhabitants of Jerusalem is not to be described.

4. The *efficacy of the petition*, in securing the blessing prayed for.— — — A good man might say of his murderers as Stephen did, Lord, lay not this sin to their charge; but it would not follow that they would certainly be forgiven. But the intercession of Christ is for ever prevalent, for him the Father heareth always. The blood which then flowed from the cross gave efficacy to his prayer; the plea itself was the cry of blood, even of that which speaketh better things than the blood of Abel.— — —The plea of the suffering Saviour had an immediate reference to his death, the very design of which was to procure the forgiveness of sin. In this instance therefore he showed what was the object of his sacrifice, and how it would be carried into effect by his intercession. Luke xxiv. 46, 47.

II. THE PLEA BY WHICH THE PETITION IS ENFORCED: "THEY KNOW NOT WHAT THEY DO."

1. It is such as would *have not been found by any other advocate.*— — — Who indeed could have devised any plea whatever for such an offence, and for such sinners; or who dared so much as to think of a plea in such a case! Yet the blessed Saviour finds one, and the only one that could avail. 1 Tim. i. 13.

2. It is a plea which shows *that sin has different degrees of guilt*, according to the circumstances under which it is committed.— — —Sins com-

mitted through ignorance and unbelief, though great are not so aggravated as those committed against light and knowledge: hence it was that Paul obtained mercy, while apostates find none. 1 Tim. i. 13, Heb. x. 26—29. Heathens, though, guilty, are not so fearfully involved as those who have the gospel and reject it. Heb. ii. 3, xii. 25.

3. It is a plea which teaches us, that *for some there was no mercy*, though there might be for those on whose behalf it was offered.— — —There is a sin unto death, which has no forgiveness in this world, nor in that which is to come. Matt. xii. 32. And there were some among the Jews for whom there was no mercy for what they had done in this matter, though the populace in general, and many of the rulers, knew not what they did; and hence it was that Peter afterwards exhorted them to repentance, in the hope of their being forgiven. Acts iii. 17—19.

4. Though their ignorance afforded a plea for mercy, *they were not to be pardoned without repentance.*— — —Christ never prayed that sinners should be forgiven only in this way, nor that they should be pardoned before they repent, for this would be incompatible with the whole design of his mediation. His intercession for their pardon therefore includes repentance, and hence it was that such multitudes of the Jews were afterwards pricked to the heart under Peter's sermon. Acts ii. 37. Sinners must know what they have done, before they can expect mercy. Jer, ii. 19.

IMPROVEMENT.

1. We see there is that in the nature of sin which *surpasses all our conceptions*. When sinners offend against God, oppose the gospel, and reject the Saviour, "they know not what they do." Would any one if he knew it, offend his best friend, serve his worst enemy, and plunge himself into endless ruin? Or having brought himself into danger, would he reject the way of escape! Yet such is the case with every unbeliever.

2. Still we learn that notwithstanding the evil nature of sin, *there is no reason for despair*, not even for the chief of sinners. If Jerusalem sinners can be pardoned, there is hope for all: and it was amongst these unparalleled offenders that the mercy was to begin, as an example to all nations. Luke xxiv. 47.

3. The conduct of our blessed Lord is set before us in this instance *as an example*, teaching us what must be our spirit towards our enemies and persecutors. Stephen followed this example, and we must learn to do the same. Acts vii. 60, Matt. v. 44, 45.

THE CRUCIFIXION.

Luke xxiii. 33.—And when they were come to the place called Calvary, there they crucified him, and the malefactors; one on the right hand, and the other on the left. (Pr.)

How striking is the contrast between the conduct of Jesus, and that of his enemies. When they were come to Calvary, there they crucified him; and while they crucified him, he prayed for his murderers, saying, Father, forgive them. for they know not what they do, ver. 34.

In offering a few remarks upon the text, there are three things particularly worthy of notice—the place where our Lord suffered—the nature of his sufferings—and the company in which he suffered.

I. Observe the place where our Lord suffered.

This is called Calvary, or Golgotha, a small eminence, about half a mile distant from Jerusalem. This was the common place of execution, where the vilest offenders were put to death.

Two things may be observed concerning this, one relating to the intention of the murderers, and the other effecting the intention of the writer—

1. The place where Jesus suffered, marks *the malignant design of his enemies.*— — —It was not without some reason on their part that they fixed on Calvary; it was to render his name and character infamous, to express the greatest abhorrence of both, to sink and ruin his cause by affixing an indelible disgrace. Hence it was that the cross of Christ became a stumbling block to the Jews, and to the Greeks foolishness. But in this they were ultimately disappointed.

2. The place as mentioned by the evangelist, *marks his strong affection.* — — —The sacred writer employs but few words, his narration is slow and solemn, and expressive of the deepest feelings of the heart. He points to the spot with peculiar emphasis, as Jacob did to the field of Machpelah, saying, "*There* they buried Abraham and Sarah his wife; there they buried Isaac and Rebekah his wife; and there I buried Leah." Gen. xlix. 31. Annother instance of this form of speech occurs in the address of Ruth to Naomi: "Where thou diest, will I die, and *there* will I be buried." Ruth. i. 17. — — —Thus the evangelist points to Calvary, and with deep emotion says, *There* they crucified him.

3. We may also add that this directs us to *the place where we must look for mercy.*— — —There they crucified him, and thence our salvation comes. There the great sacrifice was offered up, the ransom price paid, and the great atonement made.

"There hangs all human hope: that nail supports the falling universe."

II. The nature of Christ's sufferings: "they crucified him."

The sin of which the Jews pretended to accuse our Lord, was that of blasphemy, because that "he being a man, made himself God; and calling God his Father, he made himself equal with God." By the Jewish law a blasphemer was to be stoned to death, and therefore they took up stones to cast at him; but being at that time under the Roman government, they had no power to put any one to death. They therefore brought him before Pilate, demanding that he should be crucified. The Roman law inflicted capital punishment by various other means, chiefly by decapitation; but crucifixion was fixed upon to gratify the malignity of the Jews, and the unrighteous judge yielded to their wishes. ——— In all this however the hand of God may be traced, and his wisdom seen in overruling these events for the accomplishment of his own purposes.

1. The death of the cross, though selected by Jewish malignity, would be *the fulfilment of prophecy,* ——— The disciples were blind to these things when they happened, but afterwards they saw plainly that thus it was written, and that thus it behoved Christ to suffer. Prophecy had foretold that they should pierce his hands and his feet, Psa. xxii. 16; and also his side, Zech. xii. 10; John xix. 34, 37. ——— Our Lord also had himself foretold, in numerous instances, that he should be betrayed into the hands of sinners, and be crucified. John iii. 14, viii. 28, xii. 32, 33. He had also

rendered the idea familiar by calling a profession of his name, with all the difficulties attending it, a bearing of the cross, in allusion to his carrying the cross to Calvary. Matt. xvi. 24, Mark x. 21, Luke ix. 23. ——— Hence also the doctrine of Christ crucified, as the only medium of our salvation, formed the very essence of the gospel itself. 1 Cor. ii. 2, Gal. iii. 1, vi. 14.

2. In our Lord's suffering the death of the cross, there was something *analogous to what we as sinners had deserved;* and probably it was with a view to represent this, that the Jews were suffered to crucify him—

1. It was a *lingering death,* and the Romans appear to have invented this mode of punishment on purpose to render death as dreadful as possible. In the case of our blessed Lord it was six hours, from the commencement to the end of the crucifixion, when, having power to lay down his life, he voluntarily gave up the ghost; but the malefactors had not then expired, and would probably have survived many hours longer. Mark xv. 44, John xix. 33. ——— All this time the sufferer would experience the most insatiate thirst, from the extreme anguish so long endured. Psa. xxii. 15, lxix. 21, John xix. 28. And in this lengthened pain and anguish there was something that represented the endless punishment of the wicked, the worm that dieth not, and the fire that is not quenched.

2. It was a most *painful death,* more so perhaps than any other that human malignity could devise. The wounds were all inflicted on the tenderest parts of the human body, but not so as to effect the seat of life. In the act of fixing the cross in the ground, with the sufferer suspended on it, his joints would be dislocated by the shock; and thus another prophecy would be fulfilled. Psa. xxii. 14. ——— These exquisite sufferings would shadow forth those torments of hell, in which the sinner shall thirst in vain for water to cool his tongue, and where the everburning sulphur is unconsumed.

3. The death of the cross was attended with *reproach and infamy;* none so painful, so ignominious as this. He was made a spectacle to angels and to men, and they that passed by wagged the head in derision and contempt. Yet he endured the cross, and despised the shame. ——— In this also there was a prefiguration of that public disgrace and overwhelming shame, which the righteous judge has awarded as the punishment of sin. Dan. xii. 2, Isa. lxvi. 24.

4. The death of the cross was an *accursed death,* both in the esteem of God and man. Gal. iii. 13. And the sentence to which sinners are doomed is, that they are to die the death, to die under the curse. Hence Jesus would come under the law, and into our place and stead, and so was made a curse for us.

III. THE COMPANY IN WHICH HE SUFFERED: THEY CRUCIFIED WITH HIM "TWO MALEFACTORS, ONE ONE THE RIGHT HAND, AND THE OTHER ON THE LEFT."

1. On the part of his enemies this was designed to render his death still *more ignominious and shameful,* and was no doubt contrived between Pilate and the chief priests. ——— Our blessed Lord was holy, harmless and undefiled, and separate from sinners; but now to overwhelm him with shame and public disgrace, they associate him with "malefactors." ——— Not content with this, they place him in the midst, to insinuate that he was the worst of the three. Here every circumstance tells, for every thing was intended to heighten the disgrace. ——— This arrangement might also be contrived for the purpose of discomposing his mind, during his last moments, by filling his ear with the blasphemies and reproaches of the dying malefac-

tors. When welcome to die, the least comfort we hope for is a peaceful pillow, and the presence of a sympathizing friend. But here is the blessed Saviour, surrounded by an enraged populace, and expiring on the cross, amidst the execrations of his enemies, and the groans of dying malefactors

2. But on the part of God we may see something of *the wisdom of this appointment.* ——— Prophecy was hereby fulfilled, which said that he should be numbered with transgressors. Isa. liii. 11, Mark xv. 27, 28. ——— By this means also the virtue of his sacrifice was made more fully to appear. Had two of his disciples been crucified with him, instead of two malefactors, it might have been imagined that they had contributed something to the efficacy of his sufferings: but as it is, it would appear that his own arm brought salvation, and his righteousness it sustained him. He trode the winepress alone, and of the people there was none with him. Isa. lxiii. 3. ——— Also by suffering in such society, an opportunity was given for the fuller display of his power and grace, in saving one of the malefactors in his last moments, and taking him from the cross to the paradise of God. ——— Moreover, the publicity of his crucifixion, rendered the evidence of his death more certain and indisputable; so that his enemies could not pretend that there was any collusion; and that which established the reality of his death, established also the reality of his subsequent resurrection, on which all the hopes of his followers depend.

THE EFFECTS OF CHRIST'S DEATH.

John xii. 31, 32.—Now is the judgment of this world: now shall the prince of this world be cast out. And I, if I be lifted up from the earth, will draw all men unto me. (H. H.)

INCONCEIVABLY arduous was the work which Christ had undertaken: yet amidst his heaviest trials his confidence never for a moment forsook him. He had just complained of the insupportable weight of his mental agonies; yet not so complained, but that he had desired his heavenly Father to glorify his own name, whatever sufferings he might have to endure for that end. For the satisfaction of those who would otherwise have drawn wrong conclusions from those sufferings, the Father answered him by a voice like thunder, "I have both glorified it, and will glorify it again:" and immediately Jesus, with his wonted calmness, resumed his discourse respecting the nature and necessity of his approaching death, and confidently predicted,

I. THE ISSUE OF HIS CONFLICTS—

The world and Satan were his great adversaries: and though by his death they would appear victorious over him, yet he declared that by his death,

1. The world would be judged—

What we are to understand by "the judgment of this world," we cannot absolutely determine: but we apprehend the import of that expression to be, that his death would be the means of exhibiting in the clearest view, first, *the wickedness*, and next, *the desert* of the ungodly world.

Who would have conceived *the wickedness* of the world to be so great as it really is? Who would have conceived, that, if God himself should become incarnate, and sojourn in a familiar manner upon earth, and cause the light of his perfections to shine around him, and diffuse innumerable blessings by the unbounded exercise of omnipotence and love, his creatures should rise up against him, and put him to death? Who would conceive too, that this should be done, not by ignorant savages, but by the people who had enjoyed the light of revelation, heard his gracious instructions, beheld his bright example, and received the benefit of his miraculous exertions: yea, that it should be done too, not by the inconsiderate vulgar, but by the rulers themselves, and by the priests and ministers of God's sanctuary? This shews what human nature itself is, even under the greatest possible advantages: and humiliating is the picture which it exhibits to us.

But *the desert* also of the world is manifested to us in the death of Christ: for Christ suffered the penalty due to sin: "to redeem us from the curse of the law, he became a curse:" and all the misery that he endured both in body and soul as our surety and substitute, was our deserved portion. He indeed, by reason of his office, could endure it but for a time: but the soul that perishes in sin, must endure it to all eternity. Death, which to him was the period of his release, will be to the condemned soul the commencement of its sorrows, of sorrows that shall endure to all eternity. The hidings of God's face and the sense of his wrath will be co-existent with the soul itself.

2. The prince thereof would be cast out—

Satan is called the prince, and the god, of this world, because he exercises an universal government over men who are his willing subjects. Eph. ii. 2; 2 Cor. iv. 4; 2 Tim. ii. 26. That which has given him this power, is *sin:* on account of *sin*, God has delivered men into his hands as their jailor and their executioner. But Jesus Christ has "finished transgression and made an end of sin, and brought in everlasting righteousness;" and has thus rescued from the hands of Satan a countless multitude, who shall be eternal monuments of his electing love and his redeeming power. Whilst yet he hanged on the cross, the Lord Jesus "bruised the serpent's head;" Gen. iii. 15; yea, "he spoiled principalities and powers, triumphing over them openly upon the cross." Col. ii. 15. At that moment did "Satan fall from heaven as lightning:" and though he still retains a sway over the children of disobedience, yet is he forced continually to give up his vassals to the Lord Jesus, and is made to flee from those, Jam. iv. 7, whom he lately "led captive at his will." Moreover, the time is shortly coming, (yea, in the divine purpose it was, as it were, then present,) when he shall be bound in chains of everlasting darkness, and be cast into that "lake of fire" which has from the beginning been "prepared for him and for his angels."

Next, our Lord predicts,

II. The triumphs of his grace—

By being "lifted up from the earth" was meant, his crucifixion. The expression refers to the lifting up the brazen serpent in the wilderness, which was a type and emblem of the death of Christ. Compare Numb. xxi. 8, 9, with John iii. 14, 15. The Evangelist himself tells us, that our Lord intended to intimate the peculiar kind of death which he was to suffer: and the people themselves understood him as speaking of his removal from them by death. Ver. 33, 34. Nor did his words convey the idea of uncertainty, which seems intimated in our translation: the event was fixed in the divine counsels from all eternity; and he spoke of it as certainly to be accomplished.*

Here then are two things to be noted;

* ἐὰν should be "*when*," and not "*if*."

1. The event predicted—

Christ will "draw all men to himself:" He is that "Shiloh, to whom the gathering of the people should be;" and we see on the day of Pentecost the commencement of this great and glorious work. Would we understand precisely the import of the expression, there we behold it exemplified in the clearest view ——— We must not indeed imagine that every individual of mankind will be drawn to Christ; for in every age many have rejected him: but some of all nations, professions, and characters, shall be drawn to him; and at last shall be found a multitude that no man can number ——— Dan. vii. 13, 14.

2. The manner in which it shall be accomplished—

Men are not drawn to him like stocks and stones, but in a way consistent with the perfect exercise of their own free will. The power indeed is Christ's; and it is exerted with effect: but it is made effectual,—

First, *by shewing men their need of him.*—The eyes of all the wounded Israelites were drawn to the brazen serpent in the wilderness: they felt that they were dying of their wounds; they knew that no human efforts could heal them; and they were assured that a sight of that brazen serpent would effect their cure. This attraction was sufficient: they looked and were healed. Thus the jailor saw his own perishing condition, and asked, "What shall I do to be saved?" and was glad to embrace the Saviour proposed to him. Acts xvi. 30, 31. This is universally the first operation of Christ's victorious grace.

Next, he draws men *by the attractive influences of his grace.*—Because men know not how the Holy Spirit works upon the souls of men, they are ready to doubt, or even deny, his operations. But who doubts the agency of the wind? yet no man knows whence it comes, or whither it goes. It is visible in its effects; and therefore its operation is acknowledged, notwithstanding it is involved in the deepest mystery. Why then should the operation of the Holy Spirit be doubted, merely because *the mode* of his agency is not understood? John iii. 8. Were it possible to question the evidence of our senses, we should deny the virtue of the loadstone, and represent any one as weak or wicked who should profess to believe it. But we behold its effects; and our incredulity is vanquished. So then must we confess the agency of the Holy Spirit upon the souls of men, though we cannot comprehend every thing respecting it. Our Lord has told us, that "no man can come unto him, except the Father draw him:" John vi. 44; and the Psalmist affirms, that God makes us "willing in the day of his power." Ps. cx. 3. It is sufficient for us to know, that he draws us rationally, "with the cords of a man, and with the bands of love."

Lastly, he draws men *by discovering to them the wonders of his love.* Let but a glimpse of his incomprehensible love be seen, and every thing in the whole creation will be darkened: just as a view of the meridian sun renders every other object invisible. Paul tells us, that "the love of Christ constrained him:" it carried him away like a mighty torrent: nor will the soul of any man who feels it be either able or desirous to withstand its influence. As well might the angels in heaven be averse to serve their God, as the man that has tasted of redeeming love.

In this way then does the grace of Christ prevail; and in this way shall it triumph to the ends of the earth.

APPLICATION:

1. Seek to experience the attractions of his grace—

Nothing unde heaven is so desirable as this ——— Say then, with the church of old, "Draw me, and I will run after thee" ———Cant. i. 4.

2. Fear not the counteracting influence of men or devils—

Men may oppose you, and vaunt themselves against you: but they are already "judged" by the word of God; and, if they repent not, they shall be judged by the same at the tribunal of their God. If they do not themselves become such despised creatures as they esteem you to be, they will ere long "awake to shame and everlasting contempt."

Satan too may harass you: but he is a vanquished enemy: yea, he too "is judged:" John xvi. 11; and though, "as a roaring lion, he seeketh to devour you," you are provided with armor, whereby you may withstand him; Eph. vi. 11–13; and you have the promise of God, that "he shall be shortly bruised under your feet" ——— Rom. xvi. 20.

THE PROPITIATION.

1 John iv. 10.—Herein is love, not that we loved God, but that he loved us, and sent his Son to be the propitiation for our sins. (Sk.)

The interesting and all-important inquiry, "What must I do to be saved?" could never have been answered by the light of nature. How guilty, polluted, and condemned creatures may be restored to the forfeited approbation of their God, is a mystery which human reason could never penetrate, as is evident from the numerous futile schemes which have been invented to regain the Divine favor.

The supposed intrinsic merit and excellence of human works—bloody sacrifices—grievous austerities, &c.,—the senseless dream of purgatory—vague and undefinable notions of Divine mercy. All these, and various other systems equally irrational and unsatisfactory, show the imperious necessity of a plan of salvation, revealed by God himself. This glorious plan is presented to our view in the words of the text. "Herein is love," &c.

The word rendered *propitiation*, signifies the *victim* or *atoning sacrifice* by which sin is expiated, and for the sake of which God can be propitious to a fallen creature—the *vicarious offering* presented in the sinner's stead. Our text therefore leads us to observe,

I. That the state of man required a propitiation. Viewing man as a moral and an accountable agent, who has offended his Maker, the need of a propitiation provided for him, will be very obvious if we reflect,

1. *On the perfection and excellence of the law which he has broken.* It is characterized as "*Holy, just, and good.*" Our Lord has comprised it in two essential points, viz. love to God, and love to our neighbor, Matt. xxii. 37—39. This law is—Divine in its *origin*—immutable in its *nature*—reasonable in its *requirements*—benevolent in its *tendency*—indispensable in its *obligations*. Such a law therefore is essentially good, and ought to be obeyed. The principle which refuses obedience is essentially evil—consequently the person who indulges it, must justly deserve punishment, even the penalty which the law denounces, viz. *death eternal*. It follows, that if man who has violated the law be saved from its malediction, while yet the law is perfectly honored, it must be through a propitiation, an atonement—a substitute offered, and suffering in his stead.

2. *On the inability of man to expiate his offences.* All his doings, sufferings, and sacrifices, can never atone for one of his sins, nor heal a single breach of the divine commands. Even repentance, though indispensable as a *means* of salvation, is in no way an expiation of guilt. It cannot undo what is already done. Its effect is rather prospective, than retrospective. It is no requisition of the law—consequently no satisfaction of its claims ; for the law demands innocence and obedience, not repentance. Hence it appears, that some other must provide the propitiation, through which guilty man can be honorably released from the direful penalty of the law.

3. *On the inflexible nature of Divine justice,* which supports the honor of the law, and enforces its claims. Justice is essential to God. Now if man justly merits punishment, justice must inflict that punishment, either on him, or on a proper and an adequate victim that may be justly substituted in its stead. Otherwise justice must relinquish its claims, and thus be proved not essential to God—or else it must be set aside by Divine mercy, and so exhibit its own weakness, and a discord among the Divine perfections. But as we cannot admit either of these blasphemous suppositions, it follows, that no way is left for the exercise of mercy in the salvation of man, but through the medium of a vicarious sacrifice, atonement, or propitiation. We will now show,

II. That Jesus Christ is the propitiation required.

Three arguments will establish this proposition :

1. *No creature could or would become a propitiation for man.* No creature can lay God under any obligation. No creature can, strictly speaking, merit any thing from God. Hence no creature can perform works of supererogation. Much less could any mere creature bear, in a limited time and capacity, the inflictions of infinite justice. And certainly no creature ever *would* (even if it were possible) make atonement for man. See this finely represented in Paradise Lost, book 3.

2. *Jesus Christ is every way adapted to become our propitiation.* "God was manifested in the flesh", &c. His obedience unto death was infinitely meritorious, as he united in himself the Divine and human natures ; by the one he was qualified to suffer—by the other infinite value and efficacy were conveyed into his sufferings ; so that the law was magnified and made honorable, and every claim of justice satisfied.

3. *The Scriptures every where testify that Jesus Christ is our propitiation.* Here we might produce the numerous *types* of the Old Testament Isa. liii. 5, 6, 7, 10; Matt. xx. 28; Rom. iii. 24, 25, iv. 25; 2 Cor. v. 21; Gal. iii. 13; Col. i. 20; 1 Tim. i. 15; Heb. ix. 22—26; 1 John ii. 2. The Father gave the Son, John iii. 16. The Son gave himself, Gal. i. 4. He offered himself through the Eternal Spirit, Heb. ix. 14. The sacred Three combine. Hence we observe,

III. That this propitiation is a glorious display of the love of God. "Herein is love," &c.

The whole Trinity concurred in the work of man's redemption, but the Father is here represented as the first mover. *He* sent his only-begotten Son. Some have exhibited Him as burning with implacable rage against mankind, till Christ died to make him merciful. How unscriptural as well horrid the idea ! Christ died because God *was* merciful—not to *render* him so ; but to prepare a channel for his mercy to flow in a stream of salvation to men. "Herein is love," &c. This love is,

1. *Unparalled in its nature.* Remark that it was wholly undeserved—entirely unsolicited—perfectly disinterested—contrary to man's own seeking

—-never invited by anything good, by any moral excellence in man. "Not that we loved God."

2. *Intense in its ardours.* Here let us regard—the dignity of the Sufferer—the depth of his degradation—the extremity of his sufferings.

3. *Immense in its extent.* It reaches to every age and every clime—to every character and every condition, even to the lowest and most abominable of the human race. It embraces all, John iii. 16.

4. *Glorious in its purpose and final issue.* It not only procured pardon for sin and present holiness—but designed nothing less than everlasting glory for all believers. Here "grace reigns through righteousness unto everlasting life by Christ Jesus our Lord."

Inferences:—

1. How pernicious is the doctrine of Socinianism, which completely destroys this only hope of a penitent, *redemption by Christ!* On the Divinity of Christ depends the atonement,—to renounce one is to renounce both. The atonement gone; either man must be absurdly made a meritorious creature, or the perfections of God must be set at variance, and one attribute must vanquish another.

2. How dangerous is the delusion of the self-righteous! They practically renounce, what Socinians professedly deny. No one can receive the atonement, who does not feel his need of it, and if it be not applied, it can be of no avail to any individual.

3. What abundant consolation does this subject afford penitent sinners. Only let them believe, and they shall see the glory of God.

4. In this love of God we are furnished with a rule and a motive for love to each other—"Beloved, if God so loved us, we out also to love one another."

THE SUFFERINGS OF CHRIST.

Isaiah liii. 10, 11.—Yet it pleased the Lord to bruise him, &c. (Sk.)

Of all the prophetic writings, none contain more clear and correct predictions of Christ, than those of Isaiah; and of all Isaiah's writings, none describe the Messiah more accurately, both in his suffering and exalted state, than this chapter. That the prophet here speaks of our Lord Jesus Christ, is evident from the words of the Holy Ghost in the New Testament. He applies verse the 4th to our Lord, Matt. viii. 16, 17; he "healed all who were sick, that it might be fulfilled which was spoken by Esaias the prophet, saying, Himself took our infirmities, and bare our sicknesses." He applies verse the 5th to him, 1 Pet. ii. 24, "Who his own self bare our sins in his own body on the tree, that we being dead unto sin, should live unto righteousness; by whose stripes ye were healed." He applies verses the 7th and 8th to him, Acts viii. 32—35, "The place of the Scripture which he read, was this, He was led as a sheep to the slaughter; and like a lamb dumb before his shearers, so opened he not his mouth. In his humiliation his judgment was taken away; and who shall declare his generation? For his life is taken from the earth. And the eunuch answered Philip, and said, I pray thee of whom speaketh the prophet this; of himself, or of some other man? Then Philip opened his mouth, and began at the same Scripture, and preached unto him Jesus." This example teaches us, that we also may, and indeed should, preach Jesus from the words now before us. For here we find a most interesting description of his character, his sufferings, and the happy effects of his sufferings. We are led to observe,

I. HIS CHARACTER. He was God's righteous servant, of whom God had before spoken by this prophet; chap. xlii. 1, "Behold," &c.

1. *He was God's servant;* who glorified God by obeying him, John xvii. 4. He served God *fully:*—his obedience was complete, Phil. ii. 8. "Being," &c. He served God *cheerfully;* with delight, Psa. xl. 7, 8; John iv. 34. He served God *constantly;* without intermission, John viii. 29. He served God *unweariedly;* till the work assigned him was done. He labored on and ceased not, till he was enabled to say, "I have glorified thee on earth, I have finished the work thou gavest me to do."

2. *He was God's righteous servant:* being unblamable in all his deportment, and never justly chargeable with sin. This appears—From the testimony of his *friends;* of Paul, 2 Cor. 21, "Who made," &c.; of Peter, 1 Pet. ii. 22, "Who did," &c.; and of John, 1 John iii. 5. "In him was no sin."—And from the testimony of his *enemies.* This was given by Judas, who betrayed him, Matt. xxvii. 3, 4, "Then Judas," &c.; by Pilate, who condemned him to death, Matt. xxvii. 24, "When Pilate saw," &c.; and by the centurion, whose soldiers crucified Christ; "Certainly," says he, "This was a righteous man; truly this man was the Son of God," Luke xxii. 47; Mark xv. 39.

3. As God's righteous servant, *he became a perfect example*, and an *acceptable mediator.* A *perfect example* to all his followers, of piety towards God; love to mankind; and personal purity, Phil. ii. 5; 1 John ii. 6. And an *acceptable mediator.* For it was requisite that our High priest should be harmless, Heb. vii. 26, "Such a highpriest," &c. And that our Advocate should be righteous, 1 John ii. 1, "We," &c. This was requisite, that God's righteousness might be declared in our salvation, Rom. iii. 25, 26, "Whom God," &c. Hence let us observe,

II. HIS SUFFERINGS. "It pleased the Lord to bruise him," &c. Here we learn,

1. *The extent of his sufferings.* He suffered,

In his *body.* He was bruised by cruel blows, Matt. xxvii. 30, "And they spit," &c.; he was wounded by the thorns, nails, and spear, ver. 5; he endured stripes by scourging, ver. 5; compare John xix. 1, "Then Pilate took Jesus and scourged him."

In his *soul.* He was put to grief by *the sins of mankind;*—the cruelty of his avowed enemies; see Psa. xxii. 14—16; and the treachery of his professing friends; of Judas, who betrayed him; of Peter, who denied him; and the other disciples who forsook him, Matt. xxvi. 56; Zech. xiii. 6. He was also put to grief *by diabolical suggestions*, Luke xxii. 53; Heb. ii. 18; and *by the suspension of divine comfort*, Matt. xxxvi. 38, and xxxvii. 46 We here learn,

2. *The singularity of his sufferings.* These being unlike those of others, he might properly adopt Jeremiah's language in another case, Lam. i. 12, for his sufferings were *unmerited.* He was perfectly righteous; and the only one who ever suffered without being sinful in nature or practice. His sufferings were *inflicted by God;* not merely by wicked men. God laid them on him, ver. 6. God bruised him; put him to grief; and made his soul an offering for sin. Wicked men indeed were the instruments of his sufferings; but God gave him up to death. Acts ii. 23; Rom. viii. 32. His suf-

ferings were *pleasing to God.* It pleased God to bruise him. He did not afflict Christ reluctantly, as he does his other children, Lam. iii. 22, 23. And yet our Lord *concurred* in his sufferings. His soul was made an offering for sin, readily, without hesitation; he poured out his soul unto death, as his own voluntary act and deed, ver. 12; he laid down his life freely, not by compulsion, John x. 15, 18; Mark x. 45. Hence let us observe,

3. *The general nature of his sufferings.* They were evidently vicarious; or sufferings endured by him as a substitute for others.

He became an *offering* for the *sin* of others, in their stead, 2 Cor. v. 21; 1 Pet. iii. 18. He bore the iniquities of *others.* "He shall bear their iniquities," or the punishment due to their iniquities, by just desert; as the loss of divine comfort, the curse and death. Gal. iii. 13, 14, "Christ hath," &c. His sufferings were a "*travail;*" this implies that they were pains endured by him, for the benefit of others:—to make them heirs of glory, Heb. ii. 10; to heal them, Isa. liii. 5; and bring them to God, 1 Pet. iii. 18. This leads us to consider,

III. THE HAPPY EFFECTS OF HIS SUFFERINGS. In consequence thereof,

1. *He shall prolong his days.* By rising from death to immortal life, Rev. i. 13. This was effected by himself; according to his own declarations, John ii. 19, and x. 13.—And it was the reward of his obedience unto death, Isa. liii. 12; Phil. ii. 8—11.

2. *He shall justify many by his knowledge.* "By his knowledge," &c. This implies, that through or by the knowledge of him, many will obtain justification.—By justification is meant the forgiveness of sins. Compare Acts xiii. 33 and 39. The knowledge of Christ includes a just view of him as the only acceptable mediator betwixt God and men, John xiv. 6; 1 Tim. ii. 5; a cordial approbation of him, 1 Cor. ii. 2; and affiance in him, Ps. ix. 10. All who thus know him, are justified through and by him, Rom. v. 1; Acts xiii. 39.

3. *He shall see his seed:* or his posterity, the fruit of his travail. This shall be a *numerous* seed, Heb. ii. 10; Psa. ii. 8, and cx. 3. And a *hopeful* seed; a general blessing, Matt. v. 13, 14; and finally happy, Isa. xxxv. 10. He shall *see* his seed: see them *flocking to him* for salvation, Isa. lx. 8; see them *saved by him* on earth, Isa. viii. 18; and *glorified with him* in heaven, Rev. iii. 21, and xvii. 14.

4. *The pleasure of the Lord shall prosper in his hand.*—The pleasure of the Lord is his Church; the object of his delight, Isa. lxii. 4; Psa. cxlvii. 11.—This is in Christ's hand; under his government and care, Deut. xxxiii. 3; John x. 27, 28.—It shall prosper there; be kept uninjured, Matt. xvi. 18, and extend universally, Dan. ii. 44.

5. *He shall see of the travail of his soul, and shall be satisfied.* He shall witness the blessings enjoyed by his redeemed servants: their interest in God's favor; their spiritual life, comfort, and honor, Rev. vii. 15—17. And seeing this he will be well pleased that he has endured the curse, death, grief, and shame for them, Psa. xxxv. 27; Zeph. iii. 17. From Christ's sufferings,

1. *Learn your obligations to cultivate a spirit of contrition*, or godly sorrow, on account of sin. Because your sins occasioned his sufferings at first, Zech. xii. 10. And they have since crucified him afresh, Heb. vi. 6; Psa. xxxviii. 18.

2. *Your encouragement, if penitent, to hope for salvation.* For Christ was *given* for your benefit, Rom. viii. 32, and is *exalted* for your benefit, Psa. lxviii. 18.

3. *God's claims on you as the subjects of redeeming grace.* On your *services*, 1 Cor. vi. 19, 20; Rom. xii. 1; Psa. cxvi. 1, 2; Rev. i. 5, 6. "Unto him that loved us," &c.

A SKETCH FOR GOOD FRIDAY.

John i. 29.—Behold the Lamb of God, which taketh away the sin of the world. (Sk.)

The death of our Lord Jesus Christ, considered as the only saving remedy for a perishing world, demands our serious attention every day in the year; but on that particular day which is set apart by the christian church for the commemoration of his last sufferings, we should examine the subject with deep seriousness and awful reverence. The results of our examinations will amply repay our careful and diligent inquiries; for thereby we shall gain clear views of a subject, which of all others, is the most important to man; we shall feel ourselves deeply humbled before God, under a sense of those sins which nailed our Saviour to the tree; and our drooping spirits will be revived and cheered with a hope of salvation, by him who suffered on the cross. Our text points out Christ as the Lamb of God; affirms that he taketh away the sin of the world: and exhorts sinful men to behold him.

I. Jesus Christ is the Lamb of God.

1. *The paschal Lamb was a type of Christ.* A parallel might be drawn in many important particulars; but we shall only mention one: by the death of that lamb, and the sprinkling of its blood upon the door posts, all the first-born of Israel were saved from death, Exod. xii. 6, 7; and we are assured by an inspired writer, that "even Christ our passover is sacrificed for us," 1 Cor. v. 7; and by his death, and the sprinkling of his blood, we are saved from wrath, Rom. v. 9.

2. *But Jesus is called the Lamb of God, especially in reference to the daily sacrifice*, which was offered up every morning and evening continually, and was a standing type of him, Exod. xxix. 38, 39. The lambs which were offered in the daily sacrifice, were to be without blemish, and our Saviour was without sin, 1 Peter i. 19; they made a *typical* atonement, but he made a *real* atonement, 1 John ii. 2; they were offered frequently, being imperfect; but our Lord was but once offered, being an *all-perfect* offering and sacrifice, Heb. ix. 25, 26.

3. *The prophet Isaiah foretold the Jewish nation, that the Messiah would be brought as a lamb to the slaughter*, and that "as a sheep before her shearers is dumb, so he would not open his mouth," chapter liii. 7. In this prediction, two things are clearly stated, first, the death of Jesus as a slaughtered lamb; and, secondly, his patience in that awful scene. He was manifested in the flesh to destroy the works of the devil, 1 John iii. 8; and to accomplish that great object, "it behoved him to suffer, and to rise from the dead," Luke xxiv. 46.

4. *Jesus now appears, as a lamb slain, in the heavenly world*, Rev. v. 6. That appearance, in all probability, is intended to remind glorified human spirits of their salvation by his atonement; and hence, while this great truth is denied by some on earth, it is celebrated with songs of praise, by the redeemed of the Lord, verse 8; and they ascribe to the Lamb who redeemed them, power and riches, strength and honor, and glory and blessing, ver. 12.

5. *Other things are affirmed of Jesus, as an atoning Lamb, which prove the propriety of this appellation.* The sanctification of the saints in heaven is ascribed to his blood, where it is said, they "have washed their robes and made them white in the blood of the Lamb," Rev. vii. 14; they overcame the accuser of the brethren, by the blood of the Lamb, chap. xii. 11; and they are made kings and priests unto God, by his blood, chap. i. 5.

II. He taketh away the sin of the world.

1. *The sin of Adam in the garden of Eden, affected the whole world of mankind*, Rom. v. 17-21; 1 Cor. xv. 21; but it is so far taken away by the Lamb of God, that all men will rise from the dead, and no man will suffer in the eternal world for what he did, 1 Cor. xv. 22; Ezek. xviii. 20.

2. *But by the sin of the world is meant, all the sins of men, whether Jews or Gentiles;* including every kind of sin, unless we may except that against the Holy Ghost, Matt. xii. 32; and every degree of sin; so that a remedy is provided for all who go astray, Isa. liii. 6.

3. *Jesus taketh away sin, by the sacrifice of himself once offered*, Heb. x. 12; 1 Peter iii. 18; and all the sin which is taken away, is through his precious blood, Heb. ix. 32; for no man can remove his own sin from his conscience, nor can any man take away the sin of his brother, or give a ransom for him, Psa. xlix. 7; neither is there salvation in any other name than that of Jesus, Acts iv. 12.

4. *When men repent and believe the gospel, the guilt of their sin is taken away, by the Lamb of God;* and they are justified, accepted, and adopted into the family of God, Mark i. 15; Rom. v. 1; Eph. i. 6; Rom. viii. 16.

5. *By faith, the pollution of sin is taken away.* It is expressly affirmed, that we are sanctified by faith in Christ Jesus, Acts xxv. 18;—that our hearts are purified by faith, Acts xv. 9;—and that "the blood of Jesus Christ cleanseth us from all sin," 1 John i. 7.

6. *Through Jesus the Lamb of God, the practice of sin is taken away:* hence his followers excel in all holy conversation and godliness, 2 Peter iii. 11;—for he saves them from their sins, Matt. i. 21. Being saved by grace, they deny "ungodliness and worldly lusts," and "live soberly, righteously, and godly in this present world," Titus ii. 12.

7. *The tormenting fears which accompany sin, are taken away by the Lamb of God, from all who are perfected in love*, 1 John iv. 18;—so that they are no longer tormented, like other men, with frightful fears of death and hell, but rejoice in hope of the glory of God, Rom. v. 2.

8. *The sad effects of sin in a future state, will be taken away by the Lamb of God, from all who die in the Lord*, Rev. xiv. 13.—They will have a blessed and glorious resurrection, 1 Cor. xv. 51, 52;—they will appear with boldness in the day of judgment, 1 John iv. 17;—and they will "be for ever with the Lord," 1 Thess. iv. 18.

9. *All the sin which was taken away before Christ suffered for men, was taken away by him.* He was to be the Saviour, and when the first promise was made, the gospel day began to dawn, Gen. iii. 15. From that day to this, men have been placed in his hands, as the only Mediator; and through his gracious undertakings, the channels of mercy were opened immediately after the fall of our first parents.

10. *And if sin be taken away in the heathen world, it is by the Lamb of God;* for, through his blood, they may come "from the east and from the west, and from the north and from the south, and sit down in the kingdom of God," Luke ix. 29. Thus, "in every nation, he that feareth God and worketh righteousness, is accepted," through him who died for all, Acts x. 35.

III. Sinful men ard exhorted to behold him.

1. *The persons to whom these words were addressed by John the Baptist, beheld the Saviour with eyes of flesh;* for he was present among them, in his human body. In this sense we cannot see him, because he has left our world, and is gone to the Father, John xvi. 28.

2. *But we behold him by the eye of faith*, which enables us to look at things which are not seen, by the eye of the body, 2 Cor. iv. 18;—but all the internal views of the mind must be directed by that which is revealed in the written word, or we shall fall into foolish imaginations, 2 Cor. x. 5.

3. *To behold him as a religious duty, is to believe in him, and to trust in him for salvation*, Isa. xlv. 22;—and this is not merely one act of the mind, at some certain period of our lives, but a continued act, expressed by *looking* to Jesus, Heb. xii. 2.

4. Behold him in his *birth* at Bethlehem, in his *holy life* among the wicked Jews, in his *death* on Mount Calvary, in his *resurrection* from the dead, and in his *ascension* to heaven, where "he ever liveth to make intercession," Heb. vii. 25. Place these wonderful events, as they are recorded in the *Book*, before the eye of contemplation.

5. *Carefully behold him in his sacred offices.*—He was a prophet to guide us into all truth, Acts iii. 22, 23;—a Priest to atone and intercede, Heb. iv. 14;—and a King to govern and protect us, Rev. xvii. 14, xix. 16. Proper views of these offices will cheer your hearts, strengthen your hands, and inspire you with a blessed hope.

6. *As christian believers, behold him in his person.* He "is over all, God blessed for ever," Rom. ix. 5; he is man, in the proper sense of the word, having a reasonable soul, and a body which died and rose again, Luke ii. 52;—and he is God-man, and Mediator between God and men, 1 Tim. ii. 5.

7. *It becomes us to behold him with profound humility.*—He had no sin of his own, either original or actual, Heb. vii. 26;—but he suffered for our sins, and was "wounded for our transgressions," Isa. liii. 5; a thought which should lay us in the dust, and keep us there all the days of our lives.

8. *But behold him with grateful feelings.*—We love him because he is lovely; but, especially, because he first loved us, 1 John iv. 19. Had he not undertaken our cause, we should have been lost, and what but love could have moved him to die for us? Rom. v. 8.

9. *Hence we may behold him with entire confidence.*—His love is a proof that he is willing to save us; and we know "he is able to save to the uttermost," Heb. vii. 25.—He offers salvation, Acts xiii. 26; he invites us to go to him, Matt. xi. 28; and he knocks at the door of our hearts, Rev. iii. 20.

10. *While we view him as our Saviour, let us also behold him as our exemplar.*—There are good examples among men, but they are all imperfect; the example of Jesus should be placed before our eyes in all states and circumstances of life; and we should endeavor to imitate him, as far as may be proper, in all our works, and in all our ways. To attempt an imitation of him in all things would be rash presumption; but while we follow his hospitality, meekness, patience, zeal, love, and obedience, we shall be both safe and happy, 1 Peter ii. 21.

We conclude by observing, that all who thus behold the Lamb of God, shall see him at the end of the world with great joy; that they shall meet him in the air, and that they shall remain with him as their bridegroom, in a blessed and glorious state of immortality, Rev. xxi. 2–9. Amen.

IT IS FINISHED.

John xix. 30.—It is finished. (P.)

THESE words may be considered as including the following particulars:

I. THE HUMILIATION AND SUFFERINGS OF THE SAVIOUR WERE FINISHED.

1. His humiliation was profound: He condescended to take humanity—was distinguished by poverty—had not where to lay his head.

2. His sufferings were intense: He was arrayed in mock royalty for the sport of a wanton crowd—suffered the excruciating death of the cross—endured the thunderbolts of divine vengeance.

3. But the sufferings and humiliation of Christ were now terminated.

II. THE PROPHECIES OF THE OLD TESTAMENT WERE NOW FULLY ACCOMPLISHED.

1. The prophets had predicted all the remarkable events in the Saviour's life: He was to be born of a virgin, at Bethlehem—to be despised and rejected by his countrymen—to bear his sufferings with meekness and resignation—to be numbered with transgressors—not a bone to be broken—to be cut off, but not for himself.

2. These prophecies receive their full accomplishment, as appears from the Evangelical history.

III. THE MOSAICAL DISPENSATION WAS NOW FOR EVER ABOLISHED.

1. This dispensation was only a typical institution.

2. It was now abolished—oblation and sacrifice were to cease—the veil of the temple was rent, as an indication of divine authority for its abolition.

3. The Jews were no longer the exclusive objects of the divine favor—the gospel was to be preached to the Gentiles also.

IV. THE REDEMPTION OF THE GUILTY WAS NOW COMPLETELY ACCOMPLISHED.

1. Man was in a state which required redemption.

2. The justice and veracity of the divine character demanded a satisfaction for sin.

3. This satisfaction was rendered by the Saviour—in the nature which had offended, and to the extent that the law required.

V. THE EMPIRE OF SATAN WAS FOR EVER DESTROYED.

1. The world was in bondage to the prince of darkness—led captive by the devil at his will.

2. This enemy was conquered by the Saviour—at his temptation in the wilderness, when he expelled him from those he possessed, and triumphed over him on his cross.

CONCLUSION.—Be grateful for the dispensation under which you live.

THE BENEFIT ARISING TO CHRIST FROM HIS OWN SUFFERINGS.

Heb. v. 7—9.—Who in the days of his flesh, when he had offered up prayers and supplications, with strong crying and tears, unto him that was able to save him from death, and was heard in that he feared, though he were a son, yet learned he obedience by the things which he suffered; and being made perfect, he became the author of eternal salvation unto all them that obey him. (S. S.)

THE priestly office, as marked out by God, belonged exclusively to the tribe of Levi—Yet our Lord, though he was not of that tribe to which the priesthood appertained, was truly and properly a High Priest—He was constituted a priest of a different order from that of Aaron—And executed the duties of the priesthood in a far different manner than it was possible for any other person to perform them—He offered not the blood of bulls and of goats, but his own body, for the sins of the world—The apostle describing the manner in which he ministered, sets before us,

I. His conduct under his sufferings.

Never were the sufferings of any creature comparable with those of Christ.

His bodily sufferings perhaps were less than many of his followers have been called to endure*—But those of his soul were infinitely beyond our conceptions, Ps. xxii. 14, 15, with Matt. xxvi. 38—The assaults of Satan, and the wrath of God, combined to produce that bloody sweat in the garden of Gethsemane—Luke xxii. 44.

Under them he poured out his heart in prayer unto his heavenly Father.

He never lost sight of God as his Father, but addressed him with the greater earnestness under that endearing title, Mark xiv. 36—He knew that his Father was "able to save him from death"—He therefore repeatedly besought him to remove the bitter cup, and urged his petitions "with strong cries and floods of tears"—Not that he repented of the work he had undertaken; but only desired such a mitigation of his sufferings as might consist with his Father's glory, and the salvation of men—†

Nor did he desist from prayer till he had obtained his request.

Him the Father always heard—Nor was an answer now denied him—He was delivered from that which he chiefly deprecated‡—Though the cup was not removed, he was not suffered to faint in drinking it—He was strengthened by an angel in answer to his prayer, Luke xxii. 43—And clearly shewed what an answer he had received. by the dignified composure with which he immediately resigned himself into the hands of his enemies—John xviii. 4—8, 11.

His sufferings indeed could not be dispensed with; but they were amply recompensed by,

II. The benefit he derived from them.

The benefits accruing to our Lord from his own sufferings were.

1. Personal.

It was necessary for him as our high Priest to experience every thing which his people are called to endure in their conflicts with sin and Satan, Heb. ii. 17—Now the difficulty of abiding faithful to God in arduous circumstances is exceeding great—This is a trial which all his people are called to sustain—And under it they more particularly need his almighty succour—This therefore he submitted to learn—Though as the Son of God he knew all things in a speculative manner, yet he could not know this *experimentally*, but by being reduced to a suffering condition—This therefore was one benefit which he derived from his sufferings—He learned by them more tenderly to sympathize with his afflicted people, and more speedily to succour them when imploring his help with strong crying and tears—Ib. ver. 18.

*It is possible indeed that the perfect temperature of his body might give a more exquisite sensibility to the organs: but this is no where affirmed in scripture.

†John xii. 27, 28.—As a *man*, he could not but feel, and as a *good* man, he could not but deprecate the wrath of God: but he desired nothing that was inconsistent with the divine will, Matt. xxvi. 39.

‡The learned differ about the sense of ἀπὸ τῆς εὐλαβείας: some translate it *pro reverentia* others *ex metu*. See Beza on Heb. v. 7.

2. Official.

As the priests were *consecrated* to their office by the blood of their sacrifices, so was Jesus by his own blood*—From that time he had a right to impart salvation—From that time also he exercised that right—The persons indeed to whom alone he is "the author of eternal salvation," are, "those who obey him"—Not that they possess this qualification *before* he vouchsafes his mercy to them—But he invariably transforms his people into his own image—And makes them, like himself, obedient unto death—Phil. ii. 8.

We may LEARN from hence.

1. What we should do under sufferings, or a dread of God's displeasure.

We should not hastily conclude that we are not his children—Heb. xii. 6, We should rather go with humble boldness to God as our Father, Luke xv. 17, 18—We should plead his gracious promises, Ps. l. 15—Nor can we possibly be too earnest, provided we be content that his will should be done—(Alas! that there should be so little resemblance between our prayers and those of Christ!)—We should however consider *that* as the best answer to prayer, which most enables us to glorify God—

2. Whither to go for salvation.

The Father was "able to save his Son from death"—And doubtless he can save *us* also—But he has exalted his Son to be a Prince and a Saviour, Acts v. 31—To Christ therefore we are to go, and *to the Father through Christ*, Eph. ii. 18—In this way we shall find him to be the author of eternal salvation to us—Heb. vii. 25.

3. What is to be our conduct when he has saved us.

Jesus died "to purchase to himself a peculiar people zealous of good works"—We must therefore *obey* him, and that too as willingly in seasons of severe trial as in times of peace—We must be content to be conformed to the likeness of our Lord and Master—Let us be faithful unto death, and he will give us a crown of life—Rev. ii. 10.

CERTAIN SUCCESS OF CHRIST'S UNDERTAKING.

Isaiah liii. 10.—And the pleasure of the Lord shall prosper in his hand. (Pr.)

In no part of the prophetic writings are the humiliation and sufferings of Christ detailed with such affecting minuteness as in this chapter, and inveterate indeed must have been the blindness and unbelief of the Jews, not to perceive and admit the force of such overwhelming evidence. The same prophecy however foretold that the report would not be believed, and that when the Saviour should appear he would be rejected and despised of men. Nevertheless he shall see his seed, he shall prolong his days, and the pleasure of the Lord shall prosper in his hand.

I. OFFER A FEW EXPLANATORY REMARKS ON THE TERMS OF THE TEXT.

1. By "the pleasure of the Lord" we are to understand, *his purposes concerning the cause of Christ.*— — —It was an important part of his good pleasure, that sinners should be redeemed by the blood of Christ, and this he delighted to accomplish. Psa. xl. 6—8. But this part of the will of God

*Τελειωθεὶς sometimes means "*consecrated*;" see Heb. vii. 28.

is supposed in the text to be already effected, and that another part is immediately to follow, relating to the progress of Christ's kingdom.

2. The success of Christ's undertaking, in the universal spread of the gospel, is called *the pleasure of the Lord*, because it is an object of his eternal purpose, and the end he had in view in the creation of the world. Col. i. 16.— — —It is true indeed, the accomplishment of God's design is said to be his pleasure, even when it relates to the punishment of his enemies; for "he will do his pleasure on Babylon, and his arm shall be on the Chaldeans;" but that in which he takes peculiar delight is the enlargement of Christ's kingdom. God takes pleasure in all his works, but more in the work of redemption than any other, and more still in rewarding the obedience and sufferings of his well-beloved Son, than in putting him to grief. John x. 17; Phil. ii. 9.

3. The great work of subduing the world is here placed *in the hand of Christ*.— — —The work of redeeming sinners was committed to him, and he succeeded in that; and now the work of subduing the nations to the obedience of faith, is put into his hand. He is head over all things to the church, and all shall be made subservient to his will. All power in heaven and earth is given unto him, and he is sending forth his armies, that he may rule in the midst of his enemies, and triumph over all the earth. Psa. xlv. 3, 4, cx. 1—3.

4. It is here foretold that the work of Christ *shall certainly succeed*, and the pleasure of the Lord "shall prosper in his hand."— — —If placed in other hands it would have failed, but with him it must prosper. Adam was constituted the federal head of his posterity, but he failed in the undertaking, and all were ruined. Moses was charged with the redemption of Israel, but he failed of bringing them into the promised land; and as to the eternal salvation of any of them, it was effected only by the death of Christ, and not by the law of Moses. All others have failed and been discouraged, but he shall set judgment in the earth, and the isles shall wait for his law. Thousands among the Jews, and tens of thousands among the Gentiles, have submitted to his authority; and he shall still go on and prosper, till the whole earth be filled with his glory.

II. Consider the reasons why the pleasure of the Lord should prosper in the hand of Christ.

Two things are generally necessary to the success of any great undertaking; one is, personal fitness or qualification, and the other, the means of accomplishing the design.

1. Christ possesses, in an eminent degree, *the qualifications* necessary to the work he has undertaken.— — —Great and unconquerable zeal is required, where the work is arduous and attended with great difficulty, and nothing can be done without it. If a man, from mere worldly motives, engages in the work of the ministry, he will not be likely to succeed; his efforts and his zeal are totally inadequate to so important an undertaking. But Christ's heart was wholly set upon what he undertook, and his zeal shall bring it to pass. Isa. lxiii. 4.— — —Wisdom also is required. A good intention, accompanied with ardent exertions, is not sufficient; wisdom and understanding are necessary to conduct things to a proper issue; and these qualifications are possessed in an eminent degree by the blessed Saviour. Isa. iii. 13.— — —Faithfulness also to his engagements was eminently verified in him. Isa. xi. 5; Heb. iii. 2.

2. Christ possesses *all the necessary means* for carrying on his own cause in the world.— — —In consequence of his death the Holy Spirit is given,

to convince the world of sin, and to give success to a preached gospel.—— Christ is able also to save to the uttermost them that come unto God by him, and that in consequence of his intercession before the throne. He can keep us from falling, and present us faultless before the presence of his glory with exceeding joy.— — —All the arrangements of providence are in his hands; the fate of kingdoms and of empires, and whatever is necessary to the prosperity of his own most righteous cause, are entirely at his command.

Let us reflect, 1. That as God has entrusted his own glory in the hands of Christ, it becomes us to commit our all to him, that he may save us in the great day. 2. That those who labor with Christ in his cause have reason to take encouragement, for it is in his hands, and must finally prevail.

THE RESURRECTION OF CHRIST, GLAD TIDINGS.

Acts xiii. 32, 33. We declare unto you glad tidings,, how that the promise which was made unto the fathers, God hath fulfilled the same unto us their children, in that he hath raised up Jesus again; as it is written in the second Psalm, Thou art my Son, this day have I begotten thee. (S. S.)

THE resurrection of Christ was the foundation, whereon the whole edifice of our religion was built. To that Jesus himself directed his diciples to look forward as the evidence of his Messiahship; and, after he had risen, he appeared to them repeatedly for the space of forty days, that they might be enabled to testify of it with the fullest assurance. A select number were chosen by him for the very purpose of bearing witness to this wonderful event: and because St. Paul had not enjoyed the same advantage as the other apostles, he was favored with a vision of his Lord long after his removal from the sight of all other mortals, in order that he, as well as the others, might be able to testify of it from ocular demonstration.

In the words before us he speaks of Christ's resurrection.

1. AS AN ACCOMPLISHMENT OF PROPHECY.

The passage quoted by the apostle is very properly applied to this subject.

The Psalms were in the apostle's days arranged in the same order as they now are. And the scope of the second Psalm is to declare the triumph of Jesus over all his enemies by means of his resurrection from the grave, and of his consequent exaltation to the right hand of God. And he might well be said to be "begotten" in the day of his resurrection, because he was then formed anew, as it were, from the earth.

It is confirmed also by many other passages that predict the same truth.

As it was foreordained by God, so it was foretold in a variety of ways. Sometimes it was exhibited in types,* and sometimes in prophecies.† In one scripture, not quoted indeed in this place, but cited no less than six times in the New Testament, this marvellous event was predicted in terms so plain

*Isaac being put to death, as it were, by his own father, was *received again from the dead* in a figure, Heb. xi. 19. Jonah was raised again on the third day from the belly of a fish, Matt. xii. 39, 40. The living bird that was let loose after having been dipped in the blood of the bird that had been slain, represented Jesus as ascending to heaven with his own blood, Lev. xiv. 51, 53, with Heb ix. 12.

†Ver. 34, 35, with Isa. lv. 3, which certainly must include the resurrection of him that was to be "the leader and commander," and Ps. xvi. 10, which is so largely commented upon by St. Peter, Acts ii, 26--31.

that none could misunderstand it, who did not obstinately shut their eyes against the truth. Ps. cxviii. 22, with Luke xx. 17.

We must not however suppose this to be an uninteresting fact: for the apostle further speaks of it.

II. As GLAD TIDINGS TO THE SOUL.

To the disconsolate disciples the tidings of Christ's resurrection were doubtless exceeding joyful. But they ought to be no less so to us, since that event ascertains.

1. The virtue of his sacrifice.

Had he not risen, his death had been in vain. 1 Cor. xv. 14, 17, 18. We could have had no evidence that our debt was discharged, if our surety had not been liberated from the prison of the grave. But his resurrection clearly proved that he had satisfied the demands of law and justice, and it thereby affords us a ground of assured hope, and triumphant exultation. Rom. iv, 25, and viii. 34.

2. His sufficiency for our help.

If he were still dead, it would be in vain to look to him for help. But, when he had raised up himself, John x. 17, 18, and spoiled all the principalities and powers of hell, Col. ii. 15, and been exalted on purpose that he might be a Prince and a Saviour to give repentance to Israel and remission of sins, Acts v. 31, what may we not expect at his hands? Surely he is declared thereby to be the Son of God with power, Rom. i. 4, and to be able to save us to the uttermost. Heb. vii. 25. Let us only seek to know him in the power of his resurrection; Phil. iii. 10; and nothing shall be impossible unto us. Mark ix. 23.

3. The certainty of our own resurrection.

Our resurrection depended altogether upon his: if he had not risen, neither should we have risen: but because he rose, we shall rise also. Christ is the first-fruits, which, while it sanctified, assured also the whole harvest. 1 Cor. xv. 20. He is our forerunner, who is gone to heaven to prepare places for us, and will come again to raise us to the possession of them. Heb. vi. 20, John xiv. 2, 3. We therefore may consider death and the grave as vanquished for us, and look forth to the complete triumph which we ourselves shall have over them in the last day. 1 Cor. xv. 53—55. Because he liveth, we may be sure that we shall live also. John xiv. 19.

As a further IMPROVEMENT of this passage, permit me to observe,

1. How deeply are we interested in the writings of the Old Testament!

In them are promises of which we receive the accomplishment. The word of God is not of private interpretation, 2 Pet. i. 20, as though it belonged only to this or that individual. Many parts doubtless had a *peculiar* reference to those to whom they were spoken; but none have an *exclusive* reference. Let us then embrace the promises as spoken to ourselves, compare Josh. i. 5, with Heb. xiii. 5, 6, and expect the fulfilment of them to our own souls.

2. What enemies are they to themselves who despise the ministry of the gospel!

Many, when the gospel is preached to them, are ready to say, like the devils, We beseech thee torment us not. Matt. viii. 29, and Luke viii. 28. Yes, they look on faithful ministers as the troublers of Israel. 1 Kings xviii. 17. But the scope of our ministry is to "*declare glad tidings*," even to proclaim a crucified, and an exalted Saviour. Let any one contemplate the foregoing subject, and see whether it do not afford matter for rejoicing. Let men only forsake their sins, and we have not a word to utter which will not administer to them an occasion of joy.

3. What a near relation subsists between believers in all ages! They are our fathers, and we their children. We are all of one family, all united to one head, Eph. i. 10, Heb. xii. 23, and all heirs of the same glory. Let us enjoy this thought, and look forward to the time when we shall sit down with all the patriarchs and prophets in the kingdom of our God. Matt. viii. 11, Luke xiii. 28.

THE MANIFESTATION OF CHRIST TO HIS DISCIPLES AFTER HIS RESURRECTION.

John xx. 19, 20.—Then the same day at evening, being the first day of the week, when the doors were shut where the disciples were assembled for fear of the Jews, came Jesus, and stood in the midst, and said unto them, Peace be unto you, &c. (Sk.)

When Paul preached before king Agrippa, concerning the sufferings of Christ and his resurrection from the dead, he made his appeal for the verity of the facts, to the publicity with which they were attended: "For the king knoweth of these things. before whom also I speak freely: for I am persuaded that none of these things are hidden from him; for this thing was not done in a corner." Jesus Christ was a public character; what he did was for the benefit of the world; and so far was he from concealing his designs, that he adopted the most successful methods to give notoriety to his acts, and extension to his plans. Multitudes heard his sermons, saw his miracles, witnessed his sufferings, and beheld his death: "And he showed himself alive after his passion, by many infallible proofs; being seen of his disciples forty days, and speaking of the things pertaining to the kingdom of God." The text furnishes us with one of these proofs, and suggests several profitable topics for discussion. In it we have,

I. The appearance of Christ to his disciples. "The same day," &c. "where the disciples were assembled, came Jesus and stood in the midst." Here notice,

1. *The disciples were assembled.* Christ's disciples are accustomed to meet together;—*love* leads them to do this; they love one another with pure hearts fervently:—*duty* binds them to come together, "Not forsaking the assembling," &c., Heb. x. 25;—*mutual benefit* excites them to associate with each other; Christ comes among them, Matt. xviii. 20. The world has its assemblies,—pleasure its assemblies,—commerce its assemblies,—and Christ's disciples their assemblies.

2. *This was a select assembly.* Promiscuous companies for the purpose of public and devotional exercises, such as singing, prayer, and preaching, have been sanctioned by the practice of all ages; but these are not meant to set aside the use of select meetings, assemblies of disciples.

3. *It was private.* "The doors were shut." The peal of slander has long been rung against private meetings, and the vilest scenes have been associated with them; but while we have such an example as this before our eyes, we may bid defiance to the revilings of men: fear of the Jews induced them to shut the doors: they had seen the storm of persecution that fell upon Christ, and fear suggested that a similar fate awaited them. Faith in God is the best antidote to the fear of man, Psa. lvi. 3;—"What time I am afraid," &c.

4. *It was in the evening.* Evenings are favorable for religious assemblies; multitudes are then at leisure, the business of the day is closed, and what can be more proper than to spend an hour, ere we retire to rest, in the worship of God?

5. *It was immediately after our Lord's resurrection.* How solicitous he was to cheer the minds of his disconsolate disciples; five distinct times he appeared to them the same day—a memorable day!—the first day of the week; what St. John calls the Lord's day;—a day which has been kept by christians to commemorate that extraordinary event, the resurrection of Christ. Though the doors were shut, yet Jesus entered: it is possible he might have done that in the ordinary way, without their observing it; or his entrance might have been miraculous,—"With God all things are possible."

II. THE BENEDICTION HE PRONOUNCED UPON THEM. He "said unto them, Peace be unto you:" this was his usual salutation. His disciples were charged to use a similar address, Luke x. 5;—Jesus Christ is the Prince of peace,—his kingdom is the kingdom of peace,—and his benediction is the blessing of peace. This benediction was designed,

1. *To dissipate their fears.* When Christ once appeared to them in a storm, they were afraid, and thought they saw a Spirit; hs then said, "Be of good cheer," &c., Matt. xiv. 27. Similar feelings were most probably excited now, but Jesus said, "Peace be unto you."

2. *To calm their troubled consciences.* The recollection of their cowardly conduct, in deserting their Master in his great extremity, must have been a source of deep anguish to them; and when they saw Christ standing personally before them, it would be natural enough to imagine thar he came with a design to upbraid them with their cowardice and crime: but he said, "Peace be unto you."

3. *As the medium of communicating good.* When Christ speaks peace, he communicates peace. When men use terms of commendation, however expressive they may be of their kindness towards us, they are mere words; but the words of Christ are the medium of communicating divine peace to us; "The words that I speak," &c., John vi. 63.

4. *As a prelude to their future success.* Peace among the Hebrews was a term of comprehensive import, including all blessings, temporal and spiritual. When Christ said "Peace be unto you," it was in effect saying—prosperity shall attend you.

III. THE SIGHT HE EXHIBITED TO THEM. "He showed unto them his hands and his side." This served to convince the disciples,

1. *That what they saw was real and not illusive.* The body which they beheld was that identical body which was laid in the sepulchre; and Christ showed unto them his hands and his side, to remove all their doubts. "Behold my hands and my feet, that it is I myself; handle me," &c., Luke xxiv. 37—40.

2. *To remind them of the love that he bore them, and the sufferings which he had endured for their sakes.* What could be more effecting? He showed unto them his hands—hands that had been transfixed to the cross—hands that still exhibited the prints of the nails; and he showed unto them his side, which had been pierced by the soldier's spear. Who can contemplate this tender and affecting scene, without exclaiming—behold how he loved them! Does the broken soldier exhibit his scars, and the marks of his wounds, to show that he has bled for his country?—so Christ showed his hands and side, to remind his disciples that he had bled for them. With the same body he now appears in the presence God for us. St. John saw in the

midst of the throne a lamb as it had been slain, &c.;—and when Christ shall come enthroned in judgment, "every eye shall see him, and they also which pierced him," &c., Rev. i. 7.

IV. The sensation they felt on beholding him. "Then were the disciples glad," &c. This gladness was,

1. *Founded in knowledge.* They knew that it was the Lord who had thus made himself visible to them;—that it was he who had borne their griefs, and carried their sorrows They *saw* the Lord, they *heard* his voice, —and were favored with his benediction:—they knew that they were not deceived; they had the demonstration of their senses. The joy which God puts into the hearts of his people now, is of a similar kind; not arising indeed from the perceptions of sense, but from the evidence of faith,—faith supplies the place of sense, Heb. xi. 1;—"Whom having not seen ye love," &c., 1 Pet. i. 8.

2. *Produced by love.* That the disciples had loved the Lord Jesus, none can doubt,—they had left all to follow him,—they had submitted to his instruction,—and continued with him in his temptation: it is true they had been scattered in a cloudy and dark day; but they were now assembled to converse of him to whom their hearts clung with the fondest attachment; and Jesus came and stood in the midst. Can we be surprised that the disciples were "glad when they saw the Lord?" Gladness is opposed to grief; they had seen the saddest sight that was ever exhibited in the world; —a sight that made the sun to blush, and hide his head beneath the sable mantle of midnight;—a sight that wrung their hearts with unutterable anguish;—but the cause of their grief was removed;—their Lord, who had been torn from them by the cruel hands of a lawless rabble, was now restored to them;—he had been dead, but he was now alive again:—and "they saw the Lord."

3. *Associated with confidence.* The disciples entertained the most exalted ideas of their Master's character, but they had considerable doubts as to the result of his undertaking; and when they saw him expire on the cross, they were almost ready to abandon hope, and sink into despair. He had indeed suggested that he should rise again from the dead, but they did not know what this rising from the dead could mean. But now "they saw the Lord," and their confidence was established; as it would be natural for them to infer, that he who could burst the barriers of the tomb—reanimate his mortal frame—and terrify and disperse the Roman soldiery, *could do* whatsoever he pleased; and that he *would* fulfil all his engagements, and accomplish all his promises.

From the text we have something,

1. *To confirm our faith.* The resurrection of Christ is attested by the most incontrovertible witnesses, who *could not* be deceived themselves, and *would not* deceive others.

2. *To guide our conduct.* Christ met his disciples when assembled; therefore let us frequent the assemblies of the saints.

3. *To excite our expectations.* Christ comes to bless his people; he said "Peace be unto you; and he showed unto them," &c. Let us expect his blessing. Have we been ungrateful, fearful, or unbelieving? So had the disciples, yet Christ blessed them;—he is the same yesterday, to-day, and for ever;—and he will bless his people with peace.

CHRIST THE RESURRECTION AND THE LIFE.

John xi. 25, 26.—Jesus said unto her, I am the resurrection and the life: he that believeth in me, though he were dead, yet shall he live: and whosoever liveth and believeth in me, shall never die. (S. S.)

In great and long continued afflictions, we are apt to entertain hard thoughts of God. But, whatever be his intention with respect to the ungodly, we are sure that he designs nothing but good to his own peculiar people, even when he appears most regardless of their supplications. There are two ends which he invariably proposes to himself in his dispensations towards them; namely, the brighter revelation of his own glory, and the fuller manifestation of it to their souls.

In the history before us we have an account of a heavy affliction that had befallen a family, through the death of one, to whom Jesus had shewn a very peculiar attachment. He had been solicited to come and help them; but he had delayed his visit till the sick person had been dead four days. This however, though liable to misconstruction, he had done intentionally, in order that he might manifest more fully to the disconsolate sisters his own power and glory. Accordingly, when they intimated their persuasion, that, if he would pray to God for the restoration of their brother to life, God would grant his request, he told them that he needed not beseech God to effect it; for that he himself was the resurrection and the life: and was able to impart either bodily or spiritual life to whomsoever he would.

In considering this most remarkable declaration, we shall notice,

I. That part which relates to himself.

Martha having, in conformity with the prevailing opinion of the Jews, expressed her expectation of a general resurrection at the last day, Jesus says to her

"I am the resurrection."

Our Lord, in his divine nature, possessed omnipotence necessarily, and of himself. In his mediatorial capacity he was invested with it by his Father, agreeably to the plan concerted in the divine counsels. To him who had undertaken to procure salvation for a fallen world, was delegated all power requisite for the full discharge of that office. The restoring of his people to a new and heavenly life after death, was essential to their complete salvation: this therefore was committed to him; John v. 21, 25—29; and he both declared he would execute this great work, John vi. 39, 40, and gave an earnest of its accomplishment in raising himself from the dead. John x. 18; 1 Cor. xv. 20.

"I am the life."

In this term our Lord proceeds further than in the former, and asserts, that as he is the author and first-fruits of the resurrection, so is he the very principle of life whereby his people live. This might indeed be collected from many figurative expressions of scripture, which represent him as the fountain of life to all his people: John xv 1; Eph. iv, 15, 16; but we are not left to gather such an important truth from mere parables; it is asserted frequently in the plainest terms: he is a quickening spirit, 1 Cor. xv. 45, that liveth in us, John xiv. 6, and vi. 57, and Gal. ii. 20, and is our very life. Col. iii. 4. He is to the soul, what the soul is to the body; he prevades, animates, and invigorates all our spiritual faculties: by his secret energy our understanding is enabled to apprehend divine truth, and our will inclined to obey it: and, without him, the soul would be as dead as the body without the soul.

Let us now prosecute our enquiries into,

II. THAT WHICH RESPECTS HIS PEOPLE.

There is a remarkable correspondence between the two latter, and the two former clauses of the text; the latter declaring the operation of the powers expressed in the former.

1. As being "the resurrection," he will raise the bodies of his people.

Judging of things according to our weak reason, we are ready to think that the restoration of bodies, which may have undergone so many changes, is impossible. But cannot he who formed the universe out of nothing, collect the atoms that constitute our identity, and reunite them to their kindred souls? he can, and will; yea, that very Jesus, who died upon the cross, has the keys of death and of hell, Rev. i. 18, and will effect this by his own almighty power. Phil. iii. 21.

This clause might further intimate, that by the first act of faith in him our souls should be made partakers of spiritual life. And this would accord with other passages of scripture, John vi. 33, 35, and vii. 38, and x. 10, and prepare us for the next clause, which, raising in a climax, declares the benefits that shall result from a continued life of faith upon him.

2. As being "the life," he will preserve the souls of his people unto everlasting life.

The bodies of the saints must undergo the sentence denounced against sin; Rom. viii. 10; (though death to *them* is scarcely worthy the name of death: it is rather a sleep, from which they shall be awakened at the morning of the resurrection,) ver. 11, Acts vii. 60, 1 Thess. iv. 14, but their souls shall never die: none shall prevail against them; Isa. liv. 17; none shall pluck them out of Christ's hands; John x. 28; their life is hid in him beyond the reach of men or devils; Col. iii. 3; the vital principle within them is an ever-living seed, 1 Pet. i. 23, an over-flowing fountain: John iv. 14; as long as Christ liveth, they shall live also. John xiv. 19. The separation that will take place between their souls and bodies will only introduce them to a higher state of existence, which they shall enjoy until the day that their bodies shall be awakened from their slumbers, to participate and enhance their bliss.

We must not however fail to notice the description given of those to whom these promises are made.

Twice, in these few words, are these blessings limited to believers: not because our Lord disregards good works, or because they shall not be rewarded; but because we cannot do any good work unless we first receive strength from Christ by faith; John xv. 5; and because, if we obtained life by working, we should have whereof to glory before God: and God has decreed that no flesh shall glory in his presence, and that we shall glory only in the Lord. Rom. iii. 27; Eph. ii. 8, 9; 1 Cor. i. 29—31. It must never be forgotten that God has caused all fulness to dwell in his Son, Jesus Christ; Col. i. 19; and that we must, by a continued exercise of faith, receive out of that fulness grace for grace. John i. 16. It is by faith that we live, Gal. iii. 11, we stand, 2 Cor. i. 24, we walk, 2 Cor. v. 7, we are saved: Gal. ii. 16; in a word, "God has given us eternal life; but this life is *in his Son:* he therefore that hath the Son, hath life; and he that hath not the Son of God, hath not life." 1 John v. 11, 12.

The pointed interrogation with which our Lord closed this address to Martha directs us how to IMPROVE this subject: it suggests to us,

1. That all persons, however eminent in their profession, or decided in their character, ought to "examine themselves whether they be in the faith."

It was to one whom he knew to be an humble and faithful disciple, that Jesus put this question: well therefore may we who are of more doubtful character, consider it as addressed to *us;* "Believest thou this?" Believest thou that Christ is the only fountain of life; and that there is no way of receiving life from him but by faith? And dost thou believe these things, not in a mere speculative manner (for *that* many do whose souls are dead before God) but in such a way as to reduce them to practice? The believing of this record forms the one line of distinction between those that shall be saved, and those that shall perish. If we truly receive it, we have already passed from death unto life: John v. 24; if we do not receive it, we are yet dead in trespasses and sins: we have not life now; we cannot have life hereafter. A resurrection indeed we shall partake of; but it is a resurrection to damnation, and not a resurrection to life: Ib. 29; we shall live; but it will be a life justly denominated death, the second death. Rev. xx. 14. Let us not then defer our enquiries into a subject which is of such infinite importance.

2. That the believing of this record is the most effectual antidote against the troubles of life, or the fears of death.

If Martha had felt the full influence of these truths, she would have moderated her sorrows, under the persuasion that her loss was her brother's gain; and that, if her brother were not restored to life, she should soon meet him in a better world. Thus in every state the consideration of these truths will afford to us also unspeakable consolation: for, if we believe in Christ, and have through him the possession of spiritual, and the prospect of eternal life, what cause can we have to complain; what cause to fear? The world will be divested of its allurements, and death of its terrors. Satisfied that all events are under the control of our best friend, we shall commit them cheerfully to his wise disposal: and looking forward to the day in which he will call us from our graves, we shall expect his summons with composure at least, if not also with a holy impatience. Let us then live by faith on our divine Saviour, assured that he will keep us unto eternal life, and exalt us, both in body and soul, unto the everlasting enjoyment of his presence and glory.

A SKETCH FOR EASTER SUNDAY.

Collossians iii. 1.—"If ye then be risen with Christ, seek those things which are above, where Christ sitteth at the right hand of God." (Sk.)

The festival of our Lord's resurrection is called Easter, from the *goddess Eoster*, whose festival was held by her idolatrous worshippers, in the month of April. The Greekes call it κασχα, and the Latins *pascha*, from *Pasah* a Hebrew word which is applied to the Jewish passover. The Asiatic churches kept this festival on the very day that the Jews observed their passover; others the first Sunday after the first full moon following the vernal equinox; and this, after a sharp controversy, which cost many lives, was settled by the Council of Nice. But though the christian churches differed about the *time* of keeping this festival; yet they all agreed in showing particular respect and honor to the *feast;* and surely it is a day of joy and gladness, of holy triumph and of blessed hope. Our Lord is risen from the dead; and those who are risen with him, should seek those things which are above.

1. Our Lord is risen from the dead.

1. The *death* of Jesus is affirmed by all the Evangelists. This is important; for if he did not really die, it would be trifling to argue on his resurrection. *Matthew* informs us that "he cried with a loud voice and yielded up the ghost," chap. xxvii, 50; *Mark* says, "Jesus cried with a loud voice, and gave up the ghost," chap. xv. 37; *Luke* states, that, "when Jesus had cried with a loud voice, he said. Father, into thy hands I commend my spirit. And having said thus he gave up the ghost," chap. xxiii. 46; and *John* affirms, that "he bowed the head, and gave up the ghost," chap. xix. 30. And as a proof of his death, it is observed, that "one of the soldiers with a spear pierced his side, and forthwith came there out blood and water." John xix. 34.

2. The body of Jesus was *laid in a sepulchre, and means were used by his enemies to keep it there.* The Jews recollected "that he said, while he was yet alive, After three days I will rise again," Matt. xxvii. 36; therefore they requested a *watch* to guard the body lest it should be stolen away, ver. 64; and Pilate gave orders to make it as sure as they could, ver. 65; "so they went and made the sepulchre sure, sealing the stone, and setting a watch," ver. 66.

3. Every attempt of his enemies, *to prevent his resurrection, was baffled and confounded.* There was a great earthquake, Matt. xxviii. 2; "the angel of the Lord descended from heaven, and rolled back the stone from the door and sat upon it; his countenance was like lightning. and his raiment white as snow; and for fear of him the keepers did shake, and became as dead men," ver. 4.

4. After his passion, he showed himself alive by many *infallible proofs.* He was seen of his disciples forty days, speaking of the things pertaining to the kingdom of God, Acts, iii. 4. He showed himself to Mary, Mark xvi. 9; to other women, Matt. xxviii. 9; to two disciples going to Emmaus, Mark xvi. 12; to Peter Luke xxiv. 34; to all the disciples, John xx. 19; to them again, chap. xx. 26; to the disciples at the sea of Tiberias, chap. xxi. 1; to the disciples in Galilee, Matt. xxviii. 16, 17; to James, 1 Cor. xv. 7; to the eleven, Mark xvi. 14; and to above five hundred brethren at once, 1 Cor. xv. 6.

5. The disciples *could not be deceived in those appearances.* They knew his person, his voice, and his usual manner of address. They were not credulous; hence they rejected the story of the women concerning his being risen, Luke xxiv. 11; and one of them would not believe without the most substantial proofs of his resurrection, John xx. 25. They saw him *often;* they heard him *speak;* they handled his body, ver. 27; they ate and drank with him: and they saw him ascend to heaven, Acts i. 9–11.

6. In relating the resurrection of Jesus, *the disciples had no design to deceive others.* They were plain honest men; they told a plain and unvarnished tale; they were all of one mind; by their testimony of Jesus, they exposed themselves to dangers, toils, and death; the whole world, whether Jews or Gentiles, were opposed to them; of themselves they were weak and feeble, and yet they never deviated from the truth, but many of them sealed it with their blood. Thus the resurrection of our Lord, on which the whole of Christianity stands, is supported by such proofs, that the man who denies it must be pronounced either insane or abominably wicked.

7. In the resurrection of Jesus, *prophesies were fulfilled.* It was foretold

that he should not see corruption, Psa. xvi. 10; and our Lord himself, who was a true prophet, predicted his resurrection on the third day, Matt. xii. 40; John ii. 19. Had he risen sooner, his death might have deen doubted by some; and had he remained longer in the grave, he would have seen corruption. It is true he was not three whole days and nights in the sepulchre, but he rose on the third day, for having been buried on Friday, he rose on the Sunday, or the first day of the week.

8. The resurrection of our Saviour is ascribed to the FATHER, Acts ii. 32; and to HIMSELF, John x. 18; a proof that he and the Father are ONE, in a higher sense than some professing christians are willing to allow, John x. 30.

9. *He rose on the first day of the week:* hence that has been called the Lord's day, Rev. i. 10; and has been observed as the christian sabbath, Acts xx. 7; and this is highly proper, because his resurrection was the commencement of the new creation, Col. i. 18.

10. His resurrection proves, beyond a doubt, that *all his undertakings for man were accepted.* Had he been what the Jews called him, a *deceiver*, he would never have risen from the dead. Omnipotent power could not have been exerted to restore the life of an imposter, after it had been justly taken away. In that case, his disciples would have been finally scattered, and christianity would have been unknown; but the seal of divine approbation was put upon him when he rose again, so that all he had said was confirmed, and all he had done was approved.

11. Death was *conquered* by his resurrection. There had been instances before of persons rising from the dead; but they only rose to a state of mortality. Jesus was the first who rose from thedead to die no more; and is on this account, "the first fruits of them that slept," 1 Cor. xv. 20. Death, the last enemy, has been forced to deliver up his prey; the grave, his prison house, has been thrown open; and this foe has yielded to the mighty conqueror.

12. Finally, *The resurrection of our Lord is a proof that we shall rise from the dead;* "but every man in his own order: Christ the first fruits; afterwards they that are Christ's at his coming," 1 Cor. xv. 23. The resurrection will be general, "for as in Adam all die, even so in Christ shall all be made alive," ver. 22. Had not our Lord risen from the dead, we might have thought that event *incredible;* but fact has put this subject out of doubt, Acts xxvi. 8.

II. THOSE WHO ARE RISEN WITH CHRIST, SHOULD SEEK THE THINGS WHICH ARE ABOVE.

1. While we remain in a state of nature, *we are spiritually dead.* We have no union with God, Eph. ii. 12; we have no relish for divine things, Rom. viii. 5; we are at enmity against God, ver. 7; and of course, we are dead in trespasses and sins, Ephesians ii. 1.

2. When we hear the voice of the Son of God, and obey it, *we are brought into spiritual life*, John v. 25. We are called to repent and believe the gospel; Mark i. 15; and when we do so, by that power which accompanies the call, we rise into life, John iii. 36; 1 John v. 12.

3. This blessed change implies a *quickening*, Col. ii. 13; a *new birth*, John iii. 3; a new *creation*, 2 Cor. v. 17; and in our text, a *resurrection* with Christ: and it is as much the work of God, though in concurrence with the will of man, as the creation of the world, or the resurrection of the dead.

4. When we feel this saving change, we are "begotten again to a *lively hope*, by the resurrection of Jesus Christ from the dead," 1 Pet. i. 3; and this blessed hope has for its object a glorious immortality, and "an inheritance incorruptible, undefiled, and that fadeth not away."

5. We cannot be at a loss to know what is meant by *the things which are above;* because they are said to be in that world where Christ sitteth at the right hand of God. Those things include all the light, all the glory, and all the felicity of the heavenly state. There we shall be completely happy; our companions will be saints and angels; our employment will be praise; and we shall have "fulness of joy," and pleasures for evermore, Psa. xvi. 11.

6. Much is implied in *seeking* those things: particularly a *knowledge* of them; a *love* for them; and an *ardent desire* to be put in the possession of those ineffable glories. With these dispositions, we should use all the appointed means; for those things must be sought with diligence, in the way of christian duty.

7. But let us seek in a *right way:* first, in the name of Jesus, John xiv. 6; secondly, by faith in him, Rom. ix. 32; thirdly, with earnestness or holy strivings, Luke xiii. 24; and, lastly, with steady perseverence to the end, 1 Cor. xv. 58.

8. On this plan, we shall soon find *a better world*, and be for ever with the Lord, 1 Thess. iv. 17. The crown will be given to us, Rev. ii. 10. White raiment will be put upon us, Rev. vii. 13. Palms of victory will be put into our hands, ver. 9; and "God shall wipe away all tears from our eyes," ver. 17.

INFERENCES.

1. The resurrection of Jesus is a subject of *vast importance* to us and to all mankind. If true christianity stands on a rock which cannot be shaken, and all the hopes of christians will be realized; but "if Christ be not risen," preaching is vain, and the faith of christians is also vain, 1 Cor. xv. 14.

2. But *of his resurrection there can be no doubt*, in the mind of any one who examines the subject with candour. To such a one, the proofs are *irresistible* and certain; unless we could admit that the apostles were *ignorant* of what they *knew;* that they *told lies for the sake of reproach and suffering;* and that they *united* to maintain, and died to confirm a most shameful falsehood. Surely it requires more faith to be an infidel than a christian.

3. Those who believe in his resurrection and session at the right hand of God, should rise above the world; keep heaven in their view: and urge their way forward to the celestial city. There they will overtake the Saviour; behold him in his glory; and enjoy him for ever and ever. Amen.

THE ASCENSION OF CHRIST.

Mark xvi. 9.—So then after the Lord had spoken to them, he was received up into heaven, and sat on the right hand of God. (Sk.)

The life of Christ was the most extraordinary and eventful life, that was ever led upon earth: a life anticipated by saints—poutrayed by prophets—prefigured by types, and in the fulness of time exhibited to the world. Every circumstance, therefore, that was disclosed in a life which was eminently designed to be the pattern and the price of ours, excites a peculiarity of interest, which admits of no comparison; and if any event in such a life merits more than usual attention, it is unquestionably that which closed the impressive scene, and terminated the Saviour's mortal pilgrimage. We cannot contemplate the characters of men who have benefitted the world by the splendor of their talents, or the lustre of their lives, without feeling a spirit of inquisitive solicitude, to know how they finished their course, parted with their friends, and made their exit. We labor to catch the last glance of departing worth; and sigh to think that an impenetrable veil is thrown over that world of spirits to which we are rapidly tending. The text directs our thoughts to the ascension of our Saviour, a scene which cannot fail to excite our attention; we have here,

I. THE PERIOD WHEN CHRIST ASCENDED—"After the Lord had spoken." &c.

II. THE MANNER—"He was received up into heaven."

III. HIS SUBSEQUENT SITUATION—"And sat on the right hand of God."

I. THE PERIOD WHEN CHRIST ASCENDED—"After the Lord had spoken to them." The substance of this speech is related in the preceding verses: Christ had *reproved*, *directed*, and *comforted* his disciples.

1. *He upbraided them with their unbelief and hardness of heart.* Unbelief involves us in moral blame, and merits the reprehension of him who judgeth righteously It supposes facts that deserve credit,—evidences to support them,—and disregard to those evidences. The fact here was the resurrection of Christ; a fact of the highest importance, "For if Christ be not risen, preaching is vain, and faith is vain, and the apostles were false witnesses of God," 1 Cor. xv. 14, 15. *This fact was supported by evidence.* Christ had previously intimated it, Mark ix. 9; John ii. 19—22. Mary Magdalene had seen him, Mark xvi. 9—11. He had also appeared unto two of his disciples, who had told it unto the residue, v. 13. *These witnesses deserved credit*, as they were competent to judge of what they had seen and heard; and it was not probable that they would seek to deceive others by a false testimony.—*But this fact was discredited.* Here we may see the na ture of unbelief generally. Truths of the most important character are presented to us,—evidences of the most indisputable kind are afforded, but unbelief refuses to admit these evidences. Christ also upbraided his disciples *with hardness of heart;* this not unfrequently gives birth to unbelief. Faith refers as much to the disposition of the heart, as to the assent of the understanding; and where the heart is hard and unfeeling, the importance of divine truth will be unperceived, and its evidences unexamined.

2. *He said unto them, "Go ye into all the world,"* &c. *This was the direction which he gave his disciples.* The work assigned them was, "Preach the gospel;" not false doctrines, not human opinions, nor Jewish ceremonies. The sphere of their operation was, "all the world;" and their commission was "to every creature." Hence we infer, that the gospel is suited to the circumstances of all—designed for the benefit of all—and that the ministers of truth should aim at preaching it to all.

3. *Christ also comforted his disciples, by the promise of a miraculous influence, with which they should be invested.* "These signs shall follow," &c. "In my name shall they cast out devils." Devils had previously been subject to them, Luke x. 17; and according to the primitive fathers, the power of casting out devils was continued in the church for many years.—"They shall speak with new tongues:" this promise was remarkably fulfilled on the day of Pentecost, Acts ii. 4—12.—"They shall take up ser pents," Acts xxviii. 5;—"If they drink any deadly thing," either by acci dent or compulsion, "it shall not hurt them." "They shall lay hands on the sick," &c., James v. 14, 15. Such was the *reproof*, *direction*, and *encour*

agement which Christ administered to his disciples, previously to his ascension; let us notice,

II. The manner. "He was received," &c.

1. *The ascension of Christ was accomplished by his own eternal power.* "Thou hast ascended on high," &c., Psa. lxviii. 18;—"When he ascended up on high," &c., Eph. iv. 8;—"They looked steadfastly toward heaven as he went up," &c., Acts i. 10. The acts of redemption were Christ's personal acts;—at his death he laid down his life for us, no man took it from him;—his resurrection was effected by his own infinite energy;—"Christ died, and rose again," &c., Rom. xiv. 9;—and at his ascension, "he went up to heaven," not in appearance only, but really and locally.

2. *The ascension of Christ was publicly witnessed by his disciples.* "While he blessed them, he was parted from them, and carried up into heaven," &c., Luke xxiv. 51;—"While they beheld he was taken up," &c. Acts i. 9;—he had previously told them, "It is expedient for you that I go away," &c., John xvi. 7. And during the forty days that he continued with them after his resurrection, when he was seen of five hundred brethren at once, and when he spake of the things pertaining to the kingdom of God, it is highly probable that he had prepared their minds for the solemn scene which they were about to witness; for they were so far from being disappointed, or even sorrowful, at his removal from them, that they "returned to Jerusalem with great joy," Luke xxiv. 52.

3. *The ascension of Christ was hailed with transport by ministering angels.* That David spoke of the ascension of Christ in Psa. lxviii. 17, 18, is clearly proved by comparing it with Eph. iv. 8;—and there the Psalmist declares, "the chariots of God are twenty thousand, even thousands of angels: the Lord is among them," &c. Does not the whole passage refer to a military triumph, where the conqueror returns victoriously from the field of battle, amid the shouts and plaudits of the inhabitants, who come forth to hail him welcome to his native place? Psa. xxiv. 7, 8, xlvii. 5, 6. That angels felt a deep interest in what Christ did upon earth, is most incontestably proved from Luke ii. 13; Matt. iv. 11; Luke xxii. 43; Matt. xxviii. 2; Acts i. 10. And having announced the birth of Christ,—ministered to him in the wilderness,—strengthened him in his agony,—attended him at his resurrection,—did not,

> "Cherubic legions guard him home,
> And shout him welcome to the skies?"

"He was received up into heaven." Who received him? Did not angels, principalities, and powers? Did not the spirits of just men made perfect receive him into that exalted state of felicity? St. Luke declares "a cloud received him;"—but who can tell what amazing scenes were unfolded beyond that cloud?

III. His subsequent situation. "He sat on the right hand of God." This is a figurative phrase; and by it we understand,

1. *The honor and dignity to which our Saviour is exalted.* When monarchs elevate their favorites to sit at their right hand, it is considered as the highest point of distinction, 1 Kings ii. 19; Psa. xlv. 9. The dignity to which Christ's human nature is raised is inconceivably glorious, especially when contrasted with that state of shame and degradation to which he voluntarily submitted;—how admirably is this illustrated by the apostle; Phil. ii. 6—11.

2. *The rule and government with which he is invested.* Thus St. Paul declares, God hath "set him at his own right hand," &c. "And hath put all things under his feet, and gave him to be head over all things to the church," Eph. i. 20—22;—"The Father loveth the Son, and hath given all things into his hand, John iii. 35, v. 27. The government of the world and the church is in the hands of Christ; and he is set at the right hand of God, to carry on his mediatorial work,—"There he makes intercession for us," Rom. viii. 34;—"There he dispenses his favors," Eph. iv. 8, 11, 12;—"There he receives our prayers," Rev. v. 8.

3. *The tranquility and happiness of which he is possessed.* He had been a man of sorrows; he had been stricken, smitten of God, and afflicted; his soul had been put to grief, and wrung with unutterable anguish. For the joy that was set before him, "He had endured the cross," &c.;—but he is now set down at the right hand of God;—this is a situation of exquisite pleasure, Psa. xvi. 11;—there he sees of the travail of his soul and is satisfied;—and there are ascribed to him, "Blessing, and glory, and wisdom," &c., Rev. vii. 12. From this subject we learn,

1. *Christ finished the work which he came upon earth to accomplish.* He made an atonement for sin,—left us an example,—raised up apostles, gave them ample instruction,—established a new dispensation,—promised the gift of the Holy Ghost, &c.

2. *Christ has highly honored human nature.* That body which was wounded, bruised and scourged upon earth, is now seated at the right hand of God.

3. *Christ is exalted for our sake.* "To appear in the presence of God," &c., Heb. ix. 24;—this should give us confidence in our prayers,—excite our emulation,—and, above all, inspire our hopes. Our forerunner is already entered, the first fruits are gathered in,—and "to him that overcometh will I grant to sit with me in my throne," &c., Rev. iii. 21.

THE INTERCESSION OF CHRIST, A DEMONSTRATION OF HIS CAPACITY TO SAVE.

Heb. vii. 25.—Wherefore, he is able to save to the uttermost, &c. (H.)

St. Paul had always expressed a constant, tender, and zealous affection for his brethren, his kinsmen according to the flesh. This epistle is a remarkable monument of it. It is directed to the believing Hebrews, and its most evident design is, to animate them to adhere resolutely to the Christian faith. The mind of this excellent man was very capacious, and continually filled with a variety of schemes for the advancement of the gospel. As it was highly probable this, rather than any of his other epistles, would fall into the hands of many as yet unconverted Jews, he not only concealeth his name, against which they were strongly prejudiced, but in a very wise and happy manner, maketh use of such sentiments and such language as might be very proper to awaken and convince the unconverted, as well as assist the faith and joy of those who had believed in Christ.

In pursuit of these great and harmonious designs, the sacred writer insists largely on the dignity of the person and offices of our great Redeemer. He represented him as far superior to the most exalted angels. Heb. i. 4. To

Moses. Heb iii. 2, 6. To Abraham. Heb. vii. 4, 7. And to Aaron. Heb. vii. 11, 24. From hence he draweth the important inference in the text, "Wherefore, he is able," &c.

Consider,

I. WHAT ARE WE TO UNDERSTAND BY CHRIST'S BEING "ABLE TO SAVE TO THE UTTERMOST."

1. It implieth the danger and calamity of those to whom he is proposed as a Saviour. All were, without him, in a state of death, 2 Cor. v. 14; in a state of ruin, Rom. v. 12; but "in due time, Christ died for us." Rom. v. 6. "Who of God is made unto us wisdom," &c. 1 Cor. i. 30. Most men are soothed into an insensibility of their danger, hence they hear not the thunder of God's law, Gal. iii. 10, nor see the flaming sword of his vengeance. They sleep on the brink of a precipice; what need of the alarm. Ephes. v. 14.

2. A power of working out complete deliverance for his people.

1. He is able to deliver them from the "curse of the law." Isa. xlii. 21; Gal. iii. 13; Acts xiii. 39.

2. From the pollution of sin. Rom. viii. 2. If he but speak, the work is done. Matt. viii. 3; 1 John i. 9.

3. From all the artifice and power of the prince of darkness. Col. i. 13. He knoweth how to deceive the deceiver, to detect every labored stratagem; and, from the most dangerous snares, to teach such useful lessons of holy prudence, as shall tend to our constant safety. Ps. lxxiii. 24; John x. 21. "We shall be more than conquerers," &c. Rom. viii. 37.

4. To support his people in death, and receive their spirits to a world of glory. Ps. lxxiii. 26; 2 Tim. i. 12; Ps. xxiii. 4.

5. To raise their bodies from the dissolution of the grave, and conduct their complete persons to the regions of eternal felicity. John xi. 25; and verses 28, 29; Phil. iii. 21.

3. That the efficacy of his saving grace continueth the same throughout all succeeding ages. His energy wrought from the date of the first promise. Gen. iii. 15. By faith in him the elders obtained a good report. Heb. xi. 2. His victorious energy still continueth the same. Heb. xiii. 8.

II. WHAT EVIDENCE WE HAVE THAT HE IS REALLY SO.

1. He was commissioned by the Father for this great work. 1 John v. 11. He is the foundation-stone of our salvation. Isa. xxviii. 16. His name is Jesus. Matt. i. 21. God declared him to be his Son, at his entrance on his public ministry. Matt. iii. 17.

2. He appeareth in his person and character eminently fitted for the work. The mysterious union of the divine and human nature in the person of our blessed Redeemer, is that which renders him the secure confidence of our souls. Heb. vi. 19. He assumed a mortal immaculate body, that he might have somewhat to offer as a sacrifice. Heb. viii. 3; Eph. v. 2; John iii. 14. He was not only an excellent and holy man, but he was God. Rom. ix. 5; Heb. i. 3; Phil. ii. 6. Therefore, "able to save to the uttermost."

3. He has done and borne all that we can imagine necessary to effect it. 2 Cor. viii. 9; Phil. ii. 7, 8. Now he appeareth in the presence of God for us. Heb. ix. 24.

4. He hath been approved by the Father, as having completely answered this glorious design. His power to save, as Mediator, is founded on the efficacy of his atonement. Rom. i. 4; Matt. xxviii. 18--20.

5. He hath made such gracious promises of salvation as imply a full pow-

er of accomplishing it. Extent of grace implieth a correspondent extent of power. Titus ii. 11; 1 Tim. i. 15, 16; and iv. 10; Rom. v. 18.

6. He hath already begun, and carried on the salvation of a multitude of souls. Facts are stubborn things. There is a cloud of witnesses of all ages, nations, and tongues, who have been "washed, justified, and sancti fied." 1 Cor. vi. 11; Rev. vii. 13, 14. This is farther confirmed by the experience of thousands in the present day.

III. The particular arguments for it: "His ever living to make intercession for them."

The intercession which Christ ever liveth to make, is a proof of his being able to save to the uttermost; especially if we consider,

1. The foundation of it, his atonement. Heb. ix. 12. Had not Christ's atonement been satisfactory, his intercession would be vain. Indeed, God could not consistently have permitted him to enter heaven, much less to take up his residence there, under the character of an Intercessor.

2. The extent of it. The intercession of Christ is not merely his appearance before God, in the body in which he suffered, but it is attended with a constant and ardent desire that his death may be effectual to the purposes designed, in bringing many sons and daughters to God.

3. The perpetuity of it: "He ever liveth." Even at this moment Christ appeareth in heaven for us. Isa. xl. 28.

IV. The character of the persons who are encouraged to expect salvation in him: such as "come unto God by him."

A sinner must come to God through Christ. His coming to God implieth,

1. A firm persuasion of his being and attributes. Heb. xi. 6.

2. An earnest desire to secure his favor. Job. x. 12; Ps. iv. 6; xxx. 5.

3. A readiness to forsake whatever cometh in competition with him. Isa. xxvi. 13.

4. A willing subjection to his service. Luke x. 27; Rom. vi. 13; Psa. cxix. 16—127.

5. A keeping up a constant correspondence with him. Ps. lxxiii. 23; 1 John i. 3.

His coming to God through Christ implieth,

1. A deep sense of his need of a Mediator, in order to a comfortable intercourse with God; christianity is the religion of sinners; self must be humbled, that Christ may be exalted. 1 Pet. v. 6. Christ is our Days's man.

2. A full persuasion of his saving power. Mark ix. 24; Matt. viii. 2.

3. A cheerful confidence in the grace of Christ. John vi. 37; vii. 37; Matt. ix. 13; xii. 20.

4. A cordial approbation of the method in which he bestows salvation. Acts xx. 21; Rom. i. 17.

5. A constant care to maintain proper regards to Christ, in the whole course of our walking with God. Eph. ii. 18; Gal. ii. 20; 1 Pet. ii. 5.

Reflections.

1. How great is that salvation which the Lord Jesus Christ hath wrought out for us. Heb. ii. 3; Isa. xliii. 11.

2. How important is it that we all seriously inquire after this great salvation.

3. How great is the danger and misery of those who reject and affront such an Almighty Saviour. Rev. vi. 15—17.

4. How admirable and amiable doth the blessed Jesus appear, when considered as the great Intercessor of his people! Cant. v. 16.

5. With what holy boldness may the sinner draw near to God, in dependence on such an Intercessor. Heb. iv. 14—16; x. 19—22.

6. Let us adore the divine goodness, that such a salvation is offered us, in so reasonable, so easy, and so gracious a way. Rom. x. 3; Luke xix. 40.

7. Let us seriously examine whether we come to God by Christ. Acts xiii. 26.

8. Let those who have come in this manner, be thankful and courageous; let them go on till the God of peace bruise Satan under their feet; give them victory over death; and finally crown them with eternal life.

REDEMPTION BY THE BLOOD OF CHRIST.

Rev. i 5, 6.—Unto him that loveth us, and washed us from our sins in his own blood, and hath made us kings and priests unto God and his Father; to him be glory and dominion for ever and ever. Amen. (Pr.)

CHRIST is the object of praise and adoration as a divine person, being himself the Son of God; and there is also a glory attributed to him as Mediator, having redeemed us unto God by his blood. It is in the latter sense that glory and dominion are here ascribed to him, and let it be so ascribed for ever and ever. Amen.

I. We are led to consider what is implied in the text, namely, OUR POLLUTED AND DEFILED CONDITION AS SINNERS.

As coming out of the hands of our Creator, man was pure and holy, made after the image of God; but by sin we are become polluted. Yet men in general think nothing of sin, in any other way than as it affects the interests of society; and if free from outward offence, they then appear pure in their own eyes. But the defilement lies deep within, and out of the heart proceed all the evils of the life. Matt. xv. 19.

In particular, all the *springs of action* are defiled, all our thoughts, motives, and desires; so defiled as to pollute all our services and duties in religion. Even our righteousnesses are as filthy rags, and we are become abominable in the sight of God. Job xv. 16. Hence all the threatenings and curses are against us.

The corruption of our nature is such, that we are totally unfit for the society of holy beings; and while unrenewed we cannot enter into the kingdom of God. Like the leprous person we are thrust out of the camp, and cannot be admitted till the moral malady is healed.

Yet sinners think but little of their condition, and feel quite easy and contented as they are. But if God shine into the heart, we shall soon begin to see and feel our vileness, and mourn over it. All that are taught of God, are made to know the plague of their own heart. We see in what a manner David loathed himself when brought to repentance, and he is only an example of what every other penitent is made to feel. Psa. li.

II. Consider what Christ has done for us: "HE LOVED US, AND WASHED US FROM OUR SINS IN HIS OWN BLOOD."

He loved us——Love is the first moving cause of all, and therefore it is first mentioned: all that follows is the proper effect and expression of this love.

Love is the most estimable of all affections, and we generally value gifts and services done for us accordingly. If a person does ever so much for us, and not from love, it is but little regarded. Christ also values our services by the same rule, and thinks nothing of what we do, except it be from love to him. In the same way we are taught to value all that he has done for us, and to conceive of it as in the highest degree interesting, because it is the effect of love.

There are two things worthy of notice in the love of Christ, and which render what he has done for us so precious and inestimable——1. Its *freeness.* The love of Christ was fixed on us while we were yet sinners, while in our sins and in our blood, and antecedently to our being washed, which therefore could not be the ground or motive of his love. Ephes. v. 25, 26; Titus iii. 5.——2. Its *strength* or fulness. The love of Christ was such, that he gave himself for us; and greater love hath no man than this, that he lay down his life for his friend. 1 John iii. 16.

Again: He hath *washed us from our sins in his own blood*——The expression is figurative, but very strong: he hath purified us at the expense of blood. By this is meant his laying down his life for us as an atoning sacrifice, and it implies that nothing short of this would take away sin.— — — All ceremonial washings, all our prayers and tears, are utterly in vain; and nothing but the gospel can teach us how we are to be purified and made holy. Had it not been for the sacrifice of Christ, he that is holy, as angels are, should have been holy still; and he that is filthy, as men and devils are, must have been filthy still.

1. But why is our cleansing from sin *ascribed to the blood of Christ?* — — —Not because of any physical or natural efficacy, but because it is the life, and it is the blood that maketh atonement. Lev. xvii. 11. The life of the sinner is forfeited, and the life of the surety must become the sacrifice. Without shedding of blood there is no remission. Heb. ix. 22. It was not the sufferings of Christ merely, but his death, that made the atonement; and it was necessary also in his death, that there should be the shedding of his most precious blood. 1 Peter i. 19. Hence the evangelist is so careful to record the identical fact, that blood flowed from the Saviour's side while hanging on the cross. John xix. 34, 35. Hence also it is that our redemption is so repeatedly and emphatically ascribed to the blood of the cross. Ephes. i. 7; Col. i. 20; 1 John i. 7; Rev. v. 9.

2. What is there especially *in the blood of Christ that tends to cleanse from sin?*— — —The blood of bulls and of goats could not take away sin; it was not therefore by blood merely as such; nor would the blood of any mere creature suffice, however exalted in the scale of being. It was the *deity* of Christ that gave it this cleansing power. 1 John i. 7. He by the sacrifice of *himself* purged our sins, who is the brightness of the Father's glory, and the express image of his person. Heb. i. 3.

3. *In what manner does the blood of Christ cleanse us?*— — —We need a double purification; the removal of the curse due to sin, and the removal of its pollution. It is for the sake of the blood of Christ that we are pardoned and accepted; and it is in virtue of this also that the Holy Spirit is given to renew and sanctify the mind, and to cleanse us from all unrighteousness. The doctrine of the cross which gives peace to the mind, imparts also a spirit of purity.

4. *What then is needful to our being actually cleansed and pardoned?* — — —Only that we believe in Jesus, and repair to the fountain open for sin and uncleanness. He is able to save all that come unto God by him, but

none else. The annual atonement made for all Israel became effectual to those only who confessed their sins, and laid their hands upon the sacrifice: and none but the comers thereunto were benefitted by it. Those who reject the sacrifice of Christ must for ever remain unsanctified, and unforgiven, for there remaineth no more sacrifice for sin.

Having loved us, and washed us from our sins in his own blood, Christ hath *made us kings and priests unto God and his Father*——This denotes not merely what we shall be, but what we now are, a royal priesthood; and to this end he has washed us in his own blood, even as the priests of old were purified in the sacred laver, previous to their entering upon the sacerdotal office. Exod. xxix. 4. All believers are thus consecrated to the Lord, to draw near unto him, and to offer up spiritual sacrifices, acceptable by Jesus Christ. 1 Pet. ii. 5. They are the only true worshippers in the spiritual temple, and it is theirs to minister before the altar, and before the throne.

Finally: For all this love and mercy we are taught to ascribe glory and dominion to Christ. To him belong the honor and the glory of our salvation, and all that we receive from him must be cast at his feet. Nothing is more congenial to the heart of a real christian, than that the Saviour should be supremely loved and adored; and in no ascription could he acquiesce with greater cordiality than this which is here given. "To him be glory and dominion for ever and ever. Amen."

CHRIST THE ONLY SOURCE OF RIGHTEOUSNESS.

Rom. x. 4.—Christ is the end of the law for righteousness to every one that believeth. (B.)

The Apostle having insinuated, ch. iii. 3, that God would cast off the Jews for their unbelief; and, ch. ix., shown that the rejection of the unbelieving Jews from being the church of God, and the reception of the believing Gentiles, to be his people, in their stead, was not contrary to the word of God, ver. 30—33, he proceeds, in this chapter, to point out the cause of these events, in the unwillingness of the Jews to accept that method of obtaining righteousness and salvation appointed by God,—Inquire we,

I. What that righteousness is, spoken of in the text.

The righeousness here spoken of is evidently that which is necessary in order to eternal life, and which infallibly leads to it. Ch. v. 17, 21. It is termed "The righteousness of God," ver. 3; ch. i. 17, and said to be by faith. Ch. iii. 21, 22; Phil. iii. 9. It implies justification; ch. iii. 24; Tit. iii. 7; without which, as guilty, condemned sinners, we can have no title to eternal life, it being the only means of cancelling our guilt, and freeing us from condemnation, and which is followed by eternal salvation.—It implies regeneration or sanctification; see Phil. iii. 9, spoken of Eph. iv. 17—24; Tit. iii. 5, 6; John iii. 5, 6; without which we are not in Christ, 2 Cor. v. 17; Gal. vi. 15, and have no fitness for heaven.—It implies practical obedience; consequent on regeneration, Eph. ii. 10, and being the grand evidence that we are righteous. Luke i. 6; 1 John iii. 7. As to the necessity of this, see ch. ii. 6, 7; Rev. xxii. 14; and especially Matt. vii. 20. 21.

II. Where and how this righteousness is to be found.

Not in, or by, the law; but in, and through, faith.—This righteousness considered in these three branches of it, is not attainable in, or by, the law moral or ceremonial. Not in, or by, the former. Ch. viii. 3. It requires perfect, constant, and persevering obedience; this we have not paid in time past, do not at present, and cannot in future, pay. Hence it finds us guilty of violating its spiritual and holy precepts, and has no pardon to give us; it finds us depraved, and has no new nature for us; it finds us weak and helpless, and has no supernatural aid to impart.—But may we not have the help we need from the ceremonial law? cannot the sacrifices of it remove our guilt? No. "It is not possible the blood of bulls and goats should take away sin." Heb. ix. 23; x. 4. Cannot the various washings, or purifications of it, renew and cleanse our souls? No: they can only impart a ceremonial cleanness, or remove "the filth of the flesh." Heb. ix. 13; 1 Pet. iii. 21. Cannot the various institutions respecting meats and drinks, and the observance of days and months, assist us to attain, at least, a practical righteousness or obedience? No: as they do not make the tree good, of course the fruit cannot be good; as they do not purify the fountain, the streams issuing thence cannot be pure. Matt. vii. 16—19. But wherefore then serve the law? why was it instituted? in order to Christ, who is "the end" of it. The end of it, here, means the *final cause.* Christ was the end for which the law was instituted; the moral law being chiefly intended to convince men of sin, ch. iii. 19, 20; vii. 7, 8, *viz.* of their guilt, depravity, and weakness, and thus to be a "schoolmaster to bring them to Christ," Gal. iii. 19—24, and the ceremonial law to shadow forth and exhibit his sacrifice and grace:—The end, may mean, *the scope;* the law continually points to Christ; the moral law directs the sinner to have recourse to him who fulfilled it, and removed the curse of it, for that justification which itself cannot give; and the ceremonial law directs him to look from its sacrifices and purifications, to the atonement and Spirit of Christ,—The end, sometimes means, the *perfection* or *completion.* Thus love is "the end," that is, the fulfilling "of the commandment;" 1 Tim. i. 5; Christ fulfilled the moral law in fully explaining its spiritual and extensive meaning, and freeing it from the corrupt glosses of the scribes; in obeying it perfectly in his holy life, in suffering its penalty, and in providing that it may be written in our hearts; he also answered in his person, all the types and shadows of the ceremonial law:—The end, means, the *period,* or *termination.* Ch. vi. 21. Thus the law, and the whole Mosaic dispensation, gives way to the gospel, ceases, and is abolished, 2 Cor. iii. 11, and the ceremonies of it are taken out of the way by Christ. Col. ii. 14.—"Christ is the end of the law for righteousness." For justification, or righteousness imputed, is only to be found in his obedience unto death. Rom, iii. 24; 1 Cor. i. 30; 2 Cor. v. 21. Regeneration, a new creation, and entire sanctification, are only to be found in Christ, by his Spirit and grace, who is made of God to us sanctification. John i. 14, 16; 2 Cor. v. 17; 1 Cor. i. 30. Practical righteousness is likewise to be had in him; his doctrine, the law of Christ, directs us how to walk; his promises and threatenings enforce his laws; his example allures us; and his grace enables us to walk in his ways. 2 Cor. xii. 9; Heb. iv. 14—16.

III. By whom this righteousness is to be found.

By "every one that believeth."

The nature of faith is described ver. 5—10; its object is, that God hath raised Christ from the dead. This demonstrated him to be the Son of God, ch. i. 3, 4, and, therefore, the Christ, the only Saviour, able and willing to save to the uttermost. Of this faith is persuaded, and, therefore, comes to him and trusts in him for salvation.—The resurrection of Christ was the broad seal of Heaven set to his doctrine, and establishes its absolute truth and deep importance beyond all doubt; of which faith is so thoroughly per suaded, as to lay it to heart, and walk according to it.—He was raised for our justification, to show that the atonement he had made for sin was sufficient, and accepted; of this faith is also persuaded, and, therefore, relies solely on the propitiation in his blood for justification. Ch. iii. 23, &c.; Gal. ii. 16—20. He was raised that he might ascend, and intercede, and receive for us "the Promise of the Father," for which faith thirsts and comes to him. John vii. 37, 38.—He rose and ascended as our forerunner This faith believes, and, consequently, anticipates immortality and glory.—He rose to give evidence that he will judge all mankind. Acts xvii. 31. Faith is persuaded of this, and prepares to meet him, desiring to be "found of him in peace, Our faith, in these respects, must be such as will enable us to "make confession with our mouth," even if that should expose us, as in the early ages, to imprisonment and martyrdom. Therefore, it must be "with the heart man believeth unto righteousness;" ver. 10; Christ must be endeared to us more than riches, honors, liberty, or even life itself, which, if we be called to it, must be parted with for his sake. As to the faith that does not part with sin, and give up every thing that stands in competition with Christ for our hearts, it is dead. James ii. 20—26 As to the origin of this faith. See ver. 11—17. It arises from the Word and Spirit of God. "The Lord opened the heart of Lydia, that she attended to the things spoken" by the Apostle. Acts xvi. 14; Eph. ii. 8, 9; Col. ii. 12. Therefore, hearing, reading, meditation, and prayer, are the important means which we must employ, with a becoming humility, seriousness, desire, and confidence of success.—And in the exercise of that measure of faith we have received, however small, it will be increased.

THE FULNESS OF CHRIST.

John i. 16.—And of his fulness have all we received, and grace for grace. (Pr.)

The other evangelists give an account of Christ's human parentage, with the circumstances of his birth: but John gives a description of his glory as the Son of God, and of what he was before the world began. He is here spoken of as the Creator of all things, and as the light and life of men. His incarnation is next described, and with this is connected the passage before us. He dwelt amongst men, full of grace and truth; and of the fulness have we all received.

I. Illustrate and explain the subject.

Three things require to be noticed—what is meant by the fulness of Christ—in what way is this fulness communicated—and in what respect may we be said to receive grace for grace?

1. What is intended by the "fulness" of Christ.— — —Not that which is essential to him as a divine person, for that is incommunicable: but that which belongs to him as Mediator, and which is communicated to all them that believe. Col. i. 19.— — —The meaning is, that the Word being made flesh, all the riches of grace designed for man were deposited in him, were given to him, and through him to us: as when Joseph was made lord of Egypt, and all were directed to go to him for the supply of their wants. Gen. xlii. 55—57. John vi. 27.

1. Christ was the covenant head of all his people, and it is out of regard to his worthiness that all his blessings are bestowed.— — —God made a

covenant with Noah, and had respect to that, in all he did for his posterity. Gen. vi. 18. Also with Abraham, Gen. xvii. 4: with David, Psal. lxxxix. 28.— — —Thus in the counsels of divine grace, God hath blessed us in Christ Jesus, Ephes. i. 3. 2 Tim. i. 9.

2. All that is given to us freely, is to him a matter of just reward. He had power to lay down his life, and to take it up again. John x. 18: power to quicken whom he will, John v. 25: power to forgive sin even on earth, Matt. ix. 6: power to give eternal life, John x. 28.— — —These things constitute the gospel, and which are denominated "the unsearchable riches of Christ." Thus it is, that through his poverty we are made rich. 2 Cor. viii. 9.

3. Though the riches of Christ are unsearchable, yet we may form some idea of their fulness by the freeness of the invitations and promises. "If any thirst, let him come unto me and drink; he that cometh unto me, I will in no wise cast out: he is able to save unto the uttermost all them that come unto God by him: able to do exceeding abundantly above all we ask or think." — — —We may also judge of this fulness by what has actually been received from it.— — —We all derive from him, but he derives nothing from us. All that his servants have ever possessed, of gifts or of grace, and all that they have done, is from him; and this, without his riches being either exhausted or diminished.— — —Had there ever been a time when the fulness of Christ should be exhausted, it was when through weakness he was dying on the cross. But lo! even then it overflowed: "Father, forgive them—This day shalt thou be with me in paradise."

2. In what way is this fulness communicated? By first receiving Christ: ver. 12.— — —The generality of mankind are like persons living near a fountain, but have nothing to draw with: they believe not in him, and so they receive nothing from him.— — —But there are some who receive him as he is revealed in the gospel, renouncing whatever stands in competition with him; and by receiving him, they receive every supply of grace from him. — — —It is also through his dwelling in our hearts by faith, that we continue to receive: and by counting all things but loss for his sake, we are made to possess all things in him. Ephes. iii. 19.

3. How is it that we may be said to "receive grace for grace?"— — — Some understand by it, a succession of blessings one after another, an abundance; others think it means grace received by us, corresponding with that which is in Christ, as a likeness is made to resemble the original. Christ was anointed, like Aron the high priest; and as the sacred unction ran down to the skirts of his garments, so the anointing which was upon the Saviour was poured down upon all the members of his mystical body. We receive as it were the overflowings of that holy unction, and every portion of grace in our measure agreeing with the grace that is in him.

II. Improve the subject.

1. We learn from hence our condition as sinners: poor and needy, destitute of all good. All the self-sufficiency of sinners is only imaginary. The Laodiceans thought themselves rich, and increased with goods, and had need of nothing: but they were poor, and wretched, miserable, blind, and naked. He who thinks he knoweth any thing, knoweth nothing as he ought to know.

2. The way in which a poor lost sinner must be saved.— — —It is by receiving Christ, and deriving from his fulness: living upon his bounty, we are not only supplied, but made rich.

3. We see whence it was that those who have been the most eminent for grace have received all their supplies; by receiving Christ and beholding his glory.- - — —This is our example, and our encouragement.

THE PRE-EMINENCE DUE TO CHRIST.

John iii. 35.—The Father loveth the Son, and hath given all things into his hand. (Pr.)

This is part of the testimony which John the Baptist bore to Christ, in answer to an insinuation suggested by the Jews, for the purpose of exciting his jealousy and suspicion, verse 26. John feels much on this occasion, that they should attempt to place him in competition with his Lord, and rejects the idea with great force of language.

1. He tells them that he could accept of *no honors* but such as God had given him, the principal of which consisted in his being the messenger of the Lord, to prepare the way before him, and to bear testimony of him; and they knew that he never professed himself to be the Messiah: verse 27, 28.

2. John makes it out that all men *coming to Christ* as they had represented, was a proof of his being the Messiah, verse 29. He is the bridegroom, and the church is his bride. John is the bridegroom's friend, acting in subserviency, and doing his will; and this was honor enough for him. Now all things are in their proper place.

3. He gives them to expect that things *would go on* in this direction, and that Christ would be more and more glorified, though he himself should not, verse 30.

4. John then illustrates the subject more fully, and *preaches Christ* to his followers, as the only way of life and salvation, verse 31—36.

We here see how much of the evangelical ministry was possessed by John the Baptist, much more indeed than by Christ's immediate disciples, previous to the day of pentecost; and those who wish to throw him back; as though he belonged to the Jewish rather than to the christian dispensation, do him great injustice. He was more than a prophet, an evangelist, and the immediate forerunner of Christ.

In the text John speaks *as an example* to his followers, that they might learn to be of God's mind, and to honor the Saviour as he had done, without being over-solicitous of the honor that might be due to himself.

I. Observe the love of the Father to Christ.

This is a subject on which the New Testament delights to dwell, and the love here mentioned relates both to the person and the work of Christ.

1. The Father loveth him *as the Son of God.*— — —Hence those terms of endearment and filiation so often applied to Christ, as God's "own Son," his "only-begotten Son," his "dear Son," and "the Son of his love."— — It is the love the Father bears to him that makes the gift of Christ for us so unspeakable, verse 16; especially the giving of him as a sacrifice for us. Rom. viii. 32; Zech. xiii. 7. Hence also the testimony given on the banks of the Jordan. Matt. iii. 17; and on mount Tabor, xvii. 5.

2. He loveth him for the sake of *his obedience unto death*, and because he gave himself for us. John x. 17.— — —Hence also he hath highly exalted him, Phil. ii. 9; and commanded that all men should honor the Son, even as they honor the Father. John v. 23.— — —So highly does he love the Son, that he will hear no petition but in his name, and pardon no sinner but for his sake. John xiv. 6.

3. The special proof of this love is, *that he hath given all things into his hand.*— — —Such universal terms are difficult to interpret, on account of their extent. We who understand so few things, cannot enumerate them all, but we may mention some. The general idea is, that the Father hath delegated to him all the great concerns of his moral empire. It is for him to

restore it to order, and the heavens must retain him unto the restitution of all things, Acts iii. 21: and when he shall have subdued all things, and put down all authority and power, he shall deliver up the kingdom to the Father, that God may be all in all, 1 Cor. xv. 24, 28.

More particularly—

1. All the dispensations of mercy are in the hands of Christ: it is for him to save or to destroy. John v. 21; xvii. 2. It pleased the Father that in him should all fulness dwell, and out of his fulness we all receive, Col. i. 19; John i. 16.

2. God has entrusted him with his honor and glory. He is the Mediator betwixt God and man, and he is to act the part of a merciful and faithful high-priest. His work was to secure the honor of the Lawgiver, while he exercised mercy as a Saviour; and he hath done it, John xvii. 1, 4.

3. The Father hath committed to him the salvation of his people, their redemption from the curse, and from the grave. John vi. 39, 40.

4. The control of the universe is in his hands, and he is Lord of all; angels, principalities, and powers being made subject unto him, Col. i. 16; ii. 10; Ephes. i. 22.

5. The government of the church is committed to him, and he is the only lawgiver in Zion. His will is the ground of all obedience, and even the moral law is under his authority, Matt. xxviii. 18—20; 1 Cor. ix. 21.

6. The administration of the final judgment. The Father judgeth no man, but hath committed all judgment unto the Son, John v. 22; 2 Cor. v. 10.

II. Consider the consequences arising out of this doctrine.

1. Whatever is given to Christ *is given to communicate*, like treasure committed to an almoner; and even the authority with which he is invested is for the good of his church and people. He hath received gifts for men, even the rebellious, that the Lord God might dwell among them, Psalm lxviii. 18.

2. If we desire mercy we must *come to Christ for it*. Go to Joseph, said Pharaoh to the poor of the land; and so the Lord says to us, Go to Jesus.

3. As the Father loveth the Son, and hath committed all things into his hands, so *we must follow his example*, and commit our all into his hands for time and eternity, 2 Tim. i. 12. Sure we cannot refuse to treat him with similar confidence; if we do, we are not of God. Jews and deists, under pretence of honoring the Father, reject the Son; but they will be found in the wrong at last, 1 John ii. 23.

4. At all events we must become *subject to Christ*, in one way or another; for to him every knee shall bow, and every tongue shall confess. He must reign till he hath put all his enemies under his feet, 1 Cor. xv. 25.

CHRIST, ALL IN ALL.

Col. iii. 11.—Christ is all and in all. (H.)

How different is the language in which the sacred writers speak of Jesus Christ, from that adopted by many modern preachers and divines! Some will hardly condescend to name him: and, if they do, it is merely as a man a good man, a moral philosopher, or at most, a prophet, who taught maxims of wisdom, and confirmed them by a virtuous example. Whereas the primitive and apostolic writers always name him with an evident glow of affection and delight. In short, with them, "Christ was all and in all."

Let us endeavor to comprehend the phrase, "All in all; or, all in every thing." Implieth that the whole of christianity is full of Christ; and so it is. The sun is all in all to our system; he diffuseth light liberally to all the planets which revolve around him, and his heat penetrates the centre of the largest globes; on our earth he paints the flowers, embalms the fruits, ripens the grain, quickens all nature into life, and thus becometh all in all to us. Jesus Christ is the Sun of Righteousness; and whatever the sun is to the material world, that, and much more, is our Redeemer to the spiritual world; he is "all in all" in the system of christianity. Let us instance in a few particulars.

I. Christ is all in the scheme of salvation, as it respects God.

He is the covenant head, both of men and angels, and every gracious decree and purpose of the divine mind towards them hath an immediate respect to Christ; so, in the actual communications of the blessings, both of providence and grace, he is the only channel by which they are conveyed. He is the spiritual ladder which Jacob saw, whereby intercourse is opened between God and us.

II. Christ is all in all in the work of redemption, as it affects man.

He paid the price of our redemption, wrought out a perfect righteousness for our justification, and communicateth his Holy Spirit for our sanctification; he sitteth both our Prince and Advocate, at the right hand of his Father, where he will wait to intercede for us, until every son of God is brought to glory.

III. Christ is all in all in the sacred scriptures.

All divine truths connect and harmonize in him, like the rays of light collected in a focus; no considerable part of holy writ has a nearer or more distant reference to him. Abraham saw him afar off, and rejoiced in the sight; Moses pointed to him in all the services of the tabernacle; the Psalmist mingled the joys and sorrows of the Messiah with his own, or rather appeareth often to have forgot his own in meditating his: "To him give all the prophets witness." John showed him with his finger, "Behold the Lamb of God!" and all the apostolic writers delight even in the repetition of his name.

IV. Christ is all in all in the life of a believer.

His faith looks with a steady eye to the atonement; his repentance floweth from a believing sight of his sufferings and death, which also filleth his heart with gratitude and love: his hope is animated by a contemplation of his victories and glory; every grace receiveth its vigor from a believing view of Jesus. In all the troubles of life, and especially in the prospect of approaching death, this alone can comfort and satisfy the christian.

Is it not the want of looking more to Christ that maketh so many of the sons of God go lean from day to day? They look around them, the world is false, and friends are fickle; they look within them, all is dark and comfortless; let them look above, where Jesus sitteth at the right hand of God: there is strength, and righteousness, and peace, and glory.

V. Christ is all in all in the enjoyment of heaven.

"The Lamb that is in the midst of the throne shall feed them, and lead them to rivers of living waters:" so is he the all in all of the celestial antherms. The Father delighteth to honor him, and beameth all his glory through his countenance; angels delight to honor him, and tune their golden harps to praise him; saints delight to honor him, and cast their starry crowns beneath his feet. Let us also delight to honor him.

THE LORD OUR RIGHTEOUSNESS.

Jeremiah xxiii. 6.—This is his name, whereby he shall be called, The Lord our Righteousness. (S. S.)

THE writings of the prophets no less than of the apostles testify of Christ: nor can we any where find a fuller exhibition of his character than in the words before us—As to *his origin*, he is "a branch from the root of David:" and, in *his character*, "a righteous" branch. *His office* is that of "a King;" and, as to *the manner in which he executes that office*, "he executes righteousness and judgment in the land." Look we for *the effects of his administration?* "In his days Judah shall be saved, and Israel shall dwell safely." Lastly, Would we know *in what light he is to be regarded?* "This is his name, whereby he shall be called, The Lord our Righteousness."

In these words the prophet sets forth,

I. THE DIGNITY OF CHRIST.

The inspired writers never seem afraid of speaking of Christ in too exalted terms—The prophet, in this very place, declares

1. His essential dignity.

There is frequent occasion to observe that, wherever the word LORD is printed in large characters, it is in the original, JEHOVAH. Now Jehovah denotes the self-existence of the Deity, and is a name incommunicable to any creature: yet is it here assigned to Christ—By comparing similar declarations in the Old Testament with the expositions given of them in the New, we know assuredly that this name belongs to Christ; and that therefore he is and must be "God over all blessed for ever,"—Isa. vi. 5, with John xii. 41, or Isa. xlv. 22, 23, with Rom. xiv. 10, 11, or Joel ii. 32, with Rom. x. 13, 14, or Mal. iii. 1, with Luke i. 76.

2. His official dignity.

The title of Jehovah belongs equally to the Father, to the Son, and to the Holy Spirit; but the additional title of "*Our Righteousness*" is peculiar to Christ alone—It imports that Christ has by his own obedience unto death wrought out a righteousness for guilty man; and that "this righteousness shall be unto all and upon all them that believe in him"—It is in this sense that St. Paul speaks of him as "made unto us righteousness,"—1 Cor i. 30.

The connexion between the different parts of this comprehensive name deserves particular notice: for, if He were not Jehovah, he could not be our Righteousness; seeing that as a creature, he could *merit* nothing; because he would *owe* to God all that he could do; and, "after he had done all, he would be only an unprofitable servant:" but as he is God, all which he does is voluntary; and his divinity stamps an infinite value upon his work; so that it may well merit, not for himself only, but for a ruined world—

Such is the dignity of our blessed Lord: He is Jehovah, one with the Father, in glory equal, in majesty co-eternal: nor is there one ransomed soul in heaven, who does not ascribe his salvation to the blood and righteousness of this our incarnate God—

While the prophet thus expatiates on the glory of Christ, he intimates also,

II. THE DUTY OF MAN.

Our duty as sinners, and as redeemed sinners, has especial respect to Christ: and it is summarily comprehended in the ascribing to Christ the honor due unto his name—But this must be done,

1. In faith.

To compliment Christ with any titles which we do not believe due to him, would be to insult him, like those who arrayed him in mock majesty, and cried, Hail, King of the Jews—We must fully believe him to be God: we must be persuaded that we neither have nor can have any righteousness of our own: and we must be assured that "He is the end of the law for righteousness to every one that believeth," Rom. x. 4.—If we entertain any idea of meriting any thing at God's hands by our own obedience, or of adding any thing of our own to his perfect righteousness, we dishonor and degrade him; and, instead of performing our duty towards him, we violate it in the most flagrant manner: and, though we may be actuated by a blind zeal for the Father's honor, or for the interest of morality, we are indeed rebels against God, since he has commanded that "all men should honor the Son as they honor the Father," and that they should call him in faith, *The Lord our Righteousness*—

2. In sincerity.

As, to give him a title which we do not believe due to him would be mockery, so, to give it without a correspondent regard to him would be hypocrisy—Do we believe him to be Jehovah? we must regard him with reverential awe, and yield ourselves up to him in unreserved obedience—Do we believe him to be the only Righteousness of the redeemed? we must renounce entirely our own righteousness, and depend on him with our whole hearts—Do we view him in his complex character as Jehovah our Righteousness? We must rejoice in having such an almighty friend, such a sure foundation—We must glory in him as "all our salvation, and all our desire"—A less regard to him than this, not only falls below our duty, but it is absolutely inconsistent with any scriptural hope, any prospect of salvation—

From this subject we may LEARN,

1. The way of salvation.

There are but *three* ways in which we can conceive it possible for any man to be saved: namely, by works, by faith *and* works, or by faith *without* works; and the subject before us plainly declares which is the true one—Are we to be saved by our works? No: for God would never have sent his Son to be our Righteousness, if we ever could have wrought out a sufficient righteousness of our own—Besides, our own works would then have been our righteousness, and the name here ascribed to Christ would not have belonged to him—Moreover, even in heaven itself, instead of ascribing "Salvation to God and to the Lamb," we must ascribe it to God and to ourselves—

Are we then to be saved by faith *and* works? We still answer, No: for in whatever degree we trust in our own works, in that degree do we rob Christ of his official dignity; and assume to ourselves the honor due to him alone—As far as our own merits are united with his as a joint ground of our acceptance with God, so far shall we have to all eternity a ground of glorying in ourselves; yea, so far salvation will cease to be of grace; whereas "it is of faith that it may be by grace, and that boasting may be for ever excluded"—Rom. iv. 16; Eph. ii. 8, 9.

Salvation must then be by faith *without* works; we must not endeavor either in whole or in part to "establish a righteousness of our own," but seek to be clothed in the unspotted robe of Christ's righteousness—This is the declaration of God himself; Rom. iv. 5; nor did the apostles themselves know any other way of salvation, Gal. ii. 16,—We must all therefore desire, with St. Paul, to be found in Christ, not having our own righteousness but his—Phil. iii. 9.

2. The excellency of that way.

What can be conceived more *comfortable to man* than to hear of such a salvation as this? Were we told that we must work out a righteousness of our own that should be commensurate with the demands of God's law, who could entertain a hope of ever affecting it?—If we were required to do something that should be worthy to be joined with the Saviour's merits in order to render them more effectual for our acceptance, where should we find one single work of ours that we could present to God as perfect, and as deserving of so great a reward?—The best man on earth must either sit down in despair, or live in continual suspense respecting his eternal welfare—But the righteousness of Jehovah appears at once, not only adequate to our wants, but to the wants of all mankind; and, by trusting in that, we find rest unto our souls—Nor can we devise any other method of acceptance so *honorable to God;* since it refers all the glory to him; and necessitates all the hosts of the redeemed to ascribe the honor of their salvation to him alone—In spite of all the objections too that are urged against it, we can affirm that it is eminently *conducive* to the practice of *holiness*—Can we think of God becoming man in order to work out a righteousness for us, and not feel a desire to serve and honor him? "Can we continue in sin that grace may abound? God forbid"—An inspired writer assures us that "the grace of God which bringeth salvation teaches us to deny ungodliness and worldly lusts, and to live righteously, soberly, and godly in this present world"—

Let us then seek our righteousness in Christ alone; but let us shew by our lives, that this doctrine of faith is indeed "a doctrine according to godliness."

CHRIST THE HEAD OF THE CHURCH.

Colossians i. 18.—And he is the head of the body the church. (Sk.)

THE Colossians had been converted to christianity, chiefly through the instrumentality of Epaphras, who was a minister of Christ, and a fellow helper with St. Paul. But they were in danger of being seduced from the simplicity of the gospel by designing or ignorant men. False teachers had crept in among them, who inculcated the worship of angels, abstinence from animal food, the observance of Jewish festivals, the mortification of the body by long continued fasting, and the conformity to external ceremonies, as necessary to salvation.—To all these things the apostle refers in different parts of this epistle. In the preceding verses to the text, he asserts the doctrine of the essential Godhead of Christ; a doctrine which he never overlooks in any of his epistles. Here he states the relation in which Christ stands to his church. "He is the head of the body," &c. Let us,

I. Describe the church. This may at first view seem a needless task What need of description on a subject so plain? Who does not know what a church is? Have we not one in every parish? But it is with the scriptural, and not the common and corrupted application of the term, that we have to do. The term church in the New Testament uniformly refers to persons, and never to places. See Acts xx. 28; Rom. xvi. 5; Gal. i. 22. But by what marks were the members of the primitive churches designated?

1. *They were a people separated from the world.* The church and the world form two distinct societies. "Ye are not of the world," said Christ to his disciples. Hence believers were charged, "Be not conformed to this world;" and to "have no communion with the unfruitful works of darkness;" and Christianity is the same through all the revolutions of time.

2. *They were a people scorned and grevіously persecuted by the world.* Saul made havoc of the church. "Herod stretched forth his hand to vex certain of the church." At that time there was a great persecution against the church at Jerusalem. And the members of the church of Christ are still scorned and contemned by the ungodly part of mankind.

3. *They were a people who gave themselves up to the practice of prayer and supplication for themselves and their neighbors.* Christ encouraged his disciples to pray, by telling them that whatsoever they asked in his name, it should be done for them: at Jerusalem they prayed so fervently, that the whole house was shaken where they were assembled. See Acts xii. 5, xvi. 25. And the members of Christ's church still live, and always will live, in in the practice of prayer.

4. *They were a people who adorned their high profession by a consistent conduct.* We do not affirm that there were none among them who scandalized their profession, no brother who walked disorderly, no busy body in other men's matters. Alas! they were plagued with such people, but when detected they were cast out of the church. O how holy were the members of the church of Christ required to be!

II. Show why called a body.

1. *To illustrate the beauty of its moral form.* The human body is the most beautiful structure in the world. Nothing is so much admired. How exquisitely beautiful is the church of Christ. Every member of it has put on Christ, and is invested with his moral image. "The King's daughter is all glorious within," &c., Psa. xlv. 13; Isa. liv. 11—13; Eph. v. 26, 27.

2. *To describe the variety of members of which it is composed.* "We have many members in the same body, but all members have not the same office." The eyes see for the body, the hands handle for the body, the feet walk for the body, the palate tastes for the body, and the nerves feel for the body. In the church there are various members. "God gave, some apostles; and some prophets; and some evangelists;" &c., Eph. iv. 11—14. In the church now, there are many members, who hold distinct offices. Some write books, some preach sermons, some serve tables, some visit the sick, &c. Every member is useful; but every member should know his place, and keep it.

3. *To display the harmony and union of all its members.* Who that contemplates his own body, can help be astonished at the union, which subsists between all the members of which it is composed! And the church, though composed of many members, is one body, one building, one temple

one flock, one family. There is not a union of circumstances, nor of sentiment; but a union of faith, of affection, and of effort. Disunion in the church the apostles deprecated, and for union they prayed, Eph. iv. 16.

III. Illustrate the office of Christ as the head of the body.

1. *The head is the seat of dignity to the body.* It is above the body in point of local situation, and it is superior to the body in dignity and authority. And Christ is above all.

2. *The head is the seat of government for the body.* There can be no government where there is no head. Christ has the sole government in his church. The laws by which our conduct is regulated are his laws. The influence by which our sins are subdued is his influence. The account we shall have to give of our conduct is to him, and the retribution we shall receive is from his hand.

3. *The head is the seat of wisdom for the body.* The head thinks for the body, and directs all its movements. And Christ is made unto us wisdom Without the direction and influence of Christ, we should be no more capable of guiding our steps aright, than a body without a head. Alas! where did we wander before Christ took us under his direction!

4. *The head is the seat of glory to the body.* Do we not honor the head peculiarly? And Christ is the glory of his church. We honor Christ by praying to him, praising him, loving him and trusting him with our all.

5. *The head is the seat of union to the body.* The origin of all sensation and motion, is in the nerves, and these proceed from the head, and unite all the parts of the body together. And Jesus Christ unites the members of his mystical body, and makes them all one in himself.

APPLICATION.

1. *Is the church a body?* Let me then inquire, Have I union with the body? Am I united to any christian society? Why not? If there were no christian societies, there would soon be no christian ministers, no fellowship of saints, and no religion in the land. Why do I not join some christian society? Am I holier than the members of which christian churches are composed? then they ought to share my counsels and prayers. Am I worse than they? then self-interest should bind me to cast in my lot among them.

2. *Is the church a body?* Then what a horrid thing is schism in the body. No man ever hated his own flesh. To see the members of a body bite and devour one another, how unnatural! O let us never permit the demon of discord to creep in amongst us!

3. *Is the church the body of Christ?* Then by helping christians we help Christ's members. Were Christ again upon earth, and to go about naked and destitute, we should rejoice to render him assistance. But he has his members, many of whom are poor, and afflicted, and forlorn; and what we do for them, he considers as being done for himself. Is one member weak? let us help him. Is another ignorant? let us instruct him," &c.

4. *Is the church the body of Christ?* Then will he not terribly punish those who insult his body? Persecutors will have a horrid hell, Zech. ii. 8; Matt. xviii. 6.

5. *Is Christ the head of the body?* Then what may not christians expect from him! What an endearing relation subsists between Christ and believers! We are members of his body, of his flesh, and of his bones. May we grow up into him in all things! Amen.

CHRIST THE PHYSICIAN OF SOULS.

Matthew ix. 12.--"But when Jesus heard that, he said unto them, They that be whole need not a physician, but they that are sick." (Sk.)

THOUGH Jesus Christ came into the world as the friend and Saviour of sinners; yet he was in general rejected as an imposter, and deceiver of the people. The Jews having expected that he would appear as a temporal and victorious conqueror, despised his humble manifestation in "the form of a servant," and sought to put him to death, because he claimed the character of the Messiah. They regarded his doctrines as blasphemy, attributed his miracles to diabolical agency, and were greatly offended at his familiarity with publicans and sinners. And hence we learn from the preceding context, that Jesus having called Matthew to follow him, he promptly obeyed the divine command, and gladly entertained the Saviour as a guest at his house. But having most probably invited some of his former associates in sin to partake of his feast, for the benefit of the Redeemer's discourse, the fastidious Pharisees were highly indignant, and "said to the disciples, Why eateth your Master with publicans and sinners?" But when Jesus heard that, "he said unto them," by way of vindicating his own character and conduct, and for the reprehension and conviction of the censorious Pharisees, "They that be whole," &c. This is supposed to have been a well known proverb among the Jews, which the divine teacher *spiritually* applies with peculiar propriety, for the instruction of his hearers; and according to this sacred application of the words, they strikingly suggest, the nature and influence of sin, the charaeter and office of Christ,—and the subjects and attainments of grace. Observe,

I. THE NATURE AND INFLUENCE OF SIN. The scriptures describe the exceeding sinfulness of sin, by every figure calculated to excite our abhorrence, and alarm our fears. And as the effects of sin on the *soul* greatly resemble the effects of disease on the *body*, it is frequently represented under this significant emblem. This is certainly the case in the text, in which the diseased state of the soul is evidently intended, by "they that are sick." The nature of this disease is truly deplorable, and replete with imminent danger.

1. *Sin is a moral disease.* It deeply affects mankind as moral and responsible creatures. It has totally destroyed original purity and happiness; filled the world with disorder, misery and death. It has spread its poisonous infection through every faculty of the soul, and passion of the mind. The understanding is blinded,—the will is perverted,—the conscience is defiled,—and the affections are alienated from God, Eph. iv. 13. Not only is our moral constitution fatally diseased, but utterly ruined; And there is neither spiritual life nor health in us. "Wo unto us that we have sinned! The whole head is sick, and the whole heart is faint."

2. *Sin is a univresal disease.* It has mortally wounded every power, both of body and soul; and disseminated its infectious influence through the whole mass of mankind. It is the natural state of every human being, Psa. li. 5. It equally affects all ranks of men, and every distinct class of character. It universally prevails in every nation, and successively extends through every period of the world. Its desolating effects reach through all gradations of society, from the greatest monarch to the meanest subject; from the imperial palace to the plebeian cottage. There is no exception, for all have sinned; and sin infects the soul with every species of spiritual malady, and baneful influence, Isa. i. 6.

3. *Sin is a mortal disease.* It brings death and all our wo. It brings temporal death to the body, and renders all men subject to pain and dissolution, Rom. v. 15.—It brings spiritual death to the soul, and separates between God and his creatures, Eph. ii. 1—3. It also brings eternal death both to body and soul, in " the lake that burneth with fire and brimstone, which is the second death," Rom. vi. 23. How dreadful then is the disease of sin! It is the *original cause* of all suffering and sorrow here, and utter ruin and endless misery hereafter. But though the moral plague of human nature is so malignant, pestilential, and destructive, it is not desperate and irremediable. A perfect cure is obtained through the Saviour of sinners, who "was wounded for our transgressions," and by "whose stripes we are healed." Let us then consider,

II. The character and office of Christ. He represented himself in the text as a divine *Physician*. And in this capacity, as well as in all others, he possesses every possible qualification, suited to all the diversified circumstances, and adequate to the innumerable necessities of mankind.

1. *He is an accessible Physician.* All are invited to come unto him, " without money, and without price." Other physicians are in many cases difficult of access; but whether rich or poor, all are welcome to come to Christ. He will never repulse the sin-sick penitents, but receive them graciously and love them freely, John vi. 37. In the days of his flesh, he went about doing good, and healing all manner of diseases; and he is still present with us by his *word* and *Spirit*, to heal the maladies of our souls, Matt. xviii. 20; Rom. x. 6—9.

2. *He is an infallible Physician.* His infinite wisdom cannot err, nor can his omnipotent power fail of success. The most skilful human physicians are imperfect and fallible, and though they frequently administer temporary relief, their wisdom is often baffled, nor can they possibly preserve from ultimate death. But the Sovereign Physician of souls possesses an unbounded plenitude of " grace and truth," and can heal the most inveterate diseases of mankind, and fully redeem his people from all their iniquities. He is a *perfect*, a *present*, and an *everlasting* Saviour, Col. i. 19; Heb. vii. 25. With Him no case is difficult, nor disease incurable. " Is any thing too hard for the Lord?"

3. *He is an unchangeable Physician.* In all ages his name has been "like ointment poured forth," to the " weary and heavy laden." When he assumed humanity, he gave sight to the blind,—cleansed the lepers,—healed the sick,—raised the dead,—bound up the broken-hearted,—and comforted the distressed, Matt. xi. 5; Luke vi. 17—19. And though he ascended to heaven, he is still the gracious benefactor and Saviour of sinners.—All other physicians are mortal and perishing, but " Jesus is the same yesterday, to-day, and for ever." The healing virtue of his name is *undiminished*, and the cleansing efficacy of his blood is *immutable*.

4. *He is the only appointed Physician.* All other helps are insufficient, and other remedies ineffectual; " for there is none other name under heaven given among men whereby we must be saved." Nor is any other Saviour necessary, for Jesus is all-sufficient, and his saving abilities are commensurate to the moral wants of the whole world. I thank God, "there is balm in Gilead, there is a Physician there," who can perfectly heal the most *protracted* and *obstinate* disorders of the soul. Unto whom then should we go, but unto Him who can save to the uttermost? and to direct and encourage our application unto him, we shall proceed to notice,

III. THE SUBJECTS AND ATTAINMENTS OF GRACE. "They that be whole," &c. This is a self-evident position, and is intended to illustrate the penitent's character, and method of coming to Christ for salvation. It evidently suggests,

1. *We must deeply feel our spiritual maladies.* Self-ignorance is a deadly and delusive disease of the mind. Under its pernicious influence, we form the most erroneous estimates of our real state and character; which generally operate as effectual barriers to the reception of Christ. We suppose that we are *comparatively* whole and good, and therefore "trust in ourselves that we are righteous;" and consequently reject the only remedy of sovereign grace. Such was manifestly the deluded state of the ancient Pharisees, and the lukewarm Laodiceans; and such is still the infatuated state of all impenitent sinners and nominal Christians, Luke xviii. 9; 2 Cor. iv. 3, 4; Rev. iii. 17.—But when the Holy Spirit convinceth us of our ignorance, guilt, depravity, and wretchedness, we become deeply conscious of the plague of our hearts, and anxiously inquire, what we shall do to be saved, Acts ii. 37, xvi 30, 31.

2. *We must sincerely renounce our sins.* The habits of impiety greatly aggravate and augment the contagious distempers of our moral nature. It is therefore absolutely necessary, not only to be convinced of our sinful state, but we must also unfeignedly repent, and utterly forsake all our iniquities, Isa. lv. 7; Acts iii. 19. And being truly sensible of our dangerously infected and perishing condition through sin, we shall earnestly desire and seek an immediate deliverance from the pestilence of moral evil, and a participation of pardoning mercy and regenerating grace, Luke xviii. 13. For this purpose, and in this contrite state of mind,

3. *We must personally apply to the Physician of souls.* This is a duty universally enjoined, and essentially connected with the attainment of salvation. As no advantage can possibly be derived from any remedy, however excellent, unless it be actually applied, neither can we obtain an interest in Christ's saving benefits, except by a personal application unto him, in the appointed means of grace, John v. 40. We should come to the heavenly Physician penitently—believingly—importunately—immediately—and perseveringly, Matt. xi. 28; Isa. xiv. 22; 2 Cor. vi. 2. In thus coming to the Saviour, he will heal our backslidings,—restore us to spiritual health,—grant us perfect soundness of mind, and ultimately crown us with immortality and eternal life. We may learn from this subject the need we have of Christ,—the reason why he is rejected,—the sufficiency of his grace, and the efficacy of his healing power. May we embrace this truth, and rejoice in his salvation.

THE EXALTATION OF CHRIST.

Phil. ii. 9—11.—Wherefore God also hath highly exalted him, and given him a name which is above every name, that at the name of Jesus every knee should bow, of things in heaven, and things in earth, and things under the earth: and that every tongue should confess that Jesus Christ is Lord, to the glory of God the Father. (H. H.)

WE are told by an inspired Apostle, that the great scope of the Prophecies related to "the sufferings of Christ, and the glory that should follow." To the same points our attention is continually turned in the New Testament.

Sometimes they are stated as an accomplishment of prophecy, and as proofs of Christ's Messiahship: sometimes as grounds of our hope before God: sometimes as motives to stimulate us to duty: sometimes as models, according to which God will work in us: and sometimes as examples, which we are bound to follow: and sometimes as encouragements to follow those examples. It is in this last view that we are to contemplate this stupendous mystery at this time. The Apostle had said, "Look not every man on his own things, but every man also on the things of others." To illustrate and enforce this exhortation, he shews how the Lord Jesus Christ had emptied himself of all his own glory, and endured death, even the accursed death of the cross, for the salvation of men: and that in consequence of it he had received such tokens of his Father's approbation as were commensurate with the sacrifice which he had made. In considering this testimony of his Father's love, let us mark,

I. The height to which he was raised—

The Lord Jesus Christ, *as God*, was incapable of elevation: but, *as man*, he was raised from the lowest degradation to the highest degrees of glory.

Amidst the depths of his humiliation he was greatly exalted—

At his baptism he received an audible testimony from heaven, together with a visible communication of the Spirit of God, in attestation of his Messiahship. In all the miracles he wrought, a further testimony was borne to him by the Father. And in his last hours, when in appearance he was even deserted by his heavenly Father, universal nature bore witness to him; the sun going down, as it were, at noon-day; the earth rending and quaking to its very centre; and the most convincing evidence being given to all, that he whom they crucified was indeed the Son of God.

But it was not till after that period that the exaltation spoken of in the text commenced—

At his resurrection, he was declared to be the Son of God with power. — — —At his ascension he led captivity itself captive, and, surrounded with myriads of holy angels, went to take possession of his Father's throne. — — —Seated on that, he is elevated above all the works of God's hand's above men, so as to be "higher than the kings of the earth," even "King of kings and Lord of lords;" Ps. lxxxix, 27; Rev. xix. 16; and above angels also, "all the principalities and powers of heaven being made subject unto him." 1 Pet. iii. 22; Heb. i. 5, 8, 9, 13.— — —

The text requires us particularly to notice,

II. The reason of his exaltation—

It was in consequence of his previous humiliation: it was,

1. As a reward of his sufferings—

In this view it had been promised to him,— — —Isai. lii. 13—15; and liii. 10—12. In this view he himself looked forward to it with intense desire,— — —Heb. xii. 2; John xvii. 4, 5. And in this view it was actually conferred upon him,— — —Dan. vii. 13, 14; Heb. i. 3, 4.

2. As the means of completing the work he had undertaken—

He was to redeem us, both by price, and by power. On this account, after he had paid the price of our redemption, he was invested with "all power both in heaven and in earth;" and "all things were given into his hands," that he might order every thing for the accomplishment of his own will, and the furtherance of the work which he had begun. In him was all fulness treasured up, that he might impart unto his people all needful supplies of grace; Eph. i. 20—22; and to him was all authority committed, that he might put all enemies under his feet. 1 Cor. xv. 25; Ps. cx. 1, 2. Thus, by his elevation, are his triumphs and the triumphs of all his people, finally and eternally secured.

But we have further to notice his exaltation in reference to,

III. The end of it—

It was that he might be the one object,

1. Of universal adoration—

Of this he is most worthy, as all the hosts of heaven testifiy.— — —Rev. v. 11—13. And it must be paid to him: for God hath sworn with an oath, that it shall be paid to him by all in heaven, earth, and hell; Rom. xiv. 11; with Isai. xlv. 23; or if we will not yield it to him as the voluntary expression of our love, we shall be constrained to acknowledge his right to it, whilst we are suffering under the stroke of his avenging rod. Ps. ii. 1—3, 6, 9—12.

2. Of unlimited affiance—

By confessing him to be both Lord and Christ, I understand such a confession as proceeds from unfeigned faith. Rom. x. 9—11. And to this full affiance is he entitled, both according to his essential nature as God, and in his Mediatorial capacity as the Saviour of the world. Isai. xlv. 22. In what way is it to be manifested, the Prophet tells us: "Surely shall one say, In the Lord have I righteousness and strength." Isai. xlv. 24. As "the Christ," who died for us, he is our righteousness; and as "the Lord," who is the Head and Governor of all, we receive out of his fulness all needful supplies of grace and strength.

Nor let it be thought that this direction of our regards to him will derogate at all from the honor of the Father: for, on the contrary, it will be "to the glory of God the Father," whose wisdom has devised, and whose love has executed, so wonderful a plan for the salvation of men. On this subject we can have no doubt; since our Lord himself had told us, That God's very design in the whole of this stupendous mystery was, "that all men should honor the Son even as they honor the Father; and That he who honoreth not the Son, honoreth not the Father who hath sent him." John v. 22, 23.

Behold then,

1. How awful is the state of those who submit not to him!

We are equally rebels against him, whether we oppose him as Lord, or as Christ; whether we refuse to submit to his righteousness, Rom. x. 3, or to his government. O reflect, ye who are going about to establish a righteousness of your own, What will ye answer to him, when he shall call you to an account for usurping his office, and making void all that he has done and suffered for you?— — —And you, who, whilst professing to trust in him as your Saviour, live in disobedience to his commands, where will you hide your heads, when he shall say, "Bring hither those mine enemies who would not that I should reign over them, and slay them before me?" Whatever ye may now think, ye cannot invalidate the oath of God: he has sworn that unto him every knee shall bow; and, if ye do it not willingly, ye shall do it against your will, to your everlasting sorrow.

2. How blessed is the state of his obedient people!

Shall Christ be exalted to the right hand of God in vain? or will he refuse to impart to you out of his fulness? Fear not: you are committed to his care; and he will not lose one of you; "not one shall ever be plucked out of his hands." Whatever you need it is treasured up in him; and "his grace shall be sufficient for you." It may be, that in his service you may be called to endure many things: but if now "he sees of the travail of his soul and is satisfied," be assured that ere long it shall be no grief to you that you were humbled for a season: for, "if you suffer with him, you shall also reign with him," and "be glorified together with him," 2 Tim. ii. 12; Rom. viii. 17; in his kingdom for evermore.

BENEFIT OF RECEIVING CHRIST.

John i. 10—12 —He was in the world, and the world was made by him, and the world knew him not. He came unto his own, and his own received him not: but as many as received him, to them gave he power to become the sons of God, even to them that believe on his name. (H. H.)

THE blessings which administer to our worldly interest or bodily comfort, are equally welcomed by persons of all ranks and conditions: but those which have relation only to our spiritual good, are despised by many, and desired by very few. The light of the sun is not less prized by one than by another: all are sensible of its benefits, and value it accordingly. But "the Sun of righteousness has arisen upon us," and the benighted world regards him not: "he shines in the darkness, and the darkness apprehends him not." Ver. 5. Some however there are, who rejoice in his advent: and as they only have learned to appreciate his worth, they only shall enjoy the full benefits he confers.

The words of the Evangelist will lead us to shew,

I. THE CONTEMPT POURED ON CHRIST BY THE UNBELIEVING WORLD—

What was said of him in that day is equally true in this:

1. His own *creatures* "do not know him"—

It was Christ who formed the universe: "the world was made by him; and without him was not any thing made that was made." Ver. 3, with the text. He has moreover "been in the world" from the very beginning, "upholding it by his power," Heb. i. 3, and ordering every thing in it by his superintending providence. Yet, before his incarnation, he was not known; neither yet now is he known, as the Creator and Governor of the world. His name indeed is known; but he is considered only as a great prophet. The generality of those who *doctrinally* maintain his proper Deity, never *practically* realize the thought, that "by him all things subsist." Col i. 17.

2. His own *people* "do not receive him"—

The Jews were called "Christ's *own*," because he had separated them from all other people, brought them out of Egypt, led them through the wilderness, and derived his human nature from the stock of Abraham, their father. Their very country was called "Emmanuel's land." Isa. viii. 8. But we are *his* in a still more appropriate sense; because he has bought us with his blood; and we have been baptized into his name; and profess ourselves his followers. Yet we "do not really receive him," any more than the Jews themselves did. We do not receive him *in the character which he bears in the holy scriptures**— — —We do not receive him *for the ends and purposes for which he came*†— — —

Alas! what contempt is this which we pour upon him! We can shudder at the indignities offered him by the Jews; but we ourselves are no less criminal than the people who crucified and slew him: they through ignorance apprehended and executed him as a malefactor: we, with our eyes open, cry, "Hail, Master," and betray him. Matt. xxvi. 49.

But that we may not continue to treat him thus, let us consider,

*He is a Prophet to teach us, a Priest to atone for us, a King to rule over us and in us. Do we receive him under these characters?

†He came to justify us by his blood, to sanctify us by his grace, and to save us with an everlasting salvation. Do we receive him for these ends?

II. The honor he confers on those who believe in him—

A "receiving of Christ," and a "believing in him," are represented in the text as of precisely the same import. It is superfluous therefore to add any thing more in explanation of the terms. The benefits accruing from faith are the objects which next demand our attention. Unspeakable is the honor of becoming a child of God: yet to every one that believes in him, our blessed Lord gives,

1. To bear this relation to God—

"To the Jews belonged the adoption," Rom. ix. 4, as far as related to the external privileges of it. But we, on believing, "are made partakers of the divine nature." 2 Pet. i. 4. We become the children of God as well by regeneration as adoption: yea, faith is at once the means, Gal. iii. 26, and the evidence, 1 John v. 1, of our sonship with God. There is no interval of time left for us to give proofs of our sincerity, before God will acknowledge us as his: but the instant we believe in Christ, we are "sons and daughters of the Lord almighty." 2 Cor. vi. 18.

2. To enjoy the privileges of this relation—

The children of a stranger are not noticed by us, while our own children are admitted freely into our presence, and are the objects of our tenderest solicitude, our unremitted attention. We feed them, we clothe them, we protect them, we provide every thing for them that is suited to our circumstances, and that will contribute to their welfare. In all these respects believers find God a Father to them. They can go into his presence, "crying, Abba, Father;" Gal. iv. 6; and obtain from him whatever is necessary either for their support or comfort.

3. To possess an inheritance worthy of that relation—

Parents account it a duty to provide for the future maintenance of their children, and not merely for their present subsistence. With this view they lay up fortunes for them, which they are to inherit after the decease of their parents. Similar to this is the provision made for those who believe in Christ. They are "begotten again to an inheritance that is incorruptible and undefiled, and never-fading." 1 Pet. i. 3. "Being sons, they are heirs, heirs of God, and joint-heirs with Christ." Rom. viii. 17. Nor shall they merely divide their Father's inheritance among them; but every one of them shall enjoy the whole, and have his happiness enlarged, rather than diminished, by the communication of it to others.

Learn then from hence,

1. The folly of unbelievers—

One would suppose, that, in calling them to believe in Jesus Christ, we urged them to make the greatest sacrifices, and to resign every thing that could conduce to their happiness. But, on the contrary, we only invite them to "*receive;*" to receive "the greatest gift" which God himself is able to bestow: John iv. 10; to receive Him, in whom they will find all that they can possibly desire. We require them to surrender nothing but what will make them miserable; and to receive nothing which will not make them happy. How unreasonable does their conduct appear when viewed in this light! If we were to offer them bags of gold, we should find them willing enough to accept as many as we could bestow. But when we exhort them to accept *Him* who is of more value than ten thousand worlds, they turn a deaf ear to our most importunate intreaties. See, ye unbelievers, see your extreme folly! and remember, that the day is coming, when that rejection of Christ, in which you now glory, will become the ground of your bitterest lamentation.

2. The unspeakable benefit of faith—

There are many things which put a considerable difference between one man and another. The influence of wealth and dignity exalts some far above the level of their fellow-creatures. The acquisition of knowledge and wisdom has no less effect in elevating the characters and conditions of men. But all the distinctions in the universe do not avail to dignify a man so much as faith. Faith brings Christ into the soul, and puts the poorest of men into the possession of "unsearchable riches." Faith makes him, from a child of the devil, a child of God; from an heir of misery, an heir of glory. Faith elevates him from death to life, from infamy to honor, from hell to heaven. "Faith, even though it be small as a grain of mustard-seed," produces all these wonderful effects. Cultivate then, my brethren, this divine principle. Labor to have it in more continued exercise. Let Christ, the greatest object of faith, be more and more precious to your soul. Thus shall you be really the most distinguished characters on earth, and ere long "inherit the kingdom prepared for you by your heavenly Father."

FAITH IN CHRIST AN ANTIDOTE TO ALL TROUBLE.

John xiv. 1.—Let not your heart be troubled: ye believe in God; believe also in me. (H. H.)

As God is eminently distinguished by that character, "The comforter of all them that are cast down," so did Jesus evince his title to it during the whole time of his sojourning on earth: there was no distress which he did not remove from those who made their application to him; and not unfrequently did he anticipate the wants, which the unbelief or ignorance of his followers made them unable to express. He had now been revealing to his disciples the things which were speedily to be accomplished: and, perceiving that they were greatly dejected by the prospect before them, he encouraged them in the words which we have read; "Let not your hearts be troubled:" and then he prescribed an antidote, sufficient to dispel all their fears: "Ye believe in God; believe also in me."

In discoursing on these words, we shall shew,

I. The troubles which he taught them to expect—

There were three in particular which seemed most to affect them;

1. Their bereavement of his presence—

This, if it had been only to a remote quarter of the globe, or after the manner of Elijah's departure, would have greatly depressed their minds; because of the love he had manifested towards them, and their entire dependence on him for instruction and support— — —but to have him withdrawn from them by cruel sufferings and an ignominious death, was distressing beyond measure; so that the very thought of it filled them with the deepest concern— — —

2. The disappointment of all their worldly hopes—

They had supposed he was about to establish an earthly kingdom, and that they should be exalted to situations of great dignity. But when they heard, that, instead of reigning over other nations, he was to be rejected by his own; and that, instead of elevating them to posts of honor, he himself was to die upon a cross; they knew not how to reconcile these things with his former professions, or how to bear the shame which such a disappointment would unavoidably occasion— — —

3. The persecutions they were to meet with from an ungodly world—

Hitherto they had been screened from persecution, their Lord and Master having borne the brunt of it in his own person: but now they understood that they were to drink of his cup, and to endure all manner of sufferings, and death itself, after his example. This excited painful apprehensions in their minds, and caused them the most serious disquietude— — —

What means he used to dissipate their fears, will be found in,

II. The remedy he proposed—

The verbs in our text may be taken either imperatively or indicatively; and many think it would be better to construe both of them alike: but the spirit of the passage seems best preserved in our translation; which acknowledges, that they *do* believe in God the Father, and exhorts them to place the same confidence in him as in the Father. They now thought they should lose him entirely and for ever. To rectify this error, he enjoins them, notwithstanding his removal from them, to believe in him,

1. As present with them in their trials—

Though he would not be present to the eye of sense, he would be really nigh to them on all occasions. Wherever they should be, there would be no bar to his admission to their souls: he would come and visit them, and dwell in them, and manifest himself to them, as he would not unto the world. This would be a far greater blessing to them than his bodily presence; so that they had no reason to regret his apparent withdrawment from them.

2. As interested in their welfare—

They had never found him indifferent about any thing that related to them: nor would he forget them after he should have been taken from them into heaven: on the contrary, he was going thither to prepare mansions for them; and he would still enter into all their concerns, sympathizing with them in their afflictions, and regarding every thing that should be done to them as done immediately to himself. If any should give them a cup of cold water only, he would acknowledge it as an obligation conferred on him; and, if any should presume to touch them in a way of injury, *he* would resent it as if they "touched the apple of *his* eye."

3. As sufficient for their support—

They had seen what wonders he had wrought during his continuance amongst them: and they must not imagine, that, because he offered up his soul a sacrifice for sin, he was therefore deprived of his power to perform them: for though he would, in appearance, be crucified through weakness, he did really posses all power in heaven and in earth. They might still look to him for the relief of every want, and support in every trial; and they should assuredly find his grace sufficient for them.

4. As coming again to recompense all that they might endure for his sake—.

He had told them, that he would come again, and *that* too in all the glory of his Father, with myriads of attendant angels, to judge the world. They need not therefore be anxious about any present trials, since he pledged himself to remember all that they should do or suffer for him, and richly compensate their fidelity to him.

These were subjects on which he had often conversed familiarly with them: and if only they would give him credit for the accomplishment of his promises, they might discard their fears, and be of good comfort.

It will be not unprofitable to consider more distinctly,

III. The sufficiency of this remedy to dispel all anxiety from their minds—

Faith in Christ is a perfect antidote against troubles of every kind. Faith has respect to him in all his glorious offices and characters:

1. As the Saviour of the soul—

What has that man to do with fear or trouble, who sees all his iniquities purged away by the blood of Jesus, and his soul accepted before God?—— If he forget these things, he may be cast down by earthly trials: but if he keep this steadily in view, the sufferings of time will be of no account in his eyes: he will feel that he has ground for nothing but unbounded and incessant joy— — —

2. As the governor of the universe—

Who that sees how perfectly every thing is under the control of Jesus, will give way to fear or grief? Not a sparrow falls, nor a hair of our head can be touched, without him: and, if he suffer any injury to be inflicted on us, he can overrule it so as to convert it into the greatest benefit. What then have we to do, but to let him work his own will, and to expect that all things shall work together for our good?— — —

3. As the head of his people—

He is to all his people the head of vital influence; and will he forget to communicate what is necessary for the welfare of his members? We are weak; and our enemies are mighty: but is that any ground for fear, whilst we remember whose members we are? Can we not do all things through Christ strengthening us?— — —

4. As the Judge of quick and dead—

The distribution of rewards and punishments is committed unto him; and he has told us what sentence he will pronounce on all his faithful people. And will not that word, "Come ye blessed," or that, "Well done good and faithful servant," richly repay all that we can do or suffer for him in this world? Can we survey the thrones of glory he has prepared for us, and be afraid of the trials that await us here?— — —

Behold then,

1. The happiness of believers—

They *may*, they *must*, have their trials; and whilst they possess the feelings of men, they will find some trials grievous to be borne: but they neither have, nor can have, any cause for anxious fear: whilst God is for them, none can be against them. Let them therefore "be careful for nothing," but "cast all their care on Him who careth for them."

2. The misery of unbelievers—

Where has God said to *them*, "Let not your hearts be troubled?" No such word can be found in all the sacred volume. They have need of continual fear and terror: for, what refuge have they, whilst they are not united unto Christ by faith? Whither can they go under the trials of this life? and what consolation can they have in the prospect of eternity? Better were it, if they die in such a state, that they had never been born. Hear then what Jesus says to you: Look unto ME, and be ye saved, all the ends of the earth; for I am God; and besides me there is none else. His address, in the text, is a proof of his Godhead, and consequently of his sufficiency to save all that come unto God by him.

CHRIST'S LOVE TO HIS PEOPLE.

Mark iii. 31--35.—There came then his brethren and his mother, and, standing without, sent unto him, calling him. And the multitude sat about him, and they said unto him, Behold, thy mother and thy brethren without seek for thee. And he answered them, saying, Who is my mother, or my brethren? And he looked round about on them which sat about him, and said, Behold my mother and my brethren! For whosoever shall do the will of God, the same is my brother, and my sister, and mother. (H. H.)

It is common for persons to feel an undue degree of solicitude for the bodily welfare of their friends, whilst they have little anxiety for the spiritual and eternal welfare of mankind at large. Hence, if a minister be in danger of impairing his health by his exertions, they are ready to say to him, "Spare thyself:" but, if thousands be perishing all around them for lack of knowledge, they are not so ready to stir him to increased activity and diligence. The near relations of our Lord were under the influence of this partial regard, when "they went out to lay hold on Jesus, and said of him, "He is beside himself;" or, as it might rather be translated, "He is transported too far." Ver. 20, 21, ὅτι ἐξέστη. It should seem that it was with that view that they called for him at this time: they were afraid that he would sink under the weight of his continued labors. But he felt, that both health, and life too, were well sacrificed in such a cause: and therefore he disregarded their message, and turned it into an occasion of expressing the greatness of his regard for his obedient followers.

From the declaration of our Lord, we shall be led to shew,

I. The character of those whom Jesus loves.

This is expressed in few, but comprehensive words: "They do the will of God." But what is this will? It includes two things:

1. They believe in Jesus Christ—

This is eminently the will of God: 1 John iii. 23, and till this be done. nothing is done to any good purpose: the persons remain, and ever must remain, objects of his wrath. John iii. 18—36. *This therefore they do in the first place*— — —And they do it humbly, renouncing utterly every other ground of hope— — —and thankfully adoring God from their inmost souls for *such* a refuge— — —

2. They seek after universal holiness—

This also is the will of God; 1 Thess. iv. 3, nor are the loudest professions of attachment to Christ of any avail without it. Matt. vii. 21. *And this also they do.* And they do it unreservedly, accounting "no commandment grievous," 1 John v. 3, and in a progressive manner, never thinking they have attained, while any thing remains to be attained. Phil. iii. 12—14.

We pass on to consider,

II. The regard he bears towards them.

Our Lord gives them the preference to his nearest relations, *as such;* and honors them with the most endearing appellations of brother, sister, mother. Now from this we must understand, that,

1. He bears the tenderest affection towards them—

We naturally expect the warmest affection to subsist between persons so closely allied to each other. But the love that is found amongst earthly relatives is but a faint image of that which both Christ and his Father feel towards all their obedient followers. John xvi. 21.

2. He will give them the most familiar access to him—

His mother and his brethren were all this time without, whilst Jesus and his attentive followers were within, the house: and, though solicited by his own mother, he would not go out to *her*, because it would deprive *them* of the instructions which they were anxious to receive. And who can tell, what gracious communications Jesus will vouchsafe to those who serve him in spirit and in truth? They shall never seek his face in vain: they shall never call for him, but he will answer them, Here I am. Compare John xiv. 24, with Isa. lviii. 9, and lxv. 24.

3. He will order every thing for their good—

Any man that is not devoid of principle will consult the good of his family, when the management of their affairs is committed to him. And will not Jesus, who is constituted "Head over all things for the express benefit of his church," Eph. i. 22, be attentive to the wants of his obedient people? Will he not supply all their wants, mitigate all their sorrows, and overrule all things for their eternal good? Rom. viii. 28.

4. He will own them as his, in the last day—

Suppose him in that day surrounded by the whole assembled universe; and many who were once related to him in the flesh, or who once professed themselves his followers, calling upon him, and saying, 'We want a nearer access to thee; "we have eaten and drunk in thy presence; we have cast out devils in thy name, and in thy name done many wonderful works;" we are your brethren, your sisters, your nearest and dearest relatives.' Methinks he will then renew the same gracious declaration that is contained in our text; "Who is my mother, or my brethren?" And then, "stretching out his hand towards his obedient followers, he will say, Behold my mother, and my brethren: for, whosoever did the will of God, the same is my brother, and sister, and mother."

INFER,

1. How reasonable are the terms on which Christ proposes to acknowledge uss a his disciples!

He requires that all who would be his disciples should *apparently* cast off all regard for their nearest friends and relatives. Luke xiv. 26. I say *apparently;* for nothing is *really* farther from his intentions, than to encourage, either by *this* declaration, or by that in the text, any disrespect to our parents: on the contrary, we are commanded to *honor* our parents; and are told by the Apostle, that "that is the first commandment with promise." But when our love or obedience to earthly parents stands in competition with our obedience to Christ, then we must resemble Levi; in commendation of whom it is said, "He said unto his father and to his mother, I have not seen him, neither did he acknowledge his brethren, nor knew his own children." Deut. xxxiii. 9, with Exod. xxxii. 26—28. And shall this appear harsh or unreasonable? See what Jesus has done for us: He knew not his mother and his brethren in comparison of his believing and obedient people: and shall we prefer our earthly relatives to him? If he has so loved us, who are altogether polluted, and deserve nothing but evil at his hands, how much more should we so love *him*, who is altogether lovely, and deserves infinitely more love at our hands than eternity will be sufficient to express!

2. What encouragement have we to comply with these terms!

In complying with the terms which Christ has proposed, and adhering to him in opposition to the will of earthly friends, we may possibly incur their displeasure, and feel to the uttermost of their power the effects of their resentment: they may frown upon us, disown us, disinherit us. But "when father and mother forsake us, the Lord will take us up." His express promise is, that for one father, mother, brother, sister, house, or estate we lose for his sake, we shall even in this life receive an hundred fathers, mothers, brothers, sisters, houses, and estates. Mark x. 29, 30. Does any one ask, How shall this be accomplished? We might answer, that it is abundantly verified in the regard shewn to us by the Lord's people: but, independen of that, we say, the Lord Jesus will give himself to us, and be to us more than ten thousand relatives, or ten thousand worlds. Let any one say, whether the love of Christ, the grace of Christ, and the glory of Christ, do not compensate an hundred-fold for all the creature-love, and all the temporal advantages, that we can lose for him? Let the determination then of Joshua be ours; that whatever course others may follow, and whatever obstacles they may lay in our way, "we, with God's help, will serve the Lord."

3. How unlike to Christ are they, to whom a compliance with these terms is odious!

None are so odious in the eyes of the ungodly world as the true, faithful, determined christian. The generality, instead of loving him in proportion to his advancement in piety, will despise him; and will make his high attainments, not only *the occasion*, but *the measure*, of their contempt. They will be ashamed to acknowledge a pious character as a relation, or friend, or even as an acquaintance. They would rather be seen in public with an infidel or a debauchee, than with one who was eminent for his love to Christ. But how unlike to Christ are *they;* when the very thing which endears them to him, renders them odious in *their* eyes. Surely it will be well for such persons to consider what Christ's views of *them* must be? for if the godly are so precious to him *because* they are godly, surely the haters and despisers of godliness must for *that very reason* be most hateful in his eyes. Accordingly he has told us, how he will resent the contempt shewn to his people; and that "it were better for a man to have a millstone hanged about his neck, and to be cast into the sea, than that he should offend one of his little ones." Matt. xviii. 6.

CHRIST'S CARE FOR HIS SHEEP.

Isa. xl. 11.—He shall feed his flock like a shepherd: he shall gather the lambs with his arm, and carry them in his bosom; and shall gently lead those that are with young. (H. H.)

The holy Psalmist, speaking of Jehovah's care of him, says, "The Lord is my Shepherd:" and then, from the union of the Godhead with the pastoral office, he infers, "Therefore I shall not want." Ps. xxiii. 1. The same incomprehensible union is mentioned by the prophet in the passage before us. The Heralds that proclaimed the advent of the Messiah were commanded to draw the attention of men to him in these words, "Behold your God!" The person thus announced, is further described in the words preceding our text; "Behold! the Lord God will come:" and then it is added, "He shall feed his flock like a shepherd." Now when it is considered how prone the Israelites were to idolatry, it cannot be conecived that the prophet should speak of the Messiah in such exalted terms, if they did not properly belong to him. But the Prophets generally, and Isaiah in particular, are very full and explicit in declaring, that Jehovah was to become incarnate, and by the sacrifice of himself to redeem and save a ruined world. It is not however of his *person* that we now propose to speak, but of his *office; that* being the particular point to which my text refers: yet it would be improper to pass over such a strong testimony to the divinity of our blessed Lord, because, in the judgment of all, but more especially of Jews, it must have the effect of silencing every doubt upon that important subject. And it adds no little interest to the description here given of him, when we know, that He who so condescends to minister as a Shepherd to the least and meanest of his flock, is the Most High God: according as it is written, "To us a child is born, to us a Son is given; and his name shall be called The Mighty God." Isai. ix. 6.

The words which form the ground-work of our discourse, will lead me to set before you,

I. A GENERAL VIEW OF OUR LORD AS A SHEPHERD—

The character of a shepherd is frequently assigned to our blessed Lord, in the Scriptures both of the Old and New Testament: Ezek. xxxvii. 24; Zech. xiii. 7; Heb. xiii. 20; 1 Pet. v. 4; and every duty pertaining to that office is executed by him:—

1. He gathers them to his fold—

They are "wandering upon the dark mountains, in a cloudy and dark day;" Ezek. xxxiv. 6; "every one going in *his own* way," Isai. liii. 6; and "after the imaginations of his own heart."— — —Jer. xxiii. 17. The paths of all, though differing from each other according as the age, the inclinations, and the diversified temptations of the different individuals may lead them, — — —all agree in this, that they are far distant from the ways of God's commandments. Rom. iii. 11, 12. But "he searches for them, and seeks them out:" he follows them by the preaching of his word, by the dispensations of his providence, by the mighty working of his Spirit; and having found them, "he apprehends them" by his pastoral crook, Phil. iii. 12; and "makes them willing" to return with him, Ps. cx. 3; and "carries them home upon his shoulders rejoicing."— — —Luke xv. 5, 6.

2. He provides for their wants—

Oh! how sweet are the pastures into which he leads them! Ezek. xxxiv.14. Who can express the delight which a converted soul experiences in feeding upon the promises, "the exceeding great and precious promises" of his God? — — —In comparison of the food provided for the sheep of Christ, all else is but as "husks on which the swine subsist." Luke xv. 16. Isai. lv 2. This is set forth in Scripture under the image of a luxurious feast: Isai. xxiv. 6; and verily it is "a feast of fat things" to all the saints; a feast on which the even angels themselves might account it a privilege to partake.— — —Ps. lxxviii. 25.

3. He affords them his effectual protection—

Weak as they are, and beset with many enemies, they are preserved in perfect safety.— — —1 Pet. i. 5. He who laid down his life for them, will suffer "none to pluck them out of his hand."— — —John x. 11, 28. "They lie down beside the still waters," Ps. xxiii. 2; which are a just emblem of the tranquility of their own souls.— — —"They are kept in perfect peace, because they trust in him." Isai. xxvi. 3.

4. He administers to them according to their diversified necessities—

Amongst them there will be some who are sick, or diseased, or injured by some misfortune: but he knows all their particular cases, and imparts to them the relief which they severally need; "bringing back those which have been driven away, binding up that which has been broken, and strengthening that which is sick;— — —Ezek. xxxiv. 16; and never intermitting his care of them, till he has brought them to his fold above.— — —Ps xxiii. 5, 6.

But our text requires us to take,

II. A MORE PARTICULAR VIEW OF HIM AS MINISTERING TO THE WEAK AND NEEDY—

Let us notice then in a more especial manner,

1. His tenderness to the weak—

The lambs which have been but recently brought forth, may be supposed incapable of proceeding with the flock to any distant pasture. But these "he will gather with his arms, and carry in his bosom." "He will not despise the day of small things." Zech. iv. 10. There is not one in all his flock so weak, but he will pay the most minute attention to its necessities. He who gave so particular a charge to Peter to "feed his *lambs*," and required this of him as a necessary proof of his love, John xxi. 15, will not himself neglect his lambs; but rather will augment his tender assiduities in proportion as the weakness of the lamb calls for more peculiar care: he will even take it up, and "carry it in his bosom." In what an endearing view does this place the character of our blessed Lord!— — —How sweetly encouraging is this consideration to those who feel their weakness, and are ready to despond because of it!— — —Let us remember, that when his disciples would have kept persons from troubling him with their little children, he reproved them, and said, "Suffer little children to come unto me, and forbid them not; for of such is the kingdom of heaven." Mark x. 14. Whether therefore you be children in respect of your natural or spiritual birth, fail not to come to him, assured, that he will bear with your infirmities, and "perfect his own strength in your weakness."— — —2 Cor. xii. 9.

2. His compassion to the afflicted—

He will have respect to the state of his flock, even as Jacob had, who "would not overdrive them one day, lest they should all die." Gen. xxxiii. 13, 14. So our blessed Lord "will gently lead that which is with young." There are amongst his people many who are weary and heavy-laden with a sense of sin, and bowed down greatly by reason of the difficulties of their way. But to the former he sends a special invitation, with an assured promise of rest: Matt. xi. 28; and to the latter he authorizes us to declare, that "he will raise them up." Ps. cxlvi. 8. In truth, he is pre-eminently distinguished by this, that "he will not break the bruised reed, nor quench the smoking flax; but will bring forth judgment unto victory." Matt. xii. 20. Consider what is implied in these metaphors: a bruised reed is, according to human appearance, incapable of even sending forth a melodious sound; and smoking flax has, as it were, but a hidden spark of fire, whilst it is sending forth whole clouds of corruption: yet will Christ fan the expiring spark to a flame, and attune the reed to send forth the most heavenly strains. Let none then despond, however destitute they may be of any thing to encourge them from within; but let them "be strong in the Lord, and in the power of his might." — — —Eph. vi. 10.

Let me now ADD a few words,

1. In commendation of this good Shepherd—

Whence is it that all do not put themselves under his care? Is there any want of love, or tenderness, or power in him? God frequently, by his prophets, called on his rebellious people to testify against him, and to say, Whether there had been any want of kindness or care in him: "O my people, what have I done unto thee? and wherein have I wearied thee? Testify against me." Mic. vi. 3; Jer. ii. 5, 31. "What could I have done more for my people than I have done?" Isai. v. 4. So do I now, in the name of this good Shepherd, call upon you all this day, to bear, if you can, your testimony against him. Whom did he ever neglect or despise? Whom that sought him, did he ever refuse to receive? Whom that trusted in him did he ever omit to supply according to his necessities?— — —If then no complaint ever was, or could be made against him from the world, let every heart appreciate his excellency, and every soul commit itself to his care.*

2. For the augmentation and encouragement of his flock—

You who have to this hour been going astray, and walking in the way of your own hearts, reflect upon your guilt and danger, and "return now without delay to the Shepherd and Bishop of your souls."— — —1 Pet. ii. 25. As employed by him, I come now to search you out, and to bring you home to his field.— — —Eph. iv. 11; Mark xvi. 15; Jer. xxiii. 4. O think, how delightful it will be to "hear his voice calling every one of you by name," John x. 3, and "going in and out with you" as long as you shall remain in this dreary wilderness, ib. ver. 9, and then performing the same office for you in the realms of bliss! Rev vii. 17. "O listen not to the voice of strangers"— — —but, follow him— — —that you may be one fold under one Shepherd for ever and ever. John x. 5, 9, 16.

SECURITY AND COMFORT IN CHRIST.

Isaiah xxxii. 2. –A man shall be as an hiding-place from the wind, and a covert from the tempest; as rivers of water in a dry place, as the shadow of a great rock in a weary land. (S. S.)

THERE is no greater blessing to a nation than a well-ordered government—The due administration of justice, together with the protection of our person and property, afford to any people a just ground of joy and thankfulness—Such a government did God promise to the Jews under Hezekiah—But a greater than Hezekiah is here—Under the figure of an earthly monarch, Christ is promised—And the text informs us,

I. WHAT BLESSINGS WE ENJOY IN AND THROUGH CHRIST.

The metaphors, though four in number, suggest but two ideas

1. Security.

We have very little conception of winds and tempests in this climate—But the wind that rent the mountains before Elijah, 1 Kings xix. 11, and the tempest that desolated the land of Egypt, Exod. ix. 23—25, may serve to shew us how welcome a secure place must be to one who is exposed to such formidable dangers—Yet no storms on earth can fully paint to us the dangers to which we are exposed by reason of sin, Ps. xi. 6.—But the Lord Jesus Christ affords us perfect security from them all—In him we have a Goshen where no hail can come, a mountain which the wind can never affect—The billows, which shall overwhelm the whole creation besides, shall not be able to destroy us—In Christ we have an ark that can never perish—

2. Comfort.

We, in this quarter of the globe, know as little of excessive drought and heat, as of overwhelming storms and tempests—But the state of the Israelites in the wilderness, Exod. xvii. 2, 3, and of Jonah at Nineveh (Jonah iv. 8,) may aid our conceptions—How delightful was the gourd to *him*, and how

*If this were a subject for an *Ordination* or *Visitation* Sermon, the Clergy should be urged to follow the example of this good Shepherd.

reviving to *them* were the streams that gushed from the rock!—And does no a soul oppressed with sin or persecution, or fainting with desire after righteousness, experience as much distress as they?—Behold then the preciousness of Christ!—He will be not only as a shade or as water to the weary and thirsting soul, but as "rivers of water" that can never be exhausted, and a "shadow of a great rock" through which the beams of the sun can never penetrate—Many can attest his excellency in these respects—Nor shall any who seek refuge in him be ever diappointed of their hope—

But as these things are spoken of Christ as "a man," it will be proper to shew,

II. How we enjoy them in him as "a man."

Christ is truly and properly God—But he is God manifest in the flesh—And it is to him as incarnate that we stand indebted for these blessings.

1. As man, he died for our sins.

To his atonement we owe all our hopes of salvation—If he had not expiated our guilt we could never have obtained mercy—If he had not purchased for us the gift of the Holy Ghost, we never could have mortified our inward corruptions—But through his death we are freed from the apprehensions of wrath; and through his Spirit we are filled with righteousness, and peace, and joy, Rom. xiv. 17,—Hence our song will ever be, To him who loved us and washed us from our sins in his own blood, be glory and honor—Rev. i. 5.

2. As man he intercedeth for us in heaven.

As our peace was effected by the death of Christ, so is it maintained by his intercession—Now it is as man that he appears in the presence of God for us; and liveth on purpose to carry on this part of his priestly office—By virtue of this our persons and services find acceptance with God—Pardon is given us for our renewed transgressions, and strength is imparted to surmount our manifold temptations—Hence is our salvation justly ascribed, and *that* in a very peculiar manner, to his intercession for us—Heb. vii. 25.

3. As man he is our head and representative

Christ is the second Adam, the Lord from heaven, 1 Cor. xv. 45, 47,—Our life is now treasured up in *him*, that it may no longer be exposed to the assaults of our great adversary, Col. iii. 3,—It has pleased the Father that in *him* should all fulness dwell; and that out of his fulness all should receive, who shall ever be partakers of his grace, or of his glory, John i. 16,—Whether we want wisdom to guide us, righteousness to justify us, or sanctification to make us holy, we must look for all of it in and through Christ—As in Adam, our first covenant-head, all died, so in Christ, our new covenant-head, shall all be made alive—1 Cor. xv. 22.

4. As man he shall judge the world in the last day.

All judgment is committed to him because he is the Son of man, John v. 27,—And what can tend more to our security and comfort than this?—Will he, who shed his blood for us, give up what he has so dearly purchased?—Or he who both interceded for us, and supplied our wants, consign us over to perdition?—Will he not rather bear testimony in opposition to our fierce accuser, and own the work he had both wrought for us and in us?—Doubtless, if we should feel a degree of security and comfort in having a very dear friend for our judge on earth, much more may we rejoice in having for our judge in the last day, him, who bought us with his blood and renewed us by his Spirit—

We do not mean to exclude his Godhead from this great work of redemption—It is that which gives efficacy to all which he did and suffered as man—

But nevertheless it is as man. that is, as the God-man, that we feel our relation to him, and have access unto him as our sympathizing friend—

INFER,

1. What objects of pity are they who have no interest in Christ!

They are exposed to all the wrath of a sin-avenging God—And where, where will they flee for safety?—Where will they even procure a drop of water in that land of drought and misery, to which they shall be banished?—Alas! there is no protection but in this city of refuge; there is no water but in this fountain—O that men would consider what they shall do in the day of their visitation!—And flee for refuge to the hope that is now set before them—Heb. vi. 18.

2. How highly privileged are they who believe in Christ!

They are not exempt from occasional distress either of soul or body—But they have an almighty friend to whom they can carry their distress—They go to him when heavy laden; and find rest unto their souls—They feel themselves secure in their blood-sprinkled dwellings—But their privileges will not be fully seen till the last day—Then how happy in having a covert from the wrath that overwhelms the ungodly world!—Then to have their Saviour both for their witness and their judge!—Let us all cleave to him with full purpose of heart; and desire to know him more and more as our friend and our beloved."

CHRIST'S EXERCISE OF SUPREME POWER OVER THE INVISIBLE WORLD.

Rev. i. 17, 18—Fear not; I am the first and the last: I am he that liveth, and was dead; and behold, I am alive for evermore, Amen; and have the keys of hell and of death. (S. S.)

MAN, while he continued in a state of innocence, communed freely with his Maker face to face: but from the time that sin entered into the world, he has dreaded the presence of the most High, and fled from it with fear and trembling. Whenever God has been pleased to appear to any of his people, the sight has uniformly filled them with terror; and in some instances, almost deprived them even of life. This was the effect produced by a vision vouchsafed to John. Our blessed Lord, in a habit somewhat resembling that of the high priest, revealed himself to his beloved disciple: and so august was his appearance, that John, unable to endure the sight, fell at his feet as dead. But our Lord, in condescension to his weakness, dispelled his fears by making known to him the perfections of his nature, and the offices which in his mediatorial capacity he sustained.

In discoursing on his words we shall consider

I. OUR LORD'S RECORD CONCERNING HIMSELF.

A more glorious description of Jesus is not to be found in all the sacred writings: he declares himself to be

1. The eternal God.

The terms, "the first and the last," are intended to express eternity: ver 8, 11, and Rev. xxii. 13, and, in this view, it is an incommunicable attribute of Jehovah. It is often used to describe God in places where he contrasts himself with the gods of the heathen: Isa. xliv. 6, and it always characterizes him as infinitely superior to all creatures. But Jesus here arrogates it to himself. Eternity had been ascrib d to him both by prophets and apostles: Prov. viii. 22—30, Mic. v. 2, John i. 1, Heb. xiii. 8, but he here claims it himself as his own prerogative; for, notwithstanding he was in the form of a servant, he thought it not robbery to be equal with God. Phil. ii. 6. Hence then it is evident that Jesus is one with the Father, "in glory equal, in majesty co-eternal," God over all, blessed for evermore.—Rom. ix. 5.

2. The living Saviour.

He, whose brightness now exceeded that of the meridian sun, once hung upon the cross. But, says he, "*though*, και, I was dead, yet I am the living One, ὁ ζῶν, possessed of life in myself, John v. 26, and the source of life to others; and immutably living, to carry on the work which I began on earth." "Behold" this with wonder, yet with a full assurance of its truth; for, I, the "Amen," "the true and faithful witness, declare it unto thee. Now as the former assertion shews us what he was in his divine nature, this informs us what he is in his mediatorial office "He died for our offences, and rose again for our justification;" and is, not only our advocate with the Father, Rom. viii. 34, but the head of vital influence to all that believe. Eph. i. 22, 23.

3. The universal Sovereign.

By "hell" we are to understand, not the habitation of the damned only, but the whole invisible world: and "death" is the door of introduction to it. Now to "have the keys" of these, is to have the power over them, together with the entire appointment of men's states in reference to them. Isa. xxii. 22. And this power does Jesus exercise. Whomsoever he will, and in whatever time or manner he sees fit, he consigns to death, and fixes instantly in heaven or hell: "He openeth and no man shutteth; he shutteth, and no man openeth." Rev. iii. 7. Hence it appears that every event in this world also, must be under his control; and consequently, that he is the universal sovereign.

From the encouraging address which accompanied this record, we are led to consider

II. Its tendency to comfort and support the soul.

When a similar vision was vouchsafed to Daniel, its effects, which were also similar, were counteracted in the same manner. Dan. x. 5—12. Now this record of our Lord was well calculated to dissipate the fears of John; and may well also be a comfort to us

1. Under apprehensions of temporal calamities.

Impending dangers and distresses will often excite terror, and overwhelm the soul with anxious dread. But what ground of fear can he have, who has the eternal God for his refuge? What injury can arise to him, whose soul is in the Redeemer's hands, and for whose benefit all things are ordered both in heaven and earth? "Not a hair of his head can perish" but by special commission from his best friend. "Thousands may fall beside him, and ten thousand at his right hand;" but "no weapon that is formed against him, can prosper." If his eyes were opened to behold his real situation, he might see himself encompassed with horses of fire, and chariots of fire: 2 Kings vi. 17, and, standing as an impregnable fortress, he might defy the assaults of men or devils. If his God and Saviour be for him, none can be against him. Rom. viii. 31.

2. Under fears of eternal condemnation.

No man can reflect upon his own character without feeling that he deserves the wrath of God: and every one that is sensible of his own demerits, mus-

tremble lest the judgments he has deserved should be inflicted on him. Yet a just view of the Saviour may dispel his fears, and cause him to rejoice with joy unspeakable." Does his guilt appear too great to be forgiven? He that offered an atonement for it, is the eternal God. Acts xx. 28. Do doubts arise respecting his acceptance with the Father? Behold, that very Jesus who made atonement for him, ever liveth to plead it as his advocate, and to present it before the mercy seat. 1 John i. 1, 2. Do death and hell appal him with their terrors? they are altogether subject to the control of Jesus, whose power and faithfulness are pledged for the salvation of all his ransomed people. John x. 28, 29. To the weakest then we say in the name of this adorable Saviour, "Fear not:" though thou art "a worm, thou shalt thresh the mountains;" Isa. xli. 10, 14, 15, and though thou art the smallest grain that has been gathered from the field, thou shalt be treasured safely in the granary of thy heavenly Father. Amos ix. 9.

APPLICATION.

We cannot conclude the subject without applying it to those who are ignorant of Christ. Surely we must not say to you, "Fear not;" but rather, "Fear and tremble," for he whom ye have despised, is the eternal God; and ever liveth to put down his enemies, and to make them his footstool. He has only, as it were, to turn the key of the invisible world, and your souls will be locked up in the prison, from whence there is no redemption. O consider this, ye that live unmindful of this adorable Saviour; and prostrate yourselves at his feet, while his offers of mercy are yet extended to you

CHAPTER V.

THE HOLY SPIRIT.

CHRIST'S OFFER OF THE SPIRIT.

John vii. 37, 38.—In the last day, that great day of the feast, Jesus stood and cried, saying, If any man thirst, let him come unto me, and drink. He that believeth on me, as the scripture hath said, out of his belly shall flow rivers of living water. (S. S.)

OUR blessed Lord incessantly labored for the salvation of men—

Nor could their ungrateful returns at all divert him from his purpose—

His life was sought, and he knew that persons were sent to apprehend him—

Yet, instead of rejecting them with abhorrence, he sought to win them by love—

And importuned them to accept his richest blessings—

His address to them on this occasion contained,

I. AN INVITATION.

The time and manner of the invitation are worthy of notice.

This was a day of peculiar sanctity, and of uncommon festivity—*

*It was the eighth and last day of the feast of tabernacles, Lev. xxiii. 34, 36.

And it seems that some customs, not required in the original institutions of the law, obtained among the Jews at that time—*

Happy to improve the opportunity, Jesus stood in the most conspicuous place, and, with an exalted voice, claimed their attention—

And, despising equally the censures of the uncharitable, and the persecutions of the proud, he made them fresh overtures of mercy—

The invitation itself was beyond measure gracious and kind.

While they only panted for his blood, he longed for their salvation—

He pointed himself out to them as the only fountain of living waters—

And assured them of his readiness to impart whatsoever they stood in need of—

He excepted none from his offers, provided they did but "thirst" for his blessings—

What could have a more conciliatory effect on his blood-thirsty murderers?—

Lest, however, his invitations should be slighted, he enforced it with,

II. A PROMISE.

He first explained what he meant by "coming to him."

It was not a mere outward, but an inward and spiritual application, that he wished them to make to him—

They were to "believe in *him*," as possessing all fulness in himself—Col. i. 19.

And as the person appointed of the Father to convey blessings to them—Ps. lxxii. 17.

In a full persuasion of this truth they were to come to him by faith—

And to "draw water with joy from this well of salvation"—

For their encouragement he promised them a rich effusion of his Spirit.

By "living water" our Lord meant the gift of his Spirit—Ver. 39.

That "rivers of this living water should flow out of his belly," imported, that the believer should have a constant spring of consolation within him, which should refresh all who came within the sphere of his influence—

Of this blessed truth the scriptures had abundantly testified—†

And our Lord now confirmed it to them by a most solemn promise—

He assured them, as he had before done the Samaritan woman, that his communications to them should prove a source of unutterable and endless joy—John iv. 10, 13, 14.

We shall further IMPROVE this subject by addressing,

1. Those who have no desire after spiritual blessings.

Alas! how many are there who are insatiable in their thirst after earthly things; but never once desire the blessings which Christ is exalted to bestow!

*It is said that on this day they went annually to the pool of Siloam, and drawing water from thence returned with it in procession to the temple, where they poured it out with all possible demonstrations of joy. At what time this custom arose, it is not easy to determine; but probably it commenced after the Babylonish captivity; and was adopted in reference to that prediction, Isaiah xii. 3. Nor is the design of it precisely known: but it seems most likely that they then commemorated the giving of water out of the rock in the wilderness; and called upon God for rain, which was so necessary to them at that season. Perhaps the more spiritual among them, might pray also for those spiritual blessings, which their promised Messiah was appointed to bestow. These circumstances serve as the foundation of our Lord's address, and reflect much light upon it.

†Some, because our Lord's words are not found in scripture, καθὼς εἶπεν η γραφη with ὁ πιστεύων εἰς ἐμὲ: (translating εἶπεν, hath *required*) but there are many passages that speak to the same effect, though not in his express terms. See Isaiah xliv. 3.

Perhaps too they think that they contract no guilt by their neglect of him—

But it is with no small indignation that God speaks of their conduct—Jer. ii. 13.

Nor would their folly be hidden from themselves, if they only considered what "broken cisterns" the sources of their comfort have invariably proved—

O that they would drink of the living fountain before they experience the want of one "drop of water to cool their tongues!"—

2. Those who desire spiritual blessings, but know not where to go for them.

Many, like those whom our Lord addressed, look no further than to the outward duty—

But he directed their eyes to himself as the true Siloam, John ix. 7, the only fountain of good—

Thus must we also direct you to faith in Christ, as the one means of obtaining blessings from him—

Whatever delight you may take in duties, you must remember that ordinances are but the medium of communication between Christ and you—

And that the benefits you receive will be proportioned to the faith you exercise on him—

3. Those who desire spiritual blessings, but fear that Christ is unwilling to impart them.

Too many are discouraged because their prayers are not answered instantly—

They conclude themselves so unworthy as to have excited nothing but aversion in the heart of Christ towards them—

But are you unworthy? and were not they also to whom the text was addressed—

Have you waited long in vain? and is there not a special promise given for your encouragement?—Isa. xli. 17, 18.

Have you nothing to present to Christ in return? Then he bids you come without money and without price—Isa. lv. 1; Rev. xxii. 17.

Will it be an unparalleled act of mercy? Then is it that new thing which he has undertaken to perform—Isa. xliii. 19, 20.

Fear not then, but renew your application to him with increased fervor—

And your soul shall ere long "be as a watered garden, and like a spring of water, whose waters fail not"—Isa. lviii. 11.

THE ENDS FOR WHICH THE HOLY SPIRIT IS GIVEN TO US.

Ezek. xxxvi. 25—27.—Then will I sprinkle clean water upon you, and ye shall be clean: from all your filthiness, and from all your idols, will I cleanse you. A new heart also will I give you, and a new spirit will I put within you: and I will take away the stony heart out of your flesh, and I will give you an heart of flesh. And I will put my spirit within you, and cause you to walk in my statutes, and ye shall keep my judgments, and do them. (S. S.)

THE promises of the Old Testament frequently refer to different and distant periods—

In these periods they receive different degrees of accomplishment—

The promise before us was partly fulfilled in the deliverance of the Jews from idolatry after their return from captivity in Babylon—

It had a further accomplishment on the day of Pentecost—
Its final completion will take place at the millenium—
This appears by its connection with the foregoing verse—
In the mean time it is daily fulfilled to the church of God—
It may lead us to consider the ends for which God gives us his Spirit—
He sends down his Spirit
I. To CLEANSE FROM SIN.
The heart of man is full of "filthiness and of idols."
There is nothing so worthless, but it is idolized by us; nothing so filthy but it is harbored and indulged—
The idols indeed are not set up in our houses, but in our hearts, Ezek. xiv. 3.
And if the filthiness appear not in open enormities, yet are our flesh and our spirit contaminated with it throughout—
Hence God pronounces the whole race of man to be "filty and abominable"—
Nor indeed can any words sufficiently represent our deformity, Jer. xvii. 9.
To cleanse us from these God imparts his Holy Spirit.
The Spirit of God is here compared to "clean water"—
He is often spoken of in Scripture under this metaphor, John vii. 38, 39.
His sprinkling of this water on us is in allusion to the sprinklings of the ceremonial law—
It was by sprinkling, that holy persons and vessels were sanctified—
It is for the same end that God sends his Holy Spirit upon us—
The blood of Christ alone can cleanse from the guilt of sin, 1 John i. 7.
But the Spirit cleanses from the love and power of it—
Nor does the operation of the Spirit supercede the atonement—
It rather presupposes an affiance in the blood of Christ*—
Though the operation of Christ's blood and spirit are distinct, yet they are never divided, 1 John v. 6.
The one is as necessary in its place, and as effectual, as the other—
By his Spirit he cleanses the soul "from all its filthiness and all its idols."
The corruption of the heart is not indeed utterly extinguished—
But the love of sin is taken away, and its power is broken—
St. Paul ascribes this effect to the Spirit in the strongest terms, Eph. v. 25—27.
In order to effeet this permanently, God sends his Spirit
II. To RENEW THE HEART.
A change must be radical, in order to be effectual, Matt. xii. 33.
The heart, by nature, is hard and insensible as a "stone"—
The soul is altogether "dead in trespasses and sins"—
The understanding is blind, the will obstinate, the conscience seared—
A dead body is insensible of its own corruption—
So is the soul insensible of its state, because it is spiritually dead—
God therefore takes away this "stony heart out of the flesh"—
He does not really alter the powers of the soul—
The faculties remain the same as they were before—

* The purifying of the Levites well illustrates this. They were cleansed by the sprinkling of water on them: yet not so cleansed but that they needed to offer an atonement. The atonement and the sprinkling *jointly* produced the *full* effect. See Numb. viii. 6, 7, 8, 12.

But a new direction is given to them—
They are also assisted by him in their respective functions—
Hence they appear to be altogether new—
He gives in exchange "an heart of flesh."
It is characteristic of the new heart that it is tender—
It is deeply affected with its own sin and misery—
It is melted with a sense of God's unbounded mercies—
Thus in fact the christian is made "a new creature"—
In this way God prevails by the Spirit
III. To SANCTIFY THE LIFE.
What was before metaphorically, is here plainly expressed—
God, by renewing the soul, changes also the life.*
The unregenerate man accounts the commandments grievous—
The renewed person longs for a perfect conformity to them, Rom. vii. 22
He henceforth "walks as Christ himself walked"—
By the indwelling of his Spirit he "causes" his people to obey him
We cannot explain the mode of the Spirit's operations—
We are sure, however, that he does not act on men as mere machines—
He draws them in a rational manner as free agents—
He constrains them by enlightening their understanding and inclining their will—
He makes them delight in receiving and obeying his influences—
Their language is invariably like that of the church of old, Cant. i. 4.
In order to IMPROVE this promise, we would lead you to contemplate
1. Its freeness.
To whom is this promise made, but to those who are filthy and idolatrous, insensible and obdurate?—
Let none put it away from them as not belonging to them—
But rather let all lay hold on it, and plead it before God—
2. Its suitableness.
What would any one, who knew his wants, ask of God?—
Can any thing be conceived more suitable than the things here promised?
Let those who feel their need of cleansing, and renovation, rejoice that God has promised them the desire of their hearts—
3. Its preciousness.
Well does the apostle say, that the "promises are precious"—
What can he want, that has this promise fulfilled to him?—
Such an one may defy either men or devils to make him miserable—
In the purification and renewal of his soul he has all that man can desire

THE GIFT OF THE HOLY SPIRIT.

Luke xi. 13.—"If ye then, being evil, know how to give good gifts unto your children: how much more shall your heavenly Father give the Holy Spirit to them that ask him." (Sk.)

In the important and instructive paragraph with which our text is connected, we find,

*The salt being cast into the fountain, the streams are henceforth salubrious. See 2 Kings ii. 21.

1. A pious request presented to our Lord by one of his disciples 1st. "Lord teach us how to pray," &c. From this request it is conjectured, that John the Baptist, according to the usual custom of the Jewish teachers, had given his disciples certain forms of prayer to guide and assist their devotion. A similar favor from our Lord appears therefore to be thus requested by his disciples.

2. Our Lord's compliance with this request. "He said unto them, When ye pray, say," &c., v. 2—4. Here we find those petitions used as a *form* of prayer, which had previously been recommended in the sermon on the mount as a *model* of prayer. Thus we have the highest authority to use this prayer as a form.

3. An exhortation is subjoined to seek the blessings of salvation by importunate prayer. This is urged by the example of a friend, prevailed on by importunity to grant a favor, v. 5—9;—by the success of all earnest persevering supplicants, v. 10;—by the natural kindness of earthly parents, who do not give their children stones for bread, serpents for fishes, nor scorpions for eggs, v. 11, 12.—And in our text, by the infinite goodness of God; "If ye then," &c. These words exhibit our privilege—prescribe our duty—and encourage our hope—as the followers of Christ.

I. These words EXHIBIT OUR PRIVILEGE as the followers of Christ. This is, to enjoy the gift of God's Holy Spirit. Here let us observe,

1. *What is meant by the Holy Spirit.* This we may learn by noticing some particulars respecting the Holy Spirit, which we find recorded in the oracles of God. These inform us—that the Holy Spirit may be grieved; for we are cautioned against grieving him, Eph. iv. 30; that he intercedes for us, Rom. viii. 26, 27; that he reproves the world, John xvi. 7, 8; that he guides, hears, speaks, and shows things to come, John xvi. 13. Now to grieve, to intercede, to reprove, to guide, hear, speak, and show things to come, are all personal acts; hence we are assured that the Holy Spirit is a *person.*

The Scriptures also inform us, that the Holy Spirit is a person against whom unpardonable sin may be committed, Matt. xii. 31, 32; and to lie to the Holy Ghost, implies lying unto God, Acts v. 3, 4; and that those in whom the Holy Ghost dwells are temples of God, 1 Cor. iii. 16. Hereby we are assured that the Holy Spirit is a *divine* person, and truly God.—And in this we are also confirmed by the divine ordinance of baptism, Matt. xxviii. 19; and by the apostolic benediction, 2 Cor. xiii. 14.

2. *That the Holy Ghost is enjoyed by all real Christians.* This is evident from the Apostle's solemn declaration, Rom. viii. 9: "If any man," &c. It therefore follows that none can be Christ's approved servants here, nor partakers of the glory hereafter, but those who have his Spirit; and that all who are truly his, enjoy this heavenly gift.—From our Lord's promise, John vii. 37—39. This assures us that all believers are invited to receive the Holy Spirit, and actually to enjoy his gracious influence. This is further evident from the description given us of gospel salvation, Tit. iii. 5, 6. Hence observe,

3. *For what purposes he is received by them.* They receive him—as a Spirit of *penitence* and *prayer;* showing them their sin and danger, Zech. xii. 10; and exciting in them desires of salvation, Matt. v. 6.—As a Spirit of *power;* strengthening them, and enabling them to renounce sin; lay hold on Christ; bear their trials; overcome their enemies; and persevere in the path of piety, Eph. iii. 16; Job xvii. 9.—As a Spirit of *comfort;* to inspire them with assurance and hope, Rom. viii. 16, 17.—As a Spirit of *purity;* to cleanse them from all sinful practices, 1 Cor. vi. 11; all sinful tempers, dis-

positions, and imaginations, Ezek. xxxvi. 25—29. As a Spirit of *wisdom;* to lead them in the way of righteousness, Rom. viii. 14.—And as a Spirit of *fruitfulness;* by which the glorify God, Gal. v. 22, 23; John xv. 8. That we may obtain this gift, the words of our text,

II. PRESCRIBE OUR DUTY. This is, to ask as God requires.

1. *Ask sincerely;* in truth. The Lord is near to such as call upon him in truth, Psalm cxlv. 18. Call upon him, as this implies,—in the spirit of true repentance; considering, lamenting, confessing, and forsaking all sin. This God commands, Prov. i. 23; and encourages, Acts ii. 38, 39.—And in the spirit of holy fervour, with desires and cries, Psalm cxlv. 19.

2. *Ask evangelically;* according to the gospel method of approaching God; with entire dependence on the mediation of Jesus Christ, John xiv. 6. For gospel salvation is the gift of God through Christ, and should be sought as such, Rom. vi. 23; Col. iii. 17; John xiv. 14—16.

3. *Ask importunately;* with unceasing application; till you are filled with this heavenly gift as a Spirit of power, of purity and of comfort, Eph. v. 18. This importunity our Lord requires, Luke xi. 9; and it appears highly proper; for the gift of the Holy Spirit is an invaluable acquisition; it may be lost after having been enjoyed, Heb. vi. 4, 6; it will be lost, if not carefully guarded, Rev. iii. 12. And most probably, it would not be prized and guarded as it ought to be, if it had been given without our earnest importunity. Therefore, in requiring this, our Lord manifests the greatest kindness to us.

4. *Ask believingly:* in confident expectation of obtaining. To ask in doubt of success, when we ask as God requires, must dishonor him; by questioning his power, or goodness, or truth. Unbelief therefore renders prayers unavailing, James i. 5—7. To ask in faith, must consequently honor God, Rom. iv. 20, 21. Hence faith in prayer is required of us, Heb. x. 19—22. Thus also the words of the text,

III. ENCOURAGE OUR HOPE. "If ye then," &c. Here we are led to notice,

1. *That mankind are naturally evil.* They are ignorant, and know but little; they are poor, and possess but little; they are selfish, and inclined to keep what they have for their own enjoyment, Tit. iii. 3.

2. *Yet they know how to give good gifts unto their children.—Good* gifts; things suitable to their wants, and conducive to their welfare.—They *give* them: freely, however unmerited; readily without delay; unweariedly, though often repeated; cheerfully, with comfort to themselves.—They *know* how to give them: they have sufficient ability to confer them; sufficient love to bestow them; sufficient wisdom to adapt them.

3. *But God is certainly your Father, if you ask the Holy Spirit as he requires.* Your Father, by regeneration, adoption, and covenant, 2 Cor. vi. 17, 18.

4. *And God being your Father, you cannot fail of obtaining the gift of his Holy Spirit.* For he is your *heavenly* Father; all-sufficient to bestow this gift upon you, Gen. xiv. 22. He is your *covenant* Father; engaged to give it, Ezek. xxxvi 27. He is a *good* Father; inclined by love to bless you, Rom. viii. 32. A *wise* Father; who knows how to adapt its various influences to your wants, Eph. i. 7, 8. And a *gracious* Father; disposed to give it freely, Rev. xxii. 17. This gift therefore is as certain as God's power, his truth, his love, his wisdom, and grace.

APPLICATION.

1. *Recollect your privilege with suitable acts of piety.* Such as—*self-examination.* Do you enjoy this gift as a Spirit of penitence, &c., 2 Cor

xiii. 5.—*Humiliation:* on account of your enjoying no more of it, James iv. 2, 8–10. *Holy care:* to cherish and improve what divine influence you enjoy. By obeying Christ, Rev. iii. 2; and imitating St. Paul, Phil. iii. 13, 14.

2. *Recollect your duty with perseverence in it*, Col. iv. 2. Neither be discouraged by seeming delays, Heb. ii. 3; nor rest in present attainments, 2 Pet. i. 5–11, and iii. 14

2. *Recollect your encouragement with steadfast hope*—of receiving the Holy Spirit in all his influences; as a Spirit of prayer, penitence, power, &c., 1 Pet. v. 10, 11.

OFFICES OF THE HOLY SPIRIT.

John xvi. 8—11.—And when he is come, he will reprove the world of sin, and of righteousness, and of judgment: of sin, because they believe not on me; of righteousness, because I go to the Father, and ye see me no more: of judgment, because the prince of this world is judged. (H. H.)

In judging of the dispensations of God's providence or grace, we are extremely apt to err—

Hence we often mourn for things, which, if we knew the end of them, would afford us occasion for joy—

This was the case with the disciples, who were dejected on account of their Lord's approaching departure from them—

To relieve their minds, our Lord not only promised them another Comforter, but told them for what ends and purposes that Comforter should come—

I. To "CONVINCE THE WORLD OF SIN."

This office the Spirit executed among the Jews—

The sin of rejecting Christ was that which the Spirit was more particularly to reveal to the world—

And he discovered it fully by his *miraculous operations* on the disciples*—and wrought an irresistible conviction of it by his *gracious influences* on the hearts of thousands—

This office too he yet executes in the christian church—

The external testimony which he gave, remains the same in all ages—

The internal witness is given to those only whom "God has ordained to life"—

To them the Spirit shews the number, the greatness, the malignity of their sins—and particularly, the guilt, and danger of that unbelief, in which they have ignorantly lain—

This is the Spirit's work; nor is it wrought in any, but by his almighty power—Zech. iv. 6; 2 Cor. v. 5; 1 Cor. xii. 11.

If he proceeded no farther, he would not be a Comforter; but it is his office also,

II. To CONVINCE THE WORLD "OF RIGHTEOUSNESS"—

This also was accomplished by him on his first descent from heaven—

*Christ had stated, as it were, the whole credit of his Messiahship on this one point: consequently, the visible descent of the Spirit, accompanied with the miraculous gift of tongues was such an attestation to Christ, as could not be doubted, and such a reproof to his murderers as could not be withstood.

Christ, though professing himself the Saviour of the world, had been crucified as a malefactor—

The Spirit therefore was to evince, both that Christ was a righteous person, and that through his righteousness others also might be saved—

Accordingly, by his descent, the Spirit proved these things beyond a doubt—

He shewed that Christ was accepted of the Father (which he would not have been, if he had been an impostor,) and had finished all that was necessary for our salvation; seeing that, if any thing had remained to have been done on earth, he must have returned hither in order to complete it—See the text.

He moreover inclined, and enabled multitudes to believe on HIM for righteousness, whom they had just before reprobated as worthy of universal execration—

And yet daily is he occupied in glorifying Christ among us—

Whomsoever the Spirit convinces thoroughly of sin, he leads also to discoveries of Christ—

He shews to the soul the suitableness and all-sufficiency of Christ's righteousness to all those who trust in it—Ver. 14.

And leads them, with holy glorying, to say, "In the Lord have I righteousness and strength"—Isa. xlv. 24.

He has yet further undertaken,

III. To CONVINCE THE WORLD OF JUDGMENT—

He shewed to the first christians that Satan was a vanquished foe—

By the descent of the Spirit it was manifest, that Christ had triumphed over sin and Satan, death and hell—Eph. iv. 8; Col. ii. 15

By his gracious influences also, he rescued myriads from their power—and inspired them with an holy confidence, that they should finally prevail over all their spiritual enemies—2 Tim. i. 12.

Thus at this day does he cause the weakest to exult over their fallen enemy—

However active and malicious Satan is, his head is bruised, Gen. iii. 15, his power is limited, Rev. ii. 10; 1 Peter v. 8, his doom is fixed—Rom xvi. 20.

Of this the Holy Spirit assures the weak and trembling believer—

And puts into his mouth, even in the midst of all his conflicts, that triumphant song—Rom. viii. 38, 39.

USES,

1. Of conviction—

All true christians have received the Spirit for the ends and purposes for which he is here promised—

In vain then will be our orthodoxy in sentiment, if we have not this evidence of our conversion to God—ib. ver. 9.

Let us pray that the Spirit may be poured out upon us—

And let our views of our guilt and weakness lead us to glory in Christ alone—

2. Of consolation—

Are we bowed down with a *sense* of sin? we may be sure that Christ has sent his Spirit to work that conviction in us; and that, if we be instant in prayer, he will, by the same Spirit, lead us also to a view of his righteousness—

Are we ready to despond by reason of the *power* of sin? the resistance which the Holy Spirit has enabled us already to make to its dominion, is a pledge that "we shall be more than conquerors, through Him that loved us." Rom. viii. 37.

Let us only seek the Spirit as our Comforter, and we need regret no loss, no pain, no trouble, that may be the means of bringing him into our hearts.

THE POURING OUT OF GOD'S SPIRIT.

Acts ii. 17.--And it shall come to pass in the last days, saith God, I will pour out of my Spirit upon all flesh. (Sk.)

In this highly interesting chapter we find an account,

1. Of the divine *testimony* borne to the truth of the gospel, by the descent of the Holy Ghost on the day of Pentecost. Here it appears, that by inspiration, the apostles were enabled at once to speak various languages which they never before understood;—that what they were thus inspired to declare, were the wonderful works of God; or the operations of his mercy, power, and wisdom, displayed in our redemption by Christ;—and that all who were then at Jerusalem heard those wonderful works of God declared in their own respective languages. This intimated that the gospel was designed for the benefit of all the human race. In the succeeding verses, we have an account,

2. Of the different *effects* which this event produced on the different characters who witnessed it. In the devout, it excited amazement, which led them to make serious inquiry respecting what was occurring, ver. 5–12. In the careless, it excited contempt; which led them to oppose the gracious designs of God, and to treat the work of God with derision and blasphemy, ver. 13. But the wrath of man, in this, as in former cases, turned to the praise of God; for in the sequel we find an account,

3. Of Peter's *discourse* in reply to those aspersions thus cast on the works of God by his wicked opposers. In this discourse Peter repels the senseless charge of drunkenness, ver. 14, 15—and shows that this remarkable occurrence is in fact the fulfilment of prophecy, ver. 16, 17. "But this is that which was spoken by the prophet Joel, And it shall come to pass, in the last days, saith God, I will pour out of my Spirit upon all flesh." In improving these words it may be proper to make some observations on them—and some application of them. Let us make,

I. Some observations on them. Here we may notice,

1. *The blessing promised; God's Spirit.* "I will pour out of my Spirit, saith God." By the Spirit here promised is certainly meant both his miraculous and saving influence. *His miraculous influence.*—This was imparted to confirm the truth of the gospel, and to promote the spread of it in the world, Heb. ii. 3, 4; 1 Cor. xiv. 22. By means of this influence, the apostles, and many primitive christians, were endued with various gifts; as the gifts of wisdom, or knowledge, or faith, or healing, or miracles, or prophecy, or discerning of spirits, or divers kinds of tongues, or the interpretation of tongues: see 1 Cor. xii. 6–11. By the Spirit here promised is also meant,—*his saving influence;* this is enjoyed by all believers in Christ, John vii. 37, 39. The effects of this influence are intimated by the testimony of John the Baptist, Matt. iii. 11. These effects are farther intimated, by the fiery appearance which the Holy Ghost was pleased to assume on his descent, verse

3. For as fire enlightens, purifies, and warms; so believing souls are *enlightened* with knowledge, *purified* from sin, and *invigorated* with power, by the influences of God's Holy Spirit, 2 Tim. i. 7. Let us notice,

2. *The manner of its dispensation;* it will be poured out. This indicates—*the prerogative of God;* that the influences of his Spirit are at his disposal. He withholds those influences, or dispenses them, or withdraws them, as he pleases, Matt. xx. 15; Eph. i. 11; Phil. ii. 12, 13. The pouring out of God's Spirit also indicates—the *special properties* of the blessing promised. For instance, that it will be *gratuitous;* or given freely, like water from a fountain, John iv. 10; Rev. xxii. 17. That it will be *abundant;* given bountifully, without restraint, Eph. v. 18; Psa. lxxxi. 10 And that it will be *perpetual;* given in unfailing succession, Tit. iii. 5, 6. Let us notice,

3. *The extent of its influence* upon all flesh. By all flesh is meant the whole human race, however distinguished, by descent, by circumstances, or by sex. However distinguished by *descent;* whether of Jewish or Gentile extraction. This appears from the gift of Christ, Isa. xlix. 6; Luke ii. 30–32, and from the gospel ministry, Luke xxiv. 47. However distinguished by *circumstances*, whether bond or free. Both may obtain it, and both need it. The slave, with this, enjoys liberty, 2 Cor. iii. 17. The master, without this, is a slave, 2 Tim. ii. 26; Col. iii. 11. Or however distinguished by *sex;* whether male or female. For however the female sex may be enslaved by savages, oppressed by the heathens, or degraded by Mohammedans, yet christianity regards both sexes with equal favor: see Gal. iii. 26–29. This promise farther intimates, that the blessing thus free for the whole human race, shall become generally enjoyed by them, Psa. lxxii. 6, 8. Hence let us notice,

4. *The season of its communication*—The last days. By the last days are certainly meant the days in which we now live. These are called the last days, because they are the days of the gospel dispensation; which is the last dispensation of grace that God will ever establish with mankind, Heb. xii. 27, 28. And during these days this general out-pouring of God's Spirit may be expected from scripture prophecy. See Psalm ii. 8; Isa. ii. 1–10; Dan. ii. 44. As these prophecies suppose the pouring out of God's Spirit, let us notice,

5. *The certainty of its effusion.* It shall come to pass, saith God, in the last days, "I will pour out of my Spirit." This event is certain—for it is *predicted*, and it will be fulfilled. The word of prophecy is sure, 2 Pet. i. 19. It is *promised*, and will be performed. The word of promise is faithful, Psa. lxxxix. 33, 34. It is predicted and promised by *God:* whose power enables him, whose truth engages him, and whose honor binds him. to accomplish his word, Num. xxiii. 19; Psa. cxvii. 2.

Having made some observations on these words, let us now make,

II. Some application of them. In doing this, consider,

1. *The strong claims which this subject has on our attention.*

It claims attention *by the importance of the blessing which it exhibits.* The importance of this blessing appears from the *effects* ascribed to it. It is by God's Spirit that we are quickened when dead in sin, Ezek. xxxvii. 14. By this Spirit we understand our duty, as prescribed by God's word, Prov. i. 23. By this Spirit we are strengthened for all pious exercises, Eph. iii. 16. By this Spirit we are delivered from the oppression of sin, Rom. viii. 2. By this Spirit we are restored to the whole image of God, 2 Cor. iii. 18. By this Spirit we are comforted, with love, hope, and joy, Rom. v 5, and xv

13, and xiv. 17. By this spirit our pious exertions are rendered successful, Ezek. xxxvii. 7–10; 1 Cor. iii. 6. Thus the influence of God's Spirit is highly important, as it is necessary to our salvation; for without it we cannot enjoy life, nor wisdom, nor liberty, nor strength, nor holiness. It is of importance, as it is necessary to our comfort; for without it we must be destitute of love, and hope, and joy. It is of importance, as it is necessary to our youthfulness; for without it we must labor in vain, Psa. cxxvii. 1. This subject claims attention, *by our interest in the season of its communication.* We live in the last days, when God's Spirit is expressly promised: when it may be confidently expected; and when it should be earnestly sought in the use of all proper means. This leads us to consider,

2. *The duties to which this subject urges us.* It particularly urges us—to *apply* for the saving influences of God's Spirit, as he requires us in his word. By repentance, Acts ii. 38, 39; by faith in Christ, John vii. 39; Gal. iii. 14; and by earnest importunate prayer, Luke xi. 13. It urges us—to employ all those *means* which the Spirit of God is known to bless, that we may be instrumental in saving those around us; as good conversation, good books, and a faithful gospel ministry, Eccles. xi. 6. To implore the *general* effusion of God's Spirit for the conversion of the whole human race. This should be done by us individually, in our secret retirements; like David, Psa. li. 18, and lxxii. 18, 19, and Isaiah lxii. 1. And it should be done by us collectively; in social worship, Psa. xc. 16, 17; Luke xi. 2. To cultivate deep *humility* of spirit; by self-diffidence in all our pious engagements, Jer. x. 23; Zech. iv. 6, and self-abasement, in our devout and grateful acknowledgments to God, 1 Cor. xv. 10, and liii. 7; Psa. cxv. 1. Let us consider,

3. *The hopes with which this subject inspires us.* On engaging in the duties to which our text urges us, it encourages us to hope—*for the saving influence of God's Spirit in our own souls:* from the equity of God as our judge, Luke xviii. 7; from the kindness of God as our friend, Luke xi. 9, 10, and from the love of God as our father, Luke xi. 11–13. Our text encourages us to hope also—*for the general effusion of God's Spirit on the human race.* This is certain; for God here promises it, "I will pour out my Spirit," &c. And this should be *expected now:* for it will be done in God's time, Isa. lx. 19. And God's time is these last days, Psa. cii. 13; Isa. xxxii. 1, 2, 15–17.

THE HOLY SPIRIT FIGURED BY LIVING WATER.

John iv. 10.—If thou knewest the gift of God, and who it is that saith to thee, Give me to drink; thou wouldest have asked of him, and he would have given thee living water. (B.)

THE circumstances under which these words were spoken are the following—

Consider,

I. What we are to understand by the gift here mentioned, and represented under the FIGURE OF LIVING WATER.

Jesus Christ, in an especial manner, is the "gift" of God. John iii. 16; Rom. viii. 32; 2 Cor. ix. 15. Though, on this occasion, suffering from natural thirst, he wished for a little water from the well of Samaria, yet he himself is "the fountain of living waters." He is the chief object of saving knowledge, both as the gift of God, and as the fountain of living water. An application to him for this water arises from a knowledge of him, in order to which we must receive "the Spirit of wisdom and revelation." Eph. i. 17. ———

But the Holy Spirit is rather intended, which is elsewhere represented under the emblem of fire; Matt. iii. 11; Isa. iv. 4; and of air, or wind; John iii. 8;—here, under that of water; and in John vii. 37, 38; because he washes and cleanses the soul from the guilt and pollution of sin: Ezek. xxxvi. 25; refreshes the thirsty; ver. 14, and chap. vii. 37; heals the sick. Rev. xxii. 1, 17. He is represented as "*living* water," as being the only source of life to the dead in sins; and, having quickened, he makes them fruitful in righteousness. Isa. xxxii. 15–18; xliv. 3, 4; li. 3; Eph. v. 9. ———

As to the necessity of this water. We are, in ourselves, filthy, and need to be cleansed;—unhappy, and need to be refreshed:—disordered, and need to be healed:—dead, and need to be made alive;—barren. and need to be made fruitful.

The excellency of this water is manifested from our Lord's words in the fourteenth verse,—"Whosoever drinketh of the water that I shall give him," will find it so reviving and satisfying to his soul, that he "will never thirst;" he will not want the means of refreshment, be dissatisfied or unhappy; that is, provided he continue to drink thereof. If ever his thirst, or his dissatisfaction and uneasiness, return, it will be the fault of the man, not of the water. But the water, the spirit of faith, love, hope, and joy, of holiness, and happiness, "shall be in him," an inward living principle, "a well;" *a fountain* "of water:" for a well is soon exhausted; "springing," (αλλομενη,) *bubbling up*, and flowing on "into everlasting life;" which is a confluence, or an ocean of streams, arising from this fountain. ———

II. Where this living water is to be had, by whom, and on what terms.

It is to be had in Christ.—Not only in the Deity, who is infinitely great, glorious, holy, and just, and, as such, far distant from us; but in "God, manifest in the flesh;" who is our friend, kinsman, and brother. It is procured for us by his death. John xvi. 7. It is received on our behalf, in consequence of his resurrection and ascension. Psa. lxviii. 18; Acts ii. 33. Hence he waits to bestow the cleansing, refreshing, life-giving water, on those who apply to him: John vii. 37; Rev. xxi. 6; and from this consideration, we have great encouragement to ask Christ for it. ———

This living water may be had by all that are poor, and need it; Isa. xli. 17; by all who thirst for it; John vii. 37; Rev. xxi. 6; xxii. 17; by all who come to Christ, "If *any man* thirst," said he, "let him come unto me;" and by all who ask, "Thou wouldest have *asked* of me." ———

Though it was purchased dear by Christ; he gave a great price that he might have a right to impart it to sinners, and that he might render them capable of receiving it, yet we may have it as a free gift, "without money, and without price." ———

III. The reason why men are indifferent about it, and either apply not to Christ for it, or apply without success.

They *know it not;* John xiv. 17; neither the nature of the blessing, nor the great value of it, nor the necessity of obtaining it.

They know not Christ in the dignity of his person,—in his great condescension and love,—in the sufferings he endured that we might have this water,—and as the fountain of it. ———

They do not apply at all; do not confess their need of, nor ask the communication of, spiritual influences. ——

Or, if they ask, they do not ask aright, sincerely, earnestly, importunately, perseveringly, believingly, consistently. ——

APPLY the subject; showing, that ignorance, arising from an aversion to saving knowledge, and the love of sin, is no excuse; Isa. v. 12, 13; Luke xix. 44;—the state and danger of those who remain destitute of the sacred influence of the Spirit;—the duty and advantage of immediate and fervent supplication for it. Prov. i. 22–28, 32.

THE WORK OF THE SPIRIT IN STRENGTHENING MEN FOR SUFFERING OR DUTY.

Rom. viii. 26.—Likewise the Spirit also helpeth our infirmities: for we know not what we should pray for as we ought: but the Spirit itself maketh intercession for us with groanings which cannot be uttered. (S. S.)

AN hope of eternal happiness is as an anchor to the troubled soul—

It enables a person to bear up under the heaviest afflictions—

But the mind of a believer would soon faint, if it were not strengthened from above—

God therefore communicates his Spirit to his people under their trials—

By his Spirit he enables them to go forward in the way of duty—

St. Paul has been speaking of sufferings as the Christian's portion here, ver. 17, 18.

He has mentioned "hope" as a principal support to the soul under them, ver. 24.

He now specifies the Holy Spirit's agency as another mean of confirming and establishing the soul—

This agency of the Spirit we may consider

I. IN SEASONS OF SUFFERING.

Men are, in themselves, too weak to sustain many or severe trials.

There is much impatience in the heart of every man—

It too often discovers itself even in those who are, on the whole, pious—

Sometimes it is called forth by small and trifling occasions—

How passionately did Jonah resent the loss of his gourd! Jonah iv. 8, 9.

How bitterly would the disciples have revenged an act of unkindness! Luke ix. 54.

There is no trial so small but it would overcome us, if we were left to ourselves—

And they who have endured heavy trials, often faint under small ones—

But God sends his Spirit to help the infirmities of his people.

We cannot exactly discriminate between the Spirit's agency and theirs—

Indeed the Spirit acts in and by their endeavors—

He leads them to see the source and tendency of their trials—

He strengthens the natural vigor of their minds—

He suggests to them many consolatory thoughts—

Thus he fulfils to them his gracious declarations, Ps. cxlvii. 3.

These operations of the Spirit are yet more manifest

II. In seasons of prayer.

God's people "know not even what to pray for."

A great variety of passions may agitate their minds—

When this is the case, their petitions may be unbecoming and sinful—

Even a sense of guilt will often stop the mouth before God; compare Ps. xxxii. 3, and 5.

Sometimes also trouble itself will utterly overwhelm the soul, and incapacitate it for prayer, Ps. lxxvii. 4.

Our Lord himself seems to have experienced such a purturbation of mind, John xii. 27.

Nor are there any praying persons who have not often found themselves straitened in the exercise of prayer—

It yet oftener happens that they know not how to pray "as they ought."

We may easily utter good and suitable words before God—

But it is by no means easy to pray with fervent importunity—

An insurmountable languor or obduracy will sometimes come upon the soul—

Nor though we were ever so fervent can we always exercise faith—

Many have felt the same workings of mind with David, Ps. lxxvii. 7—10.

At such seasons they cannot pray as they ought—

But the Holy Spirit will "make intercession for them."

Christ is properly our advocate and intercessor, 1 John ii. 1.

But the Spirit also may be said to "intercede for us"—

The Spirit intercedes *in* us at the *throne of grace*, while Christ intercedes *for* us at the *throne of glory*—

He sometimes enables us to pour out our hearts with fluency—

This he does by discovering to us our wants, quickening our affections, and testifying to us God's willingness to answer prayer—

He does not, however, always operate in this way—

He will make intercession "with unutterable groans."

The joy of christians is represented as being sometimes inexpressible, 1 Pet. i. 8.

But frequently a sense of sin overwhelms them—

Then sighs and groans are the natural language of their hearts—

Nor are such inarticulate prayers unacceptable to God—

We have a remarkable instance of their success in the history of our Lord, John xi. 33, 38, 41.

Perhaps no prayers are more pleasing to God than these, Ps. li. 17.

Infer,

1. How many are there who live all their days without prayer!

Those in whom the Spirit intercedes are often made to feel their inability to pray aright—

Under a sense of their infirmities they are constrained to cry to God for the help of his Spirit—

But many pass all their days without any painful sense of their weakness—

They satisfy themselves with a formal performance of their duties—

Such persons never pray in an acceptable manner, John iv. 23.

Real prayer implies fervor and importunity, Isa. lxiv. 7.

And it is in vain to think that we have the spirit of grace, if we have not also the spirit of supplication, Zech. xii. 10.

May we therefore never be of those who fulfil that prophecy! Matt. xv. 7, 8.

2. What comfort may this passage afford to praying people!

Many are discouraged by the difficulties which they experience in the duty of prayer—

If they feel not an enlargement of heart, they doubt whether their prayer will be accepted—

But God will notice the groaning of his people, Ps. xxxviii. 9.

Such inward desires may often be more pleasing to him than the most fluent petitions—

They are, in fact, the voice of God's Spirit within us—

Let not any then be dejected on account of occasional deadness—

Let every one rather follow the advice of the prophet, Hab. ii. 3.

God, in due time, will assuredly fulfil his promise, Ps. lxxxi. 10.

THE HOLY GHOST IS THE AUTHOR OF ALL SOLID HOPE.

Rom. xv. 13.—Now the God of hope fill you with all joy and peace in believing, that ye may abound in hope, through the power of the Holy Ghost. (S. S.)

Christians, even in the purest ages of the church, have been too ready to indulge a spirit of bigotry and contention—

The Jewish and Gentile converts in every place were much addicted to it—

St. Paul, studious to counteract it in those at Rome, shews that Christ, though a minister of the circumcision, intended to incorporate the Gentiles into his church—

And prays for both parties, that, as the means of restoring union among themselves, they might be endued with more grace—

His words shew us,

I. The privileges of true christians.

The world forms a very false estimate of the christian's portion—

And christians themselves too often live below their privileges—

It is their privilege to be filled,

1. With lively joy.

No one in the world has so much cause for joy as they ———

Nor is their joy like that of sinners, which soon expires in spleen and melancholy—Eccl. vii. 6, and Prov. xiv. 13.

They may "rejoice evermore," and that too with "joy unspeakable"—

2. With abiding peace.

It would be thought by many that "peace" should have preceded "joy"—

But the experience of God's people accords exactly with the scriptures—Compare Isa. lv. 12, with the text.

Being freed from the torment of a guilty conscience, they have peace with God—Rom. v. 1.

Christ has both purchased for them, and bequeathed to them, his peace, which passeth all understanding—John xiv. 27, and Phil. iv. 7.

Their "peace may well be as a river, since their righteousness is as the waves of the sea"—Isa. xlviii. 18.

3. With assured hope.

This is the fruit. rather than the root, of peace and joy—

They have the promise and oath of God on their side—Heb. vi. 17, 18

And have already received in their souls an earnest of their inheritance—Eph. i. 14.

Well therefore may they enjoy a confident expectation of the promised land—

All indeed are not sufficiently studious to "walk thus in the light"—

But, what the apostle prayed for on the behalf of all, all may possess—

The apostle further directs us,

II. How WE MAY ATTAIN THE ENJOYMENT OF THEM.

In this short and comprehensive prayer we are taught to seek them.

1. From God as the fountain.

God in Christ is the "God of hope," and the source of all good—James i. 17.

In vain will be the use of other means, if we apply not to him in prayer—

But nothing is too great for God to give to the believing suppliant—

2. By faith as the means.

We can receive nothing but by the exercise of faith—James i. 6, 7.

But "in believing we shall be *filled* with joy and peace"—

It is faith that enables us to realize invisible things—

And, by experiencing the joy of faith, our hope will be confirmed—Rom. v. 5.

3. Through the Holy Ghost as the agent.

There is no power less than his that will produce these things—

The whole work of grace is, not by might or by power, but by God's Spirit—Zech. iv. 6.

He will afford us clear discoveries of the heavenly glory—

He will witness to us our adoption, and seal us with God's image—1 Cor. i. 22.

And thus while he forms us to a meetness for heaven, he gives us also a foretaste of it in our hearts—

INFER,

1. How much happier is the christian than others even in this world!

2. How happy will he be when he shall receive these communications from the Deity, not through the narrow and obstructed channel of faith, but immediately at the fountain head!

3. How deservedly will they be left destitute of this happiness hereafter, who now give the pleasures of sin their decided preference!

THE HOLY SPIRIT'S APPLICATON OF THE PROMISES OF SCRIPTURE.

Ephesians i. 13, 14.—In whom also after that ye believed, ye were sealed with that Holy Spirit of promise which is the earnest of our inheritance until the redemption of the purchased possession unto the praise of his glory. (P.)

It would be quite foreign to our present purpose to enter into a particular consideration of all the several expressions which this passage of scripture contains. It may be proper, however, to observe, that the *sealing* of the spirit of which the apostle here speaks, is evidently a distinct act from *faith:* and the sealing of the Holy Spirit appears to be a metaphorical expression to denote that the same divine agent who had implanted in their souls a principle of faith, and brought this principle into exercise, had likewise produced in their minds an assurance of their interest in the promises of the gospel, and in the blessings of salvation by a Redeemer.

PRELIMINARY OBSERVATIONS.

1st *Obs.*—That there is such a being as the *Holy Spirit* how else are we to understand the following passages, and others of a similar import, which are contained in the word of God: Gen. vi. 3; Prov. i. 23: Luke xi. 13; John vii. 37—40; Rom. viii. 16, 26; Eph. iv. 30.

2nd *Obs.*—That the Holy Spirit is a *divine* person, possessed of the names, titles, and attributes of Deity, the great author of divine and glorious works, and an object of divine adoration.

3rd *Obs.*—That this divine Spirit is the subject of many revealed and precious *promises*. And this may be one reason why he is called in the text the "Holy Spirit of promise."

4th *Obs.*—That a true and saving *faith* in Christ is the special gift of the divine Spirit a principle produced by his gracious operations on the heart, and ordinarily effected by means of a preached gospel. It was by this means the Ephesians were brought to trust or believe in Christ. Read the text.

5th *Obs.*—It is the peculiar office of the Holy Spirit, to carry on and complete the work of sanctification in those who believe, and to comfort their minds by a sweet und spiritual *application* of the promises of grace in Christ Jesus to their souls. Such was the comfort imparted to the Ephesians, who, after they believed, were sealed with the Holy Spirit of promise.

6th *Obs.*—That it is a matter of unspeakable importance to *know* and believe, on substantial evidence, that we are the subjects of the Spirit's sanctifying and comforting influences; or, in other words, that we are interested in the promises of scripture, by an application of them to our souls, through the agency of the Holy Spirit. By this remark we are led to inquire

How we may know when a promise of scripture is applied to the mind by the Holy Spirit?

This is an inquiry which is highly interesting, and of the greatest consequence; an inquiry on which many, it is to be feared, have too hastily decided. They have cried, "Peace, peace to themselves," when in reality they have had no peace. The *presumption* of some, and the *enthusiasm* of others, have led them to draw conclusions for which they have had no substantial evidences, to the dishonor of God, and to the injury of their own souls. That we may guard against those dangerous rocks on which thousands, alas! nave split, we shall do well to remember, that,

No attainments in religious *knowledge*, however extensive, which are merely speculative and natural, will warrant us to conclude, that any particular promise belongs to us.

No distinctions of *birth* or *station:* no moral virtues or moral qualifications, however amiable and praiseworthy in themselves, can authorize us to believe that this or the other promise of the gospel is ours.

No external *profession* of religion, however flaming that profession may be, is of itself sufficient to entitle us to what may be termed a personal and possessive interest in the promises of scripture.

No inward *suggestions* of the promises of scripture to the mind, however powerful; no pretended visions, or dreams, or revelations from heaven, however extraordinary, can lead us with safety to conclude on a spiritual application of the promises of scripture to our hearts. Even the devil may bring texts of scripture to the mind, and misapply them to deceive persons; and in dreams, and visions, and revelations, there may be found some cheat or imposture of the devil; but the Spirit's witness to the heart, suitable to the revelations in scripture, cannot deceive us. In order, therefore, to know that a promise of scripture is applied to the heart by the Holy Spirit, it is neeessary to ascer tain,

1st. That our *characters* answer to the characters of those who have a right to claim an interest in the promises, viz. that we are believers in Christ —that we are real christians—that we are the disciples of Christ indeed. They only who are brought to believe or trust in Christ, are sealed with the "Holy Spirit of promise."

2nd. To know that a promise of scripture is applied to the mind by the Holy Spirit, we must be led to *see our need of his assistance*, and to implore his gracious influences, to apply to our hearts those promises which may be suited to our particular circumstances. This, it appears, was the conduct of David when he had provoked the Holy Spirit to withdraw for a season his comforting influcnces. He humbly draws near to God in the exercise of prayer, and expresses his reliance on the Spirit of grace to visit him again with that holy joy and peace in believing which he had formerly experienced; [see Psalm li. 9—13.] And the apostle Paul, in praying for the Ephesians, declares his own sentiments, and at the same time directs them in what manner they should act, as the means of obtaining and enjoying this exalted privilege (Eph. i. 15, ad finem.)

3rd. The Holy Spirit, in applying the promise of scripture to the heart, enables us to discover a similarity between our *state* and the state of those for whom the promises are expressly designed. For example, the promises of divine forgiveness are made to the subjects of true evangelical repentance, and to excite us to repentance is the work of the Spirit; but if the Spirit has never led us to sorrow for sin after a godly sort, we can have no right to the promises of pardoning mercy. Those promises of scripture, likewise, which speak of the special favor, protection, and love of God, belong *exclusively* to those who are enabled to fear him, to make him their trust, and to set their hope in him and love him, (Psalm xxxi. 19; xxvii. 14; xviii. 30; xxxvii. 40; xxxii 10; cxii. 7.) But if God be not the object of our fear and confidence, and love, these promises do not belong to us.

4th. In the application of a promise of scripture to the heart, the Holy Spirit impresses the mind with a *conviction that the promise is true*, and gives the soul a persuasion on scriptural grounds, that God is both able and willing to perform it. "I know," says the believer, in glancing at a promise of the divine word, "that this is the promise of God, my father and friend, with whom there is no variableness nor shadow of turning. To his people in general this promise belongs; and having a good hope, through grace, to believe that I am one of his people, this gracious promise belongs to me."

5. We may know that a promise of scripture is applied to the mind by the Holy Spirit, when, upon a strict and impartial examination, we are directed to conclude, that we are possessed of those several *qualifications and graces of the christian life* which are inseparably connected with a right application of the promises to the heart. What these graces are the apostle particularly enumerates, Gal. v. 22, 23. These graces are not the *causes*, but the necessary *evidences* of an interest in the promises.

6th There is ground to believe that we are interested in the promises, when our *general conduct*, both personally and relatively, answers to the rules and obligations prescribed in the word of God. "Without *holiness*," it is written, "no man shall see the Lord;" and if no man without holiness shall be permitted to see the Lord in heaven, no man without holiness can really enjoy the promises of God on earth.

Inferences.—Let us rejoice in the promises of revelation, and bless God for them. They all proceed from him, are made sacred by an oath, and ratified by the death of Christ.

It becomes us also to examine, with the strictest and closest attention, what is the foundation of our title to the promises? Do we judge of our interest in them by our *frames* and *feelings*, or by the evidences of a work of grace in our souls? O let us beware of a false application of the promises! To misapply them is exceedingly dangerous.

To you who have reason to hope that the promises are yours, but whose minds respecting this matter are yet in a state of doubt and uncertainty, it may be said, because you are thus suffered to walk in darkness, and have no light, it is no proof that you are uninterested in the promises. Many good men are in a similar state. The servants of God do not all attain to an equal degree of assurance; but it is what you should seek after, and never be satisfied without it.

Finally—Let those who have felt and enjoyed the application of the promises to their souls, remember their obligations to sovereign Mercy; and "having these promises, dearly beloved, cleanse yourselves from all filthiness of the flesh and spirit, perfecting holiness in the fear of God."

THE WITNESS OF THE SPIRIT.

Rom. viii. 16.—The Spirit itself beareth witness with our spirit, that we are the children of God. (S. S.)

There is a tribunal before which we must all appear at the last day—

But we need not wait till that time to ascertain our true character—

Every man has a tribunal erected in his own bosom—

The conscience, according to the light it has received, accuses or excuses, those who will listen to its voice—

This is common to heathens as well as christians—Rom. ii. 15.

But God's people are favored with the additional testimony of the Holy Spirit—

Of this the apostle speaks in the passage before us—

We shall endeavor to shew,

I. What is the witness here spoken of.

Witnesses imply a doubt of the thing which is to be confirmed—

The thing to be ascertained here is, "That we are the children of God"—

Respecting this, many are in suspense all their days—

But God has provided means for the removal of these doubts—

He has been pleased to give us the witness of his Spirit.

1. Through the medium of rational deduction.

We may judge of our state by comparing it with the declarations of scripture—

God has given many marks and characters of his own people—e. g. 1 John iii. 10.

We may examine by these how far our practice corresponds with our duty—

And know from the testimony of an enlightened conscience our real state

This is a scriptural way of judging—

St. Paul used it;* and exhorts us to use it—2 Cor. xiii. 5.

St. Peter represents the attainment of this as a principal part of our baptismal engagement—1 Peter iii. 21.

St. John also assures us, that this is the way in which God would have us to know our state—†

2. In a way of immediate impression.

The Spirit, as a "Spirit of adoption," testifies to the believer's soul, that he belongs to God—

Not that this testimony is given without *any* reference to the scripture—

Yet it is imparted in a more instantaneous manner, and in a far higher degree, at some times than at others—

God by his Spirit sometimes "sheds abroads his love in the heart" in such a measure, and shines so clearly on the work he has already wrought there, as to convey immediately a full persuasion and assurance of an interest in his favor—

As by "the sealing of the Spirit" he stamps his own image on his children for the conviction of others, so by "the witness of the Spirit" he testifies of their adoption for the more immediate comfort of their own souls—

These manifestations are vouchsafed, for the most part, to prepare the soul for trials, to support it under them, or to comfort it after them—

But they cannot be explained for the satisfaction of others—

Yet may they be sufficiently proved from scripture to be the privilege and portion of true believers—‡

To guard the doctrine against every species of delusion, we shall shew,

II. HOW TO DISTINGUISH IT FROM ALL FALSE AND ENTHUSIASTIC PRETENTIONS.

Many, it must be confessed, have pretended to this witness on false grounds—‖

And Satan is ready enough to help forward such delusions—

But the witness of the Spirit may be distinguished from all enthusiastic pretentions to it, if we consider attentively—

1. What precedes it.

Conviction of our lost estate—faith in the Redeemer—and devotedness to God as our rightful Sovereign, must precede it—

If we have not these things, we cannot be God's children; and we may be sure the Spirit will never attest a falsehood—

2. What accompanies it.

Humility of mind—a jealous fear of ourselves—and a love to the weakest of God's people, attended these divine communications—

*He knew that God required real integrity of heart. Psa. li. 6. He therefore labored to attain it, Acts xxiv. 16. He had the testimony of his conscience that he had attained it, Heb. xiii. 18. And this testimony was a ground of joy before God, 2 Cor. i. 12.

†We cannot convey to any man a just idea of sensations which he has never felt; they must be experienced in order to be understood. The work of the Spirit in regeneration is not fully understood even by those who are the subjects of it, notwithstanding its effects are as visible as those of the wind, John iii. 8. We cannot expect, therefore, that this less visible operations should be more intelligible to those who have never experienced them at all. See Rev. ii. 17.

‡See Rom. viii. 15. 2 Cor. i. 21, 22; and Eph. iv. 30; which clearly shew, that the Holy Spirit does operate on the souls of God's people, and perform towards them the office both of a sanctifier and a comforter.

‖Some have fancied that the Spirit witnessed their adoption because they have had a singular dream, or a portion of scripture has been suddenly and strongly impressed upon their minds, or they have enjoyed peculiar comfort in their souls.

Whereas prid and conceit, with a presumptuous confidence, and a contempt of others, are ever found in deluded enthusiasts—

3. What follows it.

Manifestations of God to the soul always produce zeal in his service—victory over sin—and a longing for the enjoyment of him in heaven—

But supineness, subjection to evil tempers, and a forgetfulness of the eternal world, generally characterize the self-deceiving professor—

Let every one therefore examine his pretentions by these marks ——

ADDRESS,

1. Those who know nothing of this testimony of the Spirit.

You probably do not understand the regenerating influences of the Spirit; and yet you see them manifested in the lives of many around you—

Do not then condemn the witness of the Spirit merely because you cannot comprehend it—

Rather pray to God that you yourselves may be his children—

In this way you may hope that the Spirit will testify of your adoption—

2. Those who profess to have received it.

A delusion in this is above all things to be guarded aga nst—

If your dispositions be habitually bad, your pretensions are all a delusion—

Where the witness of the Spirit is, there will the fruits also of the Spirit be—

3. Those who long to receive it.

To have the full witness of the Spirit is desirable, but not necessary—

It is a great mercy if we enjoy his lower attestations in a good conscience—

Let us labor to serve God, and leave to him the time, manner, and degree, in which he shall reveal himself to us—

4. Those who now enjoy this witness.

The manifestations of God to the soul are a very heaven upon earth—

Let them therefore be duly esteemed and diligently improved—

But beware lest you "grieve the Spirit by whom you are sealed"—

Be looking forward with increasing earnestness to your inheritance—

And while you enjoy the inward witness that you are the children of God, let the world have an outward evidence of it in your lives.

THE SEALING OF THE SPIRIT.

Eph. i. 13, 14.—In whom also after that ye believed, ye were sealed with the Holy Spirit of promise, which is the earnest of our inheritance, until the redemption of the purchased possession, unto the praise of his glory. (S. S.)

THE blessings which we receive through Christ are innumerable—

Many are mentioned in the preceding part of this chapter—

One of the last and greatest blessings which we receive in this life, is the sealing of the Holy Spirit—

This was vouchsafed to many of the saints at Ephesus—

We shall shew,

1. What the sealing of the Spirit is.

The metaphor of sealing conveys no inadequate idea of the Spirit's operations.

A seal stamps its own image on the wax that is impressed by it; and marks the thing sealed to be the property of him that sealed it—

And the Holy Spirit forms all the lineaments of the divine image on the soul that is sealed by him; and shews that it belongs to God—

But the text itself affords us the best explanation of this term.

The future inheritance of the saints consists in a perfect conformity to God's image, and a perfect enjoyment of his love—

The sealing of the Spirit is an "earnest of that inheritance," or, in other words, *a part* of that inheritance already vouchsafed to the soul, and *a pledge* that the remainder shall in due time be given to it—

This gift of the Spirit is to be continued to the church till the final consummation of all things—*

The experience of individuals may vary with respect to it; but there shall always be some in the church who possess and enjoy it—

We are also informed respecting,

II. The manner in which it is effected.

The *agent* is none other than the Holy Ghost.

It is not in man's power to sanctify his own soul—

Nor can any one assure himself that he is the Lord's—

To impart these blessings is the prerogative of God alone—2 Cor. i. 21, 22.

The *subjects* of this work are true believers.

An unbeliever cannot possibly be sealed; because the Holy Spirit would never mark those as God's property, who do not really belong to him—

Nor are persons usually sealed on their first believing in Christ—

This higher state of sanctification and assurance is reserved for those, who, "after having believed," have maintained a close walk with God—

They must first be "in Christ," and then for Christ's sake this benefit shall be vouchsafed unto them—

The *means* by which it is effected, are the promises.

We do not presume to limit the Spirit's operations—

But his usual method of sealing is by applying the "promises" to the soul—1 Cor. ii. 4; 1 Thes. i. 5.

Of themselves, the promises can accomplish nothing; but, through his divine power, they have a comforting and transforming efficacy—2 Pet. i. 4.

The apostle further specifies,

III. Its proper tendency and operation.

The sealing of the Spirit will never elate a man with pride.

It may seem indeed that such distinguishing mercies would puff us up—

But their invariable effect is to humble those who receive them—

All the saints of old abased themselves in proportion as they were favored of God—Job xlii. 5, 6, and Isa. 6, 5.

Nor can there be any stronger evidence that a work is not of God, than its producing a contrary effect upon us—

It is intended solely to honor and glorify God.

Every work of grace should lead the mind to God as the author of it—

And the more exalted the mercy, the more powerful should this effect be—

Now this, above all, administers to us the greatest cause of thankfulness—

And will certainly incline us to love and serve him from whom it has been derived—

*The church is Christ's "purchased possession," Acts xx. 28. And its complete "redemption" from all the penal effects of sin will be at the day of judgment, Rom. viii. 23.

ADDRESS.

1. To those who are ignorant of this sublime subject.

To many, alas! the sealing of the Spirit is mere foolishness—

But those who account it so, "speak evil of things that they understand not"—

Let us seek to experience it ourselves, instead of censuring those who do—

2. To those who desire to be sealed.

God is willing to bestow this blessing on all who seek it—

If we possess it not, we should enquire what there is in us which has occasioned God to withhold it from us—

And live more on the promises, that by them it may be imparted to our souls—

3. To those who are sealed.

What a mercy is it, that you, who might long since have been sealed for condemnation, have, according to the good pleasure of God, been sealed for heaven!

Be thankful to God for this unspeakable gift—

Be careful too that you grieve not him by whom you have been sealed—Eph. iv. 30.

But improve the promises yet further for your progressive advancement in true holiness—2 Cor. vii. 1.

CHAPTER VI.

GOOD ANGELS.

THE NATURE AND MINISTRY OF ANGELS.

Psalm xxxiv. 7.—The angel of the Lord encampeth round about them that fear him, and delivereth them. (H.)

THIS psalm is supposed to have been penned by David when he changed his behavior before Achish, the king of Gath, called in the title of this psalm, Abimelech, this being a common name for all the kings of the Philistines; as Pharaoh was common to the kings of Egypt; and as Cæsar was common to the Roman emperors. The history of David's situation is recorded. 1 Sam. xxi. 10. The means of his deliverance is particularly noticed, in the text and context. He prayed to his God. Verse 4–6. His friends also prayed for him. Verse 5. And the angels of God encamped round about him. The angel, or angels of the Lord encampeth round about them that fear him, &c. Such is the love of God to his children, that he appoints many angels, on particular occasions, no less than a host, enough to form an encampment, to save his servants. I shall,

I. OFFER A FEW REMARKS RELATIVE TO THOSE BEINGS WHO TEND THE RIGHTEOUS, and,

1. They are real beings, not imaginary beings, or apparitions only. This was the error of the Sadducees. Acts xxiii. 8. But the scripture declares them to have a personal subsistence. Hence they are said to be sent forth. Heb. i. 14. They are spirits that speak. Acts x. 19. They are living

creatures; Ezek. i. 5; by which are meant angels, as they are called cherubim. Ezek. x. 16. And they are called authorities and powers. 1 Peter iii. 22. And as such possessing understanding and will; and they do such things as none but reasonable agents can do. They admire God's wisdom. Eph. iii. 10. They converse with each other; and excite each other to glorify God. Isa. vi. 3.

2. They are secondary beings. Some heathen philosophers supposed the angels to be co-eternal with God; but this cannot be. There cannot be but one first, one eternal Being. This is God's prerogative. Heb. i. 12. God created them. Col. i. 15. In one of the six days, during which all things were created. Exod. xx. 11. For before the seventh day, the heavens and all the hosts thereof, were created. Gen. ii. 1, 2. The stars are the hosts of that heaven which we behold; but the angels are the hosts of the third heaven, which to us on earth is invisible; they are so called. Neh. ix. 6. They were created before the earth; therefore before the third day of the week, for on that day the earth was created, when the sons of God shouted for joy. Job xxxviii. 7. In the Septuagint, it is all the angels. It is probable they were created, with the light, on the first day of the week, hence called morning stars, not only stars, in respect to their brightness and glory but morning stars, as being formed in the morning, the very beginning of creation.

3. They are most excellent and glorious creatures. Man is the most excellent creature upon earth; but inferior to angels even in his best estate. Ps. viii. 5. Solomon calls them higher than the greatest tyrants that oppress the earth. Eccl. v. 8. Of all creatures, they most resemble God. They resemble God in being spiritual beings, not clothed with flesh and blood as we are. They are immortal beings, and what they now are, they shall ever be. They are wise and knowing, as it respects nature and the affairs of the world. Dan. x. 13. And their natural knowledge is increased by the experience of near six thousand years. They also possess a great deal of revealed knowledge concerning the scriptures. Dan. x. 21. Also concerning individuals before they are born. Dan. xi. 6. Hence they are said to be full of eyes. Rev. iv. 6. Eyes behind, knowing what is past, and eyes before, knowing what is to come. They are holy beings, called holy ones. Dan. iv. 17. Holy angels. Matt. xxv. 31. Angels of light. 2 Cor. xi. 14. All these things show that the angels, of all other creatures, most resemble God.

4. They are very numerous. They are called a great company. Psa. lxviii. 11. There are thousands of them, ver. 17. The chariots of God are twenty thousand, even thousands of angels; nay, there are millions of them. Dan. vii. 5–10; Rev. v. 11. Nay, they are innumerable. Heb. xii. 22. Bildad asks, is there any number of his armies? Job xxv. 3. Christ tells Peter that he could call to his assistance twelve legions (a legion is 6,666) of angels, which was equal to the amount of the whole Roman army. God can spare multitudes of angels to the assistance of his servants.

5. They are very powerful. They excel in strength. Ps. ciii. 20. They are called mighty angels. 2 Thes. i. 7. One angel is able to destroy all the men in the world. Their great power is manifest by what they have done. Iron gates cannot stand before them. Acts xii. 10. An angel can make the earth shake; Matt. xxviii. 2; and occasion a most terrible destruction in a short time, as in the case of the first-born in Egypt: the army of Senacherib: Sodom and Gomorrah, &c.

6 They are orderly. Hence called an host, or an army. It is certain that some, in their employment and office, are superior to others. There are some who are captains and leaders of others, who follow them. The text says, the angel of the Lord encampeth, &c. One angel cannot make a camp, but many can, under the conduct of one, as doubtless was the case here. One particular angel announced the birth of Christ. Luke ii. 9. And a multitude under his conduct, praised God upon the occasion, ver. 13. The scriptures speak not only of angels, but also of archangels: these are styled chief princes. Dan. x. 13. We have the names of one or two. One is named Michael; Dan. xii. 1; Jude 9; 1 Thes. iv. 16; who seems to be the chief of all the angels and arch-angels of God, and who by a way of eminence is called the archangel, and the great prince. Dan. xii. 1. They are supposed to be seven in number, signified by the seven lamps in the temple, before the mercy seat. Zech. iv. 10. Hence John speaks of the seven spirits of God, &c. Rev. v. 6. Who are called seven angels. Rev. viii. 2. These seem to be the general inspectors of the whole world, and thence are said to be sent forth into all the earth.

7. They are all at God's disposal. Hence called the angels of the Lord, angels of God, and spirits of God: they are sometimes called the spirits of the Lord. 1 Kings xviii. 12; Acts viii. 39. He is their great head and leader, and is hence called, the Lord of Hosts. They stand in his presence. Luke i. 19. And do his pleasure. Ps. ciii. 20.

II. Consider who are the objects of their attention and care.

1. The world in general. Many great men have been wonderfully protected and delivered by the angels of God, out of respect to the church and people. This was the case with Darius, the Persian emperor; Dan. xi. 1; also Alexander the Great; and neither of them feared God; but they were God's instruments to accomplish his designs in the world, and as such, protected and delivered by angels.

Great mercies and judgments are dispersed by them. They are as a lamp to the righteous, to light and direct them; and as coals of fire to the wicked, to punish and consume them. David expected they would punish his enemies. Psa. xxxv. 5, 6. Sodom was destroyed by them. Gen. xix. 13. Seventy thousand Israelites fell by the plague, which was brought upon them by an angel. 2 Sam. xxiv. 16. When Jerusalem was to be destroyed, the angels forsook it, and a voice was heard saying, let us go hence. And Tacitus reports that in Jerusalem there was a voice heard, greater than human, saying the gods are departed from this place. The trumpets in the Revelation, signifying judgments on the Roman empire, were sounded by angels; and the vials, denoting judgments on the papal power, are poured out by angels, because these things are effected by their ministry.

In times of war wonderful victories are obtained by their invisible agency. They occasioned the sound in the mulberry trees, through which David obtained the victory. 2 Sam. v. 24. See also, 2 Kings vii. 6. The angels fought against the king of Persia. Dan. xi. 20. No wonder that the inconsiderable number of Grecians routed and destroyed the Persian army, which consisted of several millions, when the angels fought against them.

The great revolutions which happen in the world are effected by their ministry; when the living creatures went, then the wheels went with them. The world moved as the angels of God moved. They deposed Nebuchadnezzar, and gave his crown to another. Dan. iv. 17. When Belshazzer was slain, Babylon taken, &c., it was by their agency. An angel wrote the hand-writing on the wall, intimating to the king and his nobles the fate which awaited them

When Darius got the empire, an angel assisted him to keep it. Dan. xi. 1. The great revolution which took place in the world at the conversion of Constantine the Great, was brought about by angels. Rev. xii. 7. Thus we see, that this visible world is by God's appointment governed by the invisible world.

2. The church of God. This might be signified by the cherubim on the cu tains belonging to the tabernacle. Exod. xxvi. 1. Also by the cherubim on the walls of the temple. They promote the salvation of the church. Heb. i. 14. An angel directed Peter to Cornelius and his family. Acts x 30. Paul and others were directed by an angel to preach in Macedonia. Acts xvi. 9. When Jerusalem was besieged by the Assyrians, it is said the angel of the Lord went out, and smote the camp of the Assyrians. 1 Kings xix. 35. From which it appears, that an angel did reside in, and preside over that city, where the temple was, who, upon this occasion went out of it. So then, as one observes, angels are the guard of the queen of heaven, the Lamb's wife.

3. Individuals who fear God; such are the objects of their particular and special care. They preserve them from many evils, which otherwise would befal them. Ps. xci. 11, 12. They journey with them and protect them. Gen. xxviii. 12; xxxii. 1, 2. Paul experienced this. Acts xxvii. 23, 24. An angel appeared for Israel against Balaam. Numb. xxii. 32. And for Elisha against the king of Syria. 2 Kings vi. 17.

They convey positive blessings, by assisting God's servants in their undertakings; as in the case of Darius already mentioned, although he did not fear God; and in the case of Abraham's servant for the bood of his family. Gen. xxiv. 40. Also, by instructing them, as in the case of Dan. ix. 22; and Zech. i. 9. And the shepherds; Luke ii. 10. And Mary; John xx. 12. And Elijah; 2 Kings i. 15. And Hagar; Gen. xvi. 9. An angel smote Zechariah for his unbelief. Luke i. 20. And doubtless, they visit God's children with diseases, to correct them for some sin they have been guilty of.

They have a great influence upon the minds of men. Evil angels can suggest evil thoughts into the mind; see the case of Judas. John xiii. 2. Also Ahab. 1 Kings xxii. 22. So also good angels influence the minds of good men: and although all good thoughts are originally from God, yet he makes use of the ministry of angels for this purpose.

They stood by good men in their afflictions, to strengthen and comfort them. It was so with our Lord, in his temptation; Matt. iv. 11; and in his agony; Luke xxii. 43; also, Isaiah vi. 7; and with many of the martyrs, in the days of popery; the angels standing by them, and quenching the violence of the fire.

Angels appear in due time to deliver them. See the case of Lot and his family. Gen. xix. 16. Also, Daniel vi. 22. And Peter; Acts xii. 11. And the apostles. Acts v. 19.

They do not forsake good men at death, but carry them to heaven: it was so with Elijah. 2 Kings ii. 11. And Lazarus. Luke xvi. 22. The souls of good men pass through the devil's territory, the air, but they are safe under the convoy of angels.

They will collect all the righteous together at the great day, in order to a happy meeting with their Lord. Matt. xxiv. 31; xiii. 41.

They will also associate, and join with the redeemed of the Lord, in celebrating the praises of God and the Lamb for ever and ever. Rev. vii. 9—12.

III. What is necessary on our part that we may enjoy THE BENEFIT OF THEIR PROTECTION.

1. We must endeavor after an interest in Christ; for all the angels are at his command. It is through his mediation that we obtain the benefit of their ministry. John i. 51. If we are Christ's, all things are ours, even the angels of God.

2. We must be careful to walk in the fear of the Lord; for his angels encamp about such, says our text; this was Cornelius' character; and while he was praying, an angel came to him. Acts x. 2, 3. Also of Daniel, who was favored in the same way. Dan. ix. 20, 21. See how those who feared God were preserved. Ezek. ix. 4—6.

3. Let us imitate the angels in doing all the good we can, in every station or relation; both to the world and the church. We should strive to do the will of God on earth, as the angels do in heaven.

4. Let us remember that the eyes of angels are upon us; they witness all our actions. Eccl. v. 6. They are present at our assemblies. 1 Cor. xi. 10. Let us remember these things and act accordingly, and we shall soon associate with them in the walks of the paradise of God. Zech. iii. 7.

MINISTERING SPIRITS.

Heb. i. 14.—Are they not all ministering spirits, sent forth to minister for them who shall be heirs of salvation? (Sk.)

MAN is naturally an inquisitive creature; and under the influence of an intense thirst for the acquisition of knowledge, he is led to ask questions, read books, pursue studies, and use all the means that can augment his stock of information. On all the topics connected with our interests as citizens of the world, we gain ample information by perusing the works of men; but the Bible is the chief medium, through which information on religious subjects is freely and circumstantially communicated. Some of those subjects are frequently brought forward, largely discussed, and pointedly insisted on; others are only incidentally mentioned, as they do not form essential parts in the economy of human redemption. The text refers to one of those subjects; and though our salvation might have been secured, even if we had never known it, yet it cannot be uninteresting to men in general; and it is peculiarly calculated to administer comfort to every pious soul. We will therefore consider,

I. THE NATURE OF ANGELS;—they are *spirits*. Many of the ancient philosophers, and not a few of the christian fathers, believed that angels were clothed with some kind of bodies composed of the purest particles of matter, which they called *œtherial*; but the scriptures speak of them as spirits, Psa. civ. 4. As *spirits* they possess natural and moral perfections; of the former, they have 1st, *understandings, clear and comprehensive.* Their knowledge is vastly extended; the wisdom of an angel is proverbial. David was said to be as an angel of the Lord, to discern good and bad; and wise, according the wisdom of an angel, 2 Sam. xiv. 17—20. The angels know much of God, they behold the displays of his glory, they are his ministers to do his pleasure; they are acquainted with his works, they sang together, and shouted for joy when the foundations of the earth were laid, Job. xxxviii. 7. And they know much of what is doing in the world. 2. *As spirits they possess great power*; David declares, "they excel in strength," Psa. ciii. 20. We deem that man the strongest, who can put in motion the largest quantity of matter; what cannot an angel do? It is generally thought, that the immense slaughter of all the first-born of Egypt was accomplished by an angel. The hundred and eighty-five thousand, of the army of Sennacherib, that fell in one night, were slain by an angel, 2 Kings xix. 35. It was an angel that inflicted the pestilence upon Israel, when seventy thousand were cut off. 2 Sam. xxiv. 15. And Herod was smitten by an angel, when eaten up with worms, Acts xii. 23. 3. *As spirits they possess great activity, or swiftness of motion.* They are represented as "being full of wings;" how easily and swiftly do they transport themselves from place to place: even the finer particles of matter are amazingly volatile, how inconceivable is the velocity of light! but how tardy compared to the speed of an angel! 4. *As spirits, they are endowed with liberty.* This is essential to a moral agent; it is said of fallen angels, that they left their first estate; it was a personal act, and a matter of choice; "Freely they stood, who stood; and fell who fell; not free, what proof could they have given of true allegiance?" &c. And as spirits, they possess moral perfections; such as *purity of affections:* they are eminently termed *holy angels:—benevolence of disposition:* how ardent is their zeal for God. Some are termed seraphim, which signifies *burning*. How much they delight in our happiness. How glad to bear the tidings of peace on earth, and good will towards men.

II. The charge of angels. *Them who shall be heirs, &c.* Whether they minister to men promiscuously, I dare not say; the Bible is silent on the subject: and how far it is consistent with reason to suppose an angel ministering to a sot, or a debauchee, I leave you to judge. *The heirs of salvation* are the objects of their charge. Salvation here means that final and complete deliverance, which God will accomplish in behalf of his saints, and that ineffable glory, and inexpressible happiness, with which they will be invested. Salvation is an *inheritance*—glorious in its nature—satisfying in its enjoyment—eternal in its duration. Oh! how unlike earthly inheritances. *An heir* is a person who has a just right to a certain possession—who can make out a legal title to it—but who is in a state of minority, and not of age to possess it. All this applies to the saints; they are born of God, and "if children, then heirs, heirs of God"—this gives them a right to their heavenly inheritance—they have a legal title in the promise—but they are at present in a state of minority.

III. The character of their ministration. In considering the ministration of angels, we must be careful not to attribute to them any work that will interfere with the influence of the Holy Ghost upon the soul of man. Man is a totally depraved creature; and the whole of his salvation, from its commencement to its close, is accomplished by the Divine Spirit, without any intermediate agency. 1. *Angels minister to our instruction, when we are liable to miss our providential way.* How dark and intricate in many instances is the path we have to tread: but how clear and extended the perceptions of angels. The following scriptures sufficiently prove that they direct the *heirs of salvation* in the time of difficulty, Gen. xvi. 9; Judg. xiii. 13, 14; Matt. i. 20,—ii. 13; Acts x. 3. 2. *Angels minister to our deliverance in the times of danger*, 2 Kings vi. 17; Psa. xxxiv. 7,—xci. 11; Dan. vi. 22,—iii. 25; Acts xii. 7, 3. *Angels minister to our comfort in the seasons of distress.* In our Saviour's deepest agony, there appeared unto him an angel strengthening him, Luke xxii. 43. And as the **strength** communicated unquestionably referred to some consolatory thoughts suggested to his mind, may not we also derive *comfort* from such a source? **4.** ***Angels minister to our release from the body, and our admittance into heaven.*** Witness Lazarus, Luke xvi. 22.—See 2 Pet. i. 11.—The ministration of angels is, 1. *Divine in its authority:* they are sent. 2. *Active in its nature:* they are sent *forth.* 3. *Universal in its agency: all* ministering spirits. 4. *Benevolent in its results:* they minister to our salvation. **Infer,** 1st. The wonderful care of God over us in appointing us such ministers; how various their orders, how immense their numbers, Dan. vii. 10 2. What a motive to induce us to hate sin; the *holy* angels are with us, and how hateful must sin be in their sight. 3. From the office of angels, let us learn where true greatness lies, Matt. xx. 26. 4. From the activity and zeal of angels in doing good, let us emulate their example.

CHAPTER VII.

WICKED ANGELS.

OF EVIL ANGELS.

Eph. vi. 12.--We wrestle not against flesh and blood, but against principalities, against powers, against the rulers of the darkness of this world, against spiritual wickedness in high places.

Divine Revelation declares that all angels were originally created holy and happy, yet they did not all continue as they were created, some left their first estate. The text contains the whole scriptural doctrine concerning them. In prosecuting this important subject, I will endeavor to explain, 1. The nature and properties of evil angels; and 2. Their employment.

With regard to the first, we cannot doubt but all the angels of God were originally of the same nature.

Their original properties were, doubtless alike. There is no absurdity in supposing Satan, the chief of the wicked angels, to have been one of the first, if not the first arch-angel. Endowed with an understanding, wisdom and strength, incomprehensible to us.

We do not exactly know either what was the occasion of their apostacy, or what effect it immediately produced upon them. Some have, not improbably supposed pride, mentioned in Ps. ii. 6, 7. When they shook off their allegiance to God, they shook off all goodness, and contracted all these tempers which are most hateful to him and most opposed to his nature. Ever since, they are full of pride, envy, cruelty, and rage against the children of men.

In the prosecution of their infernal design, they are diligent in the highest degree.

One circumstance more we may learn from the scriptures concerning the evil angels; they do not wander at large, but are all united under one common head. It is Satan, that is styled by our blessed Lord, "The prince of this world;" yea, the apostle does not scruple to call him, "The god of this world." He is termed the devil by way of eminence:—Apollyon, or the destroyer;—the old serpent from his beguiling Eve under that form:—and the angel of the bottomless pit. We have reason to believe that, the other evil angels are under his command and do his pleasure.

II. THE EMPLOYMENT OF THE EVIL ANGELS.

They are as far, as God permits, governors of the world. Agreeable to which, is that expression of Satan, Matt. iv. 8, 9, when he showed our Lord all the kingdoms of the world and the glory of them: all these things will I give thee, if thou wilt fall down and worship me. It is a little more particularly expressed in Luke iv. 5, 6.—They are the rulers of the darkness of this age, of the present state of things, during which the whole world lieth in the wicked one. He is the author of all ignorance, error, folly and wickedness.

They are continually warring against the children of men. They are ever watching to see whose outward or inward circumstances, whose prosperity or adversity, whose health or sickness, whose friends or enemies, whose youth or age, whose knowledge or ignorance, whose blindness or idleness, whose joy or sorrow may lay them open to temptation. They are constantly walking about as a roaring lion, seeking whom they may devour. It is by these instruments that the foolish hearts of those that know not God are darkened; yea, they frequently darken, in a measure, the hearts of them that do know God. The god of this world knows how to blind our hearts and to obscure the lights of those truths, which at other times, shine as bright as the noon-day sun. By these means, he assaults our faith—endeavors to weaken our hopes of immortality and destroy our confidence in God.

This enemy of all righteousness is equally diligent to hinder every good word and work.

He is continually laboring with all his skill and power to infuse evil thoughts into the hearts of men.

He likewise labors to awaken evil passions or tempers in our souls. He endeavors to excite those passions and tempers, which are directly opposite to the fruit of the Spirit. He is the author of all unbelief, atheism, ill will, hatred, malice, envy.

As no good is done or spoken by any man, without the assistance of God, working together in and with those that believe in him; so there is no evil done, or spoken without the assistance of the devil, who worketh with energy, with strong, though secret power in the children of disobedience. Thus he entered into Judas, and confirmed him in the design of betraying his master; thus he put into the heart of Ananias and Sapphira, to lie unto the Holy Ghost; and, in like manner, he has a share in all the actions and words and designs of evil men. As the children of God are workers together with God in every good thought, or word, or action; so the children of the devil are workers together with him, in every evil thought, or word, or work.

It remains only to draw a few plain inferences from the doctrine which has been delivered.

As a general preservative against all the rage, the power and subtlety of your great adversary, put on the panoply, the whole armor of God. So shall ye be able to withstand all the force and all the stratagems of the enemy; so shall he be able to withstand in the evil day.

To his fiery darts and his evil suggestions, oppose the shield of faith.

If he inject doubts, whether you are a child of God: fears, lest you should not endure to the end; take to you for a helmet the hope of salvation. Hold fast that glad word. Eph i. 3.

Whenever the roaring lion, walking about and seeking whom he may devour, assaults you with all his malice, and rage and strength, resist him steadfast in the faith.

Lastly, if he transform himself into an angel of light, then are you in the greatest danger of all. Then have you need to beware, lest you also fall, when many mightier have been slain—then have you the greater need to watch and pray that ye enter not into temptation.

THE RELAPSED DÆMONIAC.

Matt. xii. 43—45.—When the unclean spirit is gone out of a man, he walketh through dry places, seeking rest, and findeth none. Then he saith, I will return into my house from whence I came out; and when he is come, he findeth it empty, swept, and garnished. Then goeth he and taketh with himself seven other spirits, more wicked than himself, and they enter in and they dwell there: and the last state of that man is worse than the first. Even so shall it be also unto this wicked generation. (S. S.)

THOUGH the general scope of the parables is, for the most part, plain and obvious, it is often difficult to see the precise meaning of some circumstances contained in them—

This is the case with the parable before us; the minuter incidents of which may be considered perhaps rather as ornamental, than as essential parts of the parable itself*—

Its import, on the whole, suggests the following observations—

I. PERSONS, ONCE DELIVERED FROM SATAN, ARE AGAIN OPEN TO HIS ASSAULTS.

Satan certainly has power over the hearts of men.

There is much ascribed to his agency in the holy scriptures—

He is said to blind the eyes of unbelievers, 2 Cor. iv. 4, and to rule in their hearts, Eph. ii. 2.

Though he has not the same power over men's bodies as he once had, he evidently possesses their souls, and drives them to perdition, Mark ix. 22

But he often loses his dominion through the preaching of the gospel.

Paul was commissioned to turn men from the power of Satan unto God, Acts xxvi. 18.

And the gospel was the weapon whereby he rescued them from his dominion, 2 Cor. x. 4.

The same divine energy also attends it, when used by us, 2 Tim. ii. 25, 26.

Though conversions are more rare than in the apostle's days, they are not less real—

Yet they who have been delivered from him, are still open to his assaults

*Our Lord had cast out a devil; and this was by the Pharisees imputed to a confederacy with Beelzebub. After shewing the absurdity of such a notion, he contrasted their state with that of the Ninevites and the Queen of Sheba; and compared them to a relapsed demoniac, who would be in a worse state than if Satan had never gone out of him at all. If we proceed to explain all that is spoken respecting the unclean spirit, we must interpret it of Satan, ejected from the Jews, and going in *dry*, that is, unfrequented places, or places *not watered by the gospel*, to find rest among the Gentiles; and, upon being pursued thither by the preaching of the apostles, returning to take more full possession of the Jews than ever; since, however reformed some of them might be, they were, as a nation, perfectly prepared, through their inveterate lusts and prejudices, to receive them

How often did he repeat his attacks on Peter! Matt. xvi. 23, Luke xxii. 31.

With what envious malice did he buffet Paul! 2 Cor. xii. 7.

How did he renew his attempts even on Christ himself! Compare Luke iv. 13, John xiv. 30, Luke xxii. 53.

Thus he still watches for his opportunity to destroy *us*, 1 Pet. v. 8.

Nor shall we be wholly out of his reach, till we are finally discharged from our warfare, Eph. vi. 11, 12.

We had need therefore to watch against this subtle enemy; for

II. IF WE BE A SECOND TIME SUBJECTED TO SATAN'S DOMINION, OUR LAST STATE WILL BE WORSE THAN THE FIRST.

It is certain that Satan can never finally prevail against the elect.

This is evidently implied in the character which is given of them, 1 John ii. 13, 14, and v. 18.

The promises of God also insure to them the victory over him, Rom. xvi. 20.

Hence they are taught to defy all the powers of darkness, Rom. viii. 38, 39.

They, into whom he may return, are described in the text.

The true children of God desire to be ever "filled with the Spirit"—

Nor will they suffer the things that please Satan to abide quietly in their hearts—

But self-deceivers are satisfied, like Herod, with a partial change, Mark vi. 20.

And continue with their old affections and lusts unmortified, Ps. lxxviii. 36, 37.

Judas, Ananias, Demas, no doubt, retained their love of this world—

Hence Satan found their hearts "swept" indeed, and "emptied" of gross sin, but still *furnished* for his reception—

And, wherever this is the case, he will surely, however expelled for a season, return ere long with increased power—

On his return to them their state will be worse than ever.

The Holy Spirit will be grieved, provoked, quenched, Eph. iv. 30, Isa. lxiii. 10, 1 Thes. v. 19.

Their consciences will be silenced, and made callous—1 Tim. iv. 2.

Their evil habits will return and gain an irresistible dominion—

They will live only to treasure up wrath against the day of wrath—

And the deliverance, which they have neglected to improve, will fearfully aggravate their final condemnation—2 Pet. ii. 20, 21.

INQUIRE,

1. Have we ever yet been delivered from Satan?

Perhaps many doubt whether they have ever been possessed by Satan—

But this alone is sufficient to prove, that they are yet under his dominion.

That usurper reigns in all till he is vanquished and expelled by Jesus Christ—

And it is only in answer to fervent prayer, that the adorable Saviour puts forth his power to drive him out—

2. Are we yet daily maintaining a strict watch against him?

If he has been cast out of us, he is seeking his opportunity to return—

Nor can he be kept away, but by constant prayer and watchfulness—

Let us then guard every avenue of our hearts—

Let us implore the aid of our divine inhabitant—

The exertion of our own power in dependence on the intercession and grace of Christ, will insure us a successful issue of the conflict, Jam. iv 7, with Luke xxii. 31, 32.

THE MEANS OF DEFEATING SATAN'S MALICE.

1 Pet. v. 8, 9.—Be sober, be vigilant: because your adversary, the devil, as a roaring lion, walketh about, seeking whom he may devour: whom resist, stedfast in the faith. (S. S.)

There are many who deny the influences of the Holy Spirit—

No wonder therefore if the agency of Satan be called in question—

But there is abundant proof in the scriptures that Satan exercises a power over the minds of men—

St. Peter had learned this truth by bitter experience—

In this view the caution he gives us is worthy of particular attention.

I. The malice of Satan.

Satan is the great adversary of mankind—

It was he who caused the fall of our first parents, Gen. iii. 1—5.

He has exerted a similar influence over all their descendants—

He still maintains his enmity against the seed of the woman, Gen. iii. 15.

He is justly compared to "a roaring lion"—

He is subtle.

The lion prowls with subtilty in search of prey—

This is noticed in David's description of wicked men, Ps. x. 9, 10.

Satan also uses many devices to destroy souls, Eph. vi. 11.

He suits his temptations to us with astonishing craft—

He draws us into his snare before we are aware of his designs, 2 Cor. ii. 11.

To be acquainted with his devices is a most eminent and useful part of christian knowledge, Ib.

He is active.

The lion ranges far and wide in search of his prey—

And Satan "walks to and fro throughout the earth" Job. i. 7, and the text.

He ceases not from his exertions day or night, Rev. xii. 10.

He is the more diligent as knowing that his time is limited, Rev. xii. 12.

He has legions of emissaries acting in concert with him, Mark v. 9.

If at any time he suspend his attacks, it is but for a season, that he may return afterwards with greater advantage, Compare Luke iv. 13, with Luke xxii. 53.

He is cruel.

The lion little regards the agonies which he occasions—

Nor has Satan any compassion for the souls which he destroys—

The savage animal kills to satisfy the calls of nature—

But our adversary reaps no benefit from the destruction of men—

His exertions serve only to increase his own guilt and misery—

Yet is he insatiable in his thirst for our condemnation—

He is powerful.

Feeble is the resistance of a lamb against the voracious lion—

Still more impotent are men before "the god of this world"—

Satan has a limited power over the elements themselves*—
The ungodly are altogether subjected to his will, Eph. ii. 2, 2 Tim. ii. 26.
Nor would the saints have the smallest power to resist him, if God should deliver them into his hands†—
If we believe this representation of Satan's malice, we cannot but desire to know
II. THE MEANS OF DEFEATING IT.
Our adversary, though great, is not invincible—
There is one stronger than he, that can overcome him, Luke xi. 21, 22.
And God has prescribed means whereby *we* also may vanquish him.
Moderation
An undue attachment to the things of time and sense gives him a great advantage over us—
He will not fail to assault us on our weak side‡—
But a deadness to the world will in some measure disarm him—
He prevailed not against our Lord, because he found no irregular affection in him, John xiv. 30.
Nor could he so easily overcome us if we disregarded earthly things—
A contempt of life has been a principal mean whereby the saints and martyrs in all ages have triumphed over him, Rev. xii. 11.
Vigilance
Unwatchfulness, even in a victorious army, exposes it to defeat—
Much more must it subject us to the power of our subtle enemy—
St. Peter had experienced its baneful effects—
He had been warned of Satan's intention to assault him, Luke xxii. 31.
He had been commanded to pray lest he should fall by the temptation,—Luke xxii. 40.
But he slept when he should have been praying, Luke xxii. 45, 46.
He stands in this respect, like Lot's wife, Luke xvii. 32, a monument to future generations—
But vigilance on our part will counteract the designs of Satan—
The armed christian, watching unto prayer, must be victorious, Eph. vi. 18.
Fortitude
The timid christian falls into a thousand snares, Prov. xxix. 25.
The only way to obtain a victory is, to fight manfully—
And this is the duty of every follower of Christ, Eph. vi. 10, 13
We must never give way to Satan, Eph. iv. 27.
We are called to wrestle and contend with him, Eph. vi. 12.
Nor shall our resistance be in vain‖—
Faith
Unbelief is a powerful instrument in the hands of Satan—
He excites it in us that he may turn us from the faith—
We must therefore hold fast *the doctrines of faith*—
We should not suffer ourselves to be moved from the hope of the gospel—
This is our anchor whereby we must outride the storm, Heb. vi. 19.

* Job. i. 12. 19. He is called "the prince of the power of the air."

† Many who have appeared lights in the church have been swept away by the tail of this great dragon, Rev. xxii. 3, 4.

‡ It was he who instigated Judas to treachery, and Ananias to falsehood: but he wrought by means of their covetousness, John xiii. 2, Acts v. 3.

‖ James iv. 7. Satan is not only checked but *terrified*, and vanquished by the resistance of the weakest christian.

We must also stedfastly exercise *the grace of faith*—
This is the weapon whereby we evercome the world, 1 John v. 4.
And by this shall we triumph over Satan himself, Eph. vi. 16
APPLICATION.
Let not the ungodly despise this adversary—
But let them seek deliverance from him through the gospel, Acts xxvi. 18.
And let the godly be continually on their guard against him, 2 Cor. xi. 3.
So shall they experience that promised blessing, Rom. xvi. 20.

THE MEANS OF SECURITY FROM SATAN'S MALICE.

Luke xxii. 31, 32. And the Lord sain, Simon, Simon, behold, Satan hath desired to have you, that he may sift you as wheat: but I have prayed for thee, that thy faith fail not. (S. S.)

THE agency, or even the existence, of evil spirits is scarcely credited amongst us—

But there is nothing more certain than that they exist, and act in the world—

To conflict with them constitutes a principal part of the Christians warfare, Eph. vi. 12.

And to be aware of their devices is no inconsiderable attainment in Christian knowledge, 2 Cor. ii. 11.

There is however a Being who is able to counteract their agency—

Of this we have a proof in the history before us—

Satan, the prince of the devils, meditated the destruction of Peter—

Our Lord with affection and earnestness warned Peter of his designs—

And, by his own intercession, secured him against his assaults.

I. THE MALICE OF SATAN.

Satan is the great adversary of mankind.

He was once as bright a morning star as any in heaven—But he rebelled against the Most High, and incurred his displeasure, 2 Pet. ii. 4.

Full of hatred against God, he sought to efface his image from our first parents—

Through subtilty he prevailed to the destruction of them and us, 2 Cor xi. 3.

Nor does he cease to assault those who through grace are restored—

He desires to agitate and distress them.

This is evidently implied in the expression in the text—

He has various ways of effecting his purpose—

He may harass us with temptations and persecutions—

He may perplex us by artful insinuations and suggestions—

His efforts were exerted against all the apostles—*

But the more eminent any are, the more they are hated by him—

Peter was distinguished for his knowledge and intrepidity, Matt. xvi. 16

Yea, he had had a peculiar honor conferred on him, Matt. xvi. 18.

On this account Satan's malice raged against him more especially—

But his ultimate end is to prove them hypocrites, or to make them apostates.

*Υμας.

This was evidently his design in assaulting Job, Job i. 9, 11; and ii. 5.

And in asking permission to try the disciples—†

Nor would he leave one faithful person upon earth—

"As a roaring lion he seeks to devour" all—

He can do nothing indeed but by divine permission—‡

But if suffered to fulfil all his will, he would destroy every soul—

His influence on the herd of swine shews what he would do to men, Matt. viii. 32.

Not one vassal of his would escape the fate of Judas, Compare Luke xxii. 3, with Matt. xxvii. 5.

But God has not left his people without means of resistance.

II. Our security.

God has both armed his people for the combat, and given them a great Deliverer—

Faith is the grace whereby he enables us to maintain our stand.

It was by faith that we were translated from Satan's kingdom into Christ's Gal. iii. 26.

It is by that also that our daily warfare is to be carried on, 2 Cor. i. 24.

Yea, through that are we to attain our full and final salvation, 1 Pet. i. 5

Faith is the shield whereby alone we can ward off the darts of Satan, Eph. vi. 16.

If that fail, we are exposed to the fiercest assaults of our enemy—

If we lose our hold of the promises, we shall be driven away as chaff—

We shall have no point around which to rally our scattered forces—

Whereas, if faith be strong, we shall hope even against hope, Rom. iv. 18, 20.

And, though wounded, we shall return with fresh vigor to the combat—

Nor shall our great adversary be able to prevail against us, Rom. x. 11

Hence that earnest caution against unbelief, Heb. iii. 12.

And that express direction respecting the mode of opposing Satan, 1 Pet. v 8, 9.

But the intercession of Christ is necessary to uphold our faith.

Peter's faith would have failed utterly if he had been left to himself—

But through the intercession of Christ he was preserved—

Thus we also should "make shipwreck of our faith"—

But our prevailing Advocate pleads for us also, John xvii. 20.

As our High-Priest he bears us on his breast-plate before the throne, Exod. xxviii. 29.

He obtains for us fresh supplies of the Spirit—

In this way he, who has been the author of our faith, will also be the finisher, Heb. xii. 2.

Hence the encouragement given us to rely on the intercession of Christ, Rom. viii. 34.

Hence the encouragement given us to regard it under every backsliding, 1 John ii. 1.

Hence the encouragement given us to rest assured of Christ's power to save, Heb. vii. 25.

Infer,

1. What need have we to be ever on our guard!

†Ἐξῃτήσατο seems to imply a kind of challenge, as in the case of Job, wherein he undertook to prove them to be but chaff, if God would suffer him to make the trial.

‡He could not afflict Job more than God saw fit to suffer him: nor could he enter into the swine without our Saviour's permission, Matt. viii. 31.

Perhaps at this moment Satan may be desiring to sift us—
And what if God should give us up into his hands?—
If suffered to exert his strength, he could soon dissipate whatever is good in us—
Nor should our past zeal in God's service remove our apprehensions—
That would rather provoke Satan to more activity against us—
Let us then "not be high-minded but fear"—
Let us follow the salutary advice which our Lord has given us, Matt. xxvi. 41.
Let us plead with fervor those important petitions, Matt. vi. 13.
At the same time let us "put on the whole armor of God"—
And prepare, as God has taught us, for the assaults of our enemy, Eph. vi. 13—18.
2. What a mercy is it to have an interest in Christ!
They who know not Chrtst are wholly under the power of Satan, 2 Tim ii. 26.
But they who are Christ's have a watchful and almighty guardian—
Our Lord provided for Peter's safety, before Peter even knew his danger—
Thus "will he keep the feet of all his saints"—
He will suffer none of them to be plucked out of his hand, John x. 28.
If he permit Satan to sift them, it shall be only for the removing of their chaff, Compare 2 Cor. xii. 7. with Heb. xii. 10, 11.
He has pledged his word for the security of the weakest of his people, Amos ix. 9.
Let us therefore commit ourselves entirely into his hands—
Let us beg him to remember our unworthy names in his intercessions—
And to deal with us as with Joshua of old, Zech. iii. 2—4.

CHAPTER VIII.

MAN.

CREATION OF MAN.

Gen. i. 26.—And God said, Let us make man in our image, after our likeness. (H. H.)

Though men constantly trace their origin to their immediate parents, and frequently to their remoter ancestors, yet they rarely consider when, or how they first came into existence, or whether any change has taken place in their nature since they came out of their Creator's hands. That there was a period when no such creature as man existed, even reason itself would teach us; for every effect must proceed from some cause: and therefore the formation of man, however remotely we trace his origin, must, in the first instance, have been the product of some intelligent Being, who was eternally self-existent. But we are not left to the uncertain deductions of reason: God has been pleased to reveal unto us (what could not otherwise have been known) Heb. xi. 3, the time and manner of our creation, together with the state in which we were created. And these are the subjects which we would now propose for your consideration:

I. THE CIRCUMSTANCES OF OUR CREATION—

We may not unprofitably notice somewhat respecting *the time*—

Five days had been occupied in reducing to order the confused chaos, and in furnishing the world with whatever could enrich or adorn it. On the sixth, God formed man, whom he reserved to the last, as being the most excellent of his works; and whose formation he delayed, till every thing in this habitable globe was fitted for his accommodation. It is not for us to inquire why God chose this space of time for the completion of his work, when he could as easily have formed it all in an instant: but one instructive lession at least we may learn from the survey which he took of every day's work; it teaches his creatures to review their works from day to day, in order that, if they find them to have been good, they may be excited to gratitude; or, if they perceive them to have been evil, they may be led to repentance. At the close of every day, God pronounced his work to be "good:" but when man was formed, and the harmony of all the parts, together with the conduciveness of each to its proper end, and the subserviency of every part to the good of the whole, were fully manifest, then he pronounced the whole to be "*very* good." From this also we learn, that it is not one work or two, however good in themselves, that should fully satisfy our minds; but a comprehensive view of all our works, as harmonizing with each other, and corresponding with all the ends of our creation.

In *the manner* of our creation there is something worthy of very peculiar attention—

In the formation of all other things God merely exercised his own sovereign will, saying, "Let there be light," "Let such and such things take place." But in the creation of man we behold the language of consultation; "Let us make man." There is not the least reason to suppose that this was a mere form of speech, like that which obtains among monarchs at this day; for this is quite a modern refinement: nor can it be an address to angels; for they had nothing to do in the formation of man: it is an address to the Son, and to the Holy Ghost, both of whom co-operated in the formation of Him who was to be the master-piece of divine wisdom and power.* This appears from a still more striking expression, which occurs afterwards; where God says, "Now man is become like *one of us*, to know good and evil." Gen. iii. 22. And it is confirmed in a variety of other passages, where God, *under the character of our "Creator," or "Maker,"* is spoken of in the plural number.†

We must not however suppose that there are three Gods: there certainly is but One God; and His unity is as clear as his existence: and this is intentionally marked in the very verse following our text; where the expressions, "*us*" and "*our*" are turned into "*he*" and "*his:*"—"God created man in *his* own image; in the image of God created *he* him."

Here, then, we may see an early intimation of the *Trinity in Unity;* a doctrine which pervades the whole Bible, and is the very corner-stone of our holy religion. And it is deserving of particular notice, that, in our dedication to our Creator at our baptism, we are expressly required to acknowledge this mysterious doctrine, being "baptized in the name of the Father, and of the Son, and of the Holy Ghost." Matt. xxviii. 19.

*The work of Creation is ascribed to Jesus Christ, John i. 1—3, and to the Holy Ghost, Gen. i. 2; Job xxvi. 13; and xxxiii. 4.

†See Job xxxv. 10; Isaiah liv. 5; Eccl. xii. 1. These are all plural *in the original.*

The text informs us further respecting,

II. The state in which we were created—

There was some "likeness" to God even in the nature of man. "God is a spirit," who thinks, and wills, and acts. Man also has a spirit, distinct from his body, or from the mere animal life: he has a thinking, willing substance, which acts upon matter by the mere exercises of its own volitions, except when the material substance on which it operates is bereft of its proper faculties, or impeded in the use of them. But the image of God in which man was formed, is, properly, two-fold:

1. Intellectual—

"God is a God of knowledge." He has a perfect discernment of every thing in the whole creation. Such, too, was Adam in his first formation. Before he had had any opportunity to make observations on the beasts of the field and the birds of the air, he gave names to every one of them, suited to their several natures, and distinctive of their proper characters. But it was not merely in things natural that Adam was so well instructed; he doubtless had just views of God, his nature and perfections: he had also a thorough knowledge of himself, of his duties, his interests, his happiness. There was no one thing which could conduce either to his felicity or usefulness, which was not made known to him, as far as he needed to be instructed in it. As "God is light without any mixture or shade of darkness," 1 John i. 5, so was Adam, in reference to all those things at least which he was at all concerned to know.

2. Moral—

Holiness is no less characteristic of the Deity than wisdom. He loves every thing that is good, and infinitely abhors every thing that is evil. Every one of His perfections is holy. In this respect, also, did man bear a resemblance to his Maker. "God made him upright." Eccl. vii. 29. As he had a view of the commandment in all its breadth, so had he a conformity to it in all his dispositions and actions. He felt no reluctance in obeying it: his will was in perfect unison with the will of his Maker. All the inferior appetites were in habitual subjection to his reason, which also was in subjection to the commands of God. We are told respecting the Lord Jesus Christ, that he was "the image of God," 2 Cor. iv. 4, "the image of the invisible God," Col. i. 15, "the express image of his person." Heb. i. 3. What the Lord Jesus Christ, therefore, was upon earth, *that* was man in Paradise—"holy, harmless, undefiled." Heb. vii. 26.

That man's resemblance to his Maker did indeed consist in these two things, is manifest; because our renewal after the divine image is expressly said to be in knowledge, Col. iii. 10, and in true holiness. Eph. iv. 24. Well, therefore, does the apostle say of man, that "he is the image and glory of God." 1 Cor. xi. 7.

Infer,

1. What an awful change has sin brought into the world!

Survey the character before drawn: and compare it with men in the present state: "How is the gold become dim, and the find gold changed!" Men are now enveloped in darkness, and immersed in sin. They "know nothing as they ought to know," and do nothing as they ought to do it. No words can adequately express the blindness of their minds, or the depravity of their hearts.——— Yet all this has resulted from that one sin which Adam committed in Paradise. He lost the divine image from his own soul; and "begat a son in his own fallen likeness:" and the streams that have been flowing for nearly six thousand years from that polluted fountain, are stiii as corrupt as ever. O that we habitually considered sin in this light, and regarded it as the one source of all our miseries!

2. What a glorious change will the Holy Spirit effect in the hearts of all who seek Him!

In numberless passages, as well as in those before cited, See notes (m) and (n), the Holy Spirit is spoken of, as "renewing" our souls, and making us "new creatures." 2 Cor. v. 17. What Adam was in Paradise, *that* shall we be, "according to the measure of the gift of Christ." "Instead of the thorn shall come up the fir-tree, and instead of the brier shall grow up the myrtle-tree." Isa. lv. 13. He will "open the eyes of our understanding," and cause us to "know all things" that are needful for our salvation: 1 John ii. 20, 27; and at the same time that he "turns us from darkness unto light, he will turn us also from the power of Satan unto God:" "He will put the law in our *minds*, and write it in our *hearts*." Heb. viii. 10. Let not any imagine that their case is desperate; for He who created all things out of nothing, can easily create us anew in Christ Jesus: and He will do it, if we only direct our eyes to Christ: "We all beholding as in a glass the glory of the Lord, shall be changed into the same image from glory to glory, even as by the Spirit of the Lord." 2 Cor. iii. 18.

3. What obligations do we owe to the ever-blessed Trinity!

If we looked no further than to our first creation, we are infinitely indebted to the sacred Three, for making us the subject of their consultation, and for co-operating to form us in the most perfect manner. But what shall we say to that other consultation, respecting the restoration of our souls? Hear, and be astonished at that gracious proposal, "Let us *restore* man *to* our image." "I," says the Father, "will pardon and accept them, if an adequate atonement can be found to satisfy the demands of justice. "Then on me be their guilt," says his only dear Son: "I will offer myself a sacrifice for them, if any one can be found to apply the virtue of it effectually to their souls, and to secure to me the purchase of my blood." "*That* shall be my charge," says the blessed Spirit: "I gladly undertake the office of enlightening, renewing, sanctifying their souls; and I will "preserve every one of them blameless unto thy heavenly kingdom." Thus, by their united efforts, is the work accomplished; and "a way of access is opened for every one of us through Christ, by that one Spirit, unto the Father." Eph. ii. 18. O let every soul rejoice in this Tri-une God! and may the Father's love, the grace of Christ, and the fellowship of the Holy Ghost, be with us all evermore! Amen.

OF THE IMMORTALITY OF THE SOUL.

Gen. ii. 7.—And he became a living soul. (H.)

THOUGH the body die, and when it dies, the soul dies not; it survives the body, and not only lives after it, but lives for ever, it never dies: though the body without the soul be dead, yet the soul without the body is not dead. When the body returns to the earth and dust, from whence it sprung, the soul returns to God, its immediate author: the body may be killed by men, but not the soul: no man has any power over that, none but God that made it: the soul is immortal, it is not capable of death, that is, in a natural and proper sense.

When it is said the soul is immortal, it must be understood that it is so in its nature; and is not liable to death either from any thing within itself, or without it; but not that it has such an immortality as God himself has, "who only hath immortality;" he has it of himself. Angels, and the souls of men, have their immortality of him, who has made them immaterial and immortal spirits; his immortality is without beginning, and any prior cause of it; theirs has a beginning from God, the first cause of them: his is independent; theirs depends on him, "in whom they live, and move, and have their being." That the soul of man is immortal, may be proved,

I. From the consideration of the soul itself—its original, nature, powers, and faculties.

1. From the original of it. It is not of men: "What is born of the flesh is flesh;" and not only carnal and sinful, but frail and mortal. "All flesh is grass," withering, decaying, and corruptible; it is the very breath of God, and has a similarity to him, particularly in immortality; "God breathed into man the breath of life." Gen. ii. 7. Elihu says, Job xxxiii. 4, "The breath of the Almighty hath given me life;" a life that will never end. Hence God is described as he that "formeth the spirit of man within him." Zech. xii. 1, and as God is the former of the souls of men, so he is the supporter of them; he "upholds their souls in life." The most malicious and cruel persecutors can only kill the body, and after that they have no more that they can do; they cannot kill the soul. Luke xii. 4.

2. The immortality of the soul may be proved from its nature; which is,

1. Spiritual, of the same nature with angels, who are made spirits, spiritual substances. Heb. xii. 9—23. The souls of men are of the same nature with angels, and they die not. Ps. civ. 4; Luke xx. 36; 1 Cor. ii. 11.

2. The soul of man is simple, unmixed, and uncompounded; it is not composed of flesh and blood, &c. as the body; a spirit has none of these.

3. It is immaterial, it is not composed of matter and form; nor is it a material form, educed out of the power of matter. Matter is divisible, discerptible, may be cut to pieces: not so the soul: it is out of the reach of every slaughtering weapon; the sharp arrow cannot penetrate into it, nor the glittering spear pierce it, nor the two-edged sword divide it.

4. It has no contrary qualities which threaten with destruction; it is neither hot nor cold; neither moist nor dry.

5. The soul of man is made after the image, and in the likeness of God, which chiefly consists in that; it bears a resemblance to the Divine nature, being the breath of God, it is a likeness to him, and particularly in its immortality.

3. The immortality of the soul may be proved from its powers and faculties.

4. Its understanding. There is a spirit or soul, in man, as Elihu says. Job xxxii. 8. And the inspiration of the Almighty giveth him understanding; an intellective power and faculty of understanding things. Ps. xxxii. 9; Job xxxv. 11.

1. The understanding of man can take in, and has knowledge of, things spiritual and incorporeal, immaterial, incorruptible, and eternal; which it would not be capable of if it were not of the same nature itself: the images of these things would not be impressed on it, nor would it be susceptible of them.

2. The soul of man has knowledge of eternity itself: though it may be observed, there is great difference in its apprehension of an eternity past, and of that which is to come: when it considers the former, it is soon at a loss, and at a full stop, is obliged to return and cannot go on; it is like a bird that attempts to soar aloft, and take flights it is not used nor equal to, it flutters and hangs its wings, and is forced to descend. But when the soul fixes its thoughts on an eternity to come, how readily does it apprehend how that shall proceed without end! with what pleasure does it roll over millions of ages in it! The reason of this difference is, because the soul itself is not from eternity, but has a beginning; whereas, it will endure to eternity and have no end.

3. The knowledge which the mind and understanding of man has of things in the present state, is very imperfect, through the brevity of life; and therefore it may be reasonably concluded, that there is a future state, in which the soul will exist, and its knowledge of things be more perfect. Arts and sciences have been cultivating many thousands of years, and in some ages great improvements have been made, and especially in latter ends; and yet there is room for farther improvements still: the knowledge of the best things, which good men have, as of God, of Christ, and of the mysteries of grace, is now very imperfect; those that know most, know but in part, and see through a glass darkly; but there is a state in which their souls will exist, when they shall see God face to face, see him as he is, and know as they are known.

4. The knowledge the mind of man has of things now, is not in proportion to the powers that he possesses. How many are there that die in infancy, and as soon as they are born, whose reasoning powers are never called forth into action and exercise; and how many die in childhood and youth, before these powers ripen, and are brought to any maturity? Now can it be thought these powers are bestowed upon them in vain? There must be then an after-state.

5. Let a man know ever so much in this present life, he is desirous of knowing more; let his acquisitions of knowledge be ever so large, after a life of studious search and inquiry, he is not satisfied, he still wants to know more; and what he has arrived unto is only to know this, that he knows but little. Now this desire of knowledge is not implanted in man, by the Author of nature, in vain; wherefore the soul must remain after death, when it will arrive to a more perfect knowledge of things.

2. The will of man is another faculty of the soul, the object and actings of which show it to be immortal.

1. The will has for its object universal good. It naturally desires complete happiness, which some place in one thing and some in another, but it is not perfectly enjoyed by any. Now there must be a future state, in which true happiness will be attained, at least by some, or else the actings of the will about it will be in vain.

2. God is the summum bonum, the chief good, the will of man rightly pitches upon, nor can it be satisfied with any thing less; good men choose him as their portion; but then he is not perfectly enjoyed as such in this life. wherefore in order to this the soul must remain after death, and be immortal.

3. The will has its desires, and which desires, even the best, are not satisfied in this life. "Whom have I in heaven but thee?"

4. The actions of the will are free, not forced by any creature; its acts are independent of the body, and can live without it.

5. The will is not weakened, nor indeed any of the powers and faculties of the soul impaired, by sickness and approaching death; though the out ward man perish, the inward man is renewed day by day; yea, when the body is become speechless and near expiring, the faculties of the soul are in exercise; a man understands clearly what his friends about him say, and can by a sign, by the lifting up his hand, signify his faith, hope, joy, and comfort; all which show that the soul sickens not with the body, nor becomes languid, nor dies with it.

II. The immortality of the soul may be proved from the light of nature and reason.

1. From the consent of all nations. Cicero says, That as we know by nature that there is a God, so we judge by the consent of all nations, that souls remain after death and are immortal: and in every thing, he says, the consent of all nations is to be reckoned the law of nature: so Seneca calls it, a public persuasion or belief.

2. This may be concluded, from an extinction of man, soul and body, being abhorrent to man; the death of the body, though nature be reluctant to it; yet, in many instances there has been a voluntary and cheerful submission to it: many good men have not loved their lives unto death.

3. It may be argued, that the natural desire in men to be religious, in some way or other; this is so natural to men, that some have chose rather to define man a religious, than a rational animal. All nations have had their gods they worshipped.

4. There is a consciousness of sinning in men; guilt arises in their consciences, on account of sins; even in the very heathen there is a conscience bearing witness in their actions.

5. Not only from the stings of conscience, but from the horror and dread wicked men are sometimes siezed with, as Felix. These things not only show that there is a Divine Being to whom men are accountable for their actions; but that there is a future state after death, in which men exist, when they shall be either in happiness or in misery.

6. The belief of this may be farther argued, from the providence of God concerned in the distribution and disposal of things in this life, which is oftentimes very unequal: wicked men prosper, and good men are greatly afflicted. Ps. lxxiii. 2, 3, 12—14; Jer. xii. 1, 2. Good men if they have hope in this life only, they would be of all men the most miserable. Luke xvi. 25; 1 Cor. xv. 19. Wherefore,

7. The immortality of the soul may be concluded from the justice of God; who is the judge of all the earth; for righteous is the Lord, though his judgments are not so manifest in this life: it is a righteous thing with God to render tribulation to them that trouble his people, and to fulfil the promises he makes to his saints.

8. If the soul be not immortal, but dies with the body, the brutes, in many things, have the advantage of men; and their state and condition in this life is, in many respects, superior to ours; they are not so weak and helpless at first coming into the world; not subject to so many diseases; in some the senses are quicker, and they have more pleasure in the exercise of them.

III. The immortality of the soul may be proved from the sacred scriptures.

Eccl. xii. 7. The soul, or spirit, is said to return to God that gave it. Matt. x. 28. Fear not them which kill the body, &c. This is to be proved,

1. From scripture doctrines; as from the doctrine of God's love to his people, which is everlasting. Jer. xxxi. 3. But this would not be true, if

the souls of God's beloved died; hence it would follow, that death can, and does, separate from the love of God, contrary to the apostle's firm persuasion. Rom. viii. 38, 39. Also from the covenant of grace, which is said to be an everlasting covenant. 2 Sam. xxiii. 5. But it is well known, that in all covenants there are confederates, and if one of the parties covenanting die, the covenant is at an end. The argument used by Christ to prove the resurrection of the dead, from covenant interest, Matt. xii. 31, 32; Luke xx. 38, equally proves, or rather more clearly, the immortality of the soul. And particularly the immortality of the soul may be concluded from the grand promise of eternal life, in the covenant made before the world began. Tit. i. 2; 1 John ii. 25. But how can this promise be fulfilled, if the souls of those to whom it is made are not immortal? It may be argued from the doctrine of adoption, another blessing in the covenant; by virtue of which saints are heirs of an eternal inheritance. Likewise it may be argued from the doctrine of Christ respecting his work, the blessings of grace by him, and the services and benefits farther to be expected from him, as the redemption of the soul by the blood of Christ, which must be shed in vain: nor can it be called eternal redemption if the soul be not immortal. The doctrine of the judgment, whether particular or general, is a proof of the soul's immortality. Moreover, the doctrine of future rewards and punishments confirms this truth; for, if the soul be not immortal, a good man cannot be rewarded in a way of grace, nor enjoy happiness in consequence of his piety, since there will be no subject of it remaining; nor a wicked man punished for his sins for the same reason.

2. The immortality of the soul may be proved from scripture instances; as from the cases of Enoch and Elijah, who were translated, soul and body, that they should not see death; as not in their bodies, so not in their souls. Abraham, Isaac, and Jacob, who died, and yet after death were living, even in the times of Christ; also from the spirits in prison, in the times of the apostle Peter, who were disobedient to the warnings of Noah; and from the resurrection of some particular persons; who, after death, were raised and lived again, their souls, which die not, being returned to them; 1 Kings xvii. 21, 22, and from the souls under the altar, whose bodies were killed; Rev, vi. 9, 10, and from the instances of persons committing their spirits to God at death. Ps. xxxi. 5; Luke xxiii. 46; Acts vii. 59; 1 Pet. iv. 16, 19.—Lastly, all such scriptures which speak of the joys of heaven, and the torments of hell.

IV. Answer some objections.

1. From reason. As,

1. That which has a beginning has an end. But this is not always true; angels have a beginning, but not an end; they die not.

2. The powers of the soul are said to decay, as the body decays; but this is only true of the powers of the sensitive soul, or part of man: not of the rational soul; not of the faculties of the understanding and will.

3. When a man dies, nothing is seen to go out of him but his breath, which vanishes away: but it is no wonder the soul should not be seen at its departure, since being a spirit, incorporeal and immaterial, it is invisible.

4. Some will have it, that this is only a contrivance of men in power, a piece of state-policy to keep men in awe. But those men were either bad or good men: bad men would be unconcerned about ways and means to serve the cause of religion; and good men would never make use of a known lie, to serve such purposes.

2. From scripture As,

1. From such scriptures which threaten the soul with death in case of sin Gen. ii. 17 And it is expressly said, the soul that sins shall die. Ezek. xviii. 4. To which may be replied—That there are various sorts of death: there is a spiritual or moral death; it is a being dead in trespasses and sins; and lies, not in the substance of the soul, but in the qualities of it. And there is an eternal death, the destruction of both body and soul in hell; this lies not in the destruction of the being of either, but in the misery of both: and there is a natural death, such as of the body, which the soul is not capable of.

2. From what is said of man. Ps. lxxviii. 39, and cxlvi. 4. This is expressive of the brevity of the bodily life of man.

3. From such passages which speak of man's going at death from whence he shall not return. Job x. 21, and xiv. 10. But these are to be understood, of his returning to his house, and former manner of living and employment of life. Chap. xii, 10. And when it is asked, Where is he, when he dies? it is easily answered, He is returned to the dust; and his soul is gone to God, and is either in bliss or wo.

4. From those places which speak of the dead as NOT: Rachel was weeping for her children, because they were not. Jer. xxxi. 15. But this cannot be meant of non-existence, either of soul or body.

ORIGINAL SIN.

Genesis iii. 13.—The serpent beguiled me, and I did eat. (Sk.)

THE origin of things is frequently involved in darkness; and the more remote the period of their commencement, the greater mysteriousness envelops their origin. Things seen at a distance are usually seen indistinctly; and facts are often related without the pomp of circumstance. This is exemplified in the subject before us. The text is a brief narration of one of the most awfully portentous acts, which was ever perpetrated upon earth; to this source, we may trace back all the crimes in their endlessly diversified circumstances, which have inundated the world; and here we see the germination of a seed, which has taken deep root, and filled the earth with poisonous fruit. Had the fact recorded in the text been merely of a speculative character, it might even then have excited curoisity, and elicited inquiry; but as we have all reaped a harvest of ills, from the seed sown on that fatal occasion, it cannot be an unprofitable exercise, to spend a few moments in recalling to mind what we know of this transaction. Two things claim our attention,

I. THE ACT OF THE SERPENT. He "beguiled me."

II. THE ACT OF THE WOMAN. "I did eat."

But who, or what was the serpent? In the first verse of this chapter, the serpent is represented as a "beast of the field:" but to suppose that any beast of the field, would of his own accord, and at his own instigation, beguile the woman, and seduce her to sin, would be an absurdity too palpable to be admitted; as it would imply, that the serpent was superior to the woman in intellectual endowments; and that he meditated her ruin by carrying into effect a most mischievous design. Bnt as God made every thing very good, and as all animals were inferior to the human pair, we must refer to some other cause for the existence of this act.

The most common opinion is, that the devil animated the body of the serpent, and spoke to Eve through his organs. In reference to this, he is called the "old serpent," Rev. xii. 9. And St. Paul said to the Corinthians, "I fear as the serpent beguiled Eve," &c., 2 Cor. xi. 3; but he could not fear that that "beast of the field," described by Moses, would corrupt the christians at Corinth. That the devil can so far possess human, or animal bodies, as to act upon them and speak through them, is most satisfactorily proved from the legion who possessed the poor demoniac, and said to Jesus, "What have we to do with thee?" &c., Matt. vii. 32. And then entering into the bodies of the swine, &c. And this enemy possessed every qualification for managing the deep-laid plot which he had so artfully devised. *He was endowed with extensive knowledge.* Angels possess amazing powers of intellect, and though fallen angels lost all moral excellency by their fall, yet they most probably retained much of their original vigor of understanding. Satan knew in what part of the universe to find the original pair; he knew their circumstances—the law they were under—the misery that would ensue on their violation of that law—and probably the mischievous results in reference to posterity. *He also possessed the most consummate wickedness.* He is called the "wicked one," and "an evil spirit." The devil is a being replete with wickedness: and this was the most wicked scheme that was ever devised. What wickedness to mar such beauty, and blight so much excellence, as creation presented when adorned in all its pristine glory! What wickedness to involve innocent and holy beings in guilt and misery! beings who deserved no such treatment, and merited no such conduct! Oh how many are there in the world who too successfully imitate this arch fiend! who are wise to do mischief; who employ their exalted powers of mind in imposing on the credulous, and ruining the innocent! But how did the serpent beguile the woman?

1. *By attacking her when alone.* I infer this, not only on the ground of a commonly received opinion, but from the narrative itself. Here we see the whole of the conversation carried on between the serpent and the woman; Adam had no share in it. The devil must have known that Adam was the superior, from the circumstance of his being first formed, and Eve being made a "helpmeet for him." Had Adam been present, they would most probably have taken sweet council together, on a subject of so much consequence. How wise it is in affairs of great moment to pause, and hesitate, and deliberate, and take advice of our superiors.

2. *By directing her attention to the prohibited object.* There was much in the garden of Eden to admire, and much to enjoy: one tree only was prohibited; to this object the serpent directed the attention of the woman, and induced her to look at it. talk of it, and desire it. We have many prohibited objects. These we should fly from; never trust our eyes to gaze on objects which are likely to excite desires of an unholy nature in our hearts. "Abstain from the appearance of evil." Oh had Eve done this, how effectually would she have broken the snare of the devil!

3. *By a prospect of advantage on eating the forbidden fruit.* Nothing weighs so much with a human being as profit. What will not a man sacrifice for the distant prospect of gain? Eve expected to be like the gods, that is, as the angels. Eve must have known, that there were such beings as angels. Who can doubt but that they made their appearance to our primitive

parents in paradise, as they appeared in after times to Abraham, Lot, &c.? And it is not improbable, but that they assumed a glorious appearance; the idea of being like them, produced a most fascinating effect on the mind of Eve. But this was all mere artifice with the tempter, who knew that instead of being as gods, they would be more like fiends, by partaking of the forbidden fruit. How many of the sons and daughters of Eve have been lured by the tempting bait of ambition, and who by aping their superiors have plunged themselves into an abyss of misery!

4. *By plausibly reasoning with her on the subject.* He knew that nothing could be done by open attack; that every thing must appear plausible and imposing; he therefore began by questioning Eve, "Hath God said, ye shall not eat of every tree of the garden?" Here was just enough to excite curiosity. Hath God said such a thing? Is this reasonable? What could such fair fruit be created for, but to be eaten? It is highly probable, that more conversation ensued than is here recorded. How forcibly does this teach us to resist the first temptations to evil, to hold no parley with the enemy.

5. *By confidently asserting, that it was a mistake under which Eve was laboring.* "Ye shall not surely die." He first tempted her to doubt, by an awful insinuating question; and then to disbelieve, by a bold, daring, mischievous lie,—the first lie that ever was uttered upon earth. This is the usual process by which he carries on his dark designs, exciting men to question the truth of established opinions, &c. Confident assertions have often great weight with innocent and unsuspecting minds. "Goodness thinks no ill, where no ill seems." Here was not only a bold contradiction to the truth of God, but an artful and base insinuation, that he had prohibited this fruit through some sinister design. "For God doth know," &c., ver. 5.

II. THE ACT OF THE WOMAN. "I did eat." This was the original transgression. Here sin entered into the world, and we learn,

1. *That the sin of Eve was a personal act.* "I did eat." Whatever blame might be imputed to the serpent, still the act of eating was all her own. The sin of the tempter was a totally distinct thing from her sin. Here was no force, no constraint, nor over-ruling power to impel her to eat; the concurrence of her will—the taking of the fruit—and the eating of it, were personal acts for which Eve only was accountable. Our sins also are personal. Temptations we all have, and innate tendencies to evil; but these are not imputed to us as sin, till we give them the concurrence of our wills, and sanction them by indulgence.

2. *The sin of Eve was a carnal act.* "I did *eat*." Here was the sin, it was in *eating*. The temptation was presented to the senses; "The woman saw that the tree was good for food." It is difficult to say, how she could *see* this, unless we admit with Milton, that she had seen the serpent eat of it. What if it *were* good for food? she needed not food; there were trees in abundance all around her, laden with fruit as fair and good as that which she coveted. "And that it was pleasant to the eyes;" but must every thing be eaten that is pleasant to the eye? And "a tree to be desired to make one wise;" here "lust conceived, and brought forth sin." Most of our temptations come to us through the medium of our senses, and sin is chiefly gratifying as it affects the animal part of a man. Sinners are nominated carnal men, that is literally, fleshly men; men who are in the flesh, who live after the flesh, and who sow to the flesh: and though sin is deeply seated in the mind, yet the members of the body become its instruments.

3. *The sin of Eve was a prohibited act.* It was a direct violation of a plain, known, positive law. The law was as *plain* as language could make

it: it was *known;* for though God gave it to Adam, prior to the formation of Eve, yet God, or her husband, had revealed it to her; her whole conversation with the serpent, evinced that she knew it: and it was *positive*, "Thou shalt not eat of it." All our sins are of a similar character, as they are transgressions of laws, plain, known, and positive.

4. *The sin of Eve was a presumptuous act.* In eating of the fruit, she must have presumed that God was insincere in what he said; that his words were not the words of truth; that the death with which she was threatened would not be inflicted; that she would escape the punishment though she ventured on the sin. Such is the presumption of sinners generally: they do not dare to give the lie to God, by any verbal protestation, but they act as if they believed that God was insincere in what he has said, and many of them are given up to strong delusions to believe a lie.

5. *The sin of Eve was a ruinous act.* She no sooner became a sinner than she became a tempter; she gave unto her husband, and he did eat also; and thus ruin was entailed on their posterity. Whether Adam would have eaten without the seduction of Eve is uncertain. Adam was not deceived; he knew better: but such is the force of bad example, that Adam, intelligent and holy as he was, plunged himself into sin and misery, to follow the example of his wife. Sinners are not satisfied with standing alone; they press others into the snares by which they themselves are entangled.

From this subject we learn,

First, *The true character of original sin.* Man was created holy, but not immutable. How far immutability can be an attribute of any created being, I must leave. God gave our first parents a law, plain, positive, and easy to be kept. Could any thing be more reasonable? A being subject to no law is subject to no government, and accountable to no superior; and to suppose that God should make a being capable of obeying him, and yet give him no law as the test of his obedience, is absurd.

Secondly, *How much ought we to be on our guard against the attacks of enemies.* If Eve in Paradise met with an insidious foe, who beguiled her, how can we hope to escape temptations? "We should suspect some danger nigh, where we possess delight." "Watch and pray."

Thirdly, *That God will call us to an account for our conduct.* Eve little suspected, while feasting on the interdicted fruit, that God was near to judge her. Let us live with eternity in our view, and bring every thing to bear on the day of reckoning.

Fourthly. *To adore the mercy of God.* Man was spared, a Saviour was promised, and the designs of the devil were frustrated.

THE FIRST TRANSGRESSION CONDEMNED.

Gen. iii. 17, 18, 19. And unto Adam he said, Because thou hast hearkened unto the voice of thy wife, and hast eaten of the tree, of which I commanded thee, saying, Thou shalt not eat of it," &c. (Sk.)

In the first chapter of this book, we find the parents of our race created pure and upright, and placed on a state of trial. In the third, we are informed of their temptation and rebellion. And here we see their Maker and their Judge coming to call them to their account; to convict them of their crimes; and to pronounce their sentence. Our text more particularly records the crime proved, and the sentence pronounced.

I. THE CRIME PROVED.—Here we may remark, that the culprit does not dare to plead, "Not guilty." 'Tis true, he blames his temper, and indirectly blames God himself; yet he confesses the fact of his transgression, ver. 12. The judge condemns the criminal's conduct in several particulars. Instance,

1. *His listening and yielding to temptation;*—"Thou hast hearkened unto the voice of thy wife." From temptation none is exempt. Nor is there any sin in being tempted. See the difference between being tempted and yielding to temptation, in our Saviour's case, Matt. iv. 1—10. His resistance of *repeated* attempts was *prompt* and *firm*. By way of contrast, look at Eve, *parleying* with the tempter, and captivated by "the desire of the flesh, the desire of the eye, and the pride of life," ver. 1—6. Which of those examples should we follow? A proper answer must consist with the following observations.—*The relative situation of the tempter is no justification of our compliance.* Has he *been our benefactor?* Such was Adam's tempter. His "*help meet*," chap. ii. 13,—his only human support. The Hebrew children were *under great obligations;* yet they refused to to sin, Dan. iii. 12. Or may the person who tempts us be our friend *in future?* All Adam's hopes and expectations from human kind centered in her who offered him the forbidden fruit. But this did not excuse him. Even Balaam says, "I cannot go beyond," &c., Num. xxii. 18. See also Dan. iii. 15; Heb. xi. 24.—*The relation in which the tempter stands to us is no justification.* Earthly ties can, in no other case, be so close as those which bound the parties in this transaction here condemned. She was not only *his wife*, but literally, part of himself, ver. 20—24. Here our Lord's remarks, Matt. x. 32—36.—*The affection we may bear the tempter is no justification.* As it is now the duty of husbands to love their wives, so, without question, Adam in his best estate was not deficient in this part of his duty. Milton, indeed, supposes that his affection for "her, his sole delight," was the only cause of his fall; that

> ——————"He took and ate,
> Against his better knowledge; not deceived:
> But fondly overcome of female charm."

This view of the case seems to be supported by 1 Tim. ii. 14, "*Thou hast hearkened to the voice of thy wife.*" But

> "Consciences and souls are made,
> To be the Lord's alone."

2. *His neglect of God's word;*—"Which I commanded thee." Here is reference to *supreme authority;* "*I* commanded," who am *thy author*, &c.;—reference to *almost unlimited indulgence;* thou hast eaten of THE tree—the *only* prohibited one; and this excepted only as a test of obedience, and a means of thy confirmation in holiness, and of rising to a higher felicity;—reference to *friendly caution;* he was forewarned of danger. Yet see,

3. *His open, positive transgression of a known law;*—"I commanded thee," personally and plainly; but "*thou hast eaten.*" If, in the *first* transgression, we find, on the part of Eve, vain curiosity, sensuality, and ambition; and on that of Adam, insubordination and idolatry, we may also mark the like principles and operation in sin in general, Gen. xxxiv. 1; Deut. xxxii. 15; Rom. i. 25; James i. 14, 15.

II. The sentence pronounced;—" *Cursed is the ground*," &c. We notice here,

1. *Deprivation*—of all the *fruits and pleasures of Eden;* enjoyed while living in obedience. Man is driven forth from the garden, to procure "bread" —and "herbs" from a "*cursed*" land. Precisely the case of backsliders; who, like the prodigal, feed on husks. Hence the candid acknowledgment and prudent resolution, Hos. ii. 7.

2 *Toil;*—" In the sweat," &c. God, who made nothing in vain, intended that his creatures should exercise their powers. Holy angels are employed, Psa. ciii. 20; Heb. i. 14; so was innocent man, Gen. ii. 15. So is glorified man, Rev. vii. 15. But in sinful man, exercise degenerated into toil. So now, they who forsake God, *hew* cisterns, &c., Jer. ii. 13.

3. *Disappointment;*—" Thorns and thistles," &c. These shall interrupt thy labors, and mock thy hopes. See the effects of sin described, Haggai i. 6. Mark the caution, Prov. xxiii. 31. Whence,

4. *Sorrow;*—arising from vexatious disappointment,—from a recollection of loss,—from family feuds, chap. iv. 3,—from gloomy anticipations; and this continually: " In sorrow—all the days," &c.

5. *Increasing infirmity;*—" Till thou return," &c. Adam was created in full vigor, but now he began to "*return* to the dust." His body became the subject of dissolution; and he might look forward to the time when " the strong men should bow," &c., Eccl. xii. 2—5. " *Dying*, thou shalt die."

6. *Death itself;*—" Unto dust *shalt thou* return," &c. This the final proof of his folly. And this might be the consummation of his punishment. For,

7. *Justice is tempered with mercy.* The sentence is not immediately executed. The criminal has a *respite:* a *subsistence:* and an *opportunity of repentance.*

Let the subject teach us,

1. *A lesson of humility.* We are the degenerate children of such a parent.

2. *A lesson of caution.* Mark the *process* of falling. Satan presents some suitable object. We appear—desire—covet—throw off restraint—and transgress, in intention, and in fact. Mark the *danger* of falling. Our first parents fell from their paradisaical state, and by a small temptation. Wherefore, " watch," &c., Matt. xxvi. 41. For, mark the *consequences* of falling. All the evils we feel or fear.

3. *A lesson of encouragement.* Respited we may recover our Eden, by means of " the second Adam, the Lord from heaven." Contrast—the first involving himself and us in guilt, pollution, and misery—the second the reverse of this, Rom. v. 12—21.

THE EXTENT OF MAN'S DEPRAVITY.

Rom. iii. 10—20.—It is written, There is none righteous, no not one: there is none that understandeth, there is none that seeketh after God. They are all gone out of the way, they are together become unprofitable, there is none that doeth good, no not one. Their throat is an open sepulchre; with their tongues they have used deceit; the poison of asps is under their lips: whose mouth is full of cursing and bitterness. Their feet are swift to shed blood. Destruction and misery are in their ways: and the way of peace have they not known. There is no fear of God before their eyes. Now we know that what things soever the law saith, it saith to them who are under the law: that every mouth may be stopped, and all the world may become guilty before God. Therefore by the deeds of the law there shall no flesh be justified in his sight. (S. S)

The scriptures are the only, and infallible source of divine knowledge—
To them the apostles continually refer in support of their doctrines—
No subject is capable of more ample proof from them than that before us—
St. Paul is shewing that all mankind are guilty and depraved—
In confirmation of this he cites many passages from the Old Testament—See Ps. xiv. 1–3. Prov. i. 16, 18. Isa. lix. 7, 8.
From these, as stated and improved in the text, we are led to consider,
I. The representation which the scripture gives of our state.
The testimonies here adduced, declare, that the most lamentable depravity pervades,
1. All ranks and orders of men.
"There is none righteous, no not one"—*
Righteousness is a conformity of heart and life to the law of God—
Where is the man on earth that possesses it by nature?—
Where is the man whose deviations from this standard have not been innumerable?—
"There is none that understandeth."
The natural man has no discernment of spiritual things—1 Cor. ii. 14.
His practical judgment is in favor of sin and the world—
"There is none that seeketh after God."
The things of time and sense are diligently pursued—
But whoever cultivates divine knowledge, or seriously enquires after God? Job xxxv. 10.
"All are gone out of the way."
Men universally prefer the way of self-righteousness to that of faith in Christ—
And that of sin and self-indulgence to holiness and self-denial—
No one that sees them would imagine, that they really intended to tread in the steps of Christ and his apostles—
"They are together become unprofitable."
God has formed us for his own glory, and each others good—
But unregenerate men never attempt to answer these ends of their creation—†
Hence they are justly compared to things worthless and vile—Luke xiv 34, 35, and John xv. 6.
"There is none that doeth good, no not one."
Nothing is really good, which is not so in its principle, rule, and end—‡
But where is the action of any natural man that will stand this test?—
2. All the faculties and powers of men.
Nothing is more offensive than an open sepulchre; Matt. xxiii. 27; or more venomous than an asp—

*The apostle has so arranged his quotations as to form a beautiful climax, every subsequent passage affirming more than that which precedes it.

†They may do good to the bodies of men; but never shew any real solicitude about their souls. Indeed, how should they, when they care not for their own souls?

‡The fear and love of God are the *principle*, the scriptures the *rule*, and God's glory the *end* of Christian obedience, 1 Cor. x. 31.

Yet both the one and the other fitly represent the effusions of a carnal heart—

"Out of the abundance of the heart the mouth will speak"—

Deceit, calumny, invective, yea, in many instances, the most horrible oaths and execrations will proceed from it—*

Hence that awful description of the human tongue—James iii. 6.

From *words* we are ready also to proceed to *actions*, yea, even the most cruel and atrocious—

Who that sees with what readiness nations engage in war, will question the declaration in the text?—

Hazael revolted at the idea of murder, when warned of his propensity to commit it; yet notwithstanding his present feelings, how "*swift* were his feet to shed blood!"—2 Kings viii. 12, 13, with ib. ver. 15, and xiii. 7.

How many at this day are impelled by shame even to destroy their own offspring!—

How frequently do men engage in duels on account of the slightest injury or insult!

And in how many instances might we ourselves, when irritated and inflamed, have committed murder in an unguarded moment, exactly as others have done, who in a cooler moment would have shuddered at the thought!—

The instance of David, who, though "a man after God's own heart," murdered Uriah, and many others with him, to conceal his shame, is sufficient of itself to shew us, what the best of men might commit, if left to themselves—2 Sam. xi. 14—17.

Well we may apply to this subject that humiliating language of the prophet—Isa. i. 5, 6.

Thus, God himself being witness, instead of walking in "paths of peace" and safety, we all by nature prefer the "ways which bring destruction and misery" both on ourselves and all around us—Ps. xxxvi. 1.

The whole of our state is properly summed up in *this*, that "there is no fear of God before our eyes; so entirely are our understandings blinded, and our hearts alienated from him, by means of our innate depravity—†

This humiliating view of our state should lead us to consider,

II. The inferences to be deduced from it.

Those which the apostle suggests in the text will suffice for our attention at this time—

1. We are all "guilty before God"

It seems inconceivable to many, that they should really be obnoxious to everlasting misery in hell—

And they will plead their own cause with zeal and eloquence—

If they concede it with respect to some more heinous transgressors, they will deny it in reference to themselves—

But God has taken care that "*every* mouth should be stopped"—

It is not possible to express the universality of men's wickedness more strongly than it is expressed in the words before us—‡

*No less than four expressions, and those exceeding strong, are used to declare the evils of the tongue.

†Verse 16 and 17, relate primarly to the evil which men do to *others*, though they may include what they do to themselves. See Isaiah lix. 7, 8.

‡"None, no not one;" "none; none; none, no not one;" "all; all together;" "every mouth;" even "all the world." Can any, after this, fancy himself an exception?

All then must "become guilty before God," and acknowledge their desert of his wrath and indignation—

They must feel their desert of condemnation, as much as a man that has been condemned for parricide feels the justice of the sentence which is pronounced against him—

O that we might all be brought to such unfeigned contrition! we should "not then be far from the kingdom of God"—Ps. li. 17.

2. We can never be justified by any works of our own.

"We *know* that what the law saith, it saith unto them that are under the law"—

Now the law saith, "Do this and live: transgress it, and thou shalt die"—Rom. x. 5; Gal. iii. 10.

But it speaks not one word about mitigating its demand to the weak, or its penalties to the guilty—

How then can any man "be justified by the works of the law?"—

Can a man be guilty, and not guilty? or can he be condemned by the law and yet justified at the same time, and in the same respects?—

Let all hope then, and all thought of justification by the law be put away from us for ever—

God has provided a better way for our justification, namely, through the blood and righteousness of his dear Son—Rom. iii. 21, 22.

And to lead us into that way was the intention of the apostle in citing the passages that have already been considered—

Let us improve this humiliating representation for this salutary end—

So shall we be "justified freely by grace, through the redemption that is in Christ Jesus"—Ib. ver. 24.

UNIVERSAL CORRUPTION OF MANKIND.

Psalm liii. 2, 3.—God looked down from heaven upon the children of men, to see if there were any that did understand, that did seek God. Every one of them is gone back, they are altogether become filthy, there is none that doeth good, no not one. (Pr.)

This is not merely a description of the state of mankind in David's time, but a description of human nature at all times, and is applied by an apostle to the state of the world many hundreds of years after the words were written. Rom. iii. 10—12.

I. Seeking the Lord is here supposed to be the criterion of a good understanding.

That it is so, will easily be made apparent; and these two things are with great propriety connected together. It is only "the fool that saith in his heart, there is no God;" a true understanding sees it to be well for the universe that there is a God, and that it would be every one's interest to seek and obey him. Psa. xcvii. 1.

1. Seeking the Lord includes our *choosing the best good for our portion*, and supposes that we are seeking a happiness superior to what this world can afford. This is what the truest wisdom would dictate: but this blessedness is only to be found in God, whose lovingkindness is better than life Communion and intercourse with him is the sum of all enjoyment; his ser

vice is its own reward, and those who have truly entered into it would never wish to go out free. Psa. xix. 10, 11, xxvii. 4.

2. Seeking the Lord includes *repentance for sin;* and this is what a good understanding would lead to, for it is altogether consonant with right reason. Job. v. 8. If nothing but our own interest were consulted, it would lead to this; and hence it is said of the prodigal when he repented, that he came to himself, and he that had been lost was found. Luke xv. 17.

3. It includes the sacrifice of every earthly good *for his sake*, and accounting his favor to be better than life. This is what a good understanding would approve, it being its proper province to form a just estimate of things. Who then acted the wiser part, Esau who sold his birthright, or Jabez who desired it that he might be blessed indeed? Who gave the best proof of a good understanding, Cain in leaving his native country because God was there; or Moses in forsaking Egypt because the Lord was not there? Was the rich man in the gospel, wise in setting his heart upon the good things of this life; or David, who desired not to have his portion with the men of this world. Psa. xvii. 5.

4. Seeking the Lord includes the resting all our hopes of salvation *upon the promises of his word:* and this is what a right understanding would approve. Hence he is called a wise man who built his house upon a rock; and he whose hope is in the promises of God, to the exclusion of every other ground of confidence, is equally wise and safe. There is no other door of hope, no other way of acceptance, but what is provided in the promises of the gospel.

II. All men by nature are corrupt, and utterly destitute of this understanding. "There is none that doeth good, no not one."

1. The loss of the divine favor is *the greatest of all evils*, and yet no one lays it to heart, or is careful to seek after it.— — —It might have been expected that men would have seen their folly in forsaking him, the fountain of living waters; would have had their eyes open to behold the tempter, who at first seduced them from God, and be anxious to return unto him from whom they have deeply revolted. Instead of this, there is none that understandeth, none that seeketh after God.— — —It is also the greatest of all evils that God has departed from us, and that he hides his face in anger. His favor is lost and gone; we are now without hope, without God in the world, and have no friend in time of need. We and all that we possess, are under the curse.— — —To be contented in such a state, and indifferent about the favor of God, is truly dreadful: yet such is the case with all men by nature.

2. God visits men with *such afflictions*, and brings them into such circumstances, as are directly adapted to make them feel their need of him: and yet God is not in all their thoughts. Job. xxxiii. 15.— — —Men either imagine that God does not see the evils with which they are visited, or that it is better to seek relief from any other quarter; like Ahaziah, who sent to the God of Ekron in a time of sickness, as if there were no God in Israel. 2 Kings i. 2, 3. It might be expected that sickness and death would lead men to seek after God; but no, there is none that understandeth, and the workers of iniquity have no knowledge.

3. By nature we have *no love to God*, and therefore do not seek him.— — —The object of our affection is necessarily an object of desire; nothing but enmity, or the most perfect indifference, can render us unmindful of the

friendship of God. And what an insult is offered to the Majesty of heaven, that we have lost his favor, and are indifferent about it.

4. Men are full of *pride and self-sufficiency*, and hence they do not seek after God. Psa. x. 4. Religion is too mean for their notice, and fit only for the attention of the vulgar. Many say in their hearts with Pharaoh, who is the Lord that I should obey his voice?— — —Great things are promised to them that seek the Lord; they shall be sure to find him, and obtain the remission of their sins; yet these promises are diregarded, and God is utterly forgotten.

III. The Lord keeps a strict eye upon the conduct of men towards him: "He looked down from heaven to see if there were any that did understand, that did seek God."

But though "every one of them is gone back, and they are altogether become filthy;" yet some are distinguished by grace, and there is a generation of them that seek thy face, oh God of Jacob. Psa. xxiv. 6. His eye is upon all such, and he will be found of them in truth; they shall never seek his face in vain. Isa. xlv. 9. He heard Ephraim when he was mourning alone, and solitary; and Jonah when he cried unto him out of the belly of hell. Jer. xxxi. 18. Those who repent and return to God, shall find him like the father of the prodigal, ready to forgive.

The Lord also notices those who do not seek him, and his eye is upon all their ways. He sees the wicked preferences of the heart, all their pride and contempt of him. Awful thought, to be under his inspection while utterly regardless of his presence, and sinning against heaven and before him.

How great is the loving kindness of God in promising salvation to them that seek him; and how inexcusable to neglect and forsake so much mercy. What bitterness will it add to the reflection, that all is lost through our own wilful neglect; and that God is for ever far from us, because we desired not the knowledge of his ways. Prov. i. 28—31.

SIN THE OFFSPRING OF OUR OWN HEARTS.

Jam. i. 13—15.—Let no man say, when he is tempted, I am tempted of God: for God cannot be tempted with evil, neither tempteth he any man: but every man is tempted, when he is drawn away of his own lust, and enticed. Then when lust hath conceived, it bringeth forth sin; and sin, when it is finished, bringeth forth death. (H. H.)

There are temptations necessarily connected with the christian life, and which often, through the weakness of our nature, become the *occasions* of sin: and there are other temptations which are the direct and immediate *cause* of sin. The former are external; the latter are within a man's own bosom. The former may be referred to God as their author, and be considered as a ground of joy: the latter must be traced to our own wicked hearts; and are proper grounds of the deepest humiliation. This distinction is made in the passage before us. In the foregoing verses the former are spoken of; ver. 2, 12, in the text, the latter.

In the words of our text, we notice the *origin*, the *growth*, and the *issue of sin*. We notice,

I. ITS ORIGIN—

Many are ready to trace their sin to God himself—

This is done when we say, "I could not help it:" for then we reflect on our Make, as not enduing us with strength sufficient for our necessities. It is done also, though not quite so directly, when we ascribe our fall to those who were in some respect accessary to it: for then we blame the providence of God, as before we did his creative power. It was thus that Adam acted, when he imputed his transgression to the influence of his wife, and ultimately to God who gave her to him. Gen. iii. 12.

But God neither is, nor can be, the Author of sin—

He may, and does, try men, in order to exercise their graces, and to shew what he has done for their souls. Thus he tempted Abraham, and Job, and Joseph, and many others. But these very instances prove that he did not necessitate, or in any respect influence, them to sin; for they shone the brighter in proportion as they were tried. But he never did, nor ever will, lead any man into sin. And though he is said to have "hardened Pharaoh's heart," and to have "moved David to number the people," he did not either of these things in any other way than by leaving them to themselves. Exod. iv. 21, and 2 Sam. xxiv. 1, with 2 Chron. xxxii. 31.

All sin must be traced to the evil propensities of our own nature—

"A clean thing cannot be brought out of an unclean;" and therefore no descendant of Adam can be free from sin. We have within us a secret bias to sin; which, however good our direction appear to be, operates at last to turn us from God. That bias is called "lust," or desire, or concupiscence: and it works in all, though in a great variety of degrees and manner. All sin is fruit proceeding from this root, even from "the lust that wars in our members;" and in whatever channel our iniquity may run, it must be traced to that as its genuine and proper source.

This will appear more strongly, while we mark,

II. ITS GROWTH—

It first formation in the soul is often slow and gradual—

"Lust," or our inward propensity to sin, presents something to our imagination as likely to gratify us in a high degree. Whether it be profit, or pleasure, or honor, we survey it with a longing eye, and thereby our desire after it is inflamed. Conscience perhaps suggests that it is forbidden fruit which we are coveting; and that, as being prohibited, it will ultimately tend rather to produce misery than happiness. In opposition to this, our sinful principle intimates a doubt whether the gratification be forbidden; or at least whether, in our circumstances, the tasting of it be not very allowable: at all events, it suggests that our fellow-creatures will know nothing respecting it; that we may easily repent of the evil; and that God is very ready to forgive; and that many who have used far greater liberties are yet happy in heaven; and that consequently we may enjoy the object of our desire, without suffering any loss or inconvenience. In this manner the affections are kindled, and the will is bribed to give its consent:* then the bait is swallowed, the hook is fastened within us; and we are "dragged away"† from God, from duty, from happiness; yea, if God do not seasonably interpose, we are drawn to everlasting perdition.

Its progress to maturity is generally rapid—

The metaphor of a fetus formed in the womb, and brought afterwards to

* Isa. xliv. 20. See this whole process illustrated, Gen. iii. 1—6.

† These seems to be the precise ideas intended to be conveyed by δελεαζόμενος Σ ἐξελκόμενος.

the birth, is frequently used in scripture in reference to sin. Job xv. 35, Ps. vii. 14, with the text. When the will has consented to comply with the suggestions of the evil principle, then the embryo of sin is, if we may so speak, formed within us; and nothing remains but for time and opportunity to bring it forth. This of course must vary with the circumstances under which we are: our wishes may be accomplished, or may prove abortive: but whether our desire be fulfilled or not, sin is imputed to us, because it formally exists within us: or rather it is brought to the birth, though not altogether in the way we hoped and expected.

We proceed to notice,

III. Its issue—

Sin was never barren: its issue is numerous as the sands upon the sea-shore: but in every instance the name of its first-born has been "death." Death is,

1. Its penalty—

Death is temporal, spiritual, and eternal, was threatened as the punishment of transgression while our first parents were yet in paradise. And on many occasions has the threatening been renewed, Ezek. xviii. 4, Rom. i. 18, and vi. 21, 23, Gal. iii. 10— — —So that sin and death are absolutely inseparable.

2. Its desert—

The fixing of death as the consequence of trangression was no arbitrary appointment. The penal evil of death is no more than the moral evil of sin. Consider the extreme malignity of sin: What rebellion against God! What a dethroning of God from our hearts! What a preferring of Satan himself, and his service, to God's light and easy yoke! View it as it is seen in the agonies and death of God's only Son: Can that be of small malignity which so oppressed and overwhelmed "Jehovah's fellow?" Of those who are now suffering the torments of the damned, not one would dare to arraign the justice of God, or to say that his punishment exceeded his offence: whatever we in our present state may think, our mouths will all be shut, when we have juster views, and an experimental sense, of the bitterness of sin. Matt. xxii. 12.

3. Its tendency—

We may see the proper effect of sin in the conduct of Adam, when he fled from God, whom he had been accustomed to meet with familiarity and joy. Gen. iii. 8. He felt a consciousness that his soul was bereft of innocence; and he was unable to endure the sight of Him whom he had so greatly offended. In the same manner sin affects our minds: it indisposes us for communion with God; it unfits us for holy exercises: and, if a person under the guilt and dominion of it were admitted into heaven, he would be unable to participate the blessedness of those around him; and would rather hide himself under rocks and mountains, than dwell in the immediate presence of an holy God. Annihilation would be to him the greatest favor that could be bestowed upon him; so truly does the Apostle say, that "the motions of sin do work in our members to bring forth fruit unto death." Rom. vii. 5.

Advice—

1. Do not palliate sin—

Though circumstances doubtless may either lesson or increase the guilt of sin, nothing under heaven can render it light or venial. Our temptations may be great; but nothing can hurt us, if we do not ourselves concur with the tempter. That wicked fiend exercised all his malice against our adorable

Lord; but could not prevail, because there was nothing in him to second or assist his efforts. So neither could he overcome us, if we did not voluntarily submit to his influence. All sin therefore must be traced to the evil dispositions of our own hearts; and consequently affords us a just occasion to humble ourselves before God in dust and ashes. If we presume to reflect on God as the author of our sin, we increase our guilt an hundred-fold: it is only in abasing ourselves that we can at all hope for mercy and forgiveness.

2. Do not trifle with temptation—

We carry about with us much inflammable matter, if we may so speak; and temptation strikes the spark which produces an explosion. How readily are evil thoughts suggested by what we see or hear; and how strongly do they fix upon the mind. "Behold how great a matter a little fire kindleth!" Let us then stand at a distance from the places, the books, the company that may engender sin. And let us, in conformity with our Lord's advice, "watch and pray, that we enter not into temptation."

3. Do not for one moment neglect the Saviour—

There is none but Jesus that can stand between sin and death. Indeed even "he overcame death only by dying in our stead: and we can escape it only by believing in him. We deserve death: we have deserved it for every sin we have ever committed. Ten thousand deaths are our proper portion

Let us then look to Him who died for us. Let us look to him, not only for the sins committed long ago, but for those of daily incursion. Our best act would condemn us, if he did not "bear the iniquity of our holy things." He is our only deliverer from the wrath to come: to Him therefore let us flee continually, and "cleave unto him with full purpose of heart."

MEN'S HATRED OF THE LIGHT.

John iii. 19—21.—This is the condemnation, that light is come into the world, and men loved darkness rather than light, because their deeds were evil. For every one that doeth evil, hateth the light, neither cometh to the light, lest his deeds should be reproved. But he that doeth truth cometh to the light, that his deeds may be made manifest, that they are wrought in God. (H. H.)

It appears strange to many, that the everlasting happiness or misery of the soul should be made to depend on the exercise of faith. The declaration of our Lord, That "he that believeth shall be saved, and he that believeth not shall be damned," is regarded by them as "a hard saying:" they see no proportion between the work and the reward on the one hand, or between the offence and the punishment on the other. In the words before us we have a solution of the difficulty. We are taught that faith and unbelief are not mere operations of the mind, but exercises of the heart; the one proceeding from a love to what is good; the other from a radical attachment to evil. Our blessed Lord had repeatedly inculcated the necessity of believing in him, in order to a participation of his proffered benefits. He had also represented unbelievers as "already condemned," even like criminals reserved for execution. To obviate any objection which might arise in the mind of Nicodemus in relation to the apparent severity of this sentence, he proceeded to shew the true ground of it, namely, That, in their rejection of him, men are actuated by an invincible love of sin, and by a consequent hatred of the light which is sent to turn them from sin.

In opening the words of our text, we shall shew,

I. WHAT IS THAT LIGHT WHICH IS COME INTO THE WORLD—

Christ is called "The light of the world," "The true light," "The Day-star," and "The Sun of righteousness that arises with healing in his wings." But,

It is *the Gospel* which is here said to have "come into the world"—

The glad tidings of salvation were now published by Christ himself; and both the manner in which that salvation was to be effected, and the manner in which it was to be received, were clearly revealed. Our blessed Lord had in this very discourse with Nicodemus declared, that "the Son of Man was to be lifted up upon the cross, as the serpent had been in the wilderness," in order that all who were dying of the wounds of sin might look to him and be healed. He had repeated again and again this important truth, on which the salvation of our fallen race depends. This mystery had from eternity been hid in the bosom of the Father; but now it was made fully manifest. *This* "light was now come into the world."

The gospel, in this view of it, is fitly designated under the metaphor of "light"—

Light is that, without which no one thing can be discerned aright.— And how ignorant are we, till the light of the gospel shines in our hearts! We know nothing of ourselves, of God, of Christ, or of the way to heaven. We cannot even appreciate the value of the soul, the importance of time, the emptiness of earthly vanities. We may indeed give our assent to the statements which we hear made upon these subjects; but we cannot have an experimental and abiding sense, even of the most obvious truths, till our minds are enlightened by the gospel of Christ.

Light causes all other things to be seen in their true colors.—Thus does also the gospel: in setting forth the Son of God as dying for our sins, it shews us the malignity of sin; the justice of God which required such an atonement for it; and, above all, the wonderful love of God, in giving us his only dear Son, in order that we might have peace through the blood of his cross.

Light carries its own evidence along with it.—Thus does also that glorious gospel of which we are speaking: it is so peculiarly suited to the necessities of man, and at the same time so commensurate with his wants; it is so calculated to display and magnify all the perfections of the Deity, and is in every respect so worthy of its Divine Author; that it commends itself to us instantly as of heavenly origin, the very master-piece of Divine wisdom.

One would imagine that such light should be universally welcomed: but since this is not the case, we shall proceed to shew,

II. WHENCE IT IS THAT MEN REJECT IT—

It is but too evident, that, as in former ages, so now also, men reject the light. But whence does this arise?

It is not because they have any sufficient reason to reject it—

If there were any thing in the gospel that rendered it unworthy of men's regard, they would have some excuse for rejecting it. But,

They cannot say that it is *inapplicable in its nature.*—We will appeal to the world, and ask, What is there, that guilty and helpless sinners would desire? Would they wish for a Saviour? Would they be glad that the whole work of salvation should be committed into his hands? Would they be especially desirous that nothing should be required of them, but to receive with gratitude, and improve with diligence, what the Saviour offers them? In short, would they be glad of a free and full salvation? *This* is precisely such a salvation as is provided for them in the gospel.

They cannot say that it is *inadequate in its provisions.*—If the gospel brought salvation to those only who were possessed of some amiable qualities, or to those who had committed only a certain number of offences; if it made any limitation or exception whatever in its offers of mercy; if it provided pardon, but not strength, or grace to begin our course, but not grace to persevere; if, in short, it omitted any one thing which any sinner in the universe could need, then some persons might say, It is not commensurate with my necessities. But we defy the imagination of man to conceive any case which the gospel cannot reach, or any want which it cannot satisfy.

They cannot say that it is *unreasonable in its demands.*—It does indeed require an unreserved surrender of ourselves to God: and on this account it appears to many to be strict and severe. But let any one examine all its prohibitions and all its commands, and he will find them all amounting in fact to these two; "Do thyself no harm;" and, "Seek to be as happy as thy heart can wish." If there be any thing in the gospel which bears a different aspect, it is owing entirely to our ignorance of its real import. The more thoroughly the gospel is understood, the more worthy of acceptation will it invariably appear.

The only true reason is, that they "hate the light"—

Till men are truly converted to God, "their deeds are universally evil;" yea "every imagination of the thoughts of their hearts is evil, only evil, continually." Now the gospel is a light which shews their deeds in their proper colors.

It reproves their ways.—They have been "calling good evil, and evil good; and putting bitter for sweet, and sweet for bitter." In reference to these things, it undeceives them. It declares plainly, that they who do such things as they have done, and perhaps have accounted innocent, shall not inherit the kingdom of God.

It mortifies their pride.—It not only shews them that they are obnoxious to the wrath of God, but that they are incapable of averting his displeasure by any thing which they themselves can do. It brings down the proud Pharisee, and places him on a level with publicans and harlots. It requires every man to acknowledge himself a debtor to divine grace for every good thing that he either has or hopes for. All this is extremely humiliating to our proud nature.

It inculcates duties which they are unwilling to perform.—Humility and self-denial, renunciation of the world and devotedness to God, enduring of shame and glorying in the cross; these, and many other duties, it enjoins, which to our carnal and corrupt nature are hateful in the extreme; yet the gospel inculcates them with a strictness not to be lowered, a plainness not to be misinterpreted, and an authority not to be withstood.

These, these are the grounds on which the gospel is rejected. If it would admit of persons following their own ways, or of their accommodating its precepts to their own views or interests, they would give it a favorable reception. But as it requires all to be cast into the very mould which it has formed, and will tolerate not the smallest wilful deviation from its rules, it is, and must be, odious in the eyes of the ungodly; "they love darkness rather than it; nor will they come to it, lest their deeds should be reproved."

A just view of these things will prepare us for contemplating,

III. Their guilt and danger in rejecting it—

Doubtless every kind of sin will be a ground of "condemnation." But men's hatred of the light is that which chiefly, and above all other things,

1. Aggravates their guilt—

The gospel is a most wonderful provision for the salvation of fallen man. It is the brightest display of divine wisdom, and the most stupendous effort of divine goodness. The rejection of this therefore, especially as proceeding from a hatred of it, argues such a state of mind as no words can adequately express. The malignity of such a disposition rises in proportion to the excellence of the gospel itself. We presume not to weigh the comparative guilt of men and devils, because the scriptures have not given us sufficient grounds whereon to institute such a comparison: but the guilt of those who reject the gospel far exceeds that of the heathen world: the wickedness of Tyre and Sidon, yea, of Sodom and Gomorrah, was not equal to that of the unbelieving Jews: nor was the guilt of those Jews, who rejected only the warnings of the prophets, comparable to that of those who despised the ministry of our Lord. In like manner, they who live under the meridian light of the gospel in this day will have still more, if possible, to answer for, than the hearers of Christ himself; because his work and offices are now more fully exhibited, and more generally acknowledged. And in the day of judgment the gospel will be as a millstone round the neck of those who rejected it: not having been a savor of life unto their salvation, it will be a savor of death unto their more aggravated condemnation.

2. Insures their punishment—

If men did not hate the gospel itself, there would be some hope that they might in due time embrace it, and be converted by it. If they would even come to the light in order that the true quality of their works might be made manifest, then we might hope that they would be convinced of their wickedness, and be constrained to flee from the wrath to come. But when they dispute against the truth, and rack their invention in order to find out objections against it; when they indulge all manner of prejudices against the gospel; when they withdraw themselves from the ministry of those who faithfully preach it, and say, as it were, to their minister, "Prophesy unto us smooth things, prophesy deceits;" what hope can there be of such persons? Their hearts are so hardened, that it is scarcely possible to make any impression upon them: if a ray of light do shine into their minds, they will endeavor to extinguish it as soon as possible; they will go to business, to pleasure, to company, yea, to intoxication itself, in order to stifle the voice of conscience, and to recover their former delusive peace. Alas! they are not only perishing of a fatal disorder, but they reject with disdain the only remedy that can do them good: they therefore must die, because they persist in drinking of the poisonous cup that is in their hands, and dash from their lips the only antidote and cure.

Application—

In so saying, thou reprovest *us*—

Behold! we declare unto you, that light, even the glorious light of the gospel of Christ, is now come into the world ———

Ye *lovers of darkness*, reject not this blessed gospel. Little can sin contribute to your happiness, even while you are most capable of tasting its pleasures: but what it can do for you in a dying hour, or in the day of judgment, it is needless for me to say. Let it not then keep you from coming to the light. Surely it is better that "your deeds should be reproved," while you have opportunity to amend them, than that you should continue in them till you experience their bitter consequences. You would not travel in the dark when you could enjoy the light of day, or refuse the assistance of a guide that would lead you into the path which you professed to seek. Only then act for your souls as you would do in your temporal concerns, and all shall yet be well. Believe in Christ, and you shall yet be saved by him; as well from the commission of sin, as from the condemnation due to it.

Ye *who profess to love the light*, be careful to "walk as children of the light." Bring every thing to the touchstone of God's word. Try your spirit and temper, as well as your words and actions by this test. See whether you take the precepts of Christ as your rule, and his example as your pattern. For the sake of the world too, as well as for your own comfort, you should come continually to the light. If you would conciliate their regard for the gospel, or remove their prejudice from yourselves, you should "*make your works manifest* that they are wrought in God." You should let your light shine before men, that they, seeing your good works, may glorify your Father that is in heaven.

VILENESS AND IMPOTENCY OF THE NATURAL MAN.

Rom. viii. 7, 8. The carnal mind is enmity against God; for it is not subject to the law of God, neither indeed can be. So then they that are in the flesh cannot please God. (H. H.)

To those who know not what is in the heart of man, it must appear strange that persons not very dissimilar in their outward conduct should be adjudged to widely different states in the eternal world. But in the most imperfect of the regenerate, there is a predominant principle of love to God; whereas in the best of unregenerate men there is a rooted enmity against him: and this alone places their characters as far asunder as heaven and hell.

St. Paul has been speaking of the final issues to which a carnal and a spiritual mind will lead: and because it may seem unaccountable that the one should terminate in death, while the other is productive of eternal life and peace, he assigns the reason of it, and shews that the carnal mind is enmity against God, and that a person under its influence is incapable of rendering him any acceptable service.

In the Apostle's words there are three things to be considered,

I. His assertion—

The mind here spoken of, is that which actuates every unregenerate man—

"The carnal mind" does not necessarily imply a disposition grossly sensual; it is (as it is explained in verse 5) a savoring of earthly and carnal thing in preference to things spiritual and heavenly. And this is the disposition that rules in the heart of every Child of man— — —

This "mind is enmity against God"—

There is not one of God's perfections, to which this disposition is not adverse. It deems his holiness too strict, his justice too severe, his truth too inflexible; and even his mercy itself is hateful to them, on account of the humiliating way in which it is exercised. Even the very existence of God is so odious to them, that they say in their hearts, "I wish there were no God." Psa. xiv. 1. He did once put himself into their power; and they shewed what was the desire of their hearts by destroying his life; and, if they could have annihilated his very being, they would, no doubt, have gladly done it.

This mind is not merely inimical to God, for then it might be reconciled; but it is "enmity" itself against him, and must therefore be slain, before the soul can ever be brought to the service and enjoyment of God.

This assertion, though strong, will not be thought too strong, when we consider,

II. His proof—

The carnal mind "is not subject to the law of God"—

The law requires that we should love God supremely, and our neighbor as ourselves. But the carnal mind prefers the world before God, and self before his neighbor. There are different degrees indeed, in which a worldly and selfish spirit may prevail; but it has more or less the ascendant over every natural man; nor is there an unregenerate person in the universe who cordially and unreservedly submits to this law.

It not only is not subject to God's law, but "it cannot be"—

There is the same contrariety between the carnal mind and the law of God, as there is between darkness and light- It has been shewn before, that the carnal mind is enmity itself against God; and that the very first principle of obedience to the law is *love*. Now how is it possible that enmity should produce love? "We may sooner expect to gather grapes of thorns, or figs of thistles."

This incapacity to obey the law of God is justly adduced as a proof of our enmity against him: for if we loved him, we should love his will; and if we hate his will. whatever we may pretend, we in reality hate him.

A due consideration of the Apostle's argument will secure our assent to,

III. His inference—

We cannot please God but by obeying his law. All external compliances are worthless in his eyes, if not accompanied with the love and devotion of the soul. But such obedience cannot be rendered by the carnal mind; and consequently they who are in the flesh, that is, are under the influence of a carnal mind, "cannot please God:" they may be admired by their fellow-creatures; but whatever they do will be an abomination in the sight of God.

This is so plain, that it scarcely admits of any confirmation: yet it may be confirmed by the Articles of our Church, which plainly and unequivocally speak the same language. Art. 10th and 13th.

On the whole then we may learn, from this subject,

1. The grounds and reasons of the Gospel—

The principal doctrines of the Gospel have their foundation, not in any arbitrary appointment of the Deity, but in the nature and necessities of man. We must seek reconciliation with God through Christ, because we are "enemies to him in our minds by wicked works." We must seek the renewing influences of the Spirit, because our nature is altogether corrupt, and incapable of either serving or enjoying God. When therefore we hear of the indispensible necessity of being born again, and of the impossibility of being saved except by faith in Christ, let us remember that these are not the dogmas of a party, but doctrines consequent upon our fallen state, and therefore of universal and infinite importance: and that, if we were to be silent on these subjects, we should be unfaithful to our trust, and betray your souls to everlasting ruin.

2. The suitableness and excellence of its provisions—

If man were commanded to reconcile himself to God, or to renovate his own nature, he must sit down in despair. Darkness could as soon generate light, as fallen man could effect either of these things. But we are not left without hope: God has provided such a Saviour as we want, to mediate between him and us: and such an Agent as we want, to form us anew after the Divine image. Lt us then embrace this Gospel, and seek to experience its blessings. Let us, as guilty creatures, implore remission through the blood of Jesus; and, as corrupt creatures beg the Holy Spirit to work effectually in us, and to render us meet for a heavenly inheritance.

IMPERFECTION OF OUR BEST SERVICES.

Iasiah lxiv. 6.—We are all as an unclean thing; and all our righteousnesses are as filthy rags. (H. H.)

Humility is that grace which is most suited to our condition as fallen creatures; and, that we may be assisted in the pursuit of it, God has graciously given us, not only promises for our encouragement, but patterns for our imitation, and models for our use. We cannot have any more instructive pattern that which is exhibited in the repenting Publican, or in the returning Prodigal. Of models, that which David has left us, in the fifty-first psalm, is perhaps the most distinguished, and of most general utility: but that which is contained in this, and part of the preceding chapter, excepting only some few expressions, is almost equally applicable to the christian world. The whole of it is a prayer drawn up by the prophet for the use of the Jews, when they should be in captivity in Babylon. We shall not enter into it at large, but shall confine our attention to the passage which we have just read, which most justly describes our state before God,

I. In general terms—

There were many things considered as unclean under the Jewish dispensation: and whosoever touched them, was deemed unclean; and, till he had been purified according to the law, he was kept both from the house of God and from all his fellow-creatures, lest he should communicate to others the defilement which he had contracted. Hence, when the prophet says, "We are all as an unclean thing," he must be understood to say, that we are,

1. Unclean in ourselves—

Who can look inward for one moment, and not confess this melancholy truth?—

2. Defiling to others—

The whole of our intercourse with each other tends to foster some vile affection, some "earthly, sensual, or devilish" inclination— — —

3. In a state of separation from God and his people—

We have by nature no delight in God: we are averse to his service, his worship, his people; our "carnal minds are enmity against him," and against every thing that leads to him, or sets him before our eyes— — —We "say continually in our hearts, Depart from us; we desire not the knowledge of thy ways."

Wretched as our state appears from this representation, the prophet sets it forth in a far more humiliating view,

II. By a particular comparison—

In the former clause of the text the prophet speaks of us as we are *on the whole:* but in the latter part he speaks of our "*righteousnesses*" *only:* and these he compares to a leprous garment, which by God's express command was to be consigned to the flames. The truth of this comparison appears, in that all our best deeds are,

1. Defective—

If we measure them by a standard of our own, we may discern no flaw in them: but the perfect law of God is that by which they must be tried: and where has there been one action of our lives that has fully come up to that standard?— — —We are required to love God with all our heart, and all our mind, and all our soul, and all our strength; and our neighbor as ourselves: but what duty that we ever performed to God or man will stand this test?— — —Hence we must confess, that every thing we have done has been impure in the sight of God— — —

2. Mixed with sin—

Pride and self-righteousness cleave to us as long as we are in an unconverted state; and the more exemplary our conduct is, the more it calls forth, and seems to justify, those hateful propensities. Let the most moral person look into his own heart, and see whether, instead of being filled with self-lothing and self-abhorrence on account of his defects, he do not find a self-preference and self-complacency arising in his heart, and prompting him to say, like the elated Pharisee, "I thank thee, O God, that I am not as other men." Now this is a fly, that would render the most precious ointment offensive. Eccl. x. 1. While such a disposition as this is harbored in our hearts, we, and all that we do, must be hateful in the sight of God, and render us fit only to be cast, as most abhorred objects, into the fire of hell.*

This subject may be IMPROVED for,

1. Our conviction—

We are very backward to acknowledge ourselves so depraved as we really are. But this declaration of God is sufficient to humble the proudest heart. It is not atrocious sinners only that are thus vile, but "*all*," all without exception. Nor are our worst actions only thus defiled, but *all*, even our best; "*all* our righteousnesses are as filthy rags." Let all then, without exception, humble themselves as "unclean," Isa. vi. 5, and "vile," Job. xl. 4, and altogether destitute of any thing that is good. Rom. viii. 18.

2. Our direction—

Our own righteousness must be wholly renounced; and all of us must enter into the kingdom of heaven on the very same footing as publicans and harlots. This is humiliating to our proud nature; but it must be done: for, if it would be unseemly to introduce to an earthly monarch his bride clothed in "filty rags," much more would it be so to present our souls to the heavenly Bridegroom clad in such polluted garments as ours. St. Paul himself felt the necessity of a better righteousness than his own; Phil. iii. 9, and, if ever we would find acceptance with God, we must seek it altogether through the righteousness of Christ.

3. Our comfort—

We need not be dejected on account of the foregoing representation; since

* See Lev. xiii. 47—58, but especially ver. 55, where it was appointed, that though the plague had not spread, or changed its color, yet if it had eaten off the knap from the cloth, the cloth was to be burned, because it was "*fret inward.*" So, though the whole conversation of a man be not polluted, or even *visibly* bad in any part, yet if there be an inward disposition that is depraved, our great High Priest, when he shall inspect our hearts, will certainly pronounce us leprous, and execute the law upon us.

there is a righteousness offered to us in the gospel, even "the righteousness of Christ, which is unto all, and upon all them believe." Rom. iii. 22. This is commensurate with our wants: it is absolutely perfect; and it was wrought out by Him, Dan. ix. 24, in order that we might be clad in it, and "that the shame of our nakedness might not appear." Rev. iii. 18. Rejoice therefore all ye who are conscious of your own depravity, and pray to God that "Christ may be made righteousness unto you;" 1 Cor. i. 30, and that you, both in time and eternity, may glory in him as "the Lord your righteousness." Jer. xxiii. 6.

IGNORANCE DESTRUCTIVE.

Hos. iv. 6.—My people are destroyed for lack of knowledge. (H. H.)

Ignorance, as it respects the things of this world, is attended with many evils. It disqualifies a man for those situations in life that require the exercise of wisdom and discretion: it degrades him in society below the rank of those who would otherwise be deemed his equals or inferiors: and it not unfrequently leads to idleness, dissipation, and vice. But ignorance of religion is of infinitely worse consequence; because it insures the everlasting destruction of the soul. To this effect God speaks in the words before us; from which we shall be led to shew,

I. The ignorance of the christian world—

The Jews, as well those of the ten tribes as those who worshipped at Jerusalem, were called "the people of God," because they had received the seal of his covenant in their infancy, and professed to acknowledge him as their God. In like manner *we*, having in our infancy been baptized into the faith of Christ, may, in a lax and general sense, be called his followers, and his people. But among nominal christians there is an awful lack of knowledge; an ignorance,

1. Of themselves—

How little do they know of their *blindness!* They suppose themselves as competent to judge of spiritual as they are of carnal things; though God tells them, that they cannot comprehend the things of the Spirit for want of a spiritual discernment. 1 Cor. ii. 11, 14.

How little do they know of their *guilt!* Do they really feel themselves deserving of God's eternal wrath and indignation? They cannot cordially acquiesce in that idea, notwithstanding they are expressly said to be under the curse and condemnation of the law. Gal. iii. 10.

How little do they know of their *depravity!* They will acknowledge, that they have this or that particular infirmity: but they have no just conception of the total depravity of their hearts; or of the truth of God's testimony respecting them, that "every imagination of the thoughts of their hearts is evil, only evil, continually." Ps. xiv. 2, 3; Gen. vi. 5.

How little do they know of their utter *helplessness!* They imagine that they can exercise repentance and faith just when they please, though they are declared by God himself to be incapable of themselves to do any thing, John xv. 5, even so much as to think a good thoug t. 2 Cor. iii. 5.

2. Of God—

They may have some general notions of his power and goodness: but what know they of his *holiness?* Do they suppose that sin is so hateful in his eyes as he represents it to be? Heb. i. 13.

What know they of his *justice?* Are they persuaded that, as the moral governor of the universe, he must enforce the sanctions of his own law; and that, however merciful he may be, he neither will nor can clear the guilty? Exod. xxxiv. 7.

What know they of his *truth?* They read many threatenings in his word; but they do not believe that he will execute them. Luke xvi. 17.

3. Of Christ—

They confess perhaps his Godhead, and acknowledge him as a Saviour. But what know they of him *as he is in himself?* Do they discern his beauty, his excellency, his glory? Is He in their eyes "chiefest among ten thousand, and altogether lovely?" Cant. v. 10, 16.

What know they of him *as he is to us?* Do they comprehend any thing of the breadth and length, the depth and height, of his unsearchable love? Eph. iii. 18, 19. Have they any adequate idea of his tender sympathy and compassion? Heb. ii. 18, and iv. 15. Have they been filled with an admiration of his fulness, his suitableness, his sufficiency? 1 Cor. i. 30.

If more were necessary to confirm this melancholy truth, we would appeal to God's own assertion respecting us, that our stupidity and ignorance are more than brutish. Isa. i. 2, 3.

Lest such ignorance should be thought venial, we proceed to notice,

II. The fatal consequences of it—

Doubtless the degrees of criminality attached to ignorance must vary according to the opportunities which men have enjoyed of obtaining knowledge. But in all men who have the light of the gospel set before them, a lack of spiritual knowledge,

1. *Tends to* their destruction—

Every sin is destructive, but more especially impenitence and unbelief. And what is the occasion of these? Must they not be traced to ignorance as their true and proper source? If men knew what ignorant, guilty, depraved, and helpless creatures they are, could they refrain from sorrow and contrition?— — —If they knew what a holy, just, and immutable God they have to do with, could they do otherwise than tremble before him?— — —If they knew what a merciful, loving, and adorable Saviour there is, whose bowels are yearning over them, who is ever following them with invitations and intreaties, and who longs for nothing so much as to save their souls, could they turn their backs upon him? Could they help crying to him for mercy, and desiring an interest in his salvation?— — —If a man, feeling himself in imminent danger of perishing in the sea, cannot but avail himself of the assistance offered him for the preservation of his life, so neither can a man who feels his danger of everlasting destruction neglect and despise the salvation offered him in the gospel.

2. *Will issue in* their destruction—

God himself best knows what he has ordained and decreed: and as the fates of men will be determined by him at last, to him, and to his word, we make our appeal.

We want to ascertain the states of those who are ignorant of the gospel: God tells us plainly, "They are lost." 2 Cor. iv. 3.

We want to be informed whether their ignorance will not be considered as a sufficient plea for their rejection of the gospel? God assures us, that instead of operating in that view, and to that extent, it shall itself be the ground of their condemnation. Isa. xxvii. 11.

We would fain hope that the Lord Jesus Christ will interpose for them at the last day, to avert or mitigate their sentence. But we are told, on the contrary, that he himself will come to judgment, for the express purpose of taking vengeance on them. 2 Thes. i. 7, 8.

Here we leave the matter. If ye will not believe such plain and positive declarations of God, we shall in vain hope to make any impression on your minds by any feeble arguments of our own.

INFER,

1. How carefully should we improve the means of grace!

The ordinances are appointed of God for our instruction in spiritual knowledge. Should we then absent ourselves from them on slight occasions? or should we be content with a formal attendance on them, while yet we derive no solid benefit to our souls? O let us remember that our *all* is at stake: and whether we hear, or read, or pray, let us do it as for eternity.

2. How earnestly should we pray for the teachings of God's Spirit!

Whether we be learned or unlearned, we can know nothing but as we are taught of God. In respect of spiritual knowledge, the rich have no advantage above the poor: yea, the poor have rather the advantage of the rich, inasmuch as they have more docility of mind; and God has promised to reveal to babes the things which are hid from the wise and prudent. James ii. 5; Matt. xi. 25. Let us then beg that our eyes may be opened, and that through the influences of the Spirit we may know the things which are freely given to us of God. 1 Cor. ii. 11; Eph. i. 18.

3. How thankful should we be for any measure of divine knowledge!

To be wise unto salvation is to be wise indeed. All other knowledge is as nothing in comparison of this. Blessed then are they who can say, "This I know, that, whereas I was blind, I now see." John ix. 25; Matt. xiii. 16. Yes, believers, "blessed are your eyes, which now see:" for if ignorance is destructive to the soul, knowledge, on the other hand, provided it be spiritual and practical, will surely save it. Isa. liii. 11; John xvii. 3, with 1 John ii. 3, 4.

MORAL PRAVITY THE ORIGIN OF INFIDELITY.

John iii. 19. And this is the condemnation. that light is come into the world, and men loved darkness rather than light, because their deeds were evil. (Sk.)

We cannot attentively review mankind in general, without being compelled to admit one of the following things—either that the Governor of the world is not a *holy* Being, or that it is not his will that the subjects of his moral government should resemble him;—or if it be his will that they should resemble him, he has not clearly revealed it; or if he has clearly revealed it, that the subjects of his moral government are deeply depraved and guilty of direct rebellion against God; for nothing can be more obvious than that the world lieth in the wicked one.

To which of these causes must we ascribe this wickedness? To the first —*that God is not a holy Being?* Impossible! for He is "the high and lofty One—whose name is Holy, and who dwelleth in the high and holy place,"—and who is "glorious in holiness. Shall we ascribe it to the second—*that it is not his will that the subjects of his moral government should resemble him?* Equally impossible! This would be to suppose that *infinite wisdom* could take pleasure in *folly;*—*infinite purity*, in *pollution;*—*infinite order*, in *anarchy;*—and *infinite benevolence*, in *misery*. Shall we trace it to the third—*that he has not clearly revealed his will?* The sacred Scriptures of the Old and New Testament will render its ascription to this cause eternally impossible;—Moses and the Prophets, Jesus Christ and the Apostles, proclaim as with one voice, "Be ye holy, for the Lord your God is holy." Whence originates the wickedness which is in the world? Not in God, but in man;—"*Men love darkness* rather than light, *because their deeds are evil.*"

Our text suggests a variety of observations.

I. THAT LIGHT IS COME INTO THE WORLD.

The preceding verses determine the application of this metaphor to Christ. It is frequently applied to him both in the Old and New Testament, Isa. xlix. 6; lx. 3; John i. 4, 5, 9. The propriety of its application is obvious from various considerations.

1. *Through Christ, the evil of sin is exhibited in its strongest light.* That *sin is an evil of great magnitude* is demonstrable from the *effects already produced.* The expulsion of our first parents from Paradise, Gen. iii. 24; iii. 16—19, the pains of conception and child-birth—the noxious productions, and comparative infertility of the earth—the convulsions of nature—war, with all its infernal concomitants—an innumerable train of diseases—and death. It is also demonstrable from the punishment which awaits it hereafter.—Its wages is death eternal, Rom. vi. x3. But in *neither*, nor in *all* these put together, does its turpitude appear in so strong a light as on the cross of Christ. It is an evil so great, that nothing can expiate it but the death of the Son of God. It is a disease so inveterate and malignant, that nothing can heal it but the blood of Immanuel. It is a ruin so complete, that nothing can restore it but an omnipotent Deliverer.

2. *Through Christ, the love of God is transcendantly manifested.* God's love manifested in creation, particularly in the creation of angels and men.—More strikingly in the redemption of the human race. *In the medium of that redemption;* the incarnation, life, sufferings, death, resurrection, and intercession of Christ. *In the subjects of that redemption;* the subjects of creating power had never offended—the subjects of redeeming love have, Rom. v. 8. The former never resisted the operations of their Creator, but were as clay in the hands of the potter—the latter frequently make strong and long-continued resistance. Yet his love, in spite of unworthiness and resistance, perseveres in its operations to save.

3. *Through Christ, a flood of light is shed on the doctrine of a future state.* This doctrine not *peculiar* to Christianity—vestiges of it in both ancient and modern Paganism—believed by Jews, Matt. xxii. 32; Acts xxiii. 8, 9; but enlightened by Christ, 2 Tim. i. 10. He teaches it, Matt. xxv. Exemplifies it in his own resurrection, 1 Cor. xv. 20—22, and shows the connection between our present character and our future state. It suggests,

II. THAT MEN GENERALLY REJECT LIGHT, AND LOVE DARKNESS.

Darkness when applied to moral subjects, denotes both ignorance and sin, Rom. xiii. 12. Our text, in each of these senses, has been, and continues to be, most awfully verified.

1. *It was verified in the conduct of the Jews, in rejecting Christ.* The

glory of God less eminently displayed in the law than in the gospel.— The law gives the knowledge of sin, Rom. vii. 7. The gospel reveals salvation, Eph. i. 13. The sacrifices of the law were beasts, Heb. x. 4; of the gospel the Son of God, Heb. x. 10. The law, compared with former dispensations of mercy, was full of glory—compared with this its glory is obscured, 2 Cor. iii. 7—11.

2. *It is verified by all rejectors of divine revelation.* Every infidel dwells in a region of darkness and uncertainty: he abounds in speculations without truth, conjectures without certainty, and queries without solutions. With all his researches, he cannot answer one of the following questions:—Has man an immaterial spirit? Will this survive the dissolution of the body? If so, will its future state be like its present, or will it be a state of retribution?—And if so, "what must we do to be saved?"—The Bible answers them all, but he rejects this.

3. *It is verified by all who place religion entirely in the performance of its outward duties.* These deny the power of godliness. All pretensions to assurance of salvation, they contemn as fanaticism. But the Scriptures teach such assurance, Rom. viii. 16, 17; 1 John iii. 14, 24; iv. 6, 13; and v. 2, 19. On any other supposition than the attainableness of such assurance, many passages are not only nugatory, but absurd, 2 Cor. xiii. 5.

III. That the reason why men reject light and love darkness is moral pravity.

Bad systems are the offspring of bad hearts, while on the other hand, those systems *re-act* upon those hearts, and perpetuate and increase their depravity. It is not the deficiency of evidence, but the love of sin which,

1. *Produces atheism.* Wherever there is a creature, there is demonstration of the existence of a Creator, Psa. xix. 1; Rom. i. 20. The atheist knows that if there be a God, he must hate and punish sin. Being resolved to persist in sin, that he may proceed quietly, he persuades himself to reject his existence.

2. *Produces deism.* Deists in general have never read the Scriptures with attention;—instance Hume: nor studied the Christian and Deistical controversy.—Their hostility arises from opposition to the holiness of its requisitions.

3. *Produces opposition to the doctrine of divine influeuce.* Divine influence consistent with reason. Taught by Scripture, John xvi. 8; Eph. ii. 1; Rom. viii. 16; 2 Cor. 1, 4. Confined not to the apostolic age, but extends to the end of time, Acts ii. 39; 2 Cor. iii. 11; Heb. xii. 28.

IV. That the consequence of rejecting light and loving darkness is condemnation.

Condemnation. Implying.

1. *In this life.*—Mental perturbation, Isa. lvii. 20, 21. God's curse accompanying the dispensations of his providence, Deut. xxviii. 15—20. A fearful looking for of judgment, Heb. x. 27.

2. *In the life to come.* The final sentence. The nature of future punishment. Its duration.

Conclude with three remarks.

1. No man will be finally condemned because he was once a sinner, but because he refused a Saviour.

2. No man can be saved who rejects Christ;

3. He who receives Christ shall enjoy the Divine favor here, and glory hereafter.

MAN'S ABUSE OF GOD'S PATIENCE.

Eccl. viii. 11.—Because sentence against an evil work is not executed speedily, therefore the heart of the sons of men is fully set in them to do evil. (S. S.)

SIN is in itself an evil of a crimson dye—

Nevertheless its malignity may be greatly increased by the aggravations with which it is attended—

One can scarcely conceive any thing that can enhance its guilt so much, as the committing of it in hopes that God's mercy will pardon it—

Yet this is the very ground on which the world indulge themselves in the commission of it—"Because," &c.

I. THE EXTENT OF MAN'S WICKEDNESS.

That sin exists in the world is visible to all—

But the degree in which it prevails is very little known—Men sin

1. Habitually

All are not equally vicious in their lives—

But all forget God and neglect their own souls

Successive years serve only to confirm this habit—

We may all adopt the confession of the church of old, Jer. iii. 25.

2. Deliberately

It were well if we never sinned, but through ignorance or inadvertance—

But what schemes have we formed for the accomplishment of sinful purposes!—

How often have we seen the sinfulness of our desires, and yet gratified them! Rom. i. 32.

The very bent and inclination of our souls has been towards wickedness—Job xv. 16.

3. Without restraint.

A regard to our reputation or interest may impose some restraint—

A fear of hell may also prevent the gratification of some desires—

But few are kept from evil like Joseph, by the fear of God, Gen. xxxix. 9.

That is the only restraint which proves uniformly effectual, Jam. ii. 11.

4. Without remorse

We must at times have felt some convictions of conscience—

But we, for the most part, stifle them by company, amusements, &c.—

Many attain to dreadful hardness of heart and impenitence, 1 Tim. iv. 2.

The prophets description may well be applied to each of us, Jer. viii. 5, 6.

Thus are "men's hearts fully set in them to do evil."

They walk after the imagination of their own hearts—

Neither mercies nor judgments can prevail with them to do otherwise—

If their sins were followed by a visible and immediate punishment, men would not dare to live in this manner—

But God defers the execution of his judgments

II. THE OCCASION OF IT.

God is not an unconcerned spectator of sin.

He has appointed a day for the revelation of his righteous judgment—

At present he forbears to inflict vengeance—

This very forbearance emboldens men to sin—"*because*," "*therefore*."

From the delay of punishment men think

1. That there is but little "evil" in sin.

God indeed calls sin "an evil work"—

But his forbearance towards sinners is thought to indicate indifference—

This however is a fatal delusion—
He has marked the evil of sin in many awful instances, 2 Pet. ii. 4—6
He will soon undeceive this blind infatuated world, Eph. v. 6.
2. That there is no "sentence" gone forth against it.
Men would gladly persuade themselves that they have no cause to fear—
The temptation whereby the serpent beguiled Eve, is cherished by them, Gen. iii. 4.
But the wrath of God is indeed denounced against sin, Rom. ii. 8, 9.
Every species and degree of sin renders us obnoxious to his displeasure, Rom. i. 18.
3. That the sentence (if there be any) will never be "executed"
Since God defers punishing, it seems possible that he may decline it altogether—
The apparent disproportion between the offence and the punishment seems to countenance this idea—
To confirm our hope we are apt to compare God with ourselves, Psa. l. 21.
But, however long God delay, he will surely strike at last, Eccl. viii. 12, 13.
Thus they take occasion from God's forbearance to persist in their evil ways.
David mentions this effect as arising from it in his day, Psa. lv. 19.
St. Peter foretells the prevalence of this iniquity in the last days, 2 Pet. iii. 3, 4.
Experience proves how universally it obtains at present—
INFER
1. How great the folly, as well as wickedness, of unregenerate men!
If there were a bare possibility of eternal punishment, how mad were it to continue in sin!—
But God has pledged himself that he will inflict it on the impenitent—Matt. xxv. 46.
Every moment's continuance in sin increases the condemnation, Rom. ii. 4, 5.
What extreme folly then is it so to abuse the forbearance of God!—
May we be ashamed of ourselves, and repent in dust and ashes—
2. What need have we to be cleansed by the blood and spirit of Christ!
What but the blood of Christ can ever expiate the guilt we have contracted?—
What but the spirit of Christ can ever deliver us from such habits?—
That we can never renew our own souls is certain, Jer. xiii. 23.
Let us therefore wash in the fountain opened for us, Zech. xiii. 1.
And let us apply to God for his almighty aid, Lam. v. 21.
3. How dreadful must be the state of those who continue impenitent!
There is a certain measure of iniquity which sinners are left to fill up—Gen. xv. 16
When this is full, nothing can avert the divine vengeance, 1 Thess. ii. 16.
Already are the arrows of divine justice pointed at them, Ps. vii. 11—13.
Eternity itself will be the duration of the punishment, Mark ix. 43—48
The time is coming when Jerusalem's state will be ours, Luke xix. 42.
Let us then tremble lest we exhaust the divine patience, Zeph. ii. 2, 3.
Let us diligently improve this day of salvation, 2 Cor. vi. 2.

THE DECEITFULNESS OF THE HEART.

Jeremiah xvii. 9.—The heart is deceitful above all things and desperately wicked: who can know it?

TRUE and faithful is the testimony of God. Men may amuse themselves and their fellow creatures with empty, high-sounding descriptions of the dignity of human nature and the all-sufficient powers of man, but every humble and truly enlightened person must at once perceive and acknowledge the truth of the text, that the heart, &c.

But by the blessing of God it may be useful to turn our attention to this important subject and point out some of the plainest and most decisive evidences of the deceitfulness of the human heart, which scriptural observation and experience afford. It is demonstrable and apparent, 1. From men's general ignorance of their own character. There is nothing in the history of mankind more unaccountable and at first view more surprising than that self-partiality which prevails amongst them. One would be apt to imagine that it should not be so difficult a matter to arrive at a just knowledge of our own character, possessing as we do every possible advantage for obtaining it. We have constant access to our own bosoms and are more interested in the discovery than in the acquisition of any other kind of knowledge. But we see that in point of fact, this knowledge is the rarest and most uncommon: nor is it difficult to account for the moral phenomenon, since the heart is, &c.

2. The deceitfulness of the heart appears from men's general disposition to justify their own conduct. This disposition our first parents discovered immediately upon their eating the forbidden fruit. When Jehovah appeared to Adam and charged him with guilt, he attempted to justify himself by laying the blame upon the woman, and in the same manner, the woman blamed the serpent.

3. The deceitfulness of the heart appears from the difficulty with which men are brought to acknowledge their faults even when conscious that they have done wrong. This necessarily follows from that disposition in human nature to which we have already adverted, viz. the disposition on all occasions to justify our own conduct. Hence men are in general so backward to acknowledge their faults, and so displeased with those, who are so faithful and friendly as to point them out. How few can bear to be told their faults. This is the sure and ready way to make most men your enemies.

4. The deceitfulness of the heart appears from the disposition which men discover to rest in the mere notion and forms of religion, while they are destitute of its power. In the present age of the church there have been too many of this character: men who from selfish and worldly motives have taken up a profession of religion without understanding its nature or feeling its power; having a name to live, but being spiritually dead.

Balaam was a remarkable instance of this. He was a man of extensive knowledge and superior gifts. He was not a stranger to religious impressions for in his calm reflecting moments, he desired to die the death of the righteous.

5th, and lastly. The deceitfulness of the heart appears in the highest degree when we overlook the real motives, and mistake the workings of their own corruptions for the fruits of the spirit of God. That there is such deceitfulness in the world none can doubt, who considers the dreadful enormities that have been committed under the sound name of religion.

On the whole as the ways in which men deceive themselves are so various, can we be too jealous over our own hearts? He that trusteth to his own heart is a fool, says Solomon, and the reason is obvious, for the heart is, &c. Let us give ourselves to self-examination instead of indulging in a censorious disposition or looking abroad to discover the faults of our neighbors. Let us descend into our own breasts and observe the plagues of our own hearts. Let us look not merely to our own actions but likewise to the principles and motives from which they proceed. Let us consider our conduct not in the light, in which self-partiality would present it to our view, but in the light in which an impartial spectator would view it—in the light in which God's word teaches us to consider it and in the light in which it will be judged at last, when God will bring to light the hidden things of darkness and make manifest the councils of all hearts. We are all more or less liable to self-deceit and they who think, they have the least of it, are in general the most of all under its dominion. Let us therefore distrust our own judgments, and sensible of our own ignorance and liableness to mistakes, let us pray for the teaching of his spirit and say with Elehu, that which I see not teach thou me.

THE ENMITY OF THE CARNAL MIND.

Romans viii. 7.—The carnal mind is enmity against God. (Sk.)

In the first four chapters of this epistle, our apostle *establishes the important doctrine of justification by faith.* This he does—by showing that all mankind have sinned, and need salvation, chap. iii. 23. That being transgressors, we cannot be saved by the merit of works, iii. 28. And that all God's approved servants have been saved by faith: for Abraham was thus saved, as a specimen of the uncircumcised, iv. 1, 3, 10, 11. And David, as a specimen of those saved in circumcision, iv. 5-7. In the succeeding chapters, our apostle *guards this doctrine* against all licentious abuse, to which it might be liable through human depravity. Here he shows, that gospel liberty is freedom from sin, chap. vi. 14, 17, 18, 22. That believers are enabled to walk in this liberty, viii. 2—4. That their continued salvation depends on their thus walking, viii. 1, 13. And that a contrary deportment would imply rebellion against God. For "the carnal mind," &c. Enmity is a confirmed dislike to an object, accompanied with a disposition to oppose it, and if possible, to injure it. In improving our text, let us consider the object, the subject, and the evidences of this enmity, here spoken of.

I. The object of this enmity. This is God, who may be justly considered as the kindest, the loveliest, and the greatest of beings.

1. *God is the kindest of beings.* This appears,

From his *creating goodness.* In making us creatures capable of enjoying him; of enjoying the assurance of his favor; of bearing his holy image; of sharing in his heavenly glory; and in creating us for this benevolent purpose, Rev. iv. 11; Psa. xxxv. 27, 28.

From his *sustaining care:* by which he consults our best interests; preserves us from all evil; and constantly provides for us, Psa. viii. 4; 1 Pet v. 7.

From his *redeeming mercy;* which devised the scheme of our redemption, Psa. cxxxvi. 23; Luke i. 78, 79; and confers its benefits, Mic. vii. 18, 19.

And from his patient *long-suffering:* which is designed to promote our repentance; by exciting us to it, Rom. ii. 4; and encouraging it, 2 Peter iii. 9.

2. *God is the loveliest of beings.* This he evidently is—

For his kindness is most *extensive*, and impartial. It embraces all his creatures without exception, Psa. cxlv. 9. It is most *disinterested*, aiming not at his own profit, but ours, Psa. cxvii. 1, 2, and xxxvi. 7. It is most *prompt* in its exercises. He waits to be gracious, Isa. xxx. 18. It is most *generous* in its displays, not accompanied with upbraidings, Jam. i. 5. And most *durable* in its continuance, it will never end, Psa. ciii. 17, 18.

3. *God is the greatest of beings.* He is infinite in *wisdom*, to discern and frustrate all the devices of his enemies, Prov. xxi. 30; infinite in *power*, to execute all his purposes, Jam. iv. 12: and infinite in *happiness;* enjoying felicity, which cannot be augmented; and security, which cannot be violated. Consequently, he is incapable of error through ignorance; of selfishness through want; or of cruelty through fear. "Great is the Lord, and greatly to be praised: and his greatness is unsearchable," Psa. cxlv. 3. But though he is the kindest, and loveliest, as well as the greatest of beings, yet all do not love him. "For the carnal mind is enmity," &c. Let us therefore consider,

II. The subject of this enmity. The carnal mind.

1. *The mind*, the immortal part of man: the most noble part of the most dignified creature on earth. This the human mind must be—because it is *rational;* capable of admitting true conceptions of things; capable of retaining those conceptions, of comparing them, and of deducing just conclusions from them, Job xxxv. 10, 11. And because it is *free* in all its acts. It is capable of choosing what reason requires, and of rejecting what it forbids. This is incontestable, from God's gracious influence, Phil. ii. 13; his proposals to mankind, Deut. xxx. 19, 20; and from the complaints brought against the impenitent, John v. 40; Matt. xxiii. 37.

2. *The carnal mind:* the natural mind of man; that mind which we bring with us into the world. The uninspired, unrenewed mind, which is not enlightened, purified, and governed, by God's Holy Spirit, Jude 19. The human mind, while it remains in this state, is called carnal,—because of its *descent.* Our minds are certainly transmitted with our bodies, by what is called natural traduction. This appears from scripture: for "on the seventh day God ended his work which he had made;" that is the work of creation, Gen. ii. 2. But this he could not have done, if he continues to create human souls. It is also said, "in the day that God created man, in the image of God made he him," Gen. v. 1, but of Seth, it is said, "And Adam begat a son in his own likeness, after his image," Gen. v. 3 Hence our Lord justly concludes, "That which is born of flesh, is flesh," John iii. 6. When the tree is corrupt, the fruit must be corrupt also, Matt. vii. 17. The soul's descent by natural traduction is also evident from facts; for children resemble their parents in mental dispositions, no less than in features. The mind is also called carnal or fleshly, because of its *affections* and *exercises.* With respect to its affections, it supremely desires and delights in the things of this world. Those things which gratify the desires of the flesh, the desires of the eye, and the pride of life, 1 John ii. 15, 16; Phil. iii. 18, 19. With respect to its exercises, all its purposes, its aims, and its contrivances are employed to obey its own will, in opposition to the will of God, Gen. vi. 5.

It must therefore follow, that those who act under the influence of the carnal mind, are enemies to God by wicked works. Which leads us to observe,

III. THE EVIDENCES OF THIS ENMITY. Enmity of mind must in itself be unseen, but may be perceived by its overt acts. For instance, when a subject is at enmity against his sovereign, he manifests it by aversion from all intercourse with him, wilful disobedience to his commands, hostile opposition to him, and hatred to his friends and servants. Thus also enmity against God is manifested,

1. *By aversion from communion with him.* To this God graciously calls us, Isa. lv. 6; 2 Chron. vii. 14. But this man naturally rejects, Job xxi. 14, 15; Isa. lxiv. 7.

2. *By wilful disobedience to God's known commands.* These he sets before us in his word, and by his servants; but man rebels against them, Dan. ix. 9, 10.

3. *By hostile opposition to him. Opposition to an amicable agreement with him.* Jer. vi. 16; ii. 25; to the gracious strivings of his Spirit, Acts vii. 51: and to the interests of his kingdom; by endeavoring to prevent its extension, Matt. xxiii. 13; and to seduce its subjects, Prov. i. 10; 1 Kings xiv. 16.

4. *And by hatred to his friends and followers.* This they manifest by reviling, slandering, and tormenting them, Matt. v. 11; John xv. 19; Heb. xi. 37.

This enmity of the carnal mind against God, teaches us,

1. *That all mankind are naturally in a degenerate state.* Man, when at first created, was made *upright;* he was then just and grateful towards his Maker, Eccl. vii. 29. He was *very good*, Gen. i. 31. And he was *crowned with glory* in himself, and with *honor* by the inferior creatures, Psa. viii. 5, 6. But man, as an enemy to God, is *unjust*, for he robs God by self-desecration, Rom. vi. 13. He is *ungrateful*, for he returns the greatest evil he is capable of repaying, for the greatest good he is capable of enjoying, Isa. i. 2. He is *injurious* to his dearest connexions, Prov. iii. 33; Deut. xxviii. 18. He is *debased* by captivity to his greatest enemy, 2 Tim. ii. 26; and by condemnation to everlasting infamy, 1 Sam. ii. 30; Dan. xii. 2. To this degeneracy all mankind are naturally subject, however amiable in tempers, or polished in manners, Psa. xiv. 2, 3. This teaches us,

2. *That an entire change of mind is necessary to our eternal salvation.* Are your minds at enmity against God? Are you averse, &c.? Then consider—your enmity exposes you to certain destruction, Thes. i. 7—9; Prov. xxix. 1. This destruction is certain; from God's knowledge of your sins, Job xxxiv. 21, 22; from his justice, Rom. ii. 6, 8, 9; and from his truth, Psa. lxviii. 21; Deut. xxxii. 40, 41. A change of mind is therefore indispensably requisite; every other change is insufficient; whether it be of sentiment, name, or outward conduct, Gal. vi. 15; John iii. 7.

3. *To obtain this change should engage our most serious concern.* Seek it in God's way; by repentance, Acts iii. 19; by prayer, Psa. li. 10; for Christ's sake, Eph. iv. 32. Seek it in God's time; now, without excuse or delay, Job xxii. 21; Psa. xcv. 7, 8. Seek it with confident expectation; from the success of others, Col. i. 21; from God's amicable disposition, 2 Cor. v. 19; his entreaty, 2 Cor. v. 20; and his promises, Isa. lv. 6, 7.

A CORRECT ESTIMATE OF HUMAN LIFE.

Psalm xc. 12. So teach us to number our days, that we may apply our hearts unto wisdom. (Sk.)

Of all the blessings which the adorable author of our being has conferred upon man, there are few more important than that inestimable boon which we denominate *time;* because it is that, on the continuance of which infinite wisdom has rendered every other good in some measure dependant. Yet, alas! notwithstanding the vast importance of our fleeting moments, how few are there who attach to them a proper estimate, and improve them according to their value. This lamentable abuse of time appears to have been commensurate with the existence of moral pravity; for the apostle Paul, in two of his Epistles, reminds the churches of the importance of "redeeming the time," Eph. v. 16; Col. iv. 5. And the devout author of the psalm before us, evidently conscious of the proneness of man to neglect and abuse time, raises his pious ejaculation to heaven, and prays, "*So teach us to number our days, that we may apply our hearts unto wisdom.*" As the same disposition in the human heart is still in operation, let us endeavor to counteract its influence by considering,

I. The means of ascertaining a correct estimate of human life.

II. The particulars of which this estimate consists.

III. The important effect which it tends to produce.

I. The means of ascertaining a correct estimate of human life.

The pious psalmist was deeply sensible of his dependence upon God, and hence he "gave himself unto prayer." Prayer was the means which he used; and this powerful instrument is universally necessary, and universally applicable. This will appear if we proceed to notice,

1. *The natural indisposition of man to improve the fleeting moments of life.* This humbling and lamentable truth forces itself upon us, supported by all that weight of evidence which *personal experience* and *daily observation* regularly furnish. Multitudes of our unhappy fellow creatures are devoting their passing hours to purposes decidedly hostile to those for which time was originally designed: whilst others, in some degree persuaded of the vast importance of time, are nevertheless deferring its proper occupation and use to some uncertain future period; and thus year after year steals into eternity unimproved, charged with an awful report to the throne of the final Judge, Luke xii. 16—20; Acts xxiv. 25. Even the Christian, acting in some measure under the influence of that estimate of life which the volume of inspiration furnishes, has reason to mourn over many blanks and vacancies which occur on the pages of his history. Hence, all have need to pray, "So teach us to number our days," &c.

2. *The sovereignty of Jehovah over the human heart.* That Omnipotent Being, who is the sole object of prayer, has the entire control of man; for he reigneth in the armies above, and on the earth beneath. He can instruct the most *ignorant mind;* subdue the most *turbulent passions;* and conquer the most *obdurate heart.* By a thousand means, unknown to erring man, he can effectually impress a true estimate of time upon the human mind. The boisterous winds—the tumultuous ocean—and the hearts of the children of men, are equally subject to his almighty dominion. 1 Chron. xxix. 11. 12, 17—19.

3. *The direct appointment of infinite wisdom.* "The Father of lights," from whom proceedeth "every good gift," has in his infinitude of wisdom

appointed and sanctioned prayer as the medium between heaven and earth: and whatever blessings we may need at the hands of our beneficent Creator, we are taught to expect them only through the lively exercise of fervent prayer. This momentous truth is supported by the testimony of *the sacred Scriptures*, and by the *experience of the truly pious in every age of the church*, Ezek. xxxvi. 37; Matt. vii. 7, 8; Jam. i. 5, 6; iv. 2, 3.

4. *The tried efficacy of prayer.* If prayer were an untried experiment, then we might entertain some doubts respecting its influence, and should have a plausible reason for hesitancy in resorting to it; but doubt is precluded, and hesitation superseded, by that overpowering strength of evidence with which the efficacy of prayer is supported. Myriads of witnesses of its power encircle the throne of Jehovah in the regions of immortality; and myriads more, still on earth, are daily feasting on the bounty of their God, through this admirable medium of divine intercourse. But we need not ascend up to heaven for evidence in support of this truth; nor need we wander to distant parts of the earth to collect convincing proofs: our researches need not exceed the limits of the present congregation; here doubtless we have many witnesses that

> "Prayer ardent opens heaven, lets down a stream
> Of glory on the consecrated hour
> Of man in audience with the deity."

Exod. xxxiii. 18—23; xxxiv. 5—7; James v. 16—18.

II. THE PARTICULARS OF WHICH THIS ESTIMATE CONSISTS. By "numbering our days" we are not to understand the psalmist to mean that it is the duty of man to ascertain the period of his mortal existence; this is one of those "secret things which (exclusively) belong to the Lord." That estimate of human life referred to in our text, doubtless includes a correct idea of its importance, together with a conscientious improvement of its parts. In thus "numbering our days," it will be necessary to consider,

1. *The smallness of their number.* The life of man is circumscribed in its limit; and though we may mark its progress by certain periods, and thus divide it into small portions, yet, generally, threescore years and ten will terminate our mortal story, and consign the most athletic to the "house appointed for all living." This is a very narrow limit, compared with its *antediluvian extent*, and with *the important work which ought to be effected*, viz. the gloom of ignorance dispelled—the oppressive load of guilt removed—and the deep-fixed stain of moral pollution washed away, Psa. xxxix. 5. James iv. 14.

2. *The rapidity of their flight.* Human life is not only limited in its duration, but also fleeting in its progress. The several portions of which it is composed steal away in rapid succession; and all the boasted power and wisdom of man are insufficient either to impede their progress, or to recall them when they have passed away. The Holy Ghost has made choice of the most fleeting objects in nature, in order to impress the human mind with a correct idea of the rapid course of time, and excite the sons of Adam to the proper occupation and improvement of their fleeting moments, Job vii. 6: Job. ix. 25; Psa. xc. 10.

3. *The uncertainty of their continuance.* Although man is capable of understanding an extensive variety of interesting subjects, yet the termination of his mortal existence is a point which he can never expect to ascertain. This solemn period infinite wisdom has concealed from the most prying curiosity. This is one of those prerogatives which Jehovah has exclu-

sively reserved to himself. The mouldering, moss-grown annals of the dead in our grave yards, together with the daily occurrence of human mortality, sufficiently establish this humbling truth, Job xxi. 21, 23—25; Luke xii. 19, 20.

4. *Their influence on our eternal destiny.* The present state of man is probationary in its nature, and decisive in its influence upon his eternal condition. It is in time that the character is formed for eternity. Earth alone is the scene of operation for that mercy which is exercised through the amazing provisions of the gospel of Christ, and which is of essential importance, as a preparation for participating the felicities of the heavenly world. The unhappy being who, "driven away in his wickedness," quits the stage of life without this gospel meetness for the skies, has

> "No patron! intercessor none! Now past
> The sweet, the clement, mediatorial hour!
> For guilt no plea! to pain no pause! no bound!
> Inexorable all! and all extreme!"

Dan. xii. 2, 3. Matt. xxv. 31—46; 2 Thess. i. 7—10.

III. The important effect which it tends to produce;—"That we may apply our hearts unto wisdom." "Wisdom" is a term very frequently used, and variously applied in the sacred Scriptures; viz. to mechanical genius, Exod. xxxi. 2, 3;—general literature, Acts vii. 22:—natural instinct, Job xxix. 17;—that prudence which enables a man to discern what is proper to be done, Eccles. x. 10;—and to true religion, Psalm cxi. 10; James iii. 17. To the last two ideas or senses alone our text seems to direct our attention. 1. The term "wisdom" sometimes describes that prudence which enables a man to discern and perform those actions which accord with the fitness of things. If the days of man be so few, so fleeting, so uncertain, and so momentous, it certainly is highly proper to seize the passing moments as they fly, and conscientiously devote them to those purposes which will produce the greatest possible benefit. Preserving them with a miser's care, from being associated with unprofitable, unnecessary, and (much less with) ungodly actions. It is the distinguished prerogative of man

> "To raise
> A royal tribute from the poorest hours;
> Immense revenue! every moment pays."

Much time may be saved by guarding against *unnecessary sleep—useless commixion with ungodly men—unprofitable reading*—and, in short, every exercise and pursuit which cannot be engaged in to the "glory of God," 1 Cor. x. 31. The advice of an eminent divine of the last century on this point, is worthy of being engraven upon our hearts: "Never be unemployed a moment. Never be triflingly employed. Never while away time." 2. "Wisdom" is sometimes applied to true religion. The application of the heart to this, is the great end of life; and no man has his heart properly influenced with the shortness, uncertainty, and importance of time, who does not make this the grand business of his life. It is very possible to apply the *head* without having the *heart* influenced. The man who, under the influence of a proper estimate of time, is the subject of this important application, has experienced a general renovation of his moral nature; he is "renewed in the spirit of his mind;" he experiences a lively union with God through faith in Jesus Christ; and he is solicitous to "comprehend with all saints what is the breadth, and length, and depth, and height, and to know the love of Christ, and be filled with all the fulness of God." Influenced by a spiritual principle, he is the subject of a spiritual enjoyment, and gives proof of the whole by holiness of practice. Gal. v. 22—25.

This subject tends,

1. To detach our affections from earthly objects.
2. To excite us to diligence in our Christian calling.
3. To alarm the trifler, and awaken in him a lively sensibility of his awful condition.

THE FRAGILITY OF HUMAN LIFE.

Job xiv. 1, 2.—Man that is born of a woman is of few days, and full of trouble. He cometh forth like a flower, and is cut down: he fleeth also as a shadow, and continueth not. (Sk.)

Death is justly designated "the king of terrors:" before him the monarch trembles and the subject is afraid, and to his dread sceptre all must bow, since "it is appointed unto men once to die," Heb. ix. 27. The great duty of man, therefore, is to conduct himself as a candidate for eternity, by securing an interest in Him who conquered death in his dark domains, and is able to deliver them who through fear of death are subject to bondage, Heb. ii. 14, 15. If death plunged man into the gulf of annihilation, he might pass through life fearless of its close; but when we consider it connected with eternal results, it becomes the duty and wisdom of all to improve the present moment. With such an object in view, let us notice,

I. The important ideas suggested in our text.

II. Improve them by practical inferences.

I. The important ideas suggested. From our text we learn,

1. *That human life is flattering in its commencement:*—Man "cometh forth like a flower." Imagery more appropriate could not have been selected. Children are like flowers in the bud, unfolding their beauty as days and months increase; their innocent actions—their broken accents—the expansion of the mind, and the acquisition of new ideas, fascinate and involuntarily allure the affections of their fond parents, who watch over them with the tenderest anxiety. In one child they see a human form, which the maturity of age will render beautiful.—In another, a nerve that will riot in danger.—A third, displaying clearness of thought, and sobriety of judgment; and a fourth, manifesting a combination of qualities admirably adapted to the purposes of life. In the opening bud the father's eye discovers much to excite hope, and the mother sees with delight the child of promise; but alas!

"Nipt by the wind's unkindly blast,
Parch'd by the sun's directer ray,
The momentary glories waste,
The short-lived beauties die away."

The flower is cut down, Psa. ciii. 15, 16; Isa. xl. 6, 7; James i, 10, 11; 1 Pet. i. 24.

2. *Disastrous in its continuance:*—"Full of trouble." Misfortunes and calamities surround us on every hand, and proclaim nothing certain in this

uncertain word. To calculate on unruffled peace, or uninterrupted prosperity, in this mutable state, is presumptuous; our stay on earth is connected with trials of various kinds, and no situation can exempt us from suffering. The word of God, experience, and observation, confirm the doctrine of our text, and testify that "man is born to trouble as the sparks fly upward," Job v. 7.

3. *Contracted in its span:*—"Few days." Life, in its longest period, is but a short journey from the cradle to the tomb. This made the pious and venerable patriarch to exclaim, "Few and evil have the days of the years of my life been," Gen. xlvii. 9. Various are the figures employed to illustrate the shortness of human life; it is compared to "a step," 1 Sam. xx. 3;—"a post," Job ix. 25;—"a tale that is told," Psa. xc. 9;—"a weaver's shuttle," Job vii. 6;—and "a vapor," James iv. 14.

4. *Incessant in its course:*—"Fleeth as a shadow." Human life is measured by seconds—hours—days—weeks—months—and years. These periodical revolutions roll on in rapid succession, and are strikingly illustrated by the image in our text, which is supposed to be taken from the shadow cast by the sun on the earth. Some suppose it the shadow of the sun dial: but whether we consider it as the shadow of the evening, which is lost when night comes on; or the shadow on a dial plate, which is continually moving onward; or the shadow of a bird flying, which stays not;—the figure fully represents the life of man, which is passing away, whether we are loitering or active, careless or serious, killing or improving time.

5. *Eventful in its issue.* Death introduces us into the fixed state of eternity, and puts a final period to all earthly enjoyments and suffering: the soul dismissed from its clay tabernacle, is introduced into a world of spirits, from whence there is no return. The wicked, at death, exchange their supposed happiness for perpetual misery, and their imaginary light for thickest darkness, "where the worm dieth not," &c., Mark ix. 48. The righteous, at death, leave the wilderness, and enter the promised land; exchange a state of suffering and conflict, for an eternity of peace and rest: so that death, though terrific in any form, is the harbinger of good to the christian; proclaiming victory to the warrior, rest to the pilgrim, a crown for the conqueror, and repose for the weary.

II. Improve them by practical inferences. Such being the character of human life, it is the duty and wisdom of piety,

1. *To enrich the juvenile mind with religious instruction.* "Man cometh forth as a flower," therefore let instruction drop as the rain, and fall as the dew: no time must be lost; the bud is unfolding, and

> "If good you plant not, vice will fill the mind."

Combine your efforts, and strengthen each other's hands, since

> "Children, like tender osiers, take the bow,
> And, as they first are fashioned, still will grow."

2 *Improve the dispensations of Providence.* If your few days are crowded with troubles of various kinds, look to the Disposer of events: "all things work together for good to them that love God," Rom. viii. 28. Are you the subjects of bodily affliction? remember here "we have no continuing city," Heb. xiii. 14. Are you bereft of friends, who died in the Lord? think of that which was a solace to David under his affliction, 1 Sam. xii

23: Are you in darkness as to the design or final issue of your sufferings? "trust in the name of the Lord," &c., Isa. l. 10.

3. *Be diligent.* Your days are few; the fugitive moment refuses to stay, and each second brings you nearer either to heaven or hell. Think, mortal man, of that part which dieth not, and live for eternity: for, "behold, now is the accepted time; behold, now is the day of salvation," 2 Cor. vi. 2. "Whatsoever thy hand findeth to do, do it with all thy might," Eccles. ix. 10. Pray with Moses, Psa. xc. 12.

4. *Maintain a noble detachment from the world.* We are strangers and pilgrims on earth, dwelling "in houses of clay, whose foundation is in the dust, which are crushed before the moth," Job iv. 19; tenants at will. Why then should we be so fond of earthly toys, when

> "Each pleasure hath its poison too,
> And every sweet a snare."

Our days flee away as a shadow; it therefore "remaineth, that both they that have wives be as though they had none; and they that weep, as though they wept not; and they that buy, as though they possessed not," &c., 1 Cor. vii. 29, 30.

5. *Live in a constant readiness for your change.* The eventful hour is at hand; therefore "be ye also ready," Matt. xxiv. 48. Live as dying creatures in a dying world. Make religion the business of your lives, the controlling principle of every action. Frequently examine yourselves whether you have faith in, and love to, our Lord Jesus Christ; whether you are in possession of, or earnestly seeking, that "holiness, without which no man can see the Lord," Heb. xii. 14. "Be not deceived! God is not mocked!"

Application.

1. *To the young.* Your strength, beauty, and all other accomplishments, are only like flowers: boast not yourselves of to-morrow; rather to-day say to God, "My Father, thou shalt be the guide of my youth."

2. *To those who have escaped the dangers of infancy and inexperienced youth.* For what purpose have you been living? Has Christ had the pre-eminence, or have earthly things engrossed your affections? Forget not that you are dying creatures, and "prepare to meet your God," Amos iv. 12.

3. *To those of you whose days have dwindled to the longest span.* Your hoary locks, trembling limbs, and palsied heads, proclaim the number of your days. Are your souls ripe for the heavenly garner? If not, for once be serious; hasten to Jesus, the only shelter from the impending storm.

CHAPTER IX.

THE WAY OF SALVATION.

THE GOSPEL COVENANT.

Jeremiah xxxi. 33.--This shall be the covenant that I will make with the house of Israel: After those days, saith the Lord, I will put my law in their inward parts, and write it in their hearts, and will be their God, and they shall be my people. (Pr.

THE glorious properties and holy effects of the gospel are here described and foretold, in contradistinction from the law of Moses. God had made a covenant with Israel, of which Moses was the mediator; but that did not secure the obedience of the people. He now therefore will make a new and better covenant, of which Christ is to be the mediator: and in this, the blessings of salvation are absolutely promised and made certain: ver. 31, 32.

1. The gospel is called a "covenant," a new covenant, in distinction from the ceremonial law, which was also called a covenant. It is so denominated, to intimate the certainty of the things promised, for covenants are confirmed by an oath: hence most of God's solemn promises to his people are so called.

2. It is a covenant made with "the house of Israel;" that is, the church of God, of which Israel was a type; yet not with the church immediately, but through the blood of the Mediator. The gospel is to us a matter of free promise: but in the hands of Christ it is a covenant with us, and on our behalf. He performs the conditions of it, and seals it with his blood. Making a covenant with any one is a sign of peace between the parties; and this new covenant is a sign of good will towards the house of Israel.

3. Making it "after those days," means after the abolition of the ceremonial law, and so rendering the former covenant void. The new covenant was introduced by the ministry of John; more fully by that of Jesus; and was finally confirmed by his death. The authority of the ceremonial law ceased immediately after this event, and both Jews and gentiles were considered as under a new dispensation. This subject is fully stated in the epistle to the Hebrews.

4. This new covenant implies that what the first could not secure this is intended to accomplish; and what that only shadowed forth this actually performs. The promise it contains was made after all other means failed, and when the house of Israel was gone into captivity. God had before written the law on tables of stone, and that did not succeed: now therefore he will write it on the heart, and the consequence is, that "he will be their God, and they shall be his people."

The import of these promises, and the grace discovered in them, will form the subject of our meditation—

I. CONSIDER THE IMPORT OF THE PROMISES.

The leading promise in the text, and that which lays the foundation of all the rest is—"I will put my law in their inward parts, and write it in their hearts."

In general observe, this new inscription is not intended to render the written law useless. Some have imagined that the law written in the heart was to become the rule of duty, and that the other is thereby superseded: but the moral law is of eternal obligation, and can never be made void.— — —Writing it in the heart, denotes in general, an inward *conformity* to the divine law, and therefore it is not the law itself.— — —The law in the heart is at best imperfect, and therefore cannot be the rule of duty.

More particularly—

1. The law written in the heart is *not any new law*, but the same as was at first impressed on the soul of man, and afterwards engraven on tables of stone. — — —Man was created after the likeness of God, in righteousness and true holiness: and was therefore perfectly conformed to the law in all its parts.

The law was defaced *by sin*, and another law introduced into our members, warring against the law of the mind; so that man by nature is not subject to the law, neither indeed can be. Rom. viii. 7.— — —Regeneration therefore consists in new engraving that law, and re-impressing the divine image on the soul of man, which sin had defaced.

2. By writing the law in the heart is meant a giving an *inward knowledge and approbation of it*, as it is expressed in another passage. Isa. li. 7.— — — The heart is like the ark of the covenant, in which the tables of the law were kept; it becomes the depository of this sacred trust.— — —Where the law is thus written, there is a knowledge of its purity, extent and spirituality; an approbation of what God requires, and a devotedness to his service. Ps. xl. 8. Rom. vii. 22.

3. It includes a *supreme affection of the divine law*, and a delight in all its requirements.— — —That on which we have placed our affections is said to be in our hearts; and there it is that God has fixed his law.— — — Before this work is begun, there is nothing but enmity to God and his government: afterwards it becomes our meat and drink to do his will.— — — The obedience rendered is not merely founded on the authority of the Lawgiver; it is also excited by a view of the excellency and goodness of the law itself.— — —The law without commands, and the law within inclines to obedience; so that such persons become as it were a law unto themselves.

4. It implies a *tenderness of conscience*, and a dread of sin; a quick discernment of its evil nature, and carefulness to avoid it.— — —If the law be written in the heart, it will feel for God's honour; and like Eli, it will tremble for the ark when it seems to be in danger.— — —This law is so deeply engraven that it shall never be obliterated; but its characters shall become increasingly legible, and a conformity to the mind and will of God a matter of continual delight.

Another promise is, "I will be their God."—The sacred Lawgiver forbids our seeking any other god; but we have all rejected him and sought another portion.— — —Now therefore he will himself become our portion, and will make the matter sure: we have been servants of sin, but he will make us servants of righteousness. Lev. xi. 4. Isa. xxvi. 13. Jer. vii. 23.

It is added, "They shall be my people."— — —Israel had often promised to be his people; but they as often forsook him, and broke his covenant. Now they shall forsake him no more, nor will he forsake them forever. Heb. viii. 12. xiii. 5.

II. The grace discovered in these promises.

1. When God created man, he *made him upright;* nor could he make him otherwise.— — —Man is now corrupt and fallen: and seeing the divine law is obliterated from his heart, God might never have written it there any more. It is of free and unmerited mercy that it is otherwise.

2. Our losing the moral image of God was *a voluntary act;* if we are without it, it is what we naturally choose.— — —We love to be without God in the world, and desire not the knowledge of his ways. The carnal

mind is enmity with God, and is not subject to his law. Great therefore is the grace that could restore the divine image to such a fallen and sinful creature.

3. It is still more that he should promise to be *our God*, and ensure to us such an unspeakable inheritance— — —For God to be our friend, secures every thing: and all good is comprehendeded in it.

Inferences,

1. If ever we be saved, we see it must be by grace alone. We have nothing to glory in, for God is all in all.

2. We learn from hence, wherein true religion consists; not in being made free from the law, or treating it with indifference; but in cherishing the highest esteem for its authority.

3. The dreadful depravity of human nature, that should render an almighty work of grace necessary to restore us to a proper frame of mind, and that nothing short of our being new created should suffice.

4. Unless the divine law be written in our heart, we have no part in the covenant, and no interest in the Saviour.

SALVATION BY CHRIST ALONE.

Acts iv. 12.—Neither is there salvation in any other: for there is none other name under heaven given among men whereby we must be saved. (H. H.)

From the account given us of the miracles wrought by our blessed Lord, we should be led, not only to acknowledge him as the true Messiah, but to consider what we ourselves may expect at his hands. His apostles, Peter and John, had healed a man who had been lame from his birth. The spectators, filled with astonishment, were ready to ascribe the honor of this miracle to them: but they told them by whom it had been effected, even by Jesus, whom they had rejected; but who, notwithstanding their contempt of him, was, and by this miracle had proved himself to be, "the head stone of the corner." Ver. 11. They then directed the attention of their auditors to their own eternal interests, and assured them, that as Jesus alone restored the cripple to the use of his limbs, so Jesus alone could save them from everlasting perdition.*

In discoursing upon the words before us, it will be proper to notice,

I. What is implied—

Nothing can be more clearly implied than *that there is salvation for us in Christ.* It may be thought that it is unnecessary to insist upon so plain and obvious a truth, more especially among those who call themselves christians: but this truth is far from being universally known; and the grounds on which it stands are very little considered: and, if it were as well understood as we are apt to imagine, still there would be a necessity for dwelling frequently upon it, on account of its vast importance, and of "determining with St. Paul to know nothing among our people but Jesus Christ, and him crucified."

In confirmation of it, we shall appeal,

*It is evident that the text refers, not to bodily healing, but to a salvation which the apostles themselves, and all their hearers, stood in need of.

1. To the typical representations of Christ—

There were a great variety of sacrifices under the law, which typified the Lord Jesus Christ. The lamb that was offered every morning and evening, foreshewed "the Lamb of God that should take away the sin of the world:" and the scape-goat, which bore the iniquities of all Israel into an uninhabited wilderness, exhibited in yet more striking colors the removal of our guilt by a transfer of it to the head of Jesus. To dwell on all the ceremonies that were appointed on different occasions for the expiation of sin, is needless: suffice it to observe, that "the blood of bulls and of goats could not take away sin;" and that if those offerings had not respect to Christ, they were altogether unworthy, either to be prescribed to man, or to be accepted for him. But the efficacy of those sacrifices for the ends for which they were instituted, proves, beyond a doubt, the infinitely greater efficacy of that sacrifice which Christ in due time offered on the cross. Heb. ix. 13, 14.

2. To the positive declarations concerning him—

Nothing can be conceived more clear and strong than the scripture declarations of Christ's sufficiency to save. How forcibly has the prophet marked the extent, Isa. xlv. 22, the fulness, Isa. i. 18, and the freeness, Isa. lv. 1, 2, of his salvation! He invites "all the ends of the earth," even persons defiled "with crimson sins," to accept all the benefits of the gospel, "without money and without price." In the New Testament the same things are spoken with all the energy that language can afford. All, without exception, are exhorted to come to Christ, Matt. xi. 28; John vi. 37, with all assurance that he will cleanse them from all sin, 1 John i. 7; Acts xiii. 39, and bestow upon them freely all the blessings of grace and glory. John iv. 10, and vii. 37, 38. Is all this a mere mockery and delusion? It surely is so, if Christ be not "able to save to the uttermost all that come unto God by him." Heb. vii. 25.

3. To matter of fact—

We can draw aside the veil of heaven, and point to some before the throne of God, who are such monuments of grace, as leave no doubt respecting the sufficiency of Christ to save any others whatsoever. Behold that man, a murderer; a murderer of no common stamp: he was not satisfied with shedding the blood of a few of his fellow-creatures, or of those who were deserving of death; but he "made the very streets of Jerusalem to run down with blood, and that with the blood of innocents." Moreover, this was but a small part of the guilt he had contracted; so various and so enormous were his crimes. Yet is he, even Manasseh, a chosen vessel, in whom God is, and for ever will be, glorified. 2 Chron. xxxiii. 1—13.

Seest thou that woman also? We know not the particulars of her conduct; but she was so vile and notorious a sinner, that it was a disgrace to notice her, yea our Lord's condescending to notice her was made a ground of doubting his divine mission: nevertheless she also, though once possessed by seven devils, is now in glory. She received, while yet upon earth, an assured testimony, from our Lord himself, that her sins, numerous as they were, were all forgiven: Luke vii. 47, 48; and now is she singing the triumphs of redeeming love as loud as any in heaven.

We could easily refer to a multitude of others, whose enormities were beyond all measure great, who nevertheless were "washed, justified, and sanctified, in the name of the Lord Jesus, and by the Spirit of our God." 1 Cor. vi. 9—11. But enough has been said to put out of all question the blessed truth we are insisting on, namely, that Jesus is a Saviour, and a Great One, and able to deliver all who trust in him. Isa. xix. 20.

Let us now turn our attention to,

II. What is expressed—

What solemn asseverations are these in the text. One would have supposed that the former of them would have been quite sufficient: but the apostle thought no repetitions superfluous, nor any accumulation of words too strong, on such a subject as this. Indeed, it is of infinite importance to every one of us to know, that, as there is salvation for us in Christ, so "*there is no salvation in any other.*"

1. There is not—

In whom else can we find the requisites of a Saviour? In whom can we find a sufficiency, either of merit to justify, or of power to renew, a sinner? If we should apply to the highest angel in heaven to give us of his merit, he would tell us that "he himself is only an unprofitable servant; for that he does no more than is his duty to do." Luke xvii. 10. If we should intreat him to change our hearts, he would confess his utter inability to effect so great a work. Shall we then look to ourselves? We are full of sin. Our merit is found—where? not in heaven truly, but in the lake that burneth with fire and brimstone. Rom. iii. 19. "Nor have we in ourselves a sufficiency even to think a good thought;" 2 Cor. iii. 5; much less to renew ourselves after the divine image. None but Jesus could atone for sin: none but Jesus could yield such an obedience to the law as should be capable of being imputed to others: none but Jesus can send down the Holy Spirit into the souls of men, or say to them, "My grace is sufficient for you:" 2 Cor. xii. 9; and therefore "there is no other name under heaven given among men whereby we can be saved."

If there were any other Saviour, the most eminent of God's servants would have had some intimation of it. Abraham, the friend of God, and the father of the faithful, would probably have heard of him: but he knew of none other; for he sought acceptance through Christ alone, and was justified solely through faith in him. Rom. iv. 3–5. David too, the man after God's own heart, who was inspired to write so much respecting Christ, would probably have been acquainted with such an important fact in order to his own salvation; but he sought refuge in none but Christ; "Purge me with hyssop," says he, "and I shall be clean; wash me, and I shall be whiter than snow." Ps. li. 7. We might hope at least that some information of this kind would have been given to the apostle Paul, who was more fully instructed in the mind and will of God than any other person: yet he knew of no other name but that of Jesus; he renounced all hope "in his own righteousness that he might be found in Christ;" Phil. iii. 9; and "he determined to insist on nothing, in all his ministrations, but Jesus Christ, and him crucified." 1 Cor. ii. 2.

Whether therefore we consider the insufficiency of all the creatures to stand in the place of a Saviour to us, or the utter ignorance of all the prophets and apostles respecting the appointment of any creature to sustain that office, we may be sure that there is none other than the person mentioned in the text, who is a man indeed, but is, at the same time, "God over all blessed for evermore."

2. There cannot be—

We presume not to be wise above what is written; or to say what God might have done if he had pleased: but we are fully warranted by the scriptures to say, that, consistently with his honor, as the Moral Governor of the Universe, man could not have been saved without a Mediator: nor could any Mediator besides Jesus have been found to execute all that was necessary for our salvation. It was necessary that the justice of God should be satisfied for the violations of his law; that his holiness should be displayed in a marked abhorrence of sin; that his truth should be kept inviolate by the execution of his threatenings; and that his law should be honored, as well by an obedience to its precepts, as by an enduring of its penalties. Now none but Jesus, who was God as well as man, could effect all these things, and therefore none but he could save us.

But there is yet another ground on which we may deny that any other could save us; namely, that if we were indebted to any other, either for righteousness or strength, we could not join in the songs of the redeemed in heaven, but must separate from the heavenly choir, Rev. vii. 9, 10, and ascribe to ourselves, or to some other, (inasmuch as we were indebted to ourselves or them,) the honor of our salvation. And how would this comport with the dignity of Jehovah, who has determined "that no flesh should glory in his presence?" It is in vain to say that the glory would ultimately accrue to him: for if we be saved by, or for, any thing of our own, we may, and must, so far take the glory to ourselves: Rom. iv. 2; and that would create discord in heaven, and be irreconcileable with the honor of the Divine Majesty.

Address,

1. The careless—

Wherefore are men so indifferent about their spiritual concerns? Is it that they are in no danger of perishing? If that were the case, why is so much said respecting salvation? and why are we cautioned so strongly against relying on any but Jesus Christ? Surely the very circumstance of Christ being sent down from heaven to die for us, is enough to alarm all our fears, and to convince us, that, if the salvation offered us could be procured by none but him, the danger of those who are not interested in him must be inexpressibly great. Let the careless then consider this; and flee for refuge to the hope that is set before them.

2. The self-righteous—

It is difficult to convince those who are looking to Christ *in part*, that they are really renouncing Christ *altogether*. But the scriptures are so plain on this point, that there cannot be the smallest doubt respecting it. Salvation is "of faith, on purpose that it may be by grace:" Rom. iv. 2; and if it be, whether in whole or in part, by our own works, it ceases to be of grace: it must be wholly of grace, or wholly of works: Rom. iv. 16; it must exclude boasting altogether, or else admit it. But boasting must be excluded wholly: Rom. xi. 6; and therefore all dependence whatsoever on our own works must be wholly and for ever renounced. Rom. iii. 27. If we will not accept salvation on these terms, "Christ shall profit us nothing." Ib. ver. 8.

3. The desponding—

The person healed by Peter and John was a very fit emblem of our state by nature and practice. "We are transgressors from the womb." But, desperate as in appearance our condition is, there is in Jesus a sufficiency of power and grace to make us whole: "his name, through faith in his name, shall give us a perfect soundness, in the presence" of God and man. Gal. v. 2, 4. Let none complain as though they were beyond the reach of mercy: for there is nothing impossible with Jesus: "with him there is mercy; with him is plenteous redemption; and he shall redeem Israel from all his sins." Acts iii. 16, and iv. 10.

THE WAY OF SALVATION.

Titus iii. 15. Not by works of righteousness which we have done, but according to his mercy he saved us, by the washing of regeneration, and renewing of the Holy Ghost. (Sk.)

If human language present us with any word with which we should become familiar, any subject we should be concerned to understand, or any enjoyment we should be anxious to realize; that word, that subject, that enjoyment, is salvation. Salvation is the noblest science, the most invaluable acquisition, and the highest happiness. Without salvation, life is a maze of error, death a gulf of horror, and eternity a scene of punishment. Considering how important a part of a minister's duty it is to explain the nature of salvation, to correct the mistakes so common concerning salvation, and to urge upon his hearers the necessity of securing salvation, I cannot do better than recommend the text to your most serious attention. The doctrines contained in it are,

I. That salvation is not effected by human agency. "Not by works of righteousness which we have done," &c. Does this position require evidence? Then consider,

1. *Where there is no salvation there are no works of righteousness.* Man is a totally depraved creature; "the imagination of the thoughts of his heart is only evil continually," Gen. vi. 5. Where then are his "works of righteousness?" Are works of righteousness the genuine effects of righteous principles? In the carnal mind these principles have no existence. For man "is very far gone from original righteousness, and of his own nature inclined to evil, so that the flesh lusteth always contrary to the spirit;" and the works of the flesh are, "adultery, fornication," &c., Gal. v. 19—21.

2. *Works of righteousness, even where they exist, possess no saving effect.* They are the evidences of salvation, and not the causes of it. They show that men are saved, but they do not operate in producing salvation. They accompany salvation, but they do not precede it. Works of righteousness possess no saving efficacy: they can never control one evil thought, conquer one evil habit, nor extirpate one evil temper; nor has God ever saved one sinner by works of righteousness.

3. *The Bible disclaims the merit of human agency in salvation,* Isa. lxiv. 6; Dan. ix. 7; Rom. iii. 20—28; xi. 5, 6; Gal. ii. 21; Eph. ii. 8, 9.

II. That salvation originates in the divine compassion. "According to his mercy he saved us," &c. Mercy is a certain modification of love, and is that sensation of mind which inclines us to pity and relieve the subjects of misery. Love regards pleasing objects, mercy miserable objects. Adam, when he fell from God, plunged himself into misery·—His misery arose from the forfeiture of his original innocency—from the absence of his God—from his irregular and depraved passions—and from the "fearful looking for of judgment and punishment." His salvation could not originate in himself, as he could neither make an atonement for his offence, nor eradicate the principles of corruption which had taken deep root in his nature. Our salvation is according to God's mercy: it

1. *Accords with the tender sympathies attributed to that mercy.* Read the descriptions which are given of God, Psa. xxv. 6; li. 6; Isa. lxiii. 15; Luke i. 78; James v. 11. Had man been suffered to perish without an offer of salvation, his destruction might have accorded with the justice of God; but

there would have been no perceptible harmony between *his* punishment and God's *tender mercy*.

2. *It accords with the readiness ascribed to that mercy*, Neh. ix. 17. God is represented as being ready to pardon, Isa. xxx. 18. Waiting to be gracious, Micah vii. 18, delighting in mercy. Oh with what readiness did the mercy of God provide a Saviour for man, and with what willingness does the Father run to meet the returning prodigal.

3. *It accords with the descriptions given of the greatness, fullness, and extent of that mercy*, Num. xiv. 19; we read of "the greatness of God's mercy," Psa. v. 7; of "the multitude of his mercy," Neh. ix. 19; of "his manifold mercies," Psa. cxix. 64; the "earth being full of his mercy," Psa. cxlv. 8. "His tender mercies being over all his works." Our salvation accords with these descriptions, in the great and tremendous evils from which we are delivered—in the immensity of blessedness to which we are raised—in the extended and universal offers made of this salvation to mankind, and in its suitability to the unnumbered necessities of our nature.

4. *It accords with the perpetuity of that mercy*. Oh how often does that delightful sentence occur; "His mercy endureth for ever," Psa. cxviii. 1. Our salvation harmonizes with that mercy. Eternal salvation is obtained for us.

III. That salvation is attended by an important change. "By the washing of regeneration." This term is very important and expressive; it is used to describe that inward and radical change which takes place in the human soul when it becomes the subject of salvation. This is variously represented, John iii. 3, by "born again;" Eph. ii. 10, "created in Christ Jesus;" iv. 24, "created in righteousness," &c.; ver. 23, "renewed in the spirit of your mind." But nothing can be more expressive than regeneration, which implies a reproduction or a *new regeneration*. The soul in its essence and faculties remains the same; but it has a new generation of perceptions, feelings, tendencies, and habits. This is called *washing*, perhaps in reference to baptism, which was an initiatory ordinance, to which all submitted who became proselytes to the christian religion; or to signify that regeneration purifies the soul from moral pollution, as washing does the body from the "filth of the flesh." We are saved "by the washing of regeneration," that is, delivered from sin and all its tremendous consequences in the other world.

1. Delivered from the *love* of sinful pleasures and carnal delights, by having the "love of God shed abroad in our hearts."

2. From the *guilt* of sinful practices, by having a knowledge of salvation by the remission of our sins.

3. From the *prevalence* of sinful habits, by the principles of holiness, and the power of the Divine Spirit.

4. From the *commission* of sinful acts, by the total regeneration of our natures, 1 John v. 18.

IV. That salvation is accomplished by a divine influence. "By the renewing of the Holy Ghost." All the influences of God upon the human soul, are effected by the agency of the Holy Ghost.

1. The light and information which we receive on divine subjects, are communicated by the Holy Ghost, John xiv. 26; 1 Cor. ii. 11, 12; 1 John ii. 20.

2. The conviction we have of our personal danger is derived from the same source, John xvi. 8.

3. The change which is produced in the minds of christian believers is attributed to the Holy Ghost, John iii. 5—8; 1 Cor. vi. 11; 2 Cor. iii. 18

4. The assurance of salvation is by the witness of the Holy Ghost. For this reason he is called the Comforter, John xiv. 16; Rom. viii. 16.

Inferences :—

1. How awful the delusion of those who depend on themselves or their works for salvation.

2. How deeply we are indebted to the divine mercy for salvation! Let us sing of the mercies of the Lord for ever.

3. How indispensible is regeneration! Salvation without it is impossible.

4. How deeply anxious should we be to secure the influences and agency of the Holy Ghost, Luke xi. 13.

NO REMISSION WITHOUT BLOOD.

Heb. ix. 22.—Without shedding of blood there is no remission. (S. S.)

THE external administration of religion has been extremely different in different ages of the world: but the method of acceptance with God has been invariably the same. Before the Mosaic ritual was formed, pardon was dispensed through the blood of sacrifies: and since it was abolished, men obtain mercy through that blood, which the sacrifies both before and under the law were intended to prefigure.

To mark the correspondence between the sacrifices under the law, and that offered by Jesus on the cross, is the great scope of the Epistle to the Hebrews. In the preceding context it is observed, that the tabernacle and all the vessels of the ministry were purged with blood; and then it is asserted as an universal truth, "that without shedding of blood there is no remission."

This assertion being of infinite importance, we shall

I. ESTABLISH IT.

The observances of the ceremonial law shew that men were saved by blood under the Mosaic dispensation

For every offence, sacrifices were to be offered according to the rank and quality of the offender: and whatever animals were sacrificed, whether bullocks, goats, lambs, or pigeons, they were to be slain, and their blood was to be sprinkled both on the altar, and on the offerer: and it was by the blood so sprinkled, that the offerer was cleansed from guilt. If a person were so poor that he could not bring a pair of young pigeons, he was at liberty to offer a measure (about five pints) of fine flour: a portion of which, answerably to the destruction of the beasts, was to be burnt, in order to shew the offender what he merited at the hands of God. Lev. v. 6—13.

There were indeed other purifications, some by fire, and others by water: but these were for ceremonial only, and never for moral, defilement.

Thus, the law, with the one exception above mentioned, spake exactly the language of the text.

The same way of salvation still obtains under the gospel

The typical sacrifices are indeed superseded by the one sacrifice of Christ But it is through his sacrifice, and through it alone, that any man is saveu

This is capable of *direct* proof from scripture.

The warning which Eli gave to his sons, when they poured contempt upon the sacrifices, and caused them to be abhorred by the people, not obscurely intimated, that acts of injustice towards men might be punished by the magistrate, and yet be forgiven through the great sacrifice: but that, if any person poured contempt upon the sacrifices, he rejected the only means of salvation, and must therefore inevitably perish. 1 Sam. ii. 17, 25.

There is yet a stronger assertion to this effect in the chapter following the text, where it is said in the most express terms, that they who reject this sacrifice have nothing to expect but wrath and fiery indignation; Heb. x. 26, 27, which could not be true if there were any other way of salvation provided for us.

It may be yet further proved by arguments, which, though of an *indirect* nature, are not the less satisfactory than the foregoing.

If salvation be not by blood *the whole Mosaic ritual was absurd.*

For what end could so many innocent beasts be slaughtered, and consumed by fire, if it were not to prefigure the great sacrifice? If they were intended to shadow forth the way of salvation through the sacrifice of Christ, there was abundant reason for such observances: and the lives of myriads of beasts were well bestowed in such a cause. But on any other supposition the legal sacrifices, having no typical reference, were unworthy of God to institute, or of man to offer.

If salvation be not by blood, *the prophets grossly misrepresented their Messiah.*

Christ was spoken of as "making his soul an offering for sin;" as having "our iniquities laid upon him;" as "wounded for our transgressions," that he might "heal us by his stripes:" Isa. liii. it was foretold that he should "be cut off: but not for himself;" that he should "finish transgression, make reconciliation for iniquity, make an end of sin, and bring in an everlasting righteousness:" Dan. ix. 24, 26. Yea, he was prophesied of as "a fountain that should be opened for sin and uncleanness:" Zech xiii. 1, and John, who was more than a prophet, pointed him out as that very Lamb of God, that should take away the sins of the world. John i. 29. Now what can be the meaning of these passages? how are they applicable to Christ, if they do not mark out his atonement? and what truth is there in such representations, if we are not to seek remission through his atoning blood?

If salvation be not by blood, *the declarations of the apostles, yea, and of Christ himself, are far more likely to mislead, than to instruct the world.*

Christ expressly told his disciples, that his "blood was shed for the remission of sins." Matt. xxvi. 28. And the apostles uniformly declare, that God purchased the church with his own blood; Acts xx. 28; that our reconciliation to God, Eph. ii. 16. Col. i. 20, and our justification before him, Rom. v. 9, together with our complete redemption, Eph. i. 7. Rev. v. 9, are by blood, even by the blood of Christ, that spotless Lamb. 1 Pet. i. 19. Is this the way to teach men that they shall be saved by their works? Must we not utterly despair of understanding any thing they have said, if we are not to expect salvation by the blood of Christ?

The apostle's assertion being thus fully established, we shall

II. Improve it.

The death of Christ has an aspect upon every thing that relates to our souls. But, not to enumerate many points. let us reflect on

1. The evil of sin

We are assured that not one sin could have been forgiven without shedding of blood. Nor was it the blood of bulls and of goats only that was necessary, but the blood of God's dear Son, even of Jehovah's Fellow; what then must sin be, that required such a sacrifice? We behold the evil of it in the miseries that are in the world; and still more in the torments of the damned: but most of all do we see its malignity in the sufferings of the Son of God: without which not the smallest transgression could ever have been expiated Let us then view sin in this light, and we shall no more account it a small and venial evil.

2. The folly of self-righteousness.

Self-righteousness consists in substituting something of our own in the place of the atonement, or in blending something of our own with it. In either case we utterly make void the death of Christ. Gal. ii. 21. And what madness is this! It is, in fact, to shut ourselves out from all hope of pardon, and to rivet our sins upon our souls for ever.

It may be thought indeed that Christ died to purchase us a right and power to save ourselves by our works. But if this was the case, why did St. Paul impute the rejection of his own nation to their going about to establish their own righteousness? Rom. ix. 31, 32, and x. 3, and why did he desire to be found in Christ, *not having his own righteousness?* Phil. iii. 9. Why did he declare that if any man were circumcised with a view to obtain justification by the law, Christ should profit him nothing? Gal. v. 2, 4. Why did he contrast salvation by grace, and salvation by works, so as to shew that they could not be blended or consist together? Rom. xi. 6. This alas! is a refuge of lies, which, together will all who flee to it, with be swept away with the besom of destruction.

Let us not then dare to put ourselves in that way, wherein God declares there is no remission.

3. The encouragement which the gospel affords to sinners

When it is said that "without shedding of blood there is no remission," it is doubtless implied, that through shedding of blood there is remission. And what a glorious truth is this? how refreshing to the weary soul! Let it be contemplated with holy joy and wonder. There is no sin, however great, from which the blood of Christ will not cleanse the soul. 1 John i. 7. David, after contracting the foulest guilt, was yet able to say, Purge me with hyssop, and I shall be clean; wash me and I shall be whiter than snow. Ps. li. 7. Let every one then go to the fountain opened for sin; let him plunge, as it were, beneath that sacred flood; and he shall instantly become pure and spotless in the sight of God. Eph. v. 25, 27.

4. The wonderful love of Christ

He knew that sin could not be forgiven, unless he would take upon him our nature, and make atonement for us by his own blood. And rather than leave us to perish as the fallen angels, he accepted the hard conditions. left the bosom of his Father, put himself in our place, and submitted to endure the penaly due to sin. O what transcendant love! how inconceivable its heights, how unsearchable its depths! Eph. iii. 18, 19, Let our minds dwell upon it continually; that our hearts being warmed with this mysterious, incomprehensible love, we may be ever vying with the hosts of heaven in singing, To him who loved us and washed us from our sins in his own blood, be glory and dominion for ever and ever. Rev, i. 5, 6.

SINNERS BROUGHT NIGH BY THE BLOOD OF CHRIST.

Ephes. ii. 13.—But now in Christ Jesus, ye who sometimes were afar off, are made nigh by the blood of Christ. (Sk.)

The Ephesian christians, previous to their conversion, were Gentiles, ver. 11; and thus were aliens from the commonwealth of Israel, and strangers from the covenants of promise, verse 12. The prophets had foretold that Jesus should be given "for a light to the Gentiles,"—for God's salvation to the ends of the earth, Isa. xlix. 6. Jesus came,—the Gentiles were enlightened:—the ends of the earth saw the salvation of God; and "in Christ Jesus those who had been far off, were made nigh by the blood of Christ."

The language of our text is as applicable to the state of the converted among *us* Gentiles, as it was to the case of the converts at Ephesus—for all such among us—"*Were far off,—are made nigh—in Christ Jesus,—by the blood of Christ.*"

I. We were sometimes far off. This intimates *distance*, and signifies that we were ignorant of God, chap. iv. 18. Destitute of his image, chap. v. 22—24. Under his displeasure, chap. ii. 1—3. Unconnected with his church, ver. 11, 12.

What a significant idea! How far were we from a true, an experimental knowledge, of God,—of the things of God: how far from any resemblance to his moral image; from any conduct, but such as merited his displeasure! And we were in disposition, in affection, equally distant from his church,—his people.

The apostle's words include another idea connected with this distance; namely, the time.

Ye were *sometimes* far off. It was with many of us a long time; with all a *miserable* time, and a *dangerous* time.

But thanks be to God! these times are passed away; our text says ye *were* far off.

Here let us pause, and think on what we *were*.

What the *peculiar nature* of our erroneous path, our remote situation, was, is comparatively of little consequence. Some of us were lost in the cares of the world. Some were deluded by the deceitfulness of riches. The lust of other things held some captive. While others were intoxicated by pleasure, or enchanted by worldly science, or drawn away by the meaner things which attract the attention of sordid souls. It is enough, more than enough, *that we were far from God*. Let us now turn our attention to our present situations.

II. Now are we made nigh. These words convey to the mind, ideas of *Relationship,—Friendship,—Union,*—and *Communion.*

Relationship. Real christians are children of God, 2 Cor. vi. 17, 18; Gal. iii. 26. They are brethren, Matt. xxiii. 8. And they are as properly related, in a religious or spiritual sense, both to God and to each other, as men are related to each other by natural ties, see John i. 12, 13; Gal. iii. 26.

Friendship. Among men of the world, all relatives are not friends; but christians are in a state of friendship with God, with Christ, and with each other, John xv. 14, 15; 1 John iii. 14.

Union. Jesus is the vine; christians are the branches, John xv. 5. He is the body; they are the members, chap. v. 30. They are the members, too, one of another, Rom. xii. 5; 1 Cor. xii. 12, 13. Again, they are represented as stones of the same building, Jesus being the chief corner stone, ver. 19—22.

Communion. They have intercourse with God, as a child with his parent, Rom. viii. 15; Gal. iv. 6, as a man with his friend. They have communion with each other, see 1 John i. 3, 6, 7; Col. iii. 16.

Thus we are made nigh; and our text leads us in the next place to consider how this blessed, this important change has been effected.

III. In Christ Jesus,—by the blood of Christ.

In Christ Jesus. He is our Mediator; God with God; man with men, see 1 Tim. ii. 5; Heb. xii. 24.

It is here the distant parties meet. Here the Gentile meets the Jew, ver. 14. Here the returning sinner meets a gracious, a merciful, a forgiving God, chap. i. 6, 7, and ver. 18. Here persons that were distant, that were hostile, meet, cordially unite, and perfectly agree, see Gal. iii. 28, 29; Col. iii. 11; John x. 16. Here even Saul of Tarsus meets the followers of Jesus of Nazareth on amicable terms; and the same mouth, which before breathed out threatening and slaughter, now breathes nothing but friendship and love. Here all *real* christians of every sect and name meet: and *here* all men may know that they are disciples of Christ, because they love one another, John xiii. 35. Here, too, they all ascribe their salvation to Jesus; and glory in being "made nigh."

By the blood of Christ. Under the old dispensation, this blood was yearly typified by that of the paschal lamb, Exod. xii. 4, 5; 1 Cor. v. 7;—daily by that of the sacrificial lamb, Exod. xxix. 38, 39; John i. 29;—and frequently by that of other sacrifices, Heb. chap. ix. and x. Covenants were ratified by blood, Exod. xxiv. 8; Heb. ix. 18—20; "and without shedding of blood is no remission," Heb. ix. 22. "We enter into the holiest by the blood of Jesus," Heb. x. 19. Almost every important circumstance connected with our salvation has reference to the blood of Christ. We are *redeemed* by his blood, chap. i. 7; Col. i. 14; 1 Peter i. 19; Rev. v. 9. *Justified* by his blood, Rom. v. 9; *washed, cleansed* by his blood, 1 John i. 7; Rev. i. 5, and vii. 14; *we conquer* through his blood, Rev. xii. 11; *we are made nigh by his blood.*

The shedding of the blood of Christ was the last grand act, as a sacrifice for the sins of mankind; a sacrifice, without which we could have no hope; without which we must have perished, Acts iv. 10, 12. Well then, may such frequent mention be made of the *blood of Christ.* It is all in vain to talk of reconciliation with God—nearest to God—to the people of God, but by the *blood of Jesus.*

Let us close the subject by inquiring.

Where are *you?* Some, I fear, are still "*afar off.*" How awful is your situation! Here you assemble with the people of God; you stand, you sit near them; perhaps you dwell under the same roof with some of them; but alas! in a religious point of view, at what a vast distance are your souls from God and his people! Perhaps you stand this moment near the verge of hell! Oh, that my voice could reach and recal you! Rather, may the voice of that "blood which speaketh better things than the blood of Abel," reach you, and bring you nigh!

Ye who are made nigh! Remember where you were; remember your deliverance, and your deliverer. Think on your present situation, thus strikingly described, Heb. xii. 22—24. Let the caution, Heb. iii. 12—14, have its proper influence on your conduct; and you may with safety and propriety adopt the following triumphant language, Rom. viii. 35, 38, 39

REPENTANCE.

Mark vi 12.—And they went out and preached that men should repent. (Sk.)

THE preachers here mentioned were our Saviour's disciples; the time referred to, was that period of Christ's ministry, when he called unto him the twelve, and sent them forth by two and two. But it is the *subject* of their preaching, which principally arrests our attention; they preached "that men should *repent*." This was exactly the manner in which the Lord Jesus, as a public teacher, began his work, ver. 14, 15, and Matt. iv. 17,—the way in which John the Baptist had commenced his, Matt. iii. 2; Mark i. 4; Luke iii. 3,—and the apostles, on the day of Pentecost, and afterwards, proceeded in the very same manner, Acts ii. 38, and iii. 19, and xxvi. 20. We infer, that the doctrince of repentance is of primary importance; and that we should frequently make it the subject of our ministry. Allow me to occupy the present time, in describing its *nature*, and enforcing its *necessity*.

I. THE NATURE OF REPENTANCE. The term repentance, when religiously applied, signifies a change in the disposition of the mind from what is bad, towards that which is good, Ezek. xviii. 30; Jer. xxv. 5. It must, indeed, be allowed that the word has a somewhat different meaning in certain passages of the Holy Scriptures; as when God is said to repent, &c.; but the former is its usual, plain, and obvious meaning; and that which I would endeavor to develop and illustrate by the following observations.

1. *Repentance begins* with a consciousness of the depravity, the guilt, and the danger connected with our fallen and unrenewed state, associated with a serious concern about the consequences, Ezek. xx. 43, and xxxvi. 31; Acts ii. 37, and xvi. 30.

2. *This view of ourselves*, if repentance be genuine, *is attended by considerable uneasiness and pain of mind*, mixed with a *godly sorrow* on account of our crimes and our danger; *sorrow*, arising as much from regret that we have offended the greatest and best of beings, as from the dread of that punishment which our sins deserve, 2 Cor. vii. 9, 10; Luke xviii. 13, 14, and xxii. 62.

3. *Another quality of true repentance* is a *hatred to sin*, shown to be real by fruits meet for repentance; such as aversion at the sight of wickedness—a constant endeavor to avoid all evil—and a sincere desire to do the will of God, Isa. lv. 7; Ezek. xviii. 21; Psa. li. 13; Acts ix. 6. This hatred to sin is uniformly accompanied by,

4. *A desire to be delivered from sin;* from its guilt—its power—its pollation—and its consequences. And this desire leads to a diligent and an earnest use of all the means calculated to secure such deliverance, Psa. li., *et passim*.

5. *Repentance is the gift of God*, Zech. xii. 10; Acts v. 31; and though in all its distinct operations, it may in various individuals, differ in degree, yet its nature is always the same; combining the above qualities, and constituting the only way to Christ, who casts out none that *thus* come to him for salvation. Let us now consider,

II. THE NECESSITY OF REPENTANCE. This may be understood from the following particulars.

1. *God commands and requires it*, Acts xvii. 30. The doctrine was delivered by the Saviour, and by the Baptist, in the form of a command: ***Repent ye***, was their mode of address.

2. *All need repentance*, because all have sinned: those who have lived lives as regular as St. Paul lived previous to his conversion, as well as those whose lives have been irregular and immoral, must repent. If there be any difference, it is this, that we are not required to repent of *such* sins as we have not committed.

3. *There can be no pardon, no salvation without repentance.* So the word of God teaches, Luke xiii. 3,—so we infer from the very nature of things. Is it rational to ask for pardon, unless there be a consciousness of guilt? Would not the circumstance of offering pardon or salvation to one who felt no need of such a favor, be absurd? Would any one prize such an inestimable blessing, unless he had previously felt guilt and sorrow, and had feared the awful consequences of dying without the forgiveness of sin, and the favor of God?

From the whole of the subject,

1. *Let the mere moralist know*, that repentance is as necessary for him, as it was for the Pharisees, in the days when Christ addressed them, as in the following passages:—Matt. iii. 7, 8, and xxiii. 27, 33; Luke xviii. 9—14.

2. *Let the Antinomian know*, that he must personally repent or perish, Psa. xxxiv. 18, and cxlvii. 3, and Isa. lxvi. 2.

3. *Let every fallen professor be aware*, that he can never be restored without repentance, Rev. ii. 5.

4. *And let every sinner under heaven be assured*, that Christ is able to save unto the uttermost, them that *thus* repent and believe the gospel.

JUSTIFICATION BY FAITH.

Rom. iii. 28. We conclude that a man is justified by faith without the deeds of the law. (B.)

These words contain a conclusion drawn from the principles laid down in the preceding context, which we must examine, if we would understand and feel the force of the inference. Having expressed his readiness to preach the Gospel at Rome, St. Paul proceeded to show the need which all have of the Gospel, the "wrath of God being revealed against all unrighteousness and ungodliness of men," and to point out the wickedness and inexcusableness of the Gentiles, and also of the Jews, in evidence of which he alleges the testimony of their own inspired writers, David and Solomon, in the best ages of their church. Hence all being sinners, and involved in guilt and condemnation, and therefore incapable of being justified by the law, natural or revealed, God has appointed another way of justification;—we say a man is "justified by faith without the deeds of the law." It will now easily appear:—

I. What is meant by justification.

The justification here meant is not that which comes upon all men, even infants, through the righteousness of Christ. Ch. v. 14, 15 18. It is not that which shall take places at the day of judgment, spoken of, ch. ii. 13—16, and by our Lord, Matt. xii. 37, which will be, not indeed by the merit, ch. vi. 23, but by the evidence of works. Rev. xx. 12; xxii. 12. It is the justification, which the true people of God experience, and possess on earth; 1 Cor. vi. 11; Tit. iii. 7; which is—not the being acquitted of all blame, or declared to be innocent, which is the meaning of the word "justi-

fied," in courts of law: Psa. cxliii. 2; ch. iii. 20:—not the being made innocent, or holy, or righteous, which would confound it with regeneration or sanctification:—But the having righteousness accounted, or imputed, to us, sin not imputed, sin pardoned, or the sentence of condemnation gone out against us reversed, and our obligation to punishment cancelled, and this by a judicial act of GOD. This implies, and draws after it, acceptance and adoption, but differs from these things, as it does also from regeneration.

II. IN WHAT SENSE WE ARE TO BE "JUSTIFIED BY FAITH."

When the Apostle says, we are "justified by faith," he does not speak of the *moving cause* of justification, which is the divine love, mercy, or grace; and hence we are said to be justified by grace; ver. 24; Tit. iii. 4—7: not of the *meritorious cause*, which is the redemption of Christ; ver. 24, 25; Isa. liii. 11; 2 Cor. v. *ult.;* and hence we are said to be "justified by Christ; Gal. ii. 17;—nor of the *efficient cause*, either of the preparation necessary, as conviction and repentance for sin, or of a sense of this justification; this is the Holy Spirit, and may be meant, Tit. iii. 7:—nor of the *instrumental cause on the part of* God, which is his Word, viz. his declarations and promises respecting pardoning the penitent: of this our Lord speaks, John xv. 3:—But of the *instrumental cause on our part*, which is faith—in Christ, as the Son of God, the Messiah, the Saviour, able and willing to save: John iii. 16—18; Gal. ii. 16; this implies that we come to him; John vi. 37; vii. 37; Matt. xi. 28; that we trust in him, as "delivered for our offences," ch. iv. 25, trust in his blood, ch. iii. 25, and that we receive him, John i. 12,—in God, ch. iv. 24,—in his mercy and promises through Christ, ch. iv. 17—23. Those who have this faith are justified, and none without it. Thus, in different senses, we are justified, by grace, by Christ, by the spirit, by the word, by faith.

III. HOW THIS IS "WITHOUT THE DEEDS OF THE LAW."

The law meant here, is chiefly the moral law, ch. ii. 17, 18, 21—23, 25. The sins mentioned in this chapter, ver 10, 18, are all breaches of the moral law; it is this also which is meant, ch. vii.—The deeds of this law are the obedience required in it, viz. in the Ten Commandments, or in those two respecting love to God and our neighbor, which comprise all the rest. These deeds cannot merit our justification, because they cannot precede it, we neither do, nor can do them till we are justified; then only do we begin to love and serve a pardoning God.—But how does this consist with St. James' doctrine? ch. ii. 14—26. Abraham was justified years before Isaac was born, but his offering him up at God's command, showed the reality and power of his faith, that it wrought by love, a love to God greater than to Isaac. Thus it declared and evidenced his faith. So was Rahab's faith evidenced, and in this way our faith must be made manifest; for the works of the law must follow our justification. Our faith must "work," Gal. v. 6; 1 Thess. i. 3; the law must be "established," ver. 31, and its "righteousness fulfilled in us," by love, ch. viii. 3, 4; xiii, 10; Gal. v. 14. We must make the law a rule of life, must view ourselves in it as in a glass, that we may see our great deficiency, and be kept in an humble disposition; must consider it as holding out to our view that "holiness without which no man shall see the Lord."—But our obedience to the law can never merit our acceptance even after our justification; we can claim this aud eternal life solely on the ground of our justification through Christ's merits.

INFERENCES.

No one that is penitent need despair on account of his sins—no one should presume on account of his righteousness.—If we be justified by faith, we may be justified *now*.

NATURE OF REGENERATION.

John iii. 3.—Verily, verily, I say unto thee, Except a man be born again, he cannot see the kingdom of God. (Pr.)

In the conduct of Nicodemus, to whom these words were addressed, there are several things worthy of notice—

1. He had a *general conviction* of the truth of christianity, though ignorant of some of its leading principles. He knew that Christ was sent of God, and yet could not understand the doctrine of the new birth. This is a very common case; there are many who know that the gospel is true, who are yet unacquainted with its sanctifying and renovating influence.

2. Nicodemus being a great man, a ruler of the Jews, was in part ashamed to *own the truth*, and to be seen amongst its decided friends. He did not like to appear in the daytime, and therefore "came to Jesus by night;" but it would have been to his honor openly to have owned the cause of Christ.

3. He came to Jesus for *instruction*, but our Lord intimates that instruction was not all he needed; he must be "born again," and could not receive instruction to any saving purpose without it. Herein lies the fitness and propriety of our Lord's answer. The plainest truths are full of darkness to an unrenewed mind, because they can only be spiritually discerned. 1 Cor. ii. 14. Nicodemus however was at length brought to receive the truth in love, and he became a disciple of the Lord Jesus. John xix. 39.

I. Endeavor to explain the nature of the change mentioned in the text, or what it is to be "BORN AGAIN."

The expression is figurative, but denotes a real and important change. It is sometimes called a being "created anew" in Christ Jesus; being "quickened" from a death in sin: giving a "new heart," and putting a "right spirit" within us: being called out of "darkness," into his marvellous "light;" putting off the "old man," and putting on the "new man," and becoming "new creatures" in Christ Jesus. By these, and a variety of similar expressions, this great moral change is denoted.

1. From all these we may see, that it means something more than a bare *reformation of conduct*.— — —Such language as that in the text would not have been employed to express a mere outward change, for that may take place without any renovation of the heart.— — —Besides, Nicodemus need not have "marvelled," if this had been all; for every one would admit that some sort of morality attaches to the profession of religion.— — —Nor does it appear that Nicodemus himself needed such a change as this. He was a "pharisee," and therefore had to boast of his own righteousness; and like Paul, as touching the law he was blameless.— — —Neither was it needful for the Holy Spirit to produce such a change as this, for it might exist without his special influence, and has existed where that influence is denied.— — —The change insisted on by our Lord is effected by the agency of the Holy Spirit: it is therefore an internal change wrought upon the soul, a being "born of water, and of the Spirit."

2. Nor does it consist merely in having *the understanding enlightened*, for Nicodemus was possessed of some religious light, and yet he must be "born again."— — —There may be a great deal of light in the head, and yet the heart remain the same. Many are enlightened in hearing the word, and yet are far enough from being new creatures in Christ Jesus. They are still estranged from the life of God, and from the power of religion, notwith-

standing their superior means of information.— — —Wherein then does this change consist, and what is it to be born again?

3. To be born of the Spirit consists in *a change of heart* respecting God and the things of God. It is a change in the disposition and temper of the mind, or the turning of the heart to God; a change in the judgment and affections, effected by the agency of the Holy Spirit. It is that change which produces repentance and faith, and from which every holy exercise of the mind proceeds, as streams from the fountain, and as branches from the root.

More particularly—

1. To be born again is to have *the image of God restored in the soul,* and to be created anew in righteousness and true holiness. As in our natural birth we are made to bear the image of the earthly, so in this the image of the heavenly.— — —Man was once in the image of his Maker; he was made upright, in the likeness of God created he him: but that image was defaced by sin, and totally lost by the fall.— — —Man in his original state was what he ought to be; his understanding was all light, without any darkness at all; his will was all rectitude, without any deviation from the standard of truth: his affections all purity, without the least defilement, and his heart was wholly on the side of God.— — —But now all is lost and gone, and we are by nature children of wrath. Regeneration is the re-impression of this image upon us, bearing a resemblance to the moral perfections of God, and being changed into the same image from glory to glory, as by the Spirit of the Lord

2. Regeneration is *the commencement of a new life in the soul,* the beginning of a new state of things. It is to become new creatures; old things are passed away, and behold all things become new, and we enter as it were into a new world.

1. It is accompanied with a new set of *thoughts and sentiments,* so that no one object of a moral kind now appears in the same light as before. All the views and prospects of the mind are changed, and we begin to know things after a different manner. We begin to have new thoughts of ourselves as sinners, and of Christ as the Saviour; new thoughts of God and his righteous government, of the law and of the gospel, of this world and that which is to come.— — —Or if our thoughts be not materially altered on these subjects generally, we are very differently affected with them, and feel a new interest in them, unknown to ourselves before.

2. It is accompanied with a new set of *affections and attachments.* We had hopes and fears, joys and griefs, pleasure and pain before; but now they are derived from a different source. We have now very different objects of desire and of dread, and sources of pleasure totally unknown before. It is all a new state, and a new world. The Lord hath led us by a way that we knew not, and in paths that we have not known. Isa. xlii. 16.

3. There is now a new set of *principles and motives.* If we attend to the same religious duties as formerly, yet it is in a very different manner. The same things which were before burdensome, are now delightful; and what was formerly done from a spirit of self-righteousness, is now done to the glory of God. Fear used to be the impelling motive, now it is love. Before, it was the hope of being delivered from misery; now it is delight in the thing itself, and the service of God is desired for its own sake.

4. There is also a new set of *companions and associates.* We had our friends and attachments, and so we have now; but they are of a different description. We are no longer strangers and foreigners, but fellow-citizens

with the saints and of the household of God. The righteous are now the excellent of the earth, in whom is all our delight.

These are some of the leading features of the change intended in the text. Let us now attempt,

II. An improvement of the subject.

1. Let us *examine ourselves*, and what we know of this change in our own souls. Are we conscious that some such change has passed upon us? Some indeed may look back to the time when they were enemies to God at heart, and others to the time when they were in a state of indifference and unconcern; but in all real believers there is a change like that which we have briefly explained, though it may be more or less evident to those who are the subjects of it.

2. We learn from hence, what is *essential to true religion*, and to its very existence in the soul. It is in vain to think ourselves christians, unless we are born again. We know nothing as we ought to know without this, and our profession is a mere delusion.

3. We see to whom we are *indebted* for this great moral change, even to the Spirit of the living God, who quickeneth whom he will. Who made thee to differ; and what hast thou, that thou hast not received? All our salvation is of God, from the foundation to the top-stone thereof. Grace, grace unto it.

NECESSITY OF REGENERATION.

John iii. 3.—Verily, Verily, I say unto thee, Except a man be born again, he cannot see the kingdom of God. (Pr.)

Having explained the nature of the change intended; that it does not consist in a mere reformation of conduct, or in the understanding being merely enlightened, but in an inward change of heart, in which we are made to bear the moral image of God, and are created anew in Christ Jesus, that it is the commencement of a new life, accompanied with new sentiments and affections, new principles and motives of conduct, and that this change is the immediate product of the Holy Spirit;—our business now will be to consider,

The necessity of this change, or why we must be born again, in order to our seeing the kingdom of God.

This necessity applies, not only to some, but to all without exception, irrespective of our former state or character, for there is no respect of persons with God.

Here it will be proper to consider a few things which render this change of heart necessary.

The solemn asseveration of our Lord, ought indeed of itself to be sufficient to convince us of its absolute necessity. As a teacher come from God, his doctrine must be true, and the peculiarly solemn manner in which he speaks on this occasion, is deserving of special regard. "Verily, verily, I say unto thee, Except a man be born again, he cannot see the kingdom of God."

Other considerations however may be added, to show the necessity of this change: some of which are the following—

1. The *depravity of human nature* affords abundant evidence, that ex-

cept a man be born again, he cannot see the kingdom of God.— — —We should not need to be regenerated, if we had not first become degenerate; if not wholly ruined by sin, we should not need to be created anew and born again. The state of human nature is like the house infected with the leprosy; repairing will not do it, it must be re-constructed.— — —That which is born of the flesh is flesh: if we had any good thing in us, we need not be created anew to good works. If not dead in trespasses and sins, and beyond the hope of recovery, we need not be quickened according to the working of his mighty power, which he wrought in Christ, when he raised him from the dead.— — —But such is our state by nature, that we are wholly corrupt; there is none that doeth good, no not one; the heart is deceitful above all things, and desperately wicked; all the imaginations of the thoughts of the heart are evil, only evil, and that continually; tne carnal mind is enmity against God, not being subject to his law, neither indeed can be.— — — Such is our moral condition, and while it continues so, we connot see the kingdom of God.

2. The *nature of the heavenly world* renders this change necessary. Flesh and blood in its present state, cannot inherit the kingdom of God. There must be a meetness, before we can be made partakers of the inheritance of the saints in light, and such a meetness as corresponds with the nature of that inheritance: all true enjoyment arises from congeniality, or an agreement in the disposition with the object to be enjoyed.

1. In order therefore to "see" the kingdom of God, there must be a *spiritual discernment.* All the objects of that kingdom are spiritual and holy, and cannot be known but by a spiritual and holy mind. The natural man receiveth not the things of the Spirit of God, for they are foolishness unto him; neither can he know them, because they are spiritually discerned. 1 Cor. ii. 14. Man is wholly blind to the equity of the law, and to the grace of the gospel; he sees no glory in the Lawgiver, and none in the Saviour. The eyes of his understanding must be enlightened, by the Spirit of wisdom and revelation, or he can have no perception of the moral beauty and excellency of heavenly things. Eph. i. 17, 18; Matt. xvi. 17.

2. To see the kingdom of God, we must have *a spiritual taste*, a holy relish for divine things, otherwise heaven could not be a place of enjoyment to us. The glory and happiness of the future state will eminently consist in a delightful and profound contemplation of God's perfections, in intimate nearness to him, and in having fellowship with the Father, Son, and Holy Spirit. But what fellowship hath righteousness with unrighteousness; and what communion hath light with darkness? 2 Cor. vi. 14. There is no entering into the kingdom, no enjoyment of its bliss, without an ardent relish for spiritual and holy things. 1 John i. 7.

3. The heavenly state requires a *disposition for holy activity*, a heart to love and serve the Lord. Though the redeemed shall cease from their present labors and sufferings, they shall not be unemployed, but shall serve God day and night in his temple. Heaven will be a place of unbounded activity; he maketh his angels spirits, and his ministers a flame of fire. There his servants shall serve him, with unwearied zeal and assiduity.— — —But how totally unfit for all this is man in his unregenerate state, having no heart for God, or for holy exercises; and to whom a Sabbath on earth is wearisome! Either heaven must cease to be what it is, or the sinner's heart must be renewed.

4. There requires a thirsting and a *longing after holiness*, not only to be free from sin, but to desire it as the perfection of bliss, the very essence of

salvation.— — —But the holiness of that world would utterly confound the sinner. Isaiah, when he had only a vision of the Holy One, cried out, I am undone, I am a man of unclean lips! And when Peter had a display of the purity and glory of the Saviour, he exclaimed, Depart from me, oh Lord, for I am a sinful man.— — —What then would the sinner do? He might have some relish for a Mahometan paradise; but how could he endure the effulgence of bliss and purity which surrounds the throne of God?

In addition to the nature of the heavenly state, as rendering regeneration necessary, we might observe,

5. The *immutability of God* shows that such a change is indispensable. A change there must be somewhere, since so solemn an asseveration has been given; and if it cannot be in him, it must take place in us. If it were possible that the nature of things might alter, or that God should cease to hate evil and love holiness, a sinner might be saved without any change of heart: otherwise it is absolutely and for ever impossible. The irrevocable sentence of God is, "there shall in no wise enter into it any thing that defileth, or that worketh abomination:" but man is all uncleanness, and therefore cannot enter. If on earth two cannot walk together except they are agreed; it is impossible that a holy God and a polluted creature should dwell together in heaven.

How utterly vain then is every hope of salvation without regenerating grace: and how needful to enquire into our own state individually, and how we stand in the sight of God.

The reality of this change must be judged of by its effects, and their accordance with the Holy Scriptures. 1 Pet. ii. 1—3.

THE IMPORTANT REQUEST.

Psalm xxv. 11.—For thy names sake, O Lord, pardon mine iniquity; for it is great. **(Sk.)**

The absolute dependance of the creature on the Creator, renders prayer equally the duty and privilege of mankind. We are therefore taught both by reason and Scripture, "that men ought always to pray and not to faint." And though the omniscient Jehovah perfectly knows our necessities, and the blessings which we desire; "yet for all these things will he be inquired of to do them for us." And hence the righteous have in all ages, cultivated a spirit of genuine devotion, and lived in habits of gratitude and praise. Thus the royal Psalmist, as "a man after God's own heart," was deeply imbued with the "spirit of grace and supplication," and enjoyed intimate intercourse and communion with "the Father of mercies." Many of his prayers and thanksgivings are recorded in this book, which are greatly diversified in their character and tendency; and eminently suited to the various states and circumstances of the saints in every succeeding period of the church. In this psalm, David lifts up his soul to the Almighty, and boldly professes unshaken confidence in his name,—gratefully acknowledges the divine goodness,—and earnestly implores, in the text, his mercy and salvation; "For thy name's sake, O Lord, pardon," &c. This important prayer contains, an ingenuous confession of sin,—an appropriate request for pardon,—and an argumen urged to obtain success.

I. An ingenuous confession of sin;—"Mine iniquity is great." Whether David here refers to his conduct in the matter of Uriah is very uncertain; but it is evident that he was deeply conscious of some defection from the Lord, which greatly distressed his mind, and led him to confess and bewail the greatness of his transgression. And as fallen and guilty sinners, we shall be induced to adopt a similar confession, if we seriously consider,

1. *Our sins are great in their number.* The scripture hath concluded all under sin, and the whole world is guilty before God. But all men do not run to the same excess in wickedness; yet the crimes of every sinner are *innumerable.* Sin is the transgression of the law, which is "holy, just, and good," and requires perfect, universal, and constant obedience. It is exceeding broad, extending to every thought, desire, purpose, word, and work of the moral creature. How often then do we all offend, and come short of the glory of God! How many have been the follies of our childhood,—the crimes of our youth,—and the backslidings of our riper age! How numerous are our sins of omission and commission; open and secret; in heart and life! Hence said Eliphaz to Job, "Is not thy wickedness great, and thine iniquities infinite?" And David declares, "Innumerable evils have compassed me about, mine iniquities are more than the hairs of mine head; therefore my heart faileth me."

2. *Our sins are great in their turpitude.* We are divinely assured, that "sin is an evil and bitter thing;" and the exceeding vileness and deformity of its nature, appear—*from the Being against whom it is committed,* who is infinitely great, good, and glorious, and delights in the happiness of his creatures, Psa. cxlv. 9; 1 Tim. ii. 4;—*from the dignity and circumstances of its subjects;* who are created, redeemed, and preserved for the glory of the Creator; and blessed with every privilege to facilitate their immortal interests, Rom. ii. 4;—*from the degrading characters which it sustains;* as ignorance, ingratitude, enmity, rebellion, bondage, folly, shame, disease, death, &c.,—and *from the awful effects which it produces;* in dishonoring the Almighty, rejecting the Saviour, destroying the sinner, filling the world with miseries, and hell with the vengeance of eternal fire! Behold then how horribly vile, malignant, and detestable is sin! Psa. v. 5; Jer. xliv. 4; Hab. i. 13.

3. *Our sins are great in their demerit.* The punishment due to sin must be in proportion to the majesty and glory of God, whose dignity it daringly insults, and whose law it impiously violates. Who then can calculate the wages of ungodliness, or the horrors of perdition! We may, however, partially discover the desert of sin, as exhibited in the doom of the fallen angels—the expulsion of man from paradise—the overthrow of Sodom and Gomorrah—the judgments inflicted on the wicked in every age—the evils and calamities which abound in the world—the sufferings and death of Christ for mankind—and the final destruction of the ungodly, "from the presence of the Lord, and from the glory of his power." But description fails; for language cannot express, nor the mind fully conceive, the just demerit and awful consequences of transgression. Tremble then, ye stout hearted sinners, and earnestly cry, "Save, Lord, or we perish!" And thank God, salvation is possible. Our text affords encouragement to the penitent, and contains,

II. An appropriate request for pardon;—"O Lord, pardon mine iniquity!" This ardent petition is highly impressive in its manner, and comprehensive in its import, and is strictly applicable to all who feel and lament the burden of sin; as,

1. *The language of genuine repentance.* The Psalmist was evidently conscious of the guilt and deformity of his iniquity, and was deeply humbled and contrite under a sense of his unfaithfulness. His backslidings reproved him, and he was penitently filled with his own ways, ver. 18. His unfeigned compunction of heart was accompanied with a penitential acknowledgment of sin, and earnest prayer for divine forgiveness, ver. 7. Repentance is absolutely necessary to obtain pardon, and is therefore sacredly enjoined as an imperious duty on all mankind, Acts xvii. 30. It is distinguished by deep conviction—sincere contrition—humble confession—gracious shame—practical fruits—and divine acceptance, Matt. iii. 8; Psa. li. 17.

2. *The language of devout solicitude.* David was well assured that God only could forgive his sin; and hence, in the text, he sincerely and fervently prays, "O Lord, pardon mine iniquity, for it is great." Faithful prayer is a sure evidence of true penitence, and is essentially connected with the attainment of mercy, and every spiritual blessing, Psa. li. 1; Ezek. xxxvi. 37. When Jesus Christ apprehended Saul of Tarsus, he assured Ananias of the *fact* of his repentance, by emphatically declaring, "Behold, he prayeth." And when the penitent publican went up to the temple to pray, he devoutly exclaimed, "God be merciful to me a sinner; and went down to his house justified." Penitential prayer is always characterized by sincerity of heart—humility of mind—agony of spirit—and fervency of manner.

3. *The language of humble confidence.* The royal suppliant was undoubtedly acquainted with the appointed method of salvation; and implicitly confided in the mercy and goodness of God, for the remission of his sins. He was therefore believingly induced to call on the name of the Lord, in full expectation of obtaining the blessing requested. Prayer always supposes a measure of confidence in the Being addressed, and an encouraging hope of succeeding in the object desired. Such a reverential boldness is highly necessary when we approach the throne of grace, to solicit mercy to pardon, "and find grace to help in time of need," Heb. x. 19—22. This appears to have been the devout state of the Psalmist's mind, when he presented the prayer in the text, which also includes,

III. An argument urged to obtain success;—"For thy *name's sake*, O Lord," &c. This plea is peculiarly appropriate and emphatic; and may be regarded as suggesting, that,

1. *The pardon of sin displays the glory of the divine perfections.* God's name signifies his nature; and this intimates that David expected forgiveness, solely on the ground of his infinite mercy and goodness. And if it be the glory of a man to pass over a transgression, it is surely much more to the glory and honor of God, to "pass by the transgression of the remnant of his heritage, because he delighteth in mercy." By the sovereign act of pardon, through the scheme of redemption, the glorious character of the Deity is eminently displayed, as a God of essential justice, holiness, goodness, faithfulness, and love, Rom. iii. 25, 26; 1 John i. 9. The perfections of Jehovah equally *co-operate* and perfectly *harmonize*, in redeeming and saving sinners, Psa. lxxxv. 10. "Who then is a God like unto thee, that pardoneth iniquity, and retaineth not his anger for ever?"

2. *The pardon of sin demonstrates the efficacy of Christ's atonement.* We are assured, that "without shedding of blood there is no remission." And hence the Jewish sacrifices were emblematic types and shadows of the sacrificial death of the "Lamb of God, which taketh away the sin of the world." Pardon therefore originates in divine love, and is procured by virtue of Christ's sufferings and mediation, Luke xxiv. 46, 47: 1 John ii. 1, 2

But a personal *apprehension* of his precious blood by faith, is necessary to obtain an experimental *realization* of his redeeming benefits, Gal. ii. 20 Believers thus individually *prove*, that "Christ our passover is sacrificed for us; in whom we have redemption through his blood, even the forgiveness of our sins."

3. *The pardon of sin exemplifies the truth of the sacred scriptures.* The Lord, throughout his word, solemnly engages, *fully* to absolve the guilt of returning penitents, Exod. xxxiv. 6, 7; Isa. i. 18; Acts xiii. 38, 39. He is ever ready to forgive, and waits that he may be exalted, and glorified in our salvation. The truth of his promise is happily realized by all the subjects of pardoning mercy, who "believe with the heart unto righteousness." They faithfully credit his declarations, trust in his goodness, and, through the pardon of sin, actually experience that "all his promises are yea and amen in Christ Jesus."

In conclusion, we may warn the careless—encourage the penitent—and congratulate the saints, who have received "the knowledge of salvation, by the remission of their sins."

THE PENITENTIAL SACRIFICE.

Psalm li. 17.—The sacrifices of God are a broken spirit; a broken and a contrite heart, ob God, thou wilt not despise. (Pr.)

David, deeply humbled for his sin, compares his present state of mind to a sacrificial victim, ready to be offered upon the altar. Such victims were separated from the flock or herd, and set apart for God. The penitent also separates himself from customary intercourse, and mourns apart. He no longer considers himself as his own, but the Lord's; to whom he now dedicates himself, by a solemn and voluntary devotion. Psa. iv. 3. Rom. xii. 1.— — And as the typical sacrifices were put to death, in order to their being offered; so the penitent becomes dead to the world, and dead to sin, and is crucified together with Christ.— — —The legal sacrifices were reiterated, year by year, and day by day, Heb. x. 11. So, though there may be special occasions for repentance as in the case of David; yet the sacrifice of a broken heart, and of a contrite spirit, must be the daily offering of every sinner who seeks acceptance with God.

I. Enquire what is included in this spiritual sacrifice.

A broken and a contrite spirit is not merely one that is distressed, nor one that is distressed for sin. Rachel was distressed for her children, and Micah about his gods; but it had nothing to do with true repentance. Cain and Judas sunk into despair, from a sense of guilt and wretchedness; but in them it was that kind of sorrow which worketh death, and not that repentance which is unto life. 2 Cor. vii. 10.

1. A truly contrite spirit is deeply affected with *the evil of sin*, as it dishonors God, and is injurious to ourselves and others.— — —This is exemplified in the case of the Prodigal, Luke xv. 21: in the case of the Publican, Luke xviii. 13: and in that of David in the context, ver. 4.— — —The conviction of such a penitent is, that he has ruined himself, beyond the power of the whole creation to redeem; that if God should utterly destroy him, the

sentence would be just; and if saved it must be of unbounded grace and love Ephes. ii. 4, 5.— — —A broken spirit is deeply contrite, and almost in danger of being swallowed up of grief. Psa. xxxviii. 3, 4; 2 Cor. ii. 7.

2. A contrite spirit groans under the burden of *inherent corruption*, as well as of sins actually committed: ver. 5, 6.— — —A true penitent is made to know the plague of his own heart, and to cry out for deliverance. Rom. vii. 23, 24. Hence some christians, after they have attained to a good hope through grace, and walked humbly with God for many years, complain more bitterly than ever of indwelling sin, and can find no relief but in the atoning blood. Those who seek justification from their own sanctification, invert the order of the gospel; and it is impossible that imperfect obedience should yield perfect peace.

3. A broken and contrite spirit trembles at the least indications of *divine displeasure*.— — —Not only judgments inflicted, but judgments threatened or only apprehended, fill it with dismay. Isa. lxvi. 2; Psa. cxix. 120.— — A true penitent trembles more at God's word than others do at his rod. 2 Chron. xxxiv. 18, 27; Job xxxi. 33.

4. A broken spirit patiently submits to the severest *chastisements*, and will bear the indignation of the Lord, from a conviction of having deserved it, and from the hope of future deliverance. Mic. vii. 9.— — —When God smites, the penitent also smites, and is at all times disposed to take part with God against himself. He giveth his cheek to him that smiteth him, and putteth his mouth in the dust. Lam. iii. 29, 30; Jer. xxxi. 18, 19.

II. God's gracious acceptance of such a sacrifice.

This is expressed negatively; "a broken and a contrite spirit, oh God, thou wilt not despise." It is so worthless in itself, consisting of nothing but the groans and tears of a broken-hearted penitent, that he might well despise it; but he will not. It is presented with so many imperfections, and in a manner so unworthy of his notice, that he might reject both the offerer and his sacrifice; but he will not—

1. Because he delights more in *showing mercy*, than in whole burnt offer ings or sacrifices. If he accepted the sacrifices under the law, it was only as they pointed to the great atonement to be made in the end of the world, and as they were accompanied with the penitential confessions of the offerer. And now especially, as these outward sacrifices have ceased, he will accept that which is spiritual. 1 Pet. ii. 5.

2. The sacrifices of a broken heart, offered up *in the name of Jesus*, cannot fail to be accepted, because they are perfumed with his incense, and presented through his intercession. Ephes. i. 6; Rev. viii. 4.

3. God has made *many promises* to the humble and the contrite, and has testified his acceptance of them and of their offering. Psa. xxxi. 20, cxlvii. 3; Isa. lvii. 13. See the case of Ephraim, Jer. xxxi. 20; of the Publican, Luke xviii. 14; and of the woman that was a sinner, vii. 50.

Let then the trembling soul be comforted: God will not despise the day of small things, nor let us despise it. Matt. xii. 20.

INVITATION TO ENLARGED PRAYER.

Psalm lxxxi. 10.—Open thy mouth wide, and I will fill it. (Pr.)

It was a heathen practice to worship the sun and the moon; the former at the time of its rising, and the latter at the time of its change. Hence some have thought, that God appointed the time of the new moon for the worship of his courts, in order to counteract the species of idolatry.

This psalm seems to have been composed for the feast of the new moon, and perhaps for the first new moon in the year.— — —This expostulation in ver. 8, 9, is very tender: the consideration by which it is enforced is what God had done, and what he would still do for his people. If he were insufficient, they might seek after a "strange god:" otherwise they were without excuse.

The "opening of the mouth," may either allude to children who cry for food, or to one who asks a favor; and it teaches us that God is able to fulfil our most enlarged desires.

I. Explain the exhortation.

"Open thy mouth wide," that is, ask much, and God will give it: expect much from him, and you shall not be disappointed.

1. Be not content with temporal blessings, but ask for those which are spiritual and eternal. It is not unlawful to desire the good things of life, but they are not chiefly to be desired. Any one spiritual blessing is of far greater magnitude than the whole world; and if we would enjoy these, we must open our mouth wide.— — —To ask for these is to desire God for our portion: it is to ask for an interest in his heart, and not merely to the bounty of his hand, but for that which shall endure for ever.— — —For example, do not be content with a reprieve from punishment, but ask for pardon. Do not ask for what is not promised, for that you may never have; but for what is promised, that you may have abundantly.— — —Do not ask for such a kind of righteousness, and for so much religion as may pass before men; but for that in which you may stand before God.— — —Do not so much desire to be delivered out of trouble, as to get good by it.

2. Be not satisfied with a small degree of religion, but aspire after and pray for much; much of the power and much of the comfort of it. He that desires so much religion as may carry him to heaven, will never come there at all. The Lord taketh pleasure in them that fear him, in them that hope in his mercy.— — —Pray not only for that faith which is saving, but for that which is strong, giving glory to God. Not only for that love which is sin cere, but for that which abounds in all knowledge, and in all judgment. Phil. i. 9. Desire to have not only peace with God, but holy freedom and intimate communion with him. 1 John i. 3.

3. Let us pray not only for those things which concern our own souls, but also for the good of the souls of others; for the good of the cause of Christ, and his kingdom at large.— — —Keep not silence, and give him no rest, until he establish and make Jerusalem a praise in the earth. Isa. lxii. 6, 7. Ask to be blessed in the blessedness of God's chosen, and to see the good of his nation. Seek the salvation of others, and you will find your own. Psa. cvi. 4, 5.

4. Ask all in faith. Faith in the divine promises is of great importance in enlarged prayer. Much of our coldness arises from unbelief: if we believe. we shall receive. John xv. 7.

II. Enforce the exhortation.

Consider what need there is for enlarged prayer, and why we should open our mouths wide in seeking God—

1. Our wants are very great and pressing. We are immortal, guilty, dying creatures. Think of what we are capable of suffering and enjoying. An eternity of bliss or woe is before us: we are candidates for the one, and if we miss it, we fall into the other.— — —How important and interesting is our situation: we are walking as it were on a narrow bridge, with an unfathomable gulf on either side. Crowns of glory are before us, and the pit of perdition is beneath us.

2. Great as our wants are, they are not too great for God to supply.— — His heart is large and he will give us according to his riches in glory. Phil. iv. 19. Open thy mouth wide, and he will fill it.

We may judge of the liberality of another, partly by his words, if he be faithful, and partly by his actions: and in this way we may know something of the divine beneficence.— — —His promises are a faithful index to his heart, and these are exceedingly great and precious. "I will be their God: their sins and iniquities will I remember no more: I will never leave them nor forsake them." Psa. xlviii. 14; Isa. xli. 10. We may also know what God will do for them that ask, by what he has done already. Consider what he did of old for the Patriarchs, and for Israel: how he pardoned, blessed, and saved them.— — —But more still since then, in the gift of his Son: and how shall he not with him also freely give us all things. Rom. viii. 32.

3. The redemption of Christ Jesus is also large. By it provision is made for all our wants, and a medium for the conveyance of every blessing. On this ground it was that our Lord encouraged his disciples to ask largely in his name. John xvi. 23, 24.— — —The love of God to sinners wanted a medium by which to express itself, like the soul of David towards Absalom; and the sufferings of Christ as our substitute sufficiently proved, that God was the enemy of sin, while he was the sinner's friend. Rom. iii. 26.— — Divine love also wanted something worthy of being rewarded. God would have given us eternal life, but there was nothing to justify its bestowment. Man by sin became utterly unworthy: but in Jesus he is well pleased: let us therefore come boldly in his name. Ephes. iii. 12; Heb. iv. 16. If we receive and enjoy but little, it is because we ask but little, and do not ask in faith. James iv. 2, 3. 1 John v. 14.

THE GOOD OLD WAY.

Jeremiah vi. 16.—Thus saith the Lord, Stand ye in the ways, and see, and ask for the old paths, where is the good way, and walk therein, and ye shall find rest for your souls.

It is the Lord that speaks in our text, and when he speaks, it is both our duty and interest to obey his voice. It is our *duty;* for he is our rightful governor: "It is he that hath made us, and not we ourselves; we are his people, and the sheep of his pasture." His hands have made and fashioned us, and we should therefore pray for understanding that we may learn his commandments. It is our *interest* to obey the Lord; because the way of holy obedience is the only way to escape eternal misery: "for unto them that are contentious, and obey not the truth, but obey unrighteousness, indignation and wrath, tribulation and anguish" will be certainly rendered by the righteous Judge of all. To obey the Lord is also conducive to our happiness; for he is the Lord our God, who teaches us to profit; and in consequence of hearkening to his commandments, our peace will flow as a river. The work of righteousness is peace; and all the ways of wisdom are ways of pleasantness. This is confirmed by the declaration in our text, "Stand ye in the way, and see," &c. That we may seek and find the rest thus promised, let us consider,

I. THE WAY HERE RECOMMENDED. Here observe,

1. *The way itself;* called the good old way. This cannot be the way of the wicked; for their way is not a good one, Ps. xxxvi. 4, Neither is it the way of peace and rest, Isa. lvii. 20, 21. It must be the way of *Scriptural piety;* that way prescribed by God in his word, Ps. cxix. 1, 165. This way, we find represented by St. Paul as comprising, "faith that worketh by love," Gal. v. 6. *Faith in Christ*, or *receiving* him in all his offices, as our Teacher, Sovereign, Redeemer, and Benefactor, Matt. xi. 28—30; John i. 12; and *walking* in him as we have received him, Col. ii. 6. *And love as the fruit and effect of this faith*, 1 Tim. i. 5. This charity includes love to God and all mankind, Matt. xxii. 36—39. And this love is the sum of all God's moral precepts, Rom. xiii. 10; Matt. xxii. 40.

2. *This course of faith and love is called a way.* It is so called, because it *leads* to the enjoyment of *eternal life*, Matt. vii. 14; Ps. xxxiv. 34. It is the *certain* way to eternal life, Rom. ii. 7; Ps. lxxxiv. 11.—And it is the *only* way to eternal life, Heb. xii. 14; Matt. vii. 21.

3. *It is called the old way.* This it certainly is with regard to us, because it is at least as old as the *reformation*. This is incontestable, when we appeal to the history and the writings of all our most renowned divines, through whose instrumentality the reformation was so happily effected.—It is as old as *Christianity*. This is evident from the doctrine of our Lord himself, John xiv. 1, and xv. 12, and of all his apostles. Witness Paul, in those passages above referred to; Peter, 2 Pet. i. 5—7; and John, 1 John iii. 23. It is as old as the *Mosaic dispensation:* For Moses himself was actuated by faith, Heb. xi. 24—27. And he repeatedly taught the way of love, both towards God and man, Deut. vi. 45; Lev. xix. 18.—It is as old as the *patriarchial ages;* as the days of Noah, Heb. xi. 7; as the days of Enoch, Gen. v. 24; Heb. xi. 5; as the days of Adam, Heb. xi. 4. And it must have been as old even as the days of Adam, when in a state of innocence: for he was made upright, Eccles. vii. 29; and as such, he could not but believe in God and love him.

4. *It is called the good way:* and this it evidently is, because *those who walk in it are good*, James iii. 17; Eph. v. 8, 9.—Because *those who walk in it do good.* They prove general blessings to their *families*, Deut. v. 29; to their *country*, Proverbs xiv. 34; and to the *world* at large. Matt. v. 13, 14.—And because the *way itself is good.* It is good in its *origin*, being prescribed by infinite goodness, Ps. cxliii. 10; and it is good in its *tendency*, leading to the happiest results, Prov. xix. 23. That we may enjoy the benefits of this way, let us consider

II. GOD'S COMMANDS RESPECTING IT. "Stand ye in the ways," &c.

1. *Stand ye in the ways and see.* In this part of God's counsel, some facts are assumed, and some duties are enjoined.—*Some facts are evidently assumed:* as that though there is but *one good* way, yet there are *many evil* ways; for instance, there are the ways of open and secret sin, of irreligion, of self-confidence, formality, and apostacy.—That *all* mankind by nature are

walking in *some* evil ways, Isa. liii. 6.—That we are naturally *ignorant* of the good old way, Jer. x. 23.—And that in the use of proper means we are capable both of *discovering* it, and *walking* in it. Hence we find in this counsel.—*Some duties evidently enjoined.* "Stand ye in the ways and see." *Stand;* make an immediate *pause* for the purpose of *consideration*, Hag. i. 5.—And *see;* seriously *examine* in what way you are walking. Is it in the way of outward or secret sin? or irreligion? or self-confidence? or formality? or apostacy? "Let every man prove his own work," 2 Cor. xiii. 5. Observe well the *tendency* of every evil way. Look before you, and consider whither it leads; it ends in death, Rom. vi. 21.

2. *Ask for the old paths: where is the good way?*—Inquire—By *searching the scriptures*, John v. 39. This is the *map* that describes it.—*By asking direction of God;* who is ready to give it, James i. 5; Prov. ii. 3–5. By *associating with the pious;* who are walking in it, Prov. xiii; 20.

3. *And walk therein.* This command requires you—*To get into it.* Do not remain out of it by delay, Job xxii. 21; and xxxvi. 18. Do not stop short of it, by resting in deficient attainments: as merely talking of it, thinking aright concerning it, and desiring it. Get into it, by coming to Christ as he invites you, Matt. ii. 29; and by coming to God by him, John xiv. 6; Heb. vii. 25.—*To keep in it*, by steadfast resistance of temptation, 1 Pet. v. 8, 9: Luke xxi. 36.—And *to go forward in it*, by improving in piety, 2 Cor. vii. 1; 2 Pet. i. 5—11. Having considered God's command respecting this way, observe

III. THE PROMISE BY WHICH HE ENCOURAGES US TO OBEY HIM:—"And ye shall find rest for your souls." Here observe,

1. *The blessing promised;*—"Rest for your souls." *Rest—gracious rest in this world;*—from the anguish of guilt, Isa. xii. 5;—from the oppression of Satan, Matt xi. 28;—from tormenting fears, Ps. xxxiv. 4:—from inward defilement, John xv. 2; 1 John i. 9;—and rest in the pleasant service of a beloved master, Matt. xi. 30; 1 John v. 3.—*Glorious rest in heaven*, Heb iv. 9;—from all temptation, Job iii. 17: from all suffering, Rev. xxi. 4:—and from all danger, Matt. vi. 20.—Rest for your souls. Rest attended with *consciousness* of enjoyment in this life, Rom. viii. 1, 2; and after death, Rev. vii. 14, 17. Rest, such as your souls require, because it is *eternal*, Ps. xvi. 11.

2. *The certainty of our obtaining it;*—"Ye *shall* find rest for your souls." On your seeking it as God requires, it is certain,—from God's *all-sufficiency:* he who promises it is the Lord, who has it to give, Gen. xiv. 22.—From his *kindness:* he calls you to enjoy it, Isa. xlv. 19;—and from his *truth:* he engages that you shall find it, 1 Thess. v. 24.

APPLICATION.

These words show us the falsehood of some common objections to a course of piety;

1. "*That this strict religion is a new way!*" No, it is the old way: sin is the new way, devised by Satan, for the purpose of leading men to hell.

2. *That it is an injurious way, unfavorable to the interests of mankind!*" No, it is the good way, and most highly beneficial, 1 Tim. iv. 8; Prov. xii. 36.

3. "*That it is a melancholy way!*" No, it is the way of peace and rest: peace through life, Luke i. 78, 79; peace in death, Ps. xxxv i; and rest for ever. Rev. xiv. 13.

THE VITAL EFFICACY OF FAITH.

James ii. 26.—For as the body without the spirit is dead, so faith without works is dead also. (Sk.)

THE subject of discussion in this chapter, is the practical tendency of genuine faith. It appears that many persons in the apostolic age perverted the doctrines of the gospel. Though they professed to embrace Christianity, their faith did not produce the fruits of a holy life and heavenly conversation. The apostle, therefore, shows them the utter insufficiency of such an empty profession; and the absolute necessity of that faith which invariably demonstrates the genuineness of its character by the efficacy of its influence. He faithfully reproves them for their unjust partiality, and affectionately inculcates the practice of piety as the result of unfeigned faith. And to enforce this impressive doctrine, he appeals to certain well known examples of faith and obedience. He distinctly specifies Abraham and Rahab, who evinced the reality of their faith by their works; the former, "when he offered Isaac his son upon the altar;" and the latter, when at the peril of her life she concealed the Jewish spies. From these premises the apostle draws the interesting conclusion in the text;—"For as the body without the spirit," &c. These words bring before us the subject of christian faith, and suggest to our consideration the necessity of its possession,—the excellency of its character,—and the efficacy of its principle.

I. THE NECESSITY OF ITS POSSESSION. This the apostle assumes; nor does he enter into any general description of its abstract nature. He simply represents it as an *essential* and *vital* principle of genuine piety, which displays the reality of its existence by the purity of its influence. And as the spirit is necessary for the existence of the body, so faith is indispensable to the possession of pure and undefiled religion. And hence,

1. *It is a duty divinely required.* It is the very foundation and principle of vital godliness. The existence and perfections of the Deity, demand its vigorous exercise: for without faith it is impossible to love or please God, Heb. xi. 6. The written revelation, also, of his will, is the *ground* and *rule* of living faith; and enjoins it as the indispensible duty of mankind, 2 Chron xx. 20; John vi. 28, 29, xx. 31; 1 John iii. 23. And whatever is *commanded* by God, is unquestionably the incumbent obligation and reasonable service of his intelligent creatures; for he requires nothing but what is perfectly wise, "holy, just, and good."

2. *It is the only way of salvation.* We are condemned by the law as transgressors; and we cannot escape its final penalties, by any thing that we can *do* or *suffer*, Rom. iii. 19, 20. But Christ hath redeemed us from the curse of the law, being made a curse for us." He is therefore the *way* to the Father, and the only medium of salvation, John xiv. 6; 1 Cor. i. 30. But it is only *by faith*, that we can realize an interest in him as *our* Saviour; "He that believeth not is condemned already," Mark xvi. 16; John iii. 16—18; Acts x. 43, xvi. 30, 31. Some, however, have thought that there is a manifest opposition between St. Paul and St. James on this subject; but this cannot exist in reality, because they both wrote by the inspiration of the same spirit. But in describing the same doctrine under *different views* and *circumstances*, they naturally adopted a different mode of expression, while they maintained perfect unity of sentiment, Rom. iv. 3; James ii. 23.

3. *It is an essential property of religion.* It is the most distinguishing principle of christianity, and the distinctive character of the righteous.

Without faith all external professions and ceremonies are vain, Gal. v. 6. It is necessary for the attainment of every spiritual blessing, and the performance of every christian duty, "for whatsoever is not of faith is sin" It is connected with every hallowed principle, disposition, enjoyment, and practice; and is the very *life*, *spirit* and *energy* of personal religion, which is significantly called, "the *work* and *profession* of faith." And as closely connected with the necessity of this gracious principle, we must consider,

II. THE EXCELLENCY OF ITS CHARACTER. This is evident from the scriptures in general, and especially from the testimonies of Jesus Christ and his apostles. It is emphatically called "precious faith," and exceeding great and glorious things are spoken of it in the inspired memorials of the saints. In this chapter, St. James admirably describes it as a principle of inestimable value, and the distinguishing excellence of our holy religion. And this will appear, if we observe,

1. *Faith is divine in its Author.* It is not the mere effort of reason; it is the special *gift* of God's grace, Eph. ii. 8; Col. ii. 12. He reveals the object—enjoins the duty—imparts the power—and inspires the grace of faith. But still it is a *personal act* of the mind, by which we credit divine truth—embrace the Saviour—and obtain salvation. No man can believe without supernatural aid; but by the ability which the Lord bestows, the obedient penitent "believes with the heart unto righteousness," and continues coming, trusting, and "looking unto Jesus, the author and finisher of faith," Heb. xii. 2.

2. *Faith is vigorous in its operations.* It is not an empty *notion*, but a living *principle.* This distinction is very important, and is clearly described by our apostle, ver. 18–20. It is possible to have many general *notions* and speculative *opinions* in religion, when we are utterly destitute of *living faith.* When faith is merely *notional*, it is fruitless; but when it is *genuine*, it produces the most gracious effects. As a principle of spiritual *life*, it quickens all the powers of the soul, and brings them into constant exertion, Gal. ii. 20. It grasps the Deity—lays hold on the Saviour—renders him precious to the soul—embraces the divine promises—resists evils and temptations—promotes stability and diligence—and endures tribulations, as "seeing him who is invisible," 2 Cor. v. 7; Heb. x. 38.

3. *Faith is consoling in its prospects.* It looks not at the things which are seen, but at those things which are not seen. It is accompanied with a consciousness of the divine favor, and an assurance that "all things will work together for our good." It affords consolation under every trial, and enables the christian to "glory in tribulations." It far exceeds the glimmering rays of reason, and mysteriously *penetrates* and *grasps* the invisible realities of immortal bliss, 2 Cor. v. 1; 1 Pet. i. 8, 9. Faith thus cheers the mind, encourages the hope, and animates the pursuit, of the believer, and supplies the place of present vision, by becoming "the *subsistence* of things hoped for, and the *demonstration* of things not seen." From this description of the excellency of faith we may easily discover,

III. THE EFFICACY OF ITS PRINCIPLE. This is distinctly asserted in the text. The comparison is peculiarly elegant and impressive. As there can be no living human body without a spirit, even so there can be no saving faith without good works;—"For as the body," &c. When faith is genuine, it always promotes,

1. *Works of purity and holiness.* It teaches its possessors to "come out from the wicked, and be separate, and touch not the unclean thing." They are deeply convinced of the exceeding sinfulness of sin, and abhor it as that

"abominable thing which the Lord hateth." They also discover the moral beauty of holiness, and practically "adorn the doctrine of their Saviour in all things," Tit. ii. 11—14. Their faith produces a hallowing influence, both on their minds and morals; and as a tree is known by its fruits, so true faith is distinguished by its legitimate effects of "holiness and righteousness of life," Matt. vii. 17—20.

2. *Works of conquest and triumph.* The warfare of christians is called "the good fight of faith." They are surrounded by numerous enemies, Eph. vi. 12. But *mighty faith* subdues sin—resists Satan—conquers the world—and triumphs over affliction, death, and the grave, 1 Cor. xv. 55–57; Heb. xi. 24, 25; 1 Pet. v. 8, 9; 1 John v. 4. Thus by faith the patriarchs, prophets, and apostles, were "more than conquerors through him that loved them," and obtained the crown of eternal life, Heb. xi. 32–39; 2 Cor. iv. 10–13.

3. *Works of love and benevolence.* When we believe in Christ, the love of God is shed abroad in our hearts; for faith works by love to God and all mankind; even to our enemies, Matt. v. 44.

4. *Works of zeal and perseverance.* The true believer is always zealously affected in the cause of Christ. He greatly rejoices in the prosperity of Zion, and mourns when she declines. He prays for the extension of the Redeemer's kingdom, and endeavors to promote the cause of righteousness and peace, Hab. iii. 2; Rom. x. 1. Under the animating influence of faith, we shall never grow weary in well-doing but "always abound in the work of the Lord, till we receive the end of our faith, even the salvation of our soul.

We may learn from this subject,

1. The necessary union between faith and works.
2. The duty and importance of self-examination.
3. The peace and felicity of "holding fast faith and a good conscience.

GOD'S METHOD OF HEALING, OFFENSIVE TO THE PRIDE OF MAN.

2 Kings v. 12.—"Are not Abana and Pharpar, rivers of Damascus, better than all the waters of Israel? may I not wash in them, and be clean?" (Sk.)

"All scripture," saith Paul, "is given by inspiration of God, and is profitable—for instruction in righteousness." *All* scripture, not particular parts or books only, but *all* and *every* part of it. Hence those who confine themselves to particular passages, and do not read the whole, deprive themselves of much important instruction. Not only may we derive profit from those facts which are immediately connected with the redemption of the soul,—or from the prominent doctrines of the gospel,—or from the precepts or promises of Christianity, but also from those parts which do not appear to have any connection with the gospel, or any particular bearing towards Christ. An attentive examination of many of these will show us how much we need Christ, and will lead us to prize his gospel. As there is no village in the kingdom from which a way may not be found to the Metropolis so there is no passage in the Bible which may not be connected with Christ.

Many of the historical parts of scripture, though they say nothing of Christ, abound in instruction. They exhibit many a beacon to admonish us of danger, and many a light to direct our course. In them we see men placed in a variety of situations, and under various aspects of providence, by which human character is developed, and the secret springs of moral actions are made manifest. Such histories instruct us in the knowledge of the human heart, a knowledge which in point of importance is second only to the knowledge of God. The history before us is of this character. Let us lift our hearts to the Father of lights, that we may be instructed. Our text suggests a variety of ideas, to which I shall call your attention in succession,

I. THAT GREAT MEN ARE NOT EXEMPTED FROM THE EVILS WHICH ATTACH TO OUR COMMON NATURE. Naaman was a great man, a commander-in-chief of the Syrian forces, a man honorable and valorous, but he was a leper. From one class of evils riches might exempt their possessors— the evils of poverty, perplexity, anxiety and embarrassment. But in many cases the opulent, through habits of vice. which are always expensive, or from a silly vanity to appear greater than they really are, participate as largely in these evils as the humblest tradesman. But from other ills they have no exemption.

1. *None from those which attach to the body.* None from *affliction* in its almost endless diversity, sometimes affecting the body, sometimes the mind-and sometimes both. None from *disappointment.* Man the is creature of hope, but his hopes are frequently not realized. His heart is fixed on a particular object, from which he expects to derive perpetual pleasure; but either it is removed out of his sight, or the supplies it sends forth are scanty, and but at intervals, or instead of being a never-failing spring of pleasure, it becomes a fountain of pain, and anguish, and misery. None from *death.* The sentence is pronounced upon all, "Dust thou art, and unto dust shalt thou return;" which with equal promptness is executed in the palace, as in the cottage, upon the prince. as upon the peasant.

2. *None from those which attach to the soul.* Great men like others are involved in the effects of the original transgression: born in sin: in whose nature is sown a corrupt seed which vegitates without the counteraction of divine grace; grows with their growth, and strengthens with their strength, till it becomes a great tree producing wild grapes. Their hearts contain a principle of rebellion, which ramifies itself through all the faculties of the soul, darkening the understanding,—perverting the will,—depraving the affections,—corrupting the memory,—and producing overt acts of rebellion in the life. *Great men*, like others, "are by nature children of wrath," and liable to eternal death. But it is pleasing to remark,

II. THAT THERE ARE NO EVILS ATTACHING EITHER TO BODY OR SOUL, WHICH GOD CANNOT REMOVE.

1. *He can heal the body.* This he can do either with or without means. Sometimes he heals miraculously,—such were many of the cures wrought by our Lord,—by his apostles,—such also was the resuscitation of the Shunamite's son by Elisha,—and of Lazarus, and the widow's son by Christ. But though he could have done every thing without means, he has chosen to do almost every thing with them both in nature, in providence, and in grace. He could have so constituted man as that food should not have been necessary to his sustenance; or he could have caused food to have been spontaneously produced without any labor on his part. But he has done neither. Man requires sustenance; and to obtain it he must plough, and sow, and reap He could have accomplished all the revolutions which have taken place in the world by his own fiat, without employing a single instrument; but instead of doing so, to accomplish the changes which have been effected, he has em-

ployed a Moses—a Cyrus—an Alexander—a Cæsar—a Titus—a Cromwell—a Bonaparte—and a Wellington. He could have irriadiated the minds of the whole human race, and perfectly instructed them in the knowledge of his character and will by the immediate inspiration of his own Spirit, without either Bibles or ministers; but he has not done so. On the contrary, in grace, as in natu·e and providence, he accomplishes the purposes of his will by a continual :nstrumentality. In conformity with his general plan, he appoints means in the case before us, verse 10.

2. *He can heal the soul.* By applying the sacred balm of pardoning mercy to the wounded conscience—by secretly, but powerfully operating upon the *will*, and giving it a new direction—by purifying and elevating the affections by strengthening *the moral powers* through the "law of the spirit of life in Christ Jesus, making us free from the law of sin and death,"—and by making the memory the depository of soul purifying truths. It is however deeply to be lamented,

III: THAT THE SIMPLICITY OF GOD'S REMEDIES ARE FREQUENTLY OFFENSIVE TO THE PRIDE OF MAN. Look at the case before us. What could be more easy than the remedy suggested? "Go, and wash in Jordon seven times." But its simplicity was that which rendered it objectionable with Naaman. Besides, he had previously arranged in his own mind how the cure was to be performed, verse 11. The patient dictated the plan of his own cure, and because the physician prescribed a different one, he was indignant. This spirit of proud dictation to God, directly opposed to that childlike docility with which we should always contemplate him, has frequently led to the rejection of his plans.

1. *It led the Jews to reject Christ.* They desired the Messiah, as Naaman desired a cure. But as Naaman had previously determined by what process the cure was to be effected, so they had formed in their minds what kind of Messiah he was to be. He was to be a great man, an illustrious prince, and a mighty warrior. He was to emancipate the Jews from vassalage, to conquer the Romans, and to extend his dominion from sea to sea, and from river to the ends of the earth. But because their carnal expectations were not realized, they put him to death.

2. *It leads many to reject the peculiar doctrines of the gospel.* The divinity of Christ,—the doctrine of the atonement,—and spiritual regeneration. Why is the divinity of Christ, for instance, rejected? Because the scriptures do not teach it? Impossible; for to him they ascribe the *name*, and *attributes*, and *works*, and *worship* of Jehovah. No, it is because men bring a previous creed to the Bible, instead of deriving their creed from it. They melt the Bible into the mould of their opinions, instead of melting their opinions into the mould of the Bible.

3. *It hinders many from closing in with God's method of justifying the ungodly.* He offers a free pardon to men as sinners, The pride of the human heart rejects this, and brings a price,—comparative innocence,—works of righteousness,—acts of charity,—or tears of penitence. The price is already paid and accepted, and the salvation already purchased can only be received by men as sinners who have nothing to pay. There is no royal road to the favor of God, any more than to learning; no, the rigid moralist and the profligate must be justified on the same terms. But,

IV. WHEN GOD'S REMEDIES ARE ADOPTED, THEY NEVER FAIL TO SUCCEED. Look at the case before us, verse 14. In the cures by the brazen serpent,—in the case of the man whose eyes were anointed with clay,—in the conversion of St. Paul,—of the Phillippian jailer,—of the great cloud of witnesses in every age, and especially of the present. Conclude,

1. *With an address to those who are insensible of their disease.* See how the moral leprosy has affected all your powers.

2. *Address those who desire to be healed.* The Jordan is flowing,—the fountain is open.—Come now, wash and be clean.

THE SINNER'S REFUGE.

Hebrews vi. 18.—That by two immutable things, in which it was impossible for God to lie, we might have a strong consolation, who have fled for refuge to lay hold upon the hope set before us. (Pr.)

THE apostle was greatly concerned for the perseverance of those who professed to believe in Jesus; when some of them seemed to turn back, he labored with all his might to reclaim them. In some parts of the epistle he appears to deal sharply with them, in the beginning of this chapter especially, he faithfully warns them of the danger of apostasy; yet towards the close, he holds up the greatest encouragement to a perseverance in faith and holiness.

I. The description given of a true believer: "HE HAS FLED FOR REFUGE."

The allusion is to the cities of refuge under the law, which were provided for the manslayer. Deut. xix. 1—6.

The words before us are full of meaning, and contain three things in particular worthy of notice—

1. *The sinner's dangerous condition* is fully implied.— — —He is exposed to some evil which threatens to overtake, and to overwhelm him with misery: this is common to all sinners.— — —Death, like the avenger of blood, is out after him, and will soon overtake him.— — —Wrath is in pursuit of him, and will finally come upon him, if he should not have reached the city in time.— — —The sinner has transgressed God's holy law, and is under condemnation. If death should overtake you, ere you reach the city of refuge, you perish forever. Do not trifle therefore, do not loiter; but flee for thy life.— — —Men would not be indifferent where life was in danger: and shall we, while our souls are in danger of the wrath to come!

2. Observe *the refuge provided.* This is called "the hope set before us." — — —There can be no doubt what this means: it might be doubtful to some under the Old Testament, but surely it is not so to us.— — —Christ crucified is the hope of the hopeless, and the only name given under heaven whereby we must be saved.— — —This is the Lamb which God has provided for a sin-offering: his death is the only source of our life: here is a full salvation, sufficient for the chief of sinners. John iii. 14.— — —If we confess our sins, he is faithful and just to forgive. 1 John i. 9. In him all the threatenings of God are turned away, and there is no more wrath; there is no objection from the nature, the number, or the aggravations of our offences. Isa. i. 18; Matt. xii. 31.

Hither it was that David fled, saying, Purge me with hyssop, and I shall be clean.— — —This is still the refuge of poor sinners, and here only can we find safety.

This hope is said to be *set before us*. God has set before us in his word, Christ and him crucified; and has called our attention to this as the only foundation of hope. Isa. xxviii. 16.

He is a refuge *near at hand*, or immediately "before us." No circuitous ways of preparation or amendment are prescribed: we are directed to look to him and be saved, to believe on him and receive eternal life.— — —Were it otherwise, what had been the condition of the dying thief. Behold, I bring near my righteousness, and my salvation shall not tarry. Isa. xlvi. 13.

The way also is *made plain*, that those who flee for refuge may not be hindered in their flight. Deut. xix. 3.— — —The sinner's refuge is set so fully in view by the gospel, that every faithful minister, every true believer can direct you to it.

3. The *state of mind necessary to our fleeing to it*.— — —Nothing indeed is nesessary as a qualification, nor as giving us a right warrant to come, but the free invitations of the gospel to the most unworthy.— — —Any sinner may come, but every sinner will not come; only those who believe in Jesus.

Fleeing to this refuge implies *a sense of our sinful and dangerous condition*.— — —This Paul had by means of the law: without this we are whole, and need not a physician. Those who flee for refuge are such as see themselves to be wholly sinful, and that God's displeasure against them is altogether just.

It implies also our understanding and *believing the gospel*. It is not merely being driven by fear, but drawn by love.— — —It is to have all our unwillingness removed, and to fall in with God's way of salvation with the whole heart.

II. The ground which God has given to such for "STRONG CONSOLATION."

Two things are mentioned, and they are both immutable; the promise, and the oath of God. Thus the Lord gave hope and comfort to Abraham, and thus he gives strong consolation to believers in Christ: ver. 13.

And why did he give the promise and the oath? He did so to *Abraham*, in order to meet all his unbelieving fears, arising from the difficulties he had to encounter, and because of the length of time he would have to wait for the performance of the promise.

To us also God has promised and sworn to give eternal life, if we believe in his dearly beloved Son.— — —Unbelief might suggest, "I am too sinful and unworthy, or there are insuperable difficulties in the way, and I shall never obtain the prize." But the promise and the oath contain an answer to every objection, and afford ground to the strongest assurance.

1. We see what encouragement there is for us as sinners to come to Christ. We come not with uncertainty, but under the sanction of a promise.

2. The motive for perseverance. If we hold out to the end, it will issue in eternal life.

THE PENITENT MALEFACTOR.

Luke xxiii. 40—43.—But the other answering, rebuked him, saying, Dost not thou fear God, seeing thou art in the same condemnation? And we indeed justly; for we receive the due reward of our deeds: but this man hath done nothing amiss. And he said unto Jesus, Lord, remember me when thou comest into thy kingdom. And Jesus said unto him, Verily I say unto thee, to-day shall thou be with me in paradise. (Pr.)

Christ is said to have triumphed over principalities and powers on his cross, and surely the conversion and salvation of this poor sinner affords a wonderful instance of it, and serves as a specimen of his mercy to future ages. Well may it be said, "this is a faithful saying, and worthy of all acceptation, that Christ Jesus came into the world to save sinners, even the chief."

This unhappy man and his fellow sufferer were "malefactors," common thieves or robbers. They had probably been partners in guilt, and both suffered for the same offence: but how great the difference between them in the final hour. The one dies in his impenitence, the other owns that he suffered justly, though at first they both railed on the dying Saviour. We may therefore well consider the penitent thief as a singular instance of the power and grace of God towards the very chief of sinners. While falling himself a sacrifice to the malice of Satan, Jesus snatches a lamb as it were out of the mouth of the lion, and takes with him to paradise, a sinner who was sinking into the pit of destruction.

I. Notice in the dying thief the operations of genuine repentance.

His situation allowed him no other opportunity of showing his grief and sorrow for sin, than by the few words which dropped from his lips while he was suspended on the cross; but these afford full proof of his sincerity. His hands and feet were nailed, but his heart was free; and his lips not being yet closed in death, he will do all he can to glorify the Saviour.

1. He begins to rebuke the reviling malefactor: "Dost not thou fear God?" ——— There were none left to defend the Saviour's cause: the disciples had all forsook him and fled, and his friends were standing afar off: the multitude around him were full of derision, and John and the woman who stood near the cross were overwhelmed with grief. ——— The dying malefactor will therefore plead for him, and boldly reproves the daring sinner at his side, whose mouth was full of cursing and bitterness. ——— This was genuine repentance, and genuine love, which could not bear that Jesus should be dishonored by railing accusations, nor that scandals should be cast on him.

2. He *confesses his sin*, and acknowledges the equity of his sentence. "We indeed," says he, "suffer justly." ——— His confession was public and open, in the presence of innumerable witnesses, and of innumerable enemies. ——— It was also of the most disinterested kind: he had nothing to hope for from man, no prospect of deliverance; there was nothing to extort his confession but the deepest sense of guilt. ——— Here could be no room for fear, for they had done their worst upon him: he was looking to Christ for salvation, but owns his condemnation to be just. ——— This indeed is confessing and giving glory to God, and that in the first place, and in the highest sense; for this confession was made *before* any plea for mercy was offered, so that whether he was saved or not, he justifies and glorifies God; and this is the spirit of genuine repentance.

3. He *vindicates* the character of Christ, while he unequivocally condemns himself. "This man has done nothing amiss." ——— Herein indeed he charged his country with the guilt of crucifying the Lord of glory; and while he himself pleads guilty, he pleads the innocence of Christ before the same tribunal. ——— This is an instance of magnanimity worthy of the character of the true penitent. "Do I not hate them, oh Lord, that hate thee; and am I not grieved with them that rise up against thee?" Psa. cxxxix. 21.

4. His repentance is accompanied with *faith in Christ:* he called him "Lord." ——— Multitudes were deriding him, his disciples had all forsaken him, and he appeared in circumstances of the deepest abasement, sinking under weakness and disgrace; yet this poor sinner owns him as the Lord, a name which implies every high idea of Christ, 1 Cor. xii. 3. ——— He also believes that Christ had a "kingdom," a kingdom not of this world, and that he was going to possess it. Though he now appeared as an outcast from heaven and earth, yet he considered him as the Lord of the invisible world. ——— He must likewise have believed that Christ, when he came to his kingdom, would there be the advocate of sinners, and would make intercession for transgressors; or had he fully known this, his prayer could not have been more appropriate.

This was great faith, especially if we consider how this poor sinner came by the knowledge of Christ. Probably he could not read, was unacquainted with the prophecies, had never seen Jesus before, nor heard any thing about him; his enemies triumphed, his friends were scattered. What he hears is only from the mouth of his accusers, and he had to collect his knowledge of Christ from the derision and scorn of the multitude; yet he realizes all that in him which they denied to him.

5. His repentance is accompanied with *earnest prayer:* "Lord, remember me." ——— This is very brief, but full and comprehensive, being the utterance of the heart. ——— He does not specify the object of his prayer, yet he selects the most appropriate terms in which to express himself, and leaves it with the Lord to give him what he needed. Lord, remember me, think of me in love, like Joseph to the butler. When it goes well with thee, remember me. ——— He might have said, Lord, pardon me, bless me, and save me; but this includes all. Let me but have a place in thy heart, and all the rest will follow. ——— The terms were also remarkably adapted to his present condition; for who would "remember" him, if Christ did not? His enemies would all forget him in a little time; and his friends, if he had any, would be glad to forget him as a reproach to them—an outcast of society, a thief and a malefactor. "*Lord*, remember me." ——— He might have thought his sin too great to be pardoned, but he does not, neither does he despair of an interest in the Saviour's love: Lord, remember *me*. ——— Self-righteous pride would have prevented his making such an application for mercy as utterly in vain, and such a spirit would have objected to prayer on account of his utter unworthiness: but he is not discouraged by the greatness of his guilt. ——— Oh what faith; what a conviction of the infine ability of the Saviour.

II. View the conduct of our Lord towards him: "VERILY I SAY UNTO THEE, TO-DAY SHALT THOU BE WITH ME IN PARADISE."

1. Though Christ would take no notice of a reviler, nor give any answer to the language of reproach, yet he would *attend to the plea of mercy;* and to the plea of one of the most unworthy, and the least likely to obtain it. ——— He would hear the prayer of a perishing sinner whose heart was contrite, even in the hour of death What condescension, and what love!

2. He answered him *without delay.* ——— He for a time deferred the request of one poor woman who sought him with great importunity, and suffered her to be repulsed; and though he answered at last, yet he kept her in long suspense. Matt. xv. 22, 23. ——— But this was an urgent case: the sinner was dying, and there was no time for delay: it was well the word was nigh him, and the Saviour so near at hand.

3. As the petition had *implied much,* so did the answer. ———To be with Jesus, to be with him in paradise, was more than he could ask or think. This would be all in all, not only including the forgiveness of sin, acceptance with God, and eternal life, but more than could enter into the heart of man to conceive. ——— The penitent had only asked of Jesus to remember him; but Jesus tells him he should be with him. He asked to be remembered at some future time, he knew not when; but Jesus tells him that "to-day" he should be blessed.

4. The promise is pronounced with a solemn *asseveration;* "Verily, I say unto thee." ——— This bears the form of an oath, and gives the fullest assurance for the performance of the promise. Heb. vi. 18.

REFLECTIONS.

1. We may observe, that there is a great difference between the conduct of this dying malefactor, and that of many dying penitents who are supposed to be converted. They often speak confidently of their state, and of their going to heaven; but this poor man did not, though Christ said so of him He prayed that he might be saved; and after what Christ said, he might believe that he should; but he himself said not a word of that. The strong language that was used was Christ's, and not his.

2. The mercy shown to the penitent thief, affords an encouraging example to perishing sinners. Christ is now in his kingdom, the Advocate is with the Father, making intercession for us; let us therefore come boldly to a throne of grace. ——— He does not forget Joseph, as the butler did. Glory and honor do not render him unmindful of his people: he is the same yesterday, to-day, and for ever.

3. There is a request on Christ's part as well as on ours: he desires to be remembered by us. 1 Cor. xi. 24. ——— He does not need it as we do but love desires it, and wishes to live in the mind of its objects.

ATTRACTIONS OF THE CROSS.

John xii. 32.—And I, if I be lifted up from the earth, will draw all men unto me. (Pr.)

John delights to dwell on the dying love of Christ, and cannot feel an equal interest on any other subject. In the last ten chapters of his gospel he narrates the principal events of the last few days of our Saviour's life on earth. In this chapter he represents him as having a conflict with nature, ver. 27; and then as uttering the language of victory and triumph: ver. 31.

1. Observe, the whole of this passage relates to *the effects* of Christ's death, which is mentioned in the present tense by way of anticipation, as if it had already taken place ver. 31.

2. *The world* is here considered as Satan's kingdom, and he is called "the prince" of it. He it is that rules and governs, both among Jews and Gentiles. ——— But now by the gospel, his kingdom should be overturned. Now is the cause of rebellion crushed, and the grand usurper is confounded.

3. The *drawing of all men* to Christ, denotes the influence of the gospel upon men of all nations, who had hitherto been led captive by the devil at his will; but they shall now become attached to Christ, as it is expressed in chap. xi. 48.

I. Consider the description given of true conversion: it consists in our being "DRAWN TO CHRIST."

We are drawn or influenced by those principles which gain an ascendency over us, or by those objects which govern our feelings or our interest. Thus the riches of the world allure the hearts of the covetous, its pleasures the mind of the sensualist, and its honors that of the ambitious. ——— By these mankind are bound to Satan's interest, and held in a state of subjection. A crown of glory has no influence on the carnal mind, which looks only at the things that are seen. ——— But when a sinner is renewed by grace, and brought to believe in Jesus, the chains are broken, and his heart is smitten with the love of a dying Saviour.

1. Religion had before *no charms*, the world being all in all. ——— Now that the sinner is converted, the Bible becomes a new book, and every thing is viewed in a new light. The law is seen to be holy, just and good; the gospel is inestimable, and all its promises are found to be exceedingly great and precious. ——— Now the sinner begins to wonder that he did not see these things before, and is at a loss to account for his past stupidity.

2. The world has now lost *its attraction*, its dominion over the heart is subdued. ——— The believer is crucified to the world, and the world is crucified to him. It is now become subordinate to higher interests, and is used without abusing it, knowing that the fashion thereof passeth away. 1 Cor. vii. 31.

3. The sinner was once drawn away by *self righteousness*, and cleaved to it as containing all his salvation. ——— He thought much of his religious attainments, and highly of himself on account of them. Luke xviii. 11. ——— But now this fine gold is become dim, and he counts all things but loss for Christ. Phil. iii. 8.

4. Once he *cleaved to flesh and blood*, and could not think of parting with friends and relations, father and mother, for Christ's sake and the gospel. He could not forget his father's house, nor think of forsaking Egypt, to endure affliction with the people of God: but like Orpah he must return to his country and to his gods, notwithstanding all his convictions of the truth. But now his heart is so attracted by the Saviour, that the ties of nature themselves begin to loosen; and like Moses and Ruth, he can forsake all for Christ. Ps. xlv. 10; Ruth i. 15, 16; Heb. xi. 24—26.

5. *Religious duties* were once *a burden to him*, and like Doeg he was detained before the Lord. His language was, what a weariness is it, and when will the Sabbath be over. ——— But now, holy duties are his delight, and his prayer is like that of the church of old, Draw me, we will run after thee. Cant. i. 4. ——— His heart is so attracted that he can find no such happiness any where else: it is good now to draw near unto God. Psalm lxxiii. 28.

Those things which before formed *the greatest objections* to religion, now become matter of choice. ——— He could not bear the reproach, the loss, the shame attending a profession of the gospel. But now like Moses, he can forsake Egypt; and with Paul, count not his life dear unto him for the name of the Lord Jesus. Acts v. 41, xxi. 13.

7. His heart is so drawn to Christ, that the thoughts of *being with him* is now the sum of his desire. Luke viii. 38. ——— Like Paul, he is even willing to depart, that he may be with Jesus. Phil. i. 23.

II. NOTICE HOW THE CROSS OF CHRIST TENDS TO EFFECT THIS.

The Jews put Christ to death in order to prevent his influence, and to make an end of his kingdom and interest in the world. John xi. 48, xii. 19. But it operated in a very different way; ch. xii. 24. ——— His glory followed up his sufferings, and was to arise out of them; the extension of his kingdom would therefore be a necessary consequence of his death. 1 Pet. i. 11.

1. Christ's being "lifted up" upon the cross would afford *the greatest possible display of love;* and love, of all principles, is the most attractive. ——— It is a melting consideration, that while we were yet enemies, he died for us. Hereby perceive we the love of God; herein indeed is love. Rom. v. 8; 1 John iii. 16, iv. 10.

2. It is through the cross of Christ that we have the words of *pardon, peace, and eternal life;* and these tidings become the grand attraction to lost sinners. ——— See how the gospel allured the hearts of John's disciples, and also those of Jesus. John i. 36—39, vi. 66—69. ——— Hence also the multitude followed him withersoever he went: this it was that drew the woman who was a sinner, to weep at his feet, and to wash them with her tears. Luke vii. 47. ——— It is by his being lifted up that he becomes the object of faith; it is by his death that death itself is destroyed, and life and immortality are brought to light. John iii. 13.

3. It was in virtue of this that *the Holy Spirit was imparted*, and this was necessary to render the gospel effectual. ——— It followed it in order of time, that it might appear in the order of nature, or to be the proper effect of it. ——— Without this all the loveliness, and all the love of the Saviour would have no influence: nor would the gospel feast be regarded, but every one would make light of it. Isa. liii. 1; Matt. xxii. 5.

III. The reason we have to expect that this INFLUENCE SHALL BE EXTENDED OVER ALL THE EARTH.

Christ's being lifted up has not yet had its full effect: he will eventually "draw all men unto himself"—

1. This is a part of *the promise* made to him by the Father, and the uttermost parts of the earth are to be his possession. Psalm ii. 8. Isaiah liii. 12.

2. It agrees with the general tenor *of prophecy*, that to him shall the gathering of the people be. Gen. xlix. 10; Dan. ii. 35; vii. 27; Mic. iv. 8; Rev. xi. 15.

We may learn from hence——1. That the way of salvation is Christ and him crucified——2. That the great object of the christian ministry is to exhibit the doctrine of the cross, as the means of converting sinners unto God ——3. That were this doctrine is faithfully preached, there is encouragement to hope it shall never be in vain.

THE CHARACTERISTIC MARKS OF TRUE PENITENCE.

Hosea vi. 1.—Come and let us return unto the Lord: for hè hath torn, and he will **heal us**, he hath smitten and he will bind us up. (S. S.)

THE spiritual dereliction which the people of God have at times experienced, has ever been considered as the most afflictive of all chastisements: but it has also been the most salutary and most effectual. The benefits arising from it were strongly exemplified in the Israelites, who after having long withstood the united efforts of all the prophets, were on a sudden constrained by it to turn to God with unfeigned contrition.

The words before us are the expressions of that repentance which was excited in the Israelites by God's departure from them, and by his grace that accompanied the affliction: Hos. v. ult. and they suggest to us a proper occasion to consider

I. THE CHARACTERISTIC MARKS OF TRUE PENITENCE

It will always be attended with

1. A sense of our departure from God

Unregenerate men live "without God in the world," and yet the thought of their being at a distance from God never enters into their minds. But as soon as the grace of repentance is given to them, they see that they "have been like sheep going astray, every one to his own way," and that they never can find happiness but in "returning to the shepherd and bishop of their souls."

2. An acknowledgement of affliction as a just chastisement for sin.

The impenitent heart murmurs and rebels under the divine chastisements: the penitent "hears the rod and him that appointed it." He blesses God for the troubles that have brought him to reflection; Ps. xvi. 7, and cxix. 67. and while he smarts under the wounds that have been inflicted on him, he regards them as the merciful tokens of parental love. Ps. cxix; 75.

3. A determination to return to God,

When a man is once thoroughly awakened to a sense of his lost condition, he can no longer be contented with a formal round of duties. He reads, hears, prays in a very different way from that to which he was wont to do. "What shall I do to be saved?" is the one thought that occupies his mind: and he is resolved through grace to sacrifice every thing that would obstruct the salvation of his soul. To hear of Christ, to seek him, to believe on him, and to receive out of his fulness, these are from henceforth his chief desire, his supreme delight. Song v. 6, 8.

4. A desire that others should return to him also.

As all the other marks, so this especially was manifested by the repenting Israelites. This is peculiarly insisted on as characteristic of the great work that shall be accomplished in the latter day. Isa. ii. 3. This has distinguished the church of God in all ages! The penitent knows how awful the state of all around him is, and how much he has contributed by his influence and example to destroy them; and therefore, though he expects nothing but "hatred for his good-will," he feels it incumbent on him to labor for their salvation: and, if it were possible, he would instruct, convert, and save the whole world.

To promote an increase of such repentance amongst us, we shall proceed to state:

II. THE GROUNDS ON WHICH A PENITENT MAY TAKE ENCOURAGEMENT OR RETURN TO GOD.

Whatever grounds of despondency we may feel within ourselves, we may take encouragement:

1. From a general view of God's readiness to heal us

God has not left himself without witness even among the heathen world; but has shewn, by his goodness to the evil and unthankful, that he is ever ready to exercise mercy. But to us who have his revealed will, he has left no possibility of doubt: for "if he spared not his own son, but delivered *him* up for us all how shall he not with him also freely give us all things." The invitations and promises with which his word is filled, are a further evidence to us, that he is willing to receive every returning prodigal, and that he will in no wise cast out any who come unto him. On this ground the whole world may adopt the words of the text, and say, "Come, let us return unto the Lord."

2. From that particular discovery of it which we have in the wounds he has inflicted on us.

The Israelites seemed to lay a peculiar stress on this, and to infer, from the very strokes of his rod, his willingness to "heal and bind them up." They even felt an assurance that his return to them would be both speedy and effectual. Ver. 2. Song i. 4. Zech. viii. 21. John i. 41, 45. Thus as soon as any person is brought to acknowledge the hand of God in his afflictions, he will improve them in this very way. Whether his troubles be of a temporal or spiritual nature, he will adore God for not leaving him in a secure and thoughtless state, and for awakening him by any means to a sense of his guilt and danger. He will begin immediately to argue as Manoah's wife: "Would the Lord have shewn me this mercy, if he had intended to destroy me?" Judg. xiii. 23. Does a father correct his child because he has *no* love to him? Are not the very expressions of his anger to be viewed as tokens of his love, Heb. xii. 6. and as *an earnest* of his returning favor as soon as the child shall have implored forgiveness.

Let those then who feel the burthen of their sins, remember, that it is God who has given them to see their iniquities; and that, the heavier their burthen is, the more abundant encouragement they have to cast it on the Lord. Matt. xi. 28.

Application.—To those who have deserted God.

Let us only reflect on the months and years that we have past without any affectionate remembrance of God, or any earnest application to Christ as our Mediator and Advocate; and we shall not need many words to convince us, that we are included in this number. But let us consider whom "we have forsaken; even God, the fountain of living waters;" and, with all our labor in pursuit of happiness, we have only "hewed out for ourselves cisterns, broken cisterns that can hold no water." Jer. ii. 13. Let our past experience suffice to shew us the vanity and folly of our ways: and let us "return unto him from whom we have deeply revolted." But let us beware lest we "heal our wounds slightly." Christ is the brazen Serpent to which all must look: He is the good Samaritan who alone can help us, and who has submitted to be himself "wounded for our transgressions," that he might "heal us by his stripes."

2. To those who are deserted by God.

God does find it necessary sometimes to withdraw the light of his countenance from his people. But, whatever he may have done on some particular occasions, we are sure that in general he does not forsake us till after we have forsaken him. Hence, when the Israelites were deserted by him they did not say, let us pray that he will return to us; but, let us return unto him:

for they were well assured that, as the alienation had begun on their part, so it would be terminated as soon as ever they should humble themselves in a becoming manner. Let those then who are under the hidings of God's face, inquire, what has occasioned his departure from them: and let them put away "the accursed thing," and turn to him with their whole hearts. Let them rest assured, that "there is balm in Gilead;" and that, if they come to him in the name of Christ, their "backslidings shall be healed," and their happiness restored." Hos. xiv. 4. Lam. iii. 31, 32. Ps. xcvii. 11, and cxlvii. 3.*

* If this were the subject of a *Fast Sermon*, the APPLICATION might be comprised in the following observations. 1. The calamities of the nation are manifest tokens of God's displeasure, and calls to repentance.—2. All the efforts of our rulers to heal our wounds will be in vain, if we do not repent.—3. A general turning unto God would bring us speedy and effectual relief.

THE USE OF COVENANTING WITH GOD.

Chronicles xxix. 10, 11.—Now it is in mine heart to make a covenant with the Lord God of Israel, that his fierce wrath may turn away from us. My sons, be not now negligent. (S. S.)

A TRULY pious man will not be satisfied with serving God in his closet—

He will exert his influence to bring others also to a sense of their duty—

The public exercise of the ministry indeed belongs to those only who are duly called to it. Heb. v. 4.—

But all who are possessed of authority (parents, masters, magistrates, and kings,) should use it for the promoting of virtue and religion—

Christians of every rank and description should exhort one another. Heb iii. 13.—

We have a noble example set before us in the conduct of Hezekiah—

As soon as he came to the throne, he set himself to restore the service of the temple—

And called upon all, both ministers and people, to make a solemn covenant with their God—

The royal proclamation for the observance of this day speaks in effect the language of the text—

I. SHEW WHEN WE HAVE REASON TO APPREHEND THAT GOD'S ANGER IS WAXED HOT AGAINST US.

We cannot in all cases determine how far a dispensation may be sent in anger or in love—

But in general we may say, that God is greatly incensed against us—

1. When our sins are multiplied against him.

Sin is invariably the object of God's abhorrence. Hab. i. 13. Ps. v. 5.—

This truth is so evident that it needs not any confirmation—

It needs only to be applied with power to our hearts and consciences—

What lamentable depravity pervades every part of the nation!—

There is no iniquity, however heinous, which is not practised without remorse—

If we look into our own bosoms, what reason for humiliation may we find!—

What ingratitude for mercies received, and impenitence for sins committed!—

What rebellion against God, what contempt of his Son, what resistance of his Spirit, have we not occasion to deplore!—

And shall not God be avenged of such a nation as this?—

Yea, have not *we* reason to fear that *we* shall be monuments of his wrath—

2. When his judgments are multiplied upon us.

God often sends *temporal* afflictions to his people in love? Heb. xii. 6.—

But *spiritual* judgments are a certain token of his wrath—

Blindness of mind, obduracy of heart, and obstinacy in sin are among his heaviest judgments. Isa. vi. 9, 10.—

And have none of us reason to fear that these are now inflicted on us?—

But it is by temporal judgments chiefly that he punishes nations—

It was from these that Hezekiah judged of God's anger against the Jews Ver. 8, 9.—

And are not these multiplied upon our land at this time?—

Surely the displeasure of God can scarcely ever be more strongly displayed, than it is in the calamities under which we now groan—

But that none may yield to desponding fears we shall,

II. Point out the best means of averting his wrath.

Repentance towards God and faith in Christ are the means prescribed by God—

But it is not a slight and superficial use of these means that will suffice—

We should solemnly devote ourselves to God in a perpetual covenant.

Not that we should attempt to renew the covenant of works—

That would make void the Gospel, and seal our eternal condemnation. Gal. iii. 10.—

Nor should we think to add any thing to the covenant of grace—

That was once made with Christ, and is ordered in all things and sure. Heb. viii. 6.

But we should patiently and deliberately renounce all our former ways—

We should seriously give up ourselves to God as his redeemed people—

And intreat him to perfect us in any way which he shall see fit—

Such covenants as these have often been made by the most eminent saints.

Under the old Testament dispensation they were judged acceptable to God—

Omitting many other instances, we may notice the solemn covenant of Asa. 2 Chron. xv. 12–15.

Nor was that less remarkable which was entered into by Josiah. 2 Kings xxiii. 3.—

Isaiah and Jeremiah speak of the making of such covenants as characteristic of the gospel times. Isa. xliv. 5. Jer. l. 4. 5.

St. Paul highly commends the conduct of the Macedonians on account of their having thus given themselves up to God. 2 Cor. viii. 5.—

And recommends a similar practice to all christians of every age and nation. Rom. xii. 1.—

Nor can we doubt of their acceptableness to God.

Hezekiah manifestly supposed that God would accept him in this duty. *The text.*—

It was recommended to Ezra in circumstances where there was but little hope remaining. Ezra x. 3.—

And God himself expressly enjoined it as the means of averting his displeasure. Jer. iv. 4.—

Not that we are to suppose that there is any thing meritorious in such an act—

But, it tends, of itself, to the humiliation and confirmation of our souls—

And will be both accepted and remembered by our covenant God and Father. Deut. xxix. 12, 13.—

These means being at once so scriptural and so important, we shall,

III. Urge upon you the adoption of them.

We admire the tender and affectionate address of Hezekiah to the priests—

And with similar concern would we now invite you to the performance of your duty—

1. There is no time for delay.

Many are "negligent" at present in expectation of a more convenient season—

But who can assure himself that he shall be alive on the morrow. James iv. 14.—

Or that, if he be, he shall have an inclination to that from which he is now averse?—

Or that God will grant him the aids of his Spirit which are now refused?—

The voice of God to every one is, Seek me to-day, while it is called to day. Heb. iii. 13, 15.—

With respect to the nation, who can tell how soon the cloud that hangs over us may burst, and overwhelm us utterly?—

Let us follow the example of the repenting Ninevites. Jonah iii. 5—9.-

If "it be in our hearts to make a covenant," let it instantly be done Ps. cxix. 60.—

And let every one, while we are yet speaking, implore help of God to do it with sincerity—

2. If we neglect this duty, we *cannot hope* to escape the wrath of God.

Sodom was destroyed, because they laughed at God's threatenings as idle tales—

And the strongest empires, in succession, have fallen a sacrifice to their sins—

Who then shall protect *us*, if we continue to provoke the Majesty of heaven?—

But, whatever be the fate of the nation, we must all appear at the judgment seat of Christ—

And there none will be acknowledged as his people, who had not voluntarily taken him for their Lord and Saviour—

If then ye have any regard for your eternal welfare, neglect him no longer—

But, in the penitent language of the prophet, devote yourselves to his service. Isa. xxvi. 13.—

3. If we heartily engage in this duty, we have *nothing to fear*.

Were such a covenant general through the nation, God would soon remove his judgments—

But whatever come upon the land, God's faithful people shall be objects of his favor—

Though they may be involved in the general calamities, they shall be comforted with the divine presence. Ps. xxxiv. 18, 19.—

They need not therefore be agitated with fear on account of God's displeasure in this world—

Nor have they any thing to dread in the eternal world. Mal. iii. 17.

Let us then enter into this matter with our whole hearts—
And pray day and night for grace to perform our vows—
Unfaithfulness to our engagements will incense God still more against us—
And provoke him to inflict yet heavier judgments upon us. Jer. xxxiv. 18–20.
It were even better never to have vowed, than to vow and not pay. Ecc. v. 5. 2. Pet. ii. 21.
He however, who puts it into our heart to make, can enable us to keep, our covenant. Jude 24.
Let us then engage simply in dependence on the divine strength—
But found all our hopes of acceptance on that better and unchangeable covenant, which Christ has entered into on our behalf—

THE REQUISITES FOR ACCEPTABLE PRAYER.

1 Kings viii. 38, 39.—What prayer and supplications soever be made by any man, or by all thy people Israel, which shall know every man the plague of his own heart, and spread forth his hands towards this house: then hear thou in heaven thy dwelling-place, and forgive, and do, and give to every man according to his ways whose heart thou knowest. (S. S.)

Religion is often thought to be an employment fit only for weak minds, or for those who have nothing else to engage their attention—
But it is worthy the pursuit of the wisest and greatest men—
Never did Solomon appear more glorious than when uttering these words—
At the head of all his subjects he dedicated his temple to God—
He set them a bright example of piety and devotion—
And interceded, not for them only, but for all succeding generations.
In this portion of his instructive prayer we may see,
I. The requisites for acceptable prayer.
An humble, upright, fervent, believing, submissive, obediential frame of mind is necessary when we approach the throne of grace—
But the most essential requisites for acceptable worship are comprised in,
1. A deep sense of our own depravity.
The "plague of one's own heart" is, one's indwelling corruption*—
"Every one" has some "sin that more easily besets him"—
Not that a mere acquaintance with this plague is sufficient—
We must know the depth and inveteracy of our disorder—
Our knowledge too must produce an unfeigned self-abhorrence—
And a full conviction of our utter helplessness—
Nor without this knowledge can we offer up acceptable prayer—
We cannot lament what we neither feel nor know—
Or seek for mercy, when we perceive not our need of it—
While ignorant of our depravity, we are not in a state to receive mercy—
We should not even be willing to accept of mercy on God's terms—

* Some understand "plague" as expressing some loathsome disorder; and the rather because it is translated "sore" in the parallel passage 2 Chron. vi. 29. This is the true sense of it when it relates to the body; but *here* the heart is represented as the seat of this disorder, and therefore it must be understood of sin. This is confirmed by what is said in the text of God's knowing the heart.

The very offers of salvation would rather excite our displeasure than our gratitude*—

2. A believing view of Christ.

The temple of Solomon was the more immediate residence of the Deity—

All were on this account directed to look towards it when they prayed—

That temple was typical of the Lord Jesus Christ†—

In him "dwells all the fulness of the Godhead bodily"—

To him our eyes are therefore to be directed. Isai. xlv. 22.

We are to offer all our petitions to him, or in his name. John xiv. 13, 14.

This regard to him is neeessary to the acceptance of our prayers—

It is through him alone that we gain access to the Deity. Eph. ii. 18.

We cannot approach the Father in any other way. John xiv. 6.

Nor is there any other channel whereby the divine blessings can flow down to us, John i. 16.

On these accounts we must "stretch out our hands towards" HIM—

We must view HIM as our only source of spiritual blessings—

They who truly seek after God will soon experience,

II. THE EFFICACY OF PRAYER WHEN ATTENDED WITH THOSE REQUISITES.

Carnal, cold, or unbelieving petitions will receive no answer, Jam. iv. 3; Matt. xv. 8, 9; Jam. i. 6, 7.

But humble and believing prayer will obtain the richest blessings.

1. National.

The passage before us relates to the whole Jewish nation—

It supposes them to have incurred the heavy displeasure of God—

And teaches them how they are to avert his wrath—

Nor did God leave them in suspense about the issue of such humiliation—

He declared in vision to Solomon that his petitions were accepted, 2 Chron. vii. 12–14.

The Jewish history affords many striking instances of deliverance vouchsafed to a repenting people.‡

Nor can we doubt but that the same means would still be crowned with the like success.‖

2. Personal.

He who "knows our heart" will grant all that we can desire, 1 John v 14, 15.

Forgiveness of sin.

Who more infamous and abandoned than that woman? Luke vii. 37, 39.

Yet she, in humility and faith, applied to Jesus, Luke vii. 38.

And received an assurance that her iniquities were forgiven, Ib. 47, 48, 50

Peace of conscience.

How troubled, almost to distraction, were the murderers of our Lord! Acts ii. 37.

*A man, not sensible that he had subjected himself to capital punishment by breaking the laws of his country, would reject with indignation, an offer of deliverance from an ignominious death: but a self-condemned criminal on the eve of his execution would receive such an offer gladly.

†See John ii. 19, 21, and compare Exod. xxiii. 21, with the expression, "My name shall be there." 1 Kings viii. 29.

‡ Jehosapht praying according to the direction in the text, 2 Chron. xx. 5—13, expressly reminded God of his promise, ver. 9. And the success of his prayer far exceeded all reasonable expectation; see ver. 22—25.

‖If this were a *Fast Sermon*, it would be proper to enlarge a little on this idea in reference to the peculiar state of the nation at the time.

But, according to Peter's direction, they looked to Jesus, Ib. 38.
And were immediately filled with "peace and joy in believing," Ib. 46.
*Deliverance from temporal troubles.
We cannot conceive greater temporal affliction than that endured by Jonah, Jonah ii. 1—3.
Yet, when to appearance irrevocably lost, he prayed in this manner, Ib. 4, 7.
And experienced a most unparalled deliverance, Ib. 10.
*Victory over our spiritual enemies.
With what vehemence did Satan assault the apostle Paul! 2 Cor. xii. 7
The afflicted saint cried with earnestness to the Lord Jesus, Ib. 8.
His troubles were immediately turned into triumphant exultations, Ib 9.
Renewal after the divine image.
Nothing on earth does a believer desire so much as this—
Yet this shall be attained in the same way—
An humble an believing view of Christ shall effect it, iii. 18.
*A peaceful death.
Stephen died by the hands of cruel and bloodthirsty enemies, Acts vii. 54
But he offered an humble and believing prayer to Christ, Ib. 59.
And his death was to him as a serene and peaceful sleep, Ib. 60.
A glorious immortality.
He who died *justly* by the hands of the public executioner must have merited in a high degree the wrath of God, Luke xxiii. 41.
Nevertheless in his last hour he directed his eyes to Christ, Ib. 42.
And that very day was he admitted with Christ to Paradise, Ib. 43.
APPLICATION.
Let none despair on account of the greatness of their sins—
Or of the judgments of God which are already inflicted on them.
God will suffer none to "seek his face in vain"—
Let every one then bewail "the plague of his own heart"—
And offer up believing prayers "towards God's holy oracle."*

* This will suffice for two Sermons, the first head being the subject of one, and the second head of the other. If it form the ground of one Sermon only, those particulars which are marked with an asterisk * under the second head may be omitted.

THE PRAYER OF JABEZ.

1 Chron. iv. 10.—And Jabez called on the God of Israel, saying, Oh, that thou wouldest bless me indeed, and enlarge my coast, and that thine hand might be with me, and that thou wouldest keep me from evil, that it may not grieve me. And God granted him that which he requested. (S. S.)

REMARKABLE is the honor which God puts upon prayer—
And numberless are the instances which are recorded of its efficacy—
Jabez is here mentioned in a long catalogue of names—
But while the names only of others are recorded, he is particularly noticed—
He is even declared to have been more honorable than all his brethren—
This distinction indeed might be given him on account of his primogeniture—
But it was certainly still more due on account of his piety—

Like the patriarch Jacob, "wrestled with God and prevailed"—

I. The import of his prayer.

In its primary sense it evidently related to *temporal* blessings.

God had promised his people an inheritance in Canaan—

But they were not able of themselves to drive out the inhabitants—

Jabez therefore, sensible of his insufficiency, prayed to God for help—

He begged for the blessing of God upon his own endeavors—

He desired to be preserved from the dangers to which his military exploits would expose him—

And to have, through the divine interposition, an enlarged inheritance in the promised land—

These requests he urged with a significant and earnest plea—

But there is reason to think it had also a *spiritual* meaning.

The earthly Canaan was typical of the heavenly kingdom—

The enemies also that were to be driven out, were typical of the enemies with whom the christian has to contend—

Moreover, the assistance, which God rendered to his people, was intended to show us what aid we might expect from him—

And what evil will a child of God deprecate so much as sin?—

Surely nothing is so "grievous" to him as the prevalence of corruption, Rom. vii. 24.

Well therefore may Jabez be considered as looking beyond this world—

And as imploring a secure possession of his heavenly inheritance—

In both these views the prayer is well worthy of our notice.

II. The excellence of it.

It is the sentiment, rather than the expression, that gives excellence to prayer—

But in both respects we may admire that before us—

It was,

Humble.

He felt his entire dependence upon the power and grace of God—

This is intimated not merely in the petitions offered, but in the very manner in which they were offered—"Oh, that," &c.

Such humility is absolutely necessary to render prayer acceptable—

The more we abase ourselves, the more will God exalt us—

Let this be remembered in all our addresses at the throne of grace—

Diffusive

Jabez did not content himself with a mere general petition—

He opened distinctly his several wants to God—

A similar conduct is proper for us also, Phil. iv. 6.

Not that God needs to be informed of our wants, or that he will hear us for our much speaking, Matt. vi. 7, 8.

But we need to recite our wants, in order to impress our own minds with a sense of our utter helplessness and unworthiness—

Importunate

He enforced his request with a very earnest plea—

Nor, in reference to sin, could any plea be more proper for *him*-

We indeed should urge the prevailing name of Jesus—

But we may also properly deprecate sin as "grievous" to our souls—

Yea, a disposition to do this is both an evidence of our sincerity, and a pledge of the divine acceptance—

And, in pleading thus, we may well adopt the words of Jacob—Gen. xxxii. 26.

Believing

The title, by which he addressed the Deity, argued his faith in God—
It expressed a confidence in God as the hearer of prayer, Ib. 28.
It is in this way that we also should approach the Deity, Heb. xi. 6.
Without such faith our petitions will have but little effect, Jam. i. 6, 7.
But with it, they shall never go forth in vain, Mark xi. 24.
Prayer possessing such qualities could not fail of success.

III. THE SUCCESS WITH WHICH IT WAS ATTENDED.

We have no detailed account of God's kindness towards him—
But we are informed that God granted him all that he requested.
If Jabez was not straitened in asking, much less was God in giving—
"The prayer of the upright is God's delight"—
We cannot possibly enlarge our requests too much—
We lose much by not using more of holy vehemence, 2 Kings xiii. 19.
The promises made to us exceed not our desires only, but our conceptions, Eph. iii. 20.
Petitions offered in faith, have, as it were, the force of commands, Isaiah xlv. 11.
The more we abound in them, the more we shall find that saying true, Ps. lxxxi. 10.
And often will God vouchsafe us an instantaneous answer, Ps. cxxxviii. 3.
Let us therefore take encouragement from this concise history.
Many and great are the blessings we need from God—
But the throne of his grace is always open to us—
Let us then spread all our sins, and wants before him—
Let us approach him as our God in Christ Jesus—
Let us view him as a gracious answerer of prayer, Ps. lxv. 2, and lvii. 2
And our success shall surely correspond with that of Jabez—
"God never did, or will, say to any, Seek ye my face in vain"—

APPLICATION.

Let all now call to mind their several wants and necessities—
Let nothing be thought too small, or too great, to ask—
Let our prayers, like that of Jabez, be daily recorded in heaven—
Let the pressure of our wants, and the richness of our prospects, stimulate us—
Let us expect the accomplishment of that glorious promise—John xiv. 13, 14.
And in due time our prayers shall be turned into everlasting praises.

HUMILIATION FOR THE SIN OF THE HEART.

2 Chron. xxxii. 26.—Hezekiah humbled himself for the pride of his heart. (S. S.)

THE best of men are liable to fall through temptation—
But they will deeply bewail any sin into which they have been betrayed—
Hezekiah was a man of very distinguished piety, 2 Kings xx. 3.
But he was not sufficiently aware, that his integrity was the effect of divine grace, and not of human power—
God therefore left him for a moment to the influence of his own heart—Ver. 31.

In consequence of this he soon gave a proof of his inherent depravity—
But, on discovering his sin, he instantly humbled himself for it before God—
We shall,

I. SHEW THE NATURE AND GROUNDS OF HEZEKIAH'S HUMILIATION.

The sin committed by him does not in human estimation appear great.
The princes of Babylon sent to congratulate him on his recovery—
He received them with all the kindness and courtesy that he could express—
And shewed them every thing in his dominions that could afford them entertainment—

But his conduct was exceeding sinful in the sight of God; for in it,

1. He sought his own glory

Hezekiah evidently thought of nothing else at that time—
He wished to shew how great a man he was, in order that his alliance might be courted, and his power feared—
Now this would have been highly criminal in any man, Prov. xxv. 27.
But it was especially so in him, at that particular juncture—
He had just been at the border of the grave; and therefore should have been more impressed with the vanity of earthly grandeur—
And should have seen the folly and wickedness of *priding himself* in things so empty, so worthless, so transient—

2. He sought his own glory in preference to God's honor.

He had now a happy opportunity of magnifying the God of Israel—
He might have told the ambassadors, what God had done for his nation in former times—
He might have recited the wonderful restoration which God had at this time afforded to himself in particular, together with the stupendous miracle with which the promise of that recovery had been confirmed, 2 Kings xx. 11.
He might have commended Jehovah as an answerer of prayer—Ib. ver. 4, 5.
And in this way have exalted him above all the gods of the heathen—
And surely the mercies that had been vouchsafed unto him, demanded such a tribute—
But he was pitifully occupied about SELF—
And basely preferred *his own* honor before God's—

3. He sought his own glory before the good of his friends

The ambassadors were shewing great kindness to him—
He should therefore have recompensed them in the best way—
He should have instructed them in the knowledge of the God of Israel—
And have told them how willing HE was to become their God—
Thus perhaps he might have converted and saved their souls—
And have spread the knowledge of the true God in Babylon—
Yea, eventually, he might have been instrumental to the salvation of thousands—
But he utterly forgot the necessities of their souls—
And was offering incense to his own vanity, when he should have been promoting their eternal welfare—
This was his sin; and God denounced a heavy judgment against him on account of it.
His riches were all to be taken away by the Chaldeans—
His own children were to be made eunuchs in the king of Babylon's palace—
And the whole nation to be led into a miserable captivity—
But, if his offence was great, his humiliation also was remarkable.

He heard with trembling the judgments which God threatened to execute—

Instead of palliating his sin, he acknowledged at once the justice of the Deity in inflicting such a punishment on account of it—

In concert with all his subjects, he implored forgiveness at God's hands—

And, having obtained a respite of the sentence, thankfully acquiesced in the determinations of heaven, Isa. xxxix. 8.

While we see in him much to shun, and much to imitate, let us,

II. ENQUIRE WHETHER WE ALSO HAVE NOT SIMILAR GROUNDS FOR HUMILIATION?

Pride is deeply rooted in the heart of fallen man—

We are prone to be lifted up on every occasion.

We are vain of any *natural endowments* of body or mind—

The strong displays his strength; the beautiful, her beauty—

A penetrating mind, or tenacious memory, are made grounds of self-admiration, and self-preference—

Any *acquired distinctions* also become food for our vanity—

The man of wealth, of honor, or of power, assumes a consequence from his elevation, and demands from others a homage as his due—

The proficient in any act or science courts applause, and delights to have his talents admired—

Even the *gifts of grace*, through the depravity of our nature, become occasions of pride—

Not only an ability to speak or pray with fluency, but even an insight into the corruption of the heart, is often exhibited more for the purpose of attracting admiration than of doing good—

Whatever we have that elevates us a little above our fellow-creatures, our proud hearts are fond of displaying it, and pleased with the flattering attentions which it procures for us—

We indulge the disposition too to the neglect of God's honor, and of the eternal welfare of those around us.

How many glorious opportunities have we of speaking for God!—

What grounds of praising him might we find in the sacred records!—

How many too might we find in our own experience!—

And what unspeakable benefit might arise to mankind, if we carefully improved these opportunities!—

But how rarely is our intercourse with each other made subservient to these ends—

We waste our time in flattering attentions and unprofitable civilities—

We are as intent on gratifying the vanity of ourselves or others, as if our social converse were capable of no better improvement—

How much then do we need to imitate Hezekiah's humiliation!

However innocent we may think such conduct, it is highly criminal in the sight of God—

It renders us justly obnoxious to God's heaviest judgments—Matt. xii. 36, 37.

Should we not then humble ourselves before him in dust and ashes?—

Should not the forbearance he has exercised call forth our devoutest acknowledgments?—

And should we not adore his goodness even if he only delay to execute his threatened vengeance?—

Let us not attempt to palliate this common, but vile, iniquity—

But rather unite in deprecating the wrath we have deserved—

INFER,

1. What dreadful evils arise from small beginnings!

Hezekiah at first probably intended only to shew civility to his friends—

But through inattention to the motions of his heart, he fell into grievous sin, and brought on the whole nation the heaviest judgments—

And what enormities have not the motions of pride, of lewdness, of covetousness, or revenge, produced amongst ourselves, when, if they had been checked at first, they might have been easily subdued?—

Let us learn then to mark the first risings of sin in our hearts—

Let us remember, that God notices and abhors sin in the heart, no less than when it is brought forth into open act—

Let us intreat him to sanctify our inward man, 1 Thess. v. 23.

And *never to leave us to ourselves for one single moment*—

2. How great is the efficacy of fervent prayer and intercession!

The judgment denounced against Hezekiah was to have been speedily inflicted—

But he and Judah sought the Lord by humble and fervent prayer—

And the Lord deferred the evil till the next generation—

Thus will he do also in answer to our prayers—

If we turned to him as a nation, he would *prolong our national* prosperity—

And would *blot out for ever* the *personal* guilt of every true penitent—

Let us then humble ourselves for our abominations both of heart and life—

So shall we find God as gracious unto us, as he was to his people of old.

THE WOMAN OF CANAAN.

Matthew xv. 25.—"Lord, help me." (Sk.)

JESUS came down from heaven to save a perishing world, and his merciful regards extended both to Jews and Gentiles; but his ministry and miracles were, generally, confined to the lost sheep of the house of Israel. Here, however, we have an exception. A poor woman of Canaan came unto him on behalf of her daughter, and after a painful trial of her faith, he mercifully granted unto her the blessing which she desired. The whole account is highly interesting, and will furnish us with many important and useful observations.

I. THE PERSON WHO APPLIED TO JESUS, WAS A "WOMAN OF CANAAN."

1. Her *ancestors were a wicked race*, Lev. xviii. 24, 25;—and were driven out of their native country, as a just punishment of their enormous crimes. Deut, iv. 38. The Israelites, under the command of Joshua, took possession of their land; and, by divine appointment, it became their inheritance, Josh. xiv. 1, 2.

2. But the character and conduct of this woman is a standing proof, that *the descendants of wicked nations may be reformed and saved:* this was the case with the Corinthians, of whom the apostle Paul said, alluding to the abominable wickedness of the heathen world, "Such were some of you; but ye are washed, but ye are sanctified" 1 Cor. vi. 11.

3 Her *faith in the Son of God put the Jewish people to shame* They despised and hated him; but she honored and adored him: and there are persons in the heathen world, in the present day, whose general conduct puts to shame the merely nominal christians of our highly favored land.

II. SHE APPLIED TO OUR LORD FOR HER DAUGHTER, WHO WAS "GREVIOUSLY VEXED WITH A DEVIL."

1. In many instances *devils have had the power over the bodies of men and women;* and that power has been exercised in tormenting those who have been under their influence. But we never read of these apostate spirits doing any good, or attempting to make any person happy. They are wicked and mischievous, and it will be dreadful to be delivered into their hands, Matt. xviii. 34, 35.

2. But *Jesus had power to cast out devils*, and to deliver men from their hellish rage and malice. A word of his terrified those foul spirits, and put whole legions of them to flight, Mark v. 9—13. This poor women had heard the fame of Jesus, Matt. iv, 24; and sought his help with humble confidence.

2. And *has he not power over devils now?* Do they not tremble at the sound of his precious name? He holds the powers of hell in chains; he destroys their influence in our hearts, Eph. ii. 1—4; and bruises Satan under our feet, Rom. xvi. 20.

III. THE WOMAN USED MEANS WHICH WERE PROPER, AND WHICH WELL BECAME HER SITUATION.

1. She addressed Jesus as the *son of David*, and thereby acknowledged that he was the Christ which should come into the world; for the Jews called their Messiah the son of David, because he was to descend from him, and to sit upon his throne, Isa. ix. 7.

2. And *she cried for mercy:* the case of her daughter required the interposition of mercy. It was wise in her to go to Jesus, for he was full of grace, John i. 14; and it will be wise in us to go to him for a complete deliverence from the power and tyranny of our adversary the devil, who "as a roaring lion, walking about seeking whom he may devour," 1 Pet. v. 8. She was not ashamed of earnest prayer, but cried aloud; let us also cry aloud, like David, out of the depths of penitential sorrow, Psa. cxxx. 1, 2.

IV. JESUS, AS IF HE DID NOT HEAR HER CRY, REMAINED SILENT, AND "ANSWERED HER NOT A WORD."

1. He seemed to treat her with *contempt;* but was trying and proving her faith, How often does he proceed on a similar plan, in his dealings with humble penitents, so that they are ready to ask, "Is his mercy clean gone for ever?" Psa. lxxvii. 8.

2. But let them *patiently wait* for his salvation, Psa. xl. 1. He may be silent for a time; but mercy is in his heart. Only remain at the throne of grace, and continue to cry for mercy, and he will give an answer of peace, Gen. xli. 16.

V. HIS DISCIPLES, WEARY OF HER NOISY CRY, BESOUGHT HIM TO SEND HER AWAY.

1. It is highly probable, from the answer of Jesus, that *they wished him to grant her request;* for, otherwise, there would be no point in his saying, "I am not sent but unto the lost sheep of the house of Israel." But allowing this, there is *no proof that they pitied her case*, as they only wanted to get rid of her, on account of the multitude of people brought about them by her loud cries.

2. But *the ministers of Jesus should pity all who are in trouble;* kindly

bear with the little improprieties of behaviour which they may fall into, in such circumstances; treat them with the utmost tenderness, weeping with them that weep, Rom. xii. 15; and, especially intercede for them with their heavenly Lord and Master. A feeling heart is a fine trait in a christian minister, Rom. ix. 1—3.

VI. In reply to his disciples, Jesus stated his mission to the house of Israel.

1. He calls them *lost sheep*, because they had gone astray, and were exposed to imminent perils. No animal in the world is more exposed to danger than a wandering sheep; and when the foolish conduct of men is set forth by this figure in the Holy Scriptures, their danger is forcibly pointed out: and were not the Jews exposed, in their wanderings, to error, sin, and punishment?

2. Jesus was sent, as a holy prophet, to *seek the wandering sheep* of the house of Israel; to bring them back to the fold of God; and to place them in safe and happy circumstances. To this he alludes in another figure, where he says, "How often would I have gathered thy children together, even as a hen gathereth her chickens under her wings, and ye would not?" Matt. xxiii. 37.

3. But *he was not sent as a prophet to the Gentiles*, nor did he send his disciples to them in the days of his flesh, Matt. x. 5, 6; but after his resurrection, he commissioned them to go "into all the world," and to "preach the gospel to every creature," Mark xvi. 15. Thus we have known the joyful sound, and we may walk in the light of the Lord's countenance, Psalms lxxxix. 15.

VII. Now the woman drew near and worshipped Jesus, saying, "Lord, help me."

1. She *paid him honor as the son of David;* but we dare not affirm that she worshipped him as God; because we are not quite sure that she was acquainted with his divinity. Kings were worshipped with *civil respect*. Thus the congregation of Israel "bowed down their heads and worshipped the Lord and the king," 1 Chron. xxix. 20. But we, who know the Saviour, as *God over all*, are bound to worship him with divine honors, Rev. v. 13.

2. The cry of the woman was, *Lord help me:* she knew he *could* help her, because he had helped others in similar circumstances; and she hoped he *would* help her, because she had heard of his wonderful compassion. With this conviction let us approach his mercy seat, resting assured that he is both able and willing to help us, in our lowest and most abject state.

3. Many persons would have been *offended* at the silence of Jesus; but this poor woman, being strong in faith, took no offence. It ill becomes a suppliant to murmur and complain, especially one who applies for blessings on the ground of mercy; and what other ground have we? We are sinners and there is no salvation for us, but by grace, Eph. ii. 8.

VIII. But when this woman paid honor to our Lord, and asked his gracious help, he spake to her with apparent unkindness.

1. He called the house of Israel *children;* but they were rebellious children, Isa. i. 2. They treated him cruelly; but he expressed tender love to them. That love continued, when their malice had brought him to the cross. There he said, "Father, forgive them; for they know not what they do," Luke xxiii. 34. He was not willing, after all, to give them up to wrath and justice, Hos. xi. 8.

2. The blessings which he was bestowing on those rebellious children, he called *bread*. By that bread he meant his wise instructions, his healing

power, and his nourishing influences. He was the bread of life, and if his own nation had received him as the true Messiah, he would have fed them with the bread of life, as he had fed their fathers by manna in the wilderness, John vi. 31—35.

3. Though his own nation despised that bread, yet he said to this Cananite, it is not meet to take it from them, and to cast it to the dogs. He did not call her countrymen dogs; but reminded her that they were viewed with *contemtp*, on account of their impurities and abominations. This was not said with a view to reproach any class of men; but to prove her faith.

IX. THE WOMAN, CONSCIOUS OF HER VILENESS, ACKNOWLEDGED THE TRUTH OF HIS OBSERVATION; BUT HUMBLY CRAVED THE CRUMBS WHICH MIGHT FALL FROM HIS TABLE.

1. Here we see a remarkable instance of *genuine humility;* the poor Canaanite did not say a word about the degrading title, only, "*Truth, Lord.*" It was as much as if she had said, "let us be called dogs, we deserve such treatment, and I will not attempt to prove that we have any just claims to thy benevolence."

2. But her remarks were *ingenious and inimitably beautiful;* and the reason assigned, why it was not meet to give her the children's bread, was made the ground of her pleading. "The Canaanites, who deserved to be called dogs, ought not to expect the bread of children; but remember, Lord, that dogs eat the crumbs which fall from their master's table; and I only ask thee for the crumbs which are given to those animals."

3, How strong was her *faith;* how *persevering* her application; how *earnest* her desire to obtain the blessing! An humbled spirit is willing to be accounted vile. Let us carefully study, and humbly own, our vileness; and while we humble ourslves before the Lord, and deem the smallest favour an undeserved boon, his mighty hand will lift us up, James iv. 10; 1 Pet. v. 6.

X. WHEN HER FAITH WAS PROVED, JESUS SAID, "BE IT UNTO THEE EVEN AS THOU WILT."

1. Her faith in the power and merciful kindness of Christ was *great.* When he was silent she was not discouraged, but waited for an answer; and when he hinted at her unworthiness to receive the children's bread, she said, "Truth, Lord." Hence we learn that a steady and strong faith in our adorable Saviour, produces persevering prayer; and the humble penitent says, "I will not let thee go, except thou bless me," Gen. xxxii. 26.

2. The poor woman was blessed; her faith and prayer were *successful;* and her daughter was made whole from that very hour. And we may boldly affirm, that all our lawful petitions, offered up in the name of Jesus, will be heared and answered; for he has said, "Ask and it shall be given you, seek and ye shall find, knock and it shall be opened unto you," Luke xi. 9.

INFERENCES.

1. The usurped dominion of the devil, and the miseries of his deluded children, demand particular notice. Let us study his devices, 2 Cor. xi. 11; and resist him that he may flee from us, James iv. 7.

2. It is a pleasing reflection, that the head of this old serpent has been bruised, agreeably to the first promise, Gen. iii. 15; and that the seed of the woman has power to bind him in chains, Rev. xx. 1–3.

3. We should go to Jesus in all our troubles; exercise ourselves in a devotional faith; expect deliverance from him alone; and when delivered, give him the glory which is due to his holy name.

4. Our griefs and sorrows will soon come to an end; we shall be removed far from our enemy, the devil; and spend a blessed eternity with God our Saviour. He is now touched with the feeling of our infirmities; he has a loving heart and a strong hand; and is mighty to save his chosen people, Isaiah lxiii. 1.

RELIGION NOT A VAIN THING.

Deuteronomy xxxii. 47.—For it is not a vain thing for you; because it is your life. (Sk.)

One of our poets has compared the exit of a good man to the sun, which seems "larger at his setting." And never was the remark more fully illustrated and confirmed, than in the character and circumstances of Moses when he delivered the text. He had been great and good through life; but now his greatness and goodness appeared in higher perfection, and shone with more than usual radiance. The closing scene drew near, his race of peril and glory was just run. He had voluntarily chosen in early life to suffer affliction with the people of God, and now he convenes them together, and delivers in their ears his solemn, his final charge; a charge which for genuine affection, deep seriousness, grand and elevated sentiment, stern fidelity, and awfully prophetic warnings, has never found a parrallel. He rehearses the righteous acts of the Lord—reminds Israel of their rebellions—warns them of their danger—instructs them in their duty, and closes the whole by saying, "Set your hearts unto all the words," &c. ver. 46, 47. We will notice,

I. The object to which Moses referred;—"It is not a vain thing," &c.

II. The affirmation which he made concerning it;—"It is your life.'

I. The object to which Moses refers. This is stated in ver. 46, "Set your hearts unto all the words," &c. Two things are included in these words, viz. *personal* and *family religion*. Israel were to set their hearts to do all the words of the law themselves, and then to command their children to do them. There were many laws, or commandments, which Moses received from God, and delivered unto Israel, with which we have nothing to do. Some were ceremonial, relating to the peculiar mode of Jewish worship. Others were judicial, referring to the administration of justice among them. But the moral law, which was amplified in the ten commandments, and epitomised in those well known precepts, "Thou shalt love the Lord," &c., Matt. xxii. 37—39, concerns us as much as it did Israel, and we remark concerning it, that—*It is imperative in its nature.* "Thou shalt love," &c. We are not lawless beings, left to live at random; nor has God given us a law, and left it optional with us to observe, or not observe it. But it is imperative upon us; we must do it, or inherit a curse for omitting to do it. *It is comprehensive in its requirements.* It binds us to love God with all our powers, passions, and affections. Our thoughts, words, and actions, are to be inspired, regulated, and ruled by love.—*It is universal in its extent.* It binds every man, in every clime, and in every station to love God, and to love his neighbor.—*It is perpetual and eternal in its obligation.* It knows no change by the revolutions of years, it never can be abrogated. Should any inquire how this law is to be kept, Moses will instruct them, "Set your hearts to all the words," &c.—*Set your hearts to consider the nature of this law.* This will instruct you, how utterly impossible is it for you to comply with the requisitions of this law, without renewing grace. "By the law is the knowledge of sin." Know the law and you will know yourselves. Counterfeit coin is best detected by comparing it with that which is genuine—*Set your hearts to pray for that grace which will enable you to love the law of the Lord.* Carnal men hate the law, because it is so holy, it allows of no unhallowed pleasures, sanctions no criminal indulgence; but good men have the law of God in their hearts, meditate in that law day and night, and are ready individually to say, "O how I love thy law!"—*Set your hearts to expect the accomplishment of that promise,* "The Lord thy God will circumcise thine heart," Deut. xxx. 6.

Family religion is also enjoined;—"Ye shall command your children to observe to do all the words of this law."—*Parental duty must be regulated by the law of God.* Have you children? Get them to read, to understand, and to do what the Bible enjoins.—*Parental duty is authorized by the command of God.* It is imperative upon parents to command their children, "Ye shall command," &c. Such is the object to which Moses referred. Let us consider,

II. The affirmation which he made concerning it;—"It is not a vain thing," &c. Here are two things to be noticed; what religion is not, and what it is.

1. *It is not an empty, airy, unsubstantial thing.* For such the word vain frequently signifies. Job calls the months of his affliction "months of vanity." Idols are called vanity, and idolaters vain men. Religion is not a vain thing, not a phantom of the brain, not a cunningly devised fable, but a substantial reality that may be felt, tasted, and enjoyed.

2. *It is not a false deceitful thing.* Vain words are false lying words. Taking the name of God in vain, is using it falsely, as well as unnecessarily. Religion is not a false thing. There are indeed false systems of religion, and lying vanities substituted for religion, but the religion of the Bible is inviolably true; it emanates from a God of truth; and it leads to truth in principle and practice. Infidels *say* it is false, but Christians *know* it is true.

3. *It is not a foolish senseless thing.* "Vain man would be wise;" and ignorant men think religion is folly; and count the lives of its professors madness. "The preaching of the cross is to them that perish foolishness," &c. But religion is the essence of true wisdom; under its influence, we aim at the noblest objects, by the adoption of the most eligible means for securing those objects.

4. *It is not a fruitless, unproductive thing.* "Vain is the help of man.' "Except the Lord keep the city," &c., Psa. cxxvii. 1. Religion is universally profitable, Prov. iii. 13—18, 1 Tim. iv. 8, vi. 6.

But the principal reason why it is not a vain thing is, "It is your life." To the Jews especially this was applicable, because,

1. *It was the means of prolonging their life.* Long life was promised to them, as the reward of obedience to the law of God. "Through this thing ye shall prolong your days," &c., Exod. xx. 12; Prov. iii. 16, x. 27; Psa. xxxiv. 12, 13. And though it may be said, that these promises do not belong to us, yet religion in numberless instances prolongs life, as it saves us from practices which tend to the extinction of life.

2. *It added to the happiness of their life.* God's design in all the dispensations of his grace is the promotion of human happiness. What a miserable kind of existence is life without religion; to live under the curse of

God, ens aved to the devil, under the dominion of guilt, tormented with fears of hell, and every day fitting for damnation. But what a happy, glorious life does that man possess who loves God, and knows that God loves him.

3. *It promoted the utility of their life.* He who lives without religion. lives uselessly. The life of a wicked man is a curse rather than a blessing; and nonenity is preferable to existence, unless the end for which it is given be answered. Religion teaches us to live to be useful. We pray for others—set them good examples—consider the poor, and minister to the necessities of the afflicted.

4. *It prepared them for eternal life.* Heaven is eternal life; not only eternal existence, but endless enjoyment. Religion prepares for this life. He who loves God with all his heart, is a vessel of honor fit for the Master's use; and God will ere long receive him into his kingdom to behold his glory.

INFERENCES.

1. *Religion consists in setting your hearts to know and to keep the commandments of God.* This will serve to reprove those who place it in frames and feelings, fanciful notions, modes of faith, dreams, visions, raptures, &c.

2. *Religion is not a vain thing.* How awfully do thousands deceive themselves. Some treat it with sovereign contempt. Others profess to know it; but their conduct belies their profession. How vain does it appear in the eyes of multitudes!

3. *Religion is your life.* Then tremble at the thought of living without it. Without it you are dead even while you live. O seek to know, love, and serve God. Then you will be "happy while on earth you live, mightier joys ordained to know."

THE PRODIGAL SON.

Luke xv. 23, 24.—Bring hither the fatted calf, and kill it; and let us eat and be merry. For this my son was dead, and is alive again; he was lost, and is found. (S. S.)

THE willingness of God to receive sinners is abundantly declared in scripture—

But in no place is it so amply, or so beautifully described as in the parable before us—

The reference which the parable has to the Jews and Gentiles will be more properly noticed, when we come to consider the conduct of the elder brother—

At present we may view it as a lively representation of a sinner's return to God—

The text leads our attention to three points (which are also the three distinguishing parts of the parable) namely, the prodigal's departure from his father, his return to him, and his reception with him—

I. HIS DEPARTURE.

He went from his father's house, litt e thinking of the ruin he should bring upon himself.

The *occasion* of his departure was, that he hated the restraint of his father's presence—

And longed for independence, that he might gratify his own inclinations—

Hence he desired his father to divide him his portion—

But little did he think to what *extent* his passions would carry him—

Scarcely had he received his portion before he left his father

And departed to a distant country, where his actions would pass unnoticed—

Having thus thrown the reins upon the neck of his appetites, he was carried on with irresistible impetuosity—

From one degree of sin to another he rushed forward without restraint—

Nor stopped till he had wasted his substance in riotous living—

At last he began to feel the *consequences* of his folly—

He was reduced to a state of extreme wretchedness—

Yet he determined to do any thing rather than return to his father—

Though a Jew, he submitted for hire to the ignominious employment of feeding swine—

His wages however, there being a grievous famine in the land, would not procure him even necessary subsistence—

In vain did he attempt to fill his belly with the husks intended for the swine—

In vain did he solicit assistance from those who had known him in his more prosperous days—

"No man," either from gratitude or compassion, "gave him" any relief—

Such is the departure of sinners from the presence of their God

They have experienced the restraints of education—

But have sighed for liberty and independence—

With their growing years, they increasingly abuse the mercies which God has bestowed upon them—

Their reason, their time, and other talents they employ in the service of sin—

Though they do not all run to the same excess of riot, they live equally at a distance from God—

At last perhaps they begin to feel the misery which their neglect of him has brought upon them—

His providence too concurs with his grace to make a deeper wound in their conscience—

But they try any carnal expedients rather than return to God—

Nor can ever be prevailed on to turn unto him, till they have fully proved the insufficiency of the creature to afford them help—

Whatever they may think of themselves in such a state, they are really "*dead*," and "*lost*"—

But the prodigal was not gone beyond recovery, as is evident from,

II. HIS RETURN.

During his departure he had been as a person destitute of reason—

At last however, "*coming to himself*," he thought of his father's house

The various steps of his return are worthy of notice.

He first reflected on the folly and madness of his former ways—

And on the incomparably happier state of those who lived under his father's roof, and whom perhaps he once despised for submitting to such restraints—

He then resolved that he would return to his father, and implore his forgiveness—

Having formed the purpose, he instantly arose to carry it into execution—

And set off, destitute as he was, to obtain, if possible, the lowest office among his father's domestics—

These exactly describe the steps of a sinner's return to God

He first begins to see how madly and wickedly he has acted—

He feels that he has reduced himself to a wretched and perishing condition—

He considers how happy are those once despised people, who enjoy the favor of his heavenly father—

And how happy he himself should be, if he might but obtain the meanest place in his family—

With these views he determines to abase himself as a vile, self-ruined creature—

There are no terms so humiliating, but he finds them suited to his case—

He is rather fearful of not humbling himself sufficiently than of aggravating his sin too much—

He resolves that he will go to a throne of grace and ask for mercy—

Nor will he wait for any more convenient season, lest he should perish before the hoped-for season arrive—

He is ashamed indeed to go in so mean and destitute a condition—

But he despairs of ever going in any other way—

He therefore breaks through all the engagements he has made with sin and Satan—

And goes, with all his guilt upon him, to his God and Saviour-

He now perhaps may be deemed *mad* by his former companions—

But he should rather be considered as now "*coming to himself*"—

The effect of the prodigal's repentance appears in,

III. His reception

His father, it seems, was wishfully looking out for him—

And, on his first appearance, ran to testify his good will towards him

The sight of the returning child caused the father's bowels to yearn over him—

Nor would he suffer an upbraiding word to escape his lips—

When the prodigal began his confession, the father interrupted him with kisses—

And not only would not hear the whole of his confession, but would not even hurt his feelings by saying that he pardoned him—

He ordered the best robe, with shoes and a ring, to be instantly put upon him—

And killed the fatted calf in order to celebrate the joyful occasion—

What a delightful representation does this give us of the reception which penitents find with God!

God longs for their salvation even while they are at a distance from him·

He notices with joy the first approaches of their souls towards him—

Instead of frowning on the prodigal he receives him with joy—

Instead of upbraiding him with his folly, he seals upon his soul a sense of pardon—

He arrays him in robes of righteousness and garments of salvation—

He adorns him in a manner suited to the relation into which he is brought—

He provides for his future comfortable and upright conversation—

He rejoices over him as recovered from the dead—

And makes it an occasion of festivity to all the angels in heaven—

Thus do even the vilest sinners find their hopes, not only realised, but far exceeded—

They come for pardon, and obtain joy; for deliverance from hell, and get a title to heaven—

Their utmost ambition is to be regarded as the meanest of God's servants: and they are exalted to all the honors and happiness of his beloved children—

APPLICATION

Who would not wish to resemble this prodigal in his reception with his father—

But, in order to it, we must resemble him in his penitence and contrition—

Let none think that, because they have been more moral than the prodigal, they do not need to repent like him—

All of us without exception have walked after the imagination of our own hearts, without any love to his presence or regard for his authority—

Let all of us then cry for mercy, as miserable sinners—

The more vile we are in our own eyes, the more acceptable shall we be to God—

Some perhaps may fear to return, because they have been so exceeding vile—

But let none imagine that they have gone beyond the reach of mercy—

The promise of acceptance extends to all without exception, John vii. 37.

"There is bread enough and to spare" for all that will go to God—

Let all then accept the Saviour's invitation, Matt. xi. 28.

Let us this day afford an occasion of joy to all the hosts of heaven—

Then shall we ourselves be soon made partakers of their joy—

And dwell, as dear children, in our Father's house for ever and ever.

THE BALM OF GILEAD, A CURE FOR DISEASED SOULS.

Jer. viii. 22.—Is there no balm in Gilead? &c. (H.)

THESE words were originally spoken of God's ancient people the Jews, who, at this time, it appears, were in a dreadfully declining state. They had provoked the Lord to anger with their graven images and strange vanities. ver. 19. The prophet Jeremiah was exceedingly affected on their account; ver. 21, and exclaims in the language of the text, "Is there no balm," &c.

I shall take occasion from these words, to consider,

I. THAT MANKIND UNIVERSALLY ARE IN A DISEASED STATE.

The soul of man is here meant, and hence the diseases alluded to are diseases of the soul. That the distempers of the mind are compared to wounds, disease, and sickness, will appear from Ps. xxxviii. 5; ciii. 3; cxlvii. 3; Ezek. xxxiv. 4; Matt. ix. 12.

We may here point out some of those diseases.

1. Atheism, infidelity, or unbelief of divine truths. This is a deadly disease, as it hinders the success of the gospel, and the saving of souls. Bad as this disease is, it is not to be found in hell. James ii. 19.

2. Ignorance of God and of gospel truths, even among those who profess to know him. Hosea iv. 6. There are multitudes living in the midst of gospel light, who are yet in gross darkness. They may be cured. Rev. iii. 17, 18; Jer. xxiv. 7.

3. Hardness of heart: hence they sit under the word, and hear the most terrible threatenings and curses denounced against their sins, and are as much unmoved as the seats they sit on. This may be cured. Ezek. xxxvi. 26; Phil. i. 6.

4. Earthly mindedness. This clogs the soul, and unfits it for spiritual exercises. The thoughts of God and eternity are thereby shut out. Other plagues kill their thousands, this kills its tens of thousands. Pharaoh's words are true of them. Exod. xiv. 3. There is help for this also. Cant. iv. 8; Col. iii. 1, 2.

5. Aversion to spiritual duties. There are thousands who would rather toil their bodies a whole day, than spend a quarter of an hour upon their knees with God in secret. Of Sabbaths and sermons they say, What a weariness is it? when will the Sabbath be gone? Mal. i. 13. For this we obtain relief. Ps. cx. 3; Isa. xl. 31; Ezek. xxxvi. 27.

6. Hypocrisy and formality in God's service: drawing near to God with our lips only; how unpleasant to God is a voice without the heart and affections. He heavily complains of it. Isa. xxix. 13. This also may be healed. Jer. xxxi. 33; Prov. iv. 18; 2 Cor. iv. 16.

7. Trusting to our own righteousness: depending upon our duties and performances for salvation, instead of believing on Christ, with the heart unto righteousness. Rom. x. 10.

8. Indwelling corruption. Sometimes it rises like a flood, swells high, and carries all before it. Ps. lxv. 3; Isa. lxiv. 6. There is help for this also. Ps. lxv. 3; Mich. vii. 19; Rom. vii. 24, 25.

9. Backsliding from the Lord: losing our spirituality and liveliness in God's service: then every grace decays in the soul, and the service of God becomes a weariness to us. This is a spiritual consumption, but it may be cured. Deut. xxx. 6; Hos. xiv. 4—6; John xiv. 19.

There are several symptoms which seem to render our diseases almost desperate and incurable.

1. When the body is *universally* affected; and with a complication of diseases, the case is truly alarming, and this is the state of the soul. Isa. i. 5, 6. Still we may be recovered. David was. Ps. ciii. 2, 3.

2. When diseases are of long continuance, and rooted in the habit. This is the case of the soul. Ps. li. 5; Deut. xxviii. 59. Yet the Lord can make their dry bones live. Ezek. xxxvii.

3. When all around consider their case as desperate. This is often the case with sinners. Ezek. xxxvii. 3. And they often say with Israel, Behold our bones are dried. Ezek. xxxvii. 11. But see the promise in this case. Jer. xxx. 17.

4. When its threatening symptoms are not observed, so as to provide timely remedies; "although the fire be kindled round about us, we lay it not to heart." Our case is not unlike that of Israel. Isa. lvii. 17. But desperate as this case may be, there is hope of deliverance. ver. 18.

When the patient loses his senses, and becomes lethargic that he cannot be awakened. And this is often the case with sinners. Isa. xxvi. 11; xxix. 40. Yet still there is hope. Jer. xxxiii. 6.

II. That there is a physician who can cure all our diseases.

God himself is our physician. Exod. xv. 26. Our cure is the work of the whole Trinity; but especially of Jesus Christ, God incarnate, who came into this world with a commission to heal souls. He opened this commission at the commencement of his ministry Luke iv. 18. And afterwards. Mal. ix. 12, 13.

In this office of healer, he was typified by the brazen serpent. John iii. 14. By the Sun of Righteousness. Mal. iv. 2. By the tree of life. Rev. xxii. 2.

The Lord Jesus Christ, being God-man, is nobly qualified to be our soul's physician. For,

1. He is infinite in knowledge, and understands all diseases, with the proper remedies, so that he can never mistake in any case, nor make wrong applications for the cure.

2. He has sovereign authority, and almighty power, whereby he can command diseases to come and go at his pleasure.

3. He hath infinite pity, and readiness to help the distressed; as he hath in him the compassion of a God, so he hath also the bowels of a man: hence he is inclined frequently to go to the sick without being sent for, and to the poor, who have nothing to give. On this account he is represented by the good Samaritan.

4. He hath wonderful patience towards the distressed, he bears with their ingratitude, and goes on with his work, till he has accomplished a perfect cure.

III. The remedy wihch he applies to effect the cure, which is his *own blood.*

This is the true balm of Gilead which cures the sick soul. Isa. liii. 5. And although the Scriptures speak of other means of healing, all these are used in subserviency to Christ's blood, the blessed meritorious means of our cure, the only balm that procures all other means of healing us. These are,

1. The Spirit of God, with his gracious operations upon the soul. Gal. iii. 13, 14.

2. The word and ordinances of Christ. These are the leaves of the tree of life, which are for the healing of the nations. Ps. cvii. 20.

3. Afflictions. He sends these to make us feel how bitter sin is, to cause us to search our wounds, to mourn over them, and apply for the remedy. Isa. xxvii. 9.

4, Faithful ministers. The great Physician sends them to dispense sound and wholesome doctrines for that end. 1 Tim. vi. 3; Titus ii. 1.

5. Pious christians, even the poorest of them, help in this blessed work by their prayers. James v. 15. May such praying souls abound in all our congregations!

As to the Physician's method of applying the remedy. He,

1. Makes sinners sensible that they are sick, before he makes them whole; by convincing them of sin and misery. that they may prize Christ and his healing balm; such are said to be sick. Matt. ix. 12. Now this preparatory sickness implies a discovery of the dangerous nature of the disease, sin; an anxious care to be delivered from it; a dissatisfaction with all earthly comforts; grief and sorrow of heart; Ps. xxxviii. 6, 18, despair of healing ourselves. Hos. xiv. 3. The absolute need of an infinitely wise and powerful Physician: a willingness to submit to his prescriptions, saying with Paul, Acts ix. 6.

2. Works faith in the soul, by his Holy Spirit; that is to say, he powerfully persuades and enables him to embrace Christ as his Saviour, and apply the balm of his blood and merits to his wounded soul, to remove guilt, to obtain pardon, and reconcile him to God. When this is done, the danger is over. John v. 24. To several diseased souls, Jesus said, "Thy faith hath made thee whole"

3. Accomplishes and perfects the cure, by the sanctifying influences of the Spirit, rooting out the very seeds of the disease, and makes the soul perfect in holiness, and meet for entering into heaven, where constant and uninterrupted health shall be enjoyed to all eternity.

IV. THE REASONS WHY SO FEW ARE HEALED, NOTWITHSTANDING THERE IS A BALM IN GILEAD, AND A PHYSICIAN TO APPLY IT.

The cause is surely in us. For,

1. Many are ignorant of their disease, and wilfully so: they have no feeling, no care, no fear; they boast the goodness of their hearts, and thank God for it.

2. Many are in love with their disease, more than with their Physician. God may say to them, as in Ps. lii. 3.

3. Many neglect the season of healing: they slight Christ and his offers in the gospel in the days of youth and health, and never inquire after him till it is too late.

4. Many will not trust wholly to Christ for healing; but Christ must have the sole honor of the cure, or he will not be their Physician.

5. Many will not submit to the prescriptions of Christ for healing; they will not submit to-self-examination, repentance, contrition, godly sorrow, mortification, or self-denial, and therefore they are unhealed.

To conclude.

1. Let those who are in a diseased state, see their danger, for it is great; and if they do not apply to this Physician, they cannot be healed. Awake, therefore, O secure your soul! consider thy case, and flee to the great Physician for help.

2. The balm of Gilead is freely offered to you in the gospel. Isa. xlv. 22; Ezek. xviii. 32.

3. Consider how long you have slighted this balm already. Now improve your day like the people of Capernaum. Luke iv. 40; 2 Cor. vi. 2

4. And those whom he has healed, manifest their gratitude by living to his glory.

THE IMPORTANT QUESTION.

John ix. 35.—Dost thou believe on the Son of God? (Sk.)

THE text contains an important question addressed by the Lord Jesus to a highly privileged individual, on a most memorable occasion. The question relates to the most essential article of the christian religion; faith in the Son of God. The individual was a man, who, though born blind, had recently received sight; and the occasion was, when the Jews had excommunicated him for attesting the truth. Whether we regard the *sentiments* which the disciples entertained concerning this blind beggar, v. 2, or the *means* used by the Redeemer to open his eyes, v. 6, 7, or the *combination* of the Jews against Christ, v. 22, or the cogent and rational argument used by the poor man in vindication of his character, v. 30–33, the whole history is remarkable, and worthy a most attentive perusal. But the text at present demands our regard, and we will consider,

I. The nature of the question:—*Dost thou believe?* &c. *To believe the Son of God* implies, 1st. Implicitly to credit the record which the inspired writers bore concerning him, especially concerning the divinity of his person, the merit of his sacrifice, and the power of his grace; that he is God over all blessed for ever—that he made his soul a sacrifice for sin—and that he is able to save them to the uttermost, that come unto God by him.

2. *To believe in the Son of God*, is to trust in him, Eph. i. 12, 13. Faith is simple credence when it refers only to a single proposition, but when it relates to a promise made by a benefactor to a starving mendicant, or a judge to a condemned culprit, it amounts to trust, confidence, and dependance. Christ is our sovereign benefactor; the benefits which he bestows are dearly purchased,—highly valued,—freely offered,—and graciously promised: but promised only to the children of faith: we must trust in Christ for their reception, and according to our faith so will it be done unto us.

3 *To believe in the Son of God*, is to receive him, John i. 12. Jesus Christ, in Matt. xii. 29, compares the soul of man to a house, and in Luke xi. 21, to a palace, a palace once glorious as the residence of the Deity, but now possessed by other inmates, and controlled by other lords, Isa. xxvi. 13; Matt. xv. 19, 20. But at the door of this palace Christ knocks for entrance, and all believers receive him, and receive him by the act of faith which perceives his excellencies, admires the suitableness of his character, and expands the powers of the soul for his reception.

4. *To believe in the Son of God*, is to realize his gracious presence; faith in this sense supplies the place of vision, by it we behold the Lamb of God, John i. 29; 2 Cor. iii. 18; Heb. xi. 27. Such is the nature of the question: let us,

II. Offer some helps, to assist you in answering it.

1. Faith is a *divine principle;* and if you *believe in the Son of God*, the power to do so was divinely bestowed, in answer to your earnest and importunate prayers. You were once without Christ; you knew him not; you reposed no confidence in him; but you was roused from your sinful slumber; your eyes were opened, you saw your dreadful danger; Christ was proposed to you in all the dignity of his person, and in all the efficacy of his sacrifice: for a while you doubted and disbelieved; but you prayed, and said, "Lord, help thou my unbelief;" and at last you were enabled to cry in the language of believing Thomas, "My Lord and my God."

2. Faith is *a self-evident principle;* and if you *believe in the Son of God*, you cannot but know it, 1 John v. 10. Is faith credence; and cannot you know whether you believe the attestation of a fact? Is faith reliance; and cannot you know whether you depend on the veracity of him who has pledged his word to you? That doctrine which teaches that a man may *believe in the Son of God*, and not know it, is as contrary to sound divinity as it is to sound sense, as the Bible uniformly attributes effects to faith; and if the effects be not produced, the cause is not in action.

3. Faith *is a victorious principle;* and if you *believe in the Son of God*, you will conquer every adverse power, and put to flight the armies of the aliens. The records in the 11th chapter of Hebrews sufficiently confirm this truth. Do the sophisms of infidelity seek to beguile you? faith will detect and dissipate them. Do the fiery darts of the devil assail you? faith will quench them. Does the world spread its allurements before your eyes? faith will vanquish them, Eph. vi. 16; 1 John v. 4.

4. Faith *is a practical principle;* and if you *believe in the Son of God*, you lives will evince the genuineness of your faith. Believe in Christ, and

you will love him, for faith worketh by love;—you will keep his commandments, for faith without works is dead;—you will endure to the end, for the end of your faith is the salvation of your souls. Believe in Christ, and his ineffable beauties will attract your desires—his spotless life will excite your emulation—his dying love will melt your hearts,—his precious blood will purge your consciences,—his meritorious death will expiate your crimes,—and his glorious resurrection will ensure your immortality.

III. State some reasons why an answer should be given.

1. The *question is important;* the person who propose it is thy Sovereign, thy Saviour, and thy Judge. He is head over all things, and therefore has an indisputable right to propose this question. It is not impertinent nor unnecessary; it concerns thy *faith*, that faith which has wrought such wonders, obtained such victories, silenced such misgivings, and without which thou must die in thy sins, and suffer the damnation of hell, John viii. 24; Mark xvi. 16.

2. The *question is personal;* "Dost *thou* believe?" &c. Do not shift it off; it is not whether thy neighbors believe, but whether *thou* believest; not whether thou hast a profession, a name, an opinion, but whether thou hast faith.

3. The *question is simple;* not complex, involving results that require the exercise of genius to solve. Many questions are so enwrapped in mystery, and have such bearings on other subjects that we are obliged to pause, hesitate, and ponder, before we can produce an appropriate answer; but the question in the text is so plain, that a child, under the influence of the Holy Ghost may answer it.

4. But *the question is doubtful:* all men have not faith, some glory in their infidelity; examine yourselves whether ye be in the faith. Dost *thou believe in the Son of God?* then worship him, verse 38.—Pray for an increase of faith, and anticipate the period when faith shall be lost in sight, and hope in all fruition.

NOAH'S FAITH AND OBEDIENCE.

Hebrews xi. 7.—"By faith Noah, being warned of God of things not seen as yet, moved with fear, prepared an ark to the saving of his house; by the which he condemned the world, and became heir of the righteousness which is by faith."

The character selected for our present consideration is particularly worthy of our attention and imitation. Though Noah lived in an age exceedingly corrupt and ungodly, he was deeply pious, and "found grace in the eyes of the Lord." He witnessed the most desolating calamity; and was placed in a situation extremely difficult and affecting:—yet, as a righteous man, he walked in holy fellowship with God;—and his eminent faith and obedience are *immortalized* in the text, for the *instruction* of all succeeding generations; "*By faith Noah*," &c.. In this illustrious example of primitive piety, we may remark,

I. The warning he received. "Noah being warned," &c. The apostle here refers to the well-known history of the destruction of the antediluvian world;—it was indeed an awful catastrophe, which was brought on mankind by their extreme corruption and abounding wickedness! But Noah, who was a faithful servant of God, was mercifully preserved from the overwhelming scourge. According to the text,

1. *He was warned of the approaching deluge.* It was an event which could not have been previously known had it not been revealed by God;—it was not the effect of a *natural cause*, but a *special judgment* of God, inflicted on incorrigible sinners. Long before its accomplishment, the Lord made known his purpose concerning it to Noah, for the instruction of himself and family, and for the warning of impenitent contemporaries. A distinct account of this revelation is found in the book of Genesis, chap. vi. 5-13.—Though these "things were *unseen as yet*," they were *certain* in their *fulfilment*:—and, in due time, fully came to pass according to the word of the Lord, Gen. vii. 17—23, &c. God is ever "slow to anger," and always *warns* before he *punishes*:—and hence,

2. *We are also warned of the impending danger.* Though we are not admonished of the same event that Noah was; yet we are warned of "unseen things," which are *equally certain*, and much more *important* to mankind. All have sinned, and all are justly liable to suffer everlasting destruction. We are, therefore, *warned* of the danger of living and dying in our sins,—and of "suffering the vengeance of eternal fire," Ezek. xviii. 30-32; 2 Thess. i. 8, 9. Though these awful calamities are "unseen as yet," they are important *realities*, of which the Lord duly *warns us* by his word,—by his ministers,—by his spirit,—and by his providence, Ezek. xxxiii. 7—9, &c. The divine warnings are faithful,—affectionate,—urgent,—and incessant;—let us, then, *attentively receive and diligently obey* them. That such was the conduct of Noah, appears from,

II. THE OBEDIENCE HE DISPLAYED. "By faith Noah, moved with fear," &c. This inspired testimony reflects great honor on the character of this excellent patriarch, and fully explains the nature of his obedience, which is here so highly commended.

1. *He exercised implicit faith in God*:—he not only believed in his existence and perfection, but also, in all the *revelations* of his *will* and the *promises* of the *Messiah*;—by *this principle* he obtained the blessings of salvation,—and was influenced in his general conduct;—and hence, his obedience is expressly attributed to the faith in the text. "By *faith* Noah," &c., ver. 6. Faith is both a *saving* and *influential* principle;—its *genuineness* must be proved by its *practical effects*;—it works by love,—purifies the heart,—regulates the life,—and grasps invisible realities. No obedience can be acceptable to God, but that which arises from unfeigned faith, Rom. xiv. 23; James ii. 17, 18, 26.

2. *He was influenced by the fear of God.* We cannot suppose he feared for the temporal safety of himself and family, for God has assured him of their preservation, Gen. vi. 18; and as a *just* and *righteous* character, he had no reason for *distressing fear* respecting his eternal welfare:—but as a man of piety, he no doubt felt greatly alarmed, by the sudden destruction of the human race. His faith produced a *reverential fear* of God;—a *compassionate fear* for perishing sinners;—and a *cautions fear* of personal vigilance and faithfulness. Genuine *faith* and holy *fear* characterize the people of God in all ages, Mal. iii. 16; Acts x. 35.

3. *He promptly obeyed the will of God.* He strictly performed the divine injunction, in "preparing an ark to the saving of his house." The Lord gave him *special directions* for this purpose, all of which he *fully* complied with, Gen. vi. 22;—he cordially believed the word of God, and his faith produced practical conformity to his will. Though we are not required

to "prepare an ark" for our safety, yet we are all commanded to seek an interest in Christ, the sinner's refuge, and "work out our salvation with fear and trembling," &c. And to encourage our imitation of Noah's character and obedience, we shall proceed to consider,

III. THE DELIVERANCE HE OBTAINED. He was greatly honored by God, and spared as a *special monument* of divine mercy in the midst of wrath.

1. *He was preserved from the general ruin.* How dreadful is the thought;—how appalling the sight!—A world deluged with sin! The earth groaning and sinking under the crimes of its guilty inhabitants! The heavens opening and pouring down the long-suspended vengeance on the incorrigible! "They were eating and drinking, marrying and giving in marriage, until the day that Noah entered into the ark; and the flood came and took them all away." How unprepared for such an awful change! Behold their frantic minds seized with unutterable horror and amazement! But where shall they look? To whom shall they go? Refuge fails!—the earth disappears!—all is gone? See them flocking around the ark—entreating, grasping, and wailing! But alas! It is all in vain; the door is shut, and the man of God, whom they had despised and insulted, is now preserved, and all his house, for his sake. "Verily there is a reward for the righteous."

2. *He condemned the impenitent world.* He did not *formally* condemn them as their *judge*,—but *ministerially*, as a "preacher of righteousness," and *practically*, by his pious example. His *faith* condemned their *unbelief*; his *obedience* condemed their *disobedience*, &c. Thus every good man *condemns* and bears witness against the follies and practices of the ungodly world, by a pious life and coversation.

2.-*He obtained the righteousness of faith.* He was not saved by *works*, but solely by *faith*. He was justified and accepted of God, through the in fintte merit of the promised Redeemer, which was imputed to him through believing. Such has ever been the only way of salvation for fallen sinners From this instructive case we should learn to consider our danger—estimate the sinner's refuge—and "believe to the saving of the soul."

THE MEANS OF GRACE.

THE ADMIRABLE NATURE OF THE DIVINE ORACLES.

Psalm cxix. 129.—Thy testimonies are wonderful; therefore doth my soul keep them. (Sk.)

The love of the marvellous is a very prevailing passion among mankind. To witness uncommon scenes, and to hear tales of wonder and amazement, generally afford them much delight. Hence artful and designing men have found it easy to impose upon the multitude the most improbable and incredible accounts of places, persons, and events. And even those who are aware of the imposture, are too frequently pleased with the enchantment of novel and romantic stories, and pursue the illusions of the imagination till they lose all relish for reality and truth. But would they read the Bible, in humble dependance upon its Author, they would there "behold wondrous things out of his law," infinitely surpassing all that the natural heart has ever conceived, even the marvellous purposes and acts of the Most High. And on every sentence of this book is impressed the seal of truth. Such was the Psalmist's view when he uttered the text; in which he expresses,

I. His profound admiration of the Divine Oracles.—"Thy testimonies are wonderful." Since David's time these testimonies have been augmented by more than two thirds of the Bible—but to the whole his emphatic declaration may with the greatest propriety be applied. They are wonderful.

1. *In their style and composition.* In this respect they are

——*Wonderfully simple and plain*—This is their general character, notwithstanding occasional obscurities—No *histories* were ever so plainly related as those of the Bible—No *precepts* were ever more clear, or *promises* less ambiguous.

——*Wonderfully grand and sublime*, wherever the matter requires it.—Witness many of the Psalms—the book of Job—the prophets—Isa. xl., and lxiii., and the Apocalypse.

——*Wonderfully concise and expressive.* The sacred writers never burden their subject with a load of words—They never need many strokes to produce the requisite effect—every word is a feature, and the moral portrait is soon complete.—Witness the Proverbs, 1 Cor. xiii., &c.

2. *In their contents.* Here are comprised,

——*The most interesting records of facts.* Creation—Fall—Flood—the Call of Abraham, &c. &c. &c. The Incarnation—Life—Death, &c. of Christ.

——*The most astonishing displays of truth.* Here the perfections, works, and will of God, are gloriously exhibited.—More especially the amazing scheme of human redemption by our Lord Jesus, and all the variety of collateral doctrines which depend upon, or are connected with this economy. Well might the discovery of these truths be called "*marvellous light.*"

——*The most admirable and perfect rules of life.* The moral law, its explication by our Lord in Matt. xxii. 37—39, and his admirable Sermon on the Mount.—The great precepts, "repent and believe,"—together with all the directions furnished by the Apostles, &c., compose a sacred code of laws —easy of comprehension—suited to our ability—harmonized with each other—happy in their tendency—and honorable to God, Psa. xix. 7—11.

——*The most animating promises,* relative to all conditions and circumstances of the people of God. Blessings temporal, spiritual, and eternal—in prosperity, adversity, temptation, death, and beyond the grave, are guaranteed to the just, Psa. lxxxiv. 11.

——*The most tremendous threatenings.*—These are addressed to the wicked, the slothful, the faithless, the backsliding, Rev. xxi. 8.

3. *Wonderful in their efficacy,* Heb. iv. 12; Jam. i. 18; 1 Pet. i. 23. This efficacy is displayed,

——In the *alarm* they spread through the sinner's conscience. The hardened and audacious rebel feels himself arraigned at the tribunal of his own conscience, where he stands accused, convicted, and condemned, by that living word which is sharper than a two-edge sword, Acts ii. 37, 38, &c.

——In the *consolation* they inspire into the mourner's bosom, Acts ii. 41—47; Matt. xi. 28, &c.

——In the *moral transformation* of the most degraded characters. Witness the murderous Jews who crucified the Saviour. When the gospel was preached to them on the day of Pentecost, it transformed them into new creatures. Witness the Corinthians, some of whom were among the vilest of men, 1 Cor. vi. 9, 10, 11.—And witness thousands in the present day, who from being worse than brutes, become eminent for every christian virtue, through the word of God.

——In the *support through life,* and the *conquest over death,* which they afford all real believers. View the christian, in labor, in temptation, difficulty, in severe affliction—the word of God affords him support, and peace, and comfort. View him in the agony of death—the divine promises are applied to his soul, and he obtains the victory.—Exulting he asks "Who shall separate," &c., Rom. viii. 35—39.

Thus then truly wonderful are the testimonies of Jehovah, and truly reasonable is the profound admiration which the Psalmist expresses.—Let us now view,

II. Their practical influence.—"Therefore doth my soul keep them." Because thy oracles are so admirable, so excellent, so worthy of thee, their adorable Author, therefore doth my soul, my rational and intellectual part, receive and keep them as an invaluable deposit. This implies,

1. *That he treasured them up in his memory.* Unlike those inattentive persons who read or hear the word of God, but are not solicitous to under stand it, or to preserve the conceptions and impressions which it conveys, (like leaky vessels, these carry nothing away,) David took care to understand and to preserve the truth.—He knew it was the noblest employment for his memory to become the depository of God's testimonies, and every one of these was too important to be forgotten.

2. *That he kept them in the exercises of faith.* He received them as *God's* testimonies, and relied upon them as an immovable foundation. By this faith they became spirit and life to him. Without this vital realizing faith, though a man could repeat the whole Bible, and had the most systematic view of its contents, all would be vain. We only feel interested in the

scriptures in proportion as we heartily believe them—and it is only in the same proportion that they become efficacious.

3. *That he held them in constant esteem, and embraced them with earnest affection.* This he often expresses in this Psalm: "How sweet are thy words unto my taste," &c.—"Thy word is pure, therefore doth thy servant love it," ver. 20, 72. This ardent love to the world results from a thorough belief of it—And is an infallible test by which we may try the genuineness of our faith.

4. *That he kept them in obedient practice.* This was undoubtedly what the Psalmist intended, as all the other particulars are necessarily pre-supposed in this. He thus kept them—*Sincerely*, ver. 80.—*Cheerfully*, ver. 47.—*Diligently*, ver. 69.—*Continually*, ver. 44.—and *Universally*, ver 6.

Infer, 1st. How wide a contrast between David's esteem for the scriptures, and that noisy empty admiration of them which so many profess, but which is so uninfluential on their hearts and lives—They make fine speeches in their praise, and even contribute towards their circulation, while they neither understand, nor believe, love, nor practise, their all-important contents.

2. How carefully should we read and hear the word of God! We should constantly drink at this sacred fountain—be always digging in this inexhaustible mine. "Search the scriptures," said our Lord. Let us then read them with *prayer*, *attention*, and *self-application*, and meditate on them like David, day and night.

3. How great are our obligations to God for sending us his word!

4. How heinous is the guilt of those who neglect and abuse it.

OF THE LAW OF GOD.

Rom. vii. 12,—Wherefore the law is holy, &c. (H.)

THE word law is variously used, sometimes for a part of the scriptures only, the Pentateuch, or five books of Moses; as when it is mentioned in the division of the scriptures by Christ, Luke xxiv. 44, and along with the prophets, and as distinct from them; John i. 45; see also chap. viii. 5, sometimes for all the books of the Old Testament, which in general go by the name of law, as does the book of Psalms on that account, as the places quoted out of it, or referred to in it, show; John x. 34; xii. 34; xv. 25; sometimes it signifies the doctrine of the scriptures in general, Ps. xix. 7, and the doctrine of the gospel in particular, Is. ii. 3; xlii. 4, called in the New Testament the law or doctrine of faith; Rom. iii. 27, and sometimes it signifies the whole body of laws given from God by Moses to the children of Israel, as distinct from the gospel of the grace of God, John i. 17, and which may be distinguished into,

1. The ceremonial law, of which this law was a shadow of good things to come by Christ, of evangelical things, and indeed was no other than the gospel veiled in types and figures.

2. Judicial, which respects the political state, or civil government of the Jews, and consists of statutes and judgments; according to which the judges of Israel determined all causes brought before them. Deut. xvii. 8—11 The government of the Jews was a very particular form of government; it was a theocracy, a government immediately under God, though he be king

of the whole world, and governor among and over the nations of it, yet he was, in a special and peculiar manner, king over Israel.

3. Moral, which lies chiefly in the Decalogue, or Ten commandments, Ex. xx. 3—17, and which our Lord has reduced, even both tables of the law, to two capital ones, love to God, and love to our neighbor; Matt. xxii. 39—40, as the apostle has reduced the commands of the second table to one, that is, love, which he calls the fulfilment of the law. Rom. xiii. 9, 10. And this law, to love God and our neighbor, is binding on every man, and is eternal, and remains invariable and unalterable; and concerning which I shall treat more largely. And consider,

I. THE AUTHOR AND GIVER OF THIS LAW.

God was the author and maker of it, Moses the giver and minister of it from God. There was a law in being before the time of Moses; or otherwise there would have been no transgression, no imputation of sin, no charge of guilt, nor any punishment inflicted; whereas death, the just demerit of sin, reigned from Adam to Moses. Besides the law given to Adam, there was the law of nature, inscribed on his heart by his Maker, as the rule of obedience to him, Rom. i. 19, 20; ii. 14, and which is reinscribed in the hearts of God's people in regeneration, according to the tenor of the covenant of grace, Jer. xxxi. 33. Now the law of Moses, for matter and substance, is the same which the law of nature, though differing in the form of administration; and this was renewed in the times of Moses, that it might be confirmed, and that it might not be forgotten, and be wholly lost out of the minds of men.

II. THE EPITHETS, OR THE PRORERTIES OF IT.

1. That it is perfect. The law of the Lord is perfect, Ps. xix. 7, which is true of the moral law, by which men come to know what is that good, and acceptable, and perfect will of God; Rom. xii. 2, what it is his will should be done, and what not be done; it takes in the whole duty of men, both to God and man; for to fear God, and keep his commandments. When the apostle John speaks of a new commandment, he means the old commandment to love one another, as he himself explains it, 1 John ii. 7, 8, and which he calls new, because enforced by a new instance and example of Christ's love in dying for his people, and by new motives and arguments taken from the same.

2. It is spiritual. "We know that the law is spiritual," says the apostle, Rom. vii. 14, which is to be understood of the moral law; for as for the ceremonial law, that is called the law of a carnal commandment, and is said to stand in carnal ordinances. Heb. vii. 16; ix. 10. The law reaches to the thoughts and intents of the heart, and the affections of the mind, and forbids and checks all irregular and inordinate motions in it, and the lusts of it. The assistance of the Spirit of God is necessary to the observance of it; and God in covenant has promised his people, that he will put his Spirit within them, and cause them to walk in his statutes, and keep his judgments, and do them. Ezek. xxxvi. 27.

3. The law is holy, and the commandment holy; it comes from a holy God, from whom nothing unholy can proceed; for holiness is his nature, and the law is a transcript of his holy will; the matter of it, or what it requires, is holy; even sanctification of the heart and life: and it directs to live holily, soberly, &c.

4. It is also just. There are no laws so righteous as the laws of God: the judgments of the Lord are true and righteous altogether. Deut iv. 8: Ps. xix. 9. It is impartial unto all, and requires the same of one as of another and renders to every man according to his works; it is just in condemning wicked men, and in justifying those that believe in Jesus.

5. The law is good; the Author of it is good only, essentially, originally, good; from whom every good and perfect gift comes. The law is materially good, it is morally good, it is pleasantly good, to a regenerate man, who, as the apostle, delights in the law of God after the inner man, and loves it, as David did, and meditates on it, as every good man does. Rom. vii. 22; Ps. cxix. 97; i. 2. And it is profitably good; not to God, Luke xvii. 10, but to men, their fellow-creatures, and fellow-christians, to whom they are serviceable, by their good works, Tit. iii. 8, and also to themselves; for though not *for*, yet *in* keeping the commands there is great reward, as peace of conscience. Ps. xix. 11; cxix. 165. The law is good, if a man use it lawfully, 1 Tim. i. 8.

III. The uses of the law both to sinners and to saints.

1. To sinners.

1. To convince of sin. Sin is a transgression of the law, by which it is known that it is sin. By the law is the knowledge of sin; not only of gross, actual sins, but of the inward lust of the mind; "I had not known lust, except the law had said, Thou shalt not covet." Rom. iii. 20; vii. 7.

2. To restrain from sin. Of this use are the laws of men; hence civil magistrates are terrors to evil doers so the law, by it menaces, deters men from sin.

3. To condemn and punish for sin. For sinners it is made, and against them it lies, to their condemnation, unless justified in Christ. 1 Tim. i. 9, 10. It accuses of sin, charges with it, brings evidence of it; stops the sinner's mouth from pleading in his own cause, pronounces guilty before God, and curses and condemns; "it is the ministration of condemnation and death.

2. It is of use to saints and true believers in Christ.

—1. To point out the will of God unto them. What is to be done by them, and what to be avoided; to inform them of, and urge them to their duty, both towards God and man.

2. To be a rule of life and conversation to them. Not a rule to obtain life, but to live according to; to direct their steps. "The commandment is a lamp, and the law is light." Prov. vi. 23. "Thy word is a lamp unto my feet." Ps. cxix. 105.

3. It is as a glass, in which a believer, by the light of the Spirit of God, may see his own face, what manner of man he is; how far short of perfection he is in himself. "I have seen an end of all perfection," &c. Hence,

4. They are led to prize the righteousness of Christ, since that is perfectly agreeable to the holy law of God; wherefore, "they desire to be found in Christ, not having on their own righteousness."

IV. The law of God continues under the present dispensation for the said uses.

Christ came not to destroy it, and loosen men's obligations to it, but to fulfil it; nor is the law made null and void by faith.

1. It does not continue as a covenant of works: and, indeed, it was not delivered to the children of Israel as such strictly and properly speaking, only in a typical sense.

2. Nor does it continue as to the form of administration of it by Moses; it is now no longer in his hands, nor to be considered as such.

3. It continues not as a terrifying law to believers, "who are not come to Mount Sinai, but they are come to Mount Sion." Nor are they awed and urged by its curses to an observance of it; but are constrained by the love of Christ.

4. Nor is it a cursing and condemning law to the saints; for "Christ had redeemed them from the curse of the law."

5. Yet it continues as a rule of walk and conversation to them, and is to be regarded by them as in the hands of Christ, their king and lawgiver. Believers, though freed from the law, in the sense before declared, yet are "not without a law to God, but under the law to Christ." 1 Cor. ix. 21.

OF THE GOSPEL.

Acts xx. 24.—The gospel of the grace of God. (H.)

THERE was gospel in the former dispensation, though called the legal dispensation; it was preached to Adam, to Abraham, and by Isaiah, and other prophets. Yet there is a clearer revelation and ministration of it under the present dispensation; as the law was, by the ministration of Moses, grace and truth; the word of grace and truth, the gospel, came by Jesus Christ, in a clearer and fuller manner than it had been made known before. John i. 17. Concerning which, the following things may be noted:

1. The name and signification of it.

The Greek word used for it signifies a good message, good news, glad tidings; the gospel is a message of good news from heaven, the far country, to sinners here on earth: such was the gospel Christ was anointed to preach; Luke iv. 18, compared with Isa. lxi. 1, and which his ministers bring, "whose feet are beautiful upon the mountains." Isa. lii. 7; Acts xiii. 32, 33. The Hebrew word used for the gospel, and the preaching of it, signifies good tidings also; and it is observed, by some, to have the signification of flesh in it which has led them to think of the incarnation of Christ; which is, undoubtedly, good news to the children of men, and a considerable branch of the gospel of Christ: and what has given Isaiah the character of an evangelical prophet, as if then present in his time; "To us a child is born:" Isa. ix. 6; see chap. vii. 14, and when the angel proclaimed the birth of Christ to the shepherds, he is said, "to bring good things." Luke ii. 10, 11. And this is one principal part of the gospel, the great mystery of godliness, "God manifest in the flesh." 1 Tim. iii. 16. Our English word gospel is of Saxon derivation; in which language, *spel* signifies speech: and so gospel is either *good speech*, which carries in it the same idea with the Greek and Hebrew words, or God's speech, which he has spoken by his Son, by his prophets, and by his ministers.

The word is variously used; sometimes it is put for the history of Christ's birth, life, and actions; such are the gospels according to Matthew, Mark, &c. Mark begins his history thus, "The beginning of the gospel of Jesus;" Mark i. 1; and Luke calls his gospel, "The former treatise he had made, of all that Jesus began, both to do and to teach:" Acts i. 1; and hence these four writers are commonly called evangelists. Sometimes the gospel is to be taken in a large sense, as including the word and ordinances: Matt. xxviii. 19, 20; Mark xvi. 15, 16, and sometimes strictly, for the doctrine of peace, pardon, &c. by Christ; hence gospel ministers, who bring good tidings of good, are said to publish peace, salvation, &c; Isa. lii. 7, the sum of which is expressed by the apostle, when he says, "This is a faithful saying," &c., 1 Tim. i. 15. Hence,

1. The gospel is called, the gospel of salvation, the word of salvation and salvation itself, Eph. i. 13; Acts xiii. 26; xxviii. 28, because it gives

an account of Christ, the author of salvation; of his appointment to it; of his mission, and coming into the world to effect it; and of his actual performance of it; of his being the able, willing, and only Saviour: and of the salvation itself, as great and glorious, perfect and complete, spiritual and everlasting; and because it describes also the persons that share in it, sinners, sensible sinners, &c.; Mark. xvi. 16: Acts xvi. 30, 31, and because it is, not only the means of revealing, but of applying salvation; for it is, to them that believe, "the power of God unto salvation."

2. The gospel of the grace of God; Acts xx. 24, because the several doctrines of it are doctrines of grace, or which exhibit blessings as flowing from the grace of God; redemption, pardon, &c.

3. The gospel of peace, the word of reconciliation; Eph. vi. 15; 2 Cor. v. 18; Acts x. 36; because it relates the steps taken in council and covenant: to form the scheme of man's peace with God; to lay the foundation of it, and to bring it about; Zech. vi. 13; Isa. liv. 10, and also relates the actual making of it; by whom, and by what means. Eph. ii. 14; Isa. liii 5; Col. i. 20; Rom. v. 10.

4. The gospel of the kingdom; Matt. iv. 23, because it treats both of the kingdom of grace here, showing wherein it lies; and of the kingdom of glory hereafter, pointing out the proper meetness for it. John iii. 5; Matt. v. 20; Luke xii. 32.

II. The author and origin of the gospel.

1. It is not of man; a device and invention of men. "I neither received it of men." Gal. i. 11, 12. It is not discoverable by the light of reason. Matt. xvi. 16, 17. Hence the gospel is frequently called, "a mystery;" the "wisdom of God in a mystery; the hidden wisdom;" and the doctrines of it, "the mysteries of the kingdom." Matt. xiii. 11.

2. The gospel is from heaven. It is good news from a far country: the gospel is, with the Holy Ghost, sent down from heaven: and Christ that spoke it, is He that speaketh from heaven. The question put concering the baptism of John, "Whence was it? from heaven, or of men?" may be put concerning the gospel, and answered as that; that is, from heaven; and not of man. 1 Pet. i. 12; Heb. xii. 25; Matt. xxi. 25. It comes also from God the Father, and is therefore called "the gospel of God." Rom. i. 1—3. It comes also from Christ, the Son of God, and is called, "the gospel of his Son, the gospel of Christ, the word of Christ, and the testimony of Christ, and the testimony of our Lord," Rom. i. 9—16; Col. iii. 16; 2 Tim. i. 8, of which Christ is the subject, sum, and substance, as well as the author. Hence the apostle says, he received it "by the revelation of Jesus Christ." Gal. i. 12. It may be said, likewise, to come from the Holy Spirit of God, the inditer of the scriptures, wherein it lies, "who searches the deep things of it, and reveals them to men."

III. The effect of the gospel, when attended with the power and Spirit of God.

1. The regeneration of men; who are said, "to be born again by the word of God," and to be "begotten again with the word of truth." 1 Pet. i. 23; James i. 18. Hence ministers of the gospel are represented as spiritual fathers. 1 Cor. iv. 15.

2. As in regeneration, souls are quickened by the Spirit and grace of God, this is ascribed to the gospel as an instrument. Hence it is called, "the Spirit which giveth life, and said to be, "the savor of life unto life." 2 Cor ii. 16, and iii. 6.

2

3. It is frequently spoken of as a light, a great light, a glorious light; and so is, in the hands of the Spirit, a means of enlightening the dark minds of men into mysteries of grace. "The entrance of thy word giveth light." Ps. cxix. 130. It is a glass, in which the glory of Christ, and of the riches of his grace, may be seen.

4. By it faith in Christ comes, and is ingenerated in the heart by the Spirit of God attending it. Hence, among other reasons, it is called "the word of faith." Rom. x. 8, 17.

5. When faith is wrought in the soul, the righteousness of Christ is revealed unto it in the gospel, and not at first believing only; it is revealed therein "from faith to faith." Rom. i. 17. Hence it is called "the word of righteousness, and the ministration of righteousness." Heb. v. 13; 2 Cor. iii. 6, 9.

6. It affords spiritual food, and is the means of feeding and nourishing souls unto everlasting life. It has in it milk for babes, and meat for strong men; and when it is found by faith, it is eaten by it with pleasure, and fills with spiritual joy. 1 Tim. iv. 6; vi. 3; Heb. v. 13, 14; Jer. xv. 16. Hence,

7. Is another effect, it yields much spiritual peace, joy, &c. The doctrines of it are calculated for such a purpose; it is glad tidings of good things; as of peace, pardon. When Philip preached Christ and his gospel in Samaria, "there was great joy in that city." Acts viii. 5, 8. All this must be understood of the gospel, not as producing these effects of itself, but as it comes, "not in word only, but with power." 1 Thess. i. 5—8; Ps. cx. 2; Rom. i. 16.

IV. The properties of the gospel.

1. It is but one; there is another, as the apostle says, Gal. i. 6, 7. The same gospel which was in the beginning, and will be to the end of the world; the same under the Old Testament as under the New; the subject of it, Christ and salvation by him; the doctrines of it, of justification, remission of sins, &c. the same, only now more clearly revealed. For it is true of the gospel, what is said of Christ, it is "the same yesterday." Heb. xiii. 8.

2. It is called, from the objects of it, the gospel of the circumcision, and the gospel of the uncircumcision. Gal. ii. 7. Not that the gospel of the one is different from that of the other; it is the same gospel, only dispensed to different persons; the circumcised Jews, and uncircumcised Gentiles.

3. It is a glorious gospel; so it is called, 2 Cor. iv. 4; 1 Tim. i. 11. It has a glory in it exceeding that of the law, and the dispensation of it, 2 Cor. iii. 11, for the clearness, fullness, suitableness of its doctrines to the state and condition of men; and in which the glory of the person of Christ, his offices, and of the blessings of grace that come by him, is held forth in great splendor and brightness.

4. It is an everlasting gospel; which is the epithet given it, Rev. xiv. 6. It was ordained in the council and covenant of God before the world was, of which it is a transcript, and so was from everlasting; 1 Pet. i 25; but "the word of the Lord endureth for ever."

THE NATURE OF THE GOSPEL.

Isaiah lii. 7.—How beautiful upon the mountains are the feet of him that bringeth good tidings, that publisheth peace; that bringeth good tidings of good, that publisheth salvation; that saith unto Zion, Thy God reigneth! (S. S.)

In order to understand the prophetic writings we must always bear in mind that they have a spiritual or mystical sense, as well as a plain and literal one—The words before us, in their primary meaning, evidently refer to the joy, with which the proclamation of Cyrus, when he permitted the captive Jews to return from Babylon to their native country, would be received—But they certainly relate also to the deliverance announced to us under the gospel dispensation; for it is in this view that they are quoted by the apostle Paul, Rom. x. 15—We shall take occasion from them to shew,

I. What the gospel is.

It is described with sufficient accuracy in the text: it is,

1. A proclamation of "peace and salvation" to man.

The gospel supposes men to have offended God, and to be obnoxious to his everlasting displeasure—It further supposes that they have no way of conciliating the divine favor, or of warding off the stroke of his indignation—Coming to men in this helpless, and hopeless state, it publisheth tidings of peace and salvation: it represents sin as expiated by the atoning blood of Jesus; and God as reconciled to all who will trust in his meritorious and all-prevailing sacrifice—This is the view which St. Paul himself gives us of the gospel; in preaching of which gospel ministers resemble the messengers sent to Babylon, who had nothing to do but to proclaim a full and free deliverance to the wretched captives, 2 Cor. v. 18–20.

2. A declaration of Christ's power and grace.

The Chaldeans, who so grievously oppressed their Jewish captives, may justly represent to us the bitter and tyrannical dominion of sin and satan; and Cyrus, who, without fee or reward, liberated them from their bondage, may be considered as the agent and representative of the Deity—As therefore the messengers would not fail to remind the Jews that Cyrus, the one author of their happiness, would continue to them his protection and favor while they maintained their allegiance to him; so, in preaching the gospel, we are to declare, that Christ, to whom we owe the beginnings of our liberty, will complete our deliverance, and continue to us all the tokens of his love, provided we yield him, as we are in duty bound, a willing and unreserved obedience—Thus did Christ himself preach the gospel, saying, Repent, for the kingdom of heaven is at hand. Comp. Mark i. 14, 15, with Matt. iv. 17.

If we view the gospel in this light, we shall see immediately,

II. That it is a ground of joy.

By a beautiful figure, the very steps of the messenger hastening over the distant mountains are represented as inspiring us with joy. That the gospel itself is a source of joy, appears in that,

1. It has been considered so from the first moment of its promulgation.

Abraham, two thousand years before its promulgation, rejoiced exceedingly in that distant prospect of it, John viii. 56,—At the birth of Jesus, our deliverer, an host of angels congratulated the world, saying, Behold, we bring you glad tidings of great joy, which shall be to all people: for unto you is born a Saviour, which is Christ the Lord, Luke ii. 10, 11,—As soon as ever the full effects of the gospel came to be experienced, the converts, filled with every malignant temper just before, were filled with joy, and eat their bread with gladness and singleness of heart, blessing and praising God, Acts ii. 46, 47,—No sooner was the gospel preached in Samaria, than there was great joy in that city: and, the instant that the eunuch had embraced it, he went on his way rejoicing, Acts viii. 8, 39,—Thus it is at this day an healing balm and a reviving cordial to all who understand and receive it—

2. It is in itself well calculated to create joy in our hearts.

Let but its blessings be felt, and it will be impossible not to rejoice—Did the Jews exult at a deliverance from a cruel yoke, and a restoration to their native country? How much more must a sinner rejoice at his deliverance from death and hell, and his restoration to the forfeited inheritance of heaven!—The transports of joy manifested by the cripple whom Peter and John had healed, were the natural effusions of a grateful heart: we should have wondered if he had not so expressed the feelings of his soul: Acts iii. 8; but he had received no benefit in comparison of that which the believer enjoys when he first embraces the gospel of Christ—Hence our prophet represents the gospel as invariably producing such sensations as the husbandman feels when bringing home the fruits of the field, or the soldier when dividing the spoils of victory, Isa. ix. 3, 6.

3. It is, and ever will be, the one subject of thanksgiving in the realms of glory.

The glorified saints never have their attention diverted from it for one single moment: day and night are they singing to him who loved them, and washed them from their sins in his own blood, Rev. i. 5, 6,—And though the angels are less interested in this subject, because they never needed redeeming grace, yet do they join the general chorus, ascribing honor and glory to him that sitteth on the throne, and to the Lamb for ever—Nor will they ever be weary of this subject, such an inexhaustible fund is it of light, and happiness, and glory—

INFER,

1. How strange is it that the gospel should be treated with indifference!

That it is so treated, needs no proof: but how amazing that it should ever be slighted by those to whom it is sent! that condemned criminals should disregard the offers of pardon sent them by their Prince!—O that there might be no more occasion for that complaint, Who hath believed our report?—Let the very feet of the messengers who bring the tidings be henceforth beautiful in our eyes—

2. Of what importance is it to distinguished between mere morality, and the gospel of Christ!

Lectures upon honesty would administer but little comfort to a person about to be executed for breaking the laws of his country: nor can mere discourses on morality administer much comfort to a self-condemning sinner: and, if he mistake such discourses for the gospel, he is fatally deceived—The gospel is a full and free offer of salvation through the blood of Christ: and this is glad tidings indeed; like "rivers of water in a dry place, or a shadow of a great rock in a weary land"—O that all who are ambassadors of God may remember the great scope of their ministry, and testify the gospel of the grace of God!—And let all who hear the joyful sound, improve the day of their visitation: blessed are they if they receive the truth in the love thereof; but most aggravated will be their condemnation if they despise the mercy so freely offered them.

THE CHANGE WROUGHT BY THE GOSPEL.

Isaiah lv. 12, 13.—For ye shall go out with joy, and be led forth with peace: the mountains and the hills shall break forth before you into singing, and all the trees of the field shall clap their hands. Instead of the thorn shall come up the fir-tree, and instead of the brier shall come up the myrtle-tree: and it shall be to the Lord for a name, for an everlasting sign that shall not be cut off. (S. S.)

THE change wrought annually on the face of nature from desolation and barrenness to beauty and fruitfulness, is a lively representation of the change effected by the gospel of Christ. "The rain and the snow descending on the earth" nourished the whole vegetable creation, and cause every part of it to spring forth in its appointed season: and, in the same manner, "the word of God, dropping as the rain and distilling as the dew" upon the souls of men, infuses life into them, and renders them fruitful in every good word and work. This is the parallel drawn by the prophet himself, who, expatiating on the subject, predicts, under the image of the Jews' return from Babylon, the progress of the gospel in renovating the intellectual and spiritual world. His words will lead us to consider

I. THE EFFECTS OF THE PREACHED GOSPEL.

The civilizing of the world is a very small part of the work which the gospel is intended to accomplish. It is sent

1. To inspire new feelings.

Man in his natural state is an entire stranger to spiritual joy, or solid peace. The peace that flows from a want of foresight or reflection, and the joy that consists in mere animal gratifications, he may possess: but he is as destitute of spiritual enjoyments, as the brute creation are of intellectual pleasure. His state however is wonderfully changed when he receives the word of God in truth. At first indeed he feels trouble and anguish; but as soon as ever he has a sense of his acceptance with God, his tears are wiped away, and "the bones which were broken rejoice." It frequently happens, especially where the preceding sorrows have been deep, that the joy which succeeds them is rapturous and abundant. The surprise of Peter, on the eve of his expected execution, was not unlike that of a new convert: suddenly, a light shone in upon him, and his chains fell off, and the prison doors flew open, and an angel conducted him out, so that he could not persuade himself that he was awake, but thought he saw a vision: thus when the new convert is first brought forth into light and liberty, and finds the obstacles, which had seemed insurmountable, removed, he is ready to think it must be all a delusion: it is with him as with those of old, "when the Lord turned again the captivity of Zion, we were like them that dream: then was our mouth filled with laughter, and our tongue with singing;" yea, "the very hills break forth before him into singing, and all the trees of the field clap their hands." We must not however suppose, that all are equally elated; or that the joy which any feel will continue with them; it will rather subside into a peaceful tranquility of mind. they may *go out with joy;* but they will be *led forth with peace.* The Saviour's joy, which is to be fulfilled in us, consisted rather in peace than exultation; and such is the legacy that he has left to us. John xvii. 13, and xiv. 27. At first we are like a stream rippling and murmuring near the fountain head; but afterwards we resemble rather the deepened river flowing with silent majesty.

2. To infuse new dispositions.

A thorny bush is unproductive and worthless; as a brier is unseemly and injurious. The one is a just image of the more decent of mankind; the other, of the more profane. All are low and groveling in their nature, having no desires beyond this present world; and too many, by their influence as well as by their example, would impede the progress of those who are walking in the good way. The fir-tree on the other hand lifts its head on high; while the myrtle diffuses its fragrance all around; and both of them retain their verdure all the year: yet such shall the vilest of mankind become, when once they embrace the gospel of Christ. They shall soar to heaven with devout affections; they shall spread around them a sweet savor of the knowledge of Christ; they shall be unfading ornaments in the place where they grow; and instead of wounding, like the brier, all that come in contact with them, they shall, like the myrtle, emit the sweeter fragrance the more they are bruised, and perfume, as it were, the very hand that bruises them.

To impress our minds with a due esteem for the gospel, let us proceed to consider

II. The excellency of those effects.

There is an inherent excellence in holy dispositions, which, independent of the consequences flowing from them to ourselves or to society, must render them amiable in our eyes. But, as the text limits our views to the honor which accrues from them to God, we shall content ourselves with observing, that the change effected by the gospel is to the Lord

1. An occasion of praise.

None who are quickened and renewed by the word ever take the honor to themselves: all with one voice cry, "He that hath wrought us for the self-same thing is God; therefore, Not unto us, O Lord, not unto us, but unto thy name be the praise." The greater the change that is wrought in any person's heart, the less will he be disposed to arrogate any thing to himself on account of it: and most of all, "when the top-stone of the spiritual building shall be brought forth, will he shout, Grace, grace unto it." From his first acquaintance with divine truth will he begin to speak of God with love and gratitude. His own experience will furnish him with an inexhaustible fund of praise and thanksgiving. Nor will his acknowledgments any longer be a dull recital of an established creed, but the lively effusions of a grateful heart.

Now if that be deemed excellent, which causes the name of any human being to be held in estimation, and to be transmitted to posterity with honor, how much more must that be excellent, which makes the name of God to be reverenced and adored!

2. A monument of glory.

It is not in this world only that God is glorified by the dispensations of his grace: at the day of judgment every saint will "be to him for a name, and for a praise and for a glory." "Christ will come to be glorified in his saints, and admired *in* all that believe." How *sovereign* will the *grace* of God appear to every one amongst them, when each sees himself as a brand plucked out of the fire! When *stupendous wisdom* will be discovered in the plan, whereby he has effected their restoration to his favor! What *marvellous patience* will he appear to have exercised towards them under all their backslidings; and what *unbounded mercy* in pardoning their multiplied transgressions! Nor will his *power* be less an object of admiration, when it is seen how *wonderfully* it has been *exerted* in converting their souls, and in preserving them unto his heavenly kingdom. Yea, as long as there shall exist one glorified saint in heaven, so long shall the perfections of the Godhead be most eminently displayed in the salvation of sinful man.

How excellent then must that change be, which to all eternity shall be the brightest mouument of the divine perfections! The work of creation is excellent, though it is so soon to pass away: but that, glorious as it is, has no glory by reason of the glory that excelleth in the new creation.

INFER,

1. What encouragement have men to hear the gospel!

As a person who had never seen the face of nature but in the depth of winter, would scarcely conceive it possible that so great an alteration could take place in it as is annually made within the space of a few weeks, so are many ready to imagine, that their hard and barren hearts are incapable of experiencing such a change as God requires. But his word is as powerful as ever: it is still "like fire, or like a hammer that breaketh the rock in pieces:" and though "it runs not, nor is glorified" to the same extent as in former days, yet wherever it is preached in sincerity and truth there are some to attest its efficacy, and to prove that "it is the power of God to the salvation of men." Let none then despair: for though "the treasure be put into an earthen vessel, God will display the excellency of his power by means of it:" he will plant the fir-tree and the myrtle where nothing grew but thorns and briers; "he will make the wilderness like Eden, and the desert like the garden of the Lord."

2. What a sure criterion have we whereby to judge of our state!

An insensibility with respect to spiritual things characterizes the natural man; and a quickness of perception with respect to them marks the person in whom the word of God has taken due effect. Have we then surrendered up our false peace, and our carnal joy? and have we attained to a scriptural "joy and peace in believing?" Have the creatures all around us been led, as it were, to sympathize with us, and congratulate us on the change? Look then next to the tempers and dispositions of the soul: have the low groveling desires of the carnal mind been made to ascend to heaven; and the natural aversion to holy exercises been exchanged for an unfeigned delight in them? In short, is God now glorified in the whole of our deportment, so that, whosoever beholds our spirit and conduct is constrained to admire the grace of God in us? Doubtless, this change is not perfect in any; nor can we expect it to be so, while we carry about with us this body of sin and death; but is the change begun? and is it carrying on towards perfection? O that on considering these questions we might have the testimony of our consciences that things are so! But if there be no evidence of these things, let us beware, lest, instead of being eternal monuments of God's love, we be objects of his everlasting displeasure.

FAITH ESTABLISHES THE LAW.

Rom. iii. 31.—Do we then make void the law through faith? God forbid: yea, we establish the law. (S. S.)

A GENERAL prejudice obtains against the way of salvation by faith—
But it prevailed equally even in the apostolic age—
Paul himself saw that his statement of the gospel did not escape censure—
He perceived that it was deemed injurious to the interests of morality—
He therefore anticipated and obviated this objection—

I. Whence it is that people suppose we make void the law through faith.

The truth, however clearly stated, is often misapprehended—

In explaining salvation by faith we affirm two things concerning the law,

1. That it has no power either to condemn or to justify believers—

It cannot *condemn* them, because Christ has redeemed them from its curse, Gal. iii. 13.

It cannot *justify* them, because they have transgressed it, and its demands of perfect obedience are unalterably the same—

Faith in Christ delivers us from the penal sanctions of the law, but does not lower its demands—

2. That our obedience to it makes no part of our justifying righteousness—

Faith and works, *as grounds of justification*, are opposite to each other, Rom. xi. 6.

If our works had any share in our justification we should have a ground of boasting, which is utterly to be excluded, Rom. iii. 27.

The smallest reliance on these makes void all hope by the gospel, Gal. v. 2, 4.

All dependence therefore on the works of the law must be entirely renounced—

These affirmations evidently exclude morality from the office of justifying—

They are therefore supposed to discountenance all practical religion—

But this mistake originates in the ignorance of the objectors themselves

II. That the believer, so far from making void the law, establishes it.

The power of the law is twofold; to command obedience, and to condemn for disobedience

The believer establishes the law in each o. these respects—

1. In its commanding power

He owns its absolute authority over him as God's creature—

All his hope is in the perfect obedience which Christ paid to it for him—

He looks upon his obligations to obey it as increased, rather than diminished, by the death of Christ—

He actually desires to obey it as much as if he were to be justified by his obedience to it—

2. In its condemning power

He acknowledges himself justly condemned by it—

He founds his hope in Christ as having borne its curse for him—

His own conscience cannot be pacified but by that atonement which satisfied the demands of the law—

Bereft of an hope in the atonement, he would utterly despair—

He flees to Christ continually "to bear the iniquity of his holiest actions"—

Thus he magnifies the law while the objector himself makes it void

III. That the person, who objects to salvation by faith alone, does indeed make void the law—

Objections against the doctrine of faith are raised from a pretended regard for the law—

But the person who blends faith and works effectually undermines the whole authority of the law—

I Its commanding power

He is striving to do something which may serve in part as a ground of his justification—

But he can do nothing which is not imperfect—

Therefore he shews that he considers the law as less rigorous in its demands than it really is—

Consequently he robs it in a measure of its commanding power—

2. Its condemning power

He never thoroughly feels himself a lost sinner—

He does not freely acknowledge that he might be justly cursed even for his most holy actions—

He even looks for justification on account of that which in itself deserves nothing but condemnation—

Thus the advocates for the law are, in fact, its greatest enemies—

Whereas the advocates for the gospel are the truest friends to the law also—

INFER,

1. How absurd is it for persons to decide on religion without ever having studied its doctrines!

In human sciences men forbear to lay down their dogmas without some previous knowledge of the points on which they decide—

But in theology all, however ignorant, think themselves competent to judge—

They indeed, who are taught of God, can judge—

But unenlightened reason does not qualify us to determine—

Let us beware of indulging prejudices against the truth—

Let us seek to be "guided into all truth by the Holy Spirit"—

2. How excellent is the salvation revealed to us in the gospel!

Salvation by faith is exactly suited to man's necessities—

It is also admirably calculated to advance the honor of God—

Every man that is saved magnifies the law, and consequently the law-giver—

The commanding and condemning power of the law are equally glorified by the sinner's dependence on the obedience and sufferings of Christ—

But in those who are condemned, *its sanctions only* are honored—

Thus is the law more honored in the salvation of one, than in the destruction of the whole human race—

Let all then admire and embrace this glorious salvation.

THE OFFICE AND OPERATION OF FAITH.

Gal. v. 6.—In Jesus Christ neither circumcision availeth any thing, nor uncircumcision, but faith, which worketh by love. (S. S.)

THE peculiar character of the gospel is, that it shews how a sinner may be justified before God—

Yet the generality of christians are far from entertaining just views of this most fundamental point—

They confound the different offices of faith and works—

But St. Paul distinguishes them with much accuracy and precision—

He invariably declares that our justification is by faith—

Yet, though he denies to works the office of justifying, he invariably insists on them as the fruits and evidences of our faith—

Nothing can be more decisive than the declaration before us—

We shall

I. Explain it

Man is prone to trust in outward rites and ceremonies

The Jews confided in the ordinance of circumcision—

The Judaizing teachers also among the christians inculcated the observance of that rite as a ground of hope—

Amongst ourselves also, many think it sufficient that they have been baptized—

Or expect to find admission into heaven because they have attended regularly at the Lord's table—

But no outward observances can avail for our salvation

An external conformity with the rule of duty may proceed from the basest principles—

It may spring from a desire to obtain man's applause, or to establish a righteousness of our own—

And it may consist with the indulgence of evil tempers and vicious appetites—

It cannot therefore of itself characterize the true christian—

Nor can it "avail *any thing*" towards procuring the divine favor—

If indeed it proceed from faith and love, it will be rewarded—

But if it be made the ground of our hope, it will prevent, rather than procure, our acceptance with God, Gal. v. 2.

That which alone can avail for our acceptance with God, is "faith"

All the promises of God are made to faith, Mark xvi. 16; Acts x. 43.

It is by faith that all the saints of old obtained salvation, Rom. iv. 3, 6, 7

St. Paul and St. James do not *really* differ respecting this—*

Nor do any passages of scripture *really* contradicts it—†

If salvation be *of grace*, it must be *by faith*, Rom. iv. 16.

Yet this faith must be productive of good works

It is not a mere notional assent to certain doctrines—

Nor is it a confident assurance respecting the safety of our own state—

But it is a living operative principle in the heart—

It is, on *our* part, the bond of union between Christ and our souls—

And it cannot but discover itself by "works of love"—

If it produce not holy tempers, and an unfeigned regard for the bodies and souls of men, it is no better than the faith of devils, Jas. ii. 19.

The declaration in the text being explained, we shall,

II. Improve it

Every part of scripture, rightly understood, is profitable for the directing both of our faith and practice, 2 Tim. iii. 16. See the Greek.

We will improve this before us,

1. "For doctrine," that is, for the establishment of true doctrine

The way of salvation is simply by faith in Christ—

* St. Paul (Rom. iv. 1—5,) speaks of Abraham as being justified before God: St. James (ii. 21—23,) speaks of Abraham as manifesting his faith before man, and as justifying his pretentions to the divine favor by a suitable conduct and conversation.

† There are many expressions both in the Old and New Testament which *seem* to assert salvation by works: but they are only declarative of the character of those that shall be finally saved, or of God's gracious determination to reward those works which flow from faith. If they were interpreted in any other way, they would invalidate the whole gospel.

And every kind of work, ceremonial or moral,* must be considered as of no avail with respect to justification before God—

However necessary, however valuable, our obedience may be if performed aright, it ceases to be valuable the moment we depend upon it—

This is clearly stated in the text and context, Gal. v. 2—6.

And St. Paul himself was practically persuaded of this doctrine—Phil. iii. 9.

Let us then renounce all confidence in our own works—

And rely wholly on the blood and righteousness of Christ—

2. "For reproof," that is, for the refuting of false doctrines

Some have argued from the text, that faith saves us *as an operative principle*—

Thus they affirm that we are justified by something *within ourselves*—

But faith, *as a principle*, is not of more value than love, 1 Cor. xiii. 13.

And if we were justified by it *as an operative principle*, we should have room to boast, just as much as we should if we were justified by love or any other principle—

The reason of our being justified by faith is, that faith unites us unto Christ, which is a property not common to any other grace—

Our works do not *make* our faith to be good or saving, but only *prove* it to be so—†

If our faith be genuine we shall discover it *to God* by a simple dependence upon Christ, and *to man* by the practice of good works—

3. "For correction" of unrighteous conduct

It must be confessed that many profess faith in Christ while their lives are unworthy of the gospel—

But such persons stand condemned even by their own profession—

No faith is of any avail, but such as "works by love"—

Let professors then weigh themselves in the balance of the sanctuary—

Let them examine their tempers, dispositions and actions—

Let them acknowledge that a proud, envious, passionate, unforgiving, covetous or selfish christian is as much a contradiction in terms, as an adulterous or murderous christian—

Let them put away either their profession or their sins—

4. "For instruction in righteousness"

To point out all the offices of love would be tedious—

But we must observe that it should operate uniformly, and respect both the bodies and souls of men—

Let us then exercise love, and abound in it more and more.‡

* The apostle does not deny that circumcision is of any avail merely because it is *a ceremonial* work, but because it is *a work*; and because dependence on it would rob Christ of his glory. His argument therefore excludes works of whatever kind they be. Compare Gal. ii. 16.

† Just as fruit does not *make* a tree good, but only *manifests* it to be so.

‡ If this were the subject of a CHARITY-SERMON, it would be proper to open *here* the nature, excellence, and importance of the particular institution which was to be benefited: and then to exhort the benevolent in general, and believers in particular, to give it their liberal support.

THE RICHES OF DIVINE GRACE DISPLAYED.

Eph. ii. 4—7.—But God, who is rich in mercy, for his great love wherewith he loved us, even when we were dead in sins, hath quickened us together with Christ . . . . . . and hath raised us up together, and made us sit together in heavenly places in Christ Jesus: that in the ages to come he might shew the exceeding riches of his grace, in his kindness towards us through Christ Jesus. (S. S.)

WHAT an accumulation of sublime ideas is here presented to our view!—

Well might the Psalmist say that the meditation of God was sweet to him—

We scarcely know whether to admire more the grace of the benefactor, or the felicity of those who participate his blessings—

But the text requires us to fix our attention on that most delightful of all subjects, the riches of divine grace—

The apostle has in the preceding verses described the state of the unregenerate world—

He now displays the grace of God towards the regenerate

I. IN ITS SOURCE.

God is "rich in mercy," and "abundant in love"

Mercy and love are, as it were, the favorite attributes of the Deity, Ex. xxxiv. 6, 7.

The exercise of these perfections is peculiarly grateful to him, Mic. vii. 18.

There is an inexhaustible fountain of them in the heart of God, Rom. x. 12.

They have flowed down upon the most unworthy of the human race—

They will flow undiminished to all eternity—

While he retains his nature he cannot but exercise these perfections, 1 John iv. 8.

These are the true sources of all the grace displayed towards fallen man

Man had nothing in him whereby he could merit the attention of his Maker—

He was fallen into the lowest state of guilt and misery—

But the bowels of his Creator yearned over him*—

God felt (if we may so speak) an irresistible impulse of compassion towards him†—

Hence was it that the Son of God was sent into the world, John iii. 16.

Hence also were so many offers of mercy made to man—

And to this alone is it owing that so much as one has ever found acceptance with God—

But, to judge how great the love was wherewith he loved us, we must trace it

II. IN ITS OPERATIONS

The grace of God has been displayed towards us in ten thousand ways—

But we must confine our attention to its operations, as they are set forth in the text—

God has "quickened us even when we were dead in sins"

What is meant by "dead in sins," appears from the preceding verses—

* In this view, God's solicitude to find Adam, and his affectionate (perhaps plaintive) inquiry after him, Gen. iii. 9, are very striking.

† We may conceive of God as expressing himself in the language of the prophet, Hos xi 8. 9.

We were walking according to the course of this world—
We were the willing servants of Satan—
We were indulging all kinds of "filthiness, both of flesh and spirit"—
We were demonstrating ourselves to be, "by nature" as well as practice, "children of wrath"—
And we were utterly destitute of all power to help and save ourselves, Rom. v. 6.
Yet *even then* did God look upon us in tender compassion*—
He quickened us by that same Spirit whereby he raised Christ from the dead, Compare 1 Pet. iii. 18, with Rom. viii. 11.
In so doing, he united us "together with Christ," and rendered us comformable to him as our head—
What an astonishing instance of divine grace was this!
He has also "raised us up, and enthroned us together with Christ in Heaven"
The apostle had before expatiated on what God had wrought for Christ, Eph. i. 19, 20.
He now draws a parallel between believers and Christ—
What was done for Christ our head and representative, may be considered as done for all the members of his mystical body—
In this view Christians may be considered *figuratively* as risen with Christ, and as already seated on his throne—
Their hearts, their conversation, their *rest*, is in Heaven, Col. iii. 1; 2 Phil. iii. 20.
How has he thus verified the declaration of Hannah! 1 Sam. ii. 8.
How has he thus discovered "the exceeding riches of his grace!"
How worthy of God such a stupendous display of grace is, we shall see if we consider it
III. In its end
God is not only the author, but also the end of all things, Rom. xi. 36.
Nor would it become him to do any thing but with a view to his own glory—
The manifestation of his own glory was the express end for which he revealed his grace, Eph. i. 6.
And this end is already in some measure attained
All ages, to the end of time, must admire the grace of God towards both the Jewish and Gentile world—
Every one, who partakes of that grace, must of necessity admire it—
The "exceeding riches of it" are unsearchable—
God's "kindness" too is infinitely enhanced by flowing to us "through Christ Jesus"—
The price paid by Christ will to eternity endear to us the blessings purchased—
At present, however, the design of God in revealing his grace is not fully answered—
But it will be completely answered in the day of judgment
Then, how exceeding rich and glorious will this grace appear!
Then the depth of misery, into which we were fallen, will be more fully known—
The spring and source of that grace will be more clearly discovered—
And all the operations will be seen in one view—

* This may be illustrated by Ezek. xvi. 4—6.

Then Christ, the one channel in which it flows, will be more intimately revealed to us—

How will every eye then admire, and every tongue then adore!

Surely nothing but such an end could account for such operations of the divine grace—

Let every one therefore seek to experience these operations in his own soul—

Let those who have been favored with them glorify God with their whole hearts.

THE REMEDY FOR THOSE WHO HAVE LOST THEIR SEASONS OF GRACE.

Jer. viii. 20—22.—The harvest is past, the summer is ended, and we are not saved. For the hurt of the daughter of my people am I hurt; I am black; astonishment hath taken hold on me. Is there no balm in Gilead? Is there no physician there? Why then is not the health of the daughter of my people recovered? (S. S.)

EVERY one acknowledges that it is his duty to trust in God—

But we are prone to creature-confidence—

Hence we are often left to faint under difficulties from which we might easily have been extricated—

Thus the Jews increased their distress by relying on the Egyptians for succor, when, if they would have trusted in God, they might have been delivered—

The prophet therefore takes up this affectionate lamentation over them—

I. WHO ARE THEY OF WHOM IT MAY BE SAID "THEIR HARVEST IS PAST, THEIR SUMMER IS ENDED, AND THEY ARE NOT SAVED?"

In its primary sense this passage is applicable only to the Jews, when they were attacked by the Babylonians—

But it may be applied to those who have lost seasons of spiritual relief—

The "summer and harvest" may be considered as seasons afforded us by God for providing for the necessities of our souls—

Many of these we have suffered to pass unimproved and unnoticed—

They therefore may be said to have lost their summer, &c. who have neglected to improve the seasons afforded

1. By nature

Youth is well fitted by nature for the work of conversion—

The mind is then more flexible, the passions more governable, and the conscience more tender—

But many have lost that favorable season—

2. By Providence

Mercies are sent by God to invite, *judgments*, to alarm—

But many who should have been drawn by them to seek after God, have remained impenitent—

The Sabbath also was instituted by God for the promoting of man's spiritual welfare—

On that day more especially God calls and converts sinners to himself—

But many have let those seasons pass, without obtaining the knowledge of salvation—

3. By grace

There are times when all experience *the strivings of God's Spirit*—
If they improved those seasons, God would "give them more grace"
But many stifle their convictions, and "resist the Holy Ghost"—
They who are in this predicament would do well to reflect on
II. THE MISERY OF THEIR STATE
The distress of the prophet's mind on account of the calamities that were coming on the Jews is most pathetically expressed—
But a view of the miseries impending over those who have lost their seasons of grace might well excite yet more painful apprehensions—
Their seasons lost are irrecoverable
Present time is often wasted, as though it were of no value—
But many would be glad on a death-bed to recall the seasons in which they had heard the tidings of salvation, or felt the motions of God's Spirit—
Such wishes, however, are all in vain—
Their seasons lost may never be renewed
We are apt to promise ourselves days and years to come, Acts xxiv. 25.
But how often does death disappoint our expectations!
Every lost season has greatly aggravated their guilt
The means of grace are most important and valuable talents—
The neglecting to improve them will be severely punished, Matt. xxv. 26, 30.
Every season they have lost has hardened their hearts
The word that does not quicken and save will stupify and condemn, Matt. xiii. 14, 15, 2 Cor. ii. 16.
Every lost season has grieved the Holy Spirit more and more
God will not alway strive with those who resist his motions, Gen. vi. 3
If he cease to strive with us, our destruction is inevitable, Hos. ix. 12.
How should we compassionate those who are in such a state!
How should every one adopt the words following my text! Jer. ix. 1.
But their condition is not desperate
III. THE REMEDY THAT YET REMAINS FOR THEM
We might be ready to suppose that such persons were incurable—
But the animated interrogatories in the text shew the contrary
Christ is a "physician" *able* and *willing* to save those who come unto him— — —
His blood is a "balm" that heals the most deadly wounds, Isa. i. 18, 1 John i. 7.
The true reason that so many die in their sins is, that they will not come to Christ for salvation, John v. 40.
Let every one then acknowledge that it is his own fault if he be not saved.

THE SCOPE AND TENDENCY OF THE GOSPEL.

Isaiah xl. 1, 2.—Comfort ye, comfort ye my people, saith your God: speak ye comfortably to Jerusalem, and cry unto her, that her warfare is accomplished, that her iniquity is pardoned; for she hath received of the Lord's hand double for all her sins. (S. S.)

THE ministerial office is fitly compared to that of a steward, who divides to every one his proper portion. 2 Tim. ii. 15. Luke xii. 42. The execution of it calls for much wisdom and discretion, because there must be a diversity both in the matter and manner of our addresses corresponding with the different states of the people to whom we minister. To some we must of necessity proclaim the terrors of God's law, however painful such a discharge of our duty may be: but the great scope of our ministry is to comfort the Lord's people, and be "helpers of their joy." The commission here given to the servants of Jehovah leads us to observe, that

I. God earnestly desires the comfort and happiness of his people

There are a people, who are eminently the Lord's people. Deut. vii. 6. 1 Pet. ii. 9. And that God is peculiarly solicitous to promote their comfort, appears,

1. From the commission which he gave to his beloved Son.

He sent his Son into the world to execute his eternal counsels—And our Lord himself, in his first public address to the people, declared, that the comfort of mourners was a principal object of his mission—Isaiah lxi. 1—3. Luke iv. 17—19.

2. From the end for which he sends his Spirit into the hearts of men.

God sends his Spirit to testify of Christ, John xv. 26, to witness our adoption into his family, Rom. viii. 15, and to seal us into the day of redemption, Eph. i. 13, 14,—In performing these offices, he comforts our souls—And he is, on that very account, distinguished by the name of "*the Comforter*," John xvi. 7.

3. From the titles which the Father himself assumes.

He calls himself "The God of consolation," Rom. xv. 5, and "the Comforter of all them that are cast down," 2 Cor. vii. 6,—He compares his concern to that of a Father pitying his child, Psa. ciii. 13, and to a mother comforting with tenderest assiduities her afflicted infant, Isa. lxvi. 13,—Yea, he assures us that his regards far exceed those of the most affectionate parent in the universe, Isa. xlix. 15.

4. From the solemn charge he gives to ministers

He sends his servants "to turn men from darkness unto light, and from the power of Satan unto God." Acts xxvi. 18. And he especially charges them to "strengthen the weak hands, to confirm the feeble knees, and to say to them that are of a fearful heart, Be strong, fear not; your God will come and save you." Isa. xxxv. 3, 4. *Thrice* is that injunction repeated in the text: and in the execution of this duty we are justly called, "The helpers of your joy." 2 Cor. i. 24.

5. From the dispensations both of his providence and grace

When he suffered his beloved Son to be tempted in all things like unto us, it was with a view to comfort us under our temptations. Heb. ii. 18. And when he comforted St. Paul under his multiplied afflictions, he still consulted the comfort of his church and people: 2 Cor. i. 3, 4; yea, however he diversified his dispensations, he had invariably the same gracious object in view. Ib. 6.

As a further proof of his regard for our comfort, we may observe that,

II. He has made abundant provision for it in his word

The message which we are commanded to deliver to his people, contains in it the richest sources of consolation. We proclaim to them, that

1. Their "warfare is accomplished."

This, as referring to the captives in Babylon, foretold their deliverance from captivity. But it chiefly relates to the deliverance of the church from the bondage and misery to which they were subject under the Mosaic dispensation. The burthensome yoke of ceremonies was to be abolished at the coming of Christ, Col. ii. 14, and to be succeeded by a "law of perfect liberty"

Jam. i. 25,—A similar deliverance every soul experiences, as soon as ever it believes in Christ: the chains of sin, wherewith it was bound, fall off; Rom. viii. 2; and, though there yet remain many conflicts to be endured, yet is Satan's power irrecoverably broken; and the once captive sinner is brought into the glorious liberty of God's children, John viii. 36,—What rich consolation must this of necessity administer to the weary, and heavy-laden!—Matt. xi. 28—30.

2. Their iniquity is pardoned.

The Lord's people, not excepting the least or meanest of them, have all their iniquities forgiven, Col. ii. 13. Ps. ciii. 12. Acts xiii. 39,—What consolation then can they want? Let their circumstances in other respects be ever so afflictive, they may "be of good cheer:" Matt. ix. 2; for we have the united testimony of prophets and apostles that they are truly blessed, Ps. xxxii. 1, 2; Rom. iv. 7, 8.

3. They have received mercies that far overbalance all their afflictions.

The prophet does not mean that the Lord's people are punished beyond their deserts (for this were contrary both to scripture and experience) Ezr. ix. 13, but that their mercies far exceed any judgments which may have been inflicted on them on account of sin. God will punish his people, (and it is necessary that he should) but their enjoying of his favor, and their prospect of his glory, are mercies, in comparison of which their troubles are not worth a thought—Indeed their very chastisements are mercies in disguise; Heb. xii. 10; and have been acknowledged as such by those who have endured them in an abundant measure. Ps. cxix. 67, 75.

Let us LEARN then from this subject,

1 The genuine tendency of the gospel.

The gospel is generally considered as a source of melancholy, and consequently, as inimical to men's happiness. But the very reverse of this is true. It calls men indeed to repentance, and, *in this view*, may be considered as an occasion of sorrow: but it is a salutary sorrow that will be followed by joy: nor can any one duly reflect on the expressions of the text, without acknowledging, that a reliance on God's promises and oath revealed in the gospel, is, as it was intended to be, a source of "strong consolation," to all the people of God. Heb. vi. 17, 18. Let this absurd prejudice then be put away, and the gospel be received by us with gratitude and joy.

2. The wonderful difference between those who embrace, and those who disregard the gospel.

Can *that* be said of carnal and worldly men, which is here spoken of the Lord's people? Are *their* chains broken? *their* sins forgiven? *their* comforts greater than any judgments that await them? No: they are yet in bondage to sin and Satan; their sins are all "sealed up in a bag" against the day of judgment; and the wrath of God is shortly coming upon them to the uttermost. Then it will appear how great a "difference there is between those who serve the Lord, and those who serve him not." Mal. iii. 18. Let not this distinction then be made a subject of profane ridicule, but a motive to seek the Lord, that we may be numbered with his people, and be made partakers of his benefits.

THE ABUNDANT GRACE OF GOD

Romans v. 20, 21.—Where sin abounded, grace did much more abound: that as sin hath reigned unto death, even so might grace reign through righteousness unto eternal life, by Jesus Christ our Lord. (S. S.)

From eternity God determined to glorify his grace—
For this end he permitted sin to enter into the world—
The publication of his law also promoted the same end—
It served to shew how awfully sin had abounded—
And consequently to magnify that grace which destroyed sin—
To this effect the apostle speaks in the text and the words preceding it—
We shall endeavor to shew,

I. How sin has abounded.

The transgression of Adam was of a very malignant nature.
In the whole preceding context *that* sin in particular is referred to—
And it may well be considered as of a crimson dye—
It argued a contempt of God's goodness, which had bestowed so much upon him, Gen. ii. 8, 9.
It argued a doubt of his veracity, which was engaged to inflict the penalty, Gen. iii. 4.
It argued a rejection of his authority, which forbad the eating of that fruit, Gen. ii. 17.
It argued an attempt to invade the peculiar prerogatives of God, Gen. iii. 5.
Surely in this single transgression sin greatly abounded—
But sin spread also over the whole world.
Adam begat sons "*in his own* fallen *likeness*"—
All his descendents inherited his corruption, Job xiv. 4.
And cast off the yoke which their Maker had imposed upon them—
There was not so much as one single exception to be found, Ps. xiv. 2, 3
On this very account God once destroyed all but one family—
It had moreover prevailed in every heart to an awful degree.
Every faculty of men's souls was debased by it—
The understanding was blinded, the will made obstinate, the conscience seared—
All the "memb rs of their bodies also were made instruments of unrighteousness"—
There was not an imagination of their thoughts that was not evil, Gen. vi. 5.
It even took occasion from the holy law of God to rage the more
God gave his law to discover and repress sin.
But sin would not endure any restraint—
It rose like water against the dam that obstructs its progress, Rom. vii. 8.
And inflamed men both against the law, and against him who gave it—
Thus, in using so good a law to so vile a purpose, it displayed its own exceeding sinfulness, Rom. vii. 13.
But God did not altogether abandon our wretched world.

II. How grace much more abounded.

God determined that his grace should be victorious—
And that it should establish its throne on the ruins of the empire which sin had erected—
For this purpose he gave us his Son to be a second Adam, Rom v. 14. 1 Cor. xv. 22, 45.
He laid on him the curse due to our iniquities—

—enabled him to "bring in an everlasting righteousness"—

—accepted us in him as our new covenant-head—

—restore us through him to eternal life—

Thus the super-abundance of his grace is manifest

1. In the object attained.

The destruction of man for sin was certainly tremendous—

Yet was it no more than what was to be expected—

The fallen angels had already been banished from heaven—

No wonder then if man was made a partaker of their misery—

But how beyond all expectation was the recovery of man!—

How wonderful that he should be restored while a superior order of beings were left to perish!—

And be exalted to a throne of glory from whence they had been cast down!—

This was indeed a manifestation of most abundant grace—

2. In the method of attaining it.

Sin had reigned unto death by means of Adam—

And certainly the destruction of the whole world for one sin argued a dreadful malignity in sin—

Yet was there nothing in this unjust or unreasonable—

But who could have thought that God should send us *his own Son?*—

That he should constitute HIM our new covenant-head and representative?—

That he should remove the curse of sin by HIS death—

———— accept sinners through HIS righteousness?—

———— remedy by a second Adam what had been brought upon us by the first?—

This was a discovery of grace that infinitely transcends the comprehension of men or angels—

3. In the peculiar advantage with which it was attained.

If Adam had retained his innocence, we also should have stood in him as our representative—

We should however have possessed only a creature's righteousness—

But in Christ we possess the righteousness of God himself, 2 Cor. v. 21.

Our reward therefore may well be augmented in proportion to the excellence of that, for which we are accepted—

Besides, the glory of God is infinitely more displayed in Christ, than ever it would have been if Adam had not fallen—

Our happiness therefore, in beholding it, must be greatly increased—

Thus our restoration through Christ will bring us to the enjoyment of far greater happiness than ever we lost in Adam, Rom. v. 15. This point is insisted on from ver. 15 to 19.

What can more fully manifest the superabounding grace of God?—

IMPROVEMENT.

1. For caution.

This doctrine seems liable to the imputation of licentiousness—

St. Paul foresaw the objection, and answered it, Rom. vi. 1, 2.

His answer should satisfy every objector—

But the reign of grace consists in destroying *every* effect of sin—

Therefore to indulge sin would be to counteract, and not to promote, the grace of God—

Let the professors of religion however be careful to give no room for this objection—

Let them "put to silence the ignorance of foolish men by well-doing"

2. For encouragement.

How strange is it that any should despair of mercy!—

The infinite grace of God has been exhibited in many striking instances. Luke vii. 47. 1 Tim. i. 14, 16.

Let us seek to become monuments of this mercy—

Let us not indeed "sin, that grace may abound"—

But let us freely acknowledge how much sin has abounded in us—

And yet expect through Christ "abundance of grace and of the gift of righteousness."

THE ABUNDANCE OF DIVINE GOODNESS.

Luke xiv. 22.—And the servant said, Lord, it is done as thou hast commanded, and yet there is room. (H.)

THESE words are part of a parable, in which much of the mystery of the gospel is contained; and the manifest design of it is, to show that, however successful the gospel of Christ has been in time past, sinners may yet come, and be received by Christ, and be for ever saved. "Wisdom hath built her house," &c.; Prov. ix. 1; and, among the highly favored guests, who are partaking of this joyful feast, "yet there is room."

Consider,

I. WHERE THERE IS ROOM.

1. In the mercy of God. It is over all his works, and from everlasting. Psa. cxlv. 9. It belongeth unto God. Psa. ciii. 17; Exod. xx. 6; Isa. xxx. 18; Psa. cxlvii. 11.

2. In the merits of Christ. He is an all-sufficient Saviour. Heb. vii. 24, 25; 1 John i. 7. The merit of his death is unbounded, as it respects man. 1 John ii. 2.

3. As to the power and efficacy of the Spirit to renew and change the hardest heart. Such a change is necessary, we have destroyed ourselves; and if ever we are recovered, it must be by help from heaven. Hos. xiii. 9. The conversion of a sinner is the Spirit's work; Titus iii. 5, 6; which the Father hath promised; Luke xxiv. 49; engaged to pour out; Zech. xii. 10; Christ died to open a way for it. Gal. iii. 13, 14.

4. In the household of faith. More members may be added to Christ's mystical body; in order to this the gospel is preached; the ministers of Christ labor, encouraged by the extensive request of their master, Christ, a little before his death. John xvii. 20. There is yet plentiful provision in our Father's house. Hosea xiv. 5. Those who come into the vineyard at the third, sixth, or ninth hour, do not hinder others from being invited and received at the eleventh; Rev. ii. 3; and we are still to pray that his kingdom may come, which is capable of increase, both as to number and perfection.

5. In the mansions of glory. They are many; John xiv. 2, 3; and all who overcome here, shall be made pillars there. Rev. iii. 12. The city is prepared for them; Heb. xi. 16; for this Jesus died; Heb. ii. 10; for this he prays. John xvii. 24. He has declared so much; John xii. 26; and when he shall appear, they also shall appear with him, &c., Col. iii. 4.

II. For whom is there room.

In general, there is room for all sorts and conditions of men; those of one kingdom and country as well as another. The gospel is sent into all the world, and to be preached to every human creature capable of hearing. Mark xvi. 15.

But more particularly.

1. There is room for the meanest and most despicable in the world. God is no respecter of persons. 1 Sam. xvi. 7. The things of the kingdom are revealed to babes. Eph. vi. 9. Not many wise or noble are called; 1 Cor. i. 26—29; the poor are chosen. James ii. 5. Lazarus in Abraham's bosom was once a beggar. Luke xv. 20. Jesus himself was poor while on earth. Matt. viii. 20.

2. The rich men are under no necessity of perishing, there is room for them. Their situation is indeed critical; Matt. xix. 24; their salvation very difficult; Mark x. 25; Luke xviii. 23; they must be delivered from trusting in riches: and with God this is possible. Matt. xix. 26.

3. The afflicted must not be forgotten, there is room for them. The pains of the body are no proof that God will not have mercy on the soul. Some of the most eminent saints have been in the furnace of affliction, as David, Hezekiah, Job: God has caused many to pass under the rod, that he might bring them into the bond of the covenant. Ezek. xx. 37.

4. There is yet room for such as have long stood out, neglecting, and making light of the invitations of the gospel. 2 Cor. vi. 2. The compassionate Redeemer is still saying, "Behold," &c., Rev. iii. 20.

5. There is yet room for such as have backslidden; having fallen into sin, after the most promising beginnings. Jer. iii. 22.

Lastly, to add no more; There is yet room for the chief of sinners. Pardon and peace were first proclaimed to those who crucified our God; Luke xxiv. 47; see 1 Tim. i. 15; and all that labor, and are heavy laden, are promised rest. Matt. xi. 28.

Application.

1. How justly may the gospel be called a joyful sound.

2. What encouragement for gospel-ministers still to preach this gospel: "Yet there is room."

3. When Satan suggests, "it is too late to repent, and be saved;" he may be silenced by the text, "Yet there is room."

4. Let none take encouragement from the text, to make light of the invitations of the gospel, or put off their repentance. For although there is room in the kingdom of grace and glory, yet we should remember there is room in the grave and in hell too: and how many have sunk into both, while neglecting their salvation.

5. This may be a source of consolation to pious souls, respecting their unconverted friends and relatives. They may yet be saved, for "yet there is room."

6. Being called into the kingdom of grace, and finding there is room, let this confirm your faith and hope, as to your reception to glory.

THE NATURE AND PROPERTIES OF THE SERVICE OF GOD.

oshua xxiv. 15.—If it seem evil unto you to serve the Lord, choose you this day whom ye will serve. (B.)

These words imply what is generally acknowledged,—That man is a rational and free creature.

Let us inquire,

I. What it is to serve the Lord; and what are the nature and properties of this service.

The foundation of the true and proper service of God must be laid in the knowledge of him, 1 Chron. xxviii. 9,—in reconciliation with him, Heb. ix. 14,—in deliverance from other masters. Matt. vi. 24. Rom. vi. 14. Luke i. 74. — — —

We must enter into his service by yielding or giving ourselves up, freely and fully to be his servants. Rom. vi. 16. This implies that we no longer yield ourselves to the world, the flesh, the devil, or sin; but to the Lord, with desire that he would accept us through his Son, and confidence that he does so. Hereby we are joined to the Lord in order to serve him. Isa. lvi. 6.

As his servants, we must be subject to his authority, and obedient to the divine will, Rom. vi. 16, including—*Holiness towards God*, which is a death to sin and deliverance from it, the being dedicated to God, employed for him, conformed to him:—And *righteousness towards our neighbors;* truth, justice, mercy, love, and its fruits.

This subjection and obedience must be constant and universal, 1 Cor. x. 31. Psa. cxix. 6.

In what sense such do, and in what sense they do not serve God, may be seen by reference to Psa. xvi. 2. Job xxii. 2, 3; xxxv. 5—8.

As to the properties of this service,—It must be *sincere* and *upright;* Jos. xxiv. 14. 1 Chron. xxviii. 9. John iv. 23, 24,—*Reverential;* Heb. xii. 28; from a sense of his presence; Luke i. 75; his glory, wisdom, power, eternity, immensity, supremacy. "Lo! God is here!"—*Fiducial* or filial, *i. e.* with confidence and hope. Luke i. 74; Rom. viii. 15; Psa. ii. 11. The foundation of this must be the mediation of Christ; justification through him; Rom. v. 1; and the testimony of our conscience. 1 John iii. 21,—*Humble*, Acts xx. 19; Mic. vi. 8; implying a deep sense of the distance between him and us, a consciousness that we are not worthy to be permitted to serve him, and that our best services are not worthy of his acceptance.—*Resigned*, *patient*, and *contented;* from a conviction that his providence is over all, and that all his dispensations are just, and wise, and kind; that his eye is on each of his servants, and that he sets each to the work which he sees he is most fit for, and puts each in the most proper place.—*Loving*, from love, Isaiah lvi. 6, a willing mind, 1 Chron. xxviii. 9, and an undivided heart. John xiv. 15; Matt. vi. 24,—*Disinterested;* with a single eye to his glory. Rom. xiv. 7—9; 1 Cor. x. 31; Col. iii. 17.

II. Whether it be evil to serve the Lord, or the reasonableness and advantages of this service.

The word *evil* is taken here in a peculiar sense, and means *unjust*, *unreasonable*, *disadvantageous*, or *unnecessary*.

Is it unjust, or unreasonable for him to demand, or for us to pay this service? He is our Creator, Preserver, and Redeemer, and ought we not to be devoted to his glory, and obedient to his will?—As to the properties of this service, since he searches the heart, is it unreasonable to serve him with sincerity? or would hypocrisy be more appropriate? He is most great and powerful; is it unreasonable to serve him with reverence and fear? Mal. i. 6. He is merciful and gracious, and the friend and father of penitent believing souls; is it unreasonable to serve him with confidence and hope? He is most just and holy; is it unreasonable to serve him with humility? He is infinite in love and goodness, and has given his only Son for our sins; 1 John iv. 8; is it unreasonable to serve him from love? He is the Lord of glory, and the centre and source of glory; is it not more reasonable we should have regard to his glory, than our own?

Is this service of God DISADVANTAGEOUS?—In *life?* Many will think so, even as many as have gained, or suppose they have gained, profit, or honor, or pleasure by sin. Sin must be renounced, and all the gains of it; our idols; our lusts, the right hand must be cut off; the right eye must be plucked out; but this is only like the being obliged not to drink poison, or stab ourselves, or parting with a gangrened member.

The service of God is sometimes attended with other consequences, as the loss of our character, our property, our liberty, our life, distress, torture; and is not this disadvantageous?

Christ makes up for these losses. Disgraced among men, we are honored before God. Deprived of the riches of this world, we are put into possession of the unsearchable riches of Christ. Denied in carnal pleasures, we enjoy spiritual. Losing a short, uncertain, vain, miserable life, we gain a durable, immortal, and most blessed life in heaven.—View also the gains of this service.

These are,—The pardon of sin,—The favor of the greatest and best Being in the universe, on whom all other beings are dependant, and to whom they are subservient,—Communion with Him,—His direction, protection, and help, with a supply of all wants,—A good conscience; the consolations of the Spirit, and the hope of eternal life.

These things are to be enjoyed in life. Is it disadvantageous then to serve God in this life? If not; surely it is not—in *death.* What can the things we are required to *give* up, when we become the servants of God, do for us in that awful moment? sin, the world, fleshly lusts?

Will it then be disadvantageous, when the world is torn from us, to have a God to fly to? When "the earthly house of this tabernacle is dissolved, to "have a building of God, a house not made with hands, eternal in the heavens?" To have no guilt, fear, or anguish but peace, hope, and joy in the Holy Ghost?

But how great the benefit arising from the service of God,—In *eternity;* the intermediate state; at the day of judgment, for ever and ever?— — —

Perhaps you say, "I own it will do a man no harm, but there is no need of it." Let us inquire therefore, is it UNNECESSARY?—Can these ends be attained without it?

Can we escape the miseries in which we are already involved, without it?—Can we shun farther, greater, and eternal miseries without it?—Can we otherwise attain the perfection and happiness of which our nature is capable, either here? or hereafter?

III. I SHALL REFER THE MATTER TO YOUR JUDGMENT AND CHOICE WHOM YOU WILL SERVE.

If you still see things in a different light, and "it seem evil unto you to serve the Lord, choose you this day whom you will serve." Will you serve the *world?* consider what is in the world: "the lust of the flesh, the lust of the eye, and the pride of life;" the emptiness, uncertainty, and short duration of these things, since the world is passing from us, and we from it. Conceive the world on fire, as it will be in the great day;—a burning God!

Will you serve the *flesh?* Your body and animal nature, infirm, afflicted, dead, corrupted,—a rotten god! Or your corrupt nature, "the flesh lusting against the Spirit," and "warring against the law of your mind, and leading you captive to the law of sin;" the greatest evil in the universe, and the fruitful source of all other evils?— — —

In serving the world and the flesh you serve *Satan*. How will he reward you? What is his inclination? Does he love and wish you well? What is his power? What has he for himself?—now?—for ever? Has he wisdom, or honor, or riches, or happiness? The poet represents him as saying, and saying truly,

"Where'er I am is hell! myself am hell."

Judge from hence what he can give you.

Bring the matter to a point this day.—You are at years to judge. You have the use of your reason; of liberty. You have had the matter fairly stated to you. Choose, therefore; find a better master, better work, and better wages if you can. If you can find a better master, Jehovah can find a servant without you. If you do not want him, he does not want you.—Why this delay? "Choose you *this day* whom ye will serve." Let me caution you against the folly and danger of procrastination in deciding a point, in which you are so materially interested.

If, after all, you choose to serve these other lords, that have had dominion over you, you must not expect me to give you directions how to serve them. There is no need I should, as your own heart, and the lives of a great majority of your fellow-sinners will sufficiently direct you. But I shall endeavor,

IV. To give some directions to those who choose to serve the Lord, with a view to assist them in that important undertaking.

Read what follows the text; "Ye cannot serve the Lord," ver. 19.—This is spoken, not of an absolute, but of a moral impossibility, or a very great difficulty, which Joshua alleges to make the people more considerate in obliging themselves, and more resolved to fulfil their obligations.—You cannot serve God, while unacquainted with him; 1 Chron. xxviii. 9;—while not reconciled to him; Heb. ix. 14;—while under the power of other masters; Luke i. 74; Rom. vi. 14;—while unchanged; Matt. vii. 17; xii. 33; Luke vi. 43—45;—while possessed only of the strength of nature. John xv. 4, 5.

Acquaint yourselves with God,—by considering his nature and attributes, and the relations in which he stands to you, as manifested by his works and word;—by prayer for the illumination of his Spirit. "I will give them a heart to know me." Jer. xxiv. 7.

Be reconciled to him, through his Son, by repentance and faith. Heb. ix. 14.

Seek deliverance out of the hands of your enemies by his Spirit. John viii. 33—36; Rom. viii. 2; 2 Cor. iii. 17.

Be born again, and made new creatures; and then, the tree being good, the fruit will be good.

Seek grace to help you in time of need. Heb. xii. 28.

In order to all these, use the means of grace in private and public, and do not rest in them; but look through them to the end.

PERSONAL AND FAMILY RELIGION.

Joshua xxiv. 15.—As for me and my house, we will serve the Lord. (B.)

THIS noble resolution of Joshua, though it has been celebrated from age to age, in all countries, where the Scriptures of the Old Testament have been known, and imitated, as well as commended by many individuals, yet has not always been understood, even by those that have undertaken to explain it, and to enforce it upon others.

I shall now add something to what has been advanced; I mean *family religion;* a necessary and important branch indeed, but one seldom treated on in public, and sadly neglected in private. And that I may lay down a proper foundation for what I have to say concerning this point I shall consider,

I. THE NATURE OF JOSHUA'S RESOLUTION.

It is a resolution of an *enlightened, awakened, justified, renewed, devoted, consistent, experienced, believer.*

Of a BELIEVER. Faith has been, and is necessary under every dispensation, Patriarchal, Mosaic, or Christian; as the Epistle to the Hebrews, ch. xi. evidently shows; it was as necessary for Joshua as for us. For, "without faith it is impossible to please God." Heb. xi. 6. It is necessary to believe in God, in his revealed will, in his declarations, promises, and threatenings. Heb. iii. 19; iv. 3. For want of this the Israelites perished in the wilderness; and for this Joshua and Caleb are so justly famed.

Of an ENLIGHTENED believer. Having a clear and distinct knowledge of him, whom he worships, 1 Chron. xxviii. 9.—A knowledge of his law, its spirituality, its great extent, and obligation. This convinces of sin.—A knowledge of the service of God, as requiring us to worship him in spirit and in truth; Matt. iv. 10; John iv. 23; to obey him Rom. vi. 16, from love; to promote his glory. 1 Cor. vi. 20. 1 Pet. ii. 2. In fine,—A knowledge of our own insufficiency, and where help may be found.

Of an AWAKENED believer.—Awakened out of the sleep of nature, Eph. v. 14, *i. e.* his insensible, unconcerned, and indolent state, as to spiritual things. Hence arises a just apprehension and sense of the majesty, power, holiness, justice, and goodness of God, producing reverence, awe, dread, fear of offending him, Josh. xxiv. 14; Heb. xii. 28; and of death, judgment, eternity, producing a deep concern and great diligence. This Joshua experienced. See the following verses.

Of a JUSTIFIED believer.—Abraham was justified, Gen. xv. 6; Rom. iv. 3, and David, Psa. xxxii., and so, undoubtedly, was Joshua. This is the foundation of that confidence, and hope, love, peace, and joy, essential to the service of God. Heb. ix. 14; iii. 6, 14. For we are to serve as *sons,* and not merely as *servants.* Rom. viii. 15. Gal. iv. 5.

Of a RENEWED believer.—Joshua was born in sin, like the rest of mankind, but born again and renewed. This is necessary: for we must "serve in newness of spirit," which we cannot do without we obtain a new spirit and a new heart. Matt. vii. 17; xii. 33. Luke vi. 43, 45.

Of a DEVOTED believer.—Sensible of God's mercy and love to him, and loving God in return, without which there can be no religion, Deut. vi. 5; xxx. 6; 1 Tim. i. 5; 1 Cor. xiii. 1, and saying, "What shall I render unto the Lord for all his benefits?"—dedicating all to him, and employing all for him.

Of a CONSISTENT believer. Walking in all God's ordinances, and worshipping him in spirit and in truth, keeping all his commandments from love, and with a single eye; endeavoring constantly to promote his glory; being "sober and righteous, as well as godly in this present world," Tit. ii. 12; serving God in righteousness towards our neighbor, as well as in holiness towards himself. Luke i. 75.

Of an EXPERIENCED believer, who has made trial of this service.—

Therefore he could resolve for himself, in dependence on the grace he had already received, and still expected. And, as to his house, he knew either that they were like-minded with himself; or he purposed to use his endeavors that they might be so, and trusted in God, he should succeed.

II. WHETHER IT WAS A RESOLUTION SO REASONABLE AND WISE, THAT IT WOULD BE WELL FOR US TO IMITATE IT.

It was reasonable and wise, because Joshua knew that he was the CREATURE of God, who had been formed, and had received all his faculties and powers for this very end. Acts xvii. 26, 27.— — —

He knew that he was a DEPENDENT creature—Living, moving and having his being in God, and that he was spared and preserved for this end; not to eat, drink, or sleep; to gratify his senses and passions, or to please himself in any way, but to serve God. Matt. iii. 10; Luke xiii. 6—9.

An OBLIGED creature.—Having received innumerable benefits and mercies for this end. Rom. xii. 1. If the ox knoweth and serveth his owner, surely Israel should know and serve God. He thought it reasonable that he should know and serve the kind hand that fed him, and the author of all his mercies.

A REDEEMED creature.—Joshua was redeemed out of Egypt, and we are redeemed from the wrath of God for this end. 2 Cor. v. 14, 15; 1 Cor. vi. 20; Tit. ii. 14, 15.

A HIGHLY PRIVILEGED creature.—A member of the visible church, and favored with the light of the revelation of Jesus Christ for this end. Eph. v. 8—10; 1 Pet. ii. 9.

An ACCOUNTABLE creature.—That must be judged, how he had answered the end of his creation, preservation, and redemption, and what use he had made of his talents.

A MORTAL creature?—Yet immortal, that must pass certainly, soon, perhaps to-morrow, from a state of trial, to a state of retribution.

He knew, therefore, that to serve God aright, was essential to his everlasting happiness; to his escaping hell and attaining heaven.

That it was essential to his present happiness; as he could not otherwise have peace of mind, a good conscience, a hope of immortality, the favor, protection, and care of God, his direction and aid, all things needful and useful, and all things working for his good.

That it was essential to his usefulness to others, and particularly to his own family, to whom, especially, God had called him to be useful.

That what was his duty and happiness was also *theirs*. Therefore, out of love, he resolves for them, that they should serve the Lord.

Nor can we doubt that it was pleasing to God that he should do his utmost to induce his family to serve God, and how certainly it was the way to the accomplishment of God's promises. Gen. xviii. 19.

Of all these accounts his resolution was reasonable and wise, therefore since we are not debarred, but at liberty so to do, we should imitate him.

III. HOW WE MAY BE ENABLED TO DO SO.

As to *ourselves*,

We must see that we lay a foundation for the service of God, in an acquaintance and reconciliation with him, adoption into his family, a new birth, in consequence of repentance and faith; whereby we receive an interest in, and union with Christ, and find in him righteousness and strength, and "grace to help in time of need."

We must make ourselves acquainted with every branch of the service of God, and of our duty.

We must not allow ourselves in the neglect of any branch of it, and, therefore, we must deny ourselves, and take up our cross.

We must be found in the constant use of the means, that the edge of our minds, when blunted, may be sharpened, and grace may be continued to us, and increased in us.

As to our *families*,

We must be deeply concerned that they should serve him.

We must set them a good example, and show,—that we serve God ourselves, and are neither hypocrites, which they may be apt to suspect, nor formalists.

We must instruct them, Deut. vi. 6—9, converse with them, read to them, make them read,—(and here we may remark the importance of children, servants, and apprentices learning to read,)—we must bring them under the word preached, if possible, on every Lord's day, and at other times, and inquire what they can remember of what they have heard. We must catechise them. This is the doctrine of the Lord. Bring up your children "in the nurture and admonition," Ephes. vi. 4. Discipline must be used by us, as it was by Abraham, "I know that he will *command* his children." Gen. xviii. 19.

We must also encourage them, and excite them every way in our power.

We must give them proof that we are actuated only by love to them.

We must pray for them; for each child by name, and must pray with them, and put them upon praying for themselves.

We must persevere in this exercise, notwithstanding all discouragements.

As a motive to this labor, for the benefit of our children, it may be mentioned, that we have been instrumental in bringing them into the world; and shall we not endeavor to save them from hell?

MORAL INABILITY COMPATIBLE WITH GOSPEL EXHORTATIONS.

Philippians ii. 12, 13.—Work out your own salvation with fear and trembling: For it is God that worketh in you both to will and to do of his good pleasure. (Pr.)

It is a happy sign that our religious sentiments are correct, when we find a use for every part of Scripture, and perceive an agreement in the whole. Some things in this passage require to be explained; and if the explanation be just, it will not be inconsistent with other parts of Scripture, which declares unequivocally that our salvation is all of grace.

"Salvation" then consists of two parts; in a deliverance from the curse of the law, and from the dominion of sin. The first was effected by the death of Christ, without us. The latter is wrought by the Holy Spirit within us, changing the dispositions of the heart The one is by price, the other by power. In the first we are wholly passive, in the latter we are active by being acted upon. Now it is of salvation in the *latter* sense that the text speaks, because it is that in which we are properly concerned. The Holy Spirit "worketh in us," but it is "to will and to do." It is we, and not the Holy Spirit that repent and believe the gospel; that mourn for sin and mortify the deeds of the body. The exhortation in the text therefore s very properly addressed to us.

To "work out" our salvation, is not meant of working in a way of merit or desert; for in this sense, salvation is not of works, but of grace. But it is to grow in grace, to perfect holiness in the fear of the Lord, to work out our way through all the difficulties that lie before us, and to endure to the end that we may be saved. We must set our feet on all our spiritual enemies, and go on mortifying the deeds of the body that we may live.

This is to be done "with fear and trembling," a disposition of mind that must accompany all our striving to enter into the kingdom of God. The work itself is great and large, and the time allowed is short, very short for so important a concern as this. While pressing into the kingdom, we have reason to fear and tremble, lest we should not finally enter in and be saved. We are like persons on a dangerous voyage, and have cause to fear lest after all we should be shipwrecked.

It is God that worketh in us "to will and to do:" he gives us a heart to seek him, he keeps up every holy resolution till it is put into actual execution. It is of God that we are at *first* made willing to submit to mercy, and to be saved in his way, by coming to Christ for life. *Now* also it is of God, who makes us willing to give up all our idols, to watch and pray against every temptation, to run in the way of his commands, and to hold out in our christian course.

If it be asked *how* the Lord worketh in us? The answer is, not by forcing us against our will, but by making us willing, and that in a way suitable to our rational nature; namely by conviction, and by the influence of motives. Hence we are led to judge of things in a measure as they are, and to act from the clearest conviction of the understanding. Only let the mind be in a proper state, and the eternal realities of religion will operate powerfully upon us, and give to the mind an impulse that is irresistible. Views of the evil nature, and awful consequences of sin will render us willing to attempt its mortification, and to submit to every species of self-denial. Proper views of the gift of God will make us thirst for that living water, and dispose us most cordially to embrace the Saviour. John iv. 10.

From the passage thus explained, we may infer,

1. That *exhortations to holy duties do not imply any self-sufficiency in us*, without the influence of the Holy Spirit. They show us what ought to be, and so are proper both to saints and sinners. But something more is necessary to make us what we ought to be, and incline us to do what God requires of us. Exhortations place before us the motives to action, but it is the Holy Spirit that prepares the mind to receive them, and to yield to their influence.

2. *That the work of the Holy Spirit does not release us from obligation*, but on the contrary, affords an additional motive for our compliance with the will of God. There is as much need for us to strive to enter in at the straight gate, as if God had never promised the aid of his Holy Spirit. It is the same in natural things as it is in spiritual things; we are as much dependent in one case as in the other; and yet that dependence does not supersede the use of ordinary means. It is "in God we live, and move

and have our being;" yet we employ means for the preservation and continuance of life, and should have no reason to expect it in any other way.

More particularly—

I. CONSIDER THE EXHORTATION ITSELF: "WORK OUT YOUR OWN SALVATION WITH FEAR AND TREMBLING."

This of necessity implies that a great part of our salvation is still to come, and is not wrought out; that much needs still be done in order to wean us from the present world, and meeten us for heaven.

1. There is much *remaining ignorance* in us, which needs to be removed. We have not yet learned to think of ourselves as we ought to think, nor of God and spiritual things as we ought. We know but in part, and see as through a glass darkly. We have made but little proficiency in divine knowledge; there are heights and depths which we have not explored.

2. Much *remaining depravity* in our hearts, many unmortified affections and lusts. There is in us a great deal of pride and vanity, love of the world, impatience and fretfulness under the dispensations of Providence, and a thousand evils which daily beset us. How important then that we watch, and pray, and strive; that we embrace every opportunity of serving the Lord, and do whatsoever our hands find to do with all our might. We are like the Israelites when they entered Canaan: we have innumerable difficulties to overcome, a host of enemies to subdue, before we can possess the land; and it is by little and little that we shall drive them out.

3. There are numerous *temptations and snares* that still await us: many as we have already escaped, there are still more in reserve. Satan will be working against us, the world will still be opposing us, and providences will still be trying. We shall need therefore great exertions, great grace, and great patience, to bear all, to overcome all, and endure to the end.—Ephes. vi. 13.

II. THE ENCOURAGEMENT GIVEN US: "FOR IT IS GOD THAT WORKETH IN YOU BOTH TO WILL AND TO DO OF HIS GOOD PLEASURE."

1. Consider *the goodness of God* in "working in us." He might have left us to get through as well as we could, and given us up to our own vileness.— — —If a nation were enslaved, and a prince sent a powerful army to their assistance, it would encourage them to renewed exertions to obtain their freedom. How much more the aid which God has promised in the spiritual warfare, which is sufficient to make us more than conquerers through him that loved us.

2. Consider *the power of God*, and of what importance it is to have such an efficient ally.— — —When we consider the strength of our enemies, and the power of indwelling sin, we are sometimes ready to despair of obtaining the victory: but the consideration that God is on our side, and working in us as well as for us, is sufficient to animate us in the conflict, and to give us the assurance of ultimate success. Joshua xxiii. 10, Hag. ii. 4.

3. The *faithfulness of God* is also encouraging. He will not forsake the work of his own hands, but will perfect that which concerneth us, for his mercy endureth forever. Psal. cxxxviii. 8. If he excite spiritual desires, it is that they may be fulfilled; if he gives repentance, it is that it may be followed with pardon and eternal life. Psal. cxlv. 19.

4. The consideration that all is wrought in us *by the Holy Spirit*, suggests a motive to fear and trembling, as well as of humble confidence and hope. This should keep us from presumption, from running into evil, or letting down our watch. If God depart from us, or withdraw the influence

of his grace, we shall perish like Samson in the midst of the Philistines. It is only by diligence and watchfulness, that we may expect God to work in us to will and to do of his good pleasure.

How lamentably deficient is that system of religion, which finds no place for the renewing influence of the Holy Ghost! It is like the earth on which neither rain nor dew descends, but is cursed with perpetual barrenness and desolation.

Let us be careful that we do not grieve the Holy Spirit by the indulgence of self-sufficiency, to the neglect of his inspiring and sanctifying grace; always remembering that he it is who worketh all our works in us. Isaiah xxvi. 12.

YOUNG PEOPLE TO BE TAUGHT THE HOLY SCRIPTURES.

2 Tim. iii. 15.—From a child thou hast known the holy Scriptures, which are able to make thee wise unto salvation, through faith which is in Christ Jesus. [Sk.]

THE Bible has by some been represented to be a book so profoundly obscure and mysterious, that none except persons of extraordinary learning and talents, can understand it. But such a representation is a libel upon the wisdom of its Author, and is equal to saying that he has given a revelation in which to the great mass of mankind, nothing is revealed. That the Bible contains mysteries, we admit—mysteries of godliness, which angels desire to look into, but which they cannot explain; profound depths which have not yet been fathomed by any created intellect. But this is not its general character. It contains much that is easy to be understood. As in a great river, which has its deep places in which the elephant might swim, and its shallow ones in which the lamb might wade, so in the Bible, whilst there is much to employ intellects of the highest order, so also is there much on a level with minds of ordinary size, and which even a way-faring man, though a fool, may understand. The apostle, who was perfectly acquainted with the character of divine revelation, was of this judgment. Instead of telling the common people that they could not understand the Scriptures, he informs them that they may even understand his knowledge in the mystery of Christ, Eph. iii. 4. And in the text he teaches that even children may know the Scriptures. I am going to show,

I. THAT THE SCRIPTURES ARE HOLY. The *Scriptures* include all the canonical books of the Old and New Testaments. To the former of these our Lord refers, John v. 39. And to these our apostle also refers in the text, and verse following. Other books have been added to these, but they are *apocryphal*, and though some of them contain some important historical information, and a richness of moral sentiment, yet they are so mixed with puerilities and absurdities, as to demonstrate their origin not to have been divine. That the Scriptures are holy, appears,

1. *From the character of their writers.* These were not wicked men, for such God never employs to declare his statutes, Psa. l. 16. To suppose otherwise would be as absurd as to suppose that he would appoint a pure stream of water to flow through a pipe polluted with the most offensive filth. God never employs the wicked in honorable work—but as pioneers to drain

bogs—to build bridges—to remove obstructions—to inflict judgments upon the beast and the false prophet,—and to be the executioners in his moral government. To the honorable parts of his work, he appoints only his own faithful servants. And for this *most* honorable, of being the medium of communication from God to man, he chose *holy men.*

2. *From their origin.* The books of Scripture are not, strictly speaking, the production of the persons whose names they bear. They are not the fruit of their learning, or genius, or talents. They were the mere amanuenses of Jehovah; for "all Scripture is given by inspiration," 2 Tim. iii. 16. Hence they contain truth without mixture of error.

3. *From their nature and tendency.* Many bad books have been written;—books awfully demoralizing;—intended and eminently calculated to destroy every pious, and moral, and virtuously social principle; and to introduce speculative and practical atheism, comprehending every species of profligacy and licentiousness. But the Scriptures are perfectly opposite to all this. He whom they reveal as *the grand object of worship is holy,* Isa. vi. 3. *His precepts are holy,* Psa. xix. 7, 8. The *sanctions* by which they are *enforced,* whether rewards or punishments, are *all promotive of holiness. His people are holy*—separated from common or sinful purposes, and set apart for God, 1 Pet. ii. 9. And the heaven which they reveal, and to which the faithful shall at last be received, is a *holy place.*

II. That the holy Scriptures may be known by young people.—Timothy had known them from a child; but as there does not appear to have been any thing in the intellectual character of Timothy, which distinguished him from others, is it fair to conclude that what *he* knew may be known by persons *now* of the same age. But to know them, we must,

1. *Be able to read them.* I do not mean, *able to read them* in the original, for though such ability has its advantages, they are not so great as some would-be linguists pretend. Linguists who are modest, will not say, that "they can furnish a better translation than we already possess." Unless we can read our own language, even this Bible thus translated will be a sealed book. There have been times when the art of reading was the privilege only of a few. Now all may acquire it, both rich and poor. The latter, if they cannot acquire it any where else, may acquire it in a Sunday School. We must,

2. *Read them in order, with deep attention and prayer.* It has been said, that "few books are more read than the Bible, and few, if any, are so little understood." It is a melancholy fact, that many who read the Scriptures, are scandalously ignorant of their sacred import. This arises partly from the *absurd* and *irregular* manner in which they search them. Instead of reading any sacred book consecutively, as they would a human composition, they read a chapter *here,* and a chapter or part of a chapter *there,* without any kind of reference either to the preceding, or intermediate, or subsequent parts. To understand them, *they must be read in regular order.—They must be read with deep attention.—The several parts must be compared*—the law with the gospel—types with their antitypes—predictions with their fulfilment. *We must avail ourselves of such helps as are within our reach*—such as ministers—well informed christians—and the works of pious and learned commentators. Above all *we must read in the spirit of prayer* for divine illumination—a sound judgment—a teachable spirit—a tenacious memory—sanctified affections—and an obedient will. To expect to become profitably acquainted with the Scriptures in any other way is enthusiasm. We proceed to show,

III. **That the knowledge of the holy Scriptures is infinitely important.** Knowledge in some cases is hurtful—in others useless—or beneficial only in particular circumstances—or its benefits are only temporary. But *this* is saving—embraces all circumstances—and extends its benefits through the whole of our existence. *The Scriptures are able to make us wise unto salvation, through faith which is in Christ Jesus.*

1. *They reveal our want of salvation.* Man sinned, Gen. iii. Through sin he forfeited the divine favor, and lost the moral image of his Creator. The forfeiture extended to all his posterity.—Hence all are *born* in sin, Psa. li. 5. All are *prone* to sin, Gen. viii. 21; Psa. xiv. 1. And hence also the seeds of mortality are sown in all, which in due time ripen into death.

2. *They reveal a Saviour.* The descriptions which they give of this Saviour, show that in him are united the divine and human natures. Of him are sometimes predicted things which can alone belong to the divinity, John i. 1, 3; Rom. ix. 5; Col. ii. 8; Rev. i. 8. At other times, those which belong only to the humanity. Such are all those texts which relate to his birth, progress in knowledge—sufferings—death, &c.—admit the twofold nature, and these are easily harmonized; reject it, and to harmonize them will be for ever impossible. Such a Saviour being infinite in wisdom, power, and goodness, must be all-sufficient.

3. *They reveal the method of salvation.* 1. *Through the death of Christ*—*Intimated* in Gen. iii. 15.—*Typified* in the offering up of Isaac, Gen. xxii.—By the various sacrifices under the law, Heb. x.—*Clearly predicted*, Psa. xl. 6—8, compared with Heb. x. 5—10; Isa. liii. Dan. ix. 26, 27.—The original law required death in case of transgression.—Christ, in dying, complied with that requisition;—declared the righteousness of God;—and obtained the remission of sins for all who have faith in his blood, Rom. iii. 25. 2. *Through faith in Christ.* The passage just quoted clearly teaches this.—Faith is the grand condition of the gospel, Mark xvi. 16; Acts xiii. 39, xvi. 31; Rom. v. 1. Without reference to Christ, and faith in him, the Old Testament Scriptures, to which our text refers, not only cannot make us wise to salvation, but the *typical*, *ceremonial*, and *prophetical* parts cannot be understood.—*Without Christ* these are destitute of meaning;—*with him* they furnish *saving instruction.*

4. *They reveal the extent of salvation.* *To all people*, Gen. xxii. 18; Luke ii. 10. *To all cases*, Isa. i. 18.—*The complete salvation of the soul from sin*—its guilt, love, power, pollution;—and of the body from the grave, and the eternal glorification of both.

From hence learn,

1. The importance of a personal acquaintance with the Scriptures.
2. The duty of parents in reference to their children.
3. The great utility of Sunday Schools.

DAVID'S ATTENTION TO HIS HOUSEHOLD.

1 Chron. xvi. 43.—And David returned to bless his house. (H. H.)

It is truly delightful to see the operation of religion on the soul of man; how it transforms him from a carnal and selfish creature, into a spiritual and heavenly Being, who, like the sun in the firmament, steadily pursues his course, and shines brighter and brighter unto the perfect day. Beautifully was it exemplified by David in the history before us; in illustration of which we shall notice,

1. The work in which he had been engaged—

This was, the bringing up of the ark from the house of Obed-edom to Jerusalem: and,

A glorious work it was—

In itself, it was a work of vast importance. For many years had the ark lain in obscurity at Kirjath-jearin, without any application being made to it for instruction from God. But, when brought up to Jerusalem, it would be accessible at all times; and, in all difficult emergencies, the will of Jehovah might be learned from it. Indeed, the whole account respecting it shews us clearly, in what light it was viewed by the nation at large — — —

As a typical act, its importance rises still higher in our estimation. It was undoubtedly typical of Christ's ascension into heaven; for in that view it is spoken of in a great variety of Psalms, Ps. xxiv. xlvii. lxviii. cxxxii., and in that view the Psalms relating to it are quoted in the New Testament. Compare Ps. lxviii. 18, with Eph. iv. 8. Let other Psalms, from the 96th to 99th, be read as referring to both these events, and they will fully illustrate the importance of the work which David had just completed— — —

And it had been performed in a manner most acceptable unto God—

In its commencement, it was begun by consulting all the great men in the nation, who were stirred up to concur in it, ch. xiii. 1—3,— — —In its progress, nothing was left to human invention, as before; but all was conducted with the strickest attention to God's revealed will. Nor did David commit the service altogether to others: no; he himself attended the procession, and played and sang with all his might; yea, and danced also before the ark with such holy ecstasies, as to subject himself to the scorn and censure of his own wife; who being a stranger to those divine raptures, imputed them, not to pious fervor, but to indecent wantonness. But his joyous exultation was such as the occasion required, and such as, though condemned by Michal, was most pleasing unto God.

Having seen the service to which he had gone forth, we proceed to notice,

II. The work to which he returned—

Though he might be well supposed at the conclusion of his service to need repose, yet he went home only to protract his labors in another way He returned to bless his house; that is,

1. To obtain blessings for them by his prayers—

He would not confine his religious exercises to public occasions, but went home to stir up in his family those blessed emotions with which his own soul was filled. He was anxious that all his wives, his children, and his servants should be partakers of his joy: and therefore he would unite with them in fervent supplication to the God of all grace, that they might themselves "know the Lord from the least even to the greatest of them," and all experience the blessedness of his salvation.

Here we behold a bright example, which it behoves us all to follow. Family prayer is, alas! too often neglected, or at best but coldly performed, by many, who profess a high regard for public ordinances: but the true child of Abraham will "command his house and children after him to fear the Lord," Gen. xviii. 19, and will say with Joshua, "Whatsoever others may do, I and my house will serve the Lord." Josh. xxiv. 15. If we have family wants, and family mercies, we should unite our prayers and our praises with our families, that God may be acknowledged as the one source from whence all good either has issued, or can be hoped for: and though we can easily imagine circumstances wherein such domestic services are impracticable, yet we cannot imagine any real piety to exist where such duties are wilfully neglected.

2. To render himself a blessing to them by his conduct—

It was promised to Abraham that he should not only be blessed himself, but be a blessing also to others: and this promise is in fact made to all the believing seed of Abraham. To make others happy was no small part of David's ambition. Hence he went to his house determining to contribute as far as possible to the edification and comfort of all connected with him. He would instruct the ignorant; and teach, not by precept only, but by example also. His determination was to "walk before his house in a perfect way" Psa. ci. 2,— — —He would not be proud, or imperious, or passionate, or fretful; but would regulate all his tempers and dispositions by the golden rule, of doing as he would be done unto: and "the law of kindness would be ever in his lips."

How different is this from the conduct of many, who from the public ordinances, in which they profess to take delight, go down to their houses to make them wretched and miserable, rather than to bless them! O let the professors of religion look well to this: for, as a consistent christian is a blessing wherever he goes, so an inconsistent christian is a curse, and a stumbling-block to all around him.

Learn then from hence,

1. How highly we are privileged—

The ark, even the Lord Jesus Christ himself, is present in the midst of us. To him we may have access; and of him we may inquire continually: and every blessing which was typically derived from the symbol of his presence, shall be really and spiritually obtained by all who seek him. If then David and the whole kingdom of Israel felt such exalted joy in the possession of that which was a mere shadow, let us not be unmindful of our privilege in possessing the substance.

2. In what way we should improve our privileges—

Let us not only rejoice in them ourselves, but endeavor to communicate the benefit of them to others. Let all who see us, be the better for us; and all who stand in any relation to us be constrained to say, that "God is with us of a truth."

THE APOSTOLIC MINISTRY.

Colossians i. 28.—Whom we preach, warning every man, and teaching every man in all wisdom; that we may present every man perfect in Christ Jesus. (Pr.)

It is one of the peculiar characteristics of the Messiah's reign, that under it the poor should have the gospel preached to them. The truth was taught in various ways before, but from hence a multitude of heralds should be sent forth to proclaim the good news of salvation.

——— The model of this practice is to be looked for in the New Testament; and in the text we see that there were three things especially pertaining to the Apostolic ministry.

I. The leading theme of it was Christ: "Whom we preach."

Preaching Christ, and the cross of Christ, is emphatically called "the gospel," 1 Cor. xv. 2—3; and "the record which God hath given of his Son." 1 John v. 11. ——— The hearers of this gospel wanted something else: "the Jews require a sign, and the Greeks seek after wisdom; but we preach Christ crucified." 1 Cor. i. 22, 23.

In justification of this practice, let us consider some of the cases to which the subject will apply—

1. There may be some who have lately been brought to a sense of *their sin and danger*, and may be come with some such question as that which filled the heart of the Phillippian jailer. ——— We preach Christ as the only hope, the only refuge of the lost.

2. Another may feel unhappy because he cannot perceive *how God can forgive sin*, consistently with justice and faithfulness. ——— The cross of Christ is the only solution of this difficulty, the only place where God and the sinner can meet and be reconciled.

3. Another having long been under conviction, is now *reformed:* he reads, and hears, and prays; but can find *no rest to his soul.* ——— Christ only is the way, and he only can give him rest. Jer. vi. 16. Matt. xi. 28.

4. Some are full of *doubts and fears*, and want to obtain an interest in the promise of eternal life. ——— We preach Christ: and if this be nothing to you, you will find nothing else to do you any real good. But if the way of salvation by him is welcome to your soul, you may dismiss your fears, for all is yours.

5. Another is bowed down under *the ills and burdens of life*, and is ready to despond and say, I shall never see good. ——— Look to Jesus, lest ye be weary and faint in your minds; consider his sorrows, and forget you own. Heb. xii. 2, 3.

6. Another is *hungering for the bread of life*, and longing to be edified and comforted. ——— The same doctrine which at first relieved us, will afterwards do to live upon, and nothing but Christ and him crucified will do us any real good. John vi. 57, 58.

7. It may be that some are *thoughtless and careless* under the word, still in a state of impenitence and unbelief. ——— But whether they will hear, or whether they will forbear, we must still go on preaching Christ and him crucified. This only is the power of God unto salvation, and this it is that furnishes motives both for repentance and faith. Isai. xlvi. 12, 13. Acts iv. 12. Rom. i. 16.

8. Some are *righteous in their own eyes*, are full, and have need of nothing; and know not that they are poor, and wretched, and blind, and naked.

——— And what can destroy these vain hopes, and lay the sinner in the dust, but the exhibition of an able and all-sufficient Saviour, and of mercy undeserved. Isai. lv. 1. Rev. iii. 17, 18.

II. The practical manner in which the apostles preached this important doctrine: "WARNING EVERY MAN, AND TEACHING EVERY MAN IN ALL WISDOM."

Warning and teaching is in some respect distinct from preaching the gospel, which properly speaking consists in proclaiming the good news of salvation; yet it is a necessary appendage to it, and essential to the christian ministry. Some men under a pretence of preaching the gospel, have neglected it, and some have denounced it as legal; but it ought to suffice for us that the apostles, in preaching Christ, "warned every man, and taught every man in all wisdom."

1. They *warned every man.* Warning is an expression of kind regard: "as my beloved sons," says Paul to the Galatians, "I warn you." Those for whom we have no regard, we generally let alone, and suffer them to have their own way. ——— Now the Scriptures makes use of warning in many cases, and we are required to do the same.—1 Where persons are in *a wrong road,* love will apprise them of it, and warn them of the danger. Exek. xxxiii. 8.—2 Where they are in a condition which exposes them to *ruin,* love will warn them to make their escape and to flee from the wrath to come. Matt. iii. 7.—3 Where men enjoy privileges and advantages which they have no heart to improve, they ought to be warned of the consequences, and exhorted to immediate repentance. Acts xiii. 41. ——— These warnings are no other than the dictates of common prudence and benevolence, and can never be excluded from any thing like a rational exercise of the christian ministry.

2. The apostles *taught every man* in all wisdom, instructing them in the first principles of the oracles of God, giving them right views of their own character and condition as sinners, and showing them the suitableness and ability of Christ as a Saviour. ——— Such also must be our labor, both in the pulpit and out of it, showing unto men the way of salvation. They are to be taught the evils they are to shun, and the good they are to choose; and this in order to their being brought to Christ, as the last and only refuge of the miserable and undone.

III. The end which the apostles had in view in the exercise of their ministry, and that is the salvation of their hearers, or "THAT THEY MIGHT PRESENT EVERY MAN PERFECT IN CHRIST JESUS."

They did not content themselves with forming the manners of their hearers nor merely with warning and teaching them: if not brought savingly to believe in Christ, they reckoned nothing to be done to any purpose. Gal. iv. 19

But how was Paul to present "every man perfect in Christ Jesus?" Did he hope to save all that heard him? Viewing them *collectively* he did not, for he knew that only a remnant would be saved. Acts xv. 14. Rom. xi. 14. But considering them *individually* he hoped for every man, and labored for their salvation.

God is not obliged to do all he is able to do to save sinners, though we are; and not knowing his counsel or design, it is for us to do our utmost, and leave the event to him. John xx. 30, 31, Rom. ix. 1—3, xi. 14.

We learn from hence, that the employment of Christ's faithful servants is to win souls to him, and it shall be their honor in the last day to present to him the fruits of their ministry. 2 Cor. xi. 2.

If this end be not answered, nothing is effected, and we shall lose our reward. A barren ministry is one of the greatest evils to be dreaded upon earth, and its consequences will be tremendous in the world to come. Ezek. xxxiv. 10. Zech. xi. 17. Matt. xxv. 30.

IMPORTANCE OF PREACHING CHRIST CRUCIFIED.

Gal. iii. 1.—Before whose eyes Jesus Christ hath been evidently set forth, crucified among you. (Pr.)

UNDER any circumstances it is both sinful and unwise to turn away from the truth as it is in Jesus; it bespeaks us blind to our own interest, as well as regardless of the glory of God. But that which rendered such conduct inexcusable in the Galatians, was the degree of evidence with which the gospel was attended, and the abundance of evangelical preaching which they enjoyed. It had been the great object of the apostles' ministry to set forth Christ, and perhaps they had done this more especially to the Galatians; so that though they had never seen Christ in the flesh, yet with such advantages as they possessed, it was as if they had actually seen him.

I. ENDEAVOR TO ASCERTAIN THE IMPORT OF THE TERMS EMPLOYED IN THE TEXT.

By "setting forth Christ crucified," is not meant a setting forth merely his bodily sufferings, or giving a tragical description of his agony in the garden or on the cross, The evangelists never attempt any thing of this kind in their narrative: on the contrary they state the circumstances with great brevity and simplicity, without any coloring or reflections of their own.—The principal reason is, that however great the sufferings which our Lord endured, the virtue of atonement did not consist in the degree of suffering, but in the dignity of him that suffered. Such a representation may indeed affect the passions, but other views of the subject are more edifying and more useful.

1. Christ is set forth in the gospel as *the great propitiation, by which God's righteousness might appear in the remission of sins.* Rom. iii. 25. ——— It was evident that God had pardoned the sins of old testament believers, and taken them to heaven, long before the true sacrifice was offered up; the righteousness of God's conduct was therefore in some degree implicated, and it was needful that it should be thoroughly cleared up. The gospel, by setting forth the death of Christ as an atonement for sin, makes a public declaration of God's righteousness, and shows at once how he can be just, and yet the justifier of him that believeth in Jesus.

2. Christ is set forth as *the great expression of divine love to a sinful and perishing world.*— — —Other proofs had been given of God's love and mercy, in his long-suffering and kindness towards men; but this is the greatest of all, and infinitely surpasses all the rest. John iii. 16. If God would give an expression of his love to sinners, it became him to do it in a manner suited to the unbounded goodness of his natnre; and herein he hath commended his love towards us. Rom. v. 8, 1 John iv. 9, 10.

3. Christ is set forth in the gospel as affording *the strongest proof of God's displeasure against sin.*— — —The wrath of God had been revealed from heaven in various forms, against the ungodliness and unrighteousness

of men; but the sufferings of Christ for us were the grand expression of God's infinite hatred of sin. In him sin was openly and publicly condemned, when he was made a curse for us. Rom. viii. 3, Gal. iii. 13.

4. Christ crucified is set forth as *the only foundation of a sinner's hope.* — — —It is the tenor and import of the whole gospel, that there is salvation in no other. As the brazen serpent was exhibited to the Israelites for their healing, even so is a crucified Saviour exhibited to us as the only medium of life and salvation. Here it is that sinners must look, and from hence alone derive their hope of acceptance with God. John i. 29, iii. 14, 15.

5. The terms in the text further denote, *the high degree of evidence which attended the ministry of the apostles*, especially among the Galatians.— — —Christ was "set forth" of old by promises, by types, and prophecies; but all this was dark and obscure. Sinners are now directed to behold the Lamb of God, and we all with open face behold, as in a glass, the glory of the Lord. There was a peculiar plainness in the preaching of the apostles, and Christ was "evidently" set forth, crucified among them. It was now shown that types and prophecies received their accomplishment in Jesus, and the fullest possible demonstration attended it. Hence those who hear the gospel are the more sinful and inexcusable, in not obeying the truth, and receiving it in love.

II. Consider the importance of setting forth Christ in the preaching of the gospel.

It was the substance of the apostolic ministry to exhibit a crucified Saviour. Paul would glory in nothing else, and determined to know nothing else; all their preaching was called, "a preaching of Christ to the people."— — — It is also a principal part of the work of the Holy Spirit to take of the things of Christ, and show them unto us; it should therefore be the great object of the christian ministry to co-operate with this design. Three important ends in particular are answered by it—

1. To exhibit Christ crucified *will tend to prove the hearts of men*, and make them manifest; and nothing besides has so direct a tendency to do it. — — —If we have any real love to God, any love to righteousness, to the souls of men, or to our own souls, the doctrine of the cross will make it evident. We shall immediately feel and discover a peculiar relish for it, it will be to us as a savor of life unto life, and the name of Jesus will be as ointment poured forth.— — —If destitute of love to God and man, and all virtuous affection, the doctrine of the cross will be to us a savor of death unto death. The preaching of Christ crucified was to the Jews a stumbling-block, and to the Greeks foolishness; but to them which are saved, Christ the wisdom of God, and the power of God, 1 Cor. i. 23, 24.

2. To set forth Christ crucified is *the only way of giving peace to souls in distress for sin.*— — —When a sinner is brought under the terrors of the law, made to see and realize his guilt and danger, and to feel his need of a Saviour, he is apt to look inward for some qualification to recommend him to Christ; but to set forth a crucified Saviour is to point him to the only refuge, and to show him at once his remedy.— — —The penitent is often led to examine himself for evidences of grace in order to obtain comfort, and is as often disappointed, while the cross of Christ is overlooked. Let the sinner then direct his eyes to Jesus, and look to Calvary, for all his help must come from thence.— — —Or if we desire a more spiritual and humble frame of mind, no means are so effectual to its production as the contemplation of a crucified Redeemer. If the doctrine of the cross will make us

happy, we have great reason to be so; if it will not, there is no help for us in God.

3. To exhibit Christ crucified is the way to draw forth and *bring into exercise all the christian graces.*— — —The doctrine of the cross furnishes fresh motives for repentance, gives a direct incentive to holy love, and lays again the foundation of our hope. If this doctrine were withheld, or only occasionally exhibited, it would becloud the whole of the christian system, and deprive it of the power of healing the broken in heart.

4. The preaching of Christ crucified is that which *leaves all unbelievers without excuse.*— — —It will be impossible for those to plead ignorance of the way of salvation, "before whose eyes" this truth has been evidently set forth. If such should eventually perish, it will not be for lack of knowledge, but for want of a heart to attend to the things which belong to their everlasting peace.

EVANGELICAL PREACHING.

Acts ii. 37.—Now when they heard this they were pricked in their heart, and said unto Peter and to the rest of the Apostles, Men and brethren, what shall we do? (Sk.)

PREACHING has ever been the principal means used for diffusing a knowledge of christianity.

It was the method adopted and enjoined by the great Author of our religion, Matt. iv. 17, and x. 7; Mark xvi. 15; and that by which his apostles succeeded in making known the gospel to the very ends of the earth, Mark xvi. 20; Acts v. 42; Rom. x. 14—18.

When engaged in properly, as to its subject and manner it is ever successful in accomplishing the great end for which it was originally adopted, 1 Cor. i. 21.——A striking instance of its early success is recorded in the chapter before us; and we are led by our text to inquire into—*the nature of that preaching which was so successful; and into the effects which followed such preaching,*

I. THE NATURE OF THE PREACHING may be understood from the context.

The subject was CHRIST.——The preacher's aim evidently was, to prove that Jesus of Nazareth was the true Messiah.

To do this *he speaks of him,* verse 22, as one that had been "approved of God among them by signs and miracles;" see John iii. 2, and xiv. 10, 11, and Acts x. 38.——*He then declares,* verse 23, that this was the person delivered to death "by the determinate counsel and foreknowledge of God;" see Luke xxiv. 26, 27, and thus introduces Christ as the Saviour,—the Sacrifice for sin, Isa. liii. 10. *He next dwells on* his resurrection, and consequent exaltation; verses 24—36, and asserts that he is both *Lord* and *Christ.* These things *he confirms*—by *Scripture,* verses 25—28,—and by sound *argument,* verses 29—36.

The *subject* was of the highest importance;——it was perfectly suitable to the audience;——

And the manner of treating it was excellent. The *discussion* was plain—concise—clear.——The *mode of address* was evidently courageous and bold.—It was such, as being equally removed from impertinence and self-confidence on the one hand, and from the fear of man on the other, such as becomes those whom God employs to speak in his name: see Prov. xxix 25; Jer. i. 17.

The *preacher* who *thus* conducted himself, demands our consideration. It was PETER, a late fisherman of Galilee, Matt. iv. 18—20, one of the lower class of society.——PETER, a poor man, who said, "Silver and gold have I none," chap. iii. 5.——PETER, whose mind had never been stored nor expanded by the knowledge of the schools.——But *Peter*, who had learned of the Lord Jesus, the Teacher who came from God, John iii. 2: he was well acquainted with the holy Scriptures;—he knew the truth experimentally;—his soul was filled with the Holy Ghost;—he had good natural sense;—he was *divinely* called to preach the Gospel;—and *thus* qualified, he preached;—power from above attended the word.

II. AND THE EFFECTS WHICH FOLLOWED well deserve our attention.

"*They were pricked in their heart.*" Hearers treat the word preached with indifference;—or feeling its force, they resist it;—or happily, like those whose case is before us, they yield to its convincing influence. These were pricked in their heart; see Heb. iv. 12. The address was made to their understanding,—their judgment,—their conscience; and being accompanied by the power of divine grace, they were rationally, Scripturally, and feelingly convinced of the error of their ways;

"*And said to Peter and to the rest of the apostles, Men and brethren, what shall we do?*" We may consider this as

The language of religious concern. They now perceived the vileness of their hearts; and the wickedness of their conduct; and the great crime of slighting, rejecting, and crucifying the Lord Jesus. particularly affected them. They saw the danger of their situation, and were alarmed about the consequences, see chap. ix. 6. Hence we cannot but view it too, as

The language of religious distress. In all cases where sinners are brought to a state of proper concern about their souls, that concern is accompanied by distress, on account of their having offended God, neglected the blessed Saviour,—grieved the Holy Spirit,—and ruined themselves; see Jer. xxxi. 18, 19; Zech. xii. 10. Such are anxious to know how they may "flee from the wrath to come;" how they may obtain salvation from sin here, and from its consequences hereafter; see Acts xvi. 30. We may therefore consider this, as

The language of humble inquiry. Such an inquiry, from such a people, is truly striking. Think on their former prejudices;—the contempt in which they had held Jesus and his followers; the probability that there were among those who thus exclaimed, some of the higher classes,—priests at least, chap. vi. 7; and it must be acknowledged, that on this occasion, the power of divine grace to convince and to humble was singularly astonishing. And we learn from the subsequent verses, that this grace was no less powerful and conspicuous, in raising there, thousands of broken-hearted penitents, from a state of godly sorrow to that of holy joy.

Such was the preaching, and such were the effects.

Our minds are farther led to the following improvement.

CHRIST CRUCIFIED *is, and ever should be, the grand subject of the Christian Ministry.* The Lord Jesus commanded his apostles to preach in *his* name; see ch. xxiv. 47. They *began* thus, as we have now seen. Thus they *continued;* see chap. iii. 12, and iv. 5—12, and v. 30, and viii. 5, 35, and ix. 20, and x. 34—43, and xi. 20, &c.—to chap. xxviii., *They preached thus* to Jews and Gentiles, 1 Cor. i. 23, 24.

There is salvation in no other,—there is no other name whereby we can be saved, chap. iv. 12. JESUS,—his Deity,—his Incarnation,—his spotless Life,—his sacrificial Death,—his Resurrection, and Intercession; JESUS, who is the author and finisher of faith,—should be, with ministers, "the first and the last,"—"all, and in all." *Most* of our discourses should be of *him* and *his salvation*;—and *none* of them should be without a voice to say, "Behold the Lamb of God!"

We are also taught to adapt our discourse to our audience;—and boldly to declare the whole counsel of God; fearing the face of no man; see Jer. i 7, 8; Ezek. ii. 6, 7.

In religion, it is of the utmost importance that the heart be affected; ("they were pricked in their hearts;") see Gen. vi. 5; Jer. xvii. 7; Joel ii. 13; Mark vii. 21; Prov. iv. 23; Psa. li. 10, 17. Sin hath its seat in the heart;—*there* the change should begin: to be effectual, it *must* begin there. ——A mere change of sentiments,—of opinions,—of profession, will avail nothing; see chap. viii. 9, 13, 18, 23.

Persons may be so affected on account of their sin and danger, that they cannot, in some cases, avoid strongly expressing what they feel. While, therefore, we cautiously guard against, and check every thing in religious profession which is unscriptural, and that would lead to disorder and confusion; we should be fully aware that there may *still* be cases in which persons religiously affected cannot help saying, "Men and brethren, What shall we do?"

The essential importance of divine influence to render the word preached successful is another idea suggested by the circumstances connected with the text. Could any argument, any eloquence of Peter's, unaccompanied by the power of divine grace, have prevailed to awaken the consciences,—to bear down the prejudices,—and to subdue the pride of those who heard him? And can preachers in our day succeed without such influence? see John xv. 5; 1 Cor. iii. 6. Though the miracle-working power of the Holy Ghost is no longer necessary to give sanction to the supernatural doctrine of salvation by faith in a *crucified Saviour*, because *such* sanction has long since been sufficient; yet the power of the Holy Ghost to assist God's ministers in their great work, and to convert and save sinners, *is ever alike necessary*, and is promised even to the end of the world, Matt. xxviii. 20; John xiv. 16; Luke xi. 13.

In the discharge of their sacred duty, let the preachers of the Gospel always seek,—always expect divine aid;—and ever look for some success. ——And though that success may not always be such as they desired, yet, doing God's work in a right disposition. they may safely console themselves with these words:—"Surely my judgment is with the Lord, and my work with my God," Isa. xlix. 4.

CHRISTIAN MINISTERS, AND THEIR WORK.

Acts xvi. 17.—These men are the servants of the most high God, which show unto us the way of salvation. (Sk.)

FROM the context we learn, that Paul and Silas were directed by a vision to go to Macedonia, ver. 6—12. Lydia, being converted to God at Philippi, received them into her house, ver. 13, 15; from whence they were followed by a female, possessed with a spirit of divination, who cried, saying, "These men," &c. This testimony, though true, had a tendency to lessen their authority, as the natural inference was, that they were in league with her. The apostle Paul, seeing it in all its bearings, expelled the demon; which occasioned violent persecution, ver. 16—24. The words of our text, however, are true, full, clear, and distinct; let us, therefore, notice,

I. THE IMPORTANT WORK OF CHRISTIAN MINISTERS; viz. to show unto mankind the way of salvation; in doing which, it is necessary that they should,

1. *Define the nature of this salvation.* It is spiritual, and imports, 1. A deliverance from *contracted guilt.* The design of the gospel is to give a knowledge of salvation by the remission of sins, Luke i. 77. Hence Peter and his coadjutors, when brought before the Sanhedrim at Jerusalem, asserted that "Jesus whom the Jews had crucified, God had exalted with his right hand to be a Prince, and a Saviour," &c., Acts v. 31; and Paul, preaching at Antioch, said, "Be it known unto you, therefore, men and brethren, that through this man is preached unto you the forgiveness of sin," &c., Acts xiii. 38, 39. 2. *The bondage of sin;* hence the gospel is the power of God to salvation, Rom. i. 16; delivering the believer from the dominion of sin, Rom. vi. 22; and empowering his feebleness to do "the good and acceptable, and perfect will of God," Rom. viii. 2, 3. 3. *Its moral pollution,* Tit. iii. 5; in which text the apostle shows that we are saved by the washing of regeneration, &c.; while John asserts, "If we walk in the light as he is in the light, we have fellowship one with another, and the blood of Jesus Christ his Son cleanseth us from all sin," 1 John i. 5. 4. *Its fatal consequences;* in the everlasting happiness of the soul. Believers are kept by the power of God through faith unto salvation," 1 Pet. i. 5; and to such Jesus will appear the second time without sin unto salvation, Heb. ix. 28. So that it imports, not only a deliverance from all moral evil and its consequences, but it secures the enjoyment of grace here, and glory hereafter, Rev. xii. 10.

2. *Develope its source;*—The pure, disinterested, unmerited, unparalleled, and unsolicited mercy of God, John iii. 16. In contemplating the scheme of redemption, which originated in the eternal mind, we may exclaim, in the language of John, "Behold *what manner* of love the Father hath bestowed upon us," 1 John iii. 1. Such love as this furnishes a subject for the everlasting contemplation of men and angels.

3. *Proclaim its Author;*—the Lord Jesus Christ: for so hath the Lord said, "I have set thee to be a light of the Gentiles, that thou shouldest be for salvation to the ends of the earth," Acts xiii. 47. "And being made perfect, he became the Author of eternal salvation unto all them that obey him," Heb. v. 9. "God hath appointed us to obtain salvation by our Lord Jesus Christ," 1 Thess. v. 9. "Neither is there salvation in any other," Acts iv. 12.

4. *Point out its necessity;*—By showing the *nature* of sin, 1 John iii. 4;—its *source,* Mark vii. 21, 22;—its *universal dominion,* Rom. v. 12, iii. 10—19;—and the irrevocable decree of God, Luke xiii. 3; John iii. 3; Heb. ii. 3, xii. 14.

5. *Explain its appointed method;*—1. *Repentance,* Mark i. 15;—originating in conviction of sin, Rom. vii. 9;—accompanied by sorrow for sin, 2 Cor. vii. 10;—manifested by reformation from sin, Luke xix. 8;—and expressed in ardent prayer to God, Luke xviii. 13. 2. *Faith towards our Lord Jesus Christ,* Acts xx. 21;—faith in his person and offices, importing

a full reliance in his merits for pardon and acceptance, Rom. iii. 24, 25:—living faith, which subjects the soul to Christ in the way of obedience, Gal. v. 6.

II. THEIR HIGH DESIGNATION;—"Servants of the most high God:" which imports,

1. *That their commission is from God.* To them he has said, "Go ye into all the world, and preach the gospel to every creature," &c., Mark xvi. 18. And their reply to the church is the language of the apostle, Eph. iii. 8. They are servants, "having this treasure in earthen vessels, that the excellency of the power may be of God," 2 Cor. iv. 7. Hence they can say, "as we were allowed of God to be put in trust with the gospel, even so we speak; not as pleasing men, but God, which trieth our hearts," 1 Thess. ii. 4.

2. *Their supplies are divine.* Their Master hath said, "Lo, I am with you alway, even unto the end of the world," Matt. xxviii. 20. In seasons of discouragement he says, "My grace is sufficient for thee," 2 Cor. xii. 9;—"Go to all that I shall send thee, and whatsoever I command thee, thou shalt speak. Be not afraid of their faces; for I am with thee to deliver thee, saith the Lord," Jer. i. 8.

3. *Their success is from God.* A minister may be sound in his judgment, orthodox in his creed, logical in his definitions, correct in his enunciation, rhetorical in his discourses, pathetic in his appeals, powerful in his application, and yet unsuccessful in winning souls; "Paul may plant, and Apollos water, but God giveth the increase," 1 Cor. iii. 7. St. Paul, who was chief of the apostles, felt this, when he said, "Brethren, pray for us, that the word of the Lord may have free course, and be glorified," 2 Thess. iii. 1. Ministers are God's servants,—to their own Master they stand or fall; they devoutly acknowledge the good done on earth, the Lord alone does it; hence their appeals to God for the aid of the Holy Ghost, without whom "nothing is wise, or strong, or good." It remains for us, therefore, to notice,

III. THE DUTY OF THOSE AMONG WHOM PROVIDENCE MAY DIRECT THEIR LABORS; which is,

1. *To receive their message.* "Whosoever," said Christ to his disciples, "shall not receive you nor hear your words, when ye depart out of that house or city, shake off the dust of your feet," &c., Matt. x. 14, 15. Need we wonder that our Lord should say, "Take heed how ye hear?" Luke viii. 18. Let no man trifle with God's message, however feeble the instrument who has delivered it.

2. *Support their characters.* "Against an elder receive not an accusation but before two or three witnesses," 1 Tim. v. 19:—"Touch not mine anointed, and do my prophets no harm," 1 Chron. xvi. 22.

3. *Respect their office.* "And we beseech you, brethren, to know them which labor among you, and are over you in the Lord, and admonish you; and esteem them very highly in love, for their works' sake," 1 Thess. v 12, 13.

4. *Supply their wants.* "For if the Gentiles have been made partakers of their spiritual things, their duty is also to minister to them in carnal things," Rom. xv. 27; 1 Tim. v. 17; 1 Cor. ix. 1—10.

5. *Facilitate their labors.* This you should do by, 1. *Your prayers*, Eph. vi. 18, 19; 1 Thess. v. 25; 2. *Your influence*, in its weight and extent.

APPLICATION.

To you is the word of this salvation sent. Have you received the truth? Do you enjoy the salvation of the gospel? If you have not obeyed the gospel, how awful your state! 1 Pet. iv. 17. "Repent ye, therefore, and be converted, that your sins may be blotted out, when the times of refreshing shall come from the presence of the Lord."

OFFICE AND RESPONSIBILITY OF MINISTERS.

Ezek. xxxiii. 8.—When I say unto the wicked, O wicked man, thou shalt surely die! if thou dost not speak to warn the wicked from his way, that wicked man shall die in his iniquity; but his blood will I require at thy hand. (H. H.)

The office of a Minister is the most important and most difficult of any that we can be called to sustain. It is the most important, because the salvation of multitudes depends upon it: and it is the most difficult, because it requires such self-denying habits, and spiritual affections. The responsibility also that attaches to it is such, that no man would dare to take it upon himself, if he had not a promise of peculiar assistance in the discharge of it. Ministers are the messengers of God to men: to them they must faithfully declare his whole counsel: however painful the truths may be which they are to deliver, and however averse men may be to hear them, they must execute their commission at the peril of their souls. To this effect God speaks in the words before us: in which we may notice,

I. What God saith to the wicked—

It is scarcely possible to conceive a more solemn declaration than that before us: "I say unto the wicked, O wicked man, thou shalt surely die!" Consider,

1. Who are the people addressed—

These are all who do not unfeignedly turn from sin to God. It matters not whether they be rich or poor, old or young, learned or unlearned. In some sense, it matters not whether their sins have been more or less heinous: for though there certainly are degrees of guilt, and some are more wicked than others, yet all are wicked, who are not following after God in righteousness and true holiness; and consequently, all such persons, however their characters may vary in other respects, are addressed in the text.

2. The declaration of God unto them—

Death is here denounced as the judgment to be inflicted on all who turn not to their God: and to the same effect the Inspired Writers uniformly speak, Isa. iii. 11, Rom. vi. 23, Jam. i. 14, 15. Nor are we at a loss to determine what is meant by "death:" it is the wrath of God, Rom. i. 18, the misery of hell, Rev. xxi. 8. This is the judgment that will come upon every individual who shall be found in the state before described. God may be considered as addressing himself to every individual of the human race; "O *thou* wicked man!" Nor is this fatal result of wickedness expressed in doubtful terms: there is no peradventure; the decree is fixed; "Thou shalt *surely* die!" Who can reflect on these words as proceeding from a God of infinite power and of inviolable truth, and not tremble?

3. The condition implied in that declaration—

If there were no condition implied in the declaration, it would have been to no purpose to make known the declaration itself; since it could have no other effect than to torment men before their time. But as in the message to Nineveh, "that in forty days Nineveh should be overthrown," there was an implied condition, that, if they repented, the threatened vengeance should be withheld; so, in this case, there is an implied assurance, that the wicked, if they will repent, shall not die. And this is expressly stated in the following context: ver. 14—16, so that, awful as this passage is, it is no less encouraging than it is awful; because it assures the contrite and believing sinner that he shall never perish.

Together with this warning, we see in the text,

II. The necessity imposed on Ministers to proclaim it—

Ministers are described as watchman, or sentinels, placed at a distance from the camp to give notice of the enemy's approach. Now this very character marks both their duty and their responsibility. But the consequences of neglect in any Minister are declared in two respects:

1. The person whom he neglects to warn, will perish—

If through the sloth or treachery of the sentinels a camp be surprised at midnight, nothing but confusion and ruin can ensue. Thus, if a person appointed to warn the wicked, neglect to do so, the wicked will continue regardless of their impending doom, till it is too late to avert it. And when the hour of vengeance is come, it will be to no purpose to say, "I was not aware of my danger; my Minister has betrayed me." No; the wicked have means of information within their own reach, independent of their Ministers; and they have secret intimations in their own consciences that they ought to repent: and therefore they must take the conseqences of their own wickedness: "they must die in their iniquity." How awful is this effect of one Minister's supineness! Alas! that hundreds, and perhaps thousands, should perish eternally, when, if he had warned them faithfully, they might have been saved for ever!

2. He himself also will be dealt with as the author of that sinner's destruction—

As a sentinel who, by neglecting to give notice of the enemy's approach, occasioned the overthrow of the army to which he belonged, would be chargeable with all the consequences of his neglect, so will the blood of all that perish through the Minister's neglect "be required at his hand." When they shall all stand before God, he will ask of the Minister, Why didst thou not warn that man, and him, and him, and him? It will be to no purpose to say, "Lord, he was rich, and I was afraid of his displeasure;" or, "Lord, he was poor, and I overlooked him;" or, "Lord, I was so engaged in business or pleasure, that I never thought about the souls committed to my charge." No: he must answer for every soul that perishes through his means, and must sink ten-fold deeper into the bottomless abyss than the most guilty of the people whom he has neglected and betrayed.

Application—

After stating these reasons for Ministerial fidelity, we need make no apology for "warning the wicked from their way:" or rather, we need apologize for not using far greater plainness of speech than we have ever yet done.

Hear then, ye wicked, with solemn awe, the voice of God to you. "O thou wicked *drunkard*, thou shalt surely die!" "O thou wicked *whoremonger*, thou shalt surely die!" "O thou wicked *swearer*, or *Sabbath-breaker*, thou shalt surely die!" Is there any one hear that, though free from gross sins, *lives in a neglect of secret prayer;* "O thou wicked man, *thou* shalt surely die!"*— — —

But while we declare these things, we would not be unmindful of the compassion which is expressed in the very mode in which God has denounced his judgments; "O thou wicked man!" This seems to intimate, that God is grieved for the misery of the wicked, even while he declares the doom that awaits them. So would we be; and the rather, because we ourselves are involved in the same condemnation, if we do not repent and turn to God.

O then, brethren, whether ye have committed gross sins or not, remember that ye all need to humble yourselves before God as condemned sinners: ye all need to wash in the fountain of the Redeemer's blood: ye all need to "turn from your transgressions, that so iniquity may not be your ruin." O that God may enable you to accept this warning with all thankfulness! We have striven, as it became us, to "deliver our own souls:" the Lord grant that, in thus endeavoring to "save ourselves, we may be instrumental to save also those that hear us!" 1 Tim. iv. 16.

THE APOSTLES CHOSEN.

Luke vi. 12, 13.—And it came to pass in those days that he went out into a mountain to pray, and continued all night in prayer to God. And when it was day, he called unto him his disciples; and of them he close twelve, whom also he named apostles. (H. H.)

The short period of our Lord's ministry on earth rendered it expedient for him to employ others as his co-adjutors in the work. Accordingly, in reference to the twelve Patriarchs, who might be considered as the fathers of the Jewish Church, he selected twelve of his disciples, who should be his instruments for planting and establishing his church. There were other seventy, whom at a later period he sent forth, two and two, for the purpose of preparing the minds of the people for his personal ministry among them; Luke x. 1: but the apostles were to be his stated servants after that he should have left this world and returned to his heavenly Father. The circumstances of their appointment were peculiar, and deserve our most attentive consideration. The night previous to their appointment he spent in prayer to his heavenly Father:† which remarkable occurrence it will be proper to notice in a threefold view:

I. As an act for our benefit—

The appointment of the apostles was a work of singular importance—

They were to be employed in the church as his messengers to declare his truth—his witnesses to attest it—as patterns also to illustrate—and martyrs to confirm it. But whence could a number of poor fishermen attain "a sufficiency for these things?"— — —

Hence our blessed Lord continued the whole night in prayer for them—

* This may be easily extended to the *formalist*, the *hppocritical professor*, &c.

† If we suppose προσευχῇ to mean "in a place of prayer," we still can have no doubt what his occupation there was.

His heavenly Father was able to furnish them for this great work, and to give them success in it; and therefore our Lord importunately sought for them the grace which they stood in need of: nor would he cease from his exertions, till he had obtained all that their necessities required. The benefit of his prayer was fully manifested as soon as they were endued with power from on high: then nothing could withstand their wisdom, or subdue their courage: they were deaf to menaces, and regardless of death. Their success was rapid, extensive, permanent: and we at this day enjoy the fruits of their labors. Through that prayer the apostles were richly furnished unto every good work; and were enabled so to establish the kingdom of our Lord, that neither earth nor hell have ever been able to prevail against it.

II. As a lesson for our instruction—

The ordination of ministers is also a most important work—

On them, under God, depends the everlasting welfare of thousands. We need only compare the state of those congregations where the gospel is faithfully preached with those which are under the superintendence of careless ministers: in the one will be found little but ignorance and irreligion; in the other, there will be many whose minds are enlightened with divine truth, and whose souls are quickened to a new and heavenly life.

But where shall persons be found duly qualified for the work—where those who will be willing to undertake it? True; if the Ministry of the Word be made a source of temporal emolument, there will be multitudes ready to engage in it: but if the "signs of a minister," or accompaniments of the ministry, be like those in the apostle's days, "reproaches, necessities, and distresses for Christ's sake," 2 Cor. xii. 10, 12, and the only *pluralities* be "labors, stripes, prisons, deaths," 2 Cor. xi. 23; ib. 24—28, there will not be many candidates for the office, nor will the qualifications for it be thought so common as they are at present. How few are ready to go and preach to the heathen, where the labor and self-denial are great, and the earthly recompence is small! Large benefices, where little is to be done, or the work can be done by proxy, are caught up with avidity: but if nothing but a future reward be held forth, and God say, "Who will go for us?" there are few indeed that will answer with the prophet, "Here am I, send me." Isa. vi. 8.

This, therefore, should be the subject of our devoutest prayers—

God himself has commanded us to commit the matter to him in prayer: "The harvest truly is plenteous, and the laborers are few; pray ye therefore the Lord of the harvest, that he will send forth *(thrust out)* ἐκβάλῃ, Matt. ix. 37, 38, laborers into his harvest." And truly, all ranks and orders of men are concerned to "labor earnestly in prayer" concerning it.

How fervently should *they* pray, *to whom the office of ordaining others is committed!* for "if they lay hands suddenly on any man, they make themselves partakers of other men's sins." 1 Tim. v. 22. Nor should *they* be less earnest *who are to be ordained.* When we consider how arduous their work is, and how great their responsibility before God; when we reflect that their word will be "a savour of life to the life and salvation of many, or a savour of death to their death" and condemnation; 2 Cor. ii. 16; and that the blood of all that perish through their neglect will be required at their hands; methinks it is a wonder that any one can be found, who, for the sake of filthy lucre, will dare to undertake it. Were the weight of the office duly considered, no one would presume to enter upon it without much prayer to God to qualify him for the discharge of it, and to bless his labors to the edification of the people.

But *the people themselves also* are no less concerned to pray, that God would "send them pastors after his own heart;" for the welfare of their souls essentially depends on the kind of ministry which they attend: if Christ be not exhibited to them in his person and offices; if they be not encouraged to receive out of his fulness all the blessings of salvation; if they be not led into discoveries of the evil of their own hearts, and instructed in the nature of that change which the Holy Spirit will effect within them; if, in short, they have not "the whole counsel of God set before them," they will be left to rest in very low attainments, if not to "perish utterly through lack of knowledge."

This lesson then should be learned by all; and so learned, as to be reduced to practice.

III. As a pattern for our imitation—

Prayer is both the duty and the privilege of all—

Our blessed Lord had doubtless more intimate communnion with his Father than we can possibly have; yet are we also authorized to call God "our Father;" yea, we are commanded to do it, and to "open our mouths wide, that he may fill them." It is not, indeed, required of us that we should spend whole nights in prayer to God; for that would probably, unless in some very peculiar circumstances, render us unfit for prosecuting the duties of the ensuing day: but we are required to "continue in prayer, and to watch thereunto with thanksgiving:" Col. iv. 2; and the more nearly we can approach to the example of our blessed Lord in the frequency and urgency of our prayers, Psa. xxii. 2; Heb. v. 7, the more remarkable will be the answers that we shall receive, and the more abundant the communications of God to our souls. If we wrestled more like Jacob, we should certainly prevail to a much greater extent than in general we do. Gen. xxxii. 34—36.

We should therefore resort to it on every particular emergency—

Though the particular object of our Lord's continuance in prayer does not occur to us, yet we all have some occasions that call for more than ordinary direction and assistance from God. On these occasions, whatever they may be, whether they relate to the body or the soul, to time or to eternity, we should go and spread our wants before God. His own command to us is, "In *every* thing, by prayer and supplication, with thanksgiving, let your requests be made known unto God." "In *all* our ways we must acknowledge him, and he will direct our paths."

In this then must all of us resemble the Lord Jesus Christ. In this has "he set us an example, that we should follow his steps:" and "we must walk as he walked." By this must all his followers be distinguished; for they are "a people near unto him." They are hypocrites of whom it is said, "They will not always call upon God:" all true christians can say, Truly our fellowship is with the Father, and with his Son Jesus Christ."

Application:

Learn hence the real state of your souls before God. Prayer has often been called the pulse of the soul: and truly it is so; for by that you may discern the state of the soul, incomparably better than you can by the pulse the state of the body. If you are prayerless people, you are dead, altogether dead in trespasses and sins. If your prayers are habitually cold and formal, they are such as God will never accept. No prayer will enter into the ears of the Lord of Hosts, but that which is offered "in spirit and in truth." Let us then beg of God to give us a spirit of grace and of supplication; and let us interest ourselves with God for the welfare of his church. Let us especially remember "those who are over us in the Lord," and "labor always fervently for them in prayer," that they may be enabled to fulfil their ministry with diligence and success. Thus shall we both insure blessings to our own souls, and be instrumental to the hastening on of that day, when "all shall know the Lord, from the least to the greatest," and "all flesh shall see the salvation of God."

THE GROUNDS OF A MINISTER'S REGARD TO HIS PEOPLE.

2 Cor. vii. 3.—You are in our hearts to die and live with you. (H. H.)

THERE is in every man a quick sensibility with respect to any thing that may affect his character: even a slight insinuation, that seems to convey reproof, is keenly felt. On this account we ought to be extremely cautious, not only when criminating others, but even when vindicating ourselves; because a necessary self-vindication may easily be construed as an oblique censure upon others. We cannot but admire the delicacy of the Apostle's mind, when asserting the integrity of his conduct towards the church at Corinth. There were some in that place who had traduced his character: for the sake of others therefore it was necessary that he should declare his innocence with respect to the things that were laid to his charge. But fearing that, in doing this, he might appear to cast a reflection indiscriminately on the whole body, he adds, with exquisite tenderness and affection, that, so far from intending to condemn them all, he was willing, if his other duties would admit of it, to live and die among them.

In order to promote in all, this amiable disposition, we shall consider,

I. THE GROUNDS OF THE APOSTLE'S LOVE—

St. Paul felt a love towards the whole human race: but he was filled with a peculiar affection towards the Corinthians on account of.

1. Their relation to God—

The Apostle had reason to believe that the Corinthians, notwithstanding some great evils which obtained among them, 1 Cor. i. 11, and iii. 1—4, and v. 1, 2, and vi. 5—8, and viii. 9—12, and xi. 18—22, and xiv. 26, were truly converted to God; and that the greater part of them were very eminent christians, 1 Cor. i. 5—7, and 2 Cor. viii. 7.

This was a just ground for loving them. Indeed, if he had not been penetrated with an unfeigned regard for them, he would have no evidence of his own love to God: for "he who loveth him that begat, must love those who are begotten of him. 1 John v. 1.

2. Their relation to himself—

Having been, in God's hand, the instrument of their conversion, he stood related to them as their spiritual father. 1 Cor. iv. 15, and 2 Cor. xii. 14, with Acts xviii. 1—18. Now, as a peculiar affection subsists between those who bear this relation according to the flesh, so it is reasonable that there should be a mutual regard between those also who are thus united in the bonds of the Spirit. Doubtless the apostle did not confine his regards to these: Col. ii. 1, but, having "travailed in birth with them," he felt all the anxieties and affections of a parent towards them.

The fervor of his love will appear from,

II. THE WAY IN WHICH HE MANIFESTED IT—

We may notice in the context,

1. His affectionate remembrance of them—

He boasted of them wherever he went: he held them up as peculiarly worthy of imitation: 2 Cor. vii. 14, and 2 Cor. viii. 24, and ix. 1, 2, and so great was the satisfaction which he felt in hearing of their welfare, that it far over-balanced all the sufferings he endured. What clearer proof could he give of his affection for them?

2. His faithful admonitions—

Though he loved them, he was not blind to their faults. When he saw them deviating from the path of duty, he performed the office of a Monitor and Guide. He changed his voice towards them, as he saw occasion: sometimes he spake with the authority of an Apostle, 1 Cor. iv. 18, 19, and sometimes with the tenderness of a friend or parent. 2 Cor. ii. 1—5, and 1 Cor. iv. 14. This was an eminent proof of his love, because it shewed that his concern for their souls swallowed up every other consideration. Lev. xix. 17 with ver. 12.

3. His devotion to their service—

He regarded not wealth, or ease, or honor; but would have been contented "to live and die with them" who had but ill requited all his past kindness: Yea, he declared, that "he would most gladly spend and be spent for them, though the more abundantly he loved them, the less he were loved." 2 Cor. xii. 15. Nothing short of laying down our life for any person could testify more love than this.

Application—

1. Let us improve our intercourse with each other in life—

It is the happiness of a minister and his people to have frequent and familiar intercourse with each other. We have through the mercy of our God enjoyed it: but alas! how little have we improved it! Let us look unto our God for his blessing upon us in future: 2 Cor. vi. 11—13, for without that "neither Paul can plant, nor Apollos water, to any good purpose." 1 Cor. iii. 5—7.

2. Let us prepare for our separation in death—

As "the Priests under the law could not continue by reason of death," so neither can we under the Gospel. We must go to give an account of our stewardship; and you to answer for the advantages you have enjoyed. Let us be looking forward to that solemn meeting which we shall have at the bar of judgment. Let us implore help from God, that we may discharge our duties towards each other aright; and meet again, not as witnesses against each other, but as fellow-heirs of his glory. And the Lord grant that we may then be your joy, and that you may be "our joy and crown of rejoicing" to all eternity! 1 Thess. ii. 19, 20, and 2 Cor. i. 14.

A MINISTER'S CHIEF JOY.

3 John 4.—I have no greater joy than to hear that my children walk in truth. (H. H.)

There subsists between a minister and his people a relation which may not unfitly be compared with that of a father and his children. The metaphorical expression of a father is more strictly applicable to those whom a minister "has begotten through the gospel;" 1 Cor. iv. 15; but it needs not to be restricted to this sense: it may be used with greater latitude in reference to those over whom a minister watches, and for whose benefit he labors with parental anxiety, especially where the person to whom the paternal relation is ascribed is somewhat advanced in years. It should seem that Gaius, to whom St. John wrote this Epistle, was converted to the faith by the ministry of Paul: 1 Cor. i. 14; yet St. John properly includes him amongst his children, because he felt the same regard for him as for those who were the more immediate seals of his own ministry; the whole body of his people being in his different epistles frequently designated by that favorite appellation. 1 John ii. 1, and iii. 18.

Respecting the state of Gaius' soul, the apostle had heard the most satisfactory account; so that he could not shew his anxiety for the bodily health of Gaius more strongly, than by wishing it to prosper *in every respect*, περὶ πάντων, ver. 2, "even as his soul prospered." Having declared the joy which this information had afforded him, he states, in general, that he had no greater joy than what arose from such tidings as these.

From hence we shall take occasion to shew,

I. WHAT IS THE GREAT OBJECT OF A MINISTER'S DESIRE IN BEHALF OF HIS PEOPLE—

To bring men to the acknowledgement of the truth is the first labor of a minister: and, till that has been effected, no other relation exists between him and them than that which he has by nature, or that which he has in common with all mankind. But when they have embraced the truth, and are become members of the family of Christ, then the minister seeks their advancement in the divine life—

Christianity, as experienced in the soul, is not a sentiment, but a habit: it not merely informs the mind, but regulates the life: and, whilst it introduces "men from darkness unto light, it turns them also from the power of Satan unto God." Having brought souls to an enjoyment of Christ, and to a conformity to his mind and will, the minister desires to see them walk in the truth.

1. Consistently—

He longs to behold in them a holy consistency; a high state of heavenly affections, and a careful attention to the duties of morality. Morality however will not satisfy him if detached from fellowship with God: nor will the most sublime intercourse with God in prayer and praise approve itself to him, if it be not accompanied with a conscientious discharge of every personal and relative duty— — —

2. Steadily—

In them he expects to find a steadiness that bids defiance to temptation, and cannot be diverted from its purpose, either by the allurements of sense or the terrors of persecution: he would have his converts to be "stedfast, immoveable, always abounding in the work of the Lord." 1 Cor. xv. 58. A fixedness of mind he regards as absolutely essential to the christian character: and he is never satisfied with the state of his people unless he find that, in the midst of the severest persecutions, they are enabled to say, "None of these things move me, neither count I my life dear unto me, so that I may but finish my course with joy"— — —

3. Progressively—

This is implied in the term "walking," which is a progressive motion necessary to the christian life. There is no possibility of standing still in religion. Our motion, if not progressive, must be retrograde. Now, as a parent wishes to see in his children a gradual advancement towards maturity both in their bodily and intellectual faculties, so does a minister long for his people's progress towards perfection. He hopes to see in them a more entire devotedness of heart unto their God and Saviour; evincing itself in a greater spirituality of mind, an increasing indifference to the things of time and sense, and a more laborious engagement in every good work— — —In a word, he wishes to see their progress like that of the sun in the firmament, "their path shining brighter and brighter unto the perfect day." Prov. iv. 18.

The emotions with which St. John beheld this conduct in Gaius were most sublime: and such they will be in every faithful minister; as will appear, whilst we shew,

II. Whence it is that the attainment of that object fills him with such exalted joy—

St. John was not inferior to any one of the apostles in holy joy. He had been pre-eminently favored by his Lord and Saviour, insomuch that he was known by the name of "the disciple whom Jesus loved." He had beheld his Lord transfigured on Mount Tabor, and shining forth in all the glory of the Godhead. He had laen in the bosom of his Lord, as on many other occasions, so especially on that evening when the commemorative ordinance of the Lord's Supper was instituted: yet even "he had no greater joy than to hear that his children walked in truth." Much more therefore may we expect that ministers, less favored than he, should have no joy more exalted than that which the sight or hearing of their people's prosperity affords them. This is their sublimest source of happiness;

1. Because it is by this only that the ends of their ministry are answered—

If the minister impart to his children "the sincere milk of the word," it is, "that they may grow thereby:" or, if he set before them "the stronger meat" of the gospel, it is, that those who are able to receive it may be the more nourished and strengthened for their future labors. If he see no growth in them, "he stands in doubt" whether they have ever been truly and savingly converted to the faith of Christ; and "he travails, as it were, a second time in birth with them, until Christ be fully and visibly formed in them." Gal. iv. 19, 20. But when he beholds the plants, which he is daily watering, thriving, and diffusing all around the fragrancy of holy and devout affections, he sees of the travail of his soul and is satisfied: and what the angels enjoyed at the first symptoms of their conversion, he enjoys from day to day: his very life is bound up in their welfare; and "he then lives, when they stand fast in the Lord." 1 Thess. iii. 8.

2. Because by this only can God be glorified—

Nothing brings more dishonor to God than an inconsistent conduct in those who profess godliness. The very name of God is often blasphemed through the misconduct of those who call themselves his peculiar people. The ungodly world are not content with condemning the offending individual; "they speak evil of the way of truth" itself, as though that countenanced and even produced the evils that have been committed. On the other hand, "the person who brings forth much fruit glorifies God," and "by his well-doing puts to silence the ignorance of foolish men." To a minister who loves the Lord Jesus Christ in sincerity, and is jealous for the honor of his name, nothing can be more delightful than to see truth triumphing over error, and the kingdom of Christ exalted on the ruins of Satan's empire. On every fresh report that is brought to his ears, he will exclaim, "Hallelujah! for the Lord God omnipotent reigneth!"— — —

3. Because without this they can have no hope of ever meeting their people in the realms of bliss—

How joyful is the thought of that hour, when the minister shall go with his people into the presence of his God, saying, "Here am I, and the children thou hast given me!" And how glorious will be the recompence of his labors, when he shall "have them as his joy and crown of rejoicing" to all eternity! 1 Thess. ii. 19, 20. If an earthly parent hear of his children, that they are advancing visibly in every thing that is good, so that, though he have no hope of seeing them in this world, he feels assured that he shall meet them again at the right hand of God, and dwell with them for ever in his immediate presence; the thought of a temporary separation from them is swallowed up in the joy that the blessed prospect affords him. So it is with the spiritual Parent, when beholding or hearing of the prosperity of his children: for he knows that he shall "rejoice in the day of Christ, that he has not run in vain, or labored in vain." Phil. ii. 16.

Permit me now to address you,

1. In a way of retrospective inquiry—

What report must I hear of you? What report have you to give me of yourselves? Has your walk been consistent, uniform, progressive?— — — Be assured, I am prepared to rejoice in your welfare with a truly paternal joy— — —

2. In a way of prospective admonition—

Great and manifold are your dangers, whatever progress you may have made. That you may escape them, "take heed to God's word," and follow the steps of your blessed Lord: and look to him for all needful strength. "Be strong in him," and you shall "be more than conquerors through him"

THE DUTY OF THOSE WHO ARE CALLED.

1 Thess. ii. 11, 12.—You know how we exhorted, and comforted, and charged every one of you, as a father doth his children, that ye would walk worthy of God, who hath called you unto his kingdom and glory. (H. H.)

Next to the example of our blessed Lord, there is none so worthy of imitation as that of St. Paul. He appears to have been so entirely cast into the mould of the gospel, that he was a living image of all that it requires. In the ministerial office especially he was almost a perfect pattern. His intrepidity, his singleness of heart, his self-denial, his fervent zeal for God, and tender love to man, never were surpassed, nor ever equalled by any human being. Respecting the purity of his intentions, and the probity of his conduct, he could appeal to all among whom he had labored, yea to God also: *no less than eight times in eleven verses does he repeat this appeal;* so conscious was he that he had exerted himself to the utmost of his power to promote the welfare of his fellow-creatures, and the glory of his God.

In the appeal before us we may notice,

I. The duty of Christians—

The first great duty of those to whom the Gospel comes, is to believe in Christ. 1 John iii. 23. and John vi. 28, 29. But yet even this is subservient to a higher end, even to the attainment of holiness, and the glorifying of God by a heavenly conversation. The christian is not to be satisfied with low attainments, but to walk worthy of his God; to walk worthy of him,

1. As his governor—

God has given us a law which is a perfect transcript of his mind and will. This law is to be the rule of our conduct. In obeying it therefore we must not select the easier parts, and overlook the precepts which are more difficult: we must not attempt to reduce the standard to our practice; but rather endeavour to raise our practice to the standard. We should not inquire, How little can I do, and yet escape punishment? but rather, What can I do to please and honour my Divine Master? How shall I commend to others his government? How shall I convince them that his service is perfect freedom. How shall I illustrate his perfections by my own conduct? How shall I make my light so to shine before them, that all who behold it shall be constrained to glorify my God, and to take upon them his light and easy yoke?

2. As his benefactor—

God has "called" his people, not by the word only, but also by "the effectual working of his power:" He has called them to be subjects of "his kingdom" on earth, and heirs of "his glory" in heaven. Eph. ii. 19. 2 Thess. ii. 13. This distinguishing grace calls for every possible expression of love and gratitude. Our one inquiry therefore should be, "What shall I render unto the Lord for all the benefits that he hath done unto me? How shall I walk worthy of such a benefactor? Shall not my soul overflow with love to him? Shall I not "delight myself in him;" and "present myself a living sacrifice to him;" and strive incessantly to "glorify his name?" Shall I think any thing too much to do or suffer, for his sake? Shall I not seek to be "pure as he is pure," and "perfect as he is perfect?" Surely, "as He who has called me is holy, so should I be holy in all manner of conversation." 1 Pet. i. 15.

This is the christian's duty; thus to argue, and thus to live.

In order to enforce this subject yet further, we will consider,

II. The duty of Ministers—

It is through the exertions of ministers that God carries on his work in the hearts of his people. Ministers are set apart on purpose to teach men their duty, and to urge them to the performance of it. They stand related to their people as a parent to his children: and in the exercise of their high office, they are to address them with parental tenderness, and parental authority.

"Suffer ye then the word of exhortation," while we endeavour to impress upon your minds a due regard for holiness: and permit me, however unworthy of the sacred office, to address you,

1. In a way of affectionate intreaty—

"God has called you unto holiness:" and "this also we wish, even your perfection." Consider then, I beseech you, how much is to be attained by your advancement in holiness.

Consider, how it will *contribute to your present happiness.*—Experience must long since have shewn you, that there is no comfort in religion, when we are living at a distance from God, or in indulgence of any besetting sin We hope too you have found how "pleasant and peaceful are the ways" of godliness, when we are steadfastly walking in them. Go on, and you will have continually increasing evidence, that "*in* keeping God's commandments there is great reward."

Consider also how your piety will *promote the good of others.*—We speak not of the benefit that will arise to society from the good offices you do them; but of the effects which your good example will produce. If your life be not "such as becometh the gospel of Christ," the world will despise religion as a worthless unproductive thing: and those who profess godliness will be apt to catch the infection, and to sink into lukewarmness. But if you "walk worthy of your vocation," you will "by your well-doing put to silence the ignorance of foolish men;" you will constrain them to confess, that the principles which operate so powerfully on your souls, must needs be good; and you will perhaps win many, who would never have been won by the word alone. 1 Pet. iii. 1.

Consider further how it will *advance your eternal happiness.*—What though there be no *merit* in your works, shall they not be rewarded? Shall not every one reap according to what he sows; Gal. vi. 7, 8. and that too, not according to the quality only, but the quantity also, of his seed? Yes; "every man shall be rewarded according to his own labour:" 1 Cor. iii. 8. he shall "reap sparingly or bountifully, according as he sowed;" 2 Cor. ix. 6. and every talent that is improved shall have a correspondent recompence in the day of judgment. Matt. xxv. 28, 29.

What further inducement can you wish for? Only reflect on these things, and surely I shall not have "exhorted" you in vain.

2. In a way of authoritative injunction—

St. Paul, when least disposed to grieve his people, said to them, "As my beloved sons, I warn you." 1 Cor. iv. 14. And in the text he tells us, that he "charged" them in a most solemn manner, and *testified* (μαρτυρούμενοι) unto them. Behold then, we testify unto you that the holiness which we inculcate is of prime importance, and indispensable necessity.

Consider that *nothing less than this will prove you to be real christians.*—If you are "Israelites indeed, you must be without guile." If fire descend from heaven into the bosom to consume your lusts, it will burn till all the fuel be consumed. The contending principles of flesh and spirit will never cease from their warfare, till the flesh be brought into subjection. Gal. v. 17. 1 Cor. ix. 27. "If you are Christ's, you have crucified the flesh with its affections and lusts." Gal. v. 24. Deceive not yourselves; for, "whomsoever you obey, his servants you are." Rom. vi. 16. If you are born of God, you will not harbour any sin. 1 John iii. 9. or be satisfied with any attainment; Phil. iii. 12—14. but will seek to be "righteous, even as God is righteous." 1 John iii. 7.

Consider that *nothing less will suffice to comfort you in a dying hour.*—When you come to that solemn season, things will appear to you in a different light from what they now do. The truths, which have now gained your assent indeed, but float in your mind as though the were devoid of interest or importance, will then present themselves to your mind as the most awful realities. What will you then think of cold and lifeless services? What bitter regret will seize yon, and terrible forebodings too perhaps, when you look back upon a partial obedience, and an hypocritical profession? O that you may not fill your dying pillow with thorns! O that you may serve the Lord in such a manner now, that in that day you may "enjoy the testimony of a good conscience," and have an abundant entrance into the kingdom of your Lord and Saviour!" 2 Pet. i. 10, 11. with Psa. xxxvii. 37.

Consider lastly, that *nothing less will avail you at the bar of judgment.* We repeat it, that you will not be saved *for* your works: but we repeat also, that you will be dealt with *according to* your works. It will be to little purpose to have cr[illegible] l 'Lord, Lord,' if you are not found to have done the things which he commanded. Matt. vii. 21—23. with Luke vi. 46. God has said, "Cursed be he that doeth the work of the Lord deceitfully;" Jer. xlviii. 10. nor will either of our self-commendations, or the applause of others, avail us, if the heart-searching God do not bear witness to our integrity. 2 Cor x. 18.

Behold then, as in the sight of God, we testify these things; and charge you all, that if you would ever behold the face of God in peace, you make it the great object of your life to walk as becometh saints, and to "adorn the doctrine of God our Saviour in all things."

APPLICATION—

The Apostle contended not himself with *general* exhortations; but addressed himself to individuals; even, as far as he could, to "*every one*" of his people. Let me then apply my subject more *particularly* to you, dispensing to each his portion in due season.

Are there among you *those who make no profession of religion?*—Think not, that you are excused from that strictness which is required of the saints. As the creatures of God, you are bound to obey him; and as "bought with the inestimable price of his Son's blood, you are bound to glorify him with your bodies and your spirits, which are his." 1 Cor. vi. 20. Nor should it be any consolation to you that you make no profession of religion, for, if you have not been called to be subjects of God's kingdom, and heirs of his glory, you are vassals of Satan, and partakers of his condemnation.

Are there *any who, by reason of their unsteady walk, are ready to doubt whether they have ever been effectually called?* Let me both "*exhort* and *charge*" them not to leave this matter in suspense; but to obtain of God that "grace that shall be sufficient for them." Let me at the same time suggest some considerations proper to "*comfort*" and support their minds. They would ask perhaps, How shall I gain the object of my wishes? How shall I walk worthy of my God? I answer, "WALK IN CHRIST," Col. ii. 6; in a continual dependence on the merit of his blood, and the assistance of his good Spirit. By his blood ye shall be cleansed from guilt: "by his Spirit ye shall be strengthened in your inner man," and be enabled to do whatever he commands. Phil. iv. 13.

Finally, let *all*, whatever they may have attained, press forward for the prize of their high calling, and endeavor to abound more and more.

DIVINE WORSHIP.

Psalm lxxxiv. 1, 2.—"How amiable are thy tabernacles, O Lord of hosts! My soul longeth, yea, even fainteth for the courts of the Lord: my heart and my flesh crieth out for the living God." (Sk.)

WHILE the Israelites were in the wilderness, on their way to Canaan, dwelling in tents, God commanded Moses to erect a tent or tabernacle for religious uses.—A part of this tent was peculiarly sacred, and called *the holy of holies;* adjoining this was *the holy place*, separated from the former by a veil; and connected with the holy place was a court where sacrifices were offered; and into which the people were occasionally permitted to enter. See Exod. xxv. 8, and xxix. 38—46; chaps. xxxvi. to xl; and Heb. chap. ix. At this tabernacle, as well as in the temple afterwards built by Solomon, the hosts of Israel assembled to worship God: here divine worship was performed according to the Jewish ritual; and here the God of Israel manifested his presence.

To a pious Israelite all these circumstances were very interesting; and these evidently were the things which excited the admiration, and called forth the warm desires of the Psalmist, when he uttered the language of the text.

Let these words lead our attention to—*The amiableness of divine worship;* and to—*The manner in which devont worshippers are drawn to its sacred exercises.*

I. THE AMIABLENESS OF DIVINE WORSHIP may be discerned, by adverting to—The persons assembled,—Their engagements,—And some interesting results, to which such engagements lead.

Behold the assembly!—It is composed of rational, immortal, accountable creatures;—of persons whose ages, relative situations, and conditions are various. They are assembled in the name of God their Maker and Preserver,—of Christ their Redeemer; their business is one, and is of everlasting importance. To adore the infinite Jehovah;—to obtain pardon, regeneration, and holiness are the purposes for which they assemble; and the Lord of Hosts is with them, Jesus is in the midst of them; and angels unperceived join their assembly.

Proceed with them in their devotions.—Psalms, hymns, divine songs,—accompanied by melodious and harmonious sounds, say, or seem to say,—"Praise waiteth for thee, O God, in Sion." And their very ears are gratified, and their spirits are exhilarated, by harmony and melody, employed in so sacred, so good a cause.

Prayer to God forms another part of their solemn exercises. They approach "the footstool of their God:" they worship, they bow down, they kneel before the Lord their Maker, Psa. xcv. 6, and speak to and commune with the Father of their spirits; and Jesus being their Advocate, their Mediator,—the petitions offered up through him are regarded; and "the fervent prayer availeth much."

The ministry of the sacred word is another interesting circumstance connected with public worship. Here the holy scriptures are read, illustrated, and suitably applied. And God opening the eyes of those present, to behold wondrous things out of his law, Ps. cxix. 18, they realize, or may realize, what is so beautifully described in the following language, Ps. xix. 7—11.

Such engagements as the above, are, with the truly devout, accompanied by dispositions, sensations, and enjoyments highly, important. "God is a spirit;" and they "worship him in spirit and in truth." They have "fellowship one with another, and with the Father, and with his Son Jesus Christ." And such a situation connected with such circumstances, is to them, "the house of God, and the gate of heaven," Gen. xxviii. 17.

Besides all this, if we look more minutely, and listen more attentively, we shall *behold* tears of penitence, and *hear* the sighing of such as are sorrowful on account of their sins, and shall have evidence that there are in the assembly, broken and contrite spirits, whom God will not despise, Ps. li. 17. To render the scene still more interesting;—see cheerful countenances, that bespeak hearts conscious of his approbation, in whose favor is life, Ps. xxx. 5, and hear the song of praise, Isa. xii. 1, 2, and the language of deliverance, Ps. xxvii. 6, and xli. 1—3, and say, are not God's tabernacles amiable? And may not those who love his worship, express their desire after it in the following language? "My soul longeth," &c. Let us examine these words, and we shall perceive,

II. THE MANNER IN WHICH DEVOUT WORSHIPPERS ARE DRAWN TO ITS SACRED EXERCISES. The Psalmist desired—The *courts of the Lord, and the living God. All his powers were drawn towards these objects; and drawn towards them in a very intense manner.*

The expressions—"*courts of the Lord*," and "*living God*," include all that is desirable in divine worship.—Some desire only the "*courts of the Lord;*" the place, the company, the outward expressions of divine worship. Others almost despise these, while they profess to desire "*the living God.*"—With the *former*, any observations about the divine presence in the place of worship, are accounted enthusiastic;—with the *latter*, public prayer,—praise, and teaching,—are almost things of nought. But mark this devout worshipper:—with him there was something very desirable in *the courts*. The social assembly,—the outward act,—the very *place* where he usually worshipped, had strong attractions; and yet these were desirable to him, only as they led to the glorious object of devotion,—*the living God*. Without his presence, all worship is a lifeless form;—but when his "power and glory are seen in the sanctuary," the place is holy;—the exercises are delightful: and such as call into action *all the powers of the truly devout*.

Observe,—"My *soul* longeth, my *heart* and my *flesh* crieth out." Surely, *soul*,—*heart*,—*flesh*, are intended to signify all those faculties which man can exercise in the worship of God. The Psalmist's understanding, his judgment, his will, his affections, and his desires, cnocurred:—all within him was drawn to the holy exercise; while his eyes were turned towards the place,—his feet were willing to convey him thither, his hands were ready to be lifted up,—and his tongue was free for prayer and praise.

Mark, too, how intensely he was drawn;—his "*soul longed*, even *fainted* for the courts of the Lord: his heart and his flesh *cried out* for the living God." We need not dwell on these expressions, they speak for themselves; rather let us strive to feel as the sacred writer felt. "Come holy Dove from the heavenly hill, and warm our frozen hearts." Think, oh think on the great, the adorable object of worship; on his power, his goodness, his mercy, his love in Christ Jesus!—and say,—Do not all these demand the *warmest* and the *strongest* exercise of all our rational, and—so far as it is necessary for the expression of our feelings and views—of all our bodily powers? See Deut, vi. 5; Matt. xxii. 37; Ps. xlii. 1, 2.

Ye formalists,—ye enthusiasts;—ye men of reason unaccompanied by affection,—of feeling unaccompanied by reason;—and ye who dispise ordinances, as well as ye who trust in them;—read this sacred book of devotion, the book of Psalms; and learn how to worship God in "the beauty of holiness,"—"in spirit and in truth!"

Let the following reflections conclude the subject.—1. Such exercises—such dispositions—and such enjoyments, as we have been considering, are congenial to the employments and the happiness of heaven, See Ps. xvi. 11; John vxii. 24; 1 Cor. xiii. 12; Rev. vii. 9—12, 15, and xxi. 3. To that state, probably, the mind of the Psalmist ascended, when he uttered the words of the text, See Ps. xxiii. 6, and xvi. 11; at least *we* may presume so far, Heb. viii. 5, and chap. ix. and think on that period, when we shall serve God day and night in his temple above; Rev. vii. 15.

2. Let the subject teach us more than ever to value divine worship;—more than ever to engage in it; and to engage in it *better* than ever.

3. Let us recollect that a meetness for heaven is as necessary as a title; and that the means of grace, when properly engaged in, are well calculated to promote that meetness.

4. And let us never forget, that if we would be benefited in divine worship we must look through the vail of outward things, and *principally* desire the presence of the *living God*.

INSTITUTION OF PUBLIC WORSHIP.

Gen. iv. 26.—Then began men to call upon the name of the Lord. (H. H.)

Of the various institutions of religion, some were clearly founded on an express appointment from God himself: others *appear* to have arisen, in the first instance, from the suggestions of holy men, and to have been afterwards authorized and established by divine authority. It is manifest that baptism was practised by the Jews long before it was appointed by Christ as the rite whereby his followers were to be consecrated to his service: but when it was first introduced, or whether by any express command of God, we know not. The change of the Sabbath from the seventh day to the first was sanctioned by the practice of the apostles: but whether they received any particular direction respecting it, we are not informed. The presumption indeed is, that all the observances which God has sanctioned, originated from him; and that men began to practise them in consequence of some intimations from him: but as this is not declared in scripture, we must be contented to leave the matter undecided. We are not any where told that God commanded men to meet together for the purposes of public worship. If we take the text in the precise sense that it bears in our translation, it should seem that public assemblies of worship were rather the offspring of necessity; and that they arose out of an increase of population, and a growing neglect of personal and family religion.

The text indeed is, in the margin of our Bibles, rendered differently: "Then began men to *call themselves by* the name of the Lord:" Nor are Commentators agreed to which of the versions we should give the preference. We shall therefore include both; and take occasion from the words to shew,

I. In what manner we should confess God—

The descendants of Cain, who had become "a fugitive and a vagabond in the earth," soon cast off all regard for God, and addicted themselves to open and shameless impiety. Lamech broke through the restraints which the Creater had imposed in relation to marriage, and "took unto him two wives;" leaving thereby an example, which in process of time effaced the very remembrance of God's original institution. From these and other abominations arose an imperious necessity for the godly to separate themselves from the ungodly, and to maintain by an open and more visible profession the honor of God in the world. This they did: and in so doing they have taught us,

1. To separate ourselves from the ungodly—

There is a certain degree of intercourse which must subsist between us and the world. But it is by no means desirable to extend it beyond that which the duties of our calling absolutely require. Our Lord repeatedly declares that his faithful followers "are not of the world, even as He was not of the world:" John xvii. 16. The apostles also with one voice guard us against cultivating the friendship of the world; James iv. 4; and teach us to come out from among them, 2 Cor. vi. 14—18, and to live as a distinct "peculiar people," 1 Pet. ii. 9, "shining among them as lights in a dark place." Phil. ii. 15. We should go to them, indeed, when duty calls, as the physician enters the infected chambers of the sick: but we should never forget, that "evil communications corrupt good manners;" 1 Cor. xv. 33, and that an undue familiarity with them is far more likely to weaken the spirituality of our own minds, than to generate a holy disposition in theirs.

In us should be verified the prophecy of Balaam, "Israel shall dwell alone, and shall not be reckoned among the nations." Numb. xxiii. 9.

To make an open profession of our attachment to Christ—

The godly, in the ante-diluvian world, called themselves children of God, as distinct from those who were only children of men: and it was foretold that a similar distinction should obtain among the followers of Christ. Isa. xliv. 5. If in one instance Peter failed in acknowledging his Lord, on other occasions he witnessed a good confession, and manfully withstood the threatenings of his enemies. Acts iv. 8, 10, 19, 20. It may be thought perhaps, that, because christianity is the established religion of the land, there is no occasion for such boldness now: but the sons of Cain and of Ishmael are yet amongst us: Jude 11; Gal. iv. 23, 29; there are in every place those who deride all vital godliness: and it requires almost as much fortitude to withstand their sneers and contempt, as it does to brave more cruel persecutions. There is the same necessity for *us* to "take up our cross and follow Christ," as there was for the primitive christians: and the command given to them to "be faithful unto death," is equally to be regarded by *us:* for the same conduct will be observed by the Judge towards men of every age and nation; "he will confess those before his Father who have confessed him in the world," and "deny before his Father those who have denied, or been ashamed of him." Matt. x. 32, 33; Mark viii. 38.

But the text instructs us also,

II. In what manner we should worship him—

We can not doubt but that Adam and his pious offspring maintained the worship of God both in their families and their closets: but till the human race were considerably multiplied, there was no occasion for what may be called *public* worship. But when the families became so numerous that they were obliged to separate, then it was necessary to call them together at stated times and seasons, that, by forming different congregations, they might all receive instruction at once, and keep up in their minds an habitual reverence for God.

The necessity for public ordinances is obvious; and the benefit arising from them is incalculable.

1. They preserve the knowledge of God in the world—

There is reason to fear, that if there were no public ordinances of religion the very name of God would be soon forgotten. Notwithstanding the establishment of such institutions, the generality are "perishing for lack of knowledge:" darkness has overspread the land, even a darkness that may be seen and felt. Exod. x. 21, with Isaiah ix. 2. But there is some light shining in the world; and *that* is diffused almost exclusively by the public ministry of the word. Occasionally, God is pleased to instruct men by his word and Spirit, without the intervention of human agents: but, as he has set apart an order of men for the express purpose of propagating his truth, so he delights to honor them as his instruments to convey his blessings to the world. Compare Zech. iv. 11—14, and 2 Cor. iv. 7, with Acts viii. 26—39, and x. 9—44. Doubtless he vouchsafes his blessing to those who read and pray in secret, provided they reverence, as far as their circumstances admit, his public institutions: but never did he, from the foundation of the world, impart his blessing to those who continued to live in an avowed contempt of his ordinances: No: "he loveth the gates of Zion more than all the dwellings of Jacob." Ps. lxxxvii. 2.

2. They are the means of perfecting his work in his people's hearts—

God has told us that this was a very principal end for his ordaining men to preach the gospel; Eph. iv. 11—15; but it is by means of the public ordinances chiefly that ministers can address the people: and consequently the ordinances themselves are the means by which God accomplishes his end. We have said before, that God will also reveal himself to his people in secret: and it sometimes happens that their communion with him in private is more sweet and intimate than in the public assembly: but may we not ask, on the other hand, whether, when the heart has been cold and formal in the closet, it has not often been warmed and animated in the church? And is not much of the enjoyment experienced in secret, the result of instructions administered in the public ordinances? In the one they gather the food; in the other they ruminate and chew the cud: but the pleasure and nourishment derived to their souls must be acknowledged, in part at least, as originating in their public duties. To these has God promised his peculiar blessing; Exod. xx. 24; Matt. xxviii. 20; and therefore we should "reverence his sanctuary," and join with one consent in a public surrender of ourselves to God. See Zeph. iii. 9. Zech. viii. 20—22.

ADDRESS,

1. Those who have others under their control—

Parents, and Masters, you are responsible to God for the exercise of your power and influence. Will you then, either by precept or example, encourage a conformity to the world, or a disregard of the worship of your God? O "destroy not their souls, for whom Christ died!" Employ your authority for God: and, whatever opposition you may meet with in the world, learn to say with Joshua, "As for me and my house, we will serve the Lord." Josh. xxiv. 15.

2. Those who are acting for themselves—

If you have "chosen the good part," be careful that it "be not taken away from you," either though the love of this world, or through the fear of man. Be steadfast, and "endure unto the end, that you may be saved at last." If you lose your life for Christ's sake, you shall find it unto life eternal. But if you are "walking in the broad road," think whither it leads: and begin to serve your God in this world, that you may be honored by him in the world to come. John xii. 26.

INDEX OF SCRIPTURE